OUR SOCIAL WORLD

5th Edition

Introduction to Sociology

CONDENSED

Our world is condensing, and it will be a different social place for our children and grandchildren.
It is in that spirit that we dedicate this book to our respective children and grandchildren:

Clay and Joanna Ballantine

Hannah and Caleb Ballantine

Andy and Sarah Jolly-Ballantine

Kai and Ayla Jolly-Ballantine

Kate Ballantine and Jason Andras

Justin and Miriam Roberts

Adina Elisabeth Roberts

Kent Roberts

Zain Blair-Roberts

Elise and Brett Weber-Roberts

Ramona June Weber-Roberts

Julie Korgen

Jessica Korgen

. . . and others who have not yet arrived on this planet.

May the condensed global society they inhabit be an increasingly humane one.

OUR SOCIAL WORLD

5th Edition

Introduction to Sociology

Jeanne H.
BALLANTINE
Wright State University

Keith A.
ROBERTS
Hanover College

Kathleen Odell
KORGEN
William Paterson University

CONDENSED

Los Angeles | London | New Delhi
Singapore | Washington DC | Melbourne

FOR INFORMATION:

SAGE Publications, Inc.
2455 Teller Road
Thousand Oaks, California 91320
E-mail: order@sagepub.com

SAGE Publications Ltd.
1 Oliver's Yard
55 City Road
London EC1Y 1SP
United Kingdom

SAGE Publications India Pvt. Ltd.
B 1/I 1 Mohan Cooperative Industrial Area
Mathura Road, New Delhi 110 044
India

SAGE Publications Asia-Pacific Pte. Ltd.
3 Church Street
#10-04 Samsung Hub
Singapore 049483

Acquisitions Editor: Jeff Lasser
Content Development Manager: Nancy Matuszak
Editorial Assistant: Adeline Wilson
Production Editor: Jane Haenel
Copy Editor: Jared Leighton
Typesetter: C&M Digitals (P) Ltd.
Proofreader: Barbara Coster
Indexer: Nancy Fulton
Cover Designer: Rose Storey
Marketing Manager: Kara Kindstrom

Printed in Canada

Library of Congress Cataloging-in-Publication Data

Names: Ballantine, Jeanne H., author. | Roberts, Keith A., author. | Korgen, Kathleen Odell, 1967- author.

Title: Our social world : condensed / Jeanne H. Ballantine, Wright State University, Keith A. Roberts, Hanover College, Kathleen Odell Korgen, William Paterson University.

Description: Fifth edition. | Thousand Oaks, CA : SAGE, 2018. | Includes bibliographical references and index.

Identifiers: LCCN 2017009804 | ISBN 9781506362021 (pbk. : alk. paper)

Subjects: LCSH: Sociology. | Sociology—Cross-cultural studies.

Classification: LCC HM586 .B352 2018 | DDC 301—dc23
LC record available at https://lccn.loc.gov/2017009804

This book is printed on acid-free paper.

17 18 19 20 21 10 9 8 7 6 5 4 3 2 1

Brief Contents

Sara Miller McCune founded SAGE Publishing in 1965 to support the dissemination of usable knowledge and educate a global community. SAGE publishes more than 1000 journals and over 800 new books each year, spanning a wide range of subject areas. Our growing selection of library products includes archives, data, case studies and video. SAGE remains majority owned by our founder and after her lifetime will become owned by a charitable trust that secures the company's continued independence.

Los Angeles | London | New Delhi | Singapore | Washington DC | Melbourne

Detailed Contents

Chapter 11 • Health Care: An Anatomy of Health and Illness   312

Chapter 12 • Politics and Economics: Probing Power, Dissecting Distribution   340

Preface

To Our Student Readers

This book will change how you view the world—and your place in it. You will gain a sociological perspective on the world that will change what you notice and how you make sense of your social world. Some of you will become sociology majors. All of you will find the subject matter of this course relevant to your personal and professional lives. You will learn how society works—and how you can influence it, develop interpersonal skills, and gain new information about social life in small groups and global social systems. As the broadest of the social sciences, sociology has a never-ending array of fascinating subjects to study.

Sociology and this book ask you to think outside the box. Why? The best way to become a more interesting person, to grow beyond the old familiar thoughts and behaviors, and to make life exciting is to explore new ways to view your social world. The world in which we live is intensely personal and individual in nature, with much of our social interaction occurring in intimate groups of friends and family. Our most intense emotions and most meaningful links to others are at this small-group "micro" level of social life.

However, these intimate micro-level links in our lives are influenced by larger social structures and global trends. The social world you face in the job markets of the 21st century is influenced by changes and forces that are easy to miss. Like the wind, which can do damage even if the air is unseen, social structures are themselves so taken for granted that it is easy to miss seeing them. However, their effects can be readily identified. Sociology's perspectives will help you to better understand your family, friends, work life, leisure time, and place in a diverse and changing world.

THE SOCIAL WORLD MODEL

A well-constructed course, like an effective essay, needs to be organized around a central question, one that leads to other subsidiary questions and intrigues the participants. For you to understand sociology as an integrated whole rather than a set of separate chapters in a book, we have organized the chapters in this book around the *social world model*: a conceptual model that demonstrates the relationships between individuals (micro level); organizations, institutions, and subcultures (meso level); and national societies and global structures (macro level). At the beginning of each chapter, a visual diagram of the model will illustrate this idea as it relates to the topic of that chapter, including how issues related to the topic have implications at various levels of analysis in the social world, influencing and being affected by other parts of society. No aspect of society exists in a vacuum. On the other hand, this model does not assume that everyone always gets along or that relationships are always harmonious or supportive. Sometimes, different parts of the society are in competition for resources and in conflict with one another.

This micro- to macro-level analysis is a central concept in the discipline of sociology. It will help you to develop a *sociological imagination*, an ability to see the complex links between various levels of the social system, from the micro level of close relationships to the macro level of globalization. Within a few months, you may not remember all of the specific concepts or terms that have been introduced, but if the way you see the world has been transformed during this course, a key element of deep learning has been accomplished. Learning to see things from alternative perspectives is a precondition for critical thinking. This entire book attempts to help you recognize connections between your personal experiences and problems and larger social forces of society. Thus, you will be learning to take a new perspective on the social world in which you live.

A key element of that social world is diversity. We live in societies in which there are people who differ in a host of ways: ethnicity, socioeconomic status, religious background, political persuasion, gender, sexual orientation, and so forth. Diversity is a blessing in many ways to a society because the most productive and creative organizations and societies are those that are highly diverse. This is the case because people with different backgrounds solve problems in very different ways. When people with such divergences come together, the outcome of their problem solving can create new solutions to vexing problems. However, diversity often creates challenges as well. Misunderstanding and us-versus-them thinking can divide people. These issues will be explored throughout this book. We now live in a global village, and in this book, you will learn something about how people on the other side of the village live and view the world.

We hope you enjoy the book and get as enthralled with sociology as we are. It genuinely is a fascinating field of study.

Jeanne H. Ballantine
Jeanne H. Ballantine
Wright State University

Keith A. Roberts
Keith A. Roberts
Hanover College

Kathleen Odell Korgen
Kathleen Odell Korgen
William Paterson University

Your authors—teaching "outside the box"

Instructors

How to Make This Book Work for You

Special features woven throughout each chapter support the theme of the book. These will help students comprehend and apply the material and make the material more understandable and interesting. These features are also designed to facilitate deep learning, to help students move beyond rote memorization, and to increase their ability to analyze and evaluate information.

For students to understand both the comparative global theme and sociology as an integrated whole rather than as a set of separate chapters in a book, we have organized this book around the *social world model:* a conceptual model that demonstrates the relationships between individuals (micro level); organizations, institutions, and subcultures (meso level); and societies and global structures (macro levels of analysis). At the beginning of each chapter, a visual diagram of the model will illustrate this idea as it relates to the topic of that chapter, including how issues related to the topic have implications at various levels of analysis in the social world.

Research indicates that unless four discrete sections of the brain are stimulated, the learning will not be long term and deep but surface and short term (Zull 2002). We have many features in this book to activate other sections of the brain, as discussed in the following sections.

"THINK ABOUT IT"

So that students can become curious, active readers, we have posed questions at the outset of each chapter that we hope are relevant to everyday life but that are also tied to the micro-meso-macro levels of analysis that serve as the theme of the book. The purpose is to transform students from passive readers who run their eyes across the words into curious, active readers who read to answer a question and to be reflective. Active or deep reading is key to comprehension and retention of reading material (Roberts and Roberts 2008). Instructors can also use this feature to encourage students to think critically about the implications of what they have read. Instructors might want to ask students to write a paragraph about one of these questions before coming to class each day. These questions might also provide the basis for in-class discussions.

We encourage students to start each chapter by reading and thinking about these questions and asking some questions of their own. This will mean that they are more likely to stay focused, remember the material in the long term, and be able to apply it to their own lives. Each chapter offers a set of learning objectives—"What You Will Learn in This Chapter"—on the title page of the chapter. Anything we can do to encourage students to take a larger view of what they are about to read and begin to ask questions will enhance comprehension and retention of the material.

A GLOBAL PERSPECTIVE AND THE SOCIAL WORLD MODEL

This book incorporates a global perspective throughout. This is done so that students can see not only how others live different but rewarding lives but also the connections between others' lives and their own. Students will need to think and relate to the world globally in future roles as workers, travelers, and global citizens. Our analysis illustrates the interconnections of the world's societies and their political and economic systems and demonstrates that what happens in one part of the world affects others.

This global approach attempts to instill interest, understanding, and respect for different groups of people and their lifestyles. Race, class, and gender are integral parts of understanding the diverse social world, and these features of social life have global implications. The comparative global theme is carried throughout the book in headings and written text, in examples, and in boxes and selection of photos. As students read this book, they should continually think about how the experiences in their private world are influenced by and may influence events at other levels: the community, organizations and institutions, the nation, and the world.

OPENING VIGNETTES

Chapters typically open with an illustration relevant to the chapter content that will grab the attention of students. For instance, in Chapter 2, "Examining the Social World," the case of Hector, a Brazilian teenager living in poverty in a *favela*, is used to illustrate research methods and theory throughout the chapter. Chapter 4, "Socialization," begins with the story of Craig Kielburger, who, at the age of 12, founded a major nonprofit organization fighting child labor practices around the world. Chapter 7 opens with the royal wedding of Prince William and Kate Middleton. Chapter 13 begins with experiences of Sally Ride, the first U.S. woman astronaut in outer space. These vignettes are meant to interest students in the upcoming subject matter by helping them relate to a personalized story. In several cases, the vignettes serve as illustrations throughout the chapters.

"THINKING SOCIOLOGICALLY" QUESTIONS

Following major topics throughout chapters, students will find thought-provoking questions that ask them to think critically and apply the material just read to some aspect of their lives or the social world. The purpose of this feature is to encourage students to apply the ideas and concepts in the text to their lives, to develop critical-thinking skills, and to use the material for better recall. These questions can be the basis for in-class discussions and can be assigned as questions to start interesting conversations with friends and families to learn how the topics relate to their own lives. Note that some of these questions have a miniature icon—a small version of the chapter-opening model—signifying that these questions reinforce the theme of micro, meso, and macro levels of social influence.

"ENGAGING SOCIOLOGY"

Perhaps the most innovative feature in this book is called "Engaging Sociology"—and the double entendre is intentional. We want students to think of sociology as engaging and fun—and to engage with the material. These features—such as applying a population pyramid to the business world, taking a survey to understand why differences in social and cultural capital can make first-generation students feel alienated on a college campus, and reading a map and learning to analyze the patterns—help students understand how interesting and useful sociology can be. There are 31 of these features in this edition.

PUBLIC SOCIOLOGY

Public Sociology has become a major initiative within sociology in the past 15 years, and students are often very interested in what can be done with sociology outside of the academy. With that in mind, this book is unlike any other introductory book in the amount of attention given to public sociologists at work. Seven "Sociologists in Action" features examine profiles of public sociologists who are working in the field.

TECHNOLOGY AND SOCIETY

Nearly every chapter examines the issues of technology as they are relevant to that chapter. We have especially sought out materials that have to do with the Internet and with communications technology.

KEY CONCEPTS, EXAMPLES, AND WRITING STYLE

Key terms that are defined and illustrated within the running narrative and that appear in the glossary appear in **purple** with an italicized definition following. Other terms that are defined but are of less significance are italicized. A list of those key concepts in bold appears at the end of the chapter. The text is rich in examples that bring sociological concepts to life for student readers. Each chapter has been student tested for readability. Both students and reviewers describe the writing style as reader friendly, often fascinating, and accessible—but not watered down.

SOCIAL POLICY AND BECOMING AN INVOLVED CITIZEN

Many chapters include discussion of some social policy issues and the relevance of sociological findings to current social debates. Furthermore, because students sometimes feel helpless and do not know what to do about social issues that concern them at macro and meso levels, we have concluded every chapter with a few ideas about how they might become involved as active citizens, even as undergraduate students. Some suggestions in the "Contributing to Our Social World: What Can We Do?" section may be assigned as extra credit, service learning, or term projects.

SUMMARY SECTIONS AND DISCUSSION QUESTIONS

Each chapter ends with review material: a "What Have We Learned?" feature that includes a bulleted key points summary of the chapter's core material. The summary is followed with probing discussion questions that ask students to go beyond memorization and apply the material in the chapter to their own lives.

A LITTLE (TEACHING) HELP FROM OUR FRIENDS

Whether the instructor is new to teaching or an experienced professor, there are some valuable ideas in this text that can help invigorate and energize the classroom. As we note earlier, substantial literature on teaching methodology tells us that student involvement is key to the learning process. In addition to the engaging sociology questions and exercises in the text, there are a number of teaching suggestions in the supplements and teaching aids for active learning in large or small classes.

INSTRUCTOR TEACHING SITE

The instructor site offers resources such as active-learning projects, collaborative-learning suggestions, options for evaluating students, and more. **SAGE edge** offers a robust online environment featuring an impressive array of tools and resources for review, study, and further exploration, keeping both instructors and students on the cutting edge of teaching and learning. SAGE edge content is open access and available on demand. Learning and teaching has never been easier!

SAGE COURSEPACKS FOR INSTRUCTORS makes it easy to import our quality content into your school's LMS. Intuitive and simple to use, it allows you to

Say NO to . . .

- required access codes
- learning a new system

Say YES to . . .

- using only the content you want and need
- high-quality assessment and multimedia exercise

For use in: Blackboard, Canvas, Brightspace by Desire2Learn (D2L), and Moodle

Don't use an LMS platform? No problem, you can still access many of the online resources for your text via SAGE edge.

SAGE coursepacks include:

- Our content delivered **directly into your LMS**
- **Intuitive, simple format** that makes it easy to integrate the material into your course with minimal effort
- Pedagogically robust **assessment tools** that foster review, practice, and critical thinking and offer a more complete way to measure student engagement, including:
  - Diagnostic chapter **pre tests and post tests** that identify opportunities for improvement, track student progress, and ensure mastery of key learning objectives
  - **Test banks** built on Bloom's Taxonomy that provide a diverse range of test items with ExamView test generation
  - **Activity and quiz options** that allow you to choose only the assignments and tests you want
  - **Instructions** on how to use and integrate the comprehensive assessments and resources provided
- **Chapter-specific discussion questions** to help launch engaging classroom interaction while reinforcing important content
- **SAGE Premium Video** (available via the interactive eBook version, linked through SAGE coursepacks) that is **assignable**, tied to learning objectives, and produced exclusively for this text to bring concepts to life and appeal to different learning styles, featuring:
  - **Corresponding multimedia assessment options** that automatically feed to your gradebook

○ Comprehensive, downloadable, easy-to-use *Media Guide in the Coursepack* for every video resource, listing the chapter to which the video content is tied, matching learning objective(s), a helpful description of the video content, and assessment questions

- **Video resources** that bring concepts to life, are tied to learning objectives and make learning easier
- EXCLUSIVE, influential SAGE **journal and reference content**, built into course materials and assessment tools, that ties important research and scholarship to chapter concepts to strengthen learning
- Editable, chapter-specific **PowerPoint®** slides that offer flexibility when creating multimedia lectures so you don't have to start from scratch but you can customize to your exact needs
- **Integrated links to the interactive eBook** that make it easy for your students to maximize their study time with this "anywhere, anytime" mobile-friendly version of the text. It also offers access to more digital tools and resources, including SAGE Premium Video
- **All tables and figures** from the textbook

STUDENT STUDY SITE

SAGE EDGE FOR STUDENTS at http://edge.sagepub .com/ballantinecondensed5e enhances learning in an easy-to-use environment that offers:

- Mobile-friendly **flashcards** that strengthen understanding of key terms and concepts and make it easy to maximize your study time, anywhere, anytime
- Mobile-friendly **practice quizzes** that allow you to assess how much you've learned and where you need to focus your attention
- A customized online **action plan** that includes tips and feedback on progress through the course and materials
- **Chapter summaries** with learning objectives that reinforce the most important material
- **SAGE Premium Video**, tied to learning objectives and produced exclusively for this text to bring concepts to life
- **Video resources** that bring concepts to life, are tied to learning objectives, and make learning easier
- **Exclusive access to influential SAGE journal and reference content** that ties important research and scholarship to chapter concepts to strengthen learning

WHAT IS NEW IN THE FIFTH CONDENSED EDITION?

In this major revision, we have reorganized several chapters and updated all data, added many new studies, and included new emphases in sociology. The following list provides a summary of key changes:

- Because a number of sociology instructors have indicated a large enrollment of nurses and with the MCAT now having sociology questions for admission to medical school, we have included a chapter on health care (instead of a religion chapter).
- Continued attention to *public sociology*, including descriptions of the work of a number of public sociologists in a feature on "Sociologists in Action."
- Ten new featured essays and six new "Sociologists in Action" features, such as a discussion of the place of sociological training in government policy work (Chapter 12).
- Revised "Engaging Sociology" features, with opportunity for data analysis by students.
- Nearly all boxed features have been shortened so they are limited to one page, and there are somewhat fewer of them.
- Scores of new examples.
- 100 new and/or updated tables and figures with nearly 500 new references.
- Fifteen new or updated maps.
- Considerable condensing of the material for more focused discussion of topics and simpler prose.
- Due to the new research on the role of W. E. B. Du Bois in sociology, he has been given a more prominent place in several discussions of theory and urban sociology.
- Several new topics have been included, such as a discussion in the family chapter (Chapter 10) on the role of social class in parenting.

The core elements of the book—with the unifying theme and the social world model at the beginning of every chapter—have not changed.

Finally, although we have been told that the writing was extraordinarily readable, we have tried to simplify sentence structure in a number of places. In short, we have tried to respond to what we heard from all of you— both students and instructors (and yes, we *do* hear from students)—to keep this book engaging and accessible.

A Personal Note to the Instructor

What is truly distinctive about this book? This is a text that tries to break the mold of the typical textbook synthesis, the cross between an encyclopedia and a dictionary. *Our Social World Condensed* is a unique course text that is *a coherent essay on the sociological imagination—understood globally*. We attempt to radically change the feel of the introductory book by emphasizing coherence, an integrating theme, and current knowledge about learning and teaching, but we also present much traditional organization and content. Instructors will not have to throw out the well-honed syllabus and begin from scratch, but they can refocus each unit so it stresses understanding of micro-level personal troubles within the macro-level public-issues framework. Indeed, in this book, we make clear that the public issues must be understood at several levels of analysis, including global.

Here is a text that engages students. *They* say so! From class testing, we know that the writing style, structure of chapters and sections, the "Thinking Sociologically" features, the wealth of examples, and other instructional aids help students stay focused, think about the material, and apply it to their lives. It neither bores them nor insults their intelligence. It focuses on deep learning rather than memorization. It develops sociological skills of analysis rather than emphasizing memorization of vocabulary. Key concepts and terms are introduced but only in the service of a larger focus on the sociological imagination. The text is both personal and global. It speaks to sociology as a science, as well as addressing public or applied aspects of sociology. It has a theme that provides integration of topics as it introduces the discipline. This text is an analytical essay, not a disconnected encyclopedia.

As one of our reviewers noted,

Unlike most textbooks I have read, the coverage in this one is very impressive. It challenges the student with college-level reading. Too many textbooks give only passing treatment to most of the topics, writing in nugget-sized blocks. More than a single definition and a few sentences of support, the text forces the student deep into the topics covered and challenges them to see interconnections.

Normally, the global perspective within textbooks, which seemed to grow in popularity in the past two decades, was implemented by using brief and exotic examples to show differences between societies—a purely comparative approach rather than a globalization treatment. They gave—and still give—a token nod to diversity. This textbook, however, forces students to take a broader look at similarities and differences in social institutions around the world and structures and processes operating in all cultures and societies in the world of which they are a part.

So our focus in this book is on deep learning, especially expansion of students' ability to role-take or "perspective-take." Deep learning goes beyond the content of concepts and terms and cultivates the habits of thinking that allow one to think critically. Being able to see things from the perspective of others is essential to doing sociology, but it is also indispensable to seeing weaknesses in various theories or recognizing blind spots in a point of view. Using the sociological imagination is one dimension of role-taking because it requires a step back from the typical micro-level understanding of life's events and fosters a new comprehension of how meso- and macro-level forces—even global ones—can shape the individual's life. Enhancement of role-taking ability is at the core of this book because it is a *prerequisite* for deep learning in sociology, and it is the core competency needed to *do* sociology. One cannot do sociology unless one can see things from various positions on the social landscape.

This may sound daunting for some student audiences, but we have found that instructors at every kind of institution have had great success with the book because of the writing style and instructional tools used throughout. We have made some strategic decisions based on these principles of learning and teaching. We have focused much of the book on higher-order thinking skills rather than memorization and regurgitation. We want students to learn to think sociologically: to apply, analyze, synthesize, evaluate, and comprehend the interconnections of the world through a globally informed sociological imagination. However, we think it is also essential to do this with an understanding of how students learn.

Many introductory-level books offer several theories and then provide critiques of the theories. The idea is to teach critical thinking. We have purposefully refrained from extensive critique of theory (although some does occur) for several reasons. First, providing critique to beginning-level students does not really teach critical thinking. It trains them to memorize someone else's critique. Furthermore, it simply confuses many of them, leaving students with the feeling that sociology is really just contradictory ideas, and the discipline really does not have anything firm to offer. Teaching critical thinking needs to be done in stages, and it needs to take curricular scaffolding into account—the building steps that occur before effective critique is possible. That is why we focus on the concept of deep learning. We are working toward building the foundations that are necessary for sophisticated critical thought at upper levels in the curriculum.

Therefore, in this beginning-level text, we have attempted to focus on a central higher-order or deep-learning skill: synthesis. Undergraduate students need to grasp this before they can fully engage in evaluation. Deep learning involves understanding of complexity, and some aspects of complexity need to be taught at advanced levels. While students at the introductory level are often capable of synthesis, complex evaluation requires some foundational skills. Thus, we offer contrasting theories in this text, and, rather than telling what is wrong with each one, we encourage students through "Thinking Sociologically" features to analyze the use of each and to focus on honing synthesis and comparison skills.

Finally, research tells us that learning becomes embedded in memory and becomes long-lasting only if it is related to something that learners already know. If they memorize terms but have no unifying framework to which they can attach those ideas, the memory will not last until the end of the course, let alone until the next higher-level course. In this text, each chapter is tied to the social world model that is core to sociological thinking. At the end of a course using this book, we believe that students will be able to explain coherently what sociology is and construct an effective essay about what they have learned from the course as a whole. Learning to develop and defend a thesis, with supporting logic and evidence, is another component of deep learning. In short, this text provides instructors with the tools to teach sociology in a way that will make a long-term impact on students.

ORGANIZATION AND COVERAGE

Reminiscent of some packaged international tours, in which the travelers figure that "it is Day 7, so this must be Paris," many introductory courses seem to operate on the principle that it is Week 4, so this must be deviance week. Students do not sense any integration, and at the end of the course, they have trouble remembering specific topics. This book is different. A major goal of the book is to show the integration between topics in sociology and between parts of the social world. The idea is for students to grasp the concept of the interrelated world. A change in one part of the social world affects all others, sometimes in ways that are mutually supportive and sometimes in ways that create intense conflict.

Although the topics are familiar, the textbook is organized around levels of analysis, explained through the social world model. This perspective leads naturally to an integrated discussion in which all topics fit clearly into an overall view, a comparative approach, and discussions of diversity and inequality. It hangs together!

As seen in the Table of Contents, the book includes 14 chapters, plus additional online materials, written to fit into a semester or quarter system. It allows instructors to use the chapters in order or to alter the order because each chapter is tied into others through the social world model. We strongly recommend that Chapter 1 be used early in the course because it introduces the integrating model and explains the theme. Also, if any institutions chapters are used, the four-page section opener on "Institutions" may be useful to include as well. Otherwise, the book has been designed for flexible use. Instructors may also want to supplement the core book with other materials, such as those suggested on the Instructor Teaching Site. Each chapter, for example, has exercises that help students grasp the practical, public implications of sociology. While covering key topics in introductory sociology, the cost and size of a condensed book allows for flexibility. Indeed, for a colorful introductory-level text, the cost of this book is remarkably low—roughly half the cost of most other very popular introductory texts.

A UNIQUE PROGRAM SUPPORTING TEACHING OF SOCIOLOGY

There is one more way in which *Our Social World* has been unique among introductory sociology textbooks. In 2007, the original authors (Ballantine and Roberts) teamed with SAGE to start a new program to benefit the entire discipline. Using royalties from *Our Social World*, we helped establish a new award program called the SAGE Teaching Innovations & Professional Development Award, designed to prepare a new generation of scholars within the teaching movement in sociology. People in their early career stages (graduate students, assistant professors, and newer PhDs) can be reimbursed $600 each for expenses entailed while attending the daylong American Sociological Association (ASA) Section on Teaching and Learning's preconference workshop. The workshop is the day before ASA meetings. In 2007, 13 young scholars—graduate students

or untenured faculty members—received this award and benefited from an extraordinary workshop on learning and teaching. Since then, more than two dozen other SAGE authors have supported this program from textbook royalties, and a total of 255 young scholars have been beneficiaries of more than $136,500 awarded as of 2017. We are pleased to have had a hand in initiating and continuing to support this program.

We hope you find this book engaging. If you have questions or comments, please contact us.

Jeanne H. Ballantine

Jeanne H. Ballantine
Wright State University
jeanne.ballantine@gmail.com

Keith A. Roberts

Keith A. Roberts
Hanover College
robertsk@hanover.edu

Kathleen Odell Korgen

Kathleen Odell Korgen
William Paterson University
korgenk@wpunj.edu

Acknowledgments

Knowledge is improved through careful, systematic, and constructive criticism. The same is true of all writing. This book is of much greater quality because we had such outstanding critics and reviewers. We, therefore, wish to honor and recognize the outstanding scholars who served in this capacity. These scholars are listed on this page and the next. We also had people who served in a variety of other capacities. Authors of short sections within the book include Kevin Bales, Thomas Horejes, Kristin Kenneavy, Elise Roberts, Brent Staples, Nancy Diggs, Ellis Jones, Anna Misleh, Jack Levin, and Lindsay Owens.

All three of us are experienced authors, and we have worked with some excellent people at other publishing houses. However, the team at SAGE Publishing is truly exceptional in support, thoroughness, and commitment to this project. Our planning meetings have been fun, intelligent, and provocative. Jeff Lasser has provided wonderful support as the SAGE Sociology Editor. Folks who have meant so much to the quality production of this book include Sheri Gilbert, permissions editor; Kara Kindstrom, senior marketing manager; and Jared Leighton, our wonderful copy editor. We have become friends and colleagues with the staff at SAGE Publishing. They are all greatly appreciated.

Thanks to the following reviewers:

Sabrina Alimahomed, *University of California, Riverside*

George Ansalone, *Florida Gulf Coast University*

Richard Ball, *Ferris State University*

Fred Beck, *Illinois State University*

Charles Bittner, *Texas Woman's University*

Stacye Blount, *Fayetteville State College*

David L. Briscoe, *University of Arkansas at Little Rock*

W. Trevor Brooks, *Austin Peay State University*

James A. Crone, *Hanover College*

April Cubbage, *Saddleback College*

David R. Dickens, *University of Nevada, Las Vegas*

Jamie M. Dolan, *Carroll College (MT)*

Amy Donley, *University of Central Florida*

Kevin Doran, *Indiana University, Bloomington*

Obi N. I. Ebbe, *The University of Tennessee at Chattanooga*

Maureen Ellis-Davis, *Bergen Community College*

Jo Ry-Anne Feller, *Palm Beach State College*

Stephanie Funk, *Hanover College*

Lance Erickson, *Brigham Young University*

Loyd R. Ganey Jr., *Western International University*

Skylar C. Gremillion, *Louisiana State University*

Mary Grigsby, *University of Missouri–Columbia*

Chris Hausmann, *University of Notre Dame*

Todd A. Hechtman, *Eastern Washington University*

Robert B. Jenkot, *Coastal Carolina University*

Keith Kerr, *Blinn College*

Lisa L. Kuecker, *Western New Mexico University*

Elaine Leeder, *Sonoma State University*

Jason J. Leiker, *Utah State University*

Stephen Lilley, *Sacred Heart University*

David A. Lopez, *California State University, Northridge*

Crystal V. Lupo, *Auburn University*

Akbar Madhi, *Ohio Wesleyan University*

Gerardo Marti, *Davidson College*

Laura McCloud, *The Ohio State University*

Meeta Mehrotra, *Roanoke College*

Melinda S. Miceli, *University of Hartford*

Leah A. Moore, *University of Central Florida*

Nirmal Niroula, *Coastal Caroline University*

Katy Pinto, *California State University at Dominguez Hills*

R. Marlene Powell, *University of North Carolina at Pembroke*

Suzanne Prescott, *Central New Mexico Community College*

Antonia Randolph, *University of Delaware*

Olga Rowe, *Oregon State University*

Paulina Ruf, *Lenoir-Rhyne University*

Sarah Samblanet, *Kent State University*

Martha L. Shockey-Eckles, *Saint Louis University*

Toni Sims, *University of Louisiana–Lafayette*

Terry L. Smith, *Harding University*

Frank S. Stanford, *Blinn College*

Tracy Steele, *Wright State University*

Rachel Stehle, *Cuyahoga Community College*

Amy Stone, *Trinity University*

John Stone, *Boston University*

Hephzibah V. Strmic-Pawl, *Manhattanville College*

Stephen Sweet, *Ithaca College*

Debra K. Taylor, *Johnson County Community College*

Ruth Thompson-Miller, *Texas A&M University*

Tim Ulrich, *Seattle Pacific University*

Thomas L. Van Valey, *Western Michigan University*

Connie Veldink, *Everett Community College*

Dennis Veleber, *Montana State University Northern*

Kristie Vise, *Northern Kentucky University*

Chaim I. Waxman, *Rutgers University*

Lisa Munson Weinberg, *Florida State University*

Debra Welkley, *California State University at Sacramento*

Matthew West, *Bevill State Community College*

Debra Wetcher-Hendricks, *Moravian College*

Deborah J. White, *Collin County Community College*

Jake B. Wilson, *University of California, Riverside*

Laurie Winder, *Western Washington University*

Robert Wonser, *College of the Canyons*

Luis Zanartu, *Sacramento City College*

John Zipp, *University of Akron*

PART **I**

Understanding Our Social World

The Scientific Study of Society

How can an individual make a difference in the world or in a community? How does your family influence your chances of gaining a college degree and a high-paying job? If you were born into a poor family, what are your chances of becoming wealthy? How does your level of education impact your likelihood of marrying—and staying married? How does the wealth of your country affect your opportunities? How can sociology help you understand your social world and be an effective member of society?

Those are some of the questions you will be able to answer as you develop a deeper understanding of our social world. Sociology is valuable because it gives us new perspectives on our personal and professional lives and because sociological insights and skills can help all of us make the world a better place. Sociology can change your life—and help you change the world.

By the time you finish reading the first two chapters, you should have an initial understanding of what sociology is, what you can gain from sociology, the roots of the sociological perspective, and how sociologists carry out research. We invite you to view our social world through a sociological lens and learn how you can use sociology to make a difference in your life, your community, and the world.

1 Sociology

A Unique Way to View the World

Sociology involves a transformation in the way one sees the world—learning to recognize the complex connections among our intimate personal lives, large organizations, and national and global systems.

MICRO

ME (MY FAMILY AND CLOSE FRIENDS)

LOCAL ORGANIZATIONS AND COMMUNITY
My school, place of worship, hangouts

MESO

NATIONAL ORGANIZATIONS, INSTITUTIONS, AND ETHNIC SUBCULTURES
My political party, ethnic affiliation

MACRO

SOCIETY
Type of national government and economic system

GLOBAL COMMUNITY
United Nations, World Bank, Doctors Without Borders, multinational corporations

This model illustrates a core idea carried throughout the book—how your own life is shaped by your family, community, society, and world and how you influence them in return. Understanding this model can help you to better understand your social world and to make a positive impact on it.

WHAT YOU WILL LEARN IN THIS CHAPTER

This chapter will help you do the following:

1.1   Explain the sociological perspective.

1.2   Describe why sociology can be useful for us.

1.3   Show how the social world model works, with examples.

THINK ABOUT IT

Micro: Local communities	How can sociology help me understand my own life in the context of my social world?
Meso: National institutions, complex organizations, and ethnic groups	How do sociologists help us understand and even improve our lives in school, work, and health care organizations?
Macro: National and global systems	How might national and global events affect my life?

The womb is apparently the setting for some great body work. It may win the prize for the strangest place to get a back massage, but, according to a recent scientific article, by the fourth month of gestation, twin fetuses begin reaching for their "womb-mates," and by 18 weeks, they spend more time touching their siblings than themselves or the walls of the uterus (Weaver 2010). Fetuses that have single-womb occupancy tend to touch the walls of the uterus a good deal to make contact with the mother. Nearly 30% of the movements of twins is directed toward their companions. Movements such as stroking the back or the head are more sustained and more precise than movements toward themselves—touching their own mouths or other facial features. As one team of scholars put it, we are "wired to be social" (Castiello et al. 2010). In short, humans are innately social creatures.

The social world is not merely something that exists outside us. As the story of the twins illustrates, the social world is also something we carry inside. We are part of it,

Within hours of their birth in October 2010, Jackson and Audrey became highly fussy if the nurses tried to put them in separate bassinets. Shortly after birth, they were both put in a warmer, and Jackson cried until he found Audrey, proceeding to intertwine his arms and legs with hers. Twins, like all humans, are hardwired to be social and in relationships with others.

we reflect on it, and we are influenced by it, even when we are alone. The patterns of the social world engulf us in ways both subtle and obvious, with profound implications for how we create order and meaning in our lives. We need others—and that is where sociology enters.

Sometimes, it takes a dramatic and shocking event for us to realize just how deeply embedded we are in our relationships in the social world that we take for granted. "It couldn't happen in the United States," read typical world newspaper accounts. "This is something you see in the Middle East, Central Africa, and other war-torn areas. . . . It's hard to imagine this happening in the economic center of the United States." Yet on September 11, 2001, shortly after 9 a.m., a commercial airliner crashed into New York City's World Trade Center, followed a short while later by another pummeling into the paired tower. This mighty symbol of financial wealth collapsed. After the dust settled and the rescue crews finished their gruesome work, nearly 3,000 people were dead and many others injured. The world as we knew it changed forever that day. This event taught U.S. citizens how integrally connected they are with the international community.

Such terrorist acts horrify people because they are unpredictable and unexpected in a normally predictable world. They violate the rules that support our connections to one another. They also bring attention to the discontent and disconnectedness that lie under the surface in many societies—discontent that can come to the surface and express itself in hateful violence. Such discontent and hostility are likely to continue until the root causes are addressed.

Terrorist acts represent a rejection of the modern civil society we know. The terrorists themselves see their acts as justifiable, as a way they can strike out against injustices and threats to their way of life. Few outside the terrorists' inner circle understand their thinking and behavior. The events of 9/11 forced U.S. citizens to realize that although they may see a great diversity among themselves, people in other parts of the world view U.S. citizens as all the same;

they are despised by some for what they represent: consumerism, individualism, freedom of religion, and tolerance of other perspectives. The United States is a world power, yet its values challenge and threaten the views of many people around the world. For many U.S. citizens, a sense of loyalty to the nation was deeply stirred by the events of 9/11. Patriotism abounded. The nation's people became more connected to one another and to their identity as U.S. citizens as a reaction to an act against the United States.

A similar sense of patriotism and connectedness arose immediately after the bombing at the Boston Marathon in 2013. First responders and marathon runners pierced with shrapnel were held up as heroes and symbols of U.S. pride and perseverance in the face of terrorist attacks. As Émile Durkheim, one of the founders of sociology, first pointed out, acts that break normal rules of behavior, as terrorism does, can unite the rule-following members of society (Durkheim [1895] 1982).

Most of the time, we live with social patterns that we take for granted as routine, ordinary, and expected. These social patterns help us to understand what is happening and to know what to expect. Unlike our innate drives, social expectations come from those around us and guide (or constrain) our behaviors and thoughts. Without shared expectations among humans about proper patterns of behavior, life would be chaotic. Our social interactions require some basic rules, and these rules create routine and normalcy in everyday interaction. It would be strange if someone broke the expected patterns. For the people in and around the World Trade Center on 9/11 and Boston on April 15, 2013, the social rules governing everyday life were brutally violated.

This chapter examines the social ties that make up our social world, as well as sociology's focus on those connections. You will learn what sociology is, what sociologists do, how sociology can be used to improve your life and society, and how the social world model helps us understand how society works.

WHAT IS SOCIOLOGY?

Sociology *is the scientific study of social life, social change, and social causes and consequences of human behavior.* Sociologists examine how society both shapes and is shaped by individuals, small groups of people, organizations, national societies, and global social networks.

The terrorist bombing of the 2013 Boston Marathon inspired residents in the Boston area and marathon runners to stand strong in the face of terrorism. The 2014 Boston Marathon attracted even more participants and spectators.

For you, this means learning how what you do affects other people and groups—and how they affect your life.

Unlike the discipline of psychology, which focuses on the attributes, motivations, and behaviors of individuals, sociology focuses on group patterns. Whereas a psychologist might try to explain behavior by examining the personality traits of individuals, a sociologist would examine the positions or tasks of different people within the group and how these positions influence what individuals think and do. Sociologists seek to analyze and explain why people interact with others and belong to groups, how groups like the family or you and your friends work together, why some groups have more power than other groups, how decisions are made, and how groups deal with conflict and change. Sociologists also examine the causes of social problems, such as child abuse, crime, poverty, and war, and ways they can be addressed.

Two-person interactions—*dyads*—are the smallest units studied by sociologists. Examples of dyads include roommates discussing their classes, a professor and student going over an assignment, a husband and wife negotiating their budget, and two children playing. Next in size are small groups consisting of three or more interacting people who know each other—a family, a neighborhood or peer group, a classroom, a work group, or a street gang. Then come increasingly larger groups—organizations such as sports or scouting clubs, neighborhood associations, and local religious congregations. Among the largest groups contained within nations are ethnic groups and national organizations or institutions, such as the auto industry, the Republican and Democratic national political parties, and national religious organizations, like the Southern Baptists. Nations themselves are still larger and can sometimes involve hundreds of millions of people. In the past several decades, social scientists have also pointed to globalization, the process by which the entire world is becoming a single interdependent entity. Of particular interest to sociologists is how these various groups are organized, how they function, why they can come into conflict, and how they influence one another.

Thinking Sociologically

Identify several dyads, small groups, and large organizations to which you belong. Did you choose to belong, or were you born into membership in these groups? How does each group influence who you are and the decisions you make? How do you influence each of the groups?

Ideas Underlying Sociology

The idea that one action can cause another is a core idea in all science. Sociologists also share several ideas that they take for granted about the social world. These ideas about humans and social life are supported by considerable evidence, and they are no longer matters of debate or controversy. They are considered to be true. Understanding these core assumptions helps us see how sociologists approach the study of people in groups.

People are social by nature. This means that humans seek contact with other humans, interact with one another, and influence and are influenced by the behaviors of others. Furthermore, humans need groups to survive. Although a few individuals may become socially isolated as adults, they could not have reached adulthood without sustained interactions with others. The central point here is that we become who we are largely because other people and groups constantly influence us.

People live much of their lives belonging to social groups. It is in social groups that we interact with family, friends, and work groups; learn to share goals and to cooperate with others in our groups; develop identities that are influenced by our group affiliations; obtain power over others—or are relatively powerless; and have conflicts with others over resources we all want. Our individual beliefs and behaviors, our experiences, our observations, and the problems we face are derived from connections to our social groups.

© iStockphoto.com/Jane

Here, children experience ordered interaction in the competitive environment of a football game. What values, skills, attitudes, and assumptions about life and social interaction do you think these young boys are learning?

Interaction between the individual and the group is a two-way process in which each influences the other. In our family or on a sports team, we can influence the shape and direction of our group, just as the group provides the rules and decides the expected behaviors for individuals.

Recurrent social patterns, ordered behavior, shared expectations, and common understandings among people characterize groups. Consider the earlier examples of the chaos created by 9/11 and the Boston Marathon bombing. These events were so troubling because they were unexpected and out of the normal range of expectations. Normally, a degree of continuity and recurrent behavior is present in human interactions, whether in small groups, large organizations, or society.

The processes of conflict and change are natural and inevitable features of groups and societies. No group can remain unchanged and hope to perpetuate itself. To survive, groups must adapt to changes in the social and physical environment, yet rapid change often comes at a price. It can lead to conflict within a society—between traditional and new ideas and between groups that have vested interests in particular ways of doing things. Rapid change can give rise to protest activities; changing in a controversial direction or failing to change fast enough can spark conflict, including revolution. The Arab Spring demonstrations illustrate the desire for rapid change from long-standing dictatorships, springing from citizens' discontent with corrupt or authoritarian rule. The problem is finding acceptable replacement governments to take over what has been overthrown.

The previous ideas underlying sociology will be relevant in each of the topics we discuss. As you read this book, keep in mind these basic ideas that form the foundation of sociological analysis: People are social; they live and carry out activities largely in groups; interaction influences both individual and group behavior; people share common behavior patterns and expectations; and processes such as change and conflict are always present. Thus, in several important ways, sociological understandings provide new lenses for looking at our social world.

Sociological Findings and Commonsense Beliefs

Through research, sociologists have shown that many commonly held beliefs are not actually true, and some "commonsense" ideas have been discredited by sociological research. Here are three examples.

Belief: Most of the differences in the behaviors of women and men are based on "human nature"; men and women are plainly very different from each other. Research shows that biological factors certainly play a part in the behaviors of men and women, but the culture (beliefs, values, rules, and way of life) that people learn as they grow up determines who does what and how biological tendencies are played out. A unique example illustrates this: In the nomadic Wodaabe tribe in Africa, women do most of the heavy work, whereas men adorn themselves with makeup, sip tea, and gossip (Cultural Survival 2010; Loftsdottir 2004). Each year, the group holds a festival where men adorn makeup and fancy hairstyles and show their white teeth and the whites of their eyes to attract a marriage partner. Such dramatic variations in the behavior of men and women around the world are so great that it is impossible to attribute behavior solely to biology or human nature alone; learned behavior patterns enter in.

Belief: Racial groupings are based on biological differences among people. Actually, racial categorizations are socially constructed (created by members of society) and vary among societies and over time within societies. A person can be seen as one race in Brazil and another in the United States. Even within the United States, racial categories have changed many times. All one has to do is look at old

© Getty Images/Oliver Strewe

In the early 20th century, immigrants to the United States who were of Irish and Italian ancestry were not considered "White" in Virginia and several other states. In some cases where parochial schools were not options, Irish and Italian children were forced to go to racially segregated public schools with Black students.

U.S. Census records and see how racial categories change over time—even within the same nation!

Belief: Most marriages in the United States do not last. The well-known divorce rate figure of 50% is misleading. To get an accurate rate, sociologist Paul Amato looked at four ways of calculating the rate: The *crude divorce rate*, or the *percentage ever divorced*, is currently 22% for women and 21% for men. The *refined divorce rate*, or the annual number of divorces per 1,000 married women, now stands at 1.9%. The *cohort measure rate* gives us the high number of 40% to 50%, but it only represents a particular time and group of people (Amato 2011). Those who marry at age 18 or younger have less education than the average person, low levels of income, and the highest divorce rates (Kennedy and Ruggles 2014). Those who are middle class or higher tend to have more stable marriages (Pew Research Center 2010; Stanton 2015).

As these examples illustrate, the discipline of sociology provides a method to assess the accuracy of our common-sense assumptions about the social world. To improve the lives of individuals in our communities and in societies around the world, decision makers must have accurate information. Sociological research can be the basis for more rational and just social policies—policies that better meet the needs of all groups in the social world. The sociological imagination, discussed next, helps us gain an understanding of social problems.

The Sociological Imagination

Events in our social world affect our individual lives. If we are unemployed or lack funds for a college education, we may say this is a personal problem. Yet broader social issues are often at the root of our situation. The sociological imagination holds that we can best understand our personal experiences and problems by examining their broader social context—by looking at the big picture.

Many individual problems (or private troubles) are rooted in social or public issues (what is happening in the social world outside one's personal control). Distinguished sociologist C. Wright Mills called *the ability to understand this complex interactive relationship between individual experiences and public issues* the **sociological imagination**. For Mills, many personal experiences can and should be interpreted in the context of large-scale forces in the wider society (C. Mills 1959).

Consider, for example, someone you know who has been laid off from a job. This personal trauma is a common

situation during a recession. Unemployed persons often experience feelings of inadequacy or lack of self-worth because of the job loss. Their unemployment, though, may be due to larger forces, such as mechanization, unsound banking practices, corporate downsizing, or a corporation taking operations to another country, where labor costs are cheaper and where there are fewer environmental regulations on companies. People may blame themselves or each other for personal troubles, such as unemployment or marital problems, believing that they did not try hard enough. Often, they do not see the connection between their private lives and larger economic and social forces beyond their control. They fail to recognize the public issues that create private troubles.

If you are having trouble paying for college, that may feel like a very personal trouble. High tuition rates, though, relate to a dramatic decline in governmental support for public higher education and financial aid for students. The rising cost of a college education is a serious public issue that our society needs to address. Individuals, alone, cannot reduce the high price of college.

As you learn about sociology, you will begin to notice how social forces shape individual lives and how this knowledge helps us understand aspects of everyday life we take for granted. In this book, we investigate how group life influences our behaviors and interactions and why some individuals follow the rules of society, and others do not. You will learn to view the social world and your place in it from a sociological perspective as you develop your *sociological imagination*. Connecting events from the global and national levels to the personal and intimate level of our own lives is the core organizing theme of this book.

● Thinking Sociologically

How has divorce, poverty, or war caused personal troubles for someone you know? Give examples of why it is inadequate to explain these personal troubles by examining only the personal characteristics of those affected.

Questions Sociologists Ask—and Don't Ask

Perhaps you have had late-night discussions with your friends about the meaning of life, the existence of God, the ethical implications of genetically modified food, or the morality of abortion. These are philosophical issues that sociologists, like other scientists, cannot answer through scientific research. What sociologists *do* ask are questions about people in social groups and organizations—questions that can be studied scientifically. Sociologists may research how people feel about such issues (the percentage of people who want genetically modified food to be labeled, for example), but sociologists do not say what are right and wrong answers to such value-driven opinions. They are more interested in how people's beliefs influence their behavior. They focus on issues that can be studied objectively and scientifically—looking for causes or consequences.

Sociologists might ask, *Who gets an abortion, why do they do so, and how does the society, as a whole, view abortion?* These are matters of fact that a social scientist can explore. However, sociologists avoid making ethical judgments about whether abortion is sometimes acceptable or always wrong. In their private lives, sociologists and other scientists may have opinions on controversial philosophical issues, but these should not enter into their scientific work.

Likewise, sociologists might ask, *What are the circumstances around individuals becoming drunk and acting drunken?* This question is often tied more to the particular social environment than to the availability of alcohol. Note that a person might become very intoxicated at a fraternity party but not at a family member's wedding reception where alcohol is served. The expectations for behavior vary in each setting. The researcher does not make judgments about whether use of alcohol is good or bad or right or wrong and avoids—as much as possible—opinions regarding responsibility or irresponsibility. The sociologist does, however, observe variations in the use of alcohol in different social situations and the resulting behaviors. The focus of sociology is on facts and what causes behaviors and their results.

Thinking Sociologically

Consider the information you have just read. What are some questions sociologists might ask about drinking and drunkenness? What are some questions sociologists would not ask about these topics, at least while in their role as researchers?

The Social Sciences: A Comparison

Not so long ago, our views of people and social relationships were based on stereotypes, intuition, superstitions, supernatural explanations, and traditions passed on from one generation to the next. Natural scientists (e.g., chemists, astronomers, biologists, and oceanographers) first used the scientific method, a model later adopted by social scientists. Social scientists, including anthropologists, psychologists, economists, cultural geographers, historians, and political scientists, as well as sociologists, apply the scientific method to study social relationships, to correct misleading and harmful misconceptions about human behavior, and to guide policy decisions. Consider the following examples of specific social science studies.

Some anthropological studies focus on garbage. They examine what people discard to understand what kind of lives they lead (Bond 2010). *Anthropology* is the study of humanity in its broadest context. It is closely related to sociology, and the two areas have common historical roots and sometimes overlapping methodologies and subject matter. However, anthropologists have four major subfields within anthropology: physical anthropology (which is related to biology), archaeology, linguistics, and cultural anthropology (sometimes called *ethnology*). This last field has the most in common with sociology. Cultural anthropologists study the culture, or way of life, of a society.

Binge drinking, losing consciousness, vomiting, or engaging in sexual acts while drunk may be sources of storytelling at a college party but can be offensive at a wedding reception.

iStock/shironosov

Getty Images/Caiaimage/Chris Ryan

iStock/zeljkosantrac

Anthropologists can learn about a society by studying what it throws away. What do you think they would learn about you from your garbage?

A psychologist may wire research subjects to a machine that measures their physiological reaction to a violent film clip and then ask them questions about what they were feeling. *Psychology* is the study of individual behavior and mental processes (e.g., sensation, perception, memory, and thought processes). It differs from sociology in that it focuses on individuals rather than on groups, institutions, and societies. Although there are different branches of psychology, most psychologists are concerned with individual motivations, personality attributes, attitudes, perceptions, abnormal behavior, mental disorders, and the stages of normal human development.

A political scientist studies opinion poll results to predict who will win the next election, how various groups of people are likely to vote, or how elected officials will vote on proposed legislation. *Political science* is concerned with government systems and power—how they work, how they are organized, the forms of government, relations among governments, who holds power and how they obtain it, how power is used, and who is politically active. Political science overlaps with sociology, particularly in the study of political theory and the nature and uses of power.

Many economists study the banking system and market trends to try to predict trends and understand the global economy. *Economists* analyze economic conditions and explore how people organize, produce, and distribute material goods. They are interested in supply and demand, inflation and taxes, prices and manufacturing output, labor organization, employment levels, and comparisons between postindustrial, industrial, and nonindustrial nations.

What these social sciences—sociology, anthropology, psychology, political science, and economics—have in common is that they study aspects of human behavior and social life. Social sciences share many common topics, methods, concepts, research findings, and theories, but each has a different focus or perspective on the social world. Each of these social sciences relates to topics studied by sociologists, but sociologists focus on human interaction, groups, and social structure, providing the broadest overview of the social world.

● Thinking Sociologically

Consider the issue of unemployment in the United States. What is one question in each discipline that an anthropologist, psychologist, political scientist, economist, and sociologist might ask about this social issue?

WHY DOES SOCIOLOGY MATTER?

Sociology is important because it helps us understand our relationships with other people and inform social policy decisions. We can also pursue a career in sociology or use skills developed through sociology in a wide range of career fields.

Why Study Sociology?

The sociological perspective helps us to be more effective as we carry out our roles as life partners, workers, friends, family members, and citizens. For example, an employee who has studied sociology may better understand how to work with groups and how the structure of the workplace affects individual behavior, how to approach problem solving, and how to collect and analyze data. Likewise, a schoolteacher trained in sociology may have a better understanding of classroom management, student motivation, the causes of poor student learning that have roots outside the school, and why students drop out.

A sociological perspective allows us to look beneath the surface of society and notice social patterns that others tend to overlook. When you view our social world with a sociological perspective, you

1. become more self-aware by understanding your social surroundings, which can lead to opportunities to improve your life;
2. have a more complete understanding of social situations by looking beyond individual explanations to include group analyses of behavior;

3. understand and evaluate problems more clearly, viewing the world systematically and objectively rather than only in emotional or personal terms;

4. gain an understanding of the many diverse cultural perspectives and how cultural differences are related to behavioral patterns;

5. assess the impact of social policies;

6. understand the complexities of social life and how to study them scientifically;

7. gain useful skills in interpersonal relations, critical thinking, data collection and analysis, problem solving, and decision making; and

8. learn how to change your local environment and the larger society.

What Do Sociologists Do?

Graduates with a bachelor's degree in sociology who seek employment immediately after college are most likely to find their first jobs in social services, administrative assistantships, sales and marketing, or management-related positions. The kinds of employment of college graduates with a sociology major are listed in Figure 1.1. With graduate degrees—a master's or a doctoral degree—sociologists usually become college teachers, researchers, clinicians, or consultants. Some work for governments while others work for businesses or public-service nonprofit organizations.

FIGURE 1.1 Occupational Categories for Sociology Graduates' First Jobs

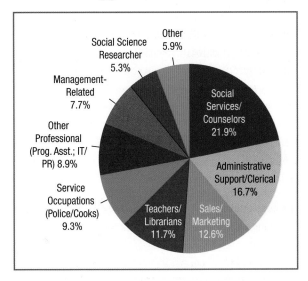

Source: Based on "21st Century Careers With an Undergraduate Degree in Sociology," American Sociological Association, 2009.

Many sociologists work outside of academia, using their knowledge and research skills to address the needs of businesses, nonprofit organizations, and government. For example, they often work in human resources departments and as consultants for businesses. In government jobs, they provide data, such as population projections for education and health care planning. In social service agencies, they help provide services to those in need, and in health agencies, they may be concerned with outreach to immigrant communities. Both sociologists who work in universities and those who work for business or government can use sociological tools to improve society. You will find examples of sociologists in the "Sociologists in Action" boxes throughout the book. In addition, at the end of some chapters, you will find a discussion of policy related to that chapter topic.

Thinking Sociologically

From what you have read so far, how might sociological tools (e.g., social interaction skills and knowledge of how groups work) be useful to you in your anticipated major and career or current job?

What Do Employers Want?

Ask employers what they want in a new hire, and the focus is likely to be on writing, speaking, and analytical skills—especially when the new employee will be faced with complex problems. Other desired skills in demand include the ability to cope with change, work effectively in diverse teams, and gather and interpret quantitative information (Miller 2015). Indeed, Deming reports that having a combination of social skills and math skills is the best predictor of landing a job that is unlikely to be replaced by technological automation and tends to do better than most other areas in pay (Deming 2015). The left column in Table 1.1 indicates what employers want from college graduates; the right column indicates the skills and competencies that are part of most sociological training. Compare the two, noting the high levels of overlap.

We now have a general idea of what sociology is and what sociologists do. It should be apparent that sociology is a broad field of interest; sociologists study all aspects of human social behavior. The next section of this chapter shows how the parts of the social world that sociologists study relate to each other, and it outlines the model you will follow as you continue to learn about sociology.

Table 1.1 What Employers Want and What Sociology Majors Can Deliver

Employers Who Want Colleges to "Place More Emphasis" on Essential Learning Outcomes		Traits and Knowledge That Are Developed in Most Sociological Training
Knowledge of Human Culture	**% Seeking**	**Skills and Competencies**
1. Global issues	72	• Knowledge of global issues • Sensitivity to diversity and differences in cultural values and traditions
2. The role of the United States in the world	60	• Sociological perspective on the United States and the world
3. Cultural values and traditions— U.S. and global	53	• Understanding diversity • Working with others (ability to work toward a common goal)
Intellectual and Practical Skills	**% Seeking**	
4. Teamwork skills in diverse groups	76	• Effective leadership skills (ability to take charge and make decisions) • Interpersonal skills (working with diverse coworkers)
5. Critical thinking and analytic reasoning	73	• Analysis and research skills • Organizing thoughts and information • Planning effectively (ability to design, plan, organize, and implement projects and to be self-motivated)
6. Written and oral communication	73	• Communication skills (listening, verbal and written communication) • Working with peers • Effective interaction in group situations
7. Information literacy	70	• Knowledge of how to find information one needs— online or in a library
8. Creativity and innovation	70	• Flexibility, adaptability, and multitasking (ability to set priorities, manage multiple tasks, adapt to changing situations, and handle pressure) • Creative ways to deal with problems
9. Complex problem solving	64	• Ability to conceptualize and solve problems • Ability to be creative (working toward meeting the organization's goals)
10. Quantitative reasoning	60	• Computer and technical literacy (basic understanding of computer hardware and software programs) • Statistical analysis
Personal and Social Responsibility	**% Seeking**	
11. Intercultural competence (teamwork in diverse groups)	76	• Personal values (honesty, flexibility, work ethic, dependability, loyalty, positive attitude, professionalism, self-confidence, willingness to learn) • Working with others; ability to work toward a common goal
12. Intercultural knowledge (global issues)	72	• Knowledge of global issues

Source: American Sociological Association (2009); Hansen and Hansen (2003); WorldWideLearn (2007). See also Association of American Colleges and Universities and Hart Research Associates (2013).

Thinking Sociologically

Imagine that you are a mayor, legislator, police chief, or another government official. You make decisions based on information gathered by social science research rather than on your own intuition or assumptions. What are some advantages to this decision-making method?

THE SOCIAL WORLD MODEL

Think about the different groups you depend on and interact with on a daily basis. You wake up to greet members of your family or your roommate. You go to a larger group—a class—that exists within an even larger organization—the college or university. Understanding sociology and the approach of this book requires a grasp of **levels of analysis**—that is, *social groups from the smallest to the largest.* It may be relatively easy to picture small groups, such as a family, a group of friends, a sports team, or a sorority or fraternity. It is more difficult to visualize large groups, such as corporations—The Gap, Abercrombie & Fitch, Eddie Bauer, General Motors Company, or Starbucks—or organizations such as local or state governments. The largest groups include nations or international organizations, such as the sprawling networks of the United Nations or the World Trade Organization. Groups of various sizes shape our lives. Sociological analysis involves an understanding of these groups that exist at various levels of analysis and the connections among them.

The **social world model** helps us picture *the levels of analysis in our social surroundings as an interconnected series of small groups, organizations, institutions, and societies.* Sometimes, these groups are connected by mutual support and cooperation, but other times, there are conflicts and power struggles over access to resources. What we are asking you to do here and throughout this book is to develop a sociological imagination—the basic lens used by sociologists. Picture the social world as connected levels of increasingly larger circles. To understand the units or parts of the social world model, look at the model shown here (and at the beginning of each chapter).

We use this social world model throughout the book to illustrate how each topic fits into the big picture: our social world. The social world includes both *social structures* and *social processes.*

Social Structures

Picture the human body, held together by bones and muscles. The organs, or *units*, that make up that body include

All social institutions are interrelated, just as the parts of the body are interdependent: If the skeletal system of the body breaks down, the muscular system and nervous system are not going to be able to get the body to do what it needs to do.

the brain, heart, lungs, and kidneys. In a similar manner, social units are *interconnected parts of the social world, ranging from small groups to societies.* These social units include dyads (two people); small groups, like the members of a family; community organizations, including schools and churches; large-scale organizations, such as political parties or state and national governments; and global societies, such as the United Nations.

All of these social units connect to make up the **social structure**—*the stable patterns of interactions, statuses (positions), roles (responsibilities), and organizations that provide stability for the society and bring order to individuals' lives.* Think about these parallels between the structure that holds together the human body and the structure that holds together societies and their units.

Sometimes, however, the units within the social structure are in conflict. For example, a religion that teaches that some forms of birth control are wrong may conflict with the health care system regarding how to provide care to women. This issue has been in the U.S. news, as many religious organizations and religious business owners have fought against the requirements of the 2010 Affordable Care Act in the United States that employers provide birth control to those who wish to receive it.

Social institutions are *organized, patterned, and enduring sets of social structures that provide guidelines for behavior and help each society meet its basic survival needs*. Think about the fact that all societies have some form of family, education, religion, politics, and economics; in more complex societies, there are also essential structures that provide science, media, health care, and a military. These are the institutions that provide the rules, roles, and relationships to meet human needs and guide human behavior. They are the units through which organized social activities take place, and they provide the setting for activities essential to human and societal survival. For example, we cannot survive without an economic institution to provide guidelines and a structure for meeting our basic needs of food, shelter, and clothing. Likewise,

society would not function without political institutions to govern and protect its members. Most social units fall under one of these institutions.

Like the human body, society and social groups have a structure. Our body's skeleton governs how our limbs are attached to the torso and how they move. Like the system of organs that make up our bodies—heart, lungs, kidneys, and bladder—all social institutions are interrelated. Just as an illness in one organ affects other organs, a dysfunction in one institution affects the other institutions. A heart attack affects the flow of blood to all other parts of the body. Likewise, if many people are unable to afford medical treatment, the society is less healthy, and there are consequences for families, schools, workplaces, and society as a whole.

The national society, one of the largest social units in our model, *includes a population of people, usually living within a specified geographic area, connected by common ideas and subject to a particular political authority*. It also features a social structure with groups and institutions. In addition to having relatively permanent geographic and political boundaries, a national society has one or more languages and a unique way of life. In most cases, national societies involve countries or large regions where the inhabitants share a common identity as members. In certain other instances, such as the contemporary United Kingdom, a single national society may include several groups of people who consider themselves distinct nationalities (Welsh, English, Scottish, and Irish). Such multicultural societies may or may not have peaceful relations.

Thinking Sociologically

How might change in one national institution, such as health care, affect change in other national institutions, such as the family and the economy? Can you think of any human activities that do not fall into one of the institutions just mentioned?

Social Processes

If social structure is similar to the human body's skeletal structure, social processes are similar to what keeps the body alive—a beating heart, the lungs processing oxygen, and the stomach processing nutrients. Social processes *take place through actions of people in institutions and other social units*. The process of socialization teaches individuals how to behave in society. It takes place through actions in families, educational systems, religious organizations, and other social units.

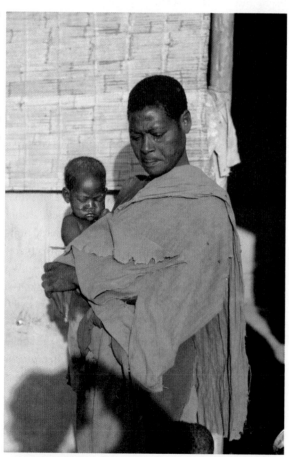

This refugee mother and child from Mozambique represent the smallest social unit, a dyad. In this case, they are trying to survive with help from larger groups, such as the United Nations.

Socialization is essential for the continuation of any society because, through this process, members of society learn the thoughts and actions needed to survive in their society. Another process, conflict, occurs between individuals or groups over money, jobs, and other needed or desired resources. The process of change also occurs continuously in every social unit; change in one unit affects other units of the social world, often in a chain reaction. For instance, change in the quality of health care can affect the workforce; a workforce in poor health can affect the economy; instability in the economy can affect families, as breadwinners lose jobs; and family economic woes can affect religious communities because devastated families cannot afford to give money to churches, mosques, or temples.

Sociologists try to identify, understand, and explain the processes that take place within social units. Picture these processes as overlying and penetrating our whole social world, from small groups to societies. Social units would be lifeless without the action brought about by social processes, just as body parts would be lifeless without the processes of electrical impulses shooting from the brain to each organ or the oxygen transmitted by blood coursing through our arteries to sustain each organ.

The Environment of Our Social World

Surrounding each social unit, whether a small family group or a large corporation, is an environment—*the setting in which the social unit operates, including everything that influences the social unit, such as its physical and organizational surroundings and technological innovations.* Just as each individual has a unique environment, including family, friends, and other social units, each social unit has an environment to which it must adjust. For example, your local church, synagogue, temple, or mosque is surrounded by its unique environment. That religious organization may seem autonomous and independent, but it depends on its national organization for guidelines and support; the local police force to protect the building from vandalism; and the local economy to provide jobs to members so that the members, in turn, can support the organization. If the religious education program is going to train children to understand the scriptures, local schools are needed to teach the children to read. A religious group may also be affected by other religious bodies, competing with one another for potential members from the community. These religious groups may work cooperatively—organizing a summer program

for children or jointly sponsoring a holy day celebration—or they may define one another as evil, each trying to malign or stigmatize the other. Moreover, one local religious group may be composed primarily of professional and businesspeople and another group mostly of laboring people. The religious groups may experience conflict, in part, because they each serve a different socioeconomic constituency. The point is that to understand a social unit or the human body, we must consider the structure and processes within the unit, as well as the interaction with the surrounding environment.

Perfect relationships or complete harmony among the social units is unusual. Social units, be they small groups or large organizations, are often motivated by self-interest and the need for self-preservation, with the result that they compete with other units for resources (time, money, skills, and the energy of members). Therefore, social units within a society are often in conflict. Whether groups are in conflict or they cooperate does not change their interrelatedness; units are interdependent and can be studied using the scientific method.

Studying the Social World: Levels of Analysis

Picture for a moment your sociology class as a social unit in your social world. Students (individuals) make up the class, the class (small group) is offered by the sociology department, the sociology department (a large group, including faculty and students) is part of the college or university, and the university (an organization) is located in a community. It follows the practices approved by the social institution (education) of which it is a part, and education is an institution located within a nation. Practices the university follows are determined by a larger accrediting agency that provides guidelines and oversight for educational institutions. The national society, represented by the national government, is shaped by global events, such as technological and economic competition among nations, natural disasters, global climate change, wars, and terrorist attacks. Such events influence national policies and goals, including policies for the educational system. Thus, global issues and conflicts may shape the content of the curriculum taught in the local classroom, from what is studied to the textbooks used.

As discussed, each of these social units is referred to as a *level of analysis* (from two students in a discussion group to a society or global system; see Table 1.2). These levels are illustrated in the social world model at the beginning of each chapter, and their relation to that chapter's content is shown through examples in the model.

Table 1.2   Levels of Analysis and Education

	Level	Parts of Education
Micro-level analysis	Interpersonal	Sociology class; professor and student interacting; study group cramming for an exam
	Local organizations	University; sociology department
Meso-level analysis	Organizations and institutions	State boards of education; National Education Association
	Ethnic groups within a nation	Islamic madrassas or Jewish yeshiva school systems
Macro-level analysis	Nations	Policy and laws governing education
	Global community	World literacy programs

Micro-Level Analysis. A focus on *individual or small-group interaction in specific situations* is called micro-level analysis. The micro level is important because one-to-one and small-group interaction form the basic foundation of all social groups and organizations to which we belong, from families to corporations to societies. We are members of many groups at the micro level.

To understand micro-level analysis, consider the problem of spousal abuse, most often involving women being abused. Why does a person remain in an abusive relationship, knowing that each year thousands of people are killed by their partners and millions more are severely and repeatedly battered? To answer this question, several possible micro-level explanations can be considered. One view is that the abusive partner has convinced the abused person that she is powerless in the relationship or that she "deserves" the abuse. Therefore, she gives up in despair of ever being able to alter the situation. The abuse is viewed as part of the interaction—of action and reaction—and some partners come to see abuse as what composes normal interaction.

Another explanation for remaining in the abusive relationship is that battering is a familiar part of the person's everyday life. However unpleasant and unnatural this may seem to outsiders, it may be seen by the abused as a normal and acceptable part of intimate relationships, especially if she grew up in an abusive family.

Another possibility is that an abused woman may fear that her children would be harmed or that she would be harshly judged by her family or religious group if she "abandoned" her mate. She may have few resources to make leaving the abusive situation possible. To study each of these possible explanations involves analysis at the micro level because each focuses on interpersonal interaction factors rather than on large, society-wide trends or

forces. Meso-level analysis leads to quite different explanations for abuse.

Meso-Level Analysis. Meso-level analysis involves looking at *intermediate-sized units smaller than the nation but larger than the local community or even the region*. This level includes national institutions (such as the economy of a country, the national educational system, or the political system within a country), nationwide organizations (such as a political party, a soccer league, or a national women's rights organization), and ethnic groups that have an identity as a group (such as Jews, Mexican Americans, or Native Americans in the United States). Organizations, institutions, and ethnic communities are smaller than the nation or global social units, but they are still beyond the everyday personal experience and control of individuals. They are intermediate in the sense of being too large to know everyone in the group, but they are not as large as nation-states. For example, state governments in the United States, provinces in Canada, prefectures in Japan, or cantons in Switzerland are at the meso level and usually more accessible and easier to change than the national bureaucracies of these countries.

In discussing micro-level analysis, we used the example of domestic violence. Recognizing that personal troubles can often be related to public issues, many social scientists look for broader explanations of spousal abuse, such as social conditions at the meso level of society (Straus, Gelles, and Steinmetz 2006). When a pattern of behavior in society occurs with increasing frequency, it cannot be understood solely from the point of view of individual cases or micro-level causes. For instance, sociological findings show that fluctuations in spousal or child abuse at the micro level are related to levels of unemployment in meso-level organizations and macro-level government economic policies.

Frustration resulting in abuse can erupt within families when poor economic conditions make it nearly impossible for people to find a stable and reliable means of supporting themselves and their families. The message here is that economic issues in the society must be addressed in order to decrease domestic violence.

Macro-Level Analysis. Studying the largest social units in the social world, called **macro-level analysis**, involves looking at *entire nations, global forces, and international social trends*. Macro-level analysis is essential to our understanding of how larger societal forces and global events shape our everyday lives. A natural disaster, such as the recent droughts and floods in North America and West Africa and massive hurricanes in Central America and the Caribbean, may change the foods we can serve at our family dinner table because much of what we consume comes from other parts of the world. (Figure 1.2 shows some of the deadliest natural disasters in 2015.) Likewise, a political conflict on the other side of the planet can lead to war, which means that a member of your family may be called to active duty and sent into harm's way more than 7,000 miles from your home. Each member of the family may experience individual stress, have trouble concentrating, and feel ill with worry. The entire globe has become an interdependent social unit. If we are to prosper and thrive

FIGURE 1.2 Natural Disasters Worldwide in 2015

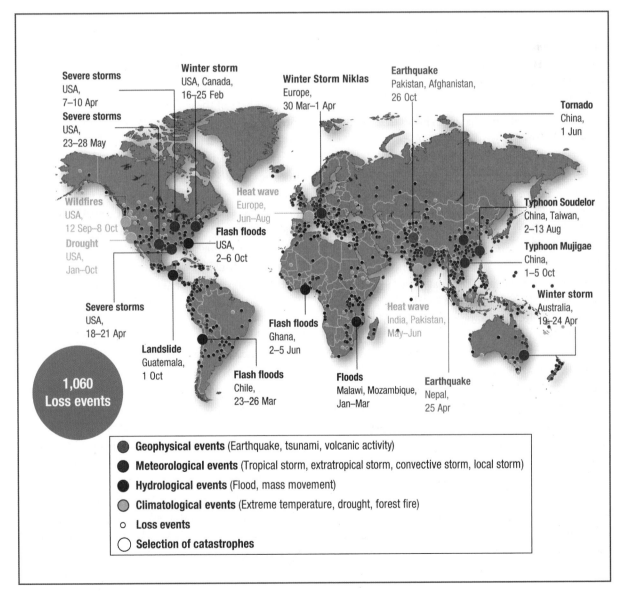

Source: Münchener Rückversicherungs-Gesellschaft (2016).

FIGURE 1.3   The Micro-to-Macro Continuum

| Micro social units | Meso social units | Macro social units |

in the world today, we need to understand connections that go beyond our local communities.

Even patterns such as domestic violence, considered as micro- and meso-level issues earlier, can be examined at the macro level. Violence against women (especially rape) occurs at different rates in different societies, with some having a *culture of rape* (Kristof and WuDunn 2009). Recent gang rapes of a Danish tourist and young teenagers became headline news and shone a spotlight on the culture and lack of law enforcement in India that encourage violence against women (McCoy 2014). The most consistent predictor of violence against women is a macho conception of masculine roles and personality. Societies or subgroups within society that teach males that the finest expression of their masculinity is physical strength and domination tend to have more battered women (Mayeda 2013).

India is far from the only nation with a culture that generates violence against women. South Africa has one of the highest levels of rape in the world, with one in four men having raped a woman and 46% of those more than once (U.S. Department of State 2015). The men tend to show no remorse because the behavior is "accepted" by their segments of society; it is "macho" (Lindow 2009).

Understanding individual human behavior often requires investigation of the larger societal beliefs and values that support that behavior. Worldwide patterns may tell us something about a social problem and offer new lenses for understanding that problem.

The social world model presented in each chapter illustrates the interplay of micro-, meso-, and macro-level forces related to that chapter's content. Figure 1.3 shows how this micro-to-macro model should be seen as a continuum.

Distinctions between each level of analysis are not always sharply delineated. The micro level shades into the meso level, and the lines between the meso level and the macro level are blurry on the continuum. Still, it is clear that in some micro-level social units, you know everyone, or at least every member of the social unit is only two degrees of separation away. In other words, every person in the social unit knows someone whom

you also know. Try the next "Engaging Sociology" to test your understanding of levels of analysis and the sociological imagination.

We all participate in meso-level social units that are smaller than the nation but that can be huge. For example, thousands or even millions of individuals join organizations such as the NRA, MoveOn.org, or the environmental group 350.org. Those involved participate in dialogues online and contribute money to these organizations. People living thousands of miles from one another united financially and in spirit to support candidates in the 2016 U.S. presidential election. We share connections with the members of these organizations, and our lives are interconnected, even if we never meet face to face.

The macro level is even more removed from the individual, but its impact can change our lives. For example, decisions by lawmakers in Washington, DC, can seem distant, but decisions by Congress and the president may determine whether your own family has health care coverage (and of what quality) and whether the United States will lead or stymie global efforts to address climate change. These government leaders will also determine whether interest rates on federal student loans for U.S. students go up.

The Social World Model and This Book

The social world engulfs each of us from the moment of our birth until we die. Throughout our lives, each of us is part of a set of social relationships that provides guidelines for how we interact with others and how we see ourselves. This does not mean that human behavior is strictly determined by our links to the social world. Humans are more than mere puppets whose behavior is programmed by social structure. It does mean, however, that the individual and the larger social world influence each other. We are influenced by and we have influence on our social environment. The social world is a human creation, and we can and do change that which we create. It acts on us, and we act on it. In this sense, social units are constantly emerging and changing in the course of human action and interaction.

ENGAGING SOCIOLOGY

Micro-Meso-Macro

The distinctions between levels of analysis are gray rather than precise. Levels of analysis should be viewed as a continuum—from micro to macro social units. Clear criteria help identify groups at each level. One criterion is size (number of people) of the group. A second is the geographic range of influence:

1. intimate or very close personal relationships (micro);

2. social units in the local community (micro);

3. social units that cover a large geographic region (like a state or commonwealth) and even nationwide groups that—despite size—are still a small portion of the entire nation (meso);

4. the nation itself (macro); and

5. units with global reach (macro).

A third criterion is degree of separation. If you know someone personally, that is one degree of separation. If you do not know the mayor of your town, but you know someone who knows the mayor, that is two degrees of separation. If you have a friend or a relative who knows someone who is a friend or relative of the governor in your state or province, that is three degrees of separation. Some research indicates that every person on the planet is within seven degrees of separation from every other human being. Let us see what these mean for various levels of analysis in our social world

Micro-level groups are small, local-community social units, such as families and school classrooms, within which everyone knows everyone else or knows someone who also knows another member. So the degree of separation is usually not more than two degrees.

Meso-level groups are social units of intermediate size, such as state governments (with limited geographic range), ethnic groups, and religious denominations (with large geographic range but population sizes that make them a minority of the entire nation). Typically, the group is large enough that members have never heard the names of many other members. Many members may have little access to the leaders, yet the group is not so large as to make the leaders seem distant or unapproachable. Almost anyone within the social unit is only three or four degrees of separation apart. Everyone in the unit knows someone who is an acquaintance of yours.

Macro-level groups are large social units, usually quite bureaucratic, that operate at a national or a global level, such as national governments or international organizations. Most members are unlikely to know or have communicated with the leaders personally or know someone who knows the leaders. The "business" of these groups is of international importance and implication. A macro-level system is one in which most of the members are at least five degrees of separation from one another—that is, they know someone who knows someone who knows someone who knows someone who knows the person in question.

* * * * * * *

Engaging With Sociology

1. Micro social units

2. Meso social units

3. Macro social units

(Continued)

(Continued)

Look at the following list of social units below. Identify which level each group is most likely to belong to: (1) micro, (2) meso, or (3) macro. Why did you answer as you did? The previous definitions should help you make your decisions. Again, some are "on the line" because this is a continuum from micro to macro, and some units could legitimately be placed in more than one group. Which ones are especially "on the line"?

___ Your nuclear family

___ The United Nations

___ A local chapter of the Lions Club or the Rotary Club

___ Your high school baseball team

___ India

___ NATO (North Atlantic Treaty Organization)

___ The First Baptist Church in Muncie, Indiana

___ The World Bank

___ A family reunion

___ Google, Inc. (international)

___ The Department of Education for the Commonwealth of Kentucky

___ The show choir in your local high school

___ African Canadians

___ The Dineh (Navajo) people

___ Canada

___ The Republican Party in the United States

___ The World Court

___ A fraternity at your college

___ The International Monetary Fund (IMF)

___ The Ministry of Education for Spain

___ The Roman Catholic Church (with its head-quarters at the Vatican in Rome)

___ Australia

___ The Chi Omega national sorority

___ Boy Scout Troop #187 in Minneapolis, Minnesota

___ Al-Qaeda (an international alliance of terrorist organizations)

___ The provincial government for the Canadian province of Ontario

___ The United States of America

See how your authors rate these at **edge.sagepub.com/ballantinecondensed5e**.

The difficulty for most of us is that we are so caught up in our daily concerns that we fail to see and understand the social forces that are at work in our personal lives. What we need are conceptual and methodological tools to help us gain a more complete and accurate perspective on the social world. The ideas, theories, methods, and levels of analysis employed by sociologists are the very tools that will help give us that perspective. To use an analogy, each different lens of a camera gives the photographer a unique view of the world. Wide-angle lenses, close-up lenses, telephoto lenses, and special filters each serve a purpose in creating a distinctive picture or frame of the world. No one lens will provide the complete picture. Yet the combination of images produced by various lenses allows us to examine, in detail, aspects of the world we might ordinarily overlook. That is what the sociological perspective gives us: a unique set of lenses to see the social world around us with deeper understanding. In seeing the social world from a sociological perspective, we are better able to understand who we are as social beings.

Throughout this book, we use the social world model as the framework for understanding the social units, processes, and surrounding environment. We look at each social unit and process. We take the unit out, examine it, and then return it to its place in the interconnected social world model so that you can comprehend the whole social world and its parts, like putting a puzzle together. Look for the model at the beginning of every chapter. We will also explain the micro-, meso-, and macro-level dimensions of issues throughout the text.

Our next chapter asks the following: When we say we know something about society, how is it that we know? What is considered evidence in sociology, and what lens (theory) do we use to interpret the data? In the next chapter, we turn to how we gather data to help us test theories to understand and influence the social world.

WHAT HAVE WE LEARNED?

How can sociology help you see new aspects of your life and change society? Throughout this book, you will find ideas and examples that will help answer these questions. You will learn how to view the social world through a sociological lens and use the *sociological imagination*. Understanding how the social world works from the micro through the meso to the macro level helps us interact more effectively in it. Using the sociological imagination enables us to see how individual troubles can be rooted in social issues and are best addressed with an understanding of the meso or macro level. This knowledge enables us to be better family members, workers, citizens, and members of the global community.

We live in a complex social world with many layers of interaction. If we really want to understand our own lives, we need to comprehend the levels of analysis that affect our lives and the connections between those levels. To do so wisely, we need both objective lenses for viewing this complex social world and valid information (facts) about the society. As the science of society, sociology can provide both tested empirical data and a broad, analytical perspective, as you will learn in the next chapter. Here is a summary of points from Chapter 1.

- Humans are, at our very core, social animals—more akin to pack or herd animals than to individualistic cats.

- Sociology is based on scientific findings, making it more predictable and reliable than opinions or commonsense beliefs in a particular culture.

- A core idea in sociology is the sociological imagination. It requires that we see how our individual lives and personal troubles are shaped by historical and structural events outside our everyday lives. It also prods us to see how we can influence our society.

- Sociology is a social science and, therefore, uses the tools of the sciences to establish credible evidence to understand our social world. As a science, sociology is scientific and objective rather than value laden.

- Sociology has practical applications, including those that are essential for the job market.

- Sociology focuses on social units or groups, on social structures such as institutions, on social processes that give a social unit its dynamic character, and on their environments.

- The social world model is the organizing theme of this book. Using the sociological imagination, we can understand our social world best by clarifying the interconnections between micro, meso, and macro levels of the social world. Each chapter of this book will examine society at these three levels of analysis.

DISCUSSION QUESTIONS

1. Think of a problem that impacts you personally (e.g., the high cost of tuition, unemployment, or divorce), and explain how you would make sense of it differently if you viewed it as (a) only a personal problem or (b) influenced by a public issue. How do possible solutions to the problem differ depending on how you view it?

2. How can sociology help you become a more informed citizen and better able to understand how government policies impact society?

3. What are three ways the sociological perspective can help you succeed in college and the workforce?

4. Think of some of the ways the social institutions of government and education are connected. Why is it in the interest of the government to support higher education? How has government support (or lack of support) impacted your college experience?

5. Imagine you would like to look at reasons behind the high college dropout rate in the United States. How might your explanations differ based on whether your analysis was on the micro, meso, or macro level? Why? Which level or levels would you focus on for your study? Why?

KEY TERMS

environment   15

levels of analysis   13

macro-level analysis   17

meso-level analysis   16

micro-level analysis   16

national society   14

social institutions   14

social processes   14

social structure   13

social units   13

social world model   13

sociological imagination   8

sociology   5

CONTRIBUTING TO OUR SOCIAL WORLD: WHAT CAN WE DO?

At the end of this and all subsequent chapters, you will find suggestions for work, service learning, internships, and volunteering that encourage you to apply the ideas discussed in the chapter. Suggestions for Chapter 1 focus on student organizations for sociology majors and nonmajors.

At the Local (Micro) Level

- *Student organizations and clubs* enable you to meet other students interested in sociology, carry out group activities, get to know faculty members, and attend presentations by guest speakers. These clubs are usually not limited to sociology majors. If no such organization exists for sociology students at your

school, consider forming one with the help of a faculty member. Sociologists also have an undergraduate honors society, Alpha Kappa Delta (AKD). Visit the AKD website at alphakappadelta.org to learn more about the society and what it takes to qualify for membership or to form a chapter.

At the Regional (Meso) Level

- *State, regional, and specialty (education, criminology, social problems, and so forth) sociological associations* are especially student friendly and feature publications and sessions at their annual meetings specifically for undergraduates. The American Sociological Association lists regional and specialty organizations and their website addresses, with direct links to their home pages at www.asanet.org/about/Aligned_Associations.cfm.

At the National and Global (Macro) Levels

- *The American Sociological Association (ASA)* is the leading professional organization of sociologists in the United States. Visit the ASA website at www .asanet.org, and take a look around it. You will find many programs and initiatives of special interest to students. If you are interested in becoming a sociologist, be sure to look at the links under the heading "News on the Profession." ASA also sponsor an Honors Program at the annual meeting that introduces students to the profession and gives students a heads-up on being successful in sociology. For more information, go to www.asanet.org/students/honors.cfm.

- *The International Sociological Association (ISA)* serves sociologists from around the world. Every four years, the ISA sponsors a large meeting (Toronto, Canada, in July 2018). Specialty groups within ISA hold smaller conferences throughout the world during the other years. Check out www.isa-sociology.org.

$SAGE edge™

Get the edge on your studies. **edge.sagepub.com/ballantinecondensed5e**

- Take a quiz to find out what you've learned.
- Review key terms with eFlashcards.
- Watch videos that enhance chapter content.

© Lisa Maree Williams / Stringer / Getty Images

Examining the Social World

How Do We Know?

Science is about knowing—through careful systematic investigation. Of course there are other ways of seeking knowledge, such as finding a good library on a beach!

MICRO

MESO

MACRO

ME (MY FAMILY AND CLOSEST FRIENDS)

LOCAL ORGANIZATIONS AND COMMUNITY
I am active in a local church, school, clubs, and sports teams.

NATIONAL ORGANIZATIONS, INSTITUTIONS, AND ETHNIC SUBCULTURES
I am active in a religious denomination, part of an educational system, and a member of an ethnic group.

SOCIETY
I am a citizen of the United States, Canada, or another country.

GLOBAL COMMUNITY
I am influenced by actions of the United Nations, the World Health Organization, or Doctors without Borders.

WHAT YOU WILL LEARN IN THIS CHAPTER

This chapter will help you do the following:

2.1 Outline the development of sociology.

2.2 Describe key theoretical perspectives.

2.3 Explain the scientific approach.

2.4 Outline the basic steps of the scientific research process.

THINK ABOUT IT

Micro: Local community	When you are trying to convince neighbors or people in your community to accept your opinion, why are facts and evidence important?
Meso: National institutions, complex organizations, and ethnic groups	How do sociologists gather accurate data about families, educational institutions, or ethnic groups?
Macro: National and global systems	How can theories about national and global processes and interactions help us understand our own lives at the micro level?

Let us travel to the Southern Hemisphere to meet a teenage boy, Hector. He is a 16-year-old, living in a *favela* (slum) on the outskirts of São Paulo, Brazil. He is a polite, bright boy, but his chances of getting an education and a steady job in his world are limited. Like millions of other children around the world, he comes from a poor rural family that migrated to an urban area in search of a better life. However, his family ended up in a crowded slum with only a shared spigot for water and one string of electric lights along the dirt road going up the hill on which they live. The sanitary conditions in his community are appalling—open sewers and no garbage collection—which makes the people susceptible to various diseases. His family is relatively fortunate, for they have cement walls and wood flooring but no bathroom, running water, or electricity. Many adjacent dwellings are little more than cardboard walls with corrugated metal roofs and dirt floors.

Hector wanted to stay in school but was forced to drop out to help support his family. Since leaving school, he has picked up odd jobs—deliveries, trash pickup, janitorial work, and gardening—to help pay for the family's dwelling and to buy food to support his parents and six siblings. Even when he was in school, Hector's experience was discouraging. He was not a bad student, and some teachers encouraged him to continue, but other students from the city teased the *favela* kids and made them feel unwelcome. Most of his friends dropped out before he did. Hector often missed school because of other obligations: looking for part-time work, helping a sick relative, or taking care of a younger sibling. The immediate need to put food on the table outweighed the long-term value of staying in school. What is the bottom line for Hector and millions like him? Because of his limited education and work skills, obligations to his family, and limited opportunities, he most likely will continue to live in poverty.

Sociologists are interested in the factors that influence the social world of children like Hector: family, friends, school, community, and the place of one's nation in the global political and economic structural systems. Sociologists use social theories and scientific methods to examine poverty and many other social issues. In this chapter, you will learn about some of the different data collection methods sociologists use to collect information and the theories they use to make sense of their data.

Sociological research helps us to understand how and why society operates and how we might change it. It can also help you make sense of why people in your family, neighborhood, college campus, and workplace act the way they do. You will, no doubt, find yourself in a situation where conducting a research study will help your organization or community.

Getty Images/Corbis Historical/Christopher Pillitz

Slum dwellers of São Paulo, Brazil. Hector lives in a neighborhood with shelters made of available materials such as boxes, with no electricity or running water and poor sanitation.

This chapter will introduce you to the basic tools used to plan studies and gather dependable information on topics of interest. It will also help you understand how sociology approaches research questions. To this end, we begin this chapter by discussing the development of sociology as a discipline and the core principles of sociology's major theoretical perspectives. We then explore sociology as a science—core ideas that underlie any science: how to collect data, ethical issues involving research, and practical applications and uses of sociological knowledge. We start with the beginnings and emergence of sociology as a field of study.

cultures encouraged at least some Europeans to learn more about the people in and around their new colonies. Second, they sought to understand the rapid changes in their own societies brought about by the Industrial Revolution (which began around the middle of the 1700s) and the French Revolution (1789–1799). Finally, advances in the natural sciences demonstrated the value of the scientific method, and some wished to apply this scientific method to social sciences and understand the social world.

In the early and mid-1800s, no one had clear, systematic explanations for why the old social structure, which

THE DEVELOPMENT OF SOCIOLOGY

Throughout recorded history, humans have been curious about how and why society operates as it does. Long before the development of science, religion and philosophy influenced the way individuals thought about the world. Both approaches to understanding society had a strong moral tone. For example, Plato's *Republic*, written around 400 BCE, outlines plans for an ideal state—complete with government, family, economic systems, class structure, and education—designed to achieve social justice. These philosophers' opinions were derived from abstract reflection about how the social world should work, but they were not tested scientifically.

The first person on record to suggest a systematic approach to explain the social world was North African Islamic scholar Ibn Khaldun (1332–1406). Khaldun was particularly interested in understanding the feelings of solidarity that held tribal groups together during his day, a time of great conflict and wars (Alatas 2006; Hozien n.d.). With this beginning came the rise of modern sociology.

The Rise of Modern Sociology

Several conditions from the 1600s to the 1800s gave rise to sociology. First, European nations were imperial powers extending their influence and control by establishing colonies in other cultures. This exposure to other

The Bastille, a state prison in Paris, France, and a symbol of oppression, was seized by the common people during the French Revolution, a social upheaval that forced social analysts to think differently about society and social stability. Today, rallying points for social movements and revolutions, such as Tahrir Square in Cairo, Egypt, illustrate that uprisings of the common people are still changing societies.

had lasted since the early Middle Ages, was collapsing or why cities were exploding with migrants from rural areas. French society was in turmoil, members of the nobility were being executed, and new rules of justice were taking hold. Churches were made subordinate to the state, equal rights under the law were established for citizens, and democratic rule emerged. These dramatic changes marked the end of the traditional monarchy and the beginning of a new social order.

It was in this setting that the scientific study of society emerged. Two social thinkers, Henri Saint-Simon (1760–1825) and Auguste Comte (1798–1857), decried the lack of systematic data collection or objective analysis in social thought. These Frenchmen argued that a science of society could help people understand and perhaps control the rapid changes and unsettling revolutions taking place.

Comte officially coined the term *sociology* in 1838. His basic premise was that religious or philosophical speculation about society did not provide an adequate understanding of how to solve society's problems. Just as the scientists compiled basic facts about the *physical* world, so too was there a need to gather scientific knowledge about the *social* world. Only then could leaders systematically apply this scientific knowledge to improve social conditions.

Comte asked two basic questions: First, what holds society together and gives rise to a stable order in lieu of anarchy? Second, why and how do societies change? Comte conceptualized society as divided into two parts: (1) *social statics*, aspects of society that give rise to order, stability, and harmony, and (2) *social dynamics*, forces that promote change and evolution (even revolution) in society. Comte was concerned with what contemporary sociologists and the social world model in this book refer to as *structure* (social statics) and *process* (social dynamics). By understanding these aspects of the social world, Comte felt that leaders could strengthen society and respond appropriately to change. His optimistic belief was that sociology would be the "queen of sciences," guiding leaders to construct a better social order (Comte [1855] 2003).

Sociology continued developing as scholars contemplated further changes brought about by the Industrial Revolution. Massive social and economic transformations in the 18th and 19th centuries brought about restructuring and sometimes the demise of political monarchies, aristocracies, and feudal lords. Scenes of urban squalor were common in Great Britain and other industrializing European nations. Machines replaced both agricultural workers and cottage (home) industries because they produced an abundance of goods faster, better, and cheaper. Peasants were pushed off the land by new technologies and

migrated to urban areas to find work; at the same time, a powerful new social class of capitalists was emerging. Industrialization brought the need for a new skilled class of laborers, putting new demands on an education system that had served only the elite. Families now depended on work and wages in the industrial sector to stay alive.

These changes stimulated other social scientists to study society and its problems. The writings of Émile Durkheim, Karl Marx, Harriet Martineau, Max Weber, W. E. B. Du Bois, and many other early sociologists set the stage for the development of sociological theories. Du Bois, an African American who had to deal with racism within and without academia, was the first scholar in North America to have a truly scientific program for the study of society, beginning prior to 1900 (A. Morris 2015). Accompanying the development of sociological theory was the use of the scientific method—the systematic gathering and recording of reliable and accurate data to test ideas. First, we turn to sociology's major theoretical perspectives.

SOCIOLOGY'S MAJOR THEORETICAL PERSPECTIVES

A *theoretical perspective* is a basic view of society that guides sociologists' research questions, methods, and analysis. They are the broadest theories in sociology, providing overall approaches to understanding the social world and social problems. Sociologists draw on major theoretical perspectives at each level of analysis to guide their research and to help them understand social interactions and social organizations. **Theories** *are statements or explanations regarding how and why two or more facts are related to each other and the connections between these facts*. A good theory also allows social scientists to make *predictions* about the social world.

Recall the description of the social world model presented in Chapter 1. It stresses the levels of analysis—smaller units existing within larger social systems. Some theories are especially useful when trying to understand small, micro-level interactions, whereas others tend to be used to make sense of large, macro-level structures. Either type of theory—those most useful at the micro or macro levels—can be used at the meso level, depending on the research question being asked. To illustrate four of the major theoretical perspectives on the social world, we delve into our examination of Hector's circumstances, introduced at the beginning of this chapter.

Micro- to Meso-Level Theories

If we wanted to study Hector's interactions with his friends and their influence on him or his school performance, we would turn to micro- and meso-level theories to guide our research. Two theories often used at the micro and meso levels of analysis are symbolic interaction theory and rational choice theory.

Symbolic Interaction Theory. Symbolic interaction theory *(also called social constructionism or interpretative theory) sees humans as active agents who create shared meanings of symbols and events and then interact on the basis of those meanings*. Through these interactions, we learn to share common ideas, understand what to expect from others, and gain the capability to shape our society. As we interact, we make use of symbols, actions, or objects that represent something else and therefore have meaning beyond their own existence—such as flags, wedding rings, words, and nonverbal gestures. Symbolic communication (e.g., language) helps people construct a meaningful world. Humans continually create and recreate society through their construction and interpretation of the social world. More than any other theory in the social sciences, symbolic interaction theory stresses human agency—the active role of individuals in creating their social environment.

George Herbert Mead (1863–1931), one of the founders of the symbolic interaction perspective, explored the mental processes associated with how humans define or make sense of situations (G. Mead [1934] 1962). He placed special emphasis on human interpretations of gestures and symbols (including language) and the meanings we attach to our actions. He also examined how we learn our social roles in society that include *expected behaviors, rights, obligations, responsibilities, and privileges assigned to a social status* (such as mother, child, teacher, and friend) and how we learn to carry out these roles. Indeed, as we will see in Chapter 4, Mead insisted that our notion of who we are—our *self*—emerges from social experience and interaction with others. Language is critical to this process, for it allows us to step outside of our own experience and reflect back on how others see us.

To summarize, the modern symbolic interaction theory emphasizes the following:

- People continually create and recreate society through interacting with one another.
- People interact by communicating with one another through the use of shared symbols.
- We learn who we are (our sense of self) and our place in society through interacting with others.

Critique of the Symbolic Interaction Theory. Each theory has its critics, those who disagree with some aspect of the theory. Although symbolic interaction theory is widely used by sociologists today, it is often criticized for neglecting the macro-level structures of society that affect human behavior. By focusing on interpersonal interactions, large-scale social forces such as an economic depression or a political revolution that shape human destinies are given less consideration. With the focus on the ability of each individual to create his or her meaning in social situations (called *agency*), symbolic interaction has often been less attuned to important macro-level issues of social class position, social power, historical circumstances, or international conflict between societies (Meltzer, Petras, and Reynolds 1975). For example, if we focused only on how Hector interacts with his family and friends in trying to determine why he dropped out of school, we would overlook macro forces (e.g., how the lack of government supports for poor families impacted his decision to drop out of school). Another critique is that it is difficult to scientifically study abstract ideas like "the development of the self," key to symbolic interaction theory.

Despite these limitations, theorists from the symbolic interaction perspective have made significant contributions to understanding the development of social identities and interactions that underlie groups, organizations, and societies. Many of these studies will be discussed in chapters throughout the book.

Rational Choice (Exchange) Theory. According to rational choice theory, *humans are fundamentally concerned with self-interests, making rational decisions based on weighing costs and rewards of the projected outcome of an action*. Someone from this perspective would say Hector would picture the situation as if it were a mental balance sheet: For example, on the plus side, staying in school may lead to future opportunities not available to the uneducated. On the minus side, school is a negative experience, and the family needs help to feed its members now, so going to school is a "waste of time." Which side will win depends on Hector's balance sheet and on family and friends' influence over the rewards versus costs.

Rational choice theory, also called *exchange theory*, has its roots in several disciplines—economics, behavioral psychology, anthropology, and philosophy (Cook, O'Brien, and Kollock 1990). Social behavior is seen as an exchange activity—a transaction in which resources are given and received (Blau 1964; Homans 1974). Every interaction involves an exchange of something valued: money, time, material goods, attention, sex, allegiance, and so on. People stay in relationships because they get something

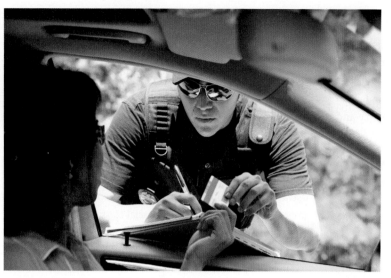

According to rational choice theory, people avoid cost or pain and seek benefits. Thus, people in authority try to control others by imposing cost for behaviors that are unwanted. The cost for this woman for speeding is an expensive ticket, and the city council and police hope it will lead to more desired behaviors.

minimize costs. They give little attention to micro-level internal mental processes, such as self-reflection. Charitable, unselfish, or altruistic behavior is not easily explained by this view. Why would a soldier sacrifice his or her life to save a comrade? Why would a starving person in a Nazi concentration camp share a crust of bread with another? Proponents of rational choice counter the criticism by arguing that if a person feels good about helping another, that, in itself, is a reward that compensates for the cost.

Thinking Sociologically

How can symbolic interaction and rational choice perspectives help explain dating behavior? For example, how might a "hookup" mean something different to females, as opposed to males? How would each of the previous micro theories answer this question a bit differently?

from the exchange, and they leave relationships that have more costs than benefits for them. They constantly evaluate whether there is reciprocity or balance in a relationship so that they are receiving as much as they give. Simply stated, people are more likely to act if they see some reward or success coming from their behavior. The implication is that self-interest for the individual is the guiding element in human interaction.

In summary, rational choice theory involves the following key ideas:

- Human beings are mostly self-centered, and self-interest drives their behavior.
- Humans calculate costs and benefits (rewards) in making decisions.
- Humans are rational in that they weigh choices in order to maximize their own benefits and minimize costs.
- Every interaction involves exchanges entailing rewards and penalties or expenditures.
- A key element in exchanges is reciprocity—a balance in the exchange of benefits.
- People keep a mental ledger in their heads about whether they owe someone else or that person owes them.

Critique of Rational Choice Theory. Rational choice theorists see human conduct as self-centered, with rational behavior implying that people seek to maximize rewards and

Meso- and Macro-Level Theories

Meso- and macro-level theories consider large units in the social world: organizations (e.g., General Motors or the Episcopal Church), institutions (such as family, education, religion, health care, politics, or economies), societies (Canada or Mexico), or global systems (the World Trade Organization or World Bank). For example, Hector's government at the national and international levels affects his life in a variety of ways. As Brazil industrializes, the nature of jobs and the modes of communication change. Local village cultures adjust as the entire nation gains more uniformity of values, beliefs, and norms. Similarly, resources such as access to clean water may be allotted at the local level, but local communities need national and sometimes international support, as illustrated by the tribal elders from Tanzania in the photo on page 31. We can begin to understand how the process of modernization influences Hector, this village in Tanzania, and other people around the globe by looking at two major macro-level perspectives: the structural-functional and conflict theories.

Structural-Functional Theory. Structural-functional theory, *also called functional theory, assumes that all parts of the social structure (including groups, organizations, and institutions), the culture (values and beliefs), and social processes (e.g., legislators working to create a law, an instructor teaching a child, or social change) work together to make the whole society run smoothly and harmoniously.* To understand the social world from this perspective, we must look at how the parts of society (structure) fit together and how each part contributes to the maintenance of society. For instance, two functions (purposes) of the family include having children and teaching them to be members of society. These and other functions help perpetuate society, for without reproducing and teaching new members to fit in, societies would collapse.

Émile Durkheim (1858–1917) was the founder of the functionalist perspective. He theorized that society is made up of necessary parts that fit together into a working whole. Durkheim believed that individuals conform to the rules of societies because of a *collective conscience*—the shared beliefs in the values of a group (Durkheim [1895] 1947). People grow up sharing the same values, beliefs, and rules of behavior as those around them. Gradually, individuals internalize these shared beliefs and rules. A person's behavior is, in a sense, governed from within because it feels right and proper to behave in accordance with what is expected. As such, the functionalist perspective of Durkheim and subsequent theorists places emphasis on social consensus, which gives rise to stable and predictable patterns of order in society. Because people need groups for survival, they adhere to the group's rules so that they do not stand apart from it. This means that most societies run in an orderly manner, with most individuals fitting into their positions in society.

Functions (consequences of an action or behavior) can be manifest or latent. **Manifest functions** are *the planned outcomes of interactions, social organizations, or institutions*. Some of the planned consequences of the microwave oven, for instance, have been to allow people to prepare meals quickly and easily, facilitating life in overworked and stressed modern families. **Latent functions** are *unplanned or unintended consequences of actions or of social structures* (Merton 1938, [1942] 1973). Some of the unplanned consequences of microwave ovens were the creation of a host of new jobs and stimulation of the economy, as people wrote new cookbooks and as businesses were formed to produce microwavable cookware and prepared foods ready for the microwave.

Latent functions can be functional or dysfunctional. Functional actions contribute to the stability or equilibrium of society, whereas **dysfunctions** are *those actions that undermine the stability or equilibrium of society* (Merton 1938). For example, by allowing people to prepare meals without using a stove or conventional oven, the microwave oven has contributed to some young people having no idea how to cook, thus making them highly dependent on expensive technology and processed foods and, in some cases, adding to problems of obesity.

The Tanzanian village elders in this photo continue to have authority to make local (micro-level) decisions about the traditional irrigation canals being improved in their village, but their expanded water supply is possible, in part, because of international financial support (meso- and macro-level decisions).

From a functionalist theory perspective, it is important to examine the possible functional and dysfunctional aspects of life in society in order to maintain harmony and balance.

In summary, the structural-functional perspective

- examines the macro-level organizations and patterns in society,
- looks at what holds societies together and enhances social continuity,
- considers the consequences, or *functions*, of each major part in society,
- focuses on the way the structure (groups, organizations, and institutions), the culture, and social processes work together to make society function smoothly, and
- notes manifest functions (which are planned), latent functions (which are unplanned or secondary), and dysfunctions (which undermine stability).

Critique of Structural-Functional Perspective. Some ideas put forth by functional theorists are so abstract that they are difficult to test with data. Moreover, functionalism does not explain social changes in society, such as conflict and revolution. As we try to understand the many societal upheavals in the world, from suicide bombings in the Middle East to the economic privatization

Getty/energy

Although the microwave oven and fast-food restaurants have had many benefits for a society in a hurry, one dysfunction is the deterioration of health, especially due to obesity.

movements in China, it is clear that dramatic social change is possible. The functionalist assumption is that if a system is running smoothly, it must be working well because it is free from conflict. It assumes that conflict is harmful, even though we know that stability may come about because of ruthless dictators suppressing the population. In short, stability is not always good.

Thinking Sociologically

Describe a manifest and a latent function of the system of higher education in the United States today. Is the latent function dysfunctional? Why, or why not?

Conflict Theory. In many ways, conflict theory turns the structural-functional theory on its head. Conflict theory contends that *conflict is inevitable in any group or society and that inequality and injustice are the source of the conflicts that permeate society*. Resources and power are distributed unequally in society, so some members have more money, goods, and prestige than others. The rich protect their positions by using the power they have accumulated to keep others in their places. From the perspective of poor people such as Hector, it seems the rich get all of the breaks. Most of us want more of the resources in society (money, good jobs, nice houses, and cars), causing the possibility of conflict between the haves and the have-nots. These conflicts sometimes bring about a change in society.

Modern conflict theory has its origins in the works of Karl Marx (1818–1883), a German social philosopher who lived in England during the height of 19th-century industrial expansion. Capitalism had emerged as the dominant economic system in Europe. *Capitalism* is an economic system in which individuals and corporations, rather than the state, own and control the means of production (e.g., factories). As they compete for profits, some win while others lose.

Marx recognized the plight of workers toiling in factories in the new industrial states of Europe and viewed the ruling elites and the wealthy industrial owners as exploiters of the working class. Marx wrote about the new working class crowded in urban slums, working long hours under appalling conditions, without earning enough money for decent housing and food. Few of the protections enjoyed by many (but not all) workers today—such as retirement benefits, health coverage, sick leave, the 40-hour workweek, and restrictions against child labor—existed in Marx's time.

Marx believed that two classes, the capitalists (also referred to as the bourgeoisie or "haves"), who owned the *means of production* (property, machinery, and other means of creating saleable goods or services), and the workers (also referred to as the proletariat or "have-nots"), would continue to live in conflict until the workers shared more equally in the profits of their labor. The more workers came to understand their plight, the more aware they would become of the injustice of the situation. Eventually, Marx believed, workers would rise up and overthrow capitalism, forming a new, classless society. Collective ownership—shared ownership of the *means of production*—would be the new economic order (Marx and Engels [1848] 1969).

The idea of the *bourgeoisie* (the capitalist exploiters who own the factories) and the *proletariat* (the exploited workers who sell their labor) has carried over to analysis of modern-day conflicts among groups in society. For example, from a conflict perspective, Hector in Brazil and millions like him in other countries are part of the reserve labor force—a cheap labor pool that can be called on when labor is needed and disregarded when demand is low, thus meeting the changing labor needs of industry and capitalism. This pattern results in permanent economic insecurity and poverty for Hector and those like him.

Many branches of the conflict perspective have grown from the original ideas of Marx. Here, we mention four contributions to conflict theory: those of American sociologists Harriet Martineau ([1837] 1962), W. E. B. Du Bois ([1899] 1967), Ralf Dahrendorf (1959), and Lewis Coser (1956). As you can see, social conflict has been a major focus of sociological investigation.

Harriet Martineau (1802–1876), generally considered the first female sociologist, wrote several books that contribute to our understanding of modern sociological research methods and provided a critique of the failure of the United States to live up to its democratic principles, especially as they related to women. She argued that social laws influence social behavior and that societies can be measured on their social progress (including how much freedom they give to individuals and how well they treat the most oppressed members of society). Her work represents the foundation of current feminist and conflict theories (Martineau 1838).

Another early American conflict theorist was W. E. B. Du Bois (1868–1963), the first African American to receive a doctorate from Harvard University. After being denied full-time positions at White universities, Du Bois founded a sociology program in 1898 at Atlanta University, a Black college. There, he established a significant research center and trained a generation of Black social scientists. In 1899, he published *The Philadelphia Negro* (one of the first truly scientific studies in North America), and in 1903, he completed a classic sociological work, *The Souls of Black Folk*. His work was truly groundbreaking (A. Morris 2015).

Du Bois, like other early sociological theorists, believed that although research should be scientifically rigorous and fair-minded, the ultimate goal of sociological work was social improvement—not just human insight. Throughout his life, Du Bois documented and lambasted the status of Black Americans, noting that African Americans were an integral part of U.S. society but not fully accepted into it.

Du Bois helped establish the National Association for the Advancement of Colored People (NAACP). He stressed the need for minority groups to become advocates for their rights—to object loudly when those in power act to disadvantage minorities—and to make society more just (Du Bois [1899] 1967). He was—and continues to be—an inspiration for many sociologists who believe that their findings should be used to create a more humane social world (C. Mills 1956).

A half-century later, in 1959, Ralf Dahrendorf (1929–2009) argued that society is always in the process of change and affected by forces that bring about change. Dahrendorf refined Marx's ideas in several ways. He pointed out that capitalism had survived, despite Marx's prediction of a labor revolt, because of improved conditions for workers (e.g., unions, the establishment of labor laws, and workplace regulations). Dahrendorf also maintained that, instead of divisions based on ownership, conflict had become based on authority.

Dahrendorf noted that those with lower-status positions, such as Hector, could form interest groups and engage in conflict with those in higher positions of authority. *Interest groups*, such as the members of Hector's *favela*, share a common situation or common interests. In Hector and his neighbors' case, these interests include a desire for sanitation, running water, electricity, jobs, and a higher standard of living. From within such interest groups, *conflict groups* arise to fight for changes. There is always potential for conflict when those without power realize their common position and form interest groups. How much change or violence is

Harriet Martineau (*left*) published a critique of the United States' failure to live up to its democratic principles 11 years before Karl Marx's most famous work, but she was not taken seriously as a scholar for more than a century because she was female—the first feminist theorist. Karl Marx (*center*) is known as the founder of conflict theory. W. E. B. Du Bois (*right*) continued the development of conflict theory and was among the first to apply that theory to U.S. society, especially to issues of race.

brought about depends on how organized those groups become.

Dahrendorf's major contribution is the recognition that conflict over resources results in a conflict not just between the proletariat and the bourgeoisie but among a multitude of interest groups, including old people versus young people, rich versus poor, one region of the country versus another, Christians versus non-Christians, and so forth. This acknowledges multiple rifts in the society based on interest groups.

Whereas Marx emphasized the divisive nature of conflict, other theorists have offered a modified theory of conflict in society. American theorist Lewis Coser took a very different approach to conflict from that of Marx, arguing that conflict can strengthen societies and the organizations within them. According to Coser, problems in a society or group lead to complaints or conflicts—a warning message to the group that all is not well. Resolution of the conflicts shows that the group is adaptable in meeting the needs of its members, thereby creating greater loyalty to the group. Thus, conflict provides the message of what is not working to meet people's needs, and the system adapts to the needs for change because of the conflict (Coser 1956; Simmel 1955).

In summary, conflict theorists advance the following key ideas:

- Conflict and the potential for conflict underlie all social relations.
- Groups of people look out for their self-interest and try to obtain resources and make sure they are distributed primarily to members of their own group.
- Social change is desirable, particularly changes that bring about a greater degree of social equality.
- The existing social order reflects powerful people imposing their values and beliefs upon the weak.

Critique of Conflict Theory. First, many conflict theorists focus on macro-level analysis and lose sight of the individuals involved in conflict situations, such as Hector and his family. Second, empirical research to test conflict theory is limited. The conflict perspective often paints a picture with rather broad brushstrokes. Research to test the picture involves interpretations of broad spans of history and is more difficult to claim as scientific. Third, conflict theorists tend to focus on social stress, power dynamics, and disharmony. Conflict theory is not very effective in explaining social cohesion and cooperation. Fourth, many critics of conflict theory argue that altruism and cooperation are common human behaviors but not recognized by conflict theory.

Thinking Sociologically

Imagine you are a legislator. You have to decide whether to cut funding for a senior citizens' program or slash a scholarship program for college students. You want to be reelected, and you know that approximately 90% of senior citizens are registered to vote, and most actually do vote. You also know that less than half of college-age people are likely to vote. These constituencies are about the same size. What would you do, and how would you justify your decision? How does this example illustrate conflict theory?

Multilevel Analysis

Many of the more contemporary theorists try to bridge the gap between micro and macro levels of analysis, offering insights relevant at each level. We examine two of these next.

Max Weber's Contributions. Max Weber (1864–1920), a German-born social scientist, has had a lasting effect on sociology and other social sciences. Weber (pronounced VAY-ber) cannot be pigeonholed easily into one of the theoretical categories or one level of analysis, for his contributions include both micro- and macro-level analyses. His emphasis on *Verstehen* (meaning deep, empathetic understanding in humans) gives him a place in micro-level theory, and his discussions of power and bureaucracies give him a place in meso- and macro-level theory (Weber 1946).

Verstehen stems from the interpretations or meanings individuals at the micro level give to their social experiences. Weber argued that to understand people's behaviors, you must step into their shoes and see the world as they do. Following in Weber's footsteps, sociologists try to understand both human behavior and the meanings that people attach to their experiences. In this work, Weber is a micro theorist who set the stage for symbolic interaction theorists.

However, the goal-oriented, efficient new organizational form called bureaucracy was the focus of much of Weber's writing at the meso level. This organizational form was based on rationality (*the attempt to reach maximum efficiency with rules that are rationally designed to accomplish goals*) rather than relying on long-standing tradition for how things should be done. As we describe in Chapter 5, Weber's ideas about society at the meso level have laid the groundwork for a theoretical understanding of modern organizations.

Weber also attempted to understand macro-level processes. For instance, in his famous book *The Protestant Ethic and the Spirit of Capitalism* (Weber [1904–1905]

1958), he asked how capitalists (those who have money and control production) understood the world around them. His work was influenced by Marx's writings, but whereas Marx focused on economic conditions as the key factor shaping history and power relations, Weber argued that Marx's focus was too narrow. Weber felt that politics, economics, religion, psychology, and people's ideas are interdependent—affecting each other. In short, Weber thought that society was more complex than Karl Marx's theory, which focused only on two groups—the haves and the have-nots—in conflict over economic resources.

Feminist Theory. Much of feminist theory has foundations in the conflict perspective. **Feminist theory** *critiques the hierarchical power structures that disadvantage women and other minorities* (Cancian 1992; P. Collins 2008). Proponents note that men form an interest group intent on preserving their privileges. Feminists also argue that sociology has been dominated by a male perspective that does not give a complete view of the social world.

Some branches of feminist theory come from interaction perspectives, emphasizing the way gender socialization, cues, and symbols shape the nature of much human interaction. Thus, feminist theory moves from meso- and macro-level analysis (e.g., looking at national and global situations that give privileges to men) to micro-level analysis (e.g., looking at inequality between husbands and wives in marriage). In particular, feminist theory points to the importance of gender as a variable influencing social patterns (Brettell and Sargent 2012; Burn 2011; Kramer and Beutel 2014; Lorber 2009).

Many people face inequality because of multiple factors; it is this interplay among factors that interests Patricia Hill Collins. An important contemporary scholar, Collins examines the discrimination and oppression people face because of their race, class, gender, sexuality, or nationality, all of which are interconnected. Collins uses the term *intersectionality*, meaning individuals have multiple identities (e.g., race, class, and gender) that intersect and impact their lives and opportunities (2005, 2008).

⬤ Thinking Sociologically

To what extent are human beings free agents who can create their own social world and come up with their own ideas about how to live their lives? To what extent are our lives determined or influenced by the social systems around us and by our positions in the economic and political system? Is this different for different people? Why?

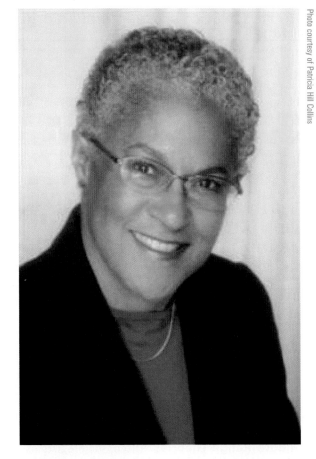

Patricia Hill Collins, an innovative feminist scholar, has challenged sociologists to look at the ways experiences of race, social class, gender, and sexuality intersect and reinforce one another.

Using Different Theoretical Perspectives

Each of the theoretical perspectives described in this chapter begins from a set of assumptions about humans. Each makes a contribution to our understanding, but each has limitations or blind spots, such as not taking into account other levels of analysis (Ritzer 2011). Figure 2.1 provides a summary of cooperative versus competitive perspectives to illustrate how the theories differ.

The strength of a theory depends on its ability to explain and predict behavior accurately. Each theoretical perspective focuses on a different aspect of society and level of analysis and gives us a different lens through which to view our social world. The social world model helps us picture the whole system and determine which theory or theories best suits our needs in analyzing a specific social process or structure.

FIGURE 2.1 Cooperative Versus Competitive Perspectives

	Macro analysis	Micro analysis
Humans viewed as cooperative (people interact with others on the basis of shared meanings and common symbols)	Structural-Functional Theory	Symbolic Interactionism Theory
Humans viewed as competitive (behavior governed by self-interest)	Conflict Theory (group interests)	Rational Choice Theory (individual interests)

Thinking Sociologically

Consider the issue of homelessness in cities around the world. How could each of the theories discussed in this chapter be used to help us understand the problem of homelessness?

Middle-Range Theories. Often, sociologists use *middle-range theories*, those theories that explain specific aspects of social life—such as deviant behavior, racial prejudice, and civic engagement—to make sense of the data they gather (Merton 1968). These theories tend to fall under the umbrella of one of the four major theoretical perspectives described earlier. For example, Erving Goffman, coming from a symbolic interactionist perspective, focused on the impact of stigma (*social disapproval that discredits a person's or group's claim to a "normal" identity*) in social interactions. His analysis of the impact of stigmas and the mid-range theory of social stigma he developed out of it provides one piece of the overall puzzle of explaining social interaction in society.

Theory and Research Methods. Scientists, including sociologists, often use theories to predict changes in society and under what conditions they are likely to occur. Theory tells the researcher what to look for and what concepts or variables need to be measured. However, explanations about the relationships between social variables need to be tested. This is where *research methods*—the procedures one uses to gather data—are relevant. Data must be carefully gathered and then used to assess the accuracy of theory. If a theory is not supported by the data, it must be reformulated or discarded. Theory and research are used together and are mutually dependent.

To study Hector's life in Brazil, researchers might focus on the micro-level interactions between Hector and his family members, peers, teachers, and employers as factors that contribute to his situation. For example, one theory could be that Hector's family has socialized him to believe that certain activities (for example, working) are more realistic or immediately rewarding than others (such as attending school). A meso-level focus might examine the influence of the organizations and institutions—such as the business world, the schools, and the religious communities in Brazil—to see how they shape the forces that affect Hector's life. Alternatively, the focus might be on macro-level analysis—the class structure (rich to poor) of the society and the global forces, such as trade relations between Brazil and other countries, that influence opportunities for Brazilians who live in poverty.

Whatever the level of analysis, as social *scientists*, sociologists use scientific methods of gathering evidence to disprove or to support theories about society.

IDEAS UNDERLYING SCIENCE

Throughout most of human history, people came to "know" the world by the traditions passed down from one generation to the next. Things were so because authoritative people in the culture said they were so. Often, there was reliance on magical, philosophical, or religious explanations of the forces in nature, and these explanations became part of tradition. For example, just 260 years ago, the conventional wisdom was that lightning storms were a sign of an angry god, not electricity caused by meteorological forces. As ways of knowing about the world shifted, tradition, religion, and magic as the primary means to understand the world were challenged. With advances in the natural sciences, observations of cause-and-effect processes became more systematic and controlled.

The scientific approach is based on several core ideas: First, there are real physical and social worlds that can be studied scientifically. Second, there is a certain order to the world, with identifiable patterns that result from a series of causes and effects. The world is not merely a collection of unrelated random events; rather, events occur in a systematic sequence and in patterns—that is, they are *causally* related. Third, the way to gain knowledge of the world is to subject it to empirical testing. **Empirical knowledge** is *founded on information gained from evidence (facts), rather than intuition. Evidence* refers to facts and observations that can be objectively observed and carefully measured using the five senses (sometimes enhanced by scientific instruments).

For knowledge to be scientific, it must come from phenomena that can be observed and measured. Phenomena that cannot be subject to measurement are not within the realm of scientific inquiry. For example, the existence of God, the devil, heaven, hell, and the soul cannot be observed and measured and therefore cannot be examined scientifically. Religion, however, can be studied scientifically by looking at the role it plays in society and our lives, its impact on our values and behavior (the sociology of religion), the historical development of specific religious traditions (the history of religion), or the emotional comfort and stability it brings to people (the psychology of religion). Social scientists do not make judgments about what religion is right or best.

Finally, science is rooted in objectivity; that is, *one must take steps to ensure that one's personal opinions or values do not bias or contaminate data collection and analysis.* Scientists are obliged not to distort their research findings so as to promote a particular point of view. Scientific research is judged first on whether it relies on careful efforts to be objective. Social scientists, like all scientists, must explain what the data reveal, not what they wish it would reveal! Researchers must be open to finding results that support *or* disprove their **hypothesis** (*an educated guess or prediction*).

Failure to meet these standards—empirical knowledge, objectivity, and scientific evidence—means that a study is not scientific. Someone's ideas can seem plausible and logical but may still not be supported by the facts. This is why evidence is so important. Sociology is concerned with using accurate evidence, and it is important to know what is or is not considered accurate. Perhaps you have seen an episode of the *CSI: Crime Scene Investigation* or *Bones* series on television. The shows in these series depict the importance of careful collection of data and commitment to objective analysis. Sociologists deal with different issues, but the same sort of concern for accuracy in gathering data guides their work. When sociologists establish theories as to why society works as it does, they must test those theories using scientific methods.

HOW SOCIOLOGISTS STUDY THE SOCIAL WORLD

Suppose you have a research question you want to answer, such as, Why do boys like Hector drop out of school? In order for your research to be scientific, you must follow the basic steps of the scientific research process.

A. PLANNING A RESEARCH STUDY
- *Step 1:* Define a topic or problem that can be studied scientifically.
- *Step 2:* Review existing relevant research studies and theory to refine the topic and define **variables**, *concepts (ideas) that can vary in frequency of occurrence from one time, place, or person to another* (such as age, ethnicity, religion, and level of education).
- *Step 3:* Formulate hypotheses or research questions, and determine how to define and measure the variables.

B. DESIGNING THE RESEARCH PLAN AND METHOD FOR COLLECTING THE DATA
- *Step 4:* Design the research plan that specifies how the data will be gathered.
- *Step 5:* Select a **sample**, *a group of systematically chosen people who represent a much larger group to study*.
- *Step 6:* Collect the data using appropriate research methods.

C. MAKING SENSE OF THE DATA
- *Step 7:* Analyze the data, and relate it to previous findings on the topic, concluding exactly what the study says about the research question(s) from Step 3.

- *Step 8:* Draw conclusions, and present the report, including suggestions for future research and policy recommendations (if appropriate). The study is then ready for peer review—critique by other social scientists. Publicize findings and recommendations supported by the peer review.

Planning a Research Study

To study Hector's situation, the researcher uses Step 1 to define a topic or problem, including the variables to be studied. Step 2 requires the researcher to review past studies on related topics to see what has been done and how variables were defined in other studies. This review provides the basis for Step 3.

In Step 3, to formulate hypotheses, researchers must link concepts, such as poverty or dropping out of school, to specific measurements. For example, the researcher could hypothesize that poverty is a major cause of *favela* teenagers dropping out of school because they need to earn money for their families. Who is a dropout might be determined by school records indicating whether that child has attended school during the past 6 months. Poverty could be defined as having a low annual income—say less than half of the average income for that size of family in the country—or by assessing ownership of property, such as cattle, automobiles, and indoor plumbing. It is important

for researchers to be clear, precise, and consistent in how they define and measure their variables.

In order to conduct research to test a theory, researchers formulate a hypothesis, a statement they can test to determine if it is true. This is called *deductive research*. It starts with a theory that you then test. *Inductive research*, on the other hand, starts with observations that then lead to hypothesis development and, potentially, theory formation. Researchers make an observation and then begin to collect more data to determine if what they witnessed initially was a social pattern. Once they start to notice social patterns, they can begin to analyze those patterns using appropriate existing theories, or they can create a new theory if existing ones do not provide needed explanations.

Thinking Sociologically

Think of a research question based on a theoretical perspective. For example, you might ask how Hector's peers affect his decisions using a micro-level theory. Then, write a hypothesis, and identify your variables in the hypothesis.

Whether you use inductive or deductive research, you must always carefully define your variables and determine how they interact with and relate to one another. The relationship between variables is central to understanding *causality*. Causal reasoning is discussed in the next "Engaging Sociology."

ENGAGING SOCIOLOGY

Being Clear About Causality

Sociology, as a science, tries to be very careful about language—more precise than we usually are in our everyday conversations. What do we really mean when we say that something *causes* something else? At the heart of the research process is the effort to find causal relationships (i.e., one variable causes another one to change). The following key terms are important in understanding how two variables (concepts that vary in frequency and can be measured) are related:

Correlation refers to a relationship between variables (such as poverty and low levels of education), with change in one variable associated with change in another. The hypothesis stated earlier predicts that poverty and teenagers dropping out of school are related and vary together. That is, when the poverty level is high, dropping out of school is also high. If we claim that there is a correlation, however, that is only the first step. We have not yet established that change in one variable *causes* a change in the other.

CORRELATION

X ←——————————————→ Y

CAUSE-AND-EFFECT VARIABLES

X ——————————————→ Y

Cause-and-effect relationships occur when there is a relationship between variables so that one variable stimulates a change in another. Once we have determined that there is probably a relationship, or correlation (the fact that the two variables, such as poverty and dropping out of school, both occur in the same situation), we need to take the next step: analyzing which comes first and seeing if one variable causes change in another. The **independent variable** *is the variable in a cause-and-effect relationship that comes first in a time sequence and causes a change in another variable*—the **dependent variable**. If we hypothesize that poverty causes Hector and others to drop out of school, *poverty* is the independent variable in this hypothesis, and *dropping out of school* is the dependent variable, dependent on the level of poverty. In determining cause and effect, the independent variable must always precede the dependent variable in time sequence if we want to try to determine whether the independent variable causes a change in the dependent variable.

SPURIOUS RELATIONSHIPS

Spurious relationships occur when there is no causal relationship between the independent and dependent variables, but they vary together, often due to a third variable affecting both of them. For example, if the quantity of ice cream consumed is highest during those weeks of the year when most drownings occur, these two events are correlated. However, eating ice cream did not *cause* the increase in deaths. Indeed, hot weather may have caused more people both to purchase ice cream and to go swimming, with the larger number of swimmers resulting in more drowning incidents. The connection between ice cream and drownings is a *spurious relationship*.

CONTROLS

Controls are steps used by researchers to eliminate all variables except those related to the hypothesis—especially those variables that might be spurious. Using controls helps ensure that the relationship is not spurious. Using the ice cream example, we might have studied beaches where lots of ice cream was sold and beaches where none was available in order to compare water death incidents. If there was no difference in death rates, the drownings could not have been caused by the ice cream.

* * * * * * *

Engaging With Sociology

1. Think of a possible cause-and-effect relationship that you would like to study.

2. Determine your independent and dependent variables.

3. What variables would you have to control for in order to determine that the relationship between your independent and dependent variables is not spurious or just a correlation?

Designing the Research Plan and Method for Collecting the Data

Researchers must always make clear how they collect their data. Every research study should be replicable—capable of being repeated—by other researchers. So enough information must be given to ensure that another researcher could repeat the study and compare results.

The appropriate data collection method depends on the level(s) of analysis of the research question (micro, meso, or macro) the researcher is asking. For example, if you want to answer a macro-level research question, such as the effect of poverty on students dropping out of school in Brazil, you should focus on large-scale social and economic data sources, such as the Brazilian census. To learn about micro-level issues, such as the influence of peers on an individual's

FIGURE 2.2   The Social World Model and Levels of Analysis

Micro Level	
Individual Small group Local community	Hector Hector's family and close friends The *favela*; Hector's local school, church, neighborhood organizations
Meso Level	
Organizations Institutions Ethnic subcultures	Brazilian corporations, Catholic Church, and local school system in Brazil Family; education; political, economic, and health systems in the region or nation of Brazil Native peoples, African-Brazilians
Macro Level	
National society Global community of nations	Social policies, trends, and programs in Brazil Status of Brazil in global economy; trade relations with other countries; programs of international organizations or corporations

decision to drop out of school, you will need to examine small-group interactions at the micro level. Figure 2.2 illustrates the different levels of analysis.

Designing the Research Plan. Step 4 is vitally important because the researcher evaluates the various methods used to collect data for research studies and selects one or more that are appropriate for the research question. These include questionnaires, interviews, observational studies, secondary data analysis, content analysis, and experiments. Some methods produce *quantitative* (numerical) data whereas others supply *qualitative* (non-numerical) data, such as individuals' responses to interviews. Questionnaires and secondary data analysis tend to be quantitative and used when conducting macro- and meso-level studies. Interviews, observational studies, and content analysis usually produce qualitative data or a blend of quantitative and qualitative data and are primarily used for micro-level research. Some studies include both quantitative and qualitative data.

Interviews are research conducted by talking directly with people and asking questions in person or by telephone. Both unstructured and semistructured interviews, which allow respondents to answer questions in a more open-ended manner, evolve in response to what the researcher learns as the research progresses.

Questionnaires contain questions and other types of items designed to solicit information appropriate to analysis of research questions (Babbie 2014). They are convenient for collecting large amounts of data because they can be distributed by mail or sent by e-mail to many respondents at once.

Observational studies (also called field research) involve systematic, planned observation and recording of interactions and other human behavior in natural settings (where the activity normally takes place, rather than in a laboratory).

They can take different forms: (1) observations in which the researcher actually participates in the activities of the group being studied or (2) observations in which the researcher is not involved in group activities but observes or videotapes the activity. It is important for observers to avoid influencing or altering group functioning and interaction by their presence.

Thinking Sociologically

If you were trying to compare how effectively two professors teach a research methods course offered in your department, what variables might you use, and what variables might you need to control? How would you set up your study? What methods would you use?

Secondary analysis uses existing data, information that has already been collected in other studies—including data banks, such as the national census. Often, large data-collecting organizations, such as the United Nations or a country's census bureau, the national education department, or a private research organization, will make data available for use by researchers. Consider the question of the dropout rate in Brazil. Researchers can learn a great deal about the behavior of school dropouts, as a group, from analysis of information gathered by ministries or departments of education. Likewise, if we want to

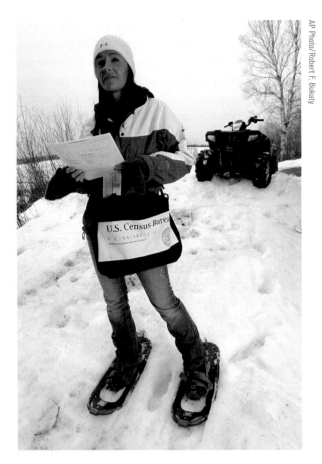

AP Photo/Robert F. Bukaty

Census questionnaires are taken in the United States and many other countries every 10 years. Sometimes, it is difficult to gather accurate data on the entire population, as in the case of homeless people or those in remote areas. Census worker Danielle Forino gathered data in Maine, where she had to use an all-terrain vehicle and sometimes snowshoes in remote sections of the North Maine Woods.

compare modern dropout rates with those of an earlier time, we may find data from previous decades to be invaluable. Secondary analysis can be an excellent way to do meso- or macro-level studies that reveal large-scale patterns in the social world.

Content analysis entails the systematic categorizing and recording of information from written or recorded sources—printed materials, videos, radio broadcasts, or artwork. With content analysis (a common method in historical research and the study of organizations), sociologists can gather the data they need from printed materials—books, magazines, newspapers, laws, letters, comments on websites, e-mails, videos, archived radio broadcasts, or even artwork. They develop a coding system to classify the source content. A researcher trying to understand shifts in Brazilian attitudes toward youth poverty in *favelas* could do a content analysis of popular magazines to see how many pages or stories were devoted to child poverty in the

Brazilian media in each decade from the 1960s to the present. Content analysis has the advantage of being relatively inexpensive and easy to do. It is also *unobtrusive*, meaning that the researcher does not influence the participants being investigated by having direct contact with them. Furthermore, examining materials in historical sequence can be effective in recognizing patterns over time.

In experiments, all variables except the one being studied are controlled so researchers can study the effects on the variable under study. An experiment usually requires an *experimental group*, in which subjects in the group are exposed to the variable being studied to test the effects of that variable on human behavior, and a control group, in which the subjects are not exposed to the variable the researcher wants to test. The control group provides a baseline with which the experimental group can be compared.

Experiments conducted in a lab can often provide the most accurate test of cause and effect. They make it possible to control most variables (eliminating irrelevant spurious variables) and determine the sequence in which variables affect each other. By separating the sample into experimental and control groups, the researcher can see if the study's independent variable makes a difference in the behavior of people who are exposed to that variable compared with those who are not. Psychologists use lab experiments, but few sociologists use this method because many sociological questions cannot be studied in controlled settings. For example, Hector's environment in the *favela* cannot be studied in a laboratory setting.

Control and experimental research projects outside of a lab setting are more common among sociologists. For example, researchers may want to determine whether a new teaching method using technology might help children from Hector's *favela*. Researchers can do so by comparing a control group, exposed to the usual teaching, and an experimental group, provided with the new method or experimental technology. We must ensure that the control and experimental groups of children are at the same academic level and that the teachers are equally motivated and prepared when teaching both classes. With this carefully designed research project, we can conclude that the new approach increases learning if the children in the experimental group score significantly higher on the final exam than those in the control group.

Triangulation refers to the use of two or more methods of data collection to enhance the amount and type of data for analysis and the accuracy of the findings. To study Hector's situation, a research study could use macro-level quantitative data on poverty and on educational statistics in Brazil and micro-level interviews with Hector and his peers to

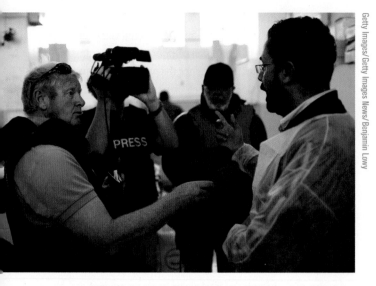

Getty Images/Getty Images News/Benjamin Lowy

Social scientists are not the only professionals who use triangulation. Journalists also consult a variety of sources, including, at times, social scientists, to put together news broadcasts.

determine their goals and their attitudes toward education. If all findings point to the same conclusion, the researcher can feel much more confident about the study results.

Selecting a Sample. It would be impossible to interview or send a questionnaire to every school dropout in Brazil to determine why the teenage dropout rate is so high. It is possible to study a portion of that population, however. In Step 5, the research design process includes determining how to make sure the study includes people who are typical—that is, representative—of the total group (or population) you want to learn about. This involves careful selection of a *sample*, a group systematically chosen to represent a much larger group.

Researchers use many types of samples. A common one, the representative sample, attempts to accurately reflect the group being studied so that the sample results can be generalized, or applied to the larger group or population. In the case of studying why so many boys from Hector's *favela* drop out of school, a representative sample for a study could be drawn from all 13- to 16-year-olds in his region or city in Brazil.

The most common form of representative sample is the *random sample*. All people in the population being studied have an equal *chance* of being selected for the study. By observing or talking with this smaller group selected from the total population under study, the researcher can get an accurate picture of the total population and have confidence that the findings apply to the larger group. Developing an effective sampling technique is often a complex process. In the case of Brazil, people constantly move in and out of the *favela*. Those who have just arrived may not have the same characteristics as

those who have been living there a long time, but it is important to have a sample that represents the whole group being studied. Samples also must be large enough to accurately represent a population and to use statistical programs to analyze the data. If you take a methods course, you will delve further into these details of sampling and data analysis discussed next.

Collecting the Data. We have now made a research plan and selected our methods to use and our sample. In Step 6, we actually collect the data following our plan. Next, we have to determine what to do with the data to answer our research problem.

Thinking Sociologically

Define and distinguish each of the following important research concepts:

- cause-and-effect relationships
- spurious relationships
- evidence
- correlation
- dependent variable
- independent variable
- hypothesis
- sample
- triangulation

Making Sense of the Data

Once you have collected your data from your sample, you have to analyze it.

Analyzing the Data. In Step 7, the researcher uses statistical and other analysis techniques to analyze what the data say in answering the research question. Imagine that you have 100 interviews from residents of Hector's *favela*, plus a notebook full of field observation notes from "hanging out" with the youth there. What do you do with the data? Social researchers use multiple techniques to analyze data, but whatever techniques they use, they look for patterns in the data and then use theories and findings from past research on the topic to make sense of those patterns.

Presenting the Findings. One of the last steps in the research process, Step 8, is to draw conclusions and present the final report. The report presents a discussion of the results, draws conclusions as to whether the hypotheses were supported or answers were found for the research question, interprets the results, and (if appropriate) makes recommendations on how to use the findings. This report is usually reviewed by other social scientists, and feedback on the study is provided to the researcher. After this step, the report (if it holds up to peer review) may be publicly disseminated. As part of the presentation and discussion of results, reports often contain tables or figures presenting summaries of data to help the reader easily understand the patterns found in the data. The next "Engaging Sociology" provides useful tips on reading research tables found in journal articles, newspapers, and magazines.

Ethical Issues in Social Research

What happens if a scientist conducts research that has negative impacts on the participants? It is due to this concern that most universities and other research organizations, especially those receiving public money, have *human subjects review boards*. The boards review the proposed research plans and methods to be sure they will *not* hurt the subjects. Of special concern are research projects in medical sciences, but social scientists must also have their research reviewed.

Sociologists and other scientists are bound by the ethical codes of conduct governing research. The American Sociological Association (ASA) code of ethics outlines standards that researchers are expected to observe when doing research, teaching, and publishing. They include

- explaining the uses and consequences of the research and gaining informed consent from respondents;
- taking steps to ensure the privacy of respondents;
- being objective, reporting findings and sources fully;
- making no promises to respondents that cannot be honored;
- accepting no support that requires violation of these principles;
- completing contracted work; and
- delineating responsibilities in works with multiple authors.

Examples of unethical research include studying people without their knowledge or consent, including only data that support the results you would like to see, and violating the confidentiality of your subjects by revealing their identities. The bottom line is that researchers must do everything they can to protect their subjects from harm.

Thinking Sociologically

Distinguish the differences in each of these approaches to gathering data in sociology, and identify a potential ethical problem in each approach:

- experiments
- observational studies
- interviews
- questionnaires
- content analysis
- secondary analysis

Putting Sociology to Work: Public Sociology

Most early sociologists—including Lester Ward, the first president of the American Sociological Association—promoted sociology as a means for improving society (Calhoun 2007). As the discipline of sociology grew from its early days and became an acknowledged social science, some sociologists advocated for "pure" research disconnected from social policy issues and the public sphere. Throughout the history of the discipline, sociologists have debated their proper role in society.

However, like physicists, chemists, and geologists, many sociologists believe that there are both important practical applications of the discipline and many policy issues that need to be informed by good social science. Today, there is a movement to recall the roots of sociology and make sociology more *public*—that is, of use to society. Public sociologists *use sociological tools to understand and inform citizens about how society operates and to improve society*. Some help create and advocate for social policies that their research indicates will make a positive impact on society. Public sociologists—whether professors or those in a variety of professions outside academia—share a common goal: to better understand how society operates *and* to make practical use of their sociological findings to better society (Pickard and Poole 2007).

Some public sociologists work outside of academia and use sociological knowledge and research skills to address organizational needs or problems in government, education, health care settings, social service agencies, and businesses. They work for clients or organizations that often determine the research questions they will address. Depending on their positions, they may be known as sociological practitioners, applied sociologists, clinical sociologists, policy analysts, program planners, or evaluation researchers, among other titles. They focus on pragmatic ways to improve organizations or society, sometimes recommending major changes and sometimes proposing modest policy proposals.

Some sociology professors build in a public sociology emphasis into their courses, hoping not only to work with students to improve the social environment in which they live but also to foster important skills for students entering the job market. The next "Sociologists in Action" feature describes one such effort.

ENGAGING SOCIOLOGY

How to Read a Research Table

A statistical table is a researcher's labor-saving device. Quantitative data presented in tabular form are clearer and more concise than the same information presented in several written paragraphs. A good table has clear signposts to help the reader avoid confusion. For instance, Table 2.1 shows many of the main features of a table, and the boxes in the margins explain how to read each feature.

HEADNOTE (or Subtitle): Many tables will have a headnote or subtitle under the title, giving information relevant to understanding the table or units in the table.

For this table, the reader is informed that it includes all persons 25 years old and over and the units will be reported in thousands.

TITLE: The title provides information on the major topic and variables in the table.

"Educational Attainment by Selected Characteristics: 2015"

HEADINGS AND STUBS: Tables generally have one or two levels of headings under the title and headnotes. These instruct the reader about what is in the columns below.

In this table, the headings indicate the level of education achieved so that the reader can identify the percentage with a specified level of education.

The table also has a stub: the far-left column under "Characteristic." This lists the items that are being compared according to the categories found in the headings. In this case, the stub indicates age, sex, and race or ethnicity.

MARGINAL TABS: In examining the numbers in the table, try working from the outside in. The marginals, the figures at the margins of the table, often provide summary information.

In this table, the first column of numbers is headed "Population (1,000)," indicating—by thousands—the total number of people in each category who were part of the database. The columns to the right indicate—by percentages—the level of educational attainment for each category.

CELLS: To make more detailed comparisons, examine specific cells in the body of the table. These are the boxes that hold the numbers or percentages.

In this table, the cells contain data on educational achievement by age, sex, and race/ethnicity (for Asians, Whites, Blacks, and Hispanics).

Table 2.1 Educational Attainment by Selected Characteristics: 2015, for Persons 25 Years Old and Over, Reported in Thousands

Characteristic	Population (1,000)	Percentage of Population—Highest Level					
		Not a High School Graduate	High School Graduate	Some College, but No Degree	Associate's Degree[1]	Bachelor's Degree	Advanced Degree
Total persons	212,312	14.3	26.5	17.7	10.0	20.5	12.0
Age							
25–34 yrs. old	43,006	12.5	22.5	18.5	10.4	25.3	10.9
35–54 yrs. old	82,715	14.0	24.9	15.8	10.6	21.9	12.8
55–64 yrs. old	86,411	15.9	30.1	16.4	9.0	16.9	11.9

UNITS: Units refer to how the data are reported. They could be in percentages, in number per 100 or 1,000, or in other units.

In this table, the data are reported first in raw numbers in thousands and then in percentages.

FACTS FROM THE TABLE: After reviewing all the above information, the reader is ready to make some interpretations about what the data mean.

In this table, the reader might note that young adults are more likely to have a college education than older citizens, though those in the middle age bracket are more likely to have graduate degrees. In addition, people with Asian background have the highest levels of education. What other interesting patterns do you see?

Characteristic	Population (1,000)	Percentage of Population—Highest Level					
		Not a High School Graduate	High School Graduate	Some College, but No Degree	Associate's Degree[1]	Bachelor's Degree	Advanced Degree
Sex							
Male	101,889	15.3	27.0	16.5	8.9	20.3	12.0
Female	110,245	13.8	26.0	16.7	10.8	20.7	12.1
Race/Ethnicity							
Asian	12,331	11.7	18.6	9.5	6.4	32.5	21.4
White[2]	140,638	10.7	26.5	16.9	10.6	22.7	11.6
Black[2]	25,420	12.9	31.0	20.5	9.9	14.6	8.2
Hispanic	31,020	36.7	26.7	14.3	7.2	10.8	4.7

Sources: U.S. Census Bureau (2016); Ryan and Bauman (2016).

1. Includes vocational degrees.

2. For persons who selected this race group only.

*Features of the table adapted from Broom and Selznick (1963).

SOURCE: The source note, found under the table, points out the origin of the data. It is usually identified by the label "Source."

Under this table, the source note says "Ryan and Bauman 2016; U.S. Census Bureau 2016."

FOOTNOTES: Some tables have footnotes, usually indicating something unusual about the data or where to find more complete data.

In this table, two footnotes are provided so that the reader does not make mistakes in interpretation.

SOCIOLOGISTS IN ACTION
KRISTIN KENNEAVY

Using Sociology to Improve Campus Life and Gain Marketable Skills

I did not become a sociologist to live in an ivory tower. Rather, I envisioned busting down the castle gate and doing work that would have a positive impact. As a result of my orientation to sociology, I created a "Public Sociologies" course in which students learn skills relevant to their careers and lives—gathering and analyzing data to understand and address social issues on our campus and in the wider community. One issue my students have worked on is interpersonal violence on campus. Students can play an important role in preventing such violence through a variety of strategies. For example, they might personally intervene if they see a couple arguing, call a resource who can diffuse the situation (such as a resident assistant or campus safety officer), or simply state their discomfort when a friend talks about women in a sexist way.

A number of bystander intervention training programs now attempt to teach these skills. Our campus chose to use the Green Dot program, a violence prevention program that focuses on peers and culture. My students and I agreed that we would help our Women's Center to evaluate the effectiveness of the Green Dot program. To do this, my students had to learn and then use research and evaluation skills.

My students designed the initial survey instrument and tested the survey with a diverse sample of their fellow students so that they could refine the measures. The following spring, my class fielded the baseline wave of the survey. They came up with a sampling strategy (using randomly selected course sections) and went through the approval process with our Institutional Review Board (IRB) to make sure that we protected our human subjects. The students distributed the surveys and entered all of the data into a computer program. Finally, we did statistical analysis of the data and prepared a report for our Women's Center and the Public Prevention and Education Committee of the New Jersey Governor's Advisory Council Against Sexual Assault.

Students in the sociology major worked on this project for over 3 years, eventually gathering three waves of data from over 1,000 students about their experiences with interpersonal violence, as well as their intentions to intervene to prevent violence. An important finding was that 1 in 5 of our female students and 1 in 10 of our male students had experienced interpersonal violence. Even more striking, two thirds of our students knew someone who had experienced interpersonal violence. We were also able to provide evidence that students who had received Green Dot training were more likely to intervene as active bystanders than students who had not. Being able to show the prevalence of the issue and the effectiveness of our prevention strategy were important for securing institutional resources to expand the program.

Through this experience, "Public Sociologies" students were able to engage in an important evaluation project that helped them develop real-world research skills. A number of my students have gone on to work in jobs that require them to consume and produce research and to bridge theory and practice (e.g., social workers, police officers, and market researchers, to name a few). You can too!

• •

Kristin Kenneavy is an associate professor of sociology at Ramapo College of New Jersey, where she works closely with the Center for Student Involvement to promote community-based learning and scholarship and continues to research interpersonal violence prevention.

So far, we have focused on what sociology is and how sociologists know what they know and do the research they do. The rest of the book examines our social world as informed by methods and theory discussed in this chapter. The next chapter explores how you can understand your culture and society at the various levels of analysis in our social world.

WHAT HAVE WE LEARNED?

The core features of *scientific* research are (1) a commitment to empirically validated evidence, facts, and information that are confirmed through systematic processes of testing using the five senses (sometimes enhanced by scientific instruments); (2) allowing ourselves to be convinced by the evidence rather than by our preconceived ideas; (3) absolute integrity and objectivity in how we conduct and report on our research; and (4) continual openness to having our findings reexamined and new interpretations proposed. We must always consider the possibility that we have overlooked alternative explanations of the data and alternative ways to view the problem.

Science—including social science—does not consist of just facts to be memorized. Science is a process that is made possible by a social exchange of ideas, a clash of opinions, and a continual search for truth. Knowledge in the sciences is created by vigorous debate. We hope you will engage in the creation of knowledge by entering into these debates.

Theories serve as lenses to help us create research questions and to make sense of the data that we gather using various research strategies. The data themselves can be used to test the theories, so there is an ongoing reciprocal relationship between theory (the lens for making sense of the data) and research (the evidence used to test the theories). The most important ideas in this chapter concern what sociology considers data or evidence and how sociology is a science. These ideas form the framework for the content of sociology.

- Attempts to understand society have existed for at least two-and-a-half millennia, but gathering of scientific evidence to test hypotheses and validate claims is a modern idea.

- Theories are especially important to science because they raise questions for research, and they explain the relationships among facts. Sociology has four primary, overriding theoretical perspectives or paradigms: symbolic interaction theory, rational choice theory, structural-functional theory, and conflict theory. Other perspectives, such as feminist theory, serve as correctives to the main paradigms. Most of these theories are more applicable at either the micro to meso level or at the meso to macro level.

- Sociology is a science used to study society, and therefore, it is essential to understand what is—and what is not—considered data or evidence. For a scientist, this means that ideas must be tested empirically—that is, scientifically.

- As social scientists, sociologists use eight systematic steps to gather data and test theories about the social world.

- The *independent variable* is the variable in a cause-and-effect relationship that comes first in a time sequence and causes a change in another variable—the *dependent variable*.

- Major methods for gathering data in sociology include questionnaires, interviews, observational studies, secondary data analysis, content analysis, and experiments.

- Quantitative data come in the form of numbers (e.g., derived from questionnaires or some secondary sources such as the census), and qualitative data come in non-numerical forms (e.g., derived from semistructured and unstructured interviews or observational studies).

- Use of multiple methods—triangulation—increases confidence in the findings.

- Scientific confidence in results requires representative samples, usually drawn randomly.

- Responsible research requires sensitivity to the ethics of research—ensuring that gathering scientific data does no one harm.

- Public sociologists use sociological tools to understand and inform citizens about how society operates and to improve society.

DISCUSSION QUESTIONS

1. If you were to examine the relationship between the government and the economy in the United States today, which of the four major theoretical perspectives outlined in the chapter would be most helpful? Why?

2. Imagine you would like to conduct a sociological study of the students with whom you attended the fourth grade to determine what key factors influenced their academic achievements. Which of the four major theoretical perspectives would you employ in your study? Why?

3. Why do research questions have to be asked in a precise way? Give an example of a precise research question. How do precise questions make it possible for you to test and measure your topic?

4. Sociologists must be continually open to having their findings reexamined and new interpretations proposed. Describe a time when you changed your mind due to new information. Was it difficult for you to change your mind? Why, or why not?

5. Why is the ability to be open to new ideas and interpretations and to be objective so vital to the scientific perspective? Do you think you could carry this aspect of the scientific process out successfully—no matter how you feel about a topic? Why, or why not?

6. If you were to conduct a study to measure student satisfaction with a particular academic department on campus, what research method(s) would you use? Why? How would the method(s) you select vary according to (a) the size of the department and (b) the type of information you sought?

KEY TERMS

conflict theory   32

dependent variable   39

dysfunctions   31

empirical knowledge   37

feminist theory   35

hypothesis   37

independent variable   39

latent functions   31

manifest functions   31

public sociologists   43

rational choice (exchange)
    theory   29

roles   29

sample   37

stigma   36

structural-functional theory   30

symbolic interaction theory   29

theories   28

variables   37

CONTRIBUTING TO OUR SOCIAL WORLD: WHAT CAN WE DO?

At the Local Level

- *Local service organizations* are found in every community and work to provide for the unmet needs of community members: housing, legal aid, medical care, elder care, and so on. United Way works with most local service organizations and may be able to let you know which ones need help in your area. Going to www.idealist.org is also a great way to find volunteer opportunities in your area. Volunteer to work with an organization in its applied needs assessment research, and practice the sociological principles and research methods described in this chapter. If your college or university has a service learning office, it will offer connections to many service opportunities, sometimes linked to specific fields of study. Many colleges and universities also offer academic service learning (ASL) credit in which course assignments include such community work under the supervision of the instructor.

At the State/Meso Level

- *State agencies* often have ongoing projects to gather data for more accurate information about the state and the needs of its citizens. Go to www.nationalservice.gov/about/contact-us/state-service-commissions to find volunteer opportunities through your state government.

At the National and Global Levels

- The *U.S. Census Bureau* is best known for its decennial (every 10 years) enumeration of the population, but its work continues each year as it prepares special reports, population estimates, and regular publications (including *Current Population Reports*). Visit the bureau's website at www.census.gov, and explore the valuable and extensive quantitative data and other information available. Visit your local Census Bureau office, or go to www.census.gov/hrd/www/jobs/student.html to find volunteer and other opportunities for students at the bureau.

$SAGE edge™

Get the edge on your studies. **edge.sagepub.com/ballantinecondensed5e**

- Take a quiz to find out what you've learned.
- Review key terms with eFlashcards.
- Watch videos that enhance chapter content.

PART II

Social Structure, Processes, and Control

Picture a house. First, there is the foundation, then the wood frame, and then the walls and roof. This provides the framework or *structure*. Within that structure, activities called *processes* take place—electricity to turn on lights and appliances, water to wash in and drink, and people to carry out these processes. If something goes wrong in the house, we take steps to control the damage and repair it.

Whether we are building a house or a society, the process of constructing our social world is parallel. *Social structure* is the framework of society with its groups and organizations; *social processes* are the dynamic activities of society. This section begins with a discussion of the structure of society, followed by the processes of culture and socialization through which individuals are taught cultural rules—how to live effectively within their society's structure. Although socialization of individuals takes place primarily at the micro level, we explore its implications at the meso and macro levels as well.

If we break the social structure into parts, such as the wood frame, walls, and roof of a house, it is the groups and organizations (including large organizations, or bureaucracies) that are parts of the social structure. To work smoothly, these organizations depend on people's loyalty so that these participants do what society and its groups need to survive. However, these components do not always work well together. Things break down. Leaders in societies try to control disruptions and deviant individuals in order to maintain control and smooth functioning in the structures.

As we explore the next few chapters, we will continue to examine social life at the micro, meso, and macro levels, for as individuals, we are profoundly shaped by social processes and structures at larger and more abstract levels, all the way to the global level.

Society and Culture

Hardware and Software of Our Social World

Depending on what resources are available where we live and what is considered usable and edible, we put something out to eat. It might be a juicy hamburger, dog meat, or bugs. What we consider food is influenced by the organization of food production, distribution, and technology and by the culture—the ideas about what is edible. In the opening photo, an international market is bustling with activity as people shop for the kinds of foods considered nutritious and tasty in their culture.

MICRO

ME (AND MY FAMILY)

LOCAL ORGANIZATIONS AND COMMUNITY
Local soccer teams and scout troops have a microculture.

MESO

NATIONAL ORGANIZATIONS, INSTITUTIONS, AND ETHNIC SUBCULTURES
Ethnic groups have a subculture.

MACRO

SOCIETY
A nation has a national culture.

GLOBAL COMMUNITY
Multinational organizations like the World Health Organization have a global culture.

WHAT YOU WILL LEARN IN THIS CHAPTER

This chapter will help you do the following:

3.1 Describe the structure (the "hardware") of our social world.

3.2 Illustrate how culture affects individuals, groups, and societies.

3.3 Provide examples of microcultures, subcultures, countercultures, and global cultures.

3.4 Compare key ideas in the symbolic interactionist, functionalist, and conflict perspectives on culture.

3.5 Explain why culture (the "software") from one society does not always "fit" with the structure ("hardware") of another society.

◑ THINK ABOUT IT

Micro: Local community	How do microcultures (such as your fraternity, study group, or athletic team) influence you?
Meso: National institutions, complex organizations, and ethnic groups	How do subcultures (such as your ethnic group) and countercultures (such as youth gangs) shape the character of your nation and influence your own life?
Macro: National and global systems	How do your nation's social structures and culture influence who you are, what opportunities are available to you, and how you dress, eat, work, and live your life?

What is considered edible, even delectable, to people in one society may be repulsive to those in another. Taste and how people eat differs greatly, depending on the culture in which one lives. Mrs. Ukita, the mom in the Ukita family, rises early to prepare a breakfast of miso soup and a raw egg on rice. The father and two daughters eat quickly and rush out to catch their early morning trains to work and school in Kodaira City, Japan. The mother cares for the house; does the shopping; and prepares a typical evening meal of fish, vegetables, and rice for the family.

The Ahmed family lives in a large apartment building in Cairo, Egypt. The 12 members of the extended family include the women who shop for and cook the food: vegetables, including peppers, greens, potatoes, squash, tomatoes, garlic, spices, and rice, along with pita bread and often fish or meat. The adult men work in shops in one of the many bazaars while the school-age children attend school, then help with the chores.

In the Breidjing refugee camp in Chad, many Sudanese refugees eat what relief agencies can get to them—and that food source is not always reliable. Typical for the Aboubakar family, a mother and five children, is rice or some other grain, oil for cooking, dried legumes, occasionally some root plants or squash that keep longer than fresh fruits and vegetables, and a few spices. The girls and women go into the desert to fetch firewood for cooking and to get water from whatever source has water at the time. This is a dangerous trip because they may be attacked and raped or even killed outside the camps.

The Walker family from Norfolk, Virginia, grabs dinner at a fast-food restaurant on their way to basketball practice and an evening meeting. Because of their busy schedules and individual activities, they cannot always find time to cook and eat together—a behavior that would be unthinkable in most societies around the world.

Although most diets include some form of grain and starch, locally available fruits and vegetables, and perhaps meat or fish, broad variations in food consumption exist even within one society. Yet all of these differences have something in common: Each represents a society with a unique culture that includes growing or buying food, preparing and eating it, storing food, and cleaning up after eating. Food is only one aspect of our way of life, common for all humans and necessary for survival. Ask yourself why you sleep on a bed, brush your teeth, or listen to music with friends. Our way of life is called culture.

Culture refers to *the way of life shared by a group of people—the knowledge, beliefs, values, rules or laws, language, customs, symbols, and material products (such as food, houses, and transportation) within a society that help meet human needs.* Culture provides guidelines for living. Learning our culture puts our social world in an understandable framework, providing a tool kit we can use to help construct the meaning of our world and behaviors in it (Bruner 1996; Nagel 1994). We compare culture with software because it is the human ideas and input that make the society work. Otherwise, society would just be structures, like the framework of a house, with no processes to bring it alive.

A **society** is *an organized and interdependent group of individuals who live together in a specific geographic area, who interact more with each other than they do with outsiders, who cooperate for the attainment of common goals, and who share a common culture over time.* Most often, societies are the same as the countries that make up the world. Each society includes key parts called institutions—family, education, religion, politics, economies, and health care or medicine—that meet basic human needs. This structure that makes up society is what we refer to here as the hardware, like the structure of a computer. Culture, the software, is learned, transmitted,

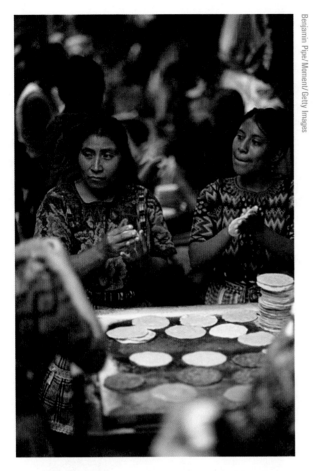

Traditional, rural Mayan women in Guatemala make tortillas, or *boxboles*. Food preparation, as well as consumption, is a deeply communal experience among these people.

shared, and reshaped from generation to generation. All activities in the society, whether educating young members, preparing and eating dinner, selecting leaders for the group, finding a mate, or negotiating with other societies, are guided by cultural rules and expectations. In each society, culture provides the social rules for how individuals carry out necessary tasks.

Society—organized groups of people—and culture—their way of life—are interdependent. The two are not the same thing, but they cannot exist without each other, just as computer hardware and software are each useless without the other.

This chapter explores the ideas of society and culture and their relation to each other, what society is and how it is organized, how it influences and is influenced by culture, what culture is, how and why culture develops, the components of culture, cultural theories, and policy issues. After reading this chapter, you will have a better idea of how you learn and make use of your society's culture.

SOCIETY: THE HARDWARE

The structures that make up society include the micro-level positions we hold (parent, student, and employee); the groups to which we belong (family, work group, and clubs); and the larger groups, organizations, or institutions in which we participate (education, political, and economic organizations). This "hardware" (structure) of our social world provides the framework for "software" (culture) to function.

Societies, usually countries but sometimes distinct sovereign groups within countries (such as Native Americans), differ because they exist in different locations with unique resources—mountains, coastal areas, jungles, and deserts. Although human societies have become more complex over time, especially in recent human history, people have been hunters and gatherers for 99% of human existence. Only a few groups remain hunters and gatherers today. As Table 3.1 illustrates, if all human history were to be compressed into the lifetime of an 80-year-old person, humans would have started cultivating crops and herding animals for their food supply only a few months ago. Note the incredible rate of change that has occurred just in the past 2 centuries.

Thinking Sociologically

What major changes took place in your grandparents' lifetimes that affect the way you and your family live today?

Societies are organized in particular patterns shaped by factors that include the way people procure food, the availability of resources, contact with other societies, and cultural beliefs. For example, people can change from herding to farming only if they have the knowledge, skills, and desire to do so and only in environments that will support agriculture. As societies develop, changes take place in the social structures and relationships between people. For example, in industrialized societies, relationships between people typically become more formal because people must interact with strangers and not just their relatives. It is important to note that not all societies go through all stages. Some are jolted into the future by political events or changes in the global system, and some resist pressures to become modernized and continue to live in simpler social systems.

Evolution of Societies

The Saharan desert life for the Tuareg tribe is pretty much as it has been for centuries. In simple traditional societies,

Table 3.1   One Million Years of Human History Compressed Into One 80-Year Lifetime

Approximate Time	Age	Event in Human History	
2.5 million years ago	Birth	*Homo habilis* is born—the first ancestor to make/use tools and have culture; evidence of sharing food, congregating, and probably sharing housing	iStockphoto.com/markichentx
2 million years ago	2 years old	*Homo erectus* shows early evidence of family structures; findings of longer life spans and three generations alive simultaneously	
15,000 years ago	79 years old	Six months ago: North America settled by early humans, hunters and gatherers	
11,000 years ago	79 years old	Five months ago: In the Middle East, the first agricultural communities, indicating food cultivation	
10,000 years ago	79 years old	Twenty weeks ago: the last ice age is over; humans spread more widely over the planet	iStockphoto.com/pius99
5,000 years ago	79 years old	Ten weeks ago: humans began to cast and use metals and built the pyramids	
2,000 years ago	79 years old	Seven weeks ago: beginning of the Common Era (under the Holy Roman Empire)	Library of Congress
220 years ago	79 years old	Two and a half weeks ago: the United States began a new experiment with democracy	
100 years ago	79 years old	Yesterday morning: the airplane was invented	Library of Congress, Prints & Photographs Division, [LC-DIG-ppprs-00626]
30–50 years ago	80th birthday	Yesterday afternoon: humans first set foot on the moon; after dinner, we broke the DNA (genetic) code and invented the first cell phone	NASA / © iStockphoto.com/pagadesign

individuals are assigned to comparatively few social positions or statuses. Today, however, few societies are isolated from global impact. Even the Tuareg are called on to escort adventurous tourists through the desert for a currency new to them and unneeded until recently. In 2012, al-Qaeda in the Islamic (or Arabian) Maghreb challenged the Tuareg's control over their desert homeland in a war in northern Mali, Africa. The Islamists have been pushed out, but the Taureg continue to struggle for autonomy as a people ("Mali 'at War' With Tuareg Rebels" 2014).

In such traditional societies, men teach their sons and nephews everything they need to know, for all men do mostly the same jobs, depending on where they live: hunting, fishing, or farming and protecting the community from danger. Likewise, daughters learn their jobs—such as childcare, fetching water, food preparation, farming, weaving, and perhaps house building—from their mothers and other female relatives. In contrast, in more complex societies, such as industrial or "modern" societies, thousands of interdependent job statuses are based on complex divisions of labor with designated tasks.

Émile Durkheim ([1893] 1947), an early French sociologist, pictured a continuum between simple and complex societies. He described simple premodern societies as held together by **mechanical solidarity**—*social cohesion and integration based on the similarity of individuals in the group, including shared beliefs, values, and emotional ties between members of the group*. Furthermore, the division of labor is based largely on male/female distinctions and age groupings; everyone fulfills his or her expected social positions. This provides the glue that holds the society together. The entire society may involve only a few hundred people, with no meso-level institutions, organizations, or subcultures. Prior to the emergence of nation-states, there was no macro level either—only tribal groupings.

According to Durkheim ([1893] 1947), as societies transformed, they became more complex through increasingly multifaceted divisions of labor and changes in the ways people carried out necessary tasks for survival. **Organic solidarity** refers to *social cohesion (glue) based on division of labor, with each member playing a highly specialized role in the society and each person being dependent on others due to interdependent, interrelated tasks*. The society has cohesion regardless of whether people have common values and shared outlooks. Prior to the factory system, for example, individual cobblers made shoes to order. With the Industrial Revolution, factories took over the process, with many individuals carrying out interdependent tasks. The division of labor is critical because it leads to new forms of social cohesion based on

interdependence, not on emotional ties. Gradual changes from mechanical (traditional) to organic (modern) society also involve harnessing new forms of energy and finding more efficient ways to use them (P. Nolan and Lenski 2014). For example, the use of steam engines and coal for fuel triggered the Industrial Revolution, leading to the development of industrial societies.

As societies changed toward organic solidarity, they added large organizations and institutions. The meso level—institutions and large bureaucratic organizations—became more influential for individuals and families. Still, as recently as 200 years ago, even large societies had little global interdependence, and life for the typical citizen was influenced mostly by events at the micro and meso levels. As communication and transportation around the world developed and expanded, the global level grew.

As you read about each of the following types of societies, from the simplest to the most complex, notice the presence of these variables: (a) division of labor, (b) interdependence of people's positions, (c) increasingly advanced technologies, and (d) new forms and uses of energy. Although none of these variables alone is *sufficient* to trigger evolution to a new type of society, they may all be *necessary* for a transition to occur.

According to Durkheim, then, in traditional societies with mechanical solidarity, interpersonal interaction and community life at the micro level were the most important aspects of social life. Meso- and macro-level societies developed as a result of changes toward more organic solidarity. As societies become more complex, meso- and macro-level institutions become more important and have increasingly profound impacts on the lives of individuals.

Hunter-Gatherer Societies. In the Kalahari Desert of southwestern Africa live hunter-gatherers known as the !Kung. (The *!* is pronounced with a click of the tongue.) The !Kung live a nomadic life, moving from one place to another as food supplies become available or are used up. As a result, they carry very few personal possessions and live in temporary huts, settling around water holes for a few months at a time. Settlements are small, rarely more than 20 to 50 people, for food supplies are not plentiful enough to support large, permanent populations (R. Lee 1984). !Kung women gather edible plants and nuts while !Kung men hunt. Beyond division of labor by gender and age, however, there are few differences in roles or status.

In *hunter-gatherer societies*, people rely on the vegetation and animals occurring naturally in their habitat to sustain life. Generally, life is organized around kinship ties and reciprocity—that is, mutual assistance—for the well-being

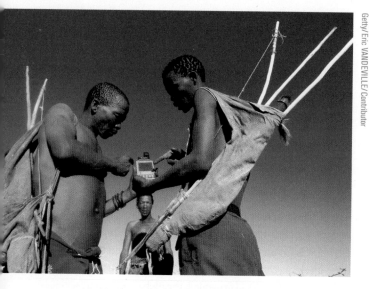

Hunting and gathering societies, like these Botswana bushmen, do still exist, but they are increasingly affected by modern societies and technologies. These hunters make notes of their most recent excursion on a GPS app on their smartphone.

of the whole community. When a large animal is killed, people gather from a wide area to share in the bounty, and great care is taken to ensure that the meat is distributed fairly. Resources are shared among the people, but sharing is regulated by a complex system of mutual obligations. A visitor who eats food at another's hearth is expected to repay that hospitality in the future.

The !Kung are a typical hunter-gatherer society. They make their clothing, shelter, and tools from available materials or obtain goods through trade with other nearby groups. People migrate seasonally to new food sources. Population size remains small, as the numbers of births and deaths in the society are balanced.

From the beginning of human experience until recently, hunting and gathering (or foraging) were the sole means of sustaining life. Other types of societies emerged only recently. Today, only a handful of societies still rely on hunting and gathering (P. Nolan and Lenski 2014). The hunter-gatherer lifestyle is becoming extinct largely because no society is isolated in today's world.

Herding and Horticultural Societies.

A seminomadic herding society, the Masai of Kenya and Tanzania move camp to find grazing land for their animals and set up semipermanent shelters for the few months they will remain in one area. Settlements consist of huts constructed in a circle with a perimeter fence surrounding the compound. At the more permanent settlements, the Masai grow short-term crops to supplement their diet.

Herding societies have food-producing strategies based on domestication of animals, whose care is the central focus of their activities. Domesticating animals has replaced hunting them. In addition to providing food and other products, cattle, sheep, goats, pigs, horses, and camels represent forms of wealth that result in more social prestige for members of the group with large herds.

Horticultural societies are those in which the food-producing strategy is based on domestication of plants, using digging sticks and wooden hoes to cultivate small gardens. They may also keep domesticated animals, but they focus on simple agriculture or gardening. They cultivate tree crops, such as date palms or bananas, and plant garden plots, such as yams, beans, taro, squash, or corn. This is more efficient than gathering wild vegetables and fruits. Both herding and horticultural societies differ from hunter-gatherer societies in that they settle in one place, make their living by cultivating food, and have some control over its production (Ward and Edelstein 2014).

The ability to control food sources was a major turning point in human history. Societies became more settled and stored surpluses of food, which led to increases in population size. A community could contain as many as 3,000 individuals. More people, surplus food, and greater accumulation of possessions encouraged the development of private property and created new status differences between individuals and families. Forms of social inequality started to become pronounced.

The technological breakthrough that moved many societies from the horticultural to the agricultural stage was the plow, introduced more than 6,000 years ago. It marked the beginning of the agricultural revolution in Europe, the Middle East, and other parts of the world, and it brought about massive changes in social structures in many societies. The end of the horticultural stage also saw advances in irrigation systems, the fertilization of land, crop rotation, more permanent settlements, land ownership, human modification of the natural environment, higher population density (cities), and power hierarchies.

Agricultural Societies.

Pedro and Lydia Ramirez, their four young children, and Lydia's parents live as an extended family in a small farming village in Nicaragua. They plow the land with the help of strong animals, such as horses and oxen, and use fertilizers and water the garden when needed. The Ramirezes' way of life is typical in an agricultural society. Agricultural societies rely primarily on raising crops for food but make use of technological advances, such as the plow, irrigation, animals, and fertilization, to continuously cultivate the same land. The continuous cultivation of the same land results in permanent settlements and greater food surpluses. Agricultural societies use energy more efficiently than foraging societies. For example, the plow circulates nutrients better than a digging stick, and when an animal pulls the plow, the farmer uses strength beyond that of a person. As increasingly sophisticated agricultural technology resulted in surplus food, the size of population centers increased to as much as a million or more.

As surpluses accumulated, land in some societies became concentrated in the hands of a few individuals. Wealthy landowners built armies and expanded their empires. During these periods, fighting for land took precedence over technological advances. War was prevalent, and societies were divided increasingly into rich and poor classes. Those who held the land and wealth could control the labor sources and acquire serfs or slaves. Thus, the feudal system was born. Serfs (the peasant class) were forced to work the land for their survival. Food surpluses also allowed some individuals to leave the land and to trade goods or services in exchange for food. For the first time, social inequality became extensive enough to divide society into social classes. At this point, religion, political power, a standing army, and other meso-level institutions and organizations came to be independent of the family. The meso level became well established.

As technology advanced, goods were manufactured in cities. Peasants moved from farming communities, where the land could not support the large population, to rapidly growing urban areas, where the demand for labor was great. It was not until the mid-1700s in England that the next major transformation of society began to take place, resulting largely from technological advances and additional harnessing of energy. (See Figure 3.1 for a timeline of this transformation.)

Industrial Societies. The Industrial Revolution involved the harnessing of steam power and the manufacture of gasoline engines, permitting machines to replace human and animal power. A tractor can plow far more land in a week than a horse, and an electric pump can irrigate more acres than an ox-driven pump. As a result of such new technologies, raw mineral products such as ores, raw plant products such as rubber, and raw animal products such as hides could be transformed into mass-produced consumer goods. The Industrial Revolution brought about enormous changes in occupations, the division of labor, production of goods, and social structures.

Industrial societies rely primarily on mechanized production, resulting in greater division of labor based on

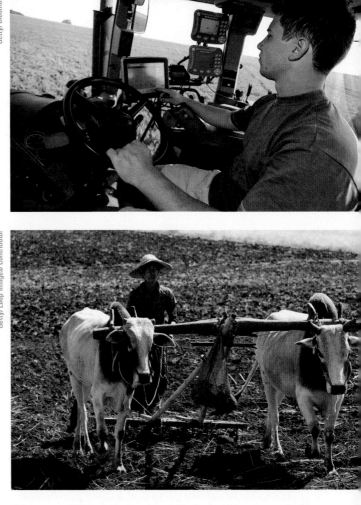

Plows, essential for agricultural societies to develop, were pushed by people and then pulled by animals and later machines. Harnessing energy ever more effectively is a prerequisite to a society becoming more complex.

expertise. Economic resources were distributed more widely among individuals in industrial societies, but inequities between owners and laborers persisted. Wage earning gradually replaced slavery and serfdom, and highly skilled workers earned higher wages, leading to the rise of a middle class. Farm workers moved from rural areas to cities to find work in factories that produced consumer goods. Cities grew, and many became populated by millions of people.

Family and kinship patterns at the micro level also changed. Agricultural societies need large, land-based extended family units to do the work of farming (recall how the Ramirez parents, grandparents, and children in

FIGURE 3.1   Timeline of the Industrial Revolution, 1712–1903

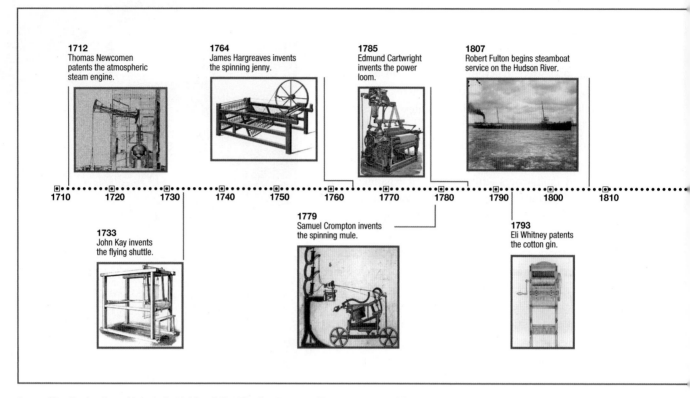

Source: Timeline is adapted from *Industrial Revolution: Timeline, Facts, and Resources,* research by B. Sobey, TheFreeResource.com.

Nicaragua all help out at harvest time), but industrial societies need individuals with specific skills, the ability to move to where the jobs are, and smaller families to support. Family roles change. Children are an asset in agricultural societies and begin work at an early age. However, from a purely economic perspective, children become a liability in an industrial society because they contribute less to the finances of the family.

Meso- and macro-level dimensions of social life expand in industrializing societies and become more influential in the lives of individuals. National institutions and multinational organizations develop. Today, for example, global organizations, such as the World Bank, the World Court, the United Nations, and the World Health Organization, address social problems and sometimes even make decisions that change national boundaries or national policies. Corporations such as Nike and Gap are multinational organizations (located in many countries). Some voluntary associations—such as Doctors Without Borders, which serves medical needs, and Amnesty International, which lobbies for human rights—do their work across the globe.

Perhaps the most notable characteristic of the industrial age is the rapid rate of change compared with other stages of societal development. The beginning of industrialization in Europe was gradual, based on years of population movement, urbanization, technological development, and other factors of modernization. Today, however, societal change occurs so rapidly that societies at all levels of development are being drawn together into a new age: the postindustrial era.

Postindustrial or Information Societies. *Postindustrial societies* are those that have moved from human labor and manufacturing to automated production and service jobs, largely processing information. Postindustrial societies require workers with high levels of technical and professional education. Those without technical education are less likely to find rewarding employment in the technological revolution. This results in new class lines being drawn, based in part on skills and education in new technologies.

The shift to an information-based society has also enhanced cross-border workplaces. As your authors finished chapters for this book, the manuscript was sent to India for typesetting in the evening and due to the time change was returned to the United States by morning. Technology, the efficiency of overnight delivery, and the lower cost of production have led many publishing companies to turn to

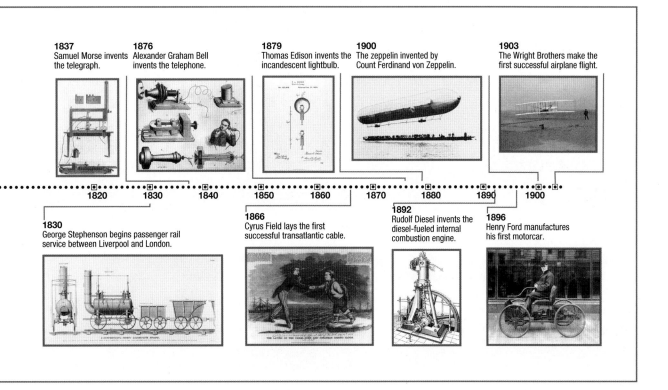

1837
Samuel Morse invents the telegraph.

1876
Alexander Graham Bell invents the telephone.

1879
Thomas Edison invents the incandescent lightbulb.

1900
The zeppelin invented by Count Ferdinand von Zeppelin.

1903
The Wright Brothers make the first successful airplane flight.

1820 1830 1840 1850 1860 1870 1880 1890 1900

1830
George Stephenson begins passenger rail service between Liverpool and London.

1866
Cyrus Field lays the first successful transatlantic cable.

1892
Rudolf Diesel invents the diesel-fueled internal combustion engine.

1896
Henry Ford manufactures his first motorcar.

businesses halfway around the world for much of the book production process. As India and other developing countries increase their trained, skilled labor force, they are being called on by national and multinational companies to carry out global manufacturing processes. India has some of the world's best technical training institutes and modern *technology*—the practical application of tools, skills, and knowledge to meet human needs and extend human abilities. Although many people in India live in poverty, a relatively new middle class is rapidly emerging in major business centers around the country.

After World War II, starting in the 1950s, the transition from industrial to postindustrial society began in the United States, Western Europe, and Japan. This shift was characterized by movement from human labor to automated production and from a predominance of manufacturing jobs to a growth in service jobs, such as computer operators, bankers, scientists, teachers, public-relations workers, stockbrokers, and salespeople. More than two thirds of all jobs in the United States now reside in organizations that produce and transmit information, thus the reference to an *information age*. Daniel Bell describes this transformation of work, information, and communication as *the third technological revolution* after industrialization based on steam (the first

This Buddhist monk uses modern technology, including a laptop that can connect him with colleagues on the other side of the globe.

technological revolution) and the invention of electricity (the second technological revolution) (D. Bell 1973, 1989). According to Bell, the third technological revolution was the development of the computer, which has led to this postindustrial era, or information age. To examine this transformation, see Table 3.2 in the next "Engaging Sociology."

ENGAGING SOCIOLOGY

Demographics of Internet Users

The following is the percentage of each group of U.S. adults who use the Internet, according to a Pew Internet and American Life Project survey. For instance, 86% of women use the Internet.

Table 3.2   Demographics of Internet Users

	Percentage Who Use the Internet
All Adults	87
Men	87
Women	86
Race/Ethnicity	
White, non-Hispanic	85
Black, non-Hispanic	81
Hispanic (English and Spanish speaking)	83
Age	
18–29	97
30–49	93
50–64	88
65+	57
Household Income	
Less than $30,000/year	76
$30,000–$49,999	83
$50,000–$74,999	95
$75,000+	99
Educational Attainment	
High school grad or less	76
Some college	91
College +	97

Source: "Internet User Demographics," Pew Research Center, Washington, DC (January, 2014). http://www.pewinternet.org/data-trend/internet-use/latest-stats/

Engaging With Sociology

Interview 10 people you know to find out about their Internet use, keeping records on the gender, age, race and ethnicity, educational attainment, and income bracket of each. Then, compare your figures with those in Table 3.2. Are they similar? If not, what possible geographic, social class, or other factors might cause your figures to be different from those in this national survey?

Postindustrial societies rely on new sources of power such as atomic, wind, thermal, and solar energy and new uses of computer automation. Computer-controlled robots have taken over many jobs once carried out by humans. The control of information and the ability to develop technologies or provide services have become key resources of money and power.

Values of 21st-century postindustrial societies favor scientific and creative approaches to problem solving, research, and development, along with attitudes that support the globalization of world economies. Satellites, cell phones, fiber optics, and especially the Internet continue to transform postindustrial societies of the information age, linking people from societies around the world.

What will the future bring? With discovery and efficient use of energy being central to sociocultural evolution and with reduction of pollution essential to stopping global climate change, alternative energy sources from wind, solar, and other forms of power will become essential. One million hydrogen-fueled cars are predicted for the United States by the year 2035 and far more for Europe and Japan. Rechargeable batteries that run for 40 hours without interruption will run many automobiles and most home appliances by 2030 (Kleinman 2014). We do not yet know how these new technologies may alter human interactions.

In much of this book, we focus on complex, multilevel societies, for this is the type of social environment in which most of us reading this book now live. Much of this book also focuses on social interaction and social structures, including interpersonal networking, the growth of bureaucratic structures, social inequality within the structure, and the core institutions necessary to meet the needs of individuals and society. In short, *hardware*— society—is the focus of many subsequent chapters. The remainder of this chapter focuses primarily on the social *software*—culture.

CULTURE: THE SOFTWARE

Culture—the ideas and "things" passed on from one generation to the next in a society, including knowledge, beliefs, values, rules and laws, language, customs, symbols, and material products—varies greatly as we travel across the globe. Each social unit of interdependent people, whether at the micro, meso, or macro level, develops a unique way of life with guidelines for expected actions and interaction of individuals and groups within society.

As you can see, the sociological definition of culture refers to far more than "high or elite culture" shared by a select few—such as fine art, classical music, opera, literature, ballet, and theater—and also far more than "popular culture"—such as reality TV, professional wrestling, YouTube, and other mass entertainment. *Popular culture* is mass produced and consumed and becomes part of everyday traditions through its practices, beliefs, and material objects. It influences public opinion and values. One type of pop culture is music in its many forms; for example, rap music often focuses on urban culture's politics, economics, and inequality and provides an outlet for frustrations through musical commentary. Much of pop culture has been shaped by technology, as we see in texting and social media. The very rapid change in this aspect of popular culture is illustrated in the next "Engaging Sociology."

Characteristics of Culture

All cultures have certain characteristics in common that define and illustrate the purposes it serves for our societies. What are these common elements?

All people share a culture with others in their society. Culture provides the rules, routines, patterns, and expectations for carrying out daily rituals and interactions. Within a society, the process of learning how to act is called socialization (discussed in Chapter 4). From birth, we learn the patterns of behavior approved in our society.

Culture evolves over time and is adaptive. What is normal, proper, and good behavior in hunter-gatherer societies, where cooperation and communal loyalty are critical to the hunt, differs from appropriate behavior in the information age, where individualism and competition are encouraged and enhance one's position and well-being.

The creation of culture is ongoing and cumulative. Individuals and societies continually build on existing culture to adapt to new challenges and opportunities. Your culture shapes the behaviors, values, and institutions that seem natural to you. Culture is so much a part of life that you may not even notice behaviors that outsiders find unusual or even abhorrent. You may not think about it when handing food to someone with your left hand, but in some other cultures, such an act may be defined as disgusting and rude.

ENGAGING SOCIOLOGY

Pop Culture Technology Timeline

Getty Images/Bernhard Lang/Iconica

How surprising to think that digital telephones, high-speed lines for computers, digitized print media, and the World Wide Web were all invented within about the past half-century, many within the last 20 years. Vinyl records, dial telephones, and VHS tapes have been surpassed by CDs, cell phones, DVDs, and streamed and downloaded movies and music. Slim laptops, iPads, and handheld computers have replaced bulky desktop computers. The following timeline shows the rapid advances of the Internet and World Wide Web in recent years; the point of this timeline is to illustrate the rapid advance of technology and the place it holds in our lives. Technology is now a primary conveyor of culture, especially pop culture.

An Internet and World Wide Web Timeline

1946: The first general-purpose computer is created, developed for military purposes.

1951: The first civilian computer is created.

1971: The first personal computer (PC) is launched.

1978: Cellular phone service begins.

1982: Invention of high-speed communications network leads to the Internet.

1984: Apple's Macintosh introduces the first PC with graphics.

1991: The Internet opens to commercial uses; the World Wide Web is launched.

1996: Google makes its debut.

2002: Amazon Web Services launched, followed in 2006 by Amazon Elastic Compute cloud.

2004: Mark Zuckerberg starts Facebook while still a college student.

2005: YouTube is created by Chad Hurley, Steve Chen, and Jawed Karim.

2009: "Killer apps," from Microsoft and Google, service delivery introduced.

2013: Wristbands to collect biological data and living, breathing running shoes launched.

2014: Video glasses with head-mounted display screen debut, and smartwatches connect to the Internet and smartphones.

2015: Three-dimensional computer cursors and robotic exoskeletons are controlled by human thoughts.

The continuing rapid advances in technology have paralleled the development of shared pop culture in the United States and around the world, culture that is accessible to everyone. Music groups from other continents have gained audiences in the United States, with some musical groups becoming instant success stories through YouTube.

* * * * * * *

Engaging With Sociology

1. Identify four of the innovations that you feel are particularly significant. What are some ways in which they have impacted your life?

2. Identify three positive and three negative ways these rapid advances in technology might impact less developed parts of the world.

3. How can the spread of pop culture across the globe (a) bring different societies closer together and (b) cause tensions within and between societies?

The transmission of culture is the feature that most separates humans from other animals. Some societies of higher primates have shared cultures but do not systematically enculturate (teach a way of life to) the next generation. Primate cultures focus on behaviors relating to obtaining food, use of territory, protection, and social status. Human cultures have significantly more content and are mediated by language. Humans are the only mammals with cultures that enable them to adapt to and even modify their environments so that they can survive on the equator, in the Arctic, or even beyond the planet.

Thinking Sociologically

Imagine playing a game of cards with four people in which each player thinks a different suit is *trump* (a rule whereby any card from the trump suit wins over any card from a different suit). In this game, one person believes hearts is trump, another assumes spades is trump, and so forth. What would happen? How would the result be similar to a society with no common culture?

Ethnocentrism and Cultural Relativity

"What's morally acceptable? It depends on where in the world you live" (Poushter 2014). In a study of 40 countries around the world about what is morally acceptable—and not—researchers at the Pew Research Center found that 78% of respondents around the world say extramarital affairs are morally unacceptable (84% in the United States), compared with 46% responding that premarital sex was unacceptable (30% in the United States). Other morality issues included gambling (62% unacceptable), abortion (56%), alcohol use (42%), divorce (24%), and contraception use (14%). The point is that what is morally acceptable varies across societies, causing judgments of others based on one's own standards. *The tendency to view one's own group and its cultural expectations as right, proper, and superior to others* is called ethnocentrism— *ethno* for ethnic group and *centrism* for centered on. As you can see, social values, beliefs, and behaviors can vary dramatically from one society to the next. These differences can be threatening and even offensive to people who judge others according to their own perspectives, experiences, and values.

If you were brought up in a society that forbids premarital or extramarital sex, for instance, you might judge many from the United States to be immoral. In a few Muslim societies, people who have premarital sex may be severely punished or even executed because such behavior is seen as an offense against the faith and the family and as a weakening of social bonds. It threatens the lineage and inheritance systems of family groups. In turn, some Americans would find such strict rules of abstinence to be strange and even wrong.

As scientists, sociologists must rely on scientific research to understand behavior. The scientific method calls for *objectivity*—the practice of considering observed behaviors independently of one's own beliefs and values. The study of social behavior, such as that cited earlier by the Pew Research Center, requires both sensitivity to a wide variety of human social patterns and a perspective that reduces bias. This is more difficult than it sounds because sociologists themselves are products of society and culture. All of us are raised in a particular culture that we view as normal or natural. Yet not every culture views the same things as "normal."

Societies instill some degree of ethnocentrism in their members because ethnocentric beliefs hold groups together and help members feel that they belong to the group. Ethnocentrism promotes loyalty, unity, high morale, and conformity to the rules of society. Fighting for one's country, for instance, requires some degree of belief in the rightness of one's own society and its causes. Ethnocentric attitudes also help protect societies from rapid, disintegrating change. If most people in a society did not believe in the rules and values of their own culture, the result could be widespread dissent, deviance, or crime.

Unfortunately, ethnocentrism can lead to misunderstandings between people of different cultures. The same ethnocentric attitudes that strengthen ties between some people may encourage hostility, racism, war, and genocide against others—even others within the society—who are different. Virtually all societies tend to "demonize" their adversary—in movies, the news, and political speeches—especially when a conflict is most intense. Dehumanizing another group with labels makes it easier to torture or kill its members or to perform acts of discrimination and brutality against them. We see this in the current conflict in Syria in which both sides in the conflict feel hatred for each other. However, as we become a part of a global social world, it becomes increasingly important to understand and accept those who are "different." Bigotry and attitudes of superiority do not enhance cross-national cooperation and trade—which is what the increasing movement toward a global village and globalization entails. The map in Figure 3.2 challenges our ethnocentric view of the world.

FIGURE 3.2   "Southside Up" Global Map

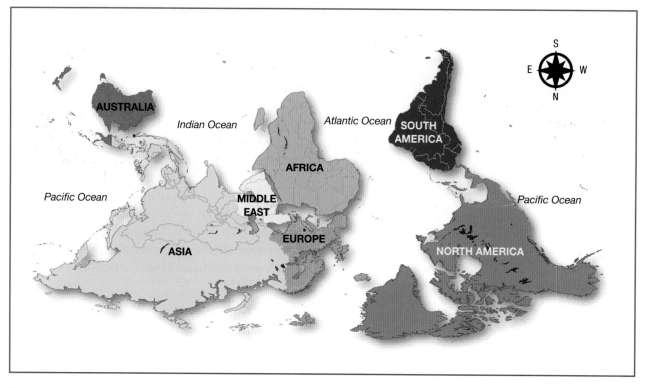

Source: Map by Anna Versluis.

Note: This map illustrates geographic ethnocentrism. U.S. citizens tend to assume it is natural that north should always be "on top." The fact that this map of the world is upside down, where south is "up," seems incorrect or disturbing to some people. Most people think of their countries or regions as occupying a central and larger part of the world.

Thinking Sociologically

What strikes you about the map? What is your reaction? How would you see this map through ethnocentric eyes and through the eyes of a cultural relativist?

U.S. foreign relations illustrate how ethnocentrism can produce hostility. Many U.S. citizens are surprised to learn that the United States—a great democracy, world power, and disseminator of food, medicine, and technological assistance to developing nations—is despised in many countries. Anti-U.S. demonstrations in South America, the Middle East, and Asia have brought this reality to life through television. The countries with the most negative feelings, over 50% of the population with an unfavorable opinion of the United States, according to polls, are Jordan (83%), Russia (81% unfavorable, up from 33% in 2010), Palestinian territories (70%), Pakistan (62%), Lebanon (60%), and Turkey (58%) (Wike, Stokes, and Poushter 2015). One cause for the unfavorable feelings in these countries is the political dominance

of the United States and the threat it poses to other people's way of life. In many places of the world, people believe the U.S. government and its citizens think only about their own welfare as their country exploits weaker nations. U.S. tourists are sometimes seen as loud-mouthed ignoramuses whose ethnocentric attitudes prevent them from seeing value in other cultures or from learning other languages.

Note that even referring to citizens of the United States as "Americans"—as though people from Canada, Mexico, Central America, and South America do not really count as Americans—is seen as ethnocentric by many people from these other countries. *America* and the *United States of America* are not the same thing, but many people in the U.S., including some presidents, fail to make the distinction. If you visit the United Mexican States (Mexico's official name), people might ask you where you are from. Say "America," and they, too, will say they are from America. Say "North America," and Mexicans will say, "From Canada or the United States of America?"

Not all ethnocentrism is hostile; some of it is just a reaction to the strange ways of other cultures. An example is making judgments about what is proper food to eat and what is just not edible. Although people everywhere eat, we can see widespread cultural differences in what people eat, as noted in the first part of this chapter. Some of the New Guinea tribes savor grasshoppers; Europeans and Russians relish raw fish eggs (caviar); Inuit children may find seal eyeballs a treat; some Indonesians eat dog; and some Nigerians prize termites. Whether it is from another time period or another society, variations in food can be shocking to us.

In contrast to ethnocentrism, cultural relativism *requires setting aside cultural and personal beliefs and prejudices to understand another group or society through the eyes of its members and using its own community standards.* Instead of judging cultural practices and social behavior as good or bad according to one's own cultural practices, the goal is to be impartial in learning the purposes and consequences of practices and behaviors of the group under study. Cultural relativism does not require that social scientists accept or agree with all of the beliefs and behaviors of the societies or groups they study. Yet it allows them to try to understand those practices in the social and cultural contexts in which they occur.

Being tolerant and understanding is not always easy. Some behaviors or ideas in other cultures can be difficult for even the most objective observer to understand. The notion of being "on time," for example, which is so much a part of the cultures of the United States, Canada, Japan, and parts of Europe, is a rather bizarre concept in some societies. Among most Native American people, such as the Dineh (Apache and Navajo), "clock time" is used when in contact with White institutions, such as schools, but of little use in their daily lives. To let a piece of machinery, such as a cell phone, govern the way one constructs and lives life is accommodated when necessary, but the Dineh orientation to time is that one should do things according to the natural rhythm of the body and other "timepieces" in nature (e.g., the moon), not according to an artificial electronic mechanism. This concept of time is difficult for many people outside some Native American cultures to grasp (E. Hall 1983; C. Wells 2008). Misunderstandings occur when North Americans think that "Native Americans are always late" and jump to the erroneous conclusion that "Indians" are undependable. Native Americans, on the other hand, think Whites are neurotic about letting some instrument control them (Basso 1996; Farrer 2011; E. Hall 1983).

⬤ **Thinking Sociologically**

Small, tightly knit societies with no meso or macro level often stress cooperation, conformity, and personal sacrifice for the sake of the community. Complex societies with established meso- and macro-level linkages tend to be more individualistic, stressing personal uniqueness, individual creativity, and critical thinking. Why do you think this is the case?

THE COMPONENTS OF CULTURE: THINGS AND THOUGHTS

Things (material objects) and thoughts (nonmaterial ideas) make up our culture. Together, they provide the guidelines for our lives.

Material Culture: The Artifacts of Life

Material culture *includes all the human-made objects we can see or touch—all of the artifacts of a group of people—*grindstones for grinding cassava root, microwave ovens for cooking, bricks of mud or clay for building shelters, hides or woven cloth for making clothing, books or computers for conveying information, tools for reshaping environments, vessels for carrying and sharing food, and weapons for dominating and subduing others.

Some material culture is from the local community; it is of micro-level origin. The kinds of materials with which homes are constructed and the materials used for clothing often reflect the geography and resources of the local area. Houses are an especially good example of material culture because they result from local ideas of what a "home" looks like and shape the interactions and attitudes of people in the society. Likewise, types of jewelry, pottery, musical instruments, or clothing reflect tastes that emerge at the micro and meso levels of family, community, and subculture. At a more macro level, national and international corporations interested in making profits work hard to establish trends in fashion and style that may cross continents and oceans.

Material culture helps drive the globalization process. Workers in Asia and Central American countries now make many of our clothes. Our shoes may come from the Philippines. The last banana you ate probably grew in Costa Rica, Guatemala, Honduras, or Panama. That

Keith Roberts

Homes are good examples of material culture. Their construction is influenced not only by local materials but also by ideas of what a home is. Homes shape the context in which family members interact, so they can influence the nonmaterial culture, including beliefs, values, and symbols. Houses, like clothes, act as symbols that communicate levels of prestige.

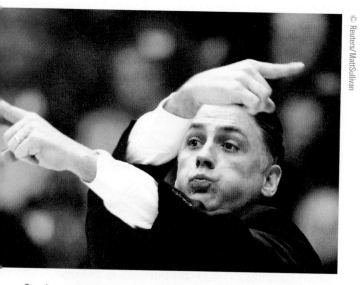

© Reuters/MattSullivan

Coaches and players use hand signals to cue each other into an upcoming play or to convey what defense or offense to set up—an example of nonverbal communication.

romantic diamond engagement ring—a symbol that represents the most intimate tie—may well be imported from a South African mine using low-paid or even slave labor. Our cars consist of parts produced on nearly every continent.

Thinking Sociologically

Think of examples of material culture that you use daily: stove, automobile, cell phone, computer, refrigerator, clock, money, and so forth. How do these material objects influence your way of life and the way you interact with others? How would your behavior be different if one of these material objects, say iPhones or money, did not exist?

Nonmaterial Culture: Beliefs, Values, Rules, and Language

Saluting the flag, saying a blessing before meals, flashing someone an obscene gesture, and a football coach signaling what defensive formation to run for the next play are all symbolic acts. In the case of the salute and the prayer, the acts undergird a belief about the nation or about a higher spiritual presence. In each case, something is communicated, yet each of these acts refers to something more abstract than any material object.

Nonmaterial culture refers to *the thoughts, language, feelings, beliefs, values, and attitudes that make up much of our culture.* They are the invisible and intangible parts of culture that involve society's rules of behavior, ideas, and beliefs that shape how people interact with others and with their environment. Although we cannot touch the nonmaterial components of our culture, they pervade our life and influence how we think, feel, and behave. Nonmaterial culture is complex, comprising four main elements: values, beliefs, norms or rules, and language.

Values are shared judgments about what is desirable or undesirable, right or wrong, and good or bad. They express the basic ideals of any group of people. In industrial and postindustrial societies, for instance, a good education is highly valued. That you are in college shows you have certain values toward learning and education. Gunnar Myrdal, a Swedish sociologist and observer of U.S. culture, referred to the U.S. value system as the *American creed,* so much a part of the way of life that it acquires the power of religious doctrine (Myrdal 1964). We tend to take our core values for granted, including freedom, equality, individualism, democracy, free enterprise, efficiency, progress, achievement, and material comfort (Macionis 2016; R. Williams 1970).

At the macro level, conflicts may arise between groups in society because of differing value systems. For example, there are major differences between the values of various Native American nations and the dominant culture—whether that dominant culture is in North, Central, or South America (R. Lake 1990; Sharp 1991). These conflicts in values have had serious consequences. For example, cooperation is a cultural value that has been passed on through generations of Native Americans. Their group survival has always depended on group cooperation in the hunt, in war, and in daily life. The value of cooperation can place native children at a disadvantage in schools that emphasize competition. Native American and Canadian First Nations children experience more success in classrooms that stress cooperation and sociability over competition and individuality (R. Lake 1990; Mehan 1992).

Beliefs are ideas we hold about life, about the way society works, and about where we fit into the world. They are expressed as specific statements that we hold to be true. Many Hindus, for example, believe that fulfilling behavioral expectations of one's own social caste will lead to rewards in one's next birth, or incarnation. In the next life, good people will be born into a higher social status. In contrast, some Christians believe that one's fate in the afterlife depends on whether one believes in certain ideas—for instance, that Jesus Christ is one's personal savior. Beliefs come from traditions established over time, sacred scriptures, experiences people have had, and lessons given by parents and teachers or other individuals in authority. Beliefs, based on values, influence the choices we make. For example, one value might be that the environment is worth preserving. A belief based on that value would be that humans should make efforts to curb global warming.

Values and beliefs, as elements of nonmaterial culture, are expressed in two forms: an ideal culture and a real culture. Ideal culture consists of *practices, beliefs, and values regarded as most desirable in society and consciously taught to children.* Not everyone, however, follows the approved cultural patterns, even though people may say they do. Sometimes, our values contradict one another. Real culture refers to *the way things in society are actually done.* For example, family time and money are both highly valued in U.S. society. However, in order to make money, we often have to sacrifice time with our families.

Norms are *rules of behavior shared by members of a society and rooted in the value system.* Examples include our rather routine behaviors, from saying "Hi" to people we meet to obeying traffic signs. Norms range from religious warnings such as, "Thou shalt not kill," to the expectation in many societies that young people will complete their high school education. Sometimes, the origins of particular norms are quite clear. Few people wonder, for instance, why there is a norm to stop and look both ways at a stop sign. Other norms, such as the rule in many societies that women should wear skirts but men should not, have been passed on through the generations and have become unconsciously accepted patterns and a part of tradition. Sometimes, we

may not know how norms originated or even be aware of norms until they are violated.

Norms generally fall into two categories—folkways and mores—based largely on their importance and people's response to the breach of those norms. *Folkways* are customs or desirable behaviors, but they are not strictly enforced. Examples of folkways include responding appropriately and politely when introduced to someone, speaking quietly in a library, not scratching your genitals in public, using proper table manners, and covering your mouth when you cough. Violation of these norms causes people to think you are weird or even uncouth but not necessarily immoral or criminal.

Mores are norms that most members observe because they have great moral significance in a society. Conforming to mores is a matter of right and wrong, and violations of many mores are treated very seriously. The person who deviates from mores is considered immoral or criminal. Being faithful in a marriage is among the stronger mores in U.S. society.

Taboos are the strongest form of mores. They concern actions considered unthinkable or unspeakable in the culture. For example, most societies have taboos that forbid incest (sexual relations with a close relative) and prohibit defacing or eating a human corpse. Taboos are most common and numerous in societies that do not have centralized governments to establish formal laws and to maintain jails.

Taboos and other moral codes are of the utmost importance to a group because they provide guidelines for what is right and wrong. Yet behaviors that are taboo in one situation may be acceptable at another time and place. The incest taboo is an example found in all cultures, yet the application of the incest taboo varies greatly across cultures (Rosman, Rubel, and Weisgrau 2009; Wolf and Durham 2004). In medieval Europe, if a man and a woman were within seven degrees of relatedness and wanted to marry, the marriage could be denied by the priest as incestuous. (Your first cousin is a third degree of relatedness from you.) Of course, in Europe, exceptions were made for the royal families, where cousins often married. By contrast, the Balinese sometimes permit twins to marry because it is believed they have already been intimately bonded together in the womb (Henley 2008; Leslie and Korman 1989). In some African and Native American societies, one cannot marry a sibling but might be expected to marry a first cousin. As Table 3.3 illustrates, the definition of what is and what is not incest varies even from state to state in the United States.

Laws are norms formally encoded by those holding political power in society, such as laws against stealing

Table 3.3   Incest Taboos in the United States: States That Allow First-Cousin Marriage

Alabama	Connecticut	Hawaii	New Mexico	South Carolina
Alaska	District of Columbia	Maryland	New York	Tennessee
California	Florida	Massachusetts	North Carolina	Vermont
Colorado	Georgia	New Jersey	Rhode Island	Virginia

States that allow first-cousin marriage only under certain conditions, such as marriage after a certain age or inability to bear children: Arizona, Illinois, Indiana, Maine, Utah, and Wisconsin.

Source: National Conference of State Legislatures (2015).

property or killing another person. The violator of a law is likely to be perceived not just as a weird or an immoral person but also as a criminal who deserves formal punishment. Many mores are passed into law, and some folkways are also made into laws, with formal punishments imposed for their violation. Behaviors may be folkways in one situation and mores or laws in another, with gradually more serious consequences. For example, nudity or various stages of near nudity may be only mildly questionable in some social settings (the beach or certain fraternity parties) but would be quite offensive in others (a four-star restaurant or a house of worship) and against the law in some situations, incurring a penalty, or sanction.

Sanctions reinforce norms through rewards and penalties. Sanctions vary with the importance of the norm and can range from a parent frowning at a child who fails to use proper table manners to a prison term or death sentence. *Formal sanctions* are rewards or punishments conferred by recognized officials. Fines for parking illegally, failing grades for plagiarism, and expulsion for bringing drugs or weapons to school are formal negative sanctions your school might impose. Positive sanctions include honors and awards. *Informal sanctions* are unofficial rewards or punishments, such as smiles, frowns, or ignoring someone. A private word of praise by your professor after class about how well you did on your exam would be an informal positive sanction; gossip or ostracism by other students because of the clothes you wear would be an informal negative sanction. Most often, adherence to norms is ingrained so deeply that our reward is simply "fitting in."

Language is the foundation of every culture. It conveys verbal, written, and nonverbal messages among members of society. The minidrama between infant and adult is played out every day around the world as millions of infants learn the language of the adults who care for them. In the process, they acquire an important part of culture, which is learned.

Although many animals can communicate with a limited repertoire of sounds, the ability to speak a language is unique to humans (R. Phillips 2013). Transport a baby from France to the Arapesh tribe in New Guinea and another baby from New Guinea to France, and each will learn to speak the language and adhere to the culture in which it is brought up. Language conveys verbal, written, and nonverbal messages among members of society.

Simply put, without language there would be little, if any, culture. Through the use of language, members of a culture can pass on essential knowledge to children and can share ideas with other members of their society. Work can be organized, and the society can build on its experiences and plan its future. Through language, members express their ideas, values, beliefs, and knowledge, a key ingredient in the ability of humans to sustain social life.

Language takes three primary forms: spoken, written, and nonverbal. There are over 7,100 languages spoken in the world, with 40% speaking one of the eight most common languages as their first tongue. About 3,700 language groups are small, with less than 10,000 native speakers. The most common first languages are Mandarin (with 1.2 billion speakers), Spanish (414 million), English (335 million), Hindi (260 million), and Arabic (237 million) (World Almanac 2015). English is the top Internet language around the world, with 536.9 million users (Internet World Statistics 2014).

Written language enables humans to store ideas for future generations, accelerating the accumulation of ideas on which to build. It also makes possible communication over distances. Members of a society learn to read these shared symbols.

Nonverbal language consists of gestures, facial expressions, and body postures. Communications scholars say this mode carries 93% of the message—55% in the facial expressions and 38% in the voice—vocal elements and intonation. That leaves 7% of the message coming from the actual words said (Debenham 2014; Fields 2015; Mehrabian 1972). Every culture uses nonverbal language to communicate, and just like verbal language, those cues may differ widely among cultures.

The power to communicate nonverbally is illustrated in American Sign Language, designed for the hearing challenged and the mute. Complex ideas can be transmitted without vocalizing a word. Indeed, one can argue that the deaf have a distinctive culture of their own, rooted in large part in the unique sign language that serves them (discussed in "Engaging Sociology" on page 74). In addition, technology has aided communication among the hearing impaired through text messaging.

Thinking Sociologically

Think about a time when you were trying to understand what someone was saying, and you could not hear the words (at a concert, a bar, or a loud party). How did you rely on the other person's nonverbal communication to interpret what he or she was trying to convey? How successful were you, and how do you know?

Language also plays a critical role in our perceptions and organization of our thoughts. The *linguistic relativity theory* posits that the people who speak a specific language make interpretations of their reality—they notice certain things and may fail to notice certain other things. Language is influenced by history and sociopolitical factors, and the structure of the language affects the conceptualization of our world (Sapir 1929, 1949; Whorf 1956). Think about this: "A person's 'picture of the universe' or 'view of the world' differs as a function of the particular language or languages that person knows" (Kodish 2003:384). Although language does not totally determine thinking, most scientists agree that it does influence thinking (Casasanto 2008; Levinson 2000). For example, recent research confirms that in some Native Alaskan cultures where life is dependent on the elements, there are more than 50 words for snow, each giving members of the group a description that could mean life or death—wet snow, dry snow, heavy snow, melting snow, and so forth (Krupnik et al. 2010; Robson 2013). The Inuit also have 17 words for various types of ice, for they must be able to distinguish types of solidified water ("Ice" 2015). Children in different cultures will learn about the world within the framework provided by their language.

In the English language, people tend to associate certain colors with certain qualities in a way that may add to the problem of racist attitudes (Levinson 2000). The definition of the word *black* includes "dismal," "boding ill," "hostile," "harmful," "inexcusable," "without goodness," "evil," "wicked," "disgrace," and "without moral light." The word *white*, on the other hand, is defined as "honest," "dependable," "morally pure," "innocent," and "without malice" (Merriam-Webster 2014; *Webster's Unabridged English Dictionary* 1989). If the linguistic relativity thesis is correct, it is more than a coincidence that bad things are associated with the *black sheep* of the family, the *blacklist*, or *Black Tuesday* (when the U.S. stock market dropped dramatically and crashed in 1929).

This association of blackness with negative images and meanings is not true of all languages. The societies that have negative images for *black* and positive images for *white* are the same societies that associate negative qualities with people of darker skin. Blackness associated with something evil is not true of many African languages (W. Jordan 2012). The use of *white* as a synonym for good or innocent—as in reference to a *white noise machine* or a *white lie*—may contribute to a cultural climate that devalues people of color. In essence, the language may influence our perception of color in a manner that contributes to racism. Interestingly, there is empirical evidence supporting this claim of color symbolism. Athletic teams that wear black uniforms have more penalties called on them than teams with lighter-colored uniforms (Frank and Gilovich 1988).

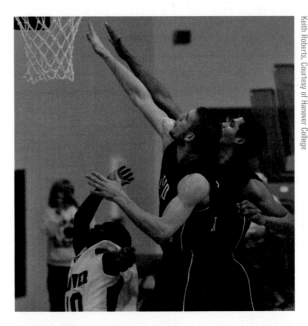

White and black as colors have symbolic meaning—with phrases like "blackballed from the club" or "black sheep of the family" indicating negative judgment associated with blackness. Research shows that teams wearing black are called for more fouls than teams wearing white.

Keith Roberts, Courtesy of Hanover College

When grouped together, material and nonmaterial components form cultural patterns. People's lives are organized around these patterns. For example, family life includes patterns of courtship, marriage, child-rearing, and care of the elderly.

We have seen that material artifacts and nonmaterial beliefs, values, norms, and language compose the basic components of culture. Next, we explore the theoretical explanations for culture.

SOCIETY, CULTURE, AND OUR SOCIAL WORLD

Whether people eat termite eggs, fish eggs, or chicken eggs, societies always have a culture, and culture is always linked to a society. Culture provides guidelines for behaviors and actions at each level of society, from the global system to the individual family. The social world model at the beginning of the chapter, with its concentric circles, represents the micro to macro levels of society. Smaller social units, such as a school, operate within a larger community that is also part of a region and the country. The culture determines what takes place in each of these units. There is a social unit—or structural "hardware"—and a cultural "software" at each level.

Microcultures: Micro-Level Analysis

Micro-level analysis focuses on social interactions in small groups. Groups of people, if those people meet with regularity and have some common interests or purpose, will develop insider language, jokes, symbols, and ways of interacting that may differ from other groups in which those same people participate. The social unit at this level of analysis only affects a portion of one's daily life (a bowling league, a book group, or a poker club) or shapes a limited time period of one's life (such as a Boy Scout troop or a soccer team for 8-year-old girls) (Gordon 1970). The social unit at the meso or macro level affects larger groups or societies and has more long-term impacts. So a microculture is *a culture that develops at the micro level in groups or organizations and affects only a segment of one's life or influences a limited period of one's life*. Other classic examples include a street gang, a college sorority, and a business office.

Hospitals are communities of people who share a microculture. People in different colored uniforms scurry around carrying out their designated tasks, part of the division of labor in the organization; each uniform has symbolic significance, indicating positions at the hospital. Hospital workers interact

© iStockphoto.com/sturti

Hospitals provide one example of a microculture. Hospital employees share terminology, rules of interaction, and values regarding objectifying human body parts so that the patient is not sexualized.

among themselves to attain goals of patient care. They have a common in-group vocabulary; a shared set of values; a hierarchy of positions, with roles and behaviors for each position; and a guiding system of regulations for the organization—all of which shape interactions during the hours when each member works in the hospital. Yet the hospital microculture may have little relevance to the rest of the employees' everyday lives. Microcultures may survive over time, with individuals coming in and leaving as workers and patients, but in a complex society, no one lives his or her entire life within a microculture. The values, rules, and specialized language used by the hospital staff continue as one shift ends and other medical personnel enter and sustain that microculture. Outside that microculture, a different set of norms takes over.

Every organization, club, and association is a social group and therefore must have a culture (a microculture) with its own set of rules and expectations. Schools develop their own unique cultures and traditions; as students graduate and move out of that microculture, others move into it and perpetuate the microculture. However, some microcultures exist for a limited period of time or for a special purpose. A summer camp microculture may develop but exists only for that summer. The following summer, a very different culture may evolve because of new counselors and campers. A girls' softball team may develop its own cheers, jokes, insider slang, and values regarding competition or what it means to be a good sport, but next year, the girls may be realigned into different teams, and the transitory culture of the previous year will change. In contrast to microcultures, subcultures continue across a person's life span.

Subcultures and Countercultures: Meso-Level Analysis

A subculture is *the culture of a meso-level group that distinguishes itself from the dominant culture of the larger society.* It is smaller than the nation but, unlike a microculture, is large enough to support people throughout the life span (Arnold 1970; Gordon 1970). Many ethnic groups within the larger society have their own subcultures, with their own sets of conventions and expectations. Picture a person, perhaps yourself, who is African Canadian, Chinese Canadian, or Hispanic Canadian, living within an ethnic community that provides food, worship, and many other resources. Despite unique cultural traits, that person is still a Canadian citizen, living within the national laws, norms, and way of life. It is just that the person's life has guidelines from the subculture, in addition to the dominant culture of the society.

Because the social unit, such as the ethnic groups mentioned earlier, plays a more long-term and pervasive role in the life span of group members than a summer camp or a sorority (microcultures), we analyze subcultures at the meso level. (Table 3.4 illustrates the connection between the social units at each level and the type of culture at that level.)

In the United States, subcultures include ethnic groups, such as Mexican American and Korean American; restricted religious groups, such as the Orthodox Jews in New York City; and social class groups, including the elite upper class on the East and West Coasts of the United States. The superwealthy have networks, exclusive clubs, and the *Social Register*, which lists the names and phone numbers of the elite, so they can maintain contact with one another. They have a culture of opulence that differs from middle-class culture, and this culture is part of their experience throughout their lives.

Note that many of the categories into which we group people are not subcultures. For example, redheads, left-handed people, tall people, individuals who read *Wired* magazine, people who are single, visitors to Chicago, and DVD watchers do not make up subcultures because they do not interact as social units or share a common way of life. A motorcycle gang, a college fraternity, and a summer camp are also not subcultures because they affect only a segment of one's life (Gordon 1970; Yablonski 1959).

Many societies have subcultures based on ethnicity or religion or other historical characteristics, but broad-based subcultures with extensive social networks can emerge in other ways as well. Perhaps the most fascinating is the deaf subculture in the United States, which is explained in the next "Engaging Sociology."

© iStockphoto.com/ Diane Diederic

Subcultures, such as the Orthodox Jewish faith community, impact their members throughout life—from infancy to death. Here, an Orthodox Jewish boy prepares to pray according to Jewish law by wrapping the leather strap of his tefillin around his arm and a tallit (prayer shawl) around his shoulders.

Table 3.4 Level of Social Units and of Culture

Social Unit (People who interact and feel they belong)	Culture (The way of life of that social unit)
Dyads, small groups, local community	Microculture
Ethnic community or social class community	Subculture
National society	Culture of a nation
Global system	Global culture

······· ENGAGING SOCIOLOGY ·······

Deaf Subculture in the United States
by Thomas P. Horejes

The deaf subculture possesses its own language, norms, and social networks that are unique to the deaf. American Sign Language (ASL) has its own conversational rules and social norms, such as mandatory eye gaze and appropriate facial expressions. Like other subcultures, the deaf subculture celebrates its own arts and entertainment, including deaf poetry, deaf music, deaf theater, and deaf cinema. The arts of the deaf subculture are often expressed visually through perspectives, experiences, and/or metaphors only understood by those who are fluent in ASL and a part of the deaf subculture. There are social gatherings and events by associations within the deaf subculture that host annual conferences and tournaments ranging from the Deaf World Softball Championships to the Rainbow Alliance of the Deaf (an LGBT organization). As with other subcultures, there is a deaf history and heritage that is passed on from generation to generation.

Many of the 5% to 10% of deaf children born to deaf parents are immediately enculturated into their own deaf subculture. In contrast, a large majority (90%–95%) of deaf children (including myself, born to hearing parents) start with an identity from the larger world (hearing society). As we progress through life, however, our identities become negotiated as we become more aware of a subculture—a deaf subculture that each of us has embraced quite differently. Some reject the deaf subculture in favor of total immersion into hearing society, whereas others navigate in the deaf subculture but in different ways. In addition to those born deaf, there are many individuals who become deaf later in life due to age, illness, or even prolonged exposure to loud sounds.

Regardless of how one becomes deaf, some individuals rely on technology (hearing aids or cochlear implants), communicate with hearing individuals via spoken or written English or through an ASL interpreter, and express willingness to work in the workplace dominated by members of the hearing society. Other deaf individuals become fully immersed into the deaf subculture, or what they call the deaf "world." They may attempt to depart from the hearing culture by rejecting values and beliefs possessed by the hearing society, such as assistive-listening devices and speech therapy, and by not placing their deaf child in hearing schools. These people typically attend only deaf plays, read about deaf history, take on jobs where communication is through sign language, and forbid any voiced language in favor of equal "access" in all aspects of their daily activities. One common denominator in shaping deaf identity and deaf subculture is language: the incorporation of sign language in the deaf individual's life.

* * * * * * *

Engaging With Sociology

1. Why does Dr. Horejes see this culture of the deaf as a subculture rather than a microculture or a counterculture?

2. Why is language the critical element in being a part of this subculture?

3. Why can a subculture exist in your own community and seemingly be invisible to you?

Thomas P. Horejes received his PhD at Arizona State University in justice studies and teaches sociology at Gallaudet University, the world's only university with programs and services specifically designed to accommodate students who are deaf or hard of hearing. He is the author of Social Constructions of Deafness: Examining Deaf Languacultures in Education.

A give-and-take exists between subcultures and the dominant culture, with each contributing to and influencing the other. Sometimes, the differences between the two lead to tension and conflict. When conflict with the larger culture becomes serious and important norms of the dominant society are violated, a different type of culture emerges.

A counterculture is *a group with expectations and values that contrast sharply with the dominant values of a particular society* (Yinger 1960). An example of a counterculture is the Old Order Amish of Pennsylvania and Ohio. The Amish drive horse-drawn buggies and seldom use electricity or modern machines. They reject many mainstream notions of success and replace them with their own work values and goals. The Old Order Amish prefer to educate their children in their own communities, insisting that their children not go beyond an eighth-grade education in the public-school curriculum. They also do not use automobiles or conventional tractors. The Amish are pacifists and will not serve as soldiers in the national military.

Other types of countercultures seek to withdraw from society, to operate outside its economic and legal systems, or even to bring about the downfall of the larger society. Examples include survivalist groups, such as racist militia and skinheads, who reject the principles of democratic pluralism. In the United States, the number of antigovernment "Patriot" groups who believe "that the federal government is conspiring to take Americans' guns and destroy their liberties as it paves the way for a global 'one-world government'" has increased dramatically over the past decade (Potok 2013c).

Some countercultures, such as the Amish, continue over time and can sustain members throughout their life cycle. Like subcultures, they may operate at the meso level, but unlike subcultures, they reject mainstream culture. Moreover, some countercultural groups, such as punk rock groups or violent and deviant teenage gangs, are short lived or are relevant to people only at a certain age. These countercultural groups operate at the micro level but are more conflictual with the dominant culture than microcultures.

Countercultures are not necessarily bad for society. According to conflict theory, which was introduced in Chapter 2, the existence of counterculture groups is clear evidence that there are contradictions or tensions within a society that need to be addressed. Countercultures often challenge the unfair treatment of groups in society that do not hold power. They sometimes develop into social organizations or protest groups. Extremist religious and political groups, whether Christian, Islamic, Hindu, or any other,

FIGURE 3.3   Cultures at Various Levels in the Social World

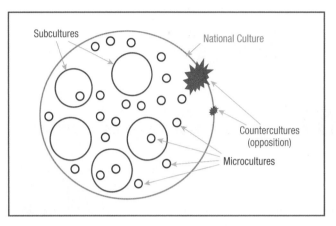

may best be understood as countercultures against Western or global influences that they perceive as threatening to their way of life. Figure 3.3 illustrates the types of cultures in the social world and the relationship between countercultures and their national culture. Countercultures, as depicted, view themselves and are viewed by others as "fringe" groups—partial outsiders within a nation.

● Thinking Sociologically

Describe a counterculture group whose goals are at odds with those of the dominant culture. Do you see any evidence to show that the group is influencing behavioral expectations and values in the larger society? What effect, if any, do countercultures have on your life?

National and Global Culture: Macro-Level Analysis

Canada is a national society, geographically bounded by the mainland United States to the south, the Pacific Ocean and Alaska to the west, the Atlantic Ocean to the east, and the Arctic to the north. The government in Ottawa passes laws that regulate activities in all provinces (which are similar to states or prefectures), and each province passes its own laws on regional matters. These geographic boundaries and political structures make up the national society of Canada.

National Society and Culture. The *national society* (introduced in Chapter 1) is a population of people, usually living within a specified geographic area, who are connected by common ideas, cooperate for the attainment of common goals, and are subject to a particular political

REUTERS/Jianan Yu

Many simple norms or beliefs about how to behave in public—like waiting in line for a train—have become accepted in cultures throughout the world.

authority. Within the nation, there may be smaller groups, such as ethnic, regional, or tribal subcultures, made up of people who identify closely with each other. Most nations have a **national culture** of *common values and beliefs that tie citizens of a nation together*. The national culture affects the everyday lives of most citizens. Within some countries of Africa and the Middle East, on the other hand, local subcultures, including ethnic or religious loyalties, are much stronger than any sense of national culture, in part because the nation-state boundaries were originally *imposed* by foreign colonial powers. Subcultural differences divide many nations. Consider the loyalties of Shi'ites, Sunnis, and Kurds in Iraq to their subcultures, where the national culture struggles for influence over its citizens through laws and military force.

In colonial America, people thought of themselves as Virginians or Rhode Islanders rather than as U.S. citizens. Even during the "War Between the States" of the 1860s, the battalions were organized by states and often carried their state banners into battle. The fact that some Southern states still call it the War Between the States rather than the Civil War communicates the struggle over whether to recognize the nation or states as the primary social unit of loyalty and identity. People in the United States today are increasingly likely to think of themselves as U.S. citizens (rather than as Iowans or Floridians), yet the national culture determines only a few of the specific guidelines for everyday life. Nonetheless, the sense of nation has grown stronger in most industrialized societies over the past century, and the primary identity is likely to be "United States" or "Canadian" citizen.

Global Society and Culture. Several centuries ago, there was no *global culture*, but with expanding travel, economic interdependence of different countries, international political linkages, global environmental concerns, and, most recently, technology allowing for communication throughout the world, people now interact across continents in seconds. **Globalization** refers to *the process by which the entire world is becoming a single sociocultural entity—more uniform, more integrated, and more interdependent*. The globalization process brings increased connectedness, uniformity, and interdependency across the planet (Eitzen and Zinn 2012; Robertson and Scholte 2007).

Western political and economic structures dominate in the development of this global society, largely as a result of the domination of Western (European and U.S.) worldviews and Western control over resources. For example, the very idea of governing a geographic region with a bureaucratic structure known as a nation-state is a fairly new notion. Formerly, many small bands and tribal groupings dominated areas of the globe. However, with globalization, nation-states now exist in every region of the world.

Global culture includes *behavioral standards, symbols, values, and material objects that have become common across the globe* (International Beliefs and Values Institute 2012). We need to understand global culture to engage in human rights issues, global education, conflict resolution, sustainability, and religious and cultural understanding. For example, beliefs that monogamy is normal; that marriage should be based on romantic love; that people have a right to life, liberty, and the pursuit of happiness; that people should be free to choose their leaders; that women should have rights, such as voting; that wildlife and fragile environments should be protected; and that everyone should have a cell phone and television set are spreading across the globe (D. Newman 2009).

During the 20th century, the idea of the primacy of individual rights, civil liberties, and human rights spread around the world, creating conflicts within nations that traditionally lack democratic institutions and processes. Backlashes against these and other Western ideas also can be seen in the acts of groups that have embraced terrorism (Eitzen and Zinn 2012; Kurtz 2007; B. Turner 1991a, 1991b). This has resulted in Western societies fighting terrorism when those groups see themselves as trying to preserve their culture (Morey and Yaqin 2011; Peek 2011).

Still, these trends are aspects of the emerging global culture. Even 100 years ago, notions of global cooperation and competition would have seemed quite bizarre (Lechner and Boli 2005). However, in nations all over the globe, people who travel by plane know they must stand in line, negotiate airport security, squeeze their bodies into confined spaces, and stay seated in the airplane until they are told they can get up (Lechner and Boli 2005). Regardless of nationality, we know how to behave in any airport in the world.

As the world community becomes more interdependent and addresses issues that can only be dealt with at the global level (such as global warming; massive human rights violations, as in the Syrian revolution or Sudanese war; international terrorism; global food shortages; and global financial crises), the idea of a common "software" of beliefs, social rules, and common interests takes on importance. Common ideas for making decisions allow for shared solutions to conflicts. Global culture at the macro level affects our individual lives, and its influence will only increase.

However, global culture is not the only pattern that is new. Today, we see a counterculture at the global level. Stateless terrorist networks such as al-Shabaab, al-Qaeda, ISIS, Boko Haram, and the Taliban reject the values of international organizations and agreements such as the World Court, the Geneva Convention, and other international systems designed to resolve disputes. Terrorists do not recognize the sovereignty of nations and do not acknowledge many values of respect for life or for civil discourse. This counterculture at the global level is a more serious threat than those at the micro and meso levels, in part because it does not fit into the global system of nations and its norms. (See the discussion of terrorism in Chapter 12.)

● Thinking Sociologically

Make a list of social units of which you are a part. Place these groups into categories of microculture, subculture, national culture, and global culture. Consider which of them affects only a portion of your day or week (such as your place of work) or only a very limited time in your entire life span. Consider which groups are smaller than the nation but will likely influence you over much of your life. To what cross-national (global) groups do you belong? Do you belong to fewer groups at the national-culture and global-culture levels or at the local microculture level? Why do you suppose that is the case?

THEORIES OF CULTURE
Cultural Theory at the Micro Level

To understand our interactions with family and friends, we turn to the micro level of analysis. Although external forces at the national and global (macro) levels shape us in

many ways, that is not the whole story, as we see when we examine the symbolic interaction approach to culture.

Symbolic Interaction Theory. How amazing it is that babies learn to share the ideas and meanings of complex cultures with others in those cultures. Symbolic interaction theory considers how we learn to share the meanings of symbols, whether material or nonmaterial. Cultures contain many symbols, such as rings, flags, and words, that stand for or represent some thing or some idea. A ring means love and commitment. A flag represents national identity and is intended to evoke patriotism and love for one's country. A term such as *middle class* conjures up images and expectations of what the term means, a meaning shared with others in our group. Together, in our groups and societies, we define what is real, normal, and good.

Symbolic interaction theory maintains that our humanness comes from the impact we have on each other through these shared understandings of symbols that humans have created. When people create symbols, such as a new greeting (e.g., a fist bump instead of a handshake) or a symbolic shield for a fraternity or sorority, they come to have an existence, meaning, and importance for the group.

Symbolic interaction theory pictures humans as consciously and deliberately creating their personal and collective histories. The theory emphasizes the part that verbal and nonverbal language and gestures play in the shared symbols of individuals and the smooth operation of society. More than any other theory in the social sciences, symbolic interaction stresses the active decision-making role of individuals—the ability of individuals to do more than conform to the larger forces of the society.

Many of our definitions of what is "normal" are shaped by what others around us define as "normal" or "good." The social construction of reality *is the process by which individuals and groups shape reality through social interaction.* Our construction of what we see as reality, influenced by our social relations, has a profound effect on our daily lives, our life chances, and what we believe is possible in our lives. One illustration of this is the notion of what is beautiful or ugly. In the late 18th and early 19th centuries, in Europe and the United States, beaches were considered eyesores because there was nothing there but crushed stone and dangerous water. A beach was not viewed as a place to relax in a beautiful environment. Likewise, when early travelers to the West encountered the Rocky Mountains, with soaring granite rising to snowcapped peaks, the idea was that these were incredibly ugly wounds in the earth's surface. The summits were anything but

Design Pics Inc/ National Geographic Creative

In the late 1700s and early 1800s, this mountain view would have been considered an eyesore—too ugly to enjoy. The social construction of reality—the definition of what is beautiful in our culture—has changed dramatically over the past 2 centuries.

appealing. Still, over time, some individuals began to redefine these crests as breathtakingly beautiful. We now see both as beautiful, but the social construction of scenery has not always been so (Lofgren 1999, 2010). So even what we experience as relaxing and peaceful in nature is shaped by how our society constructs those experiences.

This notion that individuals shape culture and that culture influences individuals is at the core of symbolic interaction theory. Other social theories tend to focus on the meso and macro levels.

Thinking Sociologically

Think about how you communicate with one or more of your close friends. What are some of the symbols you use to communicate with one another? How do these forms of communication indicate that you are close friends and help you feel connected to them?

Cultural Theories at the Meso and Macro Levels

How can we explain such diverse world practices as eating termites and worshipping cows? Why have some societies allowed men to have four wives, whereas others—such as the Shakers—have prohibited any sex between men and women? Why do some groups worship their ancestors, whereas others have many gods, and yet others believe in a single divine being? How can societies adapt to extremes of climate and geographical terrain—hot, cold, dry, wet,

mountainous, and flat? Humankind has evolved practices so diverse that it would be hard to find a practice that has not been adopted in some society at some time in history.

To explain these cultural differences, we refer to two already familiar perspectives that have made important contributions to understanding culture at the meso and macro levels: structural-functional and conflict theories.

Structural-Functional Theory. Structural-functional theorists (also called functionalists) ask why members of an ethnic subculture or a society engage in certain practices. To answer, they look at how those practices contribute to the survival or social solidarity of the group or society as a whole. An example is the reverence for cattle in India. The *sacred cow* is protected, treated with respect, and not slaughtered for food. The reasons relate to India's ancient development into an agricultural society that required sacrifices. Cattle were needed to pull plows and to provide a source of milk and dried dung for fuel. Cows gained religious significance because of their importance for the survival of early agricultural communities. They must, therefore, be protected from hungry people for the long-term survival of the group. Protecting cows was functional; that is, the practice served a purpose for society (M. Harris 1989).

Functionalists view societies as composed of interdependent parts, each fulfilling certain necessary functions or purposes for the total society (Radcliffe-Brown 1935). Shared norms, values, and beliefs, for instance, serve the function of holding a social group together. At a global, macro level, functionalists see the world moving in the direction of having a common culture, potentially reducing we-versus-they thinking and promoting unity across boundaries. Synthesis of cultures and even the loss of some cultures are viewed as a natural result of globalization.

Although most cultural practices serve positive functions for the maintenance and stability of society, some practices, such as slavery, may be functional for those in power (those using child labor) but dysfunctional for minority groups or individual members of society. The fact that some societies are weak or have died out suggests that their way of life may not have been functional in the long run. Consider the case of Haiti, a country weakened, in part, because all the forests have been cut down to provide firewood. The resulting erosion made much of the land unusable for growing crops and led to a scarcity of food (J. Diamond 2005). Add to the existing poverty and hunger the devastation brought about by two earthquakes in 2010 that damaged or destroyed most buildings, followed by a hurricane and a cholera epidemic. The country and its people must rely on external support and donations from other countries to survive as it tries to rebuild.

The functionalist perspective has been criticized because it fails to consider how much dysfunction a society has, how much conflict a society can tolerate, and how much unity is necessary for a society to survive. Some critics argue that functional theory overemphasizes the need for consensus and integration among different parts of society, thus ignoring conflicts that may point to problems such as inequality in societies (Dahrendorf 1959).

Conflict Theory. Whereas functionalists assume consensus exists because all people in society have learned the same cultural values, rules, and expectations, conflict theorists do not view culture as having this uniting effect. Conflict theorists describe societies as composed of meso-level groups—class, ethnic, religious, and political groups—vying for power. Each group protects its own self-interests and struggles to make its own cultural ways dominant in the society. Instead of consensus, the dominant groups may impose their cultural beliefs on minorities and other subcultural groups, thus laying the groundwork for conflict. Conflict theorists identify tension between meso and macro levels, whereas functionalists tend to focus on harmony and smooth integration between those levels.

Conflict theorists argue that the people with privilege and power in society manipulate institutions such as religion and education. In this way, average people learn the values, beliefs, and norms of the privileged group and accept the dominant group's beliefs, self-interests, power, and advantage. The needs of the privileged are likely to be met, and their status will be secured. For instance, schools that serve lower-class children usually teach obedience to authority, punctuality, and respect for superiors—behaviors that make for good laborers and compliant workers. The children of the affluent, meanwhile, are more likely to attend schools stressing divergent thinking, creativity, and leadership, attributes that prepare them to occupy the most professional, prestigious, and highly rewarded positions in society. Conflict theorists point to this control of the education process by those with privilege as part of the overall pattern by which the society benefits the rich.

Conflict theory can also help us understand global dynamics. Many poor nations feel that the global system protects the self-interests of the richest nations, the Global North, and that those rich nations impose their own culture, including their ideas about economics, politics, and religion, on the poorer nations of the Global South. Some scholars believe there is great richness in local customs that is lost when homogenized by cultural

Conflict theorists believe that society is composed of groups, each acting to meet its own self-interests. In Jakarta in 2016, Indonesian taxi drivers blocked a major street during a rally against car-booking companies like Uber that are cheaper because they employ mostly part-timers and do not pay benefits. According to public-transportation associations, car-booking services undermine the livelihoods of taxi drivers.

domination of the powerful nations (Eitzen and Zinn 2012; Ritzer 2007).

Conflict theory is useful for analyzing the relationships between societies (at a macro level) and between subcultures (at a meso level) within complex societies. It also helps illuminate tensions in a society when local (micro-level) cultural values clash with national (macro-level) trends. Conflict theory is not as successful, however, in explaining simple, well-integrated societies in which change is slow to come about, and cooperation is an organizing principle.

Actually, conflict may contribute to a smoother-running society in the long run. German sociologist Georg Simmel and American sociologist Lewis Coser blended insights from functional and conflict perspectives, insisting that conflict sometimes serves a positive purpose. One example is that it can alert societal leaders to problem areas that need attention; conflict can also serve to bond people together in opposition to others. Both scholars agree that some degree of conflict is essential for any group to be viable—which is a pretty strong statement about how functional conflict is (Coser 1956; Simmel 1904, 1955).

Middle-Range Theories

The perspectives just discussed are comprehensive and wide-angle in scope. They are paradigms that explain much behavior and many social patterns, but they are hard to test. *Middle-range theories* of culture bridge the gap between empirical data and abstract or broad general paradigms. R. K. Merton (1968) coined the term and argued that middle-range theories could be used to break down the abstract theories into smaller parts to test, thus providing data that could be generalized to a large group.

For example, Thomas Pettigrew et al. (2011) examined more than 500 studies that tested the intergroup contact hypothesis, a middle-range theory that maintains that intergroup contact, under appropriate conditions, can reduce prejudice. Through looking at the results of the 500-plus studies, Pettigrew showed that the positive effects of such intergroup contact are universal—across racial, ethnic, national, age, and gender groups.

THE FIT BETWEEN HARDWARE AND SOFTWARE

Computer software cannot work with incompatible machines. Some documents cannot be easily transferred to a different piece of hardware, although sometimes a transfer can be accomplished with significant modification in the formatting of the document. The same is true with the hardware of society and the software of culture. For instance, consider the size of families: The value (software) of having a large extended family, typical in agricultural

societies, does not work well in the structure (hardware) of industrial and postindustrial societies that are mostly urban and crowded. Children in urban settings are generally an economic liability compared with those who work on the farm in agricultural societies. In short, there are limits to what can be transferred from one type of society to another, and the change or "formatting" may mean the new beliefs transferred to a different social setting are barely recognizable.

Attempts to transport U.S.-style "software" (culture)—individualism, capitalism, freedom of religion, and democracy—to other parts of the world illustrate that these ideas are not always successful in other settings. The hardware of societies may be able to handle more than one type of software or set of beliefs, but there are limits to the adaptability. Thus, we should not be surprised when ideas from one society are transformed into something quite different when they are imported to another society. If we are to understand the world in which we live and if we want to improve it, we must first fully understand other societies and cultures.

Thinking Sociologically

Team sports are a core component of most societies. How does participating in team sports help prepare people to successfully navigate life in the United States? In other societies? For example, what lessons learned through playing on an organized team might be relevant to life in the competitive business world or in a cooperative, noncompetitive society?

Because there is such variation among societies and cultures in what they see as *normal*, how do we learn our particular society's expectations? The answer is addressed in the next chapter. Each society relies on the process of **socialization** to teach the culture to its members, especially new members, such as babies and immigrants. Humans go through a lifelong process of socialization to learn social and cultural expectations. The next chapter discusses the ways in which we learn our culture and become members of society.

WHAT HAVE WE LEARNED?

Individuals and small groups cannot live without the support of a larger society, the hardware of the social world. Without the software—culture—there could be no society, for there would be no norms to guide our interactions with others in society. Humans are inherently social and learn their culture from others.

Furthermore, as society has evolved into more complex and multilevel social systems, humans have learned to live in and negotiate conflicts among multiple cultures, including those at micro (microcultures), meso (subcultures), and macro (societal and global cultures) levels. Life in an information age society demands adaptability to different sociocultural contexts and tolerance of different cultures and subcultures. This is a challenge to a species that has always had tendencies toward ethnocentrism.

- *Society* refers to an organized and interdependent group of individuals who live together in a specific geographic area, interact with each other more than with outsiders, cooperate to attain goals, and share a common culture over time. Each society has a culture, the way of life shared by a group of people, including ideas and "things" that are passed on from one generation to the next; the culture has both material and nonmaterial components.

- Societies evolve from very simple to more complex, from the simple hunter-gatherer society to the information societies of the postindustrial world.

- The study of culture requires that we try to avoid ethnocentrism (judging other cultures by the standards of our culture). Instead, sociologists use the view of cultural relativism so that we can understand culture from the standpoint of those inside it.

- Just as social units exist at various levels of our social world, from small groups to global systems, cultures exist within different levels of the social system—microcultures, subcultures, national cultures, and global cultures. Some social units at the micro or meso level stand in opposition to the dominant national culture, and they are called countercultures.

- Various theories offer different lenses for understanding culture. Whereas symbolic interaction illuminates the way humans bring meaning to events (thus generating culture), the functionalist and conflict theories examine cultural harmony and conflict between cultures, respectively.

- The metaphor of hardware (society's structure) and software (culture) describes the interdependent relationship of society and culture, and as with computers, there must be some compatibility between the structure of a society and the culture. If there is none, either the cultural elements that are transported into another society will be rejected, or the culture will be "reformatted" to fit the society.

DISCUSSION QUESTIONS

1. Think about the evolution of societies described in this chapter. In which type of society (hunter-gatherer, herding, horticultural, agricultural, industrial, or postindustrial) would you prefer to live? Why? In which would you most likely be (a) economically successful and (b) content? Why?

2. This chapter points out that today, material culture "drives the globalization process." Look around at what your classmates are wearing and carrying, and come up with some examples that support that point.

3. Think of a subculture to which you belong. What are the norms, values, and material artifacts that distinguish members of your subculture from those who do not belong to it?

4. Every classroom has norms of behavior. Some are mores, and some are folkways. Describe two of each in a typical classroom at your school. How are both enforced? How do you help enforce these norms?

5. Are you part of a counterculture? Why, or why not? In what ways might a counterculture benefit a society?

KEY TERMS

counterculture 75

cultural relativism 67

culture 54

ethnocentrism 65

global culture 76

globalization 76

ideal culture 69

material culture 67

mechanical solidarity 57

microculture 72

national culture 76

nonmaterial culture 68

CONTRIBUTING TO OUR SOCIAL WORLD: *WHAT CAN WE DO?*

At the Local (Micro) Level

- *Immigrant aid groups* are ethnically oriented organizations that assist recent immigrants in dealing with adjustment to life in a new country at the local level. Contact one of these local groups, and explore the possibility of volunteering or serving as an intern. You should be able to determine if one is in your area by Googling the name of your town or city, the name of the ethnic group, and "immigrant aid group."

At the Organizational/Institutional (Meso) Level

- *Ethnic group* organizations and clubs focus on the interests of specific ethnic groups: For example, Arabic Americans, Chinese Americans, Italian Canadians, Polish Canadians, and so on. You may have one or more groups on your own campus. Contact one of these groups (of your own background or of a background that differs from your own). Arrange to attend one of the group's meetings, and learn about the subculture and activities in which its members are involved. To find an ethnic association on campus, call your campus activities office. To find one in your local area, try Googling the name of the ethnic group, "club," and the name of your town or city.

At the Global (Macro) Level

- *The United Nations Permanent Forum on Indigenous Issues* assists indigenous (native) people around the world who face threats to their cultures, languages, and basic rights as the process of globalization accelerates. We have experienced this in North America in relation to Native American and Inuit populations, but it is occurring throughout the world. Visit the forum's website at www.un.org/development/desa/indigenouspeoples, and contact the forum about the possibility of volunteering.

- *Cultural Survival* is an example of a leading nongovernmental organization (NGO) engaged in action-oriented programs. The organization partners with indigenous people to "defend their lands, languages, and cultures." Look at their website (www.culturalsurvival.org) for internship and volunteer opportunities.

$SAGE edge™

Get the edge on your studies. edge.sagepub.com/ballantinecondensed5e

- Take a quiz to find out what you've learned.
- Review key terms with eFlashcards.
- Watch videos that enhance chapter content.

4 Socialization

Becoming Human and Humane

Whether at the micro, meso, or macro level, our close associates and various organizations teach us how to be human and humane in our society. We learn skills, as well as values such as loyalty and compassion, by watching others.

ME (MY FAMILY AND CLOSEST FRIENDS)

LOCAL ORGANIZATIONS AND COMMUNITY
Families and friends serve as agents of socialization.

NATIONAL ORGANIZATIONS, INSTITUTIONS, AND ETHNIC SUBCULTURES
Citizens are socialized for national loyalty and patriotism.

SOCIETY
Political parties and religious denominations transmit values.

GLOBAL COMMUNITY
People are socialized for tolerance and respect across borders.

WHAT YOU WILL LEARN IN THIS CHAPTER

This chapter will help you do the following:

4.1 Summarize the nature-versus-nurture debate and the sociological perspective on it.

4.2 Predict the impact of isolation and neglect on children.

4.3 Defend the position that groups at each level in our social world have a stake in how we are socialized.

4.4 Describe how we develop a *self* through interacting with others.

4.5 Explain how micro- and meso-level agents of socialization influence individuals.

4.6 Discuss how macro-level agents of socialization can impact children today.

4.7 Identify policy questions that rely on an understanding of socialization.

THINK ABOUT IT

Micro: Local community	What does it mean to have a *self*? How have your family, local religious congregation, and schools shaped who you are?
Meso: National institutions, complex organizations, and ethnic groups	How do various subcultures or organizations of which you are a member (your ethnic group, political party, or religious affiliation) influence your position in the social world?
Macro: National and global systems	What would you be like if you were raised in a different country? How might globalization or other macro-level events—such as a terrorist attack on your country—impact you and your sense of self?

Canadian preteen Craig Kielburger happened to see an article about a 12-year-old boy in Pakistan, Iqbal Masih, a child who had escaped slavery and was murdered for speaking out against child labor. Iqbal was Craig's age, so the story stunned him. Curious about what child labor was, he learned that there are 250 million child laborers, ages 5 to 17, around the world. He was appalled. Although only 12, he mobilized his classmates, and they started a nonprofit called Free The Children (now WE Charity). It became an international organization that has won a number of international awards for its contributions to better the lives of oppressed children (Free The Children 2015). Craig, now 32, and his brother Marc cofounded another organization called Me to We that sells

socially conscious products and services that helps to fund WE Charity.

Many people are concerned mainly about their own self-interests, yet even as a child, Craig seemed to care about people he had never met. He was motivated to act on that concern, but why? Sociologists would point largely to his upbringing—his *socialization*. Coming from a religious background that stressed compassion and justice and being raised in a family that stressed awareness of people different from themselves, his mother, Theresa Kielburger, ensured that her children had direct experiences in the world around them. She commented to a journalist, "Kids become so desensitized by television and the media. It's important to sensitize them, and you have to do it when they are young" (Langlois 2015). She used small gestures—like stopping to have a conversation with a homeless person rather than just ignoring the person or giving away pocket change—as a way to communicate values of caring and humaneness. She often asked her boys to imagine what it feels like to be the kid in class whom everyone teases, thereby enhancing an ability to see things from the perspective of others. Craig also reported that a central family motto was, "The only failure in life is not trying," so he developed a sense of agency—of his ability to make choices and to act, even if he was still a child (Kielburger 2009: 13). Eventually, both brothers became major human rights activists in Canada, and Craig has twice been nominated for the Nobel Peace Prize (Kielburger 2009). This type of altruism clearly seems to be developed by an environment that fosters understanding, tolerance, and caring for the plight of others.

In this chapter we examine the process of *socialization*, how it involves development of our *selves*, and the many directions that process can take, depending on one's experiences in life.

Socialization is *the lifelong process of learning to become a member of the social world, beginning at birth*

REUTERS/ Finbarr O'Reilly

Unlike Craig Kielburger, who was socialized to create a gentler and more humane world, some children grow up in a world of hostility and violence. Children as young as 5 in the Democratic Republic of the Congo have been kidnapped or sold to be child soldiers in rebel armies. They are socialized through abuse by their captors and forced to obey and kill "enemies" in order to survive themselves. Their outlook is not that the world is a friendly place.

and continuing until death. It is a major part of what the family, education, religion, and other institutions do to prepare individuals to be members of their social world.

From the day they are born, infants are interactive, ready to be socialized into membership in the social world. As they cry, coo, or smile, they gradually learn that their behaviors elicit responses from other humans. This **interaction** is *the exchange of verbal and nonverbal messages*. These form the basic building block of socialization through which a child learns its culture and becomes a member of society. This process of interaction shapes the infant into a human being with a social self—the perception we have of who we are.

Three main elements provide the framework for socialization: human biological potential, culture, and individual experiences. Babies enter this world unsocialized, totally dependent on others to meet their needs and completely lacking in social awareness and an understanding of the rules of their society. Despite this complete vulnerability, they have the potential to learn the language, norms, values, and skills needed in their society. Socialization is necessary not only for the survival of the individual but also for the survival of society and its groups. The process continues in various forms throughout our lives, as we enter and exit various positions—from school to work to retirement to death.

In this chapter, we explore the nature and importance of socialization and how individuals become socialized. We also look at development of the self, who or what socializes us, macro-level issues in the socialization process, and a policy example illustrating socialization. First, we briefly examine an ongoing debate: Which is more influential in determining who we are—our genes (nature) or our socialization into the social world (nurture)?

NATURE *VERSUS* NURTURE—OR *BOTH* WORKING TOGETHER?

What is it that makes us who we are? Is it our biological makeup or the family and community in which we grow up? One side of the contemporary debate regarding nature versus nurture seeks to explain the development of the self and human social behaviors—violence, crime, academic performance, mate selection, economic success, gender roles, and other behaviors—by examining biological or genetic factors that are the basis for social behavior (J. Harris 2009; Winkler 1991). Sociologists call this sociobiology, psychologists refer

Socialization starts at the beginning of life, as babies interact intensively with their parents, observing and learning what kinds of sounds or actions elicit response from adults.

to it as evolutionary psychology, and anthropologists call it human behavioral ecology. Researchers in these fields claim that our human genetic makeup wires us for social behaviors (Pinker 2002; E. Wilson 1987, 2000).

The idea is that we perpetuate our own biological family and the human species through our social behaviors. Human groups develop power structures, are territorial, and protect their kin. Examples of behaviors that sociobiologists see as rooted in the genetic makeup of the species include a mother ignoring her own safety to help a child, soldiers dying in battle for their comrades and countries, communities feeling hostility toward outsiders or foreigners, and people defending property lines against intrusion by neighbors. Sociobiologists say that these behaviors continue because they result in an increased chance of survival of the family, one's group, and the species as a whole (Lerner 1992; Pinker 2002; E. Wilson 1980, 1987, 2000).

Most sociologists believe that sociobiology, human behavioral ecology, and evolutionary psychology explanations have flaws. Sociobiology is a *reductionist* theory; that is, it often reduces complex social behaviors to single inherited traits, such as an altruism gene, an aggression gene, or any other behavioral gene. However, evidence for such inherited traits is weak, at best. Sociologists point to the fact that there are great variations in the way members of different societies and groups behave. People born in one culture and raised in another adopt social behaviors common to the culture in which they grow up, not based on inherited traits (S. Gould 1997). If a specific social behavior is genetic, then it should be present regardless of

Getty/ Michelle Garrett

the culture in which humans are raised. What sets humans apart from other animals is not so much our biological heritage but our ability to learn the ways of our culture through socialization.

Most sociologists recognize that individuals are influenced by biology, which limits the range of human responses and creates certain needs and drives, but they believe that nurture is far more important. Some sociologists propose theories that consider both nature and nurture. Alice Rossi, former president of the American Sociological Association, has argued that we need to build both biological and social theories—or biosocial theories—into explanations of social processes, such as parenting (Rossi 1984). One group of sociologists has developed a theory called evolutionary sociology, which takes seriously the way our genetic makeup—including a remarkable capacity for language—shapes our range of behaviors. However, biological research also shows that living organisms are often modified by their environments and the behaviors of others around them—with even biological or genetic structure becoming modified due to social interaction and experiences (De Waal 2016; Dobbs 2013; Machalek and Martin 2010).

In short, biology influences human behavior, but human action and interaction can also modify biological traits. For example, the nutritional history of grandparents can affect the metabolism of their grandchildren, and what grandparents ate was largely shaped by cultural ideas about food (Freese, Powell, and Steelman 1999; "Ghost in Your Genes" 2009). Our cultural values shape what we eat today and whether we share food with the less privileged in our society. Research has shown that trauma experiences—like being in a concentration camp—can be so severe that they are passed on genetically to a next generation (Sample 2015; Thomson 2015; Yehuda et al. 2015). The bottom line is that even our biological traits may be shaped by social factors. *Socialization* is key in the process of "becoming human and becoming humane."

THE IMPORTANCE OF SOCIALIZATION

If you have lived on a farm, watched animals in the wild, or seen television nature shows, you probably have noticed that many animal young become independent shortly after birth. Horses are on their feet in a matter of hours, and by the time turtles hatch from eggs, their parents are long gone. Many species in the animal kingdom do not require contact with adults to survive because their behaviors are inborn and instinctual. Generally speaking, the more intelligent the species, the longer the period of gestation and of nutritional and social dependence on the mother and family. Humans clearly take the longest time to socialize their young and to teach them how to survive. Even among primates, human infants have the longest gestation and dependency period, generally 6 to 8 years. Chimpanzees, very similar to humans in their DNA, take only 12 to 28 months. This extended dependency period for humans—what some have referred to as the *long childhood*—allows each human being time to learn the complexities of culture. This suggests that biology and social processes work together.

Normal human development involves learning to sit, crawl, stand, walk, think, talk, and participate in social interactions. Ideally, the long period of dependence allows children the opportunity to learn necessary skills, knowledge, and social roles through affectionate and tolerant interaction with people who care about them. Yet what happens if children are deprived of adequate care or even human contact? The following section illustrates the importance of socialization by showing the effects of deprivation and isolation on normal socialization.

Getty Images/Marc Dozier/Corbis

This African family shares a playful moment together as they interact with one another. Even in such carefree moments, parents act as socializing agents for their children.

Isolated and Abused Children

What would children be like if they grew up without human contact? Among the most striking examples are the few cases we know of severely abused and neglected children whose parents kept them isolated in cellars or attics for years without providing even minimal attention and nurturing. When these isolated children were discovered, typically they suffered from profound developmental disorders that endured throughout their lives (Curtiss 1977; K. Davis 1947). Most experienced great difficulty in adjusting to their social world's complex rules of interaction, which people normally start to learn from infancy onward. Recent medical studies also show how social isolation and deprivation in early life harm brain development and can result in mental health problems (C. Johnson 2012).

In case studies comparing two girls, Anna and Isabelle, who experienced extreme isolation in early childhood, Kingsley Davis (1947) found that even minimal human contact made some difference in their socialization. Both "illegitimate" girls were kept locked up by relatives who wanted to keep their existence a secret. Both were discovered at about age 6 and moved to institutions where they received intensive training. Yet the cases were different in one significant respect: Prior to her discovery by those outside her immediate family, Anna experienced virtually no human contact. She saw other individuals only when they left food for her. Isabelle, on the other hand, lived in a darkened room with her deaf-mute mother, who provided some human contact. Anna could not sit, walk, or talk and learned little in the special school in which she was placed. When she died from jaundice at age 11, she had learned the language and skills of a 2- or 3-year-old. Isabelle, on the other hand, did progress. She learned to talk and played with her peers. After 2 years, she reached an intellectual level approaching normal for her age but remained about 2 years behind her classmates in skill and competency levels. By age 14, she was attending regular school and participating in social activities (K. Davis 1940, 1947).

Contemporary cases of children neglected or abused in their family settings or forced into slavery, prostitution, or fighting wars reinforce the importance of early social interaction. Although not totally isolated, these children also experience problems and disruptions in the socialization process. They have to deal with socially toxic abusive, violent, and dead-end environments with harmful developmental consequences for children (War Child 2014). Consider the case of child soldiers. A recent video, *Invisible Children*, went viral on YouTube, showing the plight of these children kidnapped by Joseph Kony's Lord's Resistance Army into a world of drugs, sex, and violence (Terra Networks 2013). Most will have a difficult time integrating back into society—if they have a chance to do so—although there are organizations trying to help them.

These cases illustrate the devastating effects on socialization of isolation, neglect, and abuse early in life. Humans need more from their environments than food and shelter. They need positive contact; a sense of belonging; affection; safety; and someone to teach them language, knowledge, and skills. This is children's socialization into the world, through which they develop a self. Before we examine the development of the self in depth, however, we consider the complexity of socialization in the multilevel (micro, meso, and macro) social world.

SOCIALIZATION AND THE SOCIAL WORLD

Ram, a first grader from India, had been in school in Iowa for only a couple of weeks. The teacher was giving the first test. Ram did not know much about what a test meant, but he rather liked school, and the red-haired girl next to him, Elyse, had become a friend. He was catching on to reading a bit faster than she, but she was better at the number exercises. They often helped each other learn while the teacher was busy with a small group in the front of the class. The teacher gave each child the test, and Ram saw that it had to do with numbers. He began to do what the teacher had instructed the children to do with the worksheet, but after a while, he became confused. He leaned over to look at the page Elyse was working on. She hid her sheet from him, an unexpected response. The teacher looked up and asked what was going on. Elyse said that Ram was "cheating." Ram was not quite sure what that meant, but it did not sound good. The teacher's scolding of Ram left him baffled, confused, and entirely humiliated.

This incident was Ram's first lesson in the individualism and competitiveness that govern Western-style schools. His teacher was socializing him into a new set of values. In his parents' culture, competitiveness is discouraged, and individualism is equated with selfishness and rejection of community. Often, athletic events in their culture of origin were designed to end in a tie so that no one will feel rejected. Indeed, a well-socialized person would rather lose in a competition than cause others to feel badly because they lost. Like Ram, each of us learns the values and beliefs of our culture. In Ram's case, he moved from one cultural group to another and had to adjust to more than one culture within his social world. Many migrants and immigrants around the world are going through similar experiences.

At the micro level, most parents teach children proper behaviors to be successful in life, and peers influence children to "fit in" and have fun. In fact, the process of socialization in groups allows the self to develop as individuals learn to interact with others in their culture. Interaction theory, focusing on the micro level, forms the basis of this chapter, as you will see. At the meso level, religious denominations and political groups teach their versions of the truth, and educational systems teach the knowledge and skills considered by leaders as necessary for functioning in society. At the nationwide macro level, television ads encourage viewers to be more masculine or feminine, buy products that will make them better and happier people, and join the military. From interactions with our significant others to dealing with government bureaucracy, most activities are part of the socialization experience that teaches us how to function in our society.

Keep in mind that socialization is a lifelong process. Even your grandparents are learning how to live at their stage of life. The process of socialization takes place at each level of analysis, linking the parts. Groups at each level have a stake in how we are socialized because they all need trained and loyal group members to survive. Organizations need citizens who have been socialized to devote the time, energy, and resources that these groups need to survive and meet their goals. For example, volunteer and charitable organizations cannot thrive unless people are willing to volunteer their energy, time, skills, and money. Lack of adequate socialization means social organizations will not receive the support they need to thrive—or even, possibly, survive,

Most perspectives on socialization focus on the micro level because much of socialization takes place in an individual's family, with peers, and in small groups. However, meso- and macro-level theories add to our understanding of how socialization prepares individuals for their roles in the larger social world. *Structural-functionalist perspectives* of socialization tend to see organizations at different levels supporting each other. For example, families often organize holidays around patriotic themes, such as a national independence day, or around religious celebrations. These activities can strengthen family members' commitment to the nation and buttress the moral values emphasized in churches, temples, and mosques. All of these values, in turn, help prepare individuals to support national political and economic systems.

At the meso level, the purposes and values of organizations or institutions sometimes directly contrast with one another or conflict with other parts of the social system. From the *conflict perspective*, the linkages between various parts of the social world are based on competition with or even direct opposition to another part. Socialization into a nation's military forces, for example, stresses patriotism and ethnocentrism, sometimes generating conflict and hostility toward other groups and countries. Demands from various organizations for people's time, money, and energy may leave little to give to our religious communities or even our families. Each organization and unit competes to gain our loyalty in order to claim some of our resources.

Conflict can occur in the global community as well. For example, religious groups often socialize their members to identify with humanity as a whole ("the family of God"). However, in some cases, nations do not want their citizens socialized to identify with those beyond their borders. Leaders of nations may seek to persuade Christians to kill other Christians, Jews, or Muslims, whom they define as "the enemy." If religion teaches that all people are "brothers and sisters" and if religious people object to killing, the nation may have trouble mobilizing its people to arms when the leaders call for war. Quaker, Mennonite, and Amish religious groups, among others, promote peace and refuse to engage in warfare. What would happen if all religious groups were against fighting?

Conflict theorists believe that those who have power and privilege use socialization to manipulate individuals to support the power structure and the self-interests of the elite. For example, parents decide how they would like to raise their children and what values they want to instill in them, but as their children enter school, parents must share the socialization process with school personnel who teach curricula established and approved by those in power in society. One reason why some parents choose to homeschool their children is to control external influences on the socialization process.

Whether we stress harmony in the socialization process or conflict rooted in power differences, the development of a sense of self through the process of socialization is an ongoing, lifelong process. Let us now focus on the micro level: How does the *self* develop? How did *you* develop your sense of self?

⬤ Thinking Sociologically

Although the socialization process occurs primarily at the micro level, it is influenced by events at each level in the social system. Give examples of family, community, subcultural, national, or global events that influenced how you were socialized or how you might socialize your child.

DEVELOPMENT OF THE SELF: MICRO-LEVEL ANALYSIS

Have you seen a young child, 3 years or under, using a tablet, smartphone, or other interactive device? New research shows that the impact of mobile devices on preschool children can be detrimental to their social-emotional, sensorimotor, and problem-solving skills, and empathy is not as developed as it would be through social interaction during unstructured play with peers. Using mobile devices can also affect their ability for self-regulation of behavior and early literacy skills (Walters 2015). On the other hand, educational television and mobile-device programs can help children who are closer to school age. Still, researchers suggest more direct human-to-human interaction and designated "family time" is beneficial. Children under 30 months learn primarily from human interaction. We are talking here about the development of the *self*.

A baby is born with the potential to develop a *self*, the main product of the socialization process. That self can evolve in many directions. Fundamentally, **self** refers to *the perceptions we have of who we are*. This process starts at birth. Throughout the socialization process, our self develops largely from the way others respond to us—praising us, disciplining us, ignoring us, and so on. The development of the self allows individuals to interact with other people and to learn to function at each level of the social world.

Humans are not born with a sense of self. It develops gradually, beginning in infancy and continuing throughout adulthood as we interact with others. Individual biology, culture, and social experiences all play a part in shaping the self. The hereditary blueprint each person brings into the world provides broad biological outlines, including particular physical attributes, temperament, and a maturational schedule. Each person is also born into a family that lives within a particular culture, illustrating that nature is shaped by nurture. This hereditary blueprint, in interaction with family and culture, helps create each unique person, different from any other person yet sharing the types of interactions by which the self is formed.

Most sociologists, although not all, believe that we humans are distinct from other animals in our ability to develop a self and to be aware of ourselves as individuals or objects (Irvine 2004). Consider how we refer to ourselves in the first person—*I* am hungry, *I* feel foolish, *I* am having fun, and *I* am good at basketball. We have a conception of who we are, how we relate to others, and how we differ from and are separate from others in our abilities and limitations.

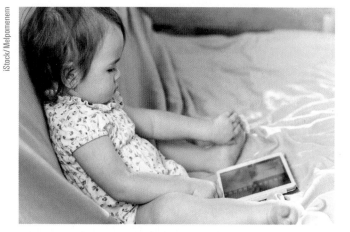

This child is learning something about technology and no doubt receiving other messages through play. Besides how to work an electronic device, what other messages might this child be learning?

We have an awareness of the characteristics, values, feelings, and attitudes that give us our unique sense of self (W. James [1890] 1934; G. Mead [1934] 1962).

Thinking Sociologically

Who are some of the people who have been most significant in shaping your *self*? How have their actions and responses helped shape your self-concept as musically talented, athletic, intelligent, kind, assertive, clumsy, or any of the other hundreds of traits that might make up your self?

The Looking-Glass Self and Role-Taking

Ty: "Hi! What's up?" (Ty has had his eye on this girl in his class, so he approaches her before class.)

Valerie: "Nothin' much."

Ty: "So what do you think of our sociology class?"

Valerie: "It's OK." (She turns around, spots a friend, and walks away.) "Hey Julie, did you get your soc assignment done?"

Ty is left to reflect on how to interpret Valerie's response. Take this common interaction, and apply it to interactions you have had. First, you approach someone and open a conversation (or someone approaches you); second, the person takes you up on the conversation—or not; third, you evaluate the individual's response and modify your behavior based on your interpretation. These steps make up the *looking-glass self*, and they are repeated many times each day. We now explore these seemingly simple interactions that are key in developing our *self* and in our socialization process.

The looking-glass self idea is part of *symbolic interaction theory* and offers important insights into how individuals develop the self. Two of the major scholars in this approach were Charles H. Cooley ([1909] 1983) and George Herbert Mead ([1934] 1962). Cooley believed that the self is a social product, shaped by interactions with others from the time of birth. He likened interaction processes to looking in a mirror, whereby each person reflects an image of the other.

> *Each to each a looking-glass*
>
> *Reflects the other that doth pass*
>
> —Cooley [1909]1983:184

For Cooley ([1909] 1983), the looking-glass self is *a reflective process that develops the self based on our interpretations and on our internalization of the reactions of others*. In this process, Cooley believed that there are three principal elements, shown in Figure 4.1: (1) We imagine how we appear to others, (2) others judge our appearance and respond to us, and (3) we react to that feedback. We experience feelings such as pride or shame based on what we imagine this judgment of others means and respond based on our interpretation. Moreover, throughout this process, we actively try to manipulate other people's view of us to serve our needs and interests. This is one of the many ways we learn to be boys or girls—the image we see reflected back to us lets us know whether we have behaved in socially acceptable ways according to gender expectations in our social setting. The issue of gender socialization, in particular, is discussed in Chapter 9. Of course, this does not mean our interpretation of the other person's response is correct, but our interpretation does determine how we respond.

Our self is influenced by the many "others" with whom we interact, and each of our interpretations of their reactions feeds into our self-concept. Recall that the isolated children failed to develop this sense of self precisely because they lacked interaction with others.

Taking the looking-glass-self idea a step further, Mead explained *that individuals take others into account by imagining themselves in the position of that other*, a process called **role-taking**. When children play mommy and daddy, doctor and patient, or firefighter, they are imagining themselves in another's shoes. Role-taking allows humans to view themselves from the standpoint of others. This requires mentally stepping out of our own experience to imagine how others experience and view the social world. Through role-taking, we begin to see who we are from the standpoint of others. In short, role-taking allows humans to view themselves as objects, as though they were looking at themselves through the eyes of another person. For Mead, role-taking is a prerequisite for the development of our sense of self.

The following "Engaging Sociology" describes a situation experienced by Brent Staples, an African American journalist. It illustrates the relationship between our development of self through the looking-glass self and role-taking, and stereotypes. Many *stereotypes*—rigid images of members of a particular group—surround young African American males in the United States. Think about the human cost of stereotypes and their effect on the socialization process as you read the following essay. If one's sense of self is profoundly influenced by how we see others respond (the looking-glass self) and one's ability to role-take by imagining oneself in another's shoes, how might the identity of a young African American boy be affected by public images of Black males?

FIGURE 4.1   The Looking-Glass Self Process of Self-Development

1. We imagine how we want to appear to others.
2. Others make judgments and respond.
3. We experience feelings and react based on our interpretations.

ENGAGING SOCIOLOGY

Black Men and Public Space

By Brent Staples

My first victim was a woman—White, well dressed, probably in her early 20s. I came upon her late one evening on a deserted street in Hyde Park, a relatively affluent neighborhood in an otherwise mean, impoverished section of Chicago. As I swung onto the avenue behind her, she cast back a worried glance. To her, the youngish Black man—broad, 6-feet, 2-inches tall, with a beard and billowing hair, both hands shoved into the pockets of a bulky military jacket—seemed menacingly close. After a few more quick glimpses, she picked up her pace and was running in earnest. Within seconds, she disappeared into a cross street.

That was more than a decade ago. I was 22 years old, a graduate student newly arrived at the University of Chicago. It was in the echo of that terrified woman's footfalls that I first began to know the unwieldy inheritance I'd come into. . . . It was clear that she thought herself the quarry of a mugger, a rapist, or worse. Suffering a bout of insomnia, however, I was stalking sleep, not defenseless wayfarers. . . . I was surprised, embarrassed, and dismayed all at once. Her flight . . . made it clear that I was indistinguishable from the muggers who occasionally seeped into the area from the surrounding ghetto. I soon gathered that being perceived as dangerous is a hazard in itself. I only needed to make an errant move after being pulled over by a policeman. Where fear and weapons meet—and they often do in urban America—there is always the possibility of death.

In that first year, my first away from my hometown, I was to become thoroughly familiar with the language of fear. At dark, shadowy intersections, I could cross in front of a car stopped at a traffic light and elicit the thunk, thunk, thunk, thunk of the driver—Black, White, male, or female—hammering down the door locks. On less traveled streets, after dark, I grew accustomed to but never comfortable with people crossing to the other side of the street rather than passing me.

After dark, on the warren-like streets of Brooklyn, where I live, I often see women who fear the worst from me. They seem to have set their faces on neutral, and with their purse straps strung across their chests bandolier style, they forge ahead as though bracing themselves against being tackled. I understand, of course, that . . . women are particularly vulnerable to street violence, and young Black males are drastically overrepresented among the perpetrators of that violence. Yet these truths are no solace against the kind of alienation that comes of being ever the suspect . . .

Over the years, I learned to smother the rage I felt at so often being taken for a criminal. Not to do so would surely have led to madness. I now take precautions to make myself less threatening. I move about with care, particularly late in the evening. . . . On late-evening constitutionals, I employ what have proven to be excellent tension-reducing measures: I whistle melodies from Beethoven and Vivaldi and the more popular classical composers. Even steely New Yorkers hunching toward nighttime destinations seem to relax, and occasionally, they even join in the tune. Virtually everybody seems to sense that a mugger wouldn't be warbling bright, sunny selections from Vivaldi's *Four Seasons*. It is my equivalent of the cowbell that hikers wear when they know they are in bear country.

* * * * * * *

Engaging With Sociology

1. Brent Staples goes out of his way to reassure others that he is harmless. What might be some other responses to this experience of having others assume one is dangerous and untrustworthy?

2. How might one's sense of self be influenced by these responses of others?

3. How are the looking-glass self and role-taking at work in this scenario?

4. Have you ever experienced a similar situation in which you felt fear or others feared you? If so, how does that affect you?

Source: Staples (2001). Reprinted with permission from Brent Staples.

Mead ([1934] 1962) also argued that role-taking is possible because humans have a unique ability to use and respond to symbols. *Symbols*, first described in Chapter 2, are actions or objects that represent something else and therefore have meaning beyond their own existence. Language and gestures are examples, for they carry specific meaning for members of a culture. Symbols such as language allow us to give names to objects in the environment and to infuse those objects with meanings. Once the person learns to symbolically recognize objects in the environment, the self can be seen as one of those objects. This starts with possessing a name that allows us to see our self as separate from other objects. If we said the name LeBron James, most people would immediately think of the same person: an extraordinary athlete who largely turned around the fortunes of the Miami Heat professional basketball team to win back-to-back NBA championships and, in 2016, brought Cleveland its first-ever NBA championship.

In the process of symbolic interaction, we take the actions of others and ourselves into account. We may blame, encourage, praise, punish, or reward ourselves. An example would be a basketball player missing the basket because the shot was poorly executed and thinking, "What did I do to miss that shot? I'm better than that!" Reflexive behavior, being able to look at oneself and one's behaviors as though from the outside looking in, includes the simple act of taking mental notes or mentally talking to one's self.

Parts of the Self

The self is composed of two distinct but related parts, according to the symbolic interaction perspective—dynamic parts in interplay with one another (Mead [1934] 1962). The most basic element of the self is what symbolic interactionist George Herbert Mead refers to as the I, *the spontaneous, unpredictable, impulsive, and largely unorganized aspect of the self*. The *I* initiates behavior without considering the possible social consequences. We can see this at work in the "I want it now" behavior of a baby or a toddler. Cookie Monster, on the children's television program *Sesame Street*, illustrates the *I* in every child, gobbling cookies at every chance and insisting on more *now*.

The *I* continues as part of the self throughout life but is controlled or tempered by the social expectations that surround individuals. In developmental stages from early childhood on, humans become increasingly influenced by interactions with others who instill society's rules. Children develop the ability to see their *self* as others see them (role-taking), allowing them to critique the behavior that was initiated by the *I*. Mead called this reflective

capacity of the self the *Me*. The **Me** is *the part of the self that has learned the rules of society through interaction and role-taking, and it controls the I and its desires*. Just as the *I* initiates the act, the *Me* gives direction to the act. In a sense, the *Me* channels the impulsive *I* in an acceptable manner according to societal rules and restraints yet meets the needs of the *I* as best it can. When we stop ourselves just before saying something and think to ourselves, "I'd better not say that," it is our *Me* monitoring and controlling the *I*. Notice that the *Me* requires the ability to take the role of the other, to anticipate the other's reaction.

Thinking Sociologically

For college students, there are many temptations that tantalize and lure the *I*. What are some of these temptations, and how does the *Me* control them (or not)?

Stages in the Development of the Self

The process of developing a social self occurs gradually and in stages, from birth to death. Mead identified three critical stages—(1) the imitation stage, (2) the play stage, and (3) the game stage—each of which requires the uniquely human ability to engage in role-taking (Mead [1934] 1962).

In the **imitation stage**, *children under 3 years old are preparing for role-taking by observing others and imitating their behaviors, sounds, and gestures*. The **play stage** *involves a child, usually from 3 to 5, having the ability to see things (role-take) from the perspective of one person at a time: simple role-taking or play-acting*. Listen to children who are 3 to 5 years old play together. You will notice that they spend most of their time telling each other what to do. One of them will say something like, "You be the mommy, and José can be the daddy, and Zoe, you be the dog. Now you say, 'Good morning, Dear,' and I'll say, 'How did you sleep?' and Zoe, you scratch at the door like you want to go out." They will talk about their little skit for 15 minutes and then enact it, with the actual enactment taking perhaps 1 minute. Small children mimic or imitate role-taking based on what they have seen as they learn and practice future roles (Handel, Cahill, and Elkin 2007).

Society and its rules are initially represented by **significant others**—*parents, guardians, relatives, siblings, or important individuals whose primary and sustained interactions are especially influential*. That is why much of the play stage involves role-taking based on these significant people in the child's life. The child does not yet understand the complex relations and multiple role players in the social world outside the immediate family. Children may have a sense of how their mommy or daddy sees them, but children are not yet able to comprehend how they are seen by the larger social world. Lack of role-taking ability is apparent when children say inappropriate things, such as, "Why are you so fat?"

The third stage in the process of developing a social self, the **game stage**, *is when a child develops the ability to take the roles of multiple others concurrently and to conform to societal expectations.* The child goes beyond the significant other, such as a parent, to value the opinions of all peers or the expectations of the community.

Have you ever watched a team of young children play T-ball (a pre–Little League baseball game in which the children hit the ball from an upright rubber device that holds the ball) or observed a soccer league made up of 6-year-olds? If so, you have seen Mead's point illustrated vividly. In soccer (or football), 5- or 6-year-old children will not play their positions despite constant urging and cajoling by coaches. They all run after the ball, with little sense of their interdependent positions. Likewise, a child in a game of T-ball may pick up a ball that has been hit, turn to the coach, and say, "Now what do I do with it?" Most still do not quite grasp throwing it to first base, and the first-base player may actually have left the base to run for the ball. It can be hilarious for everyone except the coach, as a hit that goes 7 feet turns into a home run because everyone is scrambling for the ball.

Prior to the game stage, the vision of the whole process is not possible. When children enter the game stage at about age 7 or 8, they are developmentally able to play the roles of various positions and enjoy a complex game. Each child learns what is expected and the interdependence of roles because she or he is able, at this stage, to respond to the expectations of several people simultaneously (Hewitt and Shulman 2011; Meltzer 1978). This allows the individual to coordinate his or her activity with others.

In moving from the play stage to the game stage, children's worlds expand from family and day care to neighborhood playmates, school, and other organizations. *This process gradually builds up a composite of societal expectations that the child learns from family, peers, and other organizations*, what Mead refers to as the **generalized other**. The child learns to internalize the expectations of society— the generalized other—over and above the expectations of any *significant others*. Behavior comes to be governed by abstract rules ("no running outside of the baseline" or "no touching the soccer ball with your hands unless you are the goalie") rather than guidance from and emotional ties to a significant other. Children become capable of moving into

Very young children who play soccer do not understand the role requirements of games. They all—including the goalie—want to chase after the ball. Learning to play positions and understand the roles in a complex situation is a critical step in socialization.

new social situations, such as school, organized sports, and (eventually) the workplace, to function with others in both routine and novel interactions.

The common human experience of feeling embarrassed illustrates how the *generalized other* becomes internalized into one's conception of self. Making an inappropriate remark at a party or having another call undue attention to one's appearance can cause embarrassment. Feeling embarrassed may occur when one violates a social norm and then thinks about how others view that behavior. According to this role-taking view, we see ourselves as objects from the standpoint of others, and we judge ourselves accordingly. Very young children, however, do not feel embarrassment when they do things such as soil their pants or make inappropriate comments because they have not incorporated the *generalized other*. They have not yet learned the perspective of others.

The capacity to feel embarrassed is not only an indicator of having internalized the generalized other but also a uniquely human outcome of our role-taking ability (Hewitt and Schulman 2011; Koschate-Reis 2009). Some children face challenges to their self from teasing and bullying that result in fear, shame, embarrassment, and guilt. These feelings affect the bullied child's sense of self and can influence the self into adulthood.

As children grow, they identify with new in-groups, such as a neighborhood, a college sorority, or the military. We learn new ideas and expand our understanding. Some individuals ultimately come to think of themselves as part of the global human community. Thus, for many individuals, the social world expands through socialization. However, some individuals never develop this expanded worldview, remaining narrowly confined and drawing lines between themselves and others who are different. Such narrow boundaries often result in prejudice against others.

Thinking Sociologically

Who are you? Write down 15 or 20 roles or attributes that describe who you are. How many of these items are characteristics associated with the *Me*—nouns such as *son, mother, student,* and *employee*? Which of the items are traits or attributes—adjectives such as *shy, sensitive, lonely, selfish,* and *vulnerable*? How do you think each of these was learned or incorporated into your conception of your *self*?

The Self and Connections to the Meso Level

In the preceding "Thinking Sociologically" exercise, we asked you to think about how you see yourself and what words you might use to portray yourself. If you were describing yourself for a group of people you did not know, we suspect that you would use mostly nouns describing a status or a social position within the society: *student, employee, athlete, violinist, daughter, sister, Canadian, Lutheran,* and so forth. To a large extent, our sense of who we are is rooted in social positions that are part of organizations and institutions in the society (M. Kuhn 1964; Stryker 1980). This is a key point made by what is referred to as the Iowa School of symbolic interaction: The *self* is relatively stable because we develop a core self—a stable inner sense of who we are regardless of the immediate setting in which we find ourselves. This core often centers on the most important social positions we hold in the larger structure of society. Your sense of self may shape your sexual behavior, the honesty with which you conduct business with others, and whether you are willing to cheat on an exam—even though you may not be around other people of your moral or political persuasion at the time (M. Kuhn 1964; Stryker 1980, 2000; Stryker and Stratham 1985; J. Turner 2003).

SOCIALIZATION THROUGHOUT THE LIFE CYCLE

In all societies, individuals move from one stage to the next in the socialization process. Socialization is a lifelong process with many small and large passages. Infants begin the socialization process at birth. In childhood, one rite of passage is a child's first day at school—entrance into the meso-level institution of education. This turning point marks a child's entry into the larger world. The standards of performance are now defined by the child's teachers, peers, friends, and others outside the home.

Adolescence is an important stage in Western industrial and postindustrial societies, but this stage is far from universal. Indeed, it is largely an invention of complex societies over the past 2 centuries, characterized by extensive periods of formal education and dependency on parents (Martorell, Papalia, and Feldman 2014). Adolescence is, in a sense, a structurally produced mass identity crisis because Western societies lack clear rites of passage for adolescents. Teens come to view themselves as a separate and distinct group with their own culture, slang vocabulary, clothing styles, and opinions about appropriate sexual behavior and forms of recreation.

Much of our adult years are spent in work and home life, including marriage and parenting roles for many. It is not surprising, then, that graduation from one's final alma mater (whether it be high school, college, or graduate school) and acceptance of one's first full-time job serve as rites of passage into adulthood in modern societies.

Most social scientists emphasize the importance of *rites of passage*—celebrations or public recognitions when individuals shift from one status to another—naming ceremonies, school graduations, marriages, and retirements. The importance of this shift resides in how others come to perceive the individual differently, the different expectations that others hold for the person, and changes in how the person sees himself or herself.

Thinking Sociologically

Find someone who has grown up in a different culture, and ask her or him about rites of passage from adolescence to adulthood where she or he was raised. How are the patterns similar to or different from your own?

Even the retired and elderly members of society are constantly undergoing socialization and resocialization in the process of developing their sense of self. The type of society influences the socialization experience of the elderly and how they carry out their roles, as well as their status in society. Consider the changes that have taken place in the lifetimes of those born before 1945, as described by one elder:

We were born before television, before polio shots, frozen foods, Xerox, plastic contact lenses,

Frisbees, and the Pill. . . . We never heard of artificial hearts, word processors, yogurt, and guys wearing earrings. For us time sharing means togetherness—not computers and condominiums. (Grandpa Junior 2006)

The elderly are vitally important to the ongoing group in more settled agricultural societies. They are the founts of wisdom and carry group knowledge, experiences, and traditions valued in societies where little change takes place. In industrial and postindustrial countries that continually undergo rapid changes, the wisdom is not as relevant. Yet the number of elderly people is growing rapidly as medical science keeps people alive longer, diets improve, and diseases are brought under control. Average life expectancy in all of Europe's 28 countries was 80.6 years in 2013—83.3 for women and 77.8 for men, with the highest for men in Italy at 80.3 years and for women in Spain at 86.1 years (Eurostat 2015). In 2013, the average life expectancy in the United States was 78.8 years, 76 for men and 81 for women (Centers for Disease Control and Prevention 2015d; "U.S. Life Expectancy" 2013).

In modern systems, social participation by the elderly often drops after retirement. Retirement is a rite of passage to a new status, like that of marriage or parenthood, for which there is little preparation. As a result, retired people sometimes feel a sense of uselessness when they abruptly lose their occupational status. Retirees in Western societies generally have many years of life yet to live. The most socially satisfied retirees tend to develop hobbies, enjoy sports, volunteer their time, travel, or have new jobs they can pursue after they retire.

Dying is the final stage of life (Kübler-Ross 1997). Death holds different meanings in different cultures: passing into another life, a time of judgment, a waiting for rebirth, or a void and nothingness. In some religious groups, people work hard or do good deeds because they believe that they will be rewarded in an afterlife or with rebirth to a better status in the next life on Earth. Thus, beliefs about the meaning of death can affect how people live their lives and how they cope with dying and death.

Each stage of the life cycle involves socialization into new roles in the social world. Many social scientists have studied these developmental stages and contributed insights into what happens at each stage (Clausen 1986; Gilleard and Higgs 2015; Handel et al. 2007; Papalia, Feldman, and Martorell 2015; Piaget 1989; Putt 2014). For example, some sociologists focus their research on the study of old age (gerontology) and death and dying.

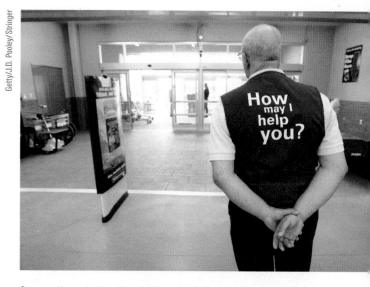

Getty/J.D. Pooley/Stringer

Some retirees, rather than taking up hobbies, decide on a part-time job, like this man, who enjoys people and is now a "greeter" at Walmart. Others take on a postretirement job because they need the income.

Death ends the lifelong process of socialization, a process of learning social rules and roles and adjusting to them. When an individual has passed on, society continues. New members are born, are socialized into the social world, pass through roles once held by others, and eventually give up those roles to younger members. Cultures provide guidelines for each new generation to follow. The social world perpetuates itself and outlives the individuals who populate it.

Thinking Sociologically

How were you socialized to view death and dying? What have you learned in your family about how to cope with death? Is death a taboo topic?

The Process of Resocialization

If you have experienced life in the military, a boarding school, a convent, a mental facility, or a prison or had a major transition in your life such as divorce or the death of a spouse or child, you have experienced resocialization. **Resocialization** is *the process of shedding one or more social positions and taking on others, which involves learning new norms, behaviors, and values suitable to the newly acquired status* (Goffman 1961). Resocialization may take place in a *total institution*—a place that cuts people off from the rest of society and totally controls their lives in the process of resocialization. These include prisons, mental hospitals, monasteries, concentration camps, boarding schools, and military barracks. Bureaucratic regimentation and the manipulation of residents for the convenience of the staff is part of the routine (Goffman 1961).

Death rituals differ depending on the culture and religion of the group. In India (*top left*), this body is being cremated next to the holy Ganges River to release the soul from earthly existence. The closest relative lights the funeral pyre. The top right photo shows the Muslim tradition of washing and wrapping the dead before burial in Najaf, Iraq. At the bottom left, a U.S. Honor Guard carries a casket with the remains of U.S. Air Force personnel at Arlington National Cemetery. A celestial burial master (*bottom right*) feeds the body of a dead Tibetan to the vultures in northwest China's Qinghai province. In Tibetan regions, the practice is known as jhator, which literally means "giving alms to the birds," as people believe in rebirth and there is no need to preserve the body.

We often associate resocialization with major developmental stages in adult life—leaving home to go to college or take a job, having a baby, divorce, retirement, and widowhood. Changes in status present opportunities to move in new and often exciting directions, such as going to college. Resocialization can also mean adjusting to living alone, raising children alone, loneliness, and possible financial problems.

Sometimes, resocialization occurs when individuals are forced to correct or reform behaviors defined as undesirable or deviant. Prison rehabilitation programs provide one example. However, research suggests that the difficulty in resocializing prisoners is rooted in the nature of the prison environment itself. Prisons are often coercive and violent environments, which may not provide the social supports necessary for bringing about positive change in a person's attitudes and behaviors.

Although resocialization is the goal of self-help groups such as Alcoholics Anonymous, Gamblers Anonymous, Parents Anonymous, drug rehabilitation groups, and weight loss groups, relapse is a common problem among participants.

Some public sociologists work on trying to understand why there are such high rates of reversion to previous patterns of behavior. Former prison inmates are at especially high risk of repeating a crime, so public sociologists want to know what might make the resocialization "stick." Clearly, not all socialization or all resocialization is positive or functional. Sometimes, resocialization alienates people from others and can contribute to violence or even terrorism.

Multiple individuals, groups, and institutions are involved in the socialization process. These socialization forces are referred to as *agents of socialization*.

AGENTS OF SOCIALIZATION: THE MICRO–MESO CONNECTION

Agents of socialization are *the transmitters of culture—the people, organizations, and institutions that help us define our identity and teach us how to thrive in our social world.* Agents are the mechanism by which the self learns the values, beliefs, and behaviors of the culture. Agents of socialization help new members find their place, just as they prepare older members for new responsibilities in society. At the micro level, one's family, one's peer group, and local groups and organizations help people know how they should behave and what they should believe. At the meso level, formal sources of learning (e.g., education and religion) and informal sources of learning (e.g., the media and books) are all agents that contribute to socialization. They transmit information to children and to adults throughout their lives.

⬤ Thinking Sociologically

As you read this section, make a list of socializing agents. Indicate two or three central messages each agent of socialization tries to instill in people. Are there different kinds of messages at the micro, meso, and macro levels? Do these messages conflict, and if so, why?

In early childhood, the family acts as the primary agent of socialization, passing on messages about respect for property and authority and the value of love and loyalty (Handel et al. 2007). **Peer groups**—*people who are roughly equal in some status within the society, such as the same age or the same occupation*—are also important, especially during the teenage years. Some writers even argue that the peer group is the most important *agent* in the socialization process of children and teens (Aseltine 1995; J. Harris 2009). Each agent has its own functions and is important at different stages of the life cycle, but meso-level institutions play a more active role as one matures. For example, schools and religious bodies become more involved in socialization as children become 6 years old and older, compared with when they were preschool age.

Formal agents of socialization are *official or legal agents (e.g., families, schools, teachers, and religious organizations) whose purpose it is to socialize the individual into the values, beliefs, and behaviors of the culture.* For example, a primary goal of families is to teach children to speak and to learn proper behavior. In addition, schoolteachers educate by giving formal instruction, and religious organizations provide moral instruction. (Schools, as formal agents of socialization, are discussed in Chapter 10.)

Informal agents of socialization are *unofficial influential agents that shape values, beliefs, and behaviors in which socialization is not the express purpose.* Examples include peers, the media, books, advertising, and the

As children become teenagers, peers become increasingly important socializing agents, shaping their norms, values, and attitudes.

Internet. They bring us continuous messages even though their primary purpose is not socialization but entertainment or selling products. Children watch countless advertisements on television, many with messages about what is good and fun to eat and how to be more attractive, more appealing, smarter, and a better person through the consumption of products. This bombardment is a particularly influential part of socialization for children and teenagers.

Lessons from one agent of socialization generally complement those from other agents. Parents work at home to support what school and religion teach. However, at times, agents provide conflicting lessons. For example, family and faith communities often give teens messages that conflict with those of peer groups regarding sexual activity and drug use. This is an example of mixed messages given by formal and informal agents.

Thinking Sociologically

What confusion might be created for children when the formal and informal agents of socialization provide different messages about values or acceptable behaviors? Is this contradiction something that parents should be concerned about? Why, or why not?

Micro-Level Socialization

Perhaps the most important micro-level formal agent of socialization is our own family—parents, siblings, and other family members. One way in which families teach children what is right and wrong is through rewards and punishments, called *sanctions*. Children who lie to their parents may receive a verbal reprimand or a slap on the hand, be sent to their rooms, have a "time-out," or receive a spanking, depending on differences in child-rearing practices among families. These are examples of negative sanctions. Conversely, children may be rewarded for good behavior with a positive sanction, such as a smile, praise, a cookie, or a special event. The number and types of sanctions dispensed in the family shape the socialization process, including development of the self and the perceptions we have of who we are and even whether we are good and clever or bad and stupid. Note that family influence varies from one culture to another.

In Japan, the mother is a key agent in the process of turning a newborn into a member of the group, passing on the strong group standards and expectations of family, neighbors, community, and society through the use of language and emotion. The child learns the importance of depending on the group and therefore fears being cast out. The need to belong creates pressure to conform to expectations, and the use of threats and the fear of shame help socialize children into Japanese ways (Brinkerhoff et al. 2014; Hendry 1987).

Nonconformity is a source of shame in Japan. The resulting ridicule is a powerful means of social control. In some cases, the outcast is physically punished by peers. Thus, to bring shame on oneself or the family is behavior to be avoided. In the most extreme cases, young people have committed suicide because they did not conform to group expectations and felt profoundly ashamed as a result.

Thinking Sociologically

How did agents of socialization influence who you are today, and how did your experience differ from that of the Japanese children just described?

In contrast to the values of conformity and fitting into the group espoused in many Asian countries, in the United States, most parents teach their children to value friendliness, cooperation, orientation toward achievement, social competence, responsibility, and independence. However, subcultural values and socialization practices may differ within the diverse groups in the U.S. population. Conceptions of what makes a "good person" or a "good citizen" and varied goals of socialization bring about differences in the process of socialization around the world.

Meso-Level Socialization

Meso-level agents also work to socialize people into specific cultural values and roles they must learn to fulfill. Education and religion are two obvious influences—both

A Japanese mother helps her son at Heian Shinto Shrine during Shichi-go-san Matsuri, also called the Seven-Five-Three Festival, a celebration with prayers of long life for children aged 3 to 7.

being institutions with primary responsibility for socialization. We discuss schools as a socializing agent in Chapter 10; here, we illustrate meso-level socialization influences with a focus on social class and the media.

Social Class. Our education level, our occupation, the house we live in, what we choose to do in our leisure time, the foods we eat, and our religious and political beliefs are just a few aspects of our lives affected by socialization. Applying what we know from sociological research, the evidence strongly suggests that socialization varies by **social class**, or *the wealth, power, and prestige rankings that individuals hold in society* (Paxton and Pearce 2009). Meso-level patterns of distribution of resources, based, in part, on the economic opportunities created by state and national policies, affect who we become.

Upper-middle-class and middle-class parents in the United States usually have above-average education and managerial or professional jobs. They tend to pass on to their children the skills and values necessary to succeed in the subculture of their social class. Subcultures, you will recall, operate at the meso level of the social system. Subcultural values such as autonomy, creativity, self-direction (the ability to make decisions and take initiative), responsibility, curiosity, and consideration of others are especially important for middle-class success and are part of middle-class subculture (Kohn 1989). If the child misbehaves, for example, middle-class parents typically analyze the child's reasons for misbehaving, and punishment is related to these reasons. Sanctions often involve instilling guilt and denying privileges.

Working-class parents tend to pass on to children their cultural values of respect for authority and conformity to rules, lessons that will be useful if the children also have blue-collar jobs (Kohn 1989). Immediate punishment with no questions asked if a rule is violated functions to prepare children for positions in which obedience to rules is important to success. They are expected to be neat, clean, well-mannered, honest, and obedient students and workers (MacLeod 2008). Socialization experiences for boys and girls are also often different, following traditional gender role expectations of the working-class subculture.

Members of each class, as you can see, socialize their children to be successful in their social class and to meet expectations for adults of that class. Schools, like families, participate in this process and socialize children to adapt to the settings in which they grow up and are likely to live. Children's social class position on entering school, in turn, has an effect on the socialization experiences they have in school (Ballantine, Hammack, and Stuber 2017). The result is the *reproduction of class*, as young people are socialized into the social class of their parents.

Social class, however, is only one of many influencing agents of socialization. As we saw in *Black Men and Public Space* (p. 93), race and ethnicity are very important factors in socialization, as is gender. We discuss gender socialization in more detail in Chapter 9, but note here that race, class, and gender act as structural constraints on some members of the population, as they receive different messages about who they are and how they should behave. Therefore, it is important to recognize the interplay of these variables in people's lives.

Electronic Media. Television and computers are important informal agents of socialization at the meso level. They are intermediate-sized social units—larger than a local community but smaller than a nation. They impact both nation-states and global agencies at the macro level by shaping public attitudes, and they affect family notions

This parent passes on a love for the piano to his young son. Because of the social class of this father, his son is likely to receive many messages about creativity, curiosity, and self-direction.

of what is normal or not normal at the micro level. In developed countries, there is scarcely a home without a television set, although viewership is dropping due to online videos (Luckerson 2014), and over 78% of homes have computers and Internet access (New Media Trend Watch 2013).

Researchers in the United States have collected nearly 5 decades of information on how television has become a way of life in homes. By the time an average child in the United States reaches age 18, he or she will have spent more time watching television than doing any other single activity besides sleeping. New findings from Great Britain indicate

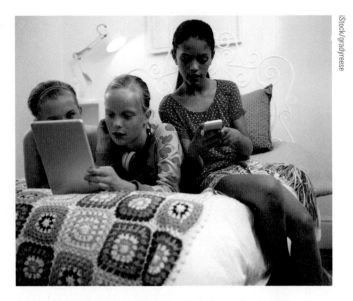

iStock/gradyreese

These children illustrate how electronic devices influence the socialization process. Notice that they are not even all sharing the same device, and this influences the way they relate to each other.

that online time (3 hours a day) now surpasses time watching TV (2.1 hours a day) for children from 5 to 15 years (J. Jackson 2016). On average, children in the U.S. between ages 8 and 18 spend 3 hours a day watching television, 1 hour and 11 minutes watching videos or DVDs, 1 hour and 44 minutes with audio media, 1 hour using computers, and 49 minutes playing video games, with a total media exposure in a typical day of 8 hours and 33 minutes (Ahuja 2013; Madden et al. 2013; Pew Research Center Internet and American Life Project 2012).

The moguls of the mass media— a meso-level social system—are able to influence socialization within the most intimate of environments. Children (in the United States) use computers at very young ages. Over "80% of children under age 5 use the Internet weekly" (Kessler 2011). Parents who play an active role in helping children understand the content of television and computer games can have a powerful effect on mitigating media's negative impacts and enhancing the positive aspects of media. The media usage habits of parents can also influence how their children respond to media (A. Jordan et al. 2006; National Consumers League 2013).

Online Social Networking. Today, almost all teens in the United States (95%) are online (Madden et al. 2013). More than 75% of teens own cell phones and text an average of 60 times a day (Ahuja 2013; Pew Research Center Internet and American Life Project 2012). Whereas just 25% of teens see friends in person every day outside of school, 55% text their friends daily (Lenhart 2015). Over half of teens (61% of boys and 52% of girls) have met a friend online through social networking sites (e.g., Instagram or Facebook) or online gaming sites. Girls who meet a friend online tend to do so through networking sites, whereas boys are about equally likely to make a friend through an online game site (Lenhart 2015). One out of five teens has met a friend in person that they got to know online.

Although social networking sites can help people meet new friends, feel connected, and gain support from others, they can also lead to some negative consequences. For teens, in particular, social media sites can be full of friendship drama. More than two out of three (68%) teen social network users say drama has arisen among their friends online. Figure 4.2 reveals some of the varying experiences of teens on social media.

The next "Engaging Sociology" looks at social network usage across various demographic groups. Examine this issue in more depth by answering the questions following Table 4.1.

FIGURE 4.2 Teens, Drama, and Support From Social Media

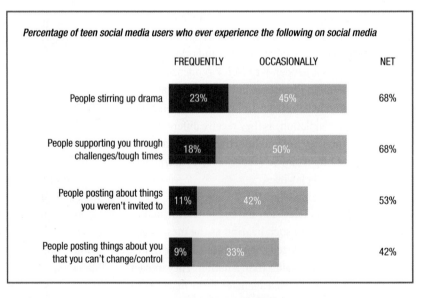

Percentage of teen social media users who ever experience the following on social media

	FREQUENTLY	OCCASIONALLY	NET
People stirring up drama	23%	45%	68%
People supporting you through challenges/tough times	18%	50%	68%
People posting about things you weren't invited to	11%	42%	53%
People posting things about you that you can't change/control	9%	33%	42%

Source: Lenhart (2015).

ENGAGING SOCIOLOGY

Uses and Consequences of Social Networking

Table 4.1   Who Uses Social Networking Sites

All Internet Users	74%
a. Men	72
b. Women	76
a. 18–29	89
b. 30–49	82
c. 50–64	65
d. 65+	49
a. High school grade or less	72
b. Some college	78
c. College+	73
a. Less than $30,000/yr	79
b. $30,000–$49,999	73
c. $50,000–$74,999	70
d. $75,000+	78

Source: Pew Research Center (2016).

Engaging With Sociology

1. Among the demographic variables of age, education, and income, which one has a significant impact on who uses social networking sites?

2. How does the impact of historical time period on the socialization process help explain the differences in social media usage described in the table?

3. Describe the possible impacts of the increased use of social networking sites. How might it affect the socialization of future generations?

4. How has your own use (or not) of social networking sites influenced (a) with whom you interact and (b) how you communicate with people? (Or if you do not use social networking sites, discuss how your nonuse of such sites has impacted your relationships with those who do.)

5. Overall, do you think the increase in the use of social networking sites has had more of a positive or negative impact on (a) your own life and (b) your society? Why?

An alarming concern with Internet socialization is its role in radicalizing some young people and involving them in terrorism. The Tsarnaev brothers—Tamerlan and Dzhokhar—were apparently well-adjusted teens while in high school, but they were deeply influenced by Internet exchanges and by political websites. Eventually, they teamed together to plot the Boston Marathon bombings on April 15, 2013. Three people were killed, and roughly 280 people were injured, many losing limbs. The actions of these young men were spawned when they adopted ideologies deeply antagonistic to the United States through Internet socialization. In a country that values free speech, controlling such antisocial influences is a real dilemma (Crary and Lavoie 2013).

Perhaps the most important aspect of television and computers is something that we do not fully understand but that has frightening potential. For the first time in human history, we have powerful agents of socialization in the home from a child's birth onward. Time spent watching television or playing computer games means less time spent engaging in interaction with family members, caregivers, and peers. Intimate family bonds formed of affection and meaningful interaction are being altered by the dominant presence of electronic media in the home. In addition, those who control the flood of mass-media messages received by children may have very different interests and concerns than parents.

Without a doubt, a significant part of the informal socialization process occurs with the assistance of electronic equipment that shares the home with parents and siblings and that commands a significant portion of a child's time and attention. We also know that macro forces, such as globalization, have influenced school curricula and media content. We move next to a discussion of some of the national and global processes that influence socialization.

SOCIALIZATION AND MACRO-LEVEL ISSUES

Sense of Self in a New Global Context

Immigration patterns and ethnic conflicts around the world have resulted in a fairly new phenomenon: transnationalism. *Transnationalism* is the process by which immigrants have multinational social relations that link together their original societies with their new locations. This means that an individual or a family has national loyalty to more than one country (Levitt 2001, 2007; Levitt and Waters 2006). Often, it occurs after the migration of war refugees, whose roots lie in their country of origin and whose close family members may continue to live there.

Consider the socialization process of transnational children raised in war-torn countries. In the Palestinian territories, especially Gaza, and in Israeli settlements along the border, children grow up with fear and hatred that result in major influences on their socialization. Some war refugees spend childhoods in refugee camps and may never return to their native countries. For people experiencing transnationalism, there are conflicting messages about culturally appropriate behaviors and the obligations of loyalty to family and nation. Events of a national or global nature directly impact how an individual is socialized—with some of the socializing influences being from outside one's country of residence.

However, one need not migrate to another country to experience global pressures and added socialization influences. The Internet and cell phones have increasingly created a sense of connectedness to other parts of the world and an awareness of global interdependencies. Mobile phones have now surpassed computers as a main means of information, education, commerce, and access to health care around the world (Bosomworth 2015). In the United States, 66% own a smartphone, and 20% use them for online services (Aaron Smith 2015).

Some commentators have even suggested that the Internet is a threat to the nation-state because it allows individuals to be socialized through friendships, loyalties, and norms that are not in the interests of the state (Drori 2006). Ideas of social justice or progress may be shaped not just by the government that rules the country but by international human rights organizations and ideas obtained from media that cross borders, such as the Internet. In recent uprisings in some Middle Eastern and North African countries, social networking kept movement participants in touch with others in the uprisings and with outside media and supporters. Socialization agents now include electronic communication beyond local and national boundaries and provide information, contacts, and friendships across borders and boundaries. Figure 4.3, on Internet use around the world, illustrates not only variability of access but also how widespread this access has become. One interesting question is how access or lack of access will influence the strength of us-versus-them feelings between citizens of different countries, insofar as sense of self is connected to belonging to a group—to a sense of *we*.

At a time when people lived in isolated rural communities and did not interact with those unlike themselves, there was little price to pay for being bigoted or chauvinistic toward those who were different. However, we now live

FIGURE 4.3 Internet Users per 100 People

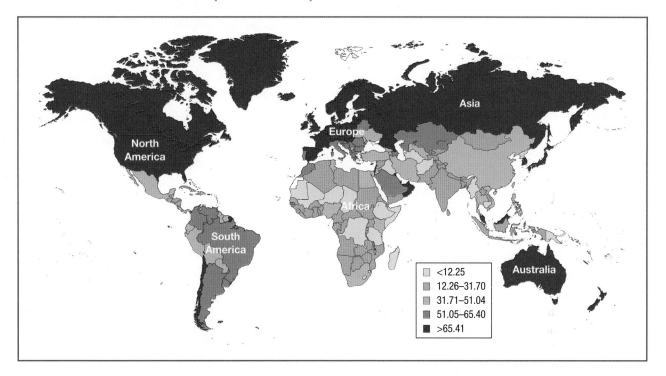

Asia

Europe

North
America

Africa

South
America

Australia

	<12.25
	12.26–31.70
	31.71–51.04
	51.05–65.40
	>65.41

Source: World Bank (2016b).

in a global village where we or our businesses will likely interact with very different people in a competitive environment. If we hold people in low regard because they are unlike us or because we think they are destined for hell, there may be a high cost for this animosity. Among other problems, terrorism is fermented when people feel alienated. Therefore, training in cultural sensitivity toward those "others" has become an economic and a political issue in many communities.

The reality is that children today live in a globalized world. An increasing number of children around the world learn multiple languages to enhance their ability to communicate with others. Some college campuses require experiences abroad as part of the standard curriculum because faculty members and administrators feel that a global perspective is essential in our world today and part of a college education. Global sensitivity and tolerance of those once considered "alien" has become a core element today.

Sometimes, global events can cause a different turn—away from tolerance and toward defensive isolation. When 19 young men from Saudi Arabia and other Middle Eastern countries crashed planes into the World Trade Center in New York City and into the Pentagon in Washington, DC, the United States was shocked and became mobilized to defend itself and its borders. The messages within schools and from the government suddenly took a more patriotic turn. So this event and other terrorist acts, clearly tragedies rooted in global political conflicts, did and can intensify the boundaries between people and loyalty to the nation-state. Global forces are themselves complex and do not always result in more tolerance.

Indeed, the only thing that we can predict with considerable certainty is that in this age of sharing a small planet, the socialization of our citizens will be influenced by events at the macro level, whether national or global.

Thinking Sociologically

How can events at the macro level (national or global) influence our individual socialization experience at the micro level?

Now that we have some understanding of the process of socialization, we look at the next level in the process of interaction and how individuals become members of small groups, networks, and large, complex organizations.

WHAT HAVE WE LEARNED?

Human socialization is pervasive, extensive, and life-long. We cannot understand what it means to be human without comprehending the impact of a specific culture on us, the influence of our close associates, and the complex interplay of pressures at the micro, meso, and macro levels. Indeed, without social interaction, there would not even be a self. We humans are, in our most essential natures, social beings. The purpose of this chapter is to open our eyes to the ways in which we become the individuals we are. We move now to a discussion of how we use our socialization in interactions with groups and organizations as members of society.

- Human beings come with their own biological makeup, but most of what makes us uniquely human we learn from our culture and society—through socialization. Humans who live in isolation from others do not receive the socialization necessary to be part of culture and are sometimes barely human.

- The self consists of the interaction of the *I*—the basic impulsive human, with drives, needs, and feelings—and the *Me*. We develop a reflective self through role-taking to see how others might view us.

- The self is profoundly shaped by others, but it also has agency—that is, it can be an initiator of action and a maker of meaning.

- The self develops through stages, from mimicking others (the play stage) to more intellectually sophisticated abilities to role-take and to see how various roles complement each other (the game stage).

- The self is modified as it moves through life stages, and some of those stages require major resocialization—shedding old roles and taking on new ones as one enters new statuses in life.

- A number of agents of socialization are at work in each of our lives, communicating messages relevant at the micro, meso, or macro level of social life. At the meso level, for example, we may receive different messages about what it means to be a "good" person depending on our ethnic, religious, or social class subculture.

- Some of these messages may be in conflict with each other, as when global messages about tolerance for those who are different conflict with a nation's desire to have absolute loyalty and a sense of superiority.

DISCUSSION QUESTIONS

1. Cooley's idea of the looking-glass self helps us understand that how we think other people view us influences our view of ourselves. How has your sense of your ability to succeed in college been influenced by the feedback you have processed from those around you (particularly teachers, peers, and family members)?

2. Socialization occurs throughout the life cycle. Into what role have you been socialized most recently? Who were the primary agents in this socialization process? Did you find the process relatively easy or difficult? Why?

3. Sociological studies have shown that middle-class and working-class parents tend to socialize their children differently. Explain the differences and describe how they relate to how you were socialized by your family of origin.

4. How has your socialization been influenced by television and video games? Do you think the extent to which these informal agents of socialization influence children these days has a positive or a negative impact on our society? Why?

5. If you were asked to create a government policy to promote positive socialization experiences that would strengthen our society, what might you propose? Why?

KEY TERMS

CONTRIBUTING TO OUR SOCIAL WORLD: WHAT CAN WE DO?

At the Local Level

In every community, numerous opportunities exist for volunteer work helping children from economically and otherwise disadvantaged backgrounds to succeed in school. *Opportunities to help disadvantaged children succeed in school include tutoring or mentoring in the local schools.*

- *Head Start centers for poor preschool children* often have opportunities to do something concrete to help children. An education faculty member at your college can give you contact information, or go to the association's website at www.nhsa.org.

- *Help in a local Boys and Girls Club* that provides socialization experiences for children through their teens. You can find a club near you by going to www.bgca.org/whoweare/Pages/FindaClub.aspx.

- *Take service-learning course* credits. Locate the service-learning office at your college or university to learn about service-learning programs on your campus that help disadvantaged children.

At the National and Global Levels

Literacy is a vital component of socialization yet remains an unmet need in many parts of the world, especially in the less developed countries of Africa and Asia.

- *World Education* provides training and technical assistance in nonformal education in economically disadvantaged communities worldwide. Go to the organization's website at www.worlded.org to learn about its wide variety of projects and volunteer or work opportunities.

- *CARE International* (www.care-international.org) and *Save the Children* (www.savethechildren.org) provide funding for families to send children to school and to receive specialized training.

- *WE Charity* (we.org), an organization that empowers young people to help other young people, has built more than 650 schools and schoolrooms for children in various parts of the world. Go to the organization's website to learn how you can work with others to help create more educational opportunities for children.

- *UNESCO (the United Nations Educational, Scientific, and Cultural Organization)* promotes literacy around the world in many ways. Learn more about its efforts at www.unesco.org/new/en/education. Opportunities exist for fundraising, internships, and eventually jobs with these organizations.

$SAGE edge™

Get the edge on your studies. edge.sagepub.com/ballantinecondensed5e

- Take a quiz to find out what you've learned.
- Review key terms with eFlashcards.
- Watch videos that enhance chapter content.

Julien Behal/ PA Wire

Interaction, Groups, and Organizations

Connections That Work

Human interactions result in connections—networks—that make life more fulfilling and our economic efforts more productive. These connections link everything from micro groups to large bureaucratic organizations. Depicted here is part of the closing ceremonies of the Olympics in London in 2012.

ME (MY FAMILY AND CLOSEST FRIENDS)

LOCAL ORGANIZATIONS AND COMMUNITY
Networks form in local organizations like civic and alumni groups.

NATIONAL ORGANIZATIONS, INSTITUTIONS, AND ETHNIC SUBCULTURES
Ethnic organizations, political parties, and religious denominations are important to many people.

SOCIETY
Citizens of a nation develop connections and a common identity.

GLOBAL COMMUNITY
The United Nations, international courts, and transnational corporations influence our lives.

WHAT YOU WILL LEARN IN THIS CHAPTER

This chapter will help you do the following:

5.1 Demonstrate the impact social networks can have on the lives of individuals.

5.2 Provide examples of how verbal and nonverbal interaction guides our behavior.

5.3 Describe the needs primary and secondary groups meet for members of society and the overall society.

5.4 Show how the characteristics of bureaucracy apply to formal organizations.

5.5 Explain why networking with people from different cultures has become increasingly important.

THINK ABOUT IT

Micro: Local community	How does interaction with family and friends affect who you are and what you believe?
Meso: National institutions, complex organizations, and ethnic groups	Is bureaucratic red tape necessary and inevitable?
Macro: National and global systems	What are some ways national trends, such as the decline in the percentage of U.S. citizens who smoke, influence your quality of life? What are some ways networks across the globe affect your daily life, your education, and your chosen profession?

Imagine that you cannot use your cell phone (or anyone else's). How would your behavior (and your mood) change? A majority of all adults tend to use their cell phones to avoid boredom, and almost all (92%) young adults ages 18–29 do so. Almost half (47%) of young adults and one out of three (32%) of those between 30 and 49 use their cell phones to avoid people around them (Aaron Smith 2015). How would you cope? Our constant access to media and communication technology has changed how we act and with whom we interact. Cell phones enable us to both connect and disconnect from others.

To use another example, Jeanne, one of the authors of this book, took a leave of absence in the mid-1980s to conduct some research in Japan. A benefit of that leave was that she escaped the distractions of ringing phones, and she could concentrate. Fax was almost unknown, and e-mail hardly existed for the civilian population. In 2016, she taught on Semester at Sea. Even in the middle of the ocean, she had instant contact with her office, publisher, and family over the international Internet superhighway. She could insert earphones into her laptop computer and have a Skype conversation by voice or pick up a mobile phone and call her family or coauthor. What a change in the span of her career! Technology is creating a smaller and different world, connected through global networks.

This chapter lays the groundwork for understanding how we fit into the structure of our social world—exploring the link between the individual and the social structure. The process starts when we are born and continues with group activities as we join playgroups, preschool, and kindergarten classes. It broadens as we become members of larger organizations and bureaucracies within universities, workplaces, national political parties, and national and international religious organizations. First, we consider how networks and connections link individuals and groups to different levels of analysis. Then, we focus on micro-level interactions, meso-level groups, and meso- and macro-level organizations and bureaucracies. Finally, we consider macro-level national and global networks.

© REUTERS/Eric Gaillard

No longer are paper and pencil the sole tools of learning. From as early as kindergarten on, students use electronic devices and the Internet at school.

NETWORKS AND CONNECTIONS IN OUR SOCIAL WORLD

Try imagining yourself at the center of a web, such as a spider's web. Attach the threads that spread from the center first to family members and close friends, on out in the web to peers, then to friends of friends. Some thread connections are close and direct. Others are more distant but connect more and more people in an ever-expanding web.

Have you ever used the "Six Degrees of Kevin Bacon" search tool? Perhaps you have heard that just about any actor can be connected to Kevin Bacon in six or fewer steps. It is also true that the typical person in the United States is now fewer than six steps (or degrees removed) from any other person in the country. Stanley Milgram and his associates studied social networks by selecting several target people in different cities (Korte and Milgram 1970; Milgram 1967; Travers and Milgram 1969). Then, they identified *starting persons* in cities more than 1,000 miles away. Each starting person was given a folder with instructions and the target person's name, address, and occupation, as well as a few other facts. The starting person was instructed to mail the folder to someone he or she knew on a first-name basis who lived closer to or might have more direct networks with the target person than the starting person had. The number of links in the chain to complete delivery ranged from two to 10, with most having five to seven intermediaries. This is the source of the reference to *six degrees of separation* and the original inspiration for the Kevin Bacon game.

More recently, research by scientists at Facebook and the University of Milan showed that the average number of acquaintances separating any two people in the world is now 4.74. Within the United States, the separation was only 4.37 people (Markoff and Sengupta 2011). Clearly, networks are powerful linkages and create a truly small world.

Our **social networks**, then, *refer to individuals linked together by one or more social relationships, connecting us to the larger society*. Our social networks provide us with **social capital**, *access to people who can help us get jobs or favors*. Networks begin with micro-level contacts and exchanges between individuals in private interactions and expand to small groups, then to large (even global) organizations (Granovetter 2007; Tolbert and Hall 2008). The stronger people's networks, the more influential they can be in a person's life (see Figure 5.1).

Networks at the Micro, Meso, and Macro Levels

As noted, networks span the micro, meso, and macro levels of analysis. For example, at the *micro level*, you develop close friends in college—bonds that may continue for the rest of your life. You introduce your friends from the student government to your roommate's friends from the soccer team, and the network expands, and your social capital increases. These acquaintances may have useful information about which professors to take, what campus organizations to join, and how to get a job in your field. You most likely carry out all of these interactions both in person and online.

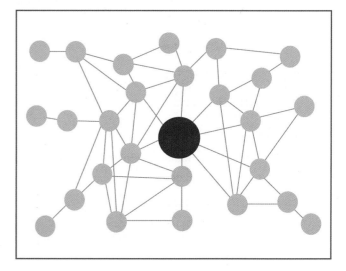

Supporters of Myanmar opposition leader Aung San Suu Kyi take a selfie as they look at the official results of the elections on a giant screen. Within seconds, their friends anywhere in the world could see them at the elections rally through the photo on their Facebook pages.

When you graduate from your university, you will be part of the university's alumni association, and this may become important to you for social contacts, business connections, or help with settling in a new location. When people refer to the old-boy network, they are talking about contacts made through general associations with people such as alumni. Men have used networks quite successfully

FIGURE 5.1 Networks: A Web of Connections

The blue circle represents an individual—perhaps you—and the yellow dots represent your friends and acquaintances. The lines represent personal relationships between individuals. Your network, then, looks a bit like a spider's web.

in the past, and networks of working women—new-girl networks—are expanding rapidly. One of the reasons for the persistent inequality in our society is that members of certain groups may not have access to these privilege-enhancing networks.

Thinking Sociologically

Map your social network web (as far as you can). What advantages do you get from your network? How might this network help you to advance in your chosen career?

Networks also link groups at different levels of analysis. In fact, you are linked through networks to (a) micro-level college, athletic, and faith communities; (b) meso-level formal, complex organizations, such as a political party or national fraternity and ethnic or social class subcultures; and (c) the macro-level nation of which you are a citizen and global entities such as the United Nations. These networks may open opportunities, but they also may create obligations that limit your freedom to make your own choices. As we move from micro-level interactions to larger meso- and macro-level organizations, interactions tend to become more formal. Formal organizations will be explored in the latter half of this chapter.

The most famous networking site is Facebook. As of the fourth quarter of 2016, Facebook had 1.86 billion active users on the site (Statistica 2016a). As a way of examining your own networks, try the exercise in the next "Engaging Sociology" feature.

ENGAGING SOCIOLOGY

Networking via Facebook

If you are on Facebook, go to your Facebook account, and note the number of friends you have listed. Then, look at them carefully to see if you can answer the following questions:

1. What is the age range of the friends on your list?

2. What is the gender composition of your list?

3. How many members of each of the following racial, ethnic, or global links are on your list?

___ African Americans

___ Whites

___ Hispanics

___ Asians

___ Other racial or ethnic group (or some combination)

___ International contacts

4. What is the socioeconomic status of your friends?

___ Blue collar (families in which the primary wage earner works for an hourly wage)

___ Middle class (families in which the primary wage earner earns a salary of less than $100,000 per year)

___ Professional (families in which the primary wage earner earns a salary of $100,000 to $500,000 per year)

___ Highly affluent corporate executive (families in which the primary wage earner earns a salary of $500,000 to $10 million per year)

___ Upper class (families in which much of the wealth is inherited and annual income is in the multimillions)

* * * * * *

Engaging With Sociology

1. Now, look at the data you have collected. What have you learned about your own networks?

2. How much socioeconomic, age, race, ethnic, and global diversity do the data reveal about your networks?

We can network through Facebook, LinkedIn, Twitter, Instagram, and other sites, and we can keep in touch constantly through text messaging. However, this means that people spend more time interacting with a piece of technology and may feel less comfortable interacting face to face with someone. Likewise, online courses are, in one sense, less intimate: The instructor and the student may never meet face to face. Yet through the Internet, more people can take college-level courses than ever before. We are only beginning to understand the implications of this technology on human interaction and on interpersonal skills.

THE PROCESS OF INTERACTION: CONNECTIONS AT THE MICRO LEVEL

Each morning as you rouse yourself, you consider what the day might bring. You evaluate what is in store for you, what roles you will play during the day, and with whom you are likely to interact.

Should you wear the ragged but comfy jeans and T-shirt? Perhaps that will not work today because there is that class trip to the courthouse. Something a bit less casual is in order. Then, you are meeting with your English professor to discuss the last essay you wrote. What approach should you take? You could act insulted that she failed to think of you as a future J. K. Rowling, Suzanne Collins, or John Green. Maybe a meek, mild "Please tell me what I did wrong; I tried so hard" approach would work. She seems a nice, sympathetic sort. After class, there is a group of students who chat in the hall. It would be nice to meet them. What strategy should you use? Tell a joke? Make small talk? Talk to the students individually so you can get to know each before engaging the whole group? Each of these responses is a strategy for interaction, and each might elicit different reactions.

The Elements of Social Interaction

"Let's have a drink!" Such a simple comment might have many different meanings. We could imagine two thirsty children playing together, men going to a bar after work, a couple of friends getting together to celebrate an event, fraternity brothers at a party, or a couple on a date. In all of these cases, **social interaction** consists of *two or more individuals purposefully relating to each other*.

"Having a drink," like all *interaction*, involves action on the part of two or more individuals, is directed toward a goal that people hope to achieve, and takes place in a social context that includes cultural norms and rules governing the situation, the setting, and other factors shaping the way people perceive the circumstances. The action, goal, and social context help us interpret the meaning of statements such as, "Let's have a drink."

The norms governing the particular social context tell us how to behave. Recall from Chapter 3 that *norms* are rules that guide human interactions. People assume that others will share their interpretation of a situation. These shared assumptions about proper behavior provide the cues for your own behavior that become a part of your social self. You look for cues to proper behavior and rehearse in your mind your actions and reactions. In the "Let's have a drink" scenario, the dress, mannerisms, speech, and actions you consider appropriate depend on expectations from your socialization and past experience in similar situations. You will, no doubt, have learned to dress and act differently depending on whether you are having the drink with an old friend or a potential romantic partner. In turn, you will expect that the person with whom you are drinking will be making the same sort of decisions on what to wear and how to behave when you get together.

Although most people assume that talking, or *verbal communication*, is the primary means of communication between individuals, words themselves are actually only a part of the message. In most contexts, they make up less than 7% of the communication, with body language, 55%, and tone of voice, 38% (Debenham 2014; Fields 2015). We communicate primarily through nonverbal communication—interactions without words, using facial expressions, the head, eye contact, body posture, gestures, touch, walk, status symbols, and personal space (Cherry 2012; Givens 2012). We learn these important elements of communication through socialization as we grow up.

People who travel to a country other than their own often use gestures as they try to be understood. Like spoken language, however, nonverbal gestures vary from culture to culture. Communicating with others in one's own language can be difficult enough. Add to this the complication of individuals with different languages, cultural expectations, and personalities using different nonverbal messages, and misunderstandings are likely. Although one may master another written and verbal language, nonverbal messages are the hardest part of another language to master because they are specific to a culture and learned through socialization.

Consider the following example: You are about to wrap up a major business deal. You are pleased with the results of your negotiations, so you give your hosts the thumb-and-finger A-OK sign. In Brazil, you have just grossly insulted your hosts—it is the equivalent of giving them "the finger." In Japan, you have asked for a small bribe. In the south of France, you have indicated the deal is worthless. Intercultural communication takes more than knowing the spoken language of a different culture.

Another example of nonverbal communication involves personal space. Most people have experienced social situations, such as parties, where someone gets too close. One person backs away, the other moves in again, and the first backs away again—into a corner or a table with nowhere else to go. Perhaps the person approaching was aggressive or rude, but it is also possible that the

In North America, friends interact at a close distance, 1.5 to 4 feet—as in the photo on the top. A more formal setting calls for a distance of 4 to 12 feet, which can feel cold and intimidating, as in the photo on the bottom.

person held different cultural norms or expectations in relation to personal space.

The amount of personal space an individual needs to be comfortable or proper varies with the cultural setting, gender, status, and social context of the interaction. Individuals from Arab countries are often comfortable at very close range. However, people from Scandinavia generally need a great deal of personal space. Consider the following four categories of social distance and social space based on a study of middle-class people in the United States, though there may be some variation within the middle class depending on ethnicity. Each category applies to particular types of activity (Hall and Hall 1992):

1. *Intimate distance:* from zero distance (touching, embracing, kissing) to 18 inches. Children may play together in such proximity, and adults and children may maintain this distance, but between adults, this intimate contact is reserved for private and affectionate relationships.
2. *Personal distance:* from 18 inches to 4 feet. This is the public distance for most friends and for informal interactions with acquaintances.
3. *Social distance:* from 4 feet to 12 feet. This is the distance for impersonal business relations, such as a job interview or class discussions between students and a professor. This distance implies a more formal interaction or a significant difference in the status of the two people.
4. *Public distance:* 12 feet and beyond. This is the distance most public figures use for addressing others, especially in formal settings and in situations in which the speaker has a very high status.

Personal space also communicates one's position in relation to others. The higher the position, the greater the control of space. In social situations, individuals with higher positions spread out, prop their feet up, put their arms out, and use more sweeping gestures.

Thinking Sociologically

Describe a time when you experienced miscommunication. Who was involved? What happened? How can what you read in this chapter help you to explain why the miscommunication occurred?

Theoretical Perspectives on the Interaction Process

Sociologists study interactions, including verbal and nonverbal communication, to better understand why people behave the way they do. Symbolic interactionists and rational choice theorists examine how and why people communicate with one another. As you will see, their different perspectives lead them to focus on different aspects of interactions and come up with distinctive conclusions as to why they occur.

Symbolic Interaction Theory. With whom do you interact? What determines whether the interaction will continue or stop? How do you know how to behave and what to say around each other? What other processes are taking place as you "talk" to each other? Why do you act differently with different people?

Symbolic interactionism is based on the idea that humans create society through interacting with one another. We act toward people and objects on the basis of the meanings those things have for us. The meanings are derived by individuals as they interact with others. Together, through our interactions with one another, we agree that objects, gestures, and phrases, like "Let's have a drink," symbolize certain things. Likewise, the word *hello* can signify the beginning of a conversation, and *goodbye* signifies the end of one because we agree on the meanings of those words and agree to act accordingly. Symbols are the key to understanding human life, and we go about the task of fitting our actions together through our shared perceptions and meanings of those symbols. Through our mental manipulation of symbols and interpretation of meaning, we *define situations* and determine how we should act in a given situation or how we should make sense of it (Charon 2010; Hewitt and Shulman 2011). More than any other theory in the social sciences, symbolic interactionism stresses the agency—the active decision-making role—of humans within their societies (Charon 2010; Hewitt and Shulman 2011).

Have you ever laughed at a joke you did not hear or understand because those around you laughed? In ambiguous situations, humans look to others to see how they have made sense of the situation or interaction taking place—do people around us look frightened, annoyed, bored, or amused? When in doubt, we tend to follow the cues of those around us. Once one person defines the situation and acts, especially if that person is highly regarded or very self-confident, others will often accept that response as "normal." This is how social interaction is involved in the social

© AP Photo/Julie Jacobson

When a U.S. presidential candidate or any possible head of state speaks, it is not only the Secret Service that keeps people at a formal distance. It is a sense of awed respect for the office: 12 feet or more is the standard distance kept between high-status public figures and other people.

construction of reality—*the process by which individuals and groups shape reality through social interaction*. This imposed notion of reality then takes on a life of its own, often constraining and even coercing people to conform (Berger and Luckmann 1966; Hewitt and Shulman 2011; J. O'Brien 2011; Ritzer 2013). For example, our career goals tend to be influenced by those with whom we interact. If you had been a woman in the United States in the 1910s, you would be unlikely to think you could pursue a career in the "male" field of engineering.

However, socially constructed constraints can be challenged by individuals and lead to different realities that, in turn, begin to influence people's perceptions of what is true and what is possible. For example, until recently, it seemed impossible for gay artists to gain acceptance in the hip-hop community. If you were gay, the choice seemed to be to choose a different genre or keep your sexual orientation hidden. This began to change when Frank Ocean publicly proclaimed in 2012 that his first love was a man, and his announcement drew support, rather than condemnation, from many other prominent hip-hop artists. The momentum for LGBT acceptance in and out of the rap world continued to grow with Macklemore, Ryan Lewis, and Mary Lambert's 2013 hit "Same Love."

A different approach to interaction analysis—called *dramaturgy*—analyzes life as a play or drama on a stage,

Keith Roberts

Depicted here are Japanese *yen*. Your local department store or restaurant will not accept *yen* in exchange for a piece of furniture or the meal you just consumed, any more than it would accept *Monopoly* money. We exchange goods and services based on some pieces of paper because we have a general agreement that this is "good currency"—a *social construction of reality*.

with scripts and props and scenes to be played. The play we put on creates an impression for our audience. In everyday life, individuals learn new lines to add to their scripts through the socialization process, including influence from family, friends, films, and television. They perform these scripts for social audiences to maintain certain images, much like the actors in a play.

Consider the following familiar example: Every day, in high schools around the world, teenagers go on stage—in the classroom or the hallway with friends and peers and with adult authorities who may later be giving grades or writing letters of reference. The props these students use include their style of clothing, a backpack, a smartphone, and a smile or a "cool" look. The set is the classroom, the cafeteria, and perhaps the athletic field. The script is shaped by the actors: Teachers and coaches may establish an authoritarian relationship with students; classmates engage in competition for grades; peers seek social status among companions. The actors include hundreds of teens struggling with issues of identity, changing bodies, and attempting to be accepted and avoid humiliation. Each individual works to assert and maintain an image through behavior, clothing, language, and friends.

Each part or character an individual plays and each audience requires a different script. For example,

interacting with peers at a bar differs from meeting a professor in her office. As we perform according to society's script for the situation, we take into consideration how our actions will influence others. By carefully managing the image we project—a process called *impression management*—we try to create an impression that works to our advantage. Most of the time, we engage in *front-stage behavior*. This is the largely scripted behavior we use with strangers or casual acquaintances. A poor or unacceptable performance, such as wearing out-of-style clothes or spilling our lunch, is embarrassing both for us and for our audience. We learn to develop strategies to cover up weaknesses or failures, such as laughing at a joke even though we do not understand it.

Sometimes, we avoid situations that will require us to play a role with which we are unfamiliar or uncomfortable. Have you ever avoided interacting with a certain group of people because you were unsure of how to act when around them or decided against trying out for a team or a theater production or running for office because you were afraid you might not make it or it was not an "in" thing to do? We learn to avoid those performance activities that are likely to result in humiliation or failure or that contradict the image we have worked to create.

At home or with close friends with whom we are more intimate, we engage in *backstage behavior*, letting our feelings show and behaving in ways that might be unacceptable for other audiences (Goffman 1967, [1959] 2001). We feel that with them, we can relax and be our "true" selves, without possible negative repercussions. So as you can see, dramaturgical analysis and its front-stage and backstage concepts can help us to better understand our interactions and how our behavior changes with the setting.

Thinking Sociologically

Describe some ways in which your life feels like a dramatic production. Identify front-stage and backstage behaviors you carry out on a daily basis.

Rational Choice Theory. Rational choice or exchange theorists look at a different aspect of interaction: why relationships continue, considering the rewards and costs of interaction for the individual. They argue that the choices we make are guided by reason (*rational choices*). If the benefits of the interaction are high and if the costs are low, the interaction will be valued and sustained. Every interaction involves calculations of self-interest, expectations of reciprocity (a mutual exchange of favors), and decisions to act in ways that have current or eventual payoff for the individual (Smelser 1992).

Reciprocity is a key concept for rational choice theorists. The idea is that if a relationship is imbalanced over a period of time, it will become unsatisfying. As theorists from this perspective see human interaction, each person tends to keep a mental ledger of who "owes" whom. If I have done you a favor, you owe me one. If you have helped me in some way, I have an obligation to you. If I then fail to comply or even do something that hurts you, you will likely view it as a breach in the relationship and have negative feelings toward me. Moreover, if one person has more power in the relationship, there is an imbalance in what each brings to the relationship.

In the study of families, scholars use the *principle of least interest*, which states that the person with the least interest in the relationship has the most power. The person with the least interest is the person who brings more resources (financial, physical, social, and personal) to the relationship and receives less. That person could easily leave. The person who offers less to the relationship or who has fewer assets is more dependent on the relationship. This person is likely to give in when there is a disagreement, so the person with less interest gets her or his way.

Sometimes, a person may engage in a behavior where there is little likelihood of reciprocity from the other person—as in cases where the behavior is altruistic or self-giving. Rational choice theorists would argue that there is still a benefit. It might be enhanced feelings of self-worth, positive recognition from others, hope for a reward in the afterlife, or just the expectation of indirect reciprocity. This latter notion is akin to the idea of *paying it forward*: The person you help might not help you, but if you are in a similar situation, you could hope for and expect someone to come to your assistance (Gouldner 1960; J. Turner 2003).

Social Status: Individuals' Link to Groups

As you will recall from Chapter 4, a status is *a social position in society*. We interact with others, and they react to us based, in part, on the statuses we hold. We interact differently when in the daughter status with our parents, in a student status with our professor, or in friend status with our peers. Each individual holds many statuses, and this combination held by any individual is called a *status set*—for instance, daughter, sister, worker, teammate, and student.

Statuses affect the type of interactions individuals have. In some interactions (as with classmates), people are equals. In other situations, individuals have interchanges with people who hold superior or inferior statuses. If you are promoted to supervisor, your interaction with former

FIGURE 5.2 Types of Status Relationships Experienced by You

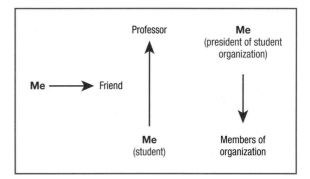

peers and subordinates will change. Consider the possible interactions shown in Figure 5.2, in which the first relationship is between equals, and the others are between those with unequal statuses.

With a friend, these status relationships are constantly being negotiated and bargained: "I'll do what you want tonight, but tomorrow, I choose." By contrast, when individuals are in dominant or subordinate positions, power or deference affects their interactions. The more powerful person, such as one who has more wealth or privilege, can interrupt in a conversation with his or her partner and show less deference in the interaction (M.-S. Kim et al. 2007; Reid and Ng 2006; J. Wood 2008).

People have no control over certain statuses they hold. These **ascribed statuses** are *often assigned at birth and do not change during an individual's lifetime*. For example, whereas a few people undergo sex transformations, for most people, sex is an ascribed characteristic. Ascribed statuses are assigned to a person without regard for personal desires, talents, or choices. In some societies, the caste or social position into which one is born (e.g., "Untouchables" or "Dalits" in India) is an ascribed status because it is usually impossible to change within one's lifetime.

Achieved status, on the other hand, *is chosen or earned by the decisions one makes and sometimes by personal ability*. Attaining a higher education, for example, improves an individual's occupational opportunities and thus his or her achieved status. Being a guitarist in a band is an achieved status and so is being a criminal, for both are earned positions based on the person's own decisions and actions.

At a particular time in life or under certain circumstances, one of an individual's statuses may become most important and take precedence over others; this is called a **master status**. Whether it is an occupation, parental status, or something else, it dominates and shapes much of an individual's life, activities, self-concept, and position in the community for a period of time. For a person who is very ill, for instance, that illness may occupy a master status, needing constant attention from doctors, influencing social relationships, and determining what that person can do in family, work, or community activities.

Thinking Sociologically

What are your statuses? Which ones are ascribed, and which are achieved statuses? Do you have a master status? How do these statuses affect the way you interact with others in your network of relationships?

The Relationship Between Status and Role

Every status (position) in your network includes certain behaviors and obligations as you carry out the roles, *the expected behaviors, rights, obligations, responsibilities, and privileges assigned to a social status*. Roles are the dynamic, action part of statuses in a society. They define how each individual in an interaction is expected to act (Linton 1937). The role of a person holding the status of *college student* includes behaviors and obligations such as attending classes, studying, taking tests, writing papers, and interacting with professors and other students. We enter most statuses with some knowledge of how to carry out the roles dictated by our culture. Through the process of socialization, we learn roles by observing others; watching television and films; reading; and being taught by family members, teachers, and others how to carry out the status.

Both statuses (positions) and roles (behavioral expectations of people holding the status) form links with other people in the social world because they must be carried out in relationships with others. For example, a father has certain obligations (or roles) toward his children and their mother. The position of father exists not on its own but in relationship to significant others who have reciprocal ties.

Your status of student requires certain behaviors and expectations, depending on whether you are interacting with a dean, a professor, an adviser, a classmate, or a prospective employer. This is because the role expectations of the status of student vary as one interacts with specific people in other statuses. In Figure 5.3, the student is the subject, and the others are those with whom the student interacts in the status of student.

Within a group, individuals may hold both formal and informal statuses. One illustration is the formal status of high school students, each of whom plays a number of informal roles in cliques that are not part of the formal

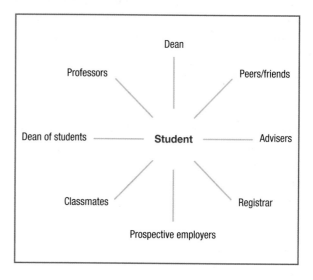

FIGURE 5.3 Types of Interactions Students Have With Reciprocal Status Holders

school structure. A student may be known, for example, as one of the popular crowd, a jock, a nerd, a loner, a goth, a clown, a prep, or an outcast. Each of these roles takes place in a status relationship with others: teacher–student, peer–peer, or coach–athlete, for example. Social networks may be based on ascribed characteristics, such as age and sex, or on achieved status, such as education, occupation, or common interests. These links, in turn, form the basis for social interactions and group structures (R. Hall 2002). However, at times, individuals cannot carry out their roles as others expect them to, creating role strain or conflict.

Role Strain and Role Conflict. Most people have faced times in their lives when they simply could not carry out all the obligations of a status, such as student—write two papers, study adequately for two exams, complete the portfolio for the studio art class, finish the reading assignments for five classes, and memorize lines for the oral interpretation class—all in the same week. Every status carries role expectations, the way the status is supposed to be carried out according to generally accepted societal or group norms. Yet in these cases, individuals face **role strain**, the *tension among roles within a status*. Role strain causes the individual to be pulled in many directions by various obligations of the single status, as in the example regarding the status of student.

To resolve role strain, individuals can cope in several possible ways, such as passing the problem off lightly (and thus not doing well in classes); considering the dilemma humorous; becoming highly focused and pulling a couple of all-nighters to get everything done; or becoming stressed, tense, fretful, and immobilized because of the strain. Most often, individuals set priorities based on their values and make decisions accordingly: "I'll work hard in the class for my major and let another one slide."

Role conflict refers to *conflict between the roles of two or more social statuses*. It differs from role strain in that it is conflict *between* the roles of two or more statuses, rather than tension among roles within one of the statuses. For example, college athletes face role conflicts from competing demands on their time. They must complete their studies on time, attend practices and be prepared for games, perhaps attend meetings of a Greek house to which they belong, and get home for a little brother's birthday. Similarly, a student may be going to school, holding down a part-time job to help make ends meet, and raising a family. If the student's child gets sick, the status of parent comes into conflict with that of student and worker. In the case of role conflict, the person may choose—or be informed by others—which status is the master status. Figure 5.4 illustrates the difference between role strain and role conflict.

Thinking Sociologically

Using Figure 5.4 as a model, write down the statuses you hold in your social world and the roles you perform in these statuses. Then, list three examples of role conflicts and three examples of role strains that you experience.

Most statuses and accompanying roles come and go. For example, you will not always be a student. You may or may not be married at different points in your life. You will retire from your job. As people grow older, they disengage from some statuses and engage in new and different statuses and roles.

Our statuses connect us to and make us integral parts of meso- and macro-level organizations. Our place within the social world, then, is guaranteed, even obligatory, because of statuses we hold—within small groups (family and peers), in larger groups and organizations (school and work organizations), in institutions (political parties or religious denominations), and ultimately as citizens of the society and the world (citizens and workers in global corporations). Each of these statuses connects us to a group setting.

GROUPS IN OUR SOCIAL WORLD: THE MICRO–MESO CONNECTION

Groups refer to *units involving two or more people who interact with each other because of shared common*

FIGURE 5.4 Role Strain and Role Conflict

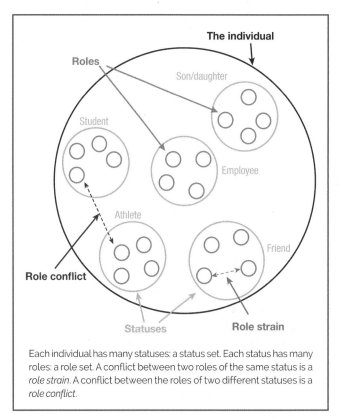

Each individual has many statuses: a status set. Each status has many roles: a role set. A conflict between two roles of the same status is a *role strain*. A conflict between the roles of two different statuses is a *role conflict*.

interests, goals, experiences, and needs (Drafke 2008). As we have seen, humans are social beings. We become members of society and gain a sense of self through social interaction. Groups meet our social needs for belonging and acceptance, support us throughout our lives, and place restrictions on us. We also need groups for protection, to obtain food, to manufacture goods, and to get jobs done. Groups can be small, intimate environments—micro-level interactions with family or friends—or they can become quite large, meso-level organizations. In any case, it is through our group memberships that the micro and meso levels are connected.

Not all collections of individuals are groups. For instance, your family is a group, but people shopping at a mall or waiting for a bus are not a group because they do not regularly interact or acknowledge shared common interests.

Groups form through a series of succeeding steps. Consider people forming a soccer team in a new league: The first step is initial interaction. If the interactions with the other members are rewarding and meet individuals' needs, the individuals will attempt to maintain the benefits the group provides and form a team (T. Mills 1984). In the second step, a collective goal emerges. For example, team members may work together to plan practice and game schedules, buy uniforms, and advertise the games. In the third and final step, the group attempts to expand its collective goals by building on the former steps and by pursuing new goals. For example, the team may reach out to new players, to coaches, and to supporters for funding.

As noted, groups impact both society and individuals. Neither would function properly without groups. The importance of groups becomes especially clear when we consider two social problems: anomie and suicide.

Group Solidarity, Anomie, and Suicide

Who commits suicide? Did you know that the answer to this is closely related to an individual's group affiliations? Early sociologist Émile Durkheim took a unique approach to making sense of suicide trends. In *Suicide*, Durkheim discussed the social factors contributing to suicide ([1897] 1964). Using existing statistical data to determine suicide rates in European populations, Durkheim looked at variables such as sex, age, religion, nationality, and the season in which the suicide was committed. His findings demonstrate that individual problems cannot be understood without also understanding the group context in which they occur.

Durkheim found that Protestants committed suicide more often than Catholics, urban folks more often than people living in small communities, people in highly developed and complex societies more frequently than those in simple societies, and people who lived alone more than those situated in families. The key variable linking these findings was the degree to which an individual was integrated into a group—that is, the extent to which they were socially bonded with others. Those who belonged to more tightly knit groups were least likely to commit suicide, whereas those whose lives were less tied to those of others were most likely to kill themselves. Durkheim described this type of suicide, when the individual feels little social bond to the group or society and lacks familial ties, as *egoistic suicide*.

A second type, *anomic suicide*, occurs when a society or one of its parts is in disorder, turmoil, or undergoing rapid change and lacks clear norms and guidelines for social behavior. With the rapid changes and continued breakdown of institutional structures in many modern and modernizing societies, religious and political groups may vie for power and offer contrasting definitions of reality. Social controls (police and military forces) may

be strained, as leaders struggle to cope with the turmoil and lack of consensus. The result of the collapse of norms is anomie, *the state of normlessness that occurs when the rules for behavior in society break down under extreme stress from rapid social change or conflict* (Merton 1938). This anomie tends to lead to higher rates of suicide.

Durkheim's third type of suicide, *altruistic suicide*, differs from the others in that it involves such a strong bond and group obligation that the individual is willing to die for the group. Self-survival becomes less important than group survival (Durkheim [1897] 1964). Examples of altruistic suicide include the young suicide bombers in Iraq, Afghanistan, and Pakistan carrying out suicide missions against their country's police forces and sometimes against NATO or American military forces, which they have defined as invading forces. U.S. military Medal of Honor recipients who sacrificed their own lives to save those of the men in their units are another example. These suicides usually include social groups that have very clear norms and high levels of consensus about values arising from their religious or political beliefs.

Durkheim's work revealed that suicide rates are strongly influenced by social and psychological factors

Suicide bombers are willing to commit altruistic suicide—to die voluntarily for the good of the group—to further their cause. Even if their behavior seems outrageous to us and injures others, it is done by people who are deeply integrated into their own social network, and the cause of the group is seen as more important than the individual's life. Reem Slaleh Raiyshi, a mother of two children from Gaza, blew herself up at the Erez Crossing between Israel and the Gaza Strip. Many in her community viewed this as altruistic.

that can operate at the meso or macro level. His findings and those of others show that groups impact our lives and even our desire to continue living (R. Hall 2002; P. Nolan, Triplett, and McDonough 2010). No individual is an island. The importance of groups and social influence at various levels in the system is an underlying theme of this text. To more fully understand the influence of groups over us, though, we must become familiar with the different types of groups in which we interact.

Types of Groups

Each of us belongs to several types of groups. Some groups provide intimacy and close relationships, whereas others do not. Some are required affiliations, and others are voluntary. Some provide personal satisfaction, and others are obligatory or necessary for survival.

Primary groups are at the most micro level and *characterized by cooperation among close, intimate, long-term relationships.* Your family members and best friends, school classmates, and close work associates are all of primary importance in your everyday life. Primary groups provide a sense of belonging and shared identity. Group members care about you, and you care about the other group members, creating a sense of loyalty. Approval and disapproval from the primary group influences the activities you choose to pursue. Belonging to the group is the main reason for membership. The group is of intrinsic value—enjoyed for its own sake—rather than for some utilitarian value, such as making money.

For individuals, primary groups provide an anchor point in society. You were raised in a primary group: your family. You hold many statuses and play a variety of roles in primary relationships: those of child, sibling, partner, parent, relative, close friend, and so on. You meet with other members face to face or keep in touch on a regular basis and know a great deal about their lives. What makes them happy or angry? What are sensitive issues? In primary groups you share values, say what you think, let down your hair, dress as you like, and share your concerns and emotions and successes and failures (Goffman 1967, [1959] 2001). Charles H. Cooley, who first discussed the term *primary group*, saw these relationships as the source of close human feelings and emotions—love, cooperation, and concern (Cooley [1909] 1983).

Secondary groups are *those with formal, impersonal, and businesslike relationships, and they are often temporary and based on a specific, limited purpose or goal.* Secondary groups are usually large and task oriented because they have a specific purpose to achieve and focus on accomplishing a goal. In the modern world, people cannot always live under the protective wing of primary-group relationships. As children grow, they move from the security and acceptance of primary groups—the home and neighborhood peer group—to a secondary group—the large school classroom, where each child is one of many students vying for the teacher's (and others') approval and competing for rewards. Similarly, the work world requires formal relations and procedures: applications, interviews, and contracts. Employment is based on specific skills, training, and job knowledge—competence to carry out the role expectations in the position.

Because each individual in a secondary group carries out a specialized task, communication between members is often specialized as well. Contacts with doctors, store clerks, and even professors are generally formal and impersonal parts of organizational life. Sometimes, associations with secondary groups are long lasting; sometimes, they are of short duration, as in the courses you are taking this term. Secondary groups operate at the meso and macro levels of our social world, but they affect individuals at the micro level.

As societies modernize, they evolve from small towns and close, primary relationships to predominantly urban areas with more formal, secondary relationships. In the postindustrial world, with family members scattered across countries and around the world, secondary relationships have come to play ever-greater roles in people's lives. Large work organizations may provide day care, health clinics, financial planning, courses to upgrade skills, and sports leagues.

Small micro-level and large macro-level groups often occur together. Behind most successful secondary groups are primary groups. Consider the small work group within a large organization that eats together or goes out for a beer on Friday afternoons. These relationships help individuals feel a part of the larger organization, just as residents of large urban areas have small groups of neighborhood friends. Table 5.1 summarizes some of the dimensions of primary and secondary groups.

Problems in primary groups can affect performance in secondary groups. Consider the problems of a student who has an argument with a partner or roommate or experiences a failure of his or her family support system due to divorce or other problems. Self-concepts and social skills diminish during times of family stress and affect group relationships in other parts of one's life (Drafke 2008).

Table 5.1   Primary- and Secondary-Group Characteristics

	Primary Group	Secondary Group
Quality of relationships	Personal orientation	Goal orientation
Duration of relationships	Usually long-term	Variable, often short-term
Breadth of activities	Broad, usually involving many activities	Narrow, usually involving a few largely goal-directed activities
Subjective perception of relationships	As an end in itself (friendship, belonging)	As a means to an end (to accomplish a task, earn money)
Typical examples	Families, close friendships	Coworkers, political organizations

Thinking Sociologically

In the past, raising children was considered a family task, done by the primary family group. Today, many children are in childcare settings, often run by secondary groups. What differences do you see between the experiences a child receives in a family and in childcare? What might be the advantages and disadvantages of each? Can a secondary group provide care comparable with that provided by a family? Can the secondary group provide better care than families? Why or why not?

Reference groups are *composed of members who act as role models and establish standards against which members measure their conduct*. Individuals look to reference

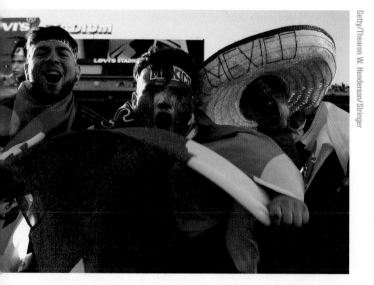

Many communities, such as colleges, find that having a sports program facilitates loyalty and sense of belonging to the in-group. Even where such an in-group does not originally exist, an athletic team can create an in-group. Here, boys anticipate the final match of the soccer World Cup between Argentina and Germany in 2014.

Getty/Thearon W. Henderson/Stringer

groups to set guidelines for behavior and decision making. Successful businesses can serve as reference groups for other businesses. The term is often used to refer to models in one's chosen career field. Ethnic groups can also be reference groups. Ethnic groups can provide adolescent members with strong reference group standards by which to judge themselves. The stronger the ethnic pride and identification, the more some teens may separate themselves from contact with members of other ethnic groups (Schaefer and Kunz 2007). This can be functional or dysfunctional for the teens, as with in-groups and out-groups.

An **in-group** is *one to which an individual feels a sense of loyalty and belonging*. It also may serve as a reference group. (Any group may fit into more than one category of group.) An **out-group** is *one to which an individual does not belong, but more than that, it is a group that competes with or acts in opposition to an in-group*.

Membership in an in-group may be based on sex, race, ethnicity, social class, religion, political affiliation, the school one attends, an interest group such as the fraternity or sorority one joins, or the area where one lives. People tend to judge others according to their own in-group identity. Members of the in-group—for example, supporters of a high school team—often feel hostility toward or reject out-group members—boosters of the rival team. The perceived outside threat or hostility is often exaggerated, but it does help create the in-group members' feelings of solidarity. Another example might be the "preps" in a high school who control many resources because they control the school's student council and many of the leadership positions in the school. They are an in-group, but the goths, punks, or burnouts (the out-group) reject the preps and seek alternatives to the activities planned by the preps. Unfortunately, these feelings of hostility can result in prejudice and ethnocentrism, overlooking the individual differences of in-group and out-group members.

Thinking Sociologically

What are some examples of your own group affiliations? Draw a diagram of your primary groups, secondary groups, peer groups, reference groups, and in-groups and out-groups.

ORGANIZATIONS AND BUREAUCRACIES: THE MESO–MACRO CONNECTION

Our days are filled with activities that involve us with complex organizations: from the doctor's appointment to college classes; from the political rally for the issue we support to worship in a church, temple, or mosque; and from paying state sales tax for our toothpaste to buying a sandwich at a fast-food franchise. Figure 5.5 shows the institutions of society, each made up of thousands of organizations (e.g., medical organizations, educational organizations, religious groups, economic corporations, political movements, and the government itself) and each following the cultural norms of the society. We have statuses and roles in each group, and these link us to networks and the larger social world. We now look at how the modern forms of these organizations developed.

Modern Organizations and Their Evolution

Recall from Chapter 3 the discussion of types of societies, from hunter-gatherer to postindustrial. Each type of society entails different organizational structures (Blau 1956; P. Nolan and Lenski 2014). The development of modern organizations and bureaucracies began with the Industrial Revolution in the 1700s and 1800s. Increasingly complex organizations required and helped create what Max Weber called the **rationalization of social life**—*the attempt to maximize efficiency by creating rules and procedures focused solely on accomplishing goals* (Weber 1947). No longer were decisions made by tradition, custom, or the whim of a despot. Instead, trained leaders planned policies to achieve organizational efficiency. Tasks became more specialized, and some manual jobs were taken over by

FIGURE 5.5   Our Social World: Institutions, Organizations, and Individual Status

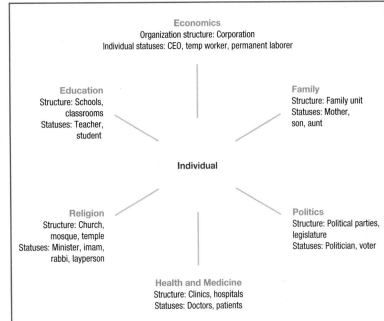

machines. People were expected to behave in purposeful, coordinated ways to advance organizational efficiency.

Formal organizations, also called *modern "rational" organizations, composed of complex secondary groups deliberately formed to pursue and achieve certain goals*, were created to standardize production and increase productivity, precision, and speed. They are called formal organizations because of the written charters, constitutions, bylaws, and procedures that govern them. Google, General Electric (GE), the Red Cross, the National Basketball Association (NBA), the Republican Party, and your university are all formal organizations.

Bureaucracies are *specific types of very large formal organizations that have the purpose of maximizing efficiency*. They are characterized by set relations among participants, clearly laid out procedures and rules, and the pursuit of stated goals. Bureaucratization evolved as the most efficient way of producing products economically for mass markets (Ritzer 2013).

An example of a bureaucratic organization can be found in the fast-food empires and chain "box" stores spreading all around the world. The next "Engaging Sociology" feature describes the trend toward the "McDonaldization of society"—sociologist George Ritzer's pop-culture term for rationalization in organizations.

ENGAGING SOCIOLOGY

The McDonaldization of Society

The process of rationalization described by Max Weber—the attempt to reach maximum bureaucratic efficiency—comes in a new modern version, expanded and streamlined, exemplified by the fast-food restaurant business that began to spread in the 1950s and chain "box" stores now found around the world. Efficient, rational, predictable sameness is sweeping the world—from diet centers such as Weight Watchers to NutriSystem to 7-Eleven and from Walmart to Gap clothing stores with their look-alike layouts. Most major world cities feature McDonald's or Kentucky Fried Chicken in the traditional main plazas of train stations for flustered foreigners and curious native consumers.

The McDonaldization of society, as George Ritzer calls it, refers to several trends: First, *efficiency* is maximized by the sameness—same store plans, same mass-produced items, and same procedures. Second is *predictability*, the knowledge that each hamburger or piece of chicken will appear and taste the same, leaving nothing to chance. Third, everything is *calculated* so that the organization can ensure that everything fits a standard—every burger is cooked the same number of seconds on each side. Fourth, there is *increased control* over employees and customers so there are fewer variables to consider—including substitution of technology for human labor as a way to ensure predictability and efficiency.

What is the result of this efficient, predictable, planned, automated new world? According to Ritzer, the world is becoming more dehumanized, and efficiency is replacing individual creativity and human interactions. The mom-and-pop grocery, bed and breakfasts, and local craft or clothing shops are rapidly becoming a thing of the past. This process of the McDonaldization of society, meaning principles of efficiency and rationalization exemplified by fast-food chains, is coming to dominate more and more sectors of our social world (Ritzer 2013). Whereas there are aspects of this predictability that we all like, it also entails a loss of the uniqueness and local flavor that individual entrepreneurs bring to a community.

Some large corporations have started a movement toward *Starbuckization* to impress consumers tired of McDonaldization. For examples, Starbucks, with its own music mixes, comfortable seats, and Wi-Fi, makes customers feel like they are purchasing a cultural product along with their coffee. This culture,

The Mall of America near Minneapolis is the largest mall in North America, with 4.3 miles of storefront footage, 520-plus stores on five stories, 4.2 million total square feet, and 25 amusement park rides. Yet many of the stores look like clones of one another, and this cathedral to consumerism can feel like an experience in the McDonaldization of society.

however, is as controlled as any other McDonaldized endeavor, making Starbucks a McClone at its core.

McDonaldization is so widespread and influential that many modern universities are now McDonaldized. A large lecture hall is a very efficient way of teaching sociology or biology to many students at once. Similarly, massive online classes, PowerPoint presentations, multiple-choice exams, and a limited choice of textbooks for professors increase the predictability of content in course offerings. Finally, grade point averages and credit hours completed are calculated—and efficient—ways to judge student accomplishments.

* * * * *

Engaging With Sociology

1. What example of McDonaldization do you see in your community? What are the pros and cons of this pattern in your locality?

2. To what extent do you think your college is McDonaldized? Why?

3. What can you and your fellow students do to address the problem of the McDonaldization of higher education?

Formal Organizations and Modern Life

Think about the many organizations that regularly affect your life: the legal system that passes laws, your college, your workplace, and voluntary organizations to which you belong. Human interactions take place in formal organizations, and formal organizations require human interaction to meet their organizational needs. Some organizations, such as the local chapter of the Rotary Club or troop of the Girl Scouts, function at the micro level. Everyone is in a face-to-face relationship with every other member of the organization. However, those local groups are part of a nationwide meso-level organization. At the macro level, the federal government in the United States is a complex formal organization that influences the lives of every citizen and organization in the nation. Meanwhile, multinational corporations and entities like the United Nations are global in their reach.

Some organizations provide us with work necessary for survival. Others are forced on us—prisons, psychiatric hospitals, military draft systems, and even education— until a certain age. Still others are organizations we believe in and voluntarily join: scouts, environmental groups, sports leagues, and religious organizations. Residents of the United States tend to join voluntary organizations at higher rates than people in many other countries (Charities Aid Foundation 2012).

Characteristics of Bureaucracy

If you have been to a Caribbean, African, Asian, or Middle Eastern market, you know that the bartering system is used to settle on a mutually agreeable price for goods. This system is more personal and involves intense interaction between the seller and the buyer, but it also takes more time and is less efficient than the buying process to which shoppers from North America are accustomed. Bartering can be frustrating to the uninitiated visitor used to the relative efficiency and predictability of bureaucracy: going to a store, selecting a product, and paying a set price. As societies become more complex, they tend to adopt bureaucratic forms of organization.

At the beginning of the 20th century, Max Weber (1864–1920) looked for the reasons behind the transition from traditional society to bureaucratic, capitalist society. He wanted to understand why bureaucracy came to dominate the forms of organization in some countries more rapidly than in others. Weber found that bureaucracies arise first in more democratic nations with capitalist, industrial economic systems. As these countries established systems of government and economics whereby positions were granted based on merit, rather than tradition, their economies could grow much faster. This growth, in turn, required more efficient and rational means of organization—bureaucratization (Weber 1947).

Weber's concept of the *ideal-type bureaucracy* refers to the dominant and essential characteristics of organizations designed for reliability and efficiency (Weber 1947). The term simply describes an organization with a particular set of traits, not a necessarily good or perfect organization. Any particular bureaucracy is unlikely to have all of the characteristics of the ideal type, but the degree of bureaucratization is measured by how closely an organization resembles the core characteristics of the ideal type. The following shows Weber's ideal-type bureaucracy with examples related to schools today:

1. *Division of labor based on technical competence:* Administrators lead but do not teach, and instructors teach only in areas of their certification; staff are assigned positions for which their credentials make them most qualified, and recruitment and promotion are governed by formal policies.

2. *Administrative hierarchy:* There are a specified chain of command and designated channels of communication, from school board to superintendent to principal to teacher.

3. *Formal rules and regulations:* Written procedures and rules—perhaps published in an administrative manual—spell out system-wide requirements, including discipline practices, testing procedures, curricula, sick days for teachers, penalties for student tardiness, field trip policies, and other matters.

4. *Impersonal relationships:* Formal relationships tend to prevail between teachers and students and between teachers and administrative staff (superintendents, principals, and counselors); written records and formal communication provide a paper trail for all decisions.

5. *Emphasis on rationality and efficiency to reach goals:* Established processes are used, based on the best interests of the school. Efficiency is defined in terms of the lowest overall cost to the organization in reaching a goal, not in terms of personal consequences.

Although the list of characteristics makes bureaucracies sound formal and rigid, informal structures allow organizational members to deviate from rules both to meet the goals of the organization more efficiently and to humanize an otherwise uncaring and sterile workplace. The *informal structure* includes the unwritten norms and the interpersonal networks that people use within an organization to carry out roles. Likewise, although bylaws, constitutions, or contracts spell out the way things are supposed to be done, people often develop unwritten shortcuts to accomplish goals. For example, the U.S. Postal Service has rules specifying that letter carriers are not supposed to walk across people's lawns, yet if they did not find shortcuts, it would take much longer for mail to be delivered.

Informal norms are not always compatible with those of the formal organization. For example, what if the norm at your organization is to do the least amount of work possible? Have you ever been pressured *not* to work hard by your coworkers? Consider the following example from a famous classical study. In the Western Electric plant near Chicago, the researchers found that new workers were quickly socialized to do "a fair day's work," and those who did more or less than the established norm—what the work group thought was fair—were considered "rate busters" or "chiselers" and experienced pressure from the group to conform. These informal norms help give workers a degree of power but make the formal goals of the organization harder to achieve (Roethlisberger and Dickson 1939). They also indicate a lack of clear communication or enforcement of the rules of the bureaucratic system.

Thinking Sociologically

How closely does each of Weber's characteristics of ideal-type bureaucracy describe your college or your work setting? Is your college highly bureaucratized, with many rules and regulations? Are decisions based on efficiency and cost-effectiveness, educational quality, or both? To what extent is your work setting characterized by hierarchy and formal rules governing your work time? To what extent is it shaped by informal relationships?

Issues in Bureaucracies

Despite the fact that some informal norms and red tape can hamper bureaucratic efficiency, bureaucracies are likely here to stay. They are the most efficient form of modern organization yet devised. Nonetheless, several individual and organizational problems created by bureaucratic structures are important to understand. These deficiencies arise from our roles in organizations or our interactions with organizations. Some examples of problems that can arise in bureaucracies are decreased levels of professionalism in bureaucracies, alienation, oligarchy, and goal displacement.

Bureaucracy, some argue, can be the number-one enemy of *professionalism*, for it reduces individuals' autonomy. First, bureaucrats insist that authority rests in the person who holds an organizational status or title in the hierarchy rather than the person with the most expertise. Second, bureaucrats tend to reward people with external rewards, such as bonuses, rather than internal motivations, such as greater freedom in how they do their work. Third, bureaucrats focus on the needs of the organization as primary rather than on the needs of the client or professional. For example, a scientist hired by a tobacco company faced a dilemma when his research findings did not support the company position that nicotine is not addictive. They wanted him to falsify his research, a violation of professional ethics. The potential clash between professionals and bureaucracy raises key concerns as universities, hospitals, and other large organizations are governed increasingly by bureaucratic principles (Roberts and Donahue 2000).

Alienation, feeling uninvolved, uncommitted, unappreciated, and unconnected to the group or the society, occurs when workers are assigned routine, boring tasks or dead-end jobs with no possibility of advancement. Marx believed that alienation is a structural feature of capitalism, with serious consequences: Workers lose their sense of purpose and become dehumanized and objectified in their work, creating a product that they often do not see completed and for which they do not get the profits (Marx [1844] 1964). Workers who see possibilities for advancement put more energy into the organization, but those stuck in their positions are less involved and put more energy into activities outside the workplace (Kanter 1977).

Thinking Sociologically

Why might giving workers increased autonomy, more participation in decision making, and stockholder shares in the company enhance commitment and productivity in your place of work? What might be some risks or downsides to such worker input and freedom?

Oligarchy, the concentration of power in the hands of a small group, is a common occurrence in bureaucratic organizations. In the early 1900s, Robert Michels, a French sociologist, wrote about the *iron law of oligarchy*, the idea that power becomes concentrated in the hands of a small group of leaders in political, business, voluntary, or other organizations. Initially, organizational needs, more than the motivation for power, cause these few stable leaders to emerge. As organizations grow, however, a division of labor emerges so that only a few leaders have access to information, resources, and the overall picture.

This, in turn, causes leaders who enjoy their elite positions of power to become entrenched (Michels [1911] 1967).

Goal displacement occurs when the original motives or goals of the organization are displaced by new, secondary goals. Organizations are formed to meet specific goals. For example, religious organizations are established to worship a deity and serve humanity on behalf of that deity, schools are founded to educate children, and social work agencies are organized to serve needy citizens. Yet over time, the original goals may not be met or become less important as other motivations and interests emerge. These organizations can sometimes become focused on the benefits they can bring to patrons or employees, rather than on fulfilling the goals for which they were established (Merton 1938; Whyte 1956). For example, in 2015, many high-ranking members of the Federation Internationale de Football Association (FIFA), international soccer's governing body, were charged with using the organization to enrich themselves through bribery, racketeering, fraud, and money laundering (C. Miller 2015).

Thinking Sociologically

In what areas of your college or workplace do you see goal displacement? In other words, where do you see decisions being driven by goals other than the original purpose of the organization?

Diversity and Equity in Organizations. In a global and diverse society, it makes sense to have a diverse workforce. The interaction of people who see things differently because of religious beliefs, ethnic backgrounds, and gender experiences increases productivity and creativity in many organizations. Having a wide range of perspectives can lead to better problem solving (Florida 2004; Molotch 2003). Successful business owners know they need to have a diverse group of employees in order to thrive. That is also one reason why colleges promote diversity on college campuses. The U.S. Supreme Court held hearings in 2013 and 2016 on affirmative action programs in higher education, programs that promote diversity on campuses and prepare a diverse workforce by actively seeking qualified underrepresented minority students for positions. Fifty large corporations, including Walmart, Pfizer, Halliburton, and American Express, joined together to write a brief in support of affirmative action programs in higher education. Although these corporations gave most of their political donations to Republicans, they supported the Obama administration's arguments in favor of affirmative action because they know a diverse workforce is good for business (M. Wilson 2012).

Despite efforts to diversify the workplace, women and other minorities in bureaucracies are underrepresented

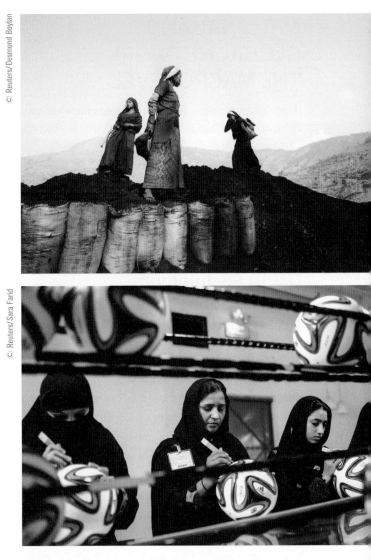

© Reuters/Desmond Boylan

© Reuters/Sara Farid

Women in many countries tend to have low-paid, dead-end jobs that result in alienation. Most, however, need the work to support themselves and their families, such as the women in these photos.

in upper-management positions (J. Berman 2015). They often find themselves with little authority and less pay than others with similar skills and credentials. It is also often much harder for minorities to even make it onto the lowest rung of bureaucratic organizations. For example, in New York City, among *equally qualified* Whites, Blacks, and Latinos applying for low-wage jobs, Latinos were less likely than Whites and Blacks were *half* as likely as White applicants to receive a job or callback. Even Whites with criminal records were just as likely as, if not more likely than, Black and Latino applicants *without* a criminal record to get a callback or job offer (Pager, Western, and Bonikowski 2009). These discriminatory actions are irrational and dysfunctional to organizations (Florida 2004, 2012; Molotch 2003).

NATIONAL AND GLOBAL NETWORKS: THE MACRO LEVEL

Understanding people unlike us, networking with people from different cultures, and being open to new ideas have become core competencies in our globalizing social world. Increasingly, colleges have study-abroad programs, and corporations seek multilingual employees with cultural competence in diverse settings. One young college graduate with a sociology degree found that she could use her sociology skills in leading groups of college-age students in international-travel experiences. She explains this use of sociology in the next "Sociologists in Action."

SOCIOLOGISTS IN ACTION
ELISE ROBERTS

Using Sociology in International Travel and Intercultural Education

After graduating from college with a bachelor's degree in sociology, I left the country to backpack through Mexico and Central America. Eventually, I found a job leading groups of teenagers on alternative-education trips abroad. What struck me on meeting my first group was that I had very few students who initially understood the sociological perspective that I took for granted and that was so helpful in dealing with others. At times, my students would make fun of the way things were done in other countries, calling them "weird" or "stupid." They would mock the local traditions, until we discussed comparable traditions in U.S. culture. These students were not mean or unintelligent. In fact, they loved the places we were seeing and the people we were meeting. They just thought everything was factually, officially weird. They had been socialized to understand their own society's ways as "right" and "normal." They were fully absorbed in the U.S. society, and they had never questioned it before.

It was rewarding to apply concepts from my textbooks in the real world. My coleaders and I learned to have fun while encouraging our students to become more socially conscious and analytical about their travel experience. They had to learn to understand "odd" gestures, like pointing with the lips or side-to-side nodding. We would use these experiences to discuss nonverbal communication and gestures that we take for granted in U.S. culture.

We would encourage our novice travelers to interact with the people around them, which helped them understand the struggles facing immigrants and non-English speakers in the United States. We would force them to have conversations while standing toe to toe with each other, and they would finish with backaches from leaning away from one another. We would not allow them to explain their behavior with "because it's creepy to stand so close together," even though this was the consensus. "Why do you feel uncomfortable?" we would ask. "Why is this weird?" The answer has to do with social constructions of what is "normal" in any society.

Of course, while traveling internationally, one is surrounded by various other sociological issues, such as different racial or ethnic conflicts, gender roles, or class hierarchies, and learning about these issues was a part of our program as well. Without realizing it, many group conversations and meetings began to remind me of some of my favorite undergraduate sociology classes. "Study sociology!" I would say. Traveling abroad on my own and leading programs overseas were extremely fascinating experiences, and it was incredibly rewarding to be able to use my sociology degree every day on my job.

• •

Elise Roberts graduated from Macalester College with a major in sociology and is now a regional organizer for Witness for Peace.

With modern communication and transportation systems and the ability to transfer ideas and money with a touch of the keyboard, global networks are superseding national boundaries. Some businesses are global and can easily move their physical headquarters from one nation to another (Ritzer 2007). This has helped many companies avoid paying millions of dollars in taxes. Apple, one of the multinational companies best at avoiding taxes, has managed to reduce its taxes by billions of dollars through "routing profits through Irish subsidiaries and the Netherlands and then to the Caribbean." This practice is now common as many corporations can move freely from nation to nation, in search of the largest profit possible (Duhigg and Kocieniewski 2013).

Profit, efficiency, and calculability are highly prized in multinational corporations. However, as these Western notions of public life are exported to other countries, a severe backlash has occurred in some nations. In many Middle Eastern Islamic countries, for example, these values clash with Muslim loyalties and priorities. The result has been high levels of anger at the United States and Western Europe. Many scholars believe that Middle Eastern anger at the United States is based not just on opposition to freedom and democracy but also on what some Middle Easterners see as the crass greed and impersonal organizational structures we try to import into their micro-, meso-, and macro-level worlds. They feel that their very culture is threatened (Ritzer 2007).

Radical fundamentalist movements—groups fueled by religious beliefs and socioeconomic stressors and that view the world in absolutes—are mostly antimodernization movements turned militant (Antoun 2008; Marty and Appleby 2004). They have emerged in Christian, Jewish, Islamic, Sikh, and other groups, largely as a response to perceived threats to their ways of life (Armstrong 2000). Some aspects of global terrorism and international conflict are a response to the way the Western world organizes its social life and exports it to other parts of the world. These conflicts, in turn, have resulted in the mobilization of the armed forces in the United States. A consequence is that members of your own family might be serving abroad even as you read these pages.

Thinking Sociologically

How has global interaction been transformed during your lifetime through Internet technology? Give an example of how you can learn about what is happening in, say, Syria right now by using the Internet. Does this make you feel more connected to people there? Why, or why not?

Our networks play a major role in setting norms and controlling our behaviors, usually resulting in our conformity to the social expectations of those in our network. This, of course, contributes to the stability of the entire social system because deviation can threaten the existence of "normal" patterns, as we see in the next chapter.

WHAT HAVE WE LEARNED?

Each of us has a network of people and groups that surround us. The scope of our networks has broadened with the increased complexity of societies and includes the global social world. Indeed, it is sometimes hard to recognize how far our networks reach. Although some of our social experiences are informal (unstructured), we are also profoundly affected by another phenomenon of the past 3 centuries: highly structured bureaucracies. As a result of both, our experiences and personal lives are far more extensively linked to meso- and macro-level events and to people and places on the other side of the globe than were those of our parents. If we hope to understand our lives, we must understand this broad context. Although it may have been possible to live without global connections and bureaucratic systems several centuries ago, these networks are intricately woven into our lifestyles and our economic systems today. The question is whether we will control these networks or they will control us.

- People in the modern world are connected through one acquaintance to another in a chain of links, referred to as networks, that can now span the globe.

- We interpret interpersonal interactions at the micro level through unspoken assumptions based on the social context, nonverbal communication, and the physical space between people.

- Many of our behaviors are shaped by the statuses (social positions) we hold and the roles (expectations associated with a status) we play. However, our multiple-status occupancy can create role conflict (between the roles of two statuses) and role strain (among the role expectations of a single status).

- When the norms of behavior are unclear, we may experience anomie (normlessness), and when anomie spreads in a society, suicide rates rise.

- Various types of groups affect our behavior—from primary and secondary groups to peer groups and reference groups.

- At the meso and macro levels, we find that formal organizations in the contemporary modern world have become bureaucratized. Bureaucratic organizations are ruled by rational calculation of the organization's goals rather than by tradition or emotional ties, tend to expand, are governed by impersonal formal rules, and stress efficiency and rational decision making.

- Bureaucracies often create particular issues that may make them inefficient or destructive, such as alienation, oligarchies, and goal displacement.

- In a global and diverse society, it makes sense to have a diverse workforce. Discrimination against minorities in promotion and hiring is irrational and dysfunctional for organizations.

- Some scholars think that this impersonal mode of organizing social life—so common in the West for several centuries now—is a critical factor in anti-American and anti-Western resistance movements.

DISCUSSION QUESTIONS

1. Think about your social network. How useful might it be in helping you get a job (or a better job) once you graduate from college? Why?

2. During a typical day, when do you engage in front-stage and backstage behavior? Why? With whom do you engage in each? Why?

3. Have you ever experienced role strain because of your status as a student? Explain why or why not. If so, how did or do you cope with it?

4. Most college students, particularly those with family, work, and/or sports team obligations, deal with role conflict. Describe a time when you dealt with a conflict between the roles you carry out. What did you do about it? How might colleges and universities diminish role conflict among students?

5. To what primary and secondary groups do you belong? How does your involvement (or lack thereof) in primary groups on your campus impact your feelings of attachment to your school?

6. Would you rather live in a bureaucratic society or in a society without bureaucratic forms of organizations? Why?

7. How does the informal structure at your college or university impact how the school functions? Does it do more to help or hurt students? Why?

KEY TERMS

CONTRIBUTING TO OUR SOCIAL WORLD: WHAT CAN WE DO?

At the Local (Micro) Level

- *Tutoring and mentoring* programs help students struggling with their studies. Contact your school's student affairs or tutoring office, and arrange to observe and/or volunteer in a program. Helping students build *social capital*, which includes knowing people who can help them to obtain the help they need, can increase their chances of success.

- Workers' Centers for employed people not represented by unions have developed in many metropolitan areas, often with the aid of local clergy. Workers' Centers help these workers to organize and develop the social capital to obtain better wages, benefits, and workplace dignity. For a list of Workers' Centers, go to www.iwj.org/worker-center-network/locations.

At the Organizational/Institutional (Meso) Level

- The social capital theory can also be applied to meso-level community organizations: *Community organizations* that work to build power and implement social change, such as *IAF (the Industrial Areas Foundation* at www.industrialareasfoundation.org), *Gamaliel* (www.gamaliel.org), and *PICO National Network* (www.piconetwork.org) provide their members with social capital. Find a group affiliated with one of these organizations near you.

- *Unions* also develop social capital for their members. Although far fewer U.S. citizens are unionized today than in past decades, membership in a union can improve the economic prospects of workers. For some workers, this can make the difference between living in poverty and obtaining a living wage. With 2 million members, the *Service Employees International Union (SEIU)* is the fastest growing union in North America. Internships with unions like SEIU are a great way to learn about organizing and social capital. You can find information about internships on the SEIU website (www.seiu.org).

- The Anti-Defamation League (www.adl.org), the Arab-American Anti-Discrimination Committee (www.adc.org), and the National Association for the Advancement of Colored People (www.naacp.org) are examples of organizations that defend the rights of minority groups. These organizations often use volunteers or interns and can provide you with the opportunity to learn about the extent to which social contacts and networks play a role in managing social conflict.

At the National/Global (Macro) Level

- Well-run *microfinance organizations* can help poor people, particularly women, gain social capital and economic independence. Three well-known and respected groups are CRS (Catholic Relief Services at crs.org/microfinance), FINCA (www.finca.org) and Kiva (www.kiva.org). Check out their websites to learn how you can support their efforts.

$SAGE edge™

Get the edge on your studies. edge.sagepub.com/ballantinecondensed5e

- Take a quiz to find out what you've learned.
- Review key terms with eFlashcards.
- Watch videos that enhance chapter content.

Julien Behal/PA Wire

6 Deviance and Social Control

Sickos, Weirdos, Freaks, and Folks Like Us

We often think of deviants as bad people who do not care about rules or other members of society; we contrast them with people like us. Sometimes, though, people need to commit deviants acts to change unjust social structures and to topple tyrants. Further, enforcement of conformity is often experienced as authoritarian.

MICRO

ME (MY FAMILY AND CLOSEST FRIENDS)

LOCAL ORGANIZATIONS AND COMMUNITY
People violate local ordinances and commit thefts.

MESO

NATIONAL ORGANIZATIONS, INSTITUTIONS, AND ETHNIC SUBCULTURES
People violate state laws, and they commit crimes using corporations.

MACRO

SOCIETY
People commit federal crimes; the national government itself may commit crimes such as torture.

GLOBAL COMMUNITY
Crimes may result in global environmental destruction or violations of human rights across national boundaries.

WHAT YOU WILL LEARN IN THIS CHAPTER

This chapter will help you do the following:

6.1 Describe who is deviant and why.

6.2 Compare key ideas in the differential association, labeling, rational choice, structural-functional, and conflict perspectives of deviance.

6.3 Provide possible explanations for why the crime rate has fallen in recent years.

6.4 Describe types of organized crime and crime by organizations prevalent today.

6.5 Give examples of crimes committed at the national and global level today.

6.6 Determine which theoretical perspective would be most useful in explaining the function of prisons in U.S. society today.

THINK ABOUT IT

Micro: Local community	Are you deviant? Who says so? Why do some people in your community become deviant, whereas others do not?
Meso: National institutions, complex organizations, and ethnic groups	What are the consequences of organized crime or occupational crime for large bureaucratic organizations?
Macro: National and global systems	What are the costs—and the benefits—of deviance for a nation? How can a global perspective on crime enhance our understanding of international and national criminal activities?

Wafa did not stand out from the girls around her as she grew up, but she was destined to make world headlines—as the first female suicide bomber in the Palestinian–Israeli conflict. She was the age of most university students reading this book, but she never had an opportunity to attend college. Her task was to smuggle explosives across the Israeli border for the intended bomber, her brother. Instead, on January 27, 2002, she blew up herself and an Israeli soldier. She was declared a martyr, a *sahida*, by the al-Aqsa Martyrs Brigade, and the organization took credit for the attack. The group's political leadership publicly approved her act, opening the way for other women to follow. Why did this happen? What motivated her to commit suicide and take another life in the process? Was she driven by ideology to participate in the Palestinian–Israeli struggle? Were there social and structural factors that affected her decision? Most importantly, was she deviant in carrying out this act, and according to whom?

Wafa Idris grew up in Palestine. She was married at a young age but did not produce children. As a result, her husband divorced her and remarried. She had no future, for who would want a barren, divorced woman in a society that values women for their purity and their childbearing ability? She was a burden to her family. Her way out of an impossible and desperate situation was to commit suicide, bringing honor and wealth to her family and redeeming herself in the process. Other women who followed Wafa have similar stories: Most shared an inability to control their own lives in the patriarchal (male-controlled) society (Gonzalez-Perez 2011; Handwerk 2004; Victor 2003).

Our question is this: Are such women deviant criminal terrorists, hapless victims of terrorist groups, mentally ill "crazies," invisible victims in a patriarchal society, or martyrs who should be honored for their acts? Who says so? Each of these views is held by someone interested in this situation. From this opening example, we can begin to see several complications that arise when defining deviance and deviants. In this chapter, we consider who is deviant, under what circumstances, and in whose eyes.

First, we discuss deviance—*the violation of social norms*—and the social control mechanisms that keep most people from becoming deviant. Occasionally, most of us violate a norm, and depending on its importance and on the severity of the violation, we may or may not be seen as deviant. Wearing strange clothes may be seen as amusing and nonconformist once in a while, but you will be labeled deviant if you do so regularly. If enough people start wearing similar clothes, however, this once deviant act will no longer be deviant. Getting a tattoo or wearing skintight jeans to school are good examples of once deviant acts now considered normal behavior in many communities. We also examine crime in this chapter, *deviant actions for which there are formal penalties imposed by the government, such as fines, jail, or prison sentences.*

You may be surprised to learn that we are all deviant at some times and in some places, and almost all of us have committed crimes. The self-test in the next "Engaging Sociology" illustrates this point.

ENGAGING SOCIOLOGY

Who Is Deviant?

Please jot down your answers to the following self-test questions. There is no need to share your responses with others.

Have you ever engaged in any of the following acts?

- ☐ stolen anything, even if its value was under $10
- ☐ used an illegal drug
- ☐ misused a prescription drug
- ☐ used tobacco prior to age 18
- ☐ drank alcohol prior to age 21
- ☐ engaged in a fistfight
- ☐ carried a concealed knife or gun without a permit
- ☐ used a car without the owner's permission
- ☐ driven a car after drinking alcohol beyond the legal limit
- ☐ forced someone to have sexual relations against her or his will
- ☐ offered sex for money
- ☐ damaged property worth more than $10
- ☐ been truant from school
- ☐ arrived home after your curfew
- ☐ accepted or transported property that you had reason to believe might be stolen
- ☐ taken a towel from a hotel room after renting the room for a night

All of these are delinquent acts (violations of legal standards), and most young people are guilty of at least one infraction. However, few teenagers are given the label of *delinquent*. If you answered yes to any of the preceding questions, you committed a crime in many states. Your penalty or sanction for the infraction could range from a stiff fine to several years in prison—*if* you got caught!

* * * * * * *

Engaging With Sociology

1. Do you think of yourself as deviant? Why, or why not?

2. Are deviants only those who get caught? For instance, if someone steals your car but avoids being caught, is he or she a deviant?

3. Who is considered deviant—and by whom?

WHAT IS DEVIANCE?

Whereas some acts, such as murder, assault, robbery, and rape, are considered deviant in almost every time and place, some deviant acts may be overlooked or even viewed as understandable under certain circumstances, such as when a family steals water and diapers from a destroyed supermarket after a natural disaster.

Some acts of deviance are considered serious offenses in one society but tolerated in another. Examples include prostitution, premarital or extramarital sex, gambling, corruption, and bribery. Even within a single society, different groups may define deviance and conformity quite differently. The state government may officially define alcohol consumption by 19-year-olds as deviant, but on a Saturday night at a fraternity party, the 19-year-old "brother" who does *not* drink may be viewed as deviant by his peers. What do these cases tell us about deviance?

Deviance is socially constructed and dependent on the time and social context. Members of groups in societies

Dressing as a medieval knight would typically be considered deviant behavior, but when the setting is a Renaissance fair, it is socially acceptable and even expected.

define (construct) what is deviant. As we noted earlier, these socially constructed definitions of deviance can change over *time* and depend on the social situation or *context* in which the behavior occurs.

If we take the same behavior and place it in a different social context, perceptions of whether the behavior is deviant may well change. For example, in Greece, Spain, and other Mediterranean countries, the clothing norms on beaches are very different from those in most of North America. Topless sunbathing by women is not at all uncommon, even on beaches designated as family beaches. The norms vary, however, even within a few feet of the beach. Women will sunbathe topless, lying only 10 feet from the boardwalk, where concessionaires sell

Deviance is *socially constructed*. Is this man deviant by virtue of his appearance? Why, or why not?

beverages, snacks, and tourist items. If these women become thirsty, they cover up, walk the 10 feet to purchase a cola, and return to their beach blankets, where they again remove their tops. To walk onto the boardwalk topless would be considered highly deviant.

Thinking Sociologically

Have you ever dressed or styled your hair in a deviant way? Why? Did you have any role models to guide you on how to do so? If so, does this mean you really were *not* being deviant? Why, or why not? Who determines whether your clothes or hairstyle are deviant?

An individual's status or group may be defined as deviant. Some individuals have a higher likelihood of being labeled deviant because of the group into which they were born, such as a particular ethnic group, or because of a distinguishing mark or characteristic, such as a deformity. Others may escape being considered deviant because of their dominant status in society. The higher one's status, the less likely that one will be suspected of violating norms and the less likely that any violations will be characterized as *criminal*. Who would suspect that a respectable, white-collar husband and father is embezzling funds from his company?

The looting that happened following Hurricane Katrina was addressed differently depending on whether it was done by Whites or African Americans (Huddy and Feldman 2006; A. C. Thompson 2009). The media showed photos of Black "looters" who "stole food," but the same media described Whites who "broke into grocery stores" in search of food as "resourceful." Likewise, gays and lesbians are often said to be deviant and accused of flaunting their sexuality. Heterosexuals are rarely accused of "flaunting" their sexuality, regardless of how overtly flirtatious or underdressed they may be. So one's group membership or ascribed traits may make a difference in whether one is defined as deviant.

Deviance can be functional for society. As structural-functionalists point out, deviance serves vital functions by setting examples of unacceptable behavior, leading to the creation of guidelines for behavior necessary to maintain social order and bonding people together through their common rejection of the deviant behavior. Deviance is also functional because it provides jobs for those who deal with deviants: police, judges, social workers, and so forth (Gans 2007). Furthermore, deviance can signal problems in society that need to be addressed and can therefore stimulate positive change.

Sometimes, deviant individuals break the model of conventional thinking, thereby opening society to new and creative paths of thinking. Scientists, inventors, activists, and artists have often been rejected in their time but have been honored later for accomplishments that positively affected society. Famous artist Vincent van Gogh, for example, lived in poverty and suffered from schizophrenia. During his life, his artistic gifts were overlooked, but he became recognized as a renowned painter after his death. His paintings now sell for millions of dollars. Likewise, Nelson Mandela, Martin Luther King Jr., and Mahatma Gandhi were once considered deviant and dangerous, but today, they are regarded as social justice heroes.

Thinking Sociologically

Think of examples in your life that illustrate the *relative nature of deviance*. For instance, which of your behaviors are deviant in one setting but not in another or were deviant when you were younger but not deviant now?

Crime: Deviance That Violates the Law

Governments create laws and impose formal sanctions—punishments—for some acts of deviance, and the social disapproval associated with being convicted of these violations results in the perpetrator being identified as *criminal. When members of society are in general agreement about the seriousness of certain crimes*, these acts are referred to as **consensus crimes** (Brym and Lie 2007; Goodman and Brenner 2002). *Predatory crimes* (crimes—usually violent—against humans, such as premeditated murder, forcible rape, and kidnapping for ransom) are consensus crimes in most nations and are described later in this chapter.

Just as what is considered deviant varies over time and place, so does what is regarded as criminal behavior. For example, at the end of the 1920s, 42 of the 48 U.S. states had laws forbidding interracial marriage (Coontz 2016; see Figure 6.1). Legislatures in half of these states removed those restrictions by the 1960s, but 16 states still had antimiscegenation laws on the books until 1967, when the U.S. Supreme Court ruling in *Loving v. Virginia* made these laws unconstitutional. Today, this legal ban on interracial marriage has been eliminated completely, illustrating that most laws change to reflect the times and sentiments of the majority of people. Likewise, the U.S. Supreme Court ruling in 2015 that same-sex marriages are legal in all states reflects an extraordinary change in the law regarding gays and lesbians (Liptak 2015).

Until recently, this same-sex couple would have been considered deviant throughout the United States. Today, the United States and Canada both recognize same-sex marriages.

We now look at theoretical perspectives that help explain deviance, how some deviant acts become crimes, and what policies might control or reduce crime.

WHAT CAUSES DEVIANT BEHAVIOR? THEORETICAL PERSPECTIVES

Helena is a delinquent. Her father deserted the family when Helena was 10, and before that, he had abused Helena and her mother. Her mother has all she can cope with; she is just trying to survive financially and keep her three children in line. Helena gets little attention and little support or encouragement in her school activities. Her grades have fallen steadily. As a young teen, she sought attention from boys, and in the process, she became pregnant. Now, the only kids who have anything to do with her are others who have been in trouble; her friends are other young people who have also been labeled delinquent. Helena's schoolmates, teachers, and mother see her as a delinquent troublemaker, and it would be hard for Helena to change their views and her status.

How did this happen? Helena's situation is, of course, only one unique case. Sociologists cannot generalize from Helena to other cases, but they do know from their studies that there are thousands of teens with problems like Helena's. We next consider some theories of deviance that help us recognize and explain patterns among delinquent teens like Helena.

FIGURE 6.1 Historical Restrictions on Interracial Marriage in the United States

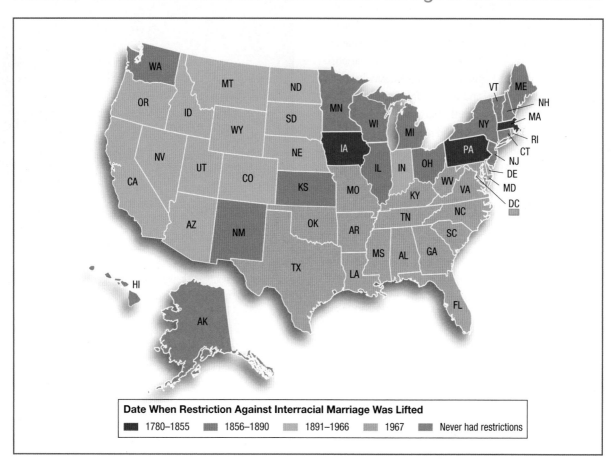

Date When Restriction Against Interracial Marriage Was Lifted
■ 1780–1855   ■ 1856–1890   ■ 1891–1966   ■ 1967   ■ Never had restrictions

Source: Wallenstein (2002). Map by Anna Versluis.

Throughout history, people have proposed explanations for why some members of society "turn bad"—from biological explanations of imbalances in hormones and claims of innate personality defects to social conditions within individual families or in the larger social structure. Biological and psychological approaches focus on personality disorders or abnormalities in the body or psyche of individuals, but they generally do not consider the social context in which deviance occurs.

Sociologists place emphasis on understanding the interactions, social structure, and social processes that lead to deviant behavior, rather than on individual characteristics. They consider the socialization process and interpersonal relationships, group and social class differences, cultural and subcultural norms, and power structures that influence individuals to conform to or deviate from societal expectations. Theoretical explanations about why people are deviant influence social policy decisions and strategies to curb deviant behavior and deal with deviants.

Some theories explain particular types of crime better than others (say, theft, as opposed to sexual assault), just as some illuminate micro-, meso-, or macro-level processes better than others. Taken together, these theories help us understand a wide range of deviant and criminal behaviors.

Micro-Level Explanations of Deviance

No one is born deviant. Individuals learn to be law-abiding citizens or to be deviant through the process of socialization. Why do some people learn to become deviant and others learn to follow the norms of society? Symbolic interaction and rational choice theories focus primarily on micro-level answers to this question.

Symbolic Interaction Approaches to Deviance: Differential Association. Symbolic interactionists focus on how our interactions with others influence whether or not we will commit deviant acts. One interactionist approach, differential association theory, describes how people learn to commit delinquent acts through their social relationships with peers and family members.

Differential association theory *focuses on the process of learning deviant behavior from those with whom we interact (e.g., family, peers, and fellow employees)* (Hagan 2011; Sutherland, Cressey, and Luckenbil 1992). Helena, for example, came to be surrounded by people who made dropping out of school and other delinquent acts seem normal. If her close friends and siblings were also sexually active as teens, her teen pregnancy might not be remarkable and might even be a source of some prestige with her group of peers.

According to differential association theory, the possibility of becoming deviant depends on four factors related to associating with a deviant group: the *duration* of time spent with the group, the *intensity* of interaction, the *frequency* of interaction, and the *priority* of the group in one's friendship network (Sutherland et al. 1992). If people have regular and frequent exposure to deviance among their longtime, close friends, they are likely to learn to behave in deviant ways.

Some theorists contend that life in poverty often involves immersion in a distinctive subculture in which poor people learn delinquent behavior patterns through socialization. The values, beliefs, norms, and practices that have evolved in poor communities over time can often encourage violation of laws. Just as upper-class youth learn norms that help them succeed in middle- and upper-class areas of society, lower-class youth may learn other behaviors that help them survive in their poor neighborhoods but that those with privilege have defined as delinquent and criminal (Bettie 2003; Chambliss 1973). The reality is that youth from all social classes commit crimes—but those crimes may be different and be perceived differently by those close to the young offenders.

Elijah Anderson's (2000) book, *Code of the Street*, describes two types of groups that coexist in poor neighborhoods: *decent people* and *street people*. *Street-oriented people* learn a code of the street that involves hanging out on the street with peers; seeking immediate gratification through sex, violence, and drugs; and adopting a certain look with their clothes and jewelry—an image expected by the group. Peers become more important than society's social control agents. *Decent families* accept mainstream values and often find support systems in church communities or other organizations. In order to survive in such neighborhoods and avoid violent sanctions from street-oriented peers, however, those from

According to differential association theory, people who abuse drugs, like this young woman, tend to learn this behavior through close associations with other illicit drug users. They come to see the drugged state as enjoyable *and* learn the techniques for using them.

decent families may dress and carry themselves in a way that conforms with the street-oriented image. The result is that other members of society, including the police, view both the street oriented and those from decent families as deviant (E. Anderson 2000).

As mentioned, we know that members of all social classes commit crimes, and no socioeconomic class has a monopoly on violence, corruption, or dishonesty. However, *labeling theory* explains why some individuals and groups are more likely to be caught and punished for deviance.

Symbolic Interaction Approaches to Deviance: Labeling. Labeling theory explains *how people can be labeled deviant after committing a deviant act, which can then lead them to carry out further acts that reflect that label.* Labels (such as *juvenile delinquent*) are symbols that have meanings affecting an individual's self-concept and the way others see the individual.

Labeling theorists define two stages in the process of becoming a deviant. **Primary deviance** is *a violation of a norm that may be an isolated act or an initial act of rule breaking*, such as a young teenager shoplifting something on a dare by friends. Most people commit acts of primary deviance. However, many of us avoid being labeled *deviant* when we commit one of these primary acts. Remember how you marked the deviant behavior test that you took at the beginning of this chapter? If you have engaged in deviant acts, you were probably not labeled deviant for

Shoplifting, when done by young people without a criminal record, provides an example of primary deviance.

the offense. If you had been so labeled, you might not be in college or taking this class.

If an individual continues to violate a norm and begins to take on a deviant identity because of being labeled as deviant, this is referred to as **secondary deviance**. Secondary deviance becomes publicly recognized, and the individual is identified as deviant, beginning a deviant career. If a teenager like Helena is caught, her act becomes known, perhaps publicized in the newspaper. She may spend time in a juvenile detention center, and parents of other teens may not want their children associating with her. Employers and store managers may refuse to hire her. Soon, there are few opportunities open to her because others expect her to be delinquent. The teen may continue performing the deviant acts and associating with delinquent acquaintances, in part because few other options are available. Society's reaction, then, is what defines a deviant person and may limit options for that person to change the label (Lemert 1951, 1972).

The process of labeling individuals and behaviors takes place at each level of analysis, from individual to society. If community or societal norms and laws define a behavior as deviant, individuals are likely to believe it is deviant. Sanctions against juvenile delinquents can have the effect of reinforcing the deviant behavior by (a) increasing alienation from the social world, (b) forcing increased interaction with deviant peers, and (c) motivating juvenile delinquents to positively value and identify with the deviant status (Kaplan and Johnson 1991).

A self-fulfilling prophecy occurs when a *belief or a prediction becomes a reality, in part because of the prediction*. A false perception of a person, perhaps based on a stereotype, can become true if it provokes behavior that fulfills that false perception or stereotype. For example, James is 8 years old and already sees himself as a "bad" kid who will end up in prison, just like his father, whom he has never met. His mother tells him he was born "bad" because he resembles his father, and his teachers and peers tell him he is "bad" because he struggles in school. In keeping with the idea of a self-fulfilling prophecy, James accepts the label and acts accordingly, refusing to do his homework and stealing other kids' lunch money. Unless someone—such as an insightful teacher—steps in to give him another image of himself, James is likely to end up in prison—not because he was born "bad" but because he was treated by others as if he were bad and learned that image of himself (Merton 1948).

Thinking Sociologically

What labels do you carry? How do you know you carry these labels? How do they affect your self-concept and behavior?

A major explanation for why certain individuals and groups are labeled deviant has to do with their status and power in society—a concern of conflict theory. Those on the fringes, away from power—the poor, minorities, members of new religious movements, or others who, in some way, do not fit into the dominant system—are more likely to be labeled as deviants. On the other hand, because the powerful have the influence to define what is acceptable, they tend to avoid the deviant label. Their behavior, even when it has a negative impact on society, is less likely to be labeled as deviant or criminal.

A study by William J. Chambliss illustrates the process of labeling in communities and groups. Perhaps during your high school years, you witnessed situations similar to that described in his study (Chambliss 1973). Chambliss looked at the behavior of two small peer groups of boys and at the reactions of community members to their behavior. The Saints, boys from "good" families, were some of the most delinquent boys at Hannibal High School. Although the Saints were constantly occupied with truancy, drinking, wild driving, petty theft, and vandalism, none was officially arrested for any misdeed during the 2-year study. The Roughnecks, who were from less affluent families, were constantly in trouble with the police and community residents, even though their rate of delinquency was about equal to that of the Saints.

What was the cause of the disparity in the labeling of these two groups? Community members, the police, and teachers alike labeled the boys based on their perceptions of the boys' family backgrounds and social class. The Saints came from stable, White, upper-middle-class families; were active in school affairs; and were precollege students who everyone expected would become professionals. In fact, the Saints almost all did become professionals, living up to their images in the community. On the other hand, the general community feeling was that the Roughnecks would amount to nothing. They carried around a negative label that was hard to change. Two Roughnecks ended up in prison, two became coaches, and little is known of the others. For a number of these boys, the prophecy became self-fulfilling (Chambliss 1973). Labels are powerful and can stigmatize an individual—branding the person with a negative mark that discredits a person's claim to a "normal" identity.

Rational Choice Approaches to Deviance. Rational choice theory, as noted in previous chapters, suggests that when individuals make decisions, they calculate the costs and benefits to themselves. They consider the balance between pleasure and pain. Turning to crime is therefore a conscious, rational, and calculated decision made after weighing the costs and benefits of alternatives. Rational choice theorists believe that punishment—imposing high "costs" for criminal behavior, such as fines, imprisonment, or even the death penalty—is the best way to dissuade criminals from choosing the path of crime. When the cost outweighs the potential benefit and opportunities are restricted, it deters people from thinking that crime is a "rational" choice (Earls and Reiss 1994; Winslow and Zhang 2008).

Positive sanctions reward those behaviors approved by society. This is the reason why schools have honor ceremonies, companies reward their top salespeople, and communities recognize civic leadership with "Citizen of the Year" awards. All these actions enhance the rewards for conventional behavior. Negative sanctions (or punishments) increase the cost to those who deviate from the norm. They range from fines for traffic violations to prison sentences for serious crimes and even death in many states for acts considered most dangerous to society.

Applying rational choice theory to crime prevention has led to measures that focus on making it harder and

Rational choice theorists would note that this little girl is weighing the costs and benefits of taking cookies, and the benefits are looking pretty sweet!

less rewarding to commit crimes. For example, improved lighting, especially at night (making it harder to commit a crime unnoticed); marking goods that may be stolen (for easy tracking and recovery); and creating positive alternatives to crime (such as summer jobs for teens) make crime both harder and less appealing (Clarke 1997).

Thinking Sociologically

Think of a time when you committed a deviant act or avoided doing so despite a tempting opportunity. What factors influenced whether you conformed to societal norms or committed the deviant act?

Meso- and Macro-Level Explanations for Deviance

Whereas micro-level interactions can lead a person to become and to be labeled as deviant, meso- and macro-level analysis can help us gain a greater understanding of the societal factors leading to deviance. As we have noted, meso-level analysis focuses on ethnic subcultures, organizations, and institutions. Macro-level analysis focuses on national and global social systems.

Structural-functional theories of deviance include (a) *social control theory*, which focuses on the processes a society or a group uses to ensure conformity to its norms and expectations; (b) *anomie*, the breakdown of societal norms guiding behavior, which leads to social disorganization;

© AP Images/Yemen Lens

The autocratic Yemeni president, *Abd Rabbuh Mansur Hadi*, claimed that the recent protests against him were leading to anomie and general social chaos. In the picture above, Yemeni army soldiers try to stop antigovernment protesters. Hadi temporarily resigned in January 2015 under siege by a rebel group called the Houthis. Social order or stability has been an issue since that time.

1. *Attachment* to other people who respect the values and rules of the society. Individuals do not want to be rejected by those to whom they are close or whom they admire.
2. *Commitment* to conventional activities (such as school and jobs) that they do not want to jeopardize.
3. *Involvement* in activities that keep them so busy with conventional roles and expectations that they do not have time for mischief.
4. *Belief* in the social rules of their culture, which they accept because of their childhood socialization and indoctrination into those conventional beliefs.

These factors decrease the likelihood that a person will commit deviant acts (Hirschi [1969] 2002).

In addition to these factors, social control theorists point out that two primary forces shape our tendency to conform. The first is internal controls—those voices within us that tell us when a behavior is acceptable or unacceptable, right or wrong. The second is external controls—society's formal or informal controls against deviant behavior. Informal external controls include smiles; frowns; hugs; and ridicule from family members, friends, and close acquaintances (Gottfredson and Hirschi 1990). Formal external controls come from the legal system through police, judges, juries, and social workers. Societies can influence both forces through societal institutions (e.g., family, education, and government) that teach us the norms of society (which we internalize) and punish those who violate the norms.

and (c) *strain theory*, which shows that the difference between definitions of success (goals) in a society and the means available to achieve those goals can lead to deviant behavior.

Structural-Functional Approaches to Deviance: Social Control. One of sociology's central concepts is social control—why people obey norms (Hagan 2011). If human beings were truly free to do whatever they wanted, they would likely commit more deviant acts. Yet to live near others and with others requires individuals to control their behaviors based on social norms and sanctions—in short, social control. Social control theory *examines the processes a society or a group uses to ensure conformity to its norms and expectations*.

The roots of social control theory can be traced back to Durkheim's work on suicide (Meier 2016). Recall that Durkheim noted that people who have more social attachments are less likely to commit suicide than those who have fewer social connections. Those who are less bonded to society are more likely to commit deviant acts, such as suicide. Travis Hirschi built on Durkheim's work on suicide to develop social control theory.

Control theory contends that people are bonded to others by four powerful factors:

Structural-Functional Approaches to Deviance: Anomie. Sociologists use the term anomie, or the state of normlessness that occurs when rules for behavior in society break down under extreme stress from rapid social change or conflict (Merton 1968). Émile Durkheim (1858–1917) first described this normlessness as a condition of weak, conflicting, or absent norms and the changes in values that arise when societies are disorganized. As discussed in Chapter 5, this situation is typical in rapidly urbanizing, industrializing societies; at times of sudden prosperity or depression; during rapid technological change; during a war; or when a government is overthrown.

Imagine you grew up in a small village where your family and all those around you have been farmers for as far back as anyone can remember. You were raised to become one yourself and thought you would raise your children to become farmers as well. Over the past few years, though, due to climate change, the rains have not come, and the fields no longer support crops. You have no choice but to leave everyone and everything you have ever known to try to find work in the nearest city. This may thrust you into a situation where norms of interaction—including mutual support and friendliness—are very different, and you might feel like you are in a different country.

Millions of people are now living out similar stories. Villagers in industrializing countries in Africa, Asia, and Latin America find themselves pushed off marginally productive rural lands and pulled into rapidly expanding cities to seek better lives and means for survival. They hope to find good jobs in these urban areas, but when they arrive, they often face disappointment. Poor, unskilled, and homeless, they move into crowded apartments or shantytowns of temporary shacks and try to adjust to the new style of life, which often includes unemployment. Old village norms that have provided the guidelines for proper behavior crumble, sometimes without clear expectations emerging to take their places. The lack of clear norms in the rapidly changing urban environment leads to high levels of social disorganization and deviant behavior.

This general idea of anomie led a group of Chicago sociologists to study the social conditions of that city that correlate with deviance. The Chicago School, as the research team is known, linked life in transitional slum areas to the high incidence of crime. Certain neighborhoods or zones in the Chicago area—generally inner-city transitional zones with recent settlers—have always had high delinquency rates, regardless of the group that occupied the area. Low economic status, ethnic heterogeneity, residential mobility, family disruption, and competing value systems (because of the constant transitions) led to community disorganization. Although new immigrant groups have replaced the older groups over time, the delinquency rate has remained high because each generation of newcomers experiences anomie (C. Shaw and McKay 1929).

Structural Functional Approaches to Deviance: Strain. What happens when you know what your goal is but you cannot find a socially acceptable path to reach it? How do you proceed? Strain theory contends that *the opportunity or limitations embedded in the structures of society may contradict and undermine the goals and aspirations society encourages for its members, creating strains that lead to deviance.*

Strain theory suggests that the gap between an individual's or a society's *goals* and the legitimate ways of attaining those goals—*the means*—can lead to strain in the society (Merton 1968). Individuals may agree with the society's *goals* for success (say, financial affluence) but may not be able to achieve them using the socially acceptable means of achieving that success. The strain created can lead to deviance. Merton uses U.S. society as an example because it places a heavy emphasis on success, as measured by wealth and social standing. He outlines five ways by which individuals adapt to the strain. Figure 6.2 shows these five types and their relationship to goals and means.

To further illustrate strain theory, we trace the choices of a lower-class student who realizes the value of an education and knows it is necessary to get ahead but has problems finding time to study because she has to work many hours a week to help support her family.

1. *Conformity* means embracing the society's definition of success and adhering to the established and approved means of achieving success. The student works hard despite the obstacles, pulling all-nighters and trying to do well in school to achieve success and a good job placement. She uses legitimate, approved means—education and hard work—to reach goals that the society views as worthy.

2. *Innovation* refers to the use of illicit means to reach approved goals. Our student uses illegitimate means to achieve her education goals. She cheats on exams or gets papers from Internet sources. Success in school is all that matters. How she attains that success does not matter.

FIGURE 6.2 Merton's Strain Theory

3. *Ritualism* involves strict adherence to the culturally prescribed rules, even though individuals give up on the goals they hoped to achieve. The student no longer thinks she can get good grades and succeed in college, but as a matter of pride and self-image, she continues to try hard and to attend school. She conforms to expectations but with no sense of purpose. She just does what she is told.

4. *Retreatism* refers to giving up on both the goals and the means. The student either bides her time, not doing well, or drops out, giving up on future job goals. She abandons or retreats from the goals of a professional position in society and the means to get there. She may even turn to a different lifestyle—for example, becoming a user of drugs and alcohol—as part of the retreat.

5. *Rebellion* entails rejecting socially approved ideas of success and the means of attaining that success. It replaces those with alternative definitions of success and alternative strategies for attaining new goals. Rebelling against the dominant cultural goals and means, our student leaves her family, abandons thoughts of college and a profession, and joins a radical political or religious group or becomes a terrorist, seeking to destabilize the government and establish a new type of society.

Deviant behavior results from retreatism, rebellion, and innovation. According to Merton, the reasons why individuals resort to these behaviors lie in the social conditions that prevent access to success, not in their individual biological or psychological makeup (Merton 1968).

The structural-functional approaches to deviance focus on what occurs if deviance disrupts the ongoing social order. They explore what causes deviance, how to prevent disruptions, how to keep change slow and nondisruptive, and how deviance can be useful to the ongoing society. However, anomie and strain theories fail to account for class conflicts and inequities that conflict theorists argue cause deviance.

Conflict Theory of Deviance. As you will recall from previous chapters, conflict theorists assume that conflict among groups is inevitable. Conflict theory focuses on a meso- and macro-level analysis of deviance, looking at deviance as the result of social inequality or of the struggle among groups for power.

Wealthy and powerful elites want to maintain their control and their high positions (Domhoff 2009). They have the power to pass laws and define what is deviant, sometimes by effectively eliminating the opposition groups. The greater the cultural difference between the dominant group and other groups in society, the greater the possibility of conflict. This is because minority groups and subcultures challenge the norms of the dominant groups and threaten the consensus in society (Huizinga, Loeber, and Thornberry 1994).

Some conflict theorists blame capitalist systems for the unjust administration of law and unequal distribution of resources, arguing that the ruling class uses the legal system to further the capitalist enterprise (Quinney 2002). The dominant or ruling class defines deviance; applies laws to protect its interests; represses efforts to make laws more just; and, in effect, may force those in subordinate classes to carry out actions that the dominant class has defined as deviant. These deviant actions become necessary for survival when the affluent restrict legitimate avenues to resources. In most cases, the dominant class consists of one racial or ethnic group that distinguishes itself from the racial or ethnic groups found in the subordinate classes. So conflict and definitions of deviance often have racial and ethnic implications, as well as social class dimensions. When people believe that those in power treat them unfairly, they have less loyalty to the society and to its rules.

To reduce deviance and crime, conflict theorists believe that we must change the structure of society. For instance, legal systems in many countries claim to support equal and fair treatment for all, but when one looks at the law in action, another picture emerges, as seen in the next "Engaging Sociology." Recall the example of the Saints and Roughnecks; the students from powerful families and higher social classes received favored treatment. Unequal treatment of groups that differ from the dominant group—the poor, the working class, and racial or ethnic minorities, in particular—is rooted in the legal, political, and occupational structures of societies.

A Multilevel Analysis of Deviance: Feminist Theories. As we have indicated in previous chapters, feminist theories sometimes take a macro approach, akin to conflict theory, and sometimes they are more micro in approach. In either case, feminist theorists consistently argue that traditional theories do not give an adequate picture or understanding of women's situations. These theorists look for explanations of violence against women and the secondary status of most women in gender relations and social structures. Although there are several branches of feminist theory, most see the macro-level causes of abuses suffered by women as rooted in the capitalist patriarchal system.

ENGAGING SOCIOLOGY

Marijuana Use Versus Marijuana Arrests

Today, we can see evidence of discrimination in the criminal justice system by comparing the treatment of Black and White Americans who use marijuana in states where it is illegal. See Figures 6.3a and 6.3b.

FIGURE 6.3a Marijuana Use by Race, 2001–2010

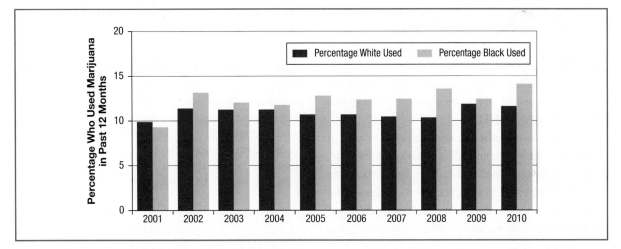

Source: Substance Abuse and Mental Health Services Administration.

FIGURE 6.3b Arrest Rates for Marijuana Possession by Race, 2001–2010

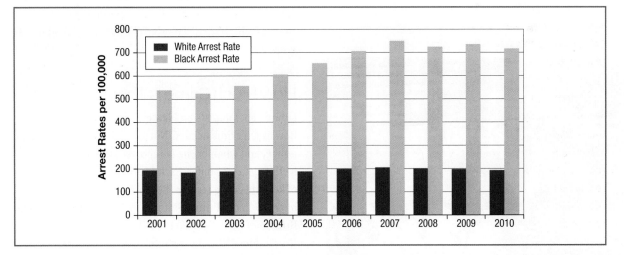

Source: FBI/Uniform Crime Reporting Program Data and U.S. Census Data.

Engaging With Sociology

1. What are the respective percentages of White and Black Americans who use marijuana?

2. What are the respective percentages of White and Black Americans arrested for marijuana use?

3. Of the theories described in this chapter, which offers the most convincing explanation for the discrepancy in the answers to Questions 1 and 2? Why?

One result of women's secondary status is that they are often victims of sexual crime, and those who commit such crimes against women do not face severe—or in some cases *any*—punishment. Criminal acts against women, including honor killings, sex trafficking, and rape, take place around the world (Bales 2012; Bales and Trodd 2008). Globally, 35% of women have experienced physical or sexual violence by an intimate partner or sexual violence by someone else at some point during their lives (United Nations Women 2015). In a few countries or regions in countries, the legal system is based on strict interpretations of religious books by those who practice rigid and literal interpretations of the faith in an attempt to maintain patriarchal control over women and their bodies. In some countries, women who are victims of rape are blamed and punished very severely while the men go free (Shackle 2012; Taseer 2011).

According to feminist theory, the work of women in the private sphere—including housework, childbearing, and childcare—is undervalued, as are the women who carry out these roles. In some societies, women are the property of their husbands, with men's strength and physical force the ultimate means of control over women. Some branches of feminist theory argue that men exploit women's labor power and sexuality to continue their dominance. The system is reproduced through new generations socialized to maintain the patriarchy and to view inequality between the sexes as "normal" and "natural." Women who deviate from the cultural expectations of "normal" behavior are condemned.

No one theory of why deviance occurs can explain all the forms of deviance. Depending on the level of analysis of the questions sociologists wish to study (micro, meso, or macro), they select the theory that best fits the data they find. In the following sections, we explore in more detail the micro–meso–macro connections as they apply to one manifestation of deviance: crime. This illustrates how the sociological imagination can be applied to deviance at each level in the social system.

● Thinking Sociologically

Meso- and macro-level social forces can be even more powerful than micro-level forces in explaining deviance. What might be the factors at the meso and macro levels that contribute to deviance such as prostitution or shoplifting? Pick a recent example of deviance now in the news. Which sociological theories help explain this deviant behavior?

CRIME AND INDIVIDUALS: MICRO-LEVEL ANALYSIS

In the United States, more than 2,800 acts are listed as federal crimes. These acts fall into several types of crime, some of which we discuss here. First, we consider how crime rates are measured.

How Much Crime Is There?

How do sociologists and law enforcement officials know how much crime occurs? Not all crime is reported to the police, and when crime is reported, the methods of collecting data may differ. Each country has its own methods of keeping crime records. For instance, the official record of crime in the United States is found in the U.S. Federal Bureau of Investigation's (FBI) *Uniform Crime Reports* (UCR). The FBI relies on information submitted voluntarily by law enforcement agencies and divides crimes into two categories: Type I and Type II offenses. Type I offenses, also known as *FBI index crimes*, include murder, forcible rape, robbery, aggravated assault, burglary, larceny theft, motor vehicle theft, and arson. Type II offenses include fraud, simple assault, vandalism, driving under the influence of alcohol or drugs, and running away from home. In fact, there are hundreds of Type II crimes. Figure 6.4, the Crime Clock, summarizes UCR

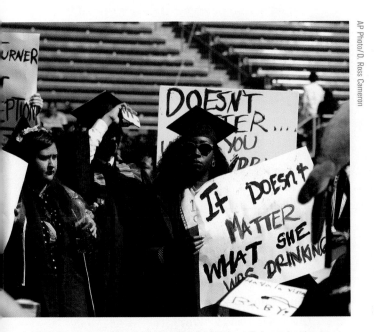

AP Photo/D. Ross Cameron

Protesters demonstrate during Stanford University's graduation in protest against a judge's decision to sentence a former Stanford University swimmer to just 6 months in jail for rape.

FIGURE 6.4   *2014 Crime Clock*

2014 CRIME CLOCK STATISTICS

A Violent Crime occurred every	26.3 seconds
One Murder every	36.9 minutes
One Rape every	4.5 minutes
One Robbery every	1.6 minutes
One Aggravated Assault every	42.5 seconds
A Property Crime occurred every	3.8 seconds
One Burglary every	18.2 seconds
One Larceny-theft every	5.4 seconds
One Motor Vehicle Theft every	45.7 seconds

Source: U.S. Department of Justice (2015).

records on Type I offenses. To examine trends in crime, social scientists calculate a rate of crime, usually per 100,000.

Although the UCR data provide a picture of how much crime gets *reported* to the police and leads to arrest, the FBI does not provide complete information on how much crime there is in the United States. The UCR does not show most corporate crimes or white-collar crimes, and *many* street crimes are not reported for a host of reasons. Further, sometimes a crime that is reported to the police does not lead to an arrest, or an arrest is made, but the case is never prosecuted in court, or a prosecutor will initiate prosecution, but the case never comes to trial. A majority of cases end in plea bargains—a suspect agrees to plead guilty in exchange for being given a lesser charge, perhaps because the suspect expresses feelings of guilt, because the person does not have the resources to fight the charges with a good attorney, or because the suspect is willing to exchange information for a lighter sentence. The reduction in the number of cases at each level of the criminal justice system contributes to the difficulty of determining accurate crime rates.

Self-reporting surveys—asking individuals what criminal acts they have committed—provide another way to measure crime rates. Criminal participation surveys typically focus on adolescents and their involvement in delinquency. *Victimization surveys* ask people how much crime they have experienced. The Bureau of Justice Statistics carries out the National Crime Victimization Survey (NCVS) each year. The NCVS indicates that the tendency to report crime to the police varies by the type of crime, with violent victimizations having the highest reporting rate.

Thinking Sociologically

Imagine that you work for the Bureau of Justice Statistics. Congress asks you to predict how many FBI agents will be needed to deal with different types of crime. How would you go about determining this, and what data sources might you use?

Although differences in crime reports are often difficult to reconcile, each measurement instrument provides a different portion of the total picture of crime. By using several data-gathering techniques (triangulation), a more accurate picture of crime begins to emerge. All data-gathering techniques indicate that the rate of violent and nonviolent crime in the United States has dropped since the mid-1990s, so we can be confident that the crime rate has really fallen. In 1991, there were 758 violent crimes per 100,000 residents, but in 2014, that number was 365.5 (Statistica 2016c). (See Figure 6.5 for the trend line since 1995.)

Researchers have yet to come to a consensus as to why crime has declined. Some ideas now under review include the following:

- Changing demographics: a decline in the number of young people (those most likely to commit crimes)
- Rising rates of incarceration (though those rates have declined over the past few years)
- New policing strategies, including computer-assisted planning and closer focus on gun use by youth

FIGURE 6.5   U.S. Violent Crime Rate Since 1995 (per 100,000 Residents)

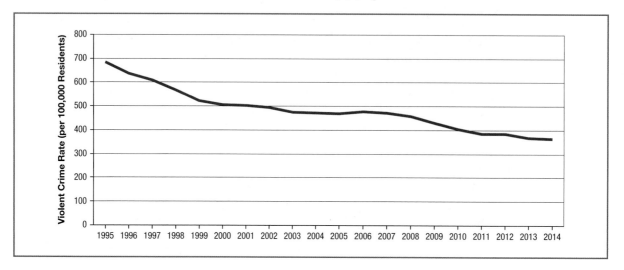

Source: Statistica (2016c).

- Greater access to abortion after the 1973 *Roe v. Wade* Supreme Court decision, which led to fewer unwanted children (relatively more likely to commit crimes due to their negative treatment)
- The phasing out of lead in gasoline in the 1970s (lead can cause brain damage related to violent behavior) (Cohn et al. 2013; R. Wilson 2015)

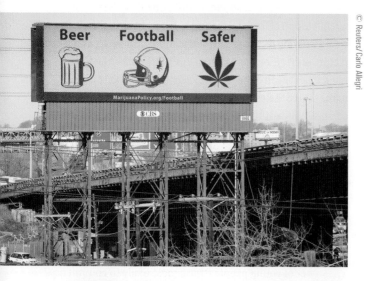

This photo shows how what we consider deviant can change over time. The people who paid for the billboard are supporting legalization of marijuana, maintaining that it is less dangerous than beer or football.

Though crime is down, it is still the common subject of news headlines. Crime reporting is relatively inexpensive, as reporters can rely on information about index crimes that officials regularly make public. So the crimes that grab the attention of average citizens of countries around the world tend to be violent crimes committed by individuals or small groups. The following are some examples of types of micro-level crimes.

Types of Crime

Predatory Crimes. Citizens of the United States tend to be most afraid of violent predatory crimes. Many citizens feel they cannot trust others. Some keep guns to protect themselves from this perceived danger. Some neighborhoods *are* dangerous; however, as noted, the total violent-crime victimization rate has declined over the past several decades. Next, we discuss more crimes committed by individuals—but stay tuned because most criminologists feel there are more serious crimes, to be discussed under meso- and macro-level deviance.

Crimes Without Victims. *Acts committed by or between individual consenting adults* are known as victimless or public-order crimes. These can include prostitution, gambling, drug use, and public drunkenness. Whereas these crimes do not result in specific victims, they are deemed harmful to society (and thus, criminal) because they violate the dominant values and norms. Though illegal, they may be tolerated (the police may look the other way) as long as they do not become highly visible. For example, it would be rare for police in the United States to crack down on a low-stakes monthly poker game friends play behind closed doors.

Victimless crimes involving drugs result in a variety of policies, from execution in Iran and hanging in Malaysia to legalization in Holland. As noted earlier, U.S. drug policies have led to huge numbers of people being imprisoned. Half of all drug arrests in 2010 were related to marijuana usage (American Civil Liberties Union 2013). However, proposals to legalize drugs in the United States have recently gained traction. As we write these words, 28 states allow for the medical use of marijuana, and eight states (Alaska, California, Colorado, Maine, Massachusetts, Nevada, Oregon, and Washington State) and Washington, DC, have legalized recreational use of the drug (Robinson and Gould 2016). A 2015 Pew poll indicated that 53% of Americans favor decriminalization of marijuana (Motel 2015).

California has the longest experience with legalization of medical marijuana—nearly 2 decades. Fears among some that legalization would lead to civic disorder, increased lawlessness, and drastic increases in other drug usage have not materialized. Due to careful monitoring of the age of buyers, teen use of marijuana in California has not increased since legalization in 1996 (Nagourney and Lyman 2013). Further, some scholars think more teen use of marijuana would not be a bad trend. When teens switch to marijuana, they tend to reduce alcohol usage, and alcohol is more likely to result in death from overuse or from drunk driving (D. M. Anderson and Rees 2013).

Thinking Sociologically

Can a person be victimized by drugs even if he willingly uses them? Many prostitutes only consent to sex acts because poverty or drug addiction leaves them with few other options and because, like many women without resources, they are vulnerable to domination by men. Are illegal drug use and prostitution really "victimless crimes," or should drug users and prostitutes be considered victims?

Hate Crimes. A hate crime is *"a criminal offense against a person or property motivated in whole or in part by an offender's bias against a race, religion,*

disability, ethnic origin or sexual orientation" (FBI 2015). The FBI reported 5,462 hate crimes in 2014, with the breakdown by bias indicated in Figure 6.6. Hate crimes are underreported, with many victims not believing the police can help them. From the data available, though, it is clear that hate crimes based on religion and sexual orientation have increased over the past few years (FBI 2015; Langton, Planty, and Sandholtz 2013; Potok 2013a).

These photos reveal how various subcultures can have sharply different views on what they consider deviant. They also help illustrate why hate crimes tend to increase as minority groups gain more power in society and their definitions of reality come to be normalized.

FIGURE 6.6   Breakdown of the 5,462 Hate Crime Incidents Reported in 2014

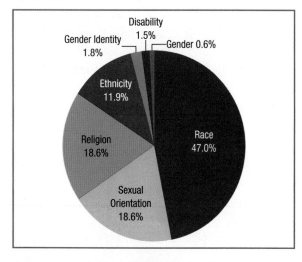

Source: FBI (2015).

Those who commit hate crimes feel rage against the victim as a representative of a group they despise. Often, they believe this group threatens their lifestyle and economic security. In the case of some White supremacy movements, philosophical, political, and even religious principles guide their group beliefs (Blee 2008). As minority groups gain notoriety *or* acceptance in society, they can face more hate crimes. For example, hate crime incidents against Muslim Americans increased after September 11, 2001, and the Boston Marathon bombing in 2013. The numbers of White supremacist groups increased dramatically after Barack Obama, the first U.S. president of color, was elected, and antigay hate crimes have become more common with the success of the same-sex marriage movement (Peek 2011).

One form of hate crime that has gotten very little attention is hostile attacks on people with one or more disabilities. Jack Levin tells of his entry into this area of research in the next "Sociologists in Action."

The aforementioned examples represent only three of the many types of micro-level crimes, characterized by individual or small-group actions. We now turn to crime in organizations and institutions at the meso level. Organizations usually commit the crimes most harmful to society.

CRIME AND ORGANIZATIONS: MESO-LEVEL ANALYSIS

Crime and organized-crime control efforts are part of the social structure of modern societies. First, as societies modernize, there is an almost universal tendency for crime rates to increase dramatically due to the anomie that new migrants and the poor experience in urban areas where old norms are no longer relevant (Merton 1938). Second, as societies become modernized and urban, they become more reliant on meso-level formal or bureaucratic mechanisms of control rather than small-community pressures and conformity. They develop a criminal justice system.

Crimes Involving Organizations and Institutions

Jeanne, one of the authors of this book, recently got a call from a fraud office at an online retailer saying that her credit card had been compromised. Someone had ordered online items from Atlanta-based Bloomingdale's, Coach, and DSW (Designer Shoe Warehouse) using her credit card—and it was not Jeanne! Credit card fraud and identity theft are two types of organized crime prevalent today.

Some crimes are committed by highly organized, hierarchically structured syndicates formed for the purpose of achieving their economic objectives through criminal behavior. On the other hand, legitimate corporations also commit crimes. Their crimes are often very serious, but the public image of such organizations is not criminal, so they are not always suspected or caught. We look first at organized criminal organizations and then at crimes committed by people within their legitimate occupations and organizations.

Organized Crime. Organized crime refers to *ongoing criminal enterprises by an organized group whose ultimate purpose is economic gain through illegitimate means* (Siegel 2011). Our image of this type of crime is sometimes glamorized in films such as *No Country for Old Men*, *The Godfather*, *Goodfellas*, and *Gangs of New York*. On television, *The Sopranos* is the ultimate media "mob" depiction. Despite the alluring view of these idealized stories, organized crime is a serious problem in many countries. It is essentially a counterculture with a hierarchical structure, from the boss down to the underlings. The organization relies on power, control, fear, violence, and

SOCIOLOGISTS IN ACTION
JACK LEVIN

Three Times the Violence

A few years ago, I was asked to serve as a speaker in England, on the topic of what the British call *disablist violence*—hate crimes committed against people with emotional, intellectual, and physical disabilities. For decades, I had studied hate crimes based on race, religion, gender, and sexual orientation, but it never occurred to me that people with disabilities might be victimized by widespread and sometimes extraordinary levels of violence. According to anonymous victim accounts from the Bureau of Justice Statistics, each year, the 54 million Americans with disabilities experience serious violence at a rate nearly 3 times that of the general population. Their rate for sexual assault is almost 4 times that of Americans who are considered to be able-bodied.

After returning from England, I decided not to just drop my newly acquired information about the plight of people with disabilities. As someone who regards himself as a public sociologist, I was eager to communicate my findings as widely as possible. First, I wrote an article titled "The Invisible Hate Crime" for an issue of *Pacific Standard* magazine (www.psmag.com/politics-and-law/the-invisible-hate-crime-27984). Then, I authored an article about the topic for the reader *Disability, Hate Crime and Violence*, edited by Roulstone and Mason-Bish.

Finally, I teamed up with producer Bill Lancaster (a colleague at Northeastern University who, years earlier, had asked me to appear on several episodes of Geraldo Rivera's then-popular talk show). We decided to produce a documentary that would help give some public visibility to what seems to be an unacknowledged hate crime.

After a couple of years gathering interviews and incidents, we put together a 15-minute film that was designed to stimulate debate and conversation among students and practitioners—especially those in or going into careers in criminal justice and social work.

The main purpose of our film, titled *Three Times the Violence* (http://original.livestream.com/webshare/video?clipId=pla_af5ee04c-ee39-4617-bbdd-48059fc22684), was to increase public and professional awareness that people with disabilities have a special vulnerability to extraordinary violence. We were intent on helping to remove disablist violence from the shadows and bring it into the spotlight. After all, the first step in combating these shameful incidents is an acknowledgment that they exist.

We don't have to change the law on hate crimes against people with disabilities—that has already happened at the federal level—but we must change the thinking of ordinary people who consider only race, religion, or sexual orientation as grounds for bigotry. Many people with disabilities are harmed more by the way others treat them than by their intellectual, psychiatric, or physical disadvantage. This unfortunate fact has been widely ignored by otherwise decent Americans, who, when they think of hate crimes, tend to focus only on people wearing sheets, armbands, steel toe boots, or Nazi tattoos.

• •

A prolific author, public speaker, and commentator, Jack Levin, PhD, is a professor emeritus at Northeastern University and codirector of the Brudnick Center on Violence and Conflict.

corruption. This type of deviance is a particular problem when societies experience rapid change and anomie and where social controls break down.

Marginalized ethnic groups that face discrimination may become involved in a quest to get ahead through organized crime. Early in U.S. history, Italians were especially prominent in organized crime, but today, many groups are involved. Organized crime around the world has gained strong footholds in countries in transition (European Commission 2014). For example, in Russia, the transition from a socialist economy to a market economy has provided many opportunities for criminal activity. The *Mafiya* is estimated to include over 90,000 people, and some estimate that the members control 70% to 80% of all private business in Russia and 40% of Russia's wealth. It is heavily involved in human trafficking and the heroin drug trade originating in Afghanistan. Estimates indicate that Russians, just half of 1% of the global population, consume 12% of the world's heroin (Lindberg and Markovic n.d.; Matthews 2014; Schmalleger 2012).

Organized crime usually takes one of three forms: (1) the sale of illegal goods and services, including gambling, loan sharking, trafficking in drugs and people, selling stolen goods, and prostitution; (2) infiltrating legitimate businesses and unions through threat and intimidation and using bankruptcy and fraud to exploit and devastate a legitimate company; and (3) racketeering—the extortion of funds in exchange for protection (i.e., not being hurt). Activities such as a casino or trash collection service often appear to be legitimate endeavors on the surface but may be cover operations for highly organized illegal crime rings.

Although the exact cost of organized crime in the United States is impossible to determine, estimates of the annual gross income of organized-crime activity range from $50 billion to $90 billion per year (CNBC 2010; Siegel 2011). Internationally, criminal proceeds for all transnational organized crime is estimated at $870 billion a year (United Nations Office on Drugs and Crime 2014a).

Transnational organized crime takes place across national boundaries, using sophisticated electronic communications and transportation technologies. The major crime clans in the world include (a) Hong Kong–based organized-crime organizations, (b) South American cocaine cartels, (c) Italian mafia, (d) Japanese *yakuza*, (e) Russian *Mafiya*, (f) West African crime groups, and (g) Mexican cartels. Each operates across borders. Organized crime is responsible for thousands of deaths every year through drug trafficking and murders and contributes to the climate of violence in many cities (Matthews 2014; Siegel 2011).

Occupational Crime. Bernard (Bernie) Madoff, a well-respected investor and former chair of the NASDAQ stock exchange, developed a Ponzi scheme that was probably the largest investment fraud Wall Street has ever seen. The scheme defrauded and wrecked thousands of investors, public pension funds, charitable foundations, and universities of billions of dollars, with more than $65 billion missing from investor accounts when the scam became public in 2008. Named after Charles Ponzi, the first to be caught (in 1919), Ponzi schemes involve promises of large returns on investments, paying old investors with money from new investors. Money is simply shifted among investors to make it appear as though the investments earn money ("Madoff Case" 2009). Meanwhile, those running the scam pocket enormous sums of the money invested.

Ponzi schemes are one example of white-collar or occupational crime, *a violation of the law committed by an individual or a group in the course of a legitimate, respected occupation or financial activity* (J. W. Coleman 2006; Hagan 2011). Occupational crime can be committed by individuals from virtually any social class, and it can occur at any organizational level. However, most often this refers to white-collar crimes.

These crimes receive less attention than violent crimes because they are less visible, do not always cause obvious physical injury to identifiable people, and are frequently committed by people in positions of substantial authority and prestige. Reports of violent crimes that appear on the television news each night attract more attention. Yet occupational crime is far more costly in money, health, and lives. Victims of financial scams who have lost their life savings or workers who have lost their good health because of unsafe and illegal work conditions are well aware of this.

Sociologists divide occupational crimes into four major categories: (1) against the company, (2) against employees, (3) against customers, and (4) against the general public or other organizations (Hagan 2011).

Crimes against the company include pilfering (using company resources, such as the photocopy machine, for personal business) and employee theft (taking company supplies for your own use, stealing from the till, and embezzlement). Those who commit occupational crimes say they do so for several reasons. First, they feel little or no loyalty to the organization, especially if it is large and impersonal. It is like stealing from nobody, they say. Second, workers feel exploited and resentful toward the company. Stealing is getting back at the company. Third, the theft is seen as a "fringe benefit" or "informal compensation" that they deserve. Such workers may spend time on a side business while at work or take paper and ink cartridges for their printer at home. Fourth, workers may steal because of the challenge. It makes the job more interesting if they can get away with it. It is important to note that these people do not see themselves as criminals, especially compared with "street" criminals (Altheide et al. 1978).

The other three types of corporate crime benefit the company at the expense of employees or members of the larger society. *Crimes against employees* refer to corporate neglect of worker safety. In 1970, the U.S. government established the Occupational Safety and Health Administration (OSHA) to help enforce regulations to protect workers, but there are still many problems. Government agencies estimate that the death rate each year from job-related illness and injuries is *5 times* the number of deaths from street crimes. For example, 1 out of every 5 cancer cases has been traced to pollutants in workplaces, and many of these cases were preventable (Simon 2006; U.S. Bureau of Labor Statistics 2014a).

Wage theft, underpaying or not paying workers, is another widespread corporate crime that harms millions of workers. Many employers do not pay workers their due wages by requiring them to work "off the clock," not paying them minimum wage, stealing their tips, not paying them overtime, refusing to give them their last check, or simply not paying them at all. A 2009 study revealed that almost half (43.6%) of low-wage, urban U.S. workers surveyed had experienced wage theft during the previous year (Bernhardt et al. 2009). In 2012 alone, nearly $1 billion was recovered for those who reported wage theft (almost 3 times the total reported stolen in robberies in 2012). This is no doubt much less than the true amount of money lost to wage theft that year, given the fact that relatively few people report wage theft (for fear of retribution) (Meixell and Eisenbrey 2014).

Neglect of worker safety is a particularly serious problem in many developing or peripheral countries trying to attract multinational corporations with low taxes, cheap labor, and few regulations. The decisions of many corporations and factory owners illustrate *rational choice theory*. Too often they decide the benefits (profit) that come from exploiting labor outweigh the costs (harm to workers). The collapse of a shoddily constructed factory building in Bangladesh that killed 1,127 workers in 2013 is a powerful example of what can result from this type of thinking.

Reuters/Andrew Biraj

Employees in the Rana Plaza building in Bangladesh made clothing for many multinational apparel companies that failed, along with the building owner, to ensure that they had a safe place to work. This is an example of corporate crime against employees.

As *strain theorists* point out, almost all corporations have the goal of making the greatest short-term profit possible, and one (deviant) method to do that is to cut expenses at the expense of worker safety. Government regulatory agencies responsible for reducing environmental hazards and workplace dangers do not have sufficient staff to police companies for adherence to laws. Internationally, there is little oversight. Multinational corporations generally look for the cheapest labor costs and fewest environmental regulations, and governments of poor countries try to attract foreign corporations to keep the poor populace employed regardless of the environmental or workplace health and safety consequences.

Since the building collapse in Bangladesh, momentum is (for the moment, at least) on the side of workers' rights organizations. After the government had done nothing following several factory fires that killed hundreds of workers, the building collapse was the last straw for many workers in Bangladesh and for millions of people seeing the carnage in the media. Protesters took to the streets in Bangladesh and across the world. This organized outrage has led to promises from the Bangladeshi government to raise the minimum wage for workers and ease antiunion laws. Many multinational corporations, fearing further negative exposure, have pledged to ensure better working conditions for Bangladeshi workers who make their products.

Consumers, as well as workers, can be victims of corporate crime. *Crimes against customers* involve acts victimizing patrons, such as selling dangerous foods or unsafe products, consumer fraud, deceptive advertising, and price-fixing (i.e., setting prices in collusion with another producer). The purpose of advertising is to convince customers to buy the product—appealing to their vanity, sexual interests, or desire to keep up with their neighbors. Sometimes, these techniques cross the line between honesty and deception, and customers purchase defective and even dangerous products—all with the full knowledge of company officials.

Crimes against the public include acts by companies that negatively affect large groups of people. One example is hospitals or medical offices that overbill the federal government's health insurance programs, Medicare and Medicaid, or insurance companies pressuring hospitals to discharge patients too early to save on costs. Surreptitiously dumping pollutants into landfills, streams, or the air is another crime against the public. Proper disposal of contaminants can be costly and time-consuming for a company, but shortcuts can cause long-term effects for the public (J. W. Coleman 2006). Pollutants from industrial wastes have caused high rates

of miscarriages, birth defects, and diseases among residents. For examples of white-collar environmental crimes, see the Environmental Protection Agency's Press page at www.justice.gov/enrd/press-room.

These examples help illustrate that white-collar crime committed by company executives is, by far, our most serious crime problem. The economic cost of white-collar crime is vastly greater than the economic cost of street crime. White-collar criminals kill considerably more people than all violent street criminals put together (J. W. Coleman 2006; Reiman and Leighton 2012).

⬤ **Thinking Sociologically**

Why are meso-level crimes (occupational/white-collar crimes) more dangerous and more costly to the public than micro-level crimes? Why do they get so much less attention?

NATIONAL AND GLOBAL CRIME: MACRO-LEVEL ANALYSIS

As we have seen, national boundaries continue to blur as people migrate around the globe and many corporations move headquarters across national lines in search of lower costs and higher profits. As we have discussed, crime syndicates, too, are multinational, as they move money, goods, and people surreptitiously across borders. Likewise, terrorist organizations have no boundaries. We now turn to the macro-level crime of terrorism.

Terrorism is *the planned use of random unlawful (or illegal) violence or the threat of violence against civilians to create (or raise) fear and intimidate citizens in order to advance the terrorist group's political or ideological goals* (U.S. Department of Defense 2011). Terrorist groups can be anarchist, state sponsored, right wing or left wing, nationalist, or religious (Rice 2013; Schmalleger 2006). Table 6.1 shows the major types of terrorist groups.

Governments can commit *state-organized crime*. Often overlooked by the public and by social scientists, this form of crime includes acts defined by law as criminal but committed by state or government officials. For example, a government might be complicit in smuggling, assassination, or torture, which is then justified in terms of "national defense." Government offices may also violate laws that restrict or limit government activities such as eavesdropping. In some countries, political prisoners, such as the Guantánamo Bay detainees held in Cuba by the

Table 6.1 Types of Terrorist Groups

Anarchist	Some contemporary antiglobalization groups
State sponsored	Hezbollah (Iran), Abu Nidal Organization (Syria)
Right wing	Neo-Nazis, skinheads, White supremacists; paramilitary groups in Colombia
Left wing	Revolutionary Armed Forces of Colombia (FARC); Revolutionary People's Liberation Party-Front, Turkey
Nationalist	Irish Republican Army, Basque Fatherland and Liberty
Religious	Al-Qaeda, Hamas, ISIS (Iraq and Syria), Aum Shinrikyo (Japan)

Sources: Rice (2013); Schmalleger (2006).

United States, are imprisoned for long periods without charges, without access to lawyers, and without trials, and some have been tortured, violating both national and international laws (Center for Constitutional Rights 2013). The U.S. Supreme Court has ruled (2006 and 2008) that the U.S. administration violated the rights of these people (Global Security 2009). The Obama administration planned to shut down the Guantánamo Bay facility in 2010, but that closure has not yet occurred, and as we write these words, 76 detainees remain at "Gitmo" (Human Rights First 2015; Savage and Erlanger 2015). Although countries may violate their own laws, it is difficult to prosecute when the guilty party is the government.

Bribery and corruption are the way of life in many governments, businesses, and police forces. The percentage of citizens who said that they had paid a bribe to obtain services is as high as 79% in Nigeria, 72% in Cambodia, and 71% in Albania. The institutions perceived to be most affected by corruption globally include political parties, the police, the judiciary, legislatures, and business (Transparency International 2012). Figure 6.7 shows an index of the perception of corruption (from 1 to 10) in various countries around the world.

⬤ Thinking Sociologically

Sometimes, government officials and even heads of state are the perpetrators of crimes. When, if ever, is it justified for a government official to violate the law of the nation?

The forms of global corruption are too extensive to catalog here, so we will settle for an illustration of one of the newest manifestations of global crime against people and property: cybercrime. Internet deviance or cyberspace crime is growing at an incredible rate. This new world of crime ranges from online identity theft and gambling to cybersex and pornography, to hate sites and stalking, to hacking into government and military files, to terrorist recruiting sites.

Corporations are finding it necessary to spend increasing amounts of money on protecting themselves from cyberattacks but still often find themselves vulnerable. Since 2012, such attacks include the following:

- Breach of Target's computer system during the Christmas shopping season of 2013 that resulted in the theft of 40 million credit card numbers (and other personal information of customers)
- Simultaneous infiltration of JPMorgan Chase and 10 other financial firms that affected 83 million households and businesses
- Attack against Adobe System's security that resulted in hackers obtaining credit card information from 2.9 million customers and passwords from 38 million users
- Theft of the usernames and passwords of 50 million users of the LivingSocial site
- Attack on Advocate Health Care's computers, resulting in the theft of 4 million patient records
- Various cyberattacks from China and Russia
- North Korea's attack against Sony Pictures after the release of the movie *The Interview* (Baker 2015; Goldstein, Perloth, and Sanger 2014; S. Kim 2014; M. Riley et al. 2014)

Law enforcement gridlock due to national and international jurisdictional confusion impedes efforts to prevent such crime. For example, as many as five U.S. agencies can be involved in preventing financial fraud on the Internet, not to mention the state and local agencies that might play a role. If the fraud involves international cybercrime, the customs services and other branches of government also

FIGURE 6.7   Corruption Percentage Index, 2015

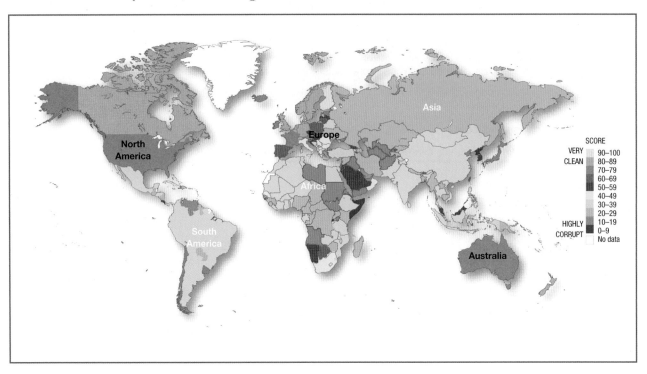

Note: Data for Africa are WHO estimates.

Source: Reprinted from CPI (2015). Copyright CPI 2015 Transparency International: the global coalition against corruption. Used with permission. For more information, visit www.transparency.org.

may enter the investigation. The resulting confusion and lack of clear authority means the federal government does not have an effective way to make companies safeguard their customers' information or to coordinate effective defenses against such illegal cyber intrusions from other nations ("Cybercrime: Smoking Gun" 2013; Perlroth and Sanger 2013). Recognizing these problems, the Obama administration pressed Congress to pass legislation to effectively deal with such crimes and also put into place an executive order that "authorizes financial and travel sanctions against anyone involved in attacks originating or directed from outside the country that pose 'a significant threat to the national security, foreign policy or economic health or financial stability of the United States'" (Baker 2015). Although systematic examination of national and international crime is important, we turn now to another macro issue: a comparison of crime across nations.

Cross-National Comparison of Crimes

The vending machine was on the corner near the Ballantines' house in Japan. The usual cola, candy, and sundries were displayed, along with cigarettes, beer, whiskey, sake, and pornographic magazines. Out of curiosity, Jeanne and her family watched to see who purchased what from the machine, and not once did they see teenagers sneaking the beer, cigarettes, or porn. It turns out that the Ballantines were not the only ones watching! The neighbors also kept an eye on who did what. Because of the stigma attached to deviant behavior in Japan, teens tend to avoid violating norms, and vigilant neighbors help keep the overall amount of deviance low. The many eyes in the neighborhood remind people that deviant behavior is unacceptable and provide informal social control over those who might be tempted to commit crimes.

Japan and the United States are both modern, urban, industrial countries, but their crime rates and the way they deal with deviant behavior and crimes differ. The overall crime rate in the United States is 3 times that of Japan, and the U.S. murder rate is almost *10 times* higher. Japan has 0.5 murders for every 100,000 people, whereas the United States has 4.6 per 100,000 residents (Cowen and Williams 2012; FBI 2014; Spacey 2012).

How can these extreme differences in crime rates be explained? Researchers look at cultural differences: Japan's low violent-crime rate is due, in part, to Japan's culturally homogeneous society and loyalty to a historic tradition of cooperation that provides a sense of moral order, a network of group relations, strong commitment to social norms, and respect for law and order. The example of vending machines in Japan illustrates this idea. In addition, guns are outlawed and much harder to come by in Japan.

Japan does not attain its lower crime rate through heavy investment in its criminal justice system. In fact, the Japanese government actually spends far less of its gross national product on the police, courts, and prisons than does the United States. For many crimes in Japan, the offender may simply be asked to write a letter of apology. This is frequently a sufficient sanction to deter the person from further violation of the law. The humiliation of writing an apology and the fear of shame and embarrassing one's family are strong enough to curb deviant behavior (Lazare 2004). Figure 6.8 provides a picture of the homicide rates per 100,000 individuals in the population in various parts of the world.

Although comparing cross-national data on crime is difficult because there are variations in the definitions of crime and the measurements used, comparisons do give us some insight into what types of crimes are committed, under what circumstances, and how often. Two sources of international data are Interpol (the International Criminal Police

Organization) and the United Nations. Although these organizations collect and present data, they have limited ways to check the accuracy of the data they receive from countries.

Global Crimes

Increasingly, crimes are global in nature. Some scholars use the *world systems theory* to understand global crime, arguing that the cause of global crime lies in the global economy, the inequalities between countries, and the competition between countries for resources and wealth. As a result of the capitalist mode of production, an unequal relationship has arisen between core nations (the developed, wealthy nations in the Global North) and peripheral nations (the Global South). Core nations often take unfair advantage of peripheral nations. Peripheral nations, in turn, must find ways to survive in this global system, and they sometimes turn to illegal methods—such as violating global environmental standards—to achieve their goals (Chase-Dunn and Anderson 2006). Some nations, though not wealthy, have many natural resources and are semiperipheral nations. Benefiting from extensive trade, they are less vulnerable than the poorest nations. Figure 6.9 helps you see where some of these core, semiperipheral, and peripheral nations are located.

FIGURE 6.8 Global Homicide Rates (per 100,000 People, by Country or Territory), 2012

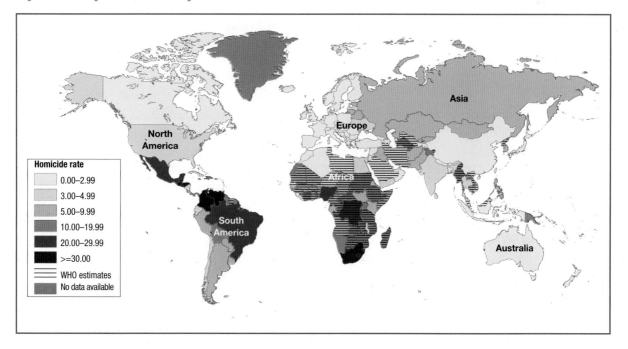

Note: Data for Africa are WHO estimates.

Source: United Nations Office on Drugs and Crime (2013). Reprinted with the permission of the United Nations.

FIGURE 6.9   Core, Semiperipheral, and Peripheral Countries of the World

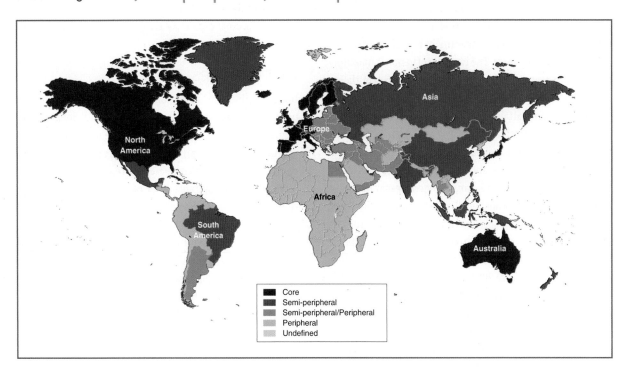

Source: Map by Anna Versluis.

As you look at this map, note that the developed or affluent countries are almost all located in the Northern Hemisphere. Although some poor countries are north of the equator, the pattern is obvious. To avoid some misleading implications of the words *developed* and *developing*, many scholars now prefer the term *Global South* to refer to less affluent nations. If you hear the term Global South, this map should help you see why it refers to developing or poor countries.

CONTROLLING CRIME: SOCIAL POLICY CONSIDERATIONS

What is the best way to control crime? Whereas all modern societies have criminal justice systems, their crime prevention strategies vary. We now look at the mechanisms used by societies to curb deviant behavior and punish deviants.

Dealing With Crime: The Criminal Justice Process

Structural-functionalists see the justice system as a crucial means of ensuring order and social control in society.

Conflict theorists, on the other hand, argue that the criminal justice system works in the interest of those in power, at the expense of the other members of society. It is in the interests of those in power to maintain the image that crime is primarily the work of outsiders and the poor. This deflects citizen discontent and hostility from the powerful and helps them retain their positions of power (Reiman and Leighton 2012). Conflict theorists point out that there will always be crime in society because the powerful will make sure that some things and some people are labeled deviant.

Depending on whether one uses a structural-functional or conflict theoretical perspective, criminal justice policy generally focuses either on how to deter deviant acts or on the injustices of the criminal justice system. In the United States today, prisons provide one of the primary means of controlling individual criminal behavior. Think about which theoretical perspective, structural-functionalism or conflict theory, you would use to better understand the function of prisons in U.S. society as you read the following section.

Prisons. Prisons are a form of *total institution* that completely controls the prisoners and regulates all of their activities. Inmates' lives are drastically changed through the processes of *degradation*, which marks the individual as deviant, and *mortification*, which breaks down the individual's original self as the inmate experiences resocialization (Goffman 1961; J. Irwin 1985; J. Irwin and Owen 2007). The inmate cannot have any personal property. Guards allow prisoners only limited communication and often verbally abuse inmates. Uniforms and standard buzz cuts (for men) are required, and inmates have strictly controlled schedules.

In a famous study that simulated a prison situation, researchers illustrated the social organization that develops and the roles that individuals play within the prison system. College students were assigned roles as prisoners or prison guards. Within a short time, the individuals in the study were acting out their roles and behaving in ways very different from their normal behavior outside of the prison situation. The students playing the role of "guard" became cruel and sadistic, causing the researcher, Philip Zimbardo, to end the experiment early. Participants had taken their roles so seriously that the abuse was beginning to have alarming consequences (Zimbardo et al. 1973). The recent abuse of prisoners in Iraq and at Guantánamo Bay prison parallels the findings from Zimbardo's earlier study of the roles that develop in these social situations (Zimbardo 2004).

Conflict theorists believe that social class and the demographic makeup of prisons reveal that prisons are mostly about controlling or "managing" minorities and poor people, not about public safety. Black males, for example, are more than 5 times more likely to be incarcerated than White men,

The U.S. has 5% of the world's population but 25% of all prisoners. Conditions—like this in Mule Creek State Prison in California—are not conducive to rehabilitation, and the incarcerated are disproportionately minorities.

and Black women are 2.5 times more likely than White women to be imprisoned (Fathi 2009; Sentencing Project 2014). Although Whites made up 63% of the overall population of the United States in 2011, just 35% of U.S. prisoners were White (Sentencing Project 2014). The makeup of U.S. prisons is presented in Table 6.2.

The recent decrease in incarceration rates in the United States stems from more people being released from prison due to overcrowding and fewer lockups for minor offenses. Still, the War on Drugs and zero-tolerance policies (which prevent judges from adjusting punishments to fit particular circumstances) keep the prison population in the United States high compared with that in any other

Table 6.2 Characteristics of People in Prison

	Percentage of U.S. Population*	Percentage of U.S. Prison Population	Ratio of the Population 30–34 Years Old in Prison	Chance of Spending Time in Prison During Lifetime
Black	12.6%	38%	1:13	32%
Hispanic	16.3%	21%	1:36	17%
White	63.7%	35%	1:90	6%

Source: Sentencing Project (2014).

*According to the 2010 U.S. Census (www.census.gov/prod/cen2010/briefs/c2010br-02.pdf).

Table 6.3 World Comparative Rates of Incarceration (per 100,000 People), 2013

Top 10 Countries (a)		Other Industrialized Countries (b)	
United States	716	England and Wales	148
St. Kitts and Nevis	649	Australia	133
Virgin Islands	539	Canada	118
Rwanda	527	France	103
Cuba	510	Italy	100
Seychelles	490	Switzerland	87
Russia	490	Netherlands	82
Anguila	487	Germany	78
Georgia	473	Sweden	60

Source: (a) Wing (2013); (b) International Center for Prison Studies (2014).

FIGURE 6.10 U.S. State and Federal Prison Population, 1925–2013

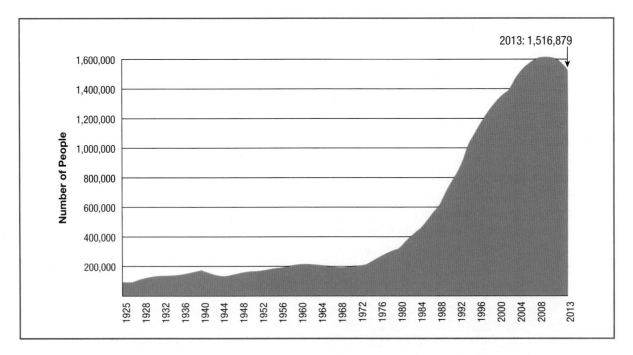

Source: Sentencing Project (2015).

Global North country and account for the highest number of causes for imprisonment (M. Alexander 2011; Guerino, Harrison, and Sabol 2011). In fact, the 2013 U.S. incarceration rate of 716 per 100,000 people is the highest in the world (Wing 2013). Although the United States contains only 5% of the world population, it has 25% of the world's prisoners (Kirchhoff 2010). Nearly half (48%) of prisoners in federal prisons were sentenced for drug offenses

(Carson and Sabol 2012). Table 6.3 compares incarceration rates among countries with the highest percentages of people in prison and among other industrialized nations. See Figure 6.10 for an illustration of the rapid growth of incarceration in the United States, despite the drop in crime rates.

Thinking Sociologically

Why do you think the United States has 5% of the world's population but 25% of the world's prisoners? How has this impacted your life? Why? How do you think your age, gender, social class, and race influenced your answer?

The Purposes of Prisons. What purpose do you believe prisons serve? From the structural-functional perspective, prisons serve several purposes for society: (a) fulfilling the desire for revenge or retribution, (b) removing dangerous people from society, (c) deterring would-be deviants, and (d) rehabilitating deviants through counseling, education, and work-training programs inside prisons (R. Johnson 2002). However, in prison, inmates are exposed to more criminal and antisocial behavior, so rehabilitation and deterrence goals are often undermined by the nature of prisons. According to a recent Bureau of Justice Statistics analysis, 4% of prison, 3.2% of jail, and 1.8% of juvenile inmates reported being sexually assaulted by other prisoners or prison guards from 2011 to 2012 (and relatively few victims actually report such assaults) (Beck et al. 2014; Bozelko 2015). This ongoing problem of assault, rape, and the threat of violence in prison so brutalizes inmates that it becomes difficult for them to reenter society as well-adjusted citizens ready to conform to societal norms (Fathi 2009; Hensley, Koscheski, and Tewksbury 2005; Liptak 2008). The federal Prison Rape Elimination Act of 2003 was supposed to curtail prison rapes, but as of 2015, only two states, New Hampshire and New Jersey, have fully followed the mandate of the act (Bozelko 2015).

Prisons and Profits. There is money to be made by locking up prisoners. All prisons can be a source of jobs for the communities in which they are located. Traditionally run by local, state, or federal governments, for-profit companies operate increasing numbers of prisons. Although privatization of prisons started in the 1980s, it has taken off in the last 2 decades. The number of people in private prisons has grown by 1,664% in the past 20 years, and today, approximately 130,000 people are in for-profit institutions (Wade 2013a). Seven states put more than 1 of every 4 of their prisoners in private prisons (Carson and Sabol 2012; S. Lee 2012).

Prison privatization advocates claim that private businesses driven by a profit motive and competition will operate prisons more efficiently. Private prisons can save on labor costs by not paying the high benefits that states must pay to employees. Those against privatization argue that incarcerating (imprisoning) people for profit is a bad idea, morally and financially. They point out that the cost per prison often rises after the initial contract with the state (Adrian Smith 2012). Some states must incarcerate a certain number of people due to contracts with private prisons, thereby manipulating the criminal justice system (Kirkham 2012). When profit motive is the bottom line, these critics argue, quality of food, training of guards, health care, educational opportunities, and other treatment of inmates can deteriorate.

Profits are also found through inmate labor. As of 2013, 37 states and Washington, DC, had legalized the contracting of prison labor to private corporations. Whereas prisoners in some state prisons receive minimum wage, many receive less. Private prisons pay workers just a pittance. CCA in Tennessee pays the most—50 cents per hour for the highest skilled positions (Pelaez 2014). These low wages lead to high profit margins for those invested in these companies, and business for such contracts is booming (Pelaez 2014). The U.S. government uses prison labor to make much of its military equipment for soldiers (e.g., helmets and bulletproof vests). U.S. corporations that use prison labor include IBM, Boeing, Motorola, Microsoft, Dell, Compaq, Honeywell, Hewlett-Packard, Nortel, Lucent Technologies, Revlon, Macy's, Pierre Cardin, and Target Stores (Pelaez 2014).

In 2016, the U.S. Justice Department announced that it would stop using private prisons. Deputy Attorney General Sally Yates announced that the decision was based on research showing private prisons are less safe, less economically efficient, and provide fewer correctional services than those run by the government (Amnesty International 2016; Zapotosky and Harlan 2016).

As one step in an effort to revamp the U.S. criminal justice system, the Obama administration proposed releasing low-level, nonviolent drug offenders who have not committed serious crimes. Thousands of federal offenders could be eligible for early release, easing overcrowding in the prison population (K. Johnson 2014). The federal government's hope is that state criminal justice systems will follow the federal lead.

The Death Penalty. Crimes of murder, assault, robbery, and rape usually receive severe penalties because citizens consider them the most dangerous crimes. The most controversial (and irreversible) method of control is for the state to put the deviant to death. The most common argument for using the death penalty, more formally known as capital punishment, is to deter people from crime. The idea is that not only will the person who has committed the crime be punished, but also others will be deterred from committing such a crime because they know that the death penalty is a possibility for them too.

However, the death penalty does not deter murder (Alarcon and Mitchell 2011; Radelet and Lacock 2009). In addition, it costs far more to use the death penalty than prison as a punishment. For example, a study in California showed that over $4 billion has been spent on 13 executions there since 1978, a cost of $308 million per execution. Because of the costs of a capital trial, various appeals processes (many of which are mandated by law to avoid mistakes), and special death row incarceration requirements, the cost is much greater than for life imprisonment (Alarcon and Mitchell 2011).

Moreover, more murders occur in states with the death penalty than in those without it. In 2015, the average murder rate in death penalty states was 5.15 per 100,000 persons, whereas the average murder rate of states without the death penalty was 4.13 (Death Penalty Information Center 2017). Thirty-two states allow the death penalty, but a movement is now underway in several states with Republican legislatures to abolish it for financial and religious reasons (Death Penalty Information Center 2016; ProCon.org 2016).

Few Global North countries use the death penalty, and in 2007, the United Nations passed a resolution calling on all nations to abolish it as "cruel and unusual punishment" (Amnesty International 2012; United Nations News Center 2010). As you can see from Figure 6.11, the United States is one of the few countries that uses the death penalty. A total of 22 countries carried out executions in 2013, with Iran and Iraq having high numbers of executions, China's true numbers unknown but suspected to be in the thousands every year, Saudi Arabia with 79, and the United States with 39 (Amnesty International 2014). Only China and Yemen officially recorded more executions in 2010 than the United States (World Coalition 2012).

Thinking Sociologically

How can you explain the higher murder rates in U.S. states that have the death penalty? Why do you think the United States still allows for the death penalty when most nations do not?

FIGURE 6.11 Global Status of the Death Penalty, 2015

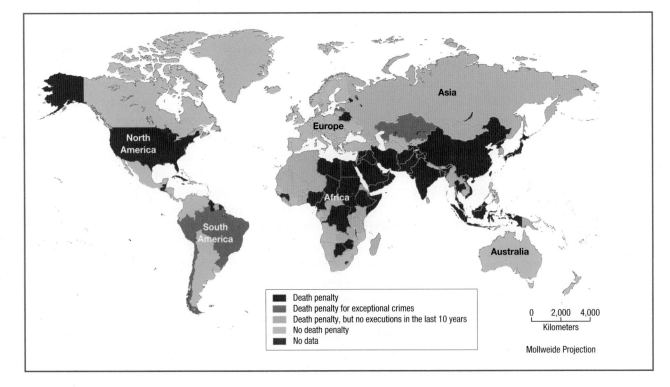

Source: Death Penalty Information Center (2015).

Race and class status relate to who receives the death penalty. In most U.S. states with capital punishment, a disproportionate number of minority and lower-class individuals are put to death. Of those executed since 1976, 56% have been White, and 34% have been Black. Yet the percentage of Blacks in the total population is less than 13%. In 2013, Maryland became the 18th state to abolish the death penalty. In describing why, the governor of the state said, "Maryland has effectively eliminated a policy that is proven not to work. Evidence shows that the death penalty is not a deterrent, it cannot be administered without racial bias, and it costs three times as much as life in prison without parole" (Sutton 2013).

These problems with the death penalty have led to a search for alternative means to deter crime and spurred policy analysts to rethink assumptions about what factors are effective in controlling human behavior.

Alternative Forms of Social Control

Recidivism rates—*the likelihood that someone who is arrested, convicted, and imprisoned will later be a repeat offender*—are very high. More than half of all men who do time in prison will be confined again for a crime (Quinney 2002; Siegel 2011). Efforts to reduce recidivism include high-quality schools, preventing young people from entering the criminal justice system in the first place, and methods of treatment other than brutalizing incarceration for those who do find themselves in trouble with the law.

It is difficult to determine how best to deter crime. Not many people think that the apology technique used in Japan would work as a deterrent to crimes in other countries. On the other hand, there is a wide range of options available for dealing with crime other than harsh (and expensive) punishments. Seeing how other countries control crime can help us take a new look at our assumptions and come up with creative new solutions that do work. For example, is the War on Drugs having more of a positive or negative impact on crime? What can we learn from how other nations deal with drugs? How might the legalization of marijuana in some U.S. states affect incarceration rates?

Sociologists use comparative studies and evaluation research of current policies to help determine the best strategies for crime and recidivism deterrence. For example, evidence shows that prison education, job training, and substance abuse programs can be used to reduce criminal justice expenses by allowing some prisoners to "earn" reduced sentences. These programs also lead to lower recidivism rates (Lawrence 2009).

Thinking Sociologically

How has what you read in this chapter affected your ideas about deviance, crime, and the criminal justice system?

One of the dominant characteristics of modern society is social inequality, and as we have seen, inequality is often an issue in criminal activity. Indeed, many of our social problems are rooted in issues of inequality. Extreme inequality may even be a threat to the deeper values and dreams of a society, especially one that stresses individualism and achievement. In the following three chapters, we look at three types of inequality: socioeconomic, ethnic or racial, and gender-based inequity.

WHAT HAVE WE LEARNED?

Deviance is socially constructed and varies across time and societies. What is considered deviant now may not be considered deviant in another place or time. All societies must fashion responses to deviant behaviors that can threaten their stability and safety. The criminal justice system tends to be a conservative force in society because of its focus on ensuring social conformity.

To make our society run more smoothly, we must understand why deviance and crime happen. Good policy must be based on accurate information and careful analysis of the information. We must also understand that deviance and conformity operate at various levels in the social world: micro, meso, and macro. In addition, it is important to understand that there may be positive aspects of deviance for any society, from uniting society against deviants to providing creative new ways to solve problems.

- Deviance—the violation of social norms, including those that are formal laws—has both positive and negative consequences for individuals and for society.

- We can use many sociological theories to explain deviance: rational choice theory and symbolic interaction's anomie and labeling theories at the micro level; structural functional theory's social control, differential association, and strain theory; and conflict and feminist theory at the meso and macro level.

- Many of the formal organizations concerned with crime (such as the FBI and the media) focus on crimes involving individuals—predatory crimes, crimes without victims, and hate crimes—but the focus on these crimes may blind us to occupational crimes that actually are more harmful and costlier to society.

- At the meso level, organized and occupational crimes cost billions of dollars and pose a great risk to thousands of lives. Occupational crime may be against the company, employees, customers, or the public.

- At the macro level, national governments sometimes commit state-organized crimes, sometimes in violation of their own laws or in violation of international laws. These crimes may be directed against their own citizens (usually minorities) or people from other countries.

- Also at the macro level, some crimes are facilitated by global networks and by global inequities of power and wealth.

- Controlling crime has generated many policy debates, from the use of prisons to the death penalty to alternative approaches to the control of deviance.

DISCUSSION QUESTIONS

1. List five acts that were once considered deviant but are now considered acceptable or even courageous. Have you ever committed a deviant act because you believed it was the moral thing to do? If yes, please explain why. If not, in what sort of situation might you consider carrying out a deviant act?

2. Have you ever been labeled deviant? Why, or why not? How does your social class, level of education, gender, race or ethnicity, and nation of origin impact the chances you will be considered deviant in your country?

3. Which of the following theories of deviance described in the chapter—rational choice, differential association, labeling theory, social control, anomie and social disorganization, strain theory, and conflict theory—best explains the recent increase in cheating among college students? Why?

4. Why is occupational crime not given as much attention as violent crime? What are some examples of occupational crimes that hurt millions of Americans every day? Have you ever been the victim of one of these crimes? What would you suggest policymakers do to curb these crimes?

5. How do conflict theorists explain the makeup of prisoners in the U.S. prison system? Do you agree with their explanation? Why, or why not?

6. How can social capital help keep people out of prison and help former prisoners avoid returning to prison? How will your social capital help you conform (or not conform) to the norms of society?

KEY TERMS

CONTRIBUTING TO OUR SOCIAL WORLD: WHAT CAN WE DO?

At the Local (Micro) Level

- *LGBT groups* support lesbian, gay, bisexual, and/or transgender students. The Consortium of Higher Education LGBT Resource Professionals, a national organization of college and university groups, maintains a website at www.lgbtcampus.org. Regardless of your own sexual identity or orientation, consider contacting your campus LGBT group, attending meetings, and participating in its support and public education activities.

- *Boys and Girls Clubs* provide local programs and services to promote healthy development by instilling a sense of competence, usefulness, and belonging in young people. Organizations for youth like Boys and Girls Clubs need interns and volunteers to provide role models for youth. Consider volunteering to help children with homework or activities. You can find a club near you by going to www.bgca.org/whoweare/Pages/FindaClub.aspx.

At the Organizational/Institutional (Meso) Level

- The extensive and rapidly growing *criminal justice system* in the United States focuses on crime prevention, law enforcement, corrections, and rehabilitation. Identify the aspect of the system that interests you most, and using faculty and community contacts, select an appropriate organization for volunteer work, an internship, or a job.

- *Criminal courts* play a central role in the administration of criminal justice, and trials are often open to the public. Attending a trial and/or contacting a judge or magistrate could provide a good introduction to the court system and some of the people who work within it.

- *Crime prevention programs* are designed to reduce crime. You can find information about such programs at the National Crime Prevention Council at www.ncpc.org/programs. In order to obtain a better understanding as to what types of crime prevention programs are most effective, go to the Center for the Study and Prevention of Violence's (CSPV) Blueprints website at www.colorado.edu/cspv/blueprints.

At the National/Global (Macro) Levels

- *The Polaris Project* works to reduce global trafficking in women and children (www.polarisproject.org). Volunteers participate in letter-writing campaigns, support antitrafficking legislation, and conduct research on the problem.

- *The Equal Justice Initiative* (EJI) works with individuals, communities, and policymakers to curb discriminatory treatment in the criminal justice system due to poverty or racial bias. You can find information about EJI internships for recent college graduates and law students at www.eji.org/fellowships-internships.

$SAGE edge™

HOMELESS AND
PREGNAT!
ANYTHING HELPS

PART III

Inequality

Why are you rich, whereas others in your sociology class or community are poor—or vice versa? Why do some people rise to the top of society with wealth, power, and prestige at their fingertips, and others languish near the bottom? Does ethnicity, race, or gender affect your position in society? What are your chances of moving out of your current social position? These are the underlying questions in the following three chapters. They focus on stratification, how individuals and groups are layered or ranked in society according to how many valued resources they possess or to which they have access (e.g., wealth, power, and prestige). **Inequality** is *a social condition in which privileges, opportunities, and substantial rewards are given to people in some positions in society but denied to others.* At the very bottom of the human hierarchy are those starving and diseased world citizens who have no hope of survival for either themselves or their families. This compares with corporate executives and some world leaders who have billions of dollars at their disposal. The implications of social stratification extend from the individual all the way to global social networks.

Sometimes the basis for social stratification and inequality is one's socioeconomic status, but other characteristics such as race, ethnicity, gender, sexual orientation, nationality, religion, or age can also help determine where you fall in the social stratification system. These differences often result in strong feelings like us-versus-them thinking.

In this section, we focus on issues of social inequality related to social class, race, ethnicity, and gender. Chapter 7 focuses on local and global socioeconomic stratification resulting in inequality; subsequent chapters examine ethnic and gender stratification.

© Reuters/Romeo Ranoco

7 Stratification

Rich and Famous—or Rags and Famine?

Will you live under the bridge or above it—rags or riches? While hard work can often make a difference, your future success also depends on your society's system of stratification and amount of inequality.

MICRO

○ ME (AND MY RAGS OR RICHES)

○ LOCAL ORGANIZATIONS
AND COMMUNITY
How I am regarded by my peers.

MESO

● NATIONAL ORGANIZATIONS,
INSTITUTIONS, AND ETHNIC
SUBCULTURES
Institutions support the privileged; ethnic
subcultures are often disadvantaged.

MACRO

● SOCIETY
The privileged control resources, health
care, economic markets, and tax rates.

● GLOBAL COMMUNITY
Rich countries have more access to
resources than poor ones.

WHAT YOU WILL LEARN IN THIS CHAPTER

This chapter will help you do the
following:

7.1 Describe what social
stratification means for
individuals and groups.

7.2 Compare key theoretical
perspectives on stratification.

7.3 Explain how achieved and
ascribed characteristics
impact individuals' life
chances.

7.4 Explain what affects your
chances for social mobility.

7.5 Compare pluralist and
power elite perspectives on
stratification.

7.6 Discuss inequality and
poverty from a sociological
perspective.

7.7 Illustrate how the digital
divide helps stratify people.

◑ THINK ABOUT IT

Micro: Local community	Why are some people in your community wealthier than others?
Meso: National institutions, complex organizations, and ethnic groups	How do institutions—such as the family, education, religion, health, politics, and the economy—help keep people in the class they were born into?
Macro: National and global systems	Why are some nations affluent and others impoverished? How does the fact that we live in a global society affect you and your social position?

Pomp and circumstance surrounded the April 2, 2011, royal wedding of William, Prince of Wales (heir to the British throne), and Catherine (Kate) Middleton. All eyes in Britain and many eyes around the world were glued to their TVs and computer monitors. Thousands waited for hours to see the happy couple in person, as they lined the royal route to the palace. The wedding for this young couple included flower arrangements for $800,000, a wedding dress that cost about $400,000, and a cake for just under $80,000. The bill for the entire wedding (security included) came in at $70 million (Mawani 2011).

Members of royal families such as Prince William and Prince Harry of Britain grow up in a privileged world, with wealth, prestige, and access to power. Their lifestyles include formal receptions, horse races, polo games, royal hunts, state visits, and other social and state functions. The family has several elegant residences at its disposal.

Prince William and Kate with their royal children (Charlotte and George), Queen Elizabeth, and Prince Philip greet crowds on the Queen's 90th birthday. Prince William is second in line to inherit the throne of England, and young George in also now in line to someday be king.

However, like most royalty, William, Harry, and now Kate Middleton also live within the confines of their elite status, with its strict expectations and limitations. They cannot show up for a beer at the local pub or associate freely with commoners. Their family problems or casual antics are subject matter for front pages of tabloids, as seen in the behavior of Prince Harry during a trip to Las Vegas that thrilled the paparazzi and dismayed the royal household. Thanks to a cell phone camera, what he did in Vegas did not stay in Vegas. Although there is no official royalty in the United States, wealthy entrepreneurs, stock brokers and bankers, and entertainment and sports figures hold positions that allow for a life of comfort similar to that of royalty.

On the other hand, rags and famine pervade the planet. Hidden from the public eye in Britain and the United States are people with no known names and no swank addresses; some have no address at all. Around the globe, wars, natural disasters, famines, economic crises, slavery, and human trafficking point to the presence of inequality. **Inequality** is *a social condition in which privileges, opportunities, and substantial rewards are given to people in some positions in society but denied to others.*

Inequality leaves many people particularly vulnerable when natural and human-made disasters strike. For example, the earthquakes in Nepal in 2015 left a population already vulnerable due to poverty and political unrest even more at risk. With human trafficking and sexual violence rates increasing in makeshift camps for survivors, women began taking self-defense classes to prepare to fight off sexual predators (Rauniyar and Burke 2015).

As noted in Chapter 6, climate change and economic hard times have pushed many low-income people from their rural homes to cities in hopes of finding jobs. However, with few jobs for unskilled and semiskilled workers in today's postindustrial service economies, many of the poor are left homeless. They live in abandoned buildings or sleep in unlocked autos, on park benches, under bridges, on beaches, or anywhere they can stretch out and hope not to be attacked or harassed. In the United States, cities such as Houston, Los Angeles, Washington, DC, and New York try to cope with the homeless by setting up sanitary facilities and temporary shelters, especially in bad weather. Cities also rely on religious and civic organizations to run soup kitchens and shelters.

In 2013, 6.3 million children under the age of 5 died. In almost half (45%) of those deaths, malnutrition was an underlying cause (World Health Organization 2014b). Extreme poverty has fallen (almost in half) over the past couple of decades, but the figures are still staggering. In 2013, 10.7 percent of the world's population lived on less than $1.90 a day (World Bank 2017). Children raised in families with the lowest incomes grow up in poverty, with lack of electricity, clean water, education, sanitation, health care, and adequate food. They die of preventable diseases.

In some areas of the world, such as India and sub-Saharan Africa, the situation is particularly desperate, and many families are starving. At daybreak, a cart traverses the city of Kolkata (Calcutta), India, picking up bodies of diseased and starved homeless people who have died on the streets during the night. Mother Teresa, who won the Nobel Peace Prize for her work with those in dire poverty, established a home in India where these people could die with dignity. She also founded an orphanage for children who would otherwise wander the streets begging or lie on the sidewalk dying. The micro- and meso-level efforts of Mother Teresa and her fellow Missionaries of Charity are noble but only a small bandage on a massive macro-level social problem.

What group of people is lower on the social hierarchy than those living in the street? That would be *slaves*. It may surprise you to know that **slavery**—*when an individual or a family is bound in servitude as the property of a person or household, bought and sold, and forced to work*—is alive and flourishing around the world (Free the Slaves 2015). An estimated 21 to 36 million people, mostly women and children from poor families in poor countries, are slaves, auctioned off or lured into slavery each year by gangs, pimps, and cross-border syndicates to work in forced labor or prostitution, as child soldiers or brides in forced marriages, or as children working on plantations or in factories (Free the Slaves 2015). Slavery caught the world's attention in April 2014 when the terrorist

The United States does not have royalty with inherited thrones and titles. However, it does have enormous gaps in wealth, with some people living in splendor and luxury beyond the imagination of the average citizen.

New York, like most cities, has a large homeless population. This person seeks shelter, and some sleep in a New York subway station.

organization Boko Haram kidnapped close to 300 Nigerian schoolgirls to sell into slavery and give to men as wives. The group argues that women are the property of men and instruments of reproduction; girls, according to Boko Haram, should not receive an education, especially not a Western education.

FIGURE 7.1   Where in the World Slaves Live

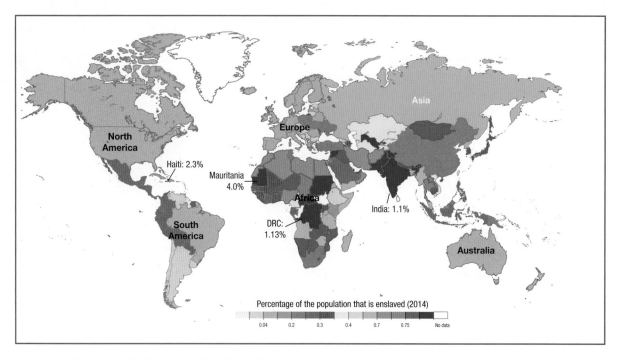

Percentage of the population that is enslaved (2014)

0.04   0.2   0.3   0.4   0.7   0.75   No data

A global phenomenon, slavery exists in all of the 162 countries studied by Walk Free Foundation (2013). Mauritania has the most slaves (1 in every 25 members of the population). Next is Haiti, with many children in slavery, followed by India and Pakistan. Sex trafficking is most common in South Asia and Eastern Europe (especially Ukraine), Myanmar (Burma), Laos, Nepal, and the Philippines. It is so profitable that businesspeople invest in involuntary brothels much as they would in a mining operation (Bales 2007, 2012; Bales and Trodd 2008). Today, approximately 60,000 people (1 in every 5,000 members of the U.S. population) are enslaved in the United States (Walk Free Foundation 2013). Figure 7.1 provides a visual image of where most slaves in the world are located.

The average U.S. citizen eats over 11 pounds of chocolate (that's 120 bars) a year, and 83% drink coffee (Perez 2013). However, the ugly side of these addictions and treats is that over 70% of the production of chocolate is from West Africa (Ivory Coast and Ghana), and most involves child labor or child slaves. Folgers, Maxwell House, Nescafe, and other major coffee companies import coffee from many plantations that use forced child labor and child slaves. Therefore, they pay very little for the coffee beans, allowing them to maintain high profit levels (Wilhoit 2014). A number of organizations, including Free the Slaves, Mercy Project, Slavery Footprint, and Ark of Hope for Children, work to stop and prevent child slavery. Buying *fair-trade certified* products means that production is free from abuse and exploitive labor practices, fair wages are paid, health and safety are observed, and sustainable methods are used. The two logos here are common ones for indicating that a product is fair trade.

As we write these words, at least 2.5 million people are suffering the abuse of *human trafficking*. A form of slavery, human trafficking consists of "the recruitment, transport, transfer, harbouring or receipt of a person by such means as threat or use of force or other forms of coercion, of abduction, of fraud or deception for the purpose of exploitation" (United Nations Office on Drugs and Crime [UNODC] 2014a). Most—but not all—victims of trafficking are women. The vast majority of trafficking (79%) results in the sexual exploitation of victims. Most other victims (18%) find themselves forced to work as slaves (UNODC 2014a).

In the slavery of the 19th century, slaves were expensive, and there was at least some economic incentive to care about their health and survival so that they could be productive workers. In the new slavery, humans are cheap and replaceable. There is little concern about working them to death, especially if they are located in remote cacao, coffee, or sugar cane plantations. By current dollars, a slave in the southern United States in the mid-1800s would have cost the equivalent of $40,000 today, but contemporary slaves are cheap. They can be procured from poor countries for an average of $90 (Bales 2012).

Many public sociologists are among those now working to address modern-day slavery. A sociologist most at the forefront of the current movement to eradicate slavery is featured in the next "Sociologists in Action."

Thinking Sociologically

Why do you think slavery exists today? List micro, meso, and macro forces at work that support modern slavery. What steps should be taken to combat each and eradicate slavery?

As we can see from the previous examples, our social world is stratified in ways that result in high levels of inequality. The rest of this chapter discusses (a) why stratification is important, (b) different systems of stratification, (c) the consequences of social rankings for individuals, (d) whether one can change social class positions (social mobility), (e) characteristics of major stratification systems, (f) poverty and social policies to address it, and (g) the global digital divide.

Child laborers fill up empty cigarettes manually with locally grown tobacco in a small bidi (cigarette) factory at Haragach in Rangpur district, Bangladesh, in 2013.

THE IMPORTANCE OF SOCIAL STRATIFICATION

Consider your own social ranking in society. You were born into a family that holds a position in society: upper, middle, or lower class. The position of your family influences the neighborhood in which you live and where you shop, go to school, play sports, engage in the arts or other activities, and attend religious services. Most likely, you and your family carry out the tasks of daily living in your community with people who share your social class status.

Your position in the stratification system affects the opportunities available to you and the choices you make in life. Note the social world model at the beginning of the chapter. It provides a visual image of the social world and socioeconomic stratification. The stratification process affects everything from individuals' social rankings at the micro level of analysis to positions of countries in the global system at the macro level.

Social stratification refers to *how individuals and groups are layered and ranked in society according to their access to and possession of valued resources*. The society's culture (rules, values, beliefs, and artifacts) determines and legitimizes the society's system of sorting its members.

SOCIOLOGISTS IN ACTION
KEVIN BALES

Stopping Slavery Today

Becoming an abolitionist sociologist crept up on me. The first tiny prodding was a leaflet I picked up at an outdoor event in London. The front of the leaflet read "There are Millions of Slaves in the World Today." I was a university professor, and I confess to an unpleasant mixture of pride and hubris in my reaction to the bold title of the leaflet. Having been involved in human rights for many years, I thought, *How could this be true if I don't know about it already?*

I came to understand why this issue was invisible. Slavery was hidden under a thick blanket of ignorance, concealed by the common assumption that it was extinct. With slavery illegal in every country, criminal slaveholders kept their activities hidden.

As I built up a picture of slavery, every new set of facts generated new questions. I began to realize that a large-scale research project was needed, and I went in search of modern slavery, traveling to India, Pakistan, Thailand, Mauritania, and Brazil—often going undercover as I studied slave-based businesses in each country. The result was the book *Disposable People: New Slavery in the Global Economy* ([1999] 2012 [3rd edition]).

In 2000, I, with three others, helped found Free the Slaves, the American sister organization of Anti-Slavery International, the world's oldest (1787) and original human rights group. Free the Slaves works with local partners to liberate slaves around the world and change the systems that allow slavery to exist. In addition to addressing the crime of enslavement, this work often involves confronting gender inequality, racism, ethnic and religious discrimination, and the negative outcomes of global economic growth. We have learned that freedom and empowerment are viral, and that freed slaves will stop at nothing to stay free and help others to liberty.

Not every part of liberation and reintegration requires sociological training, but it would be very hard to be successful without it. Without carefully constructed longitudinal surveys of villages in slavery we could never have demonstrated the *freedom dividend*, the powerful and positive economic change that comes to whole communities when slavery is abolished. Without training in the empathetic understanding of a social researcher, we could never have developed the *slavery lens*, a way of seeing this hidden crime that the U.S. government now requires of all of its foreign aid program workers. Without learning about the complex interplay of culture, society, economics, politics, and social vulnerability, we would never be able to build the unique methodologies of liberation tailored to specific and culturally rooted forms of slavery. And there is nothing like the ugly reality of a crime like slavery to push young sociologists to do their best work—using solid social science to change the world.

• •

Kevin Bales is a sociologist and professor of contemporary slavery at the Wilberforce Institute for the Study of Slavery and Emancipation (WISE) at the University of Hull, England, and cofounder of Free the Slaves in Washington, DC. This excerpt is taken from Korgen, White, and White's (2013) Sociologists in Action: Sociology, Social Change, and Social Justice.

Each society also determines what it considers to be valued resources. For example, in an agricultural society, members are ranked according to how much land or how many animals they own. In an industrial society, ownership of the *means of production* (machinery that can produce goods) and occupational skills determine class status. In postindustrial information societies, education, access to technology, and control of information dissemination are key determinants in the ranking process.

What members of each society value and the criteria they use to rank other members depends on events in the society's history, its geographic location, its level of development in the world, its political philosophy, and the decisions of those in power. The more powerful individuals tend to get the best positions, the most desirable mates, and the greatest opportunities. They may have power because of birth order, personality characteristics, age, physical attractiveness, education, intelligence, wealth, race, family background, occupation, religion, or ethnic group—whatever the basis for power is in that particular society. Those with relatively high amounts of power have advantages that perpetuate their power, and they try to hold on to those advantages through laws, customs, power, ideologies, and sometimes force. Note that each level of analysis—micro, meso, and macro—adds to our understanding of the stratification process.

Micro-Level Prestige and Influence

Remember how some of your peers on the playground were given more respect than others? Their high regard may have come from belonging to a prestigious family, having a dynamic or domineering personality, being good at games, or owning symbols that distinguished them— "cool" clothing or shoes, a desirable bicycle, or expensive toys. This is stratification at work.

Property, power, and prestige are accorded to those who have **cultural capital** (*knowledge, skills, language mastery, style of dress, and values that provide a person with access to a particular status in society*) and social capital (networks with others who have influence). Individual qualities, such as leadership skills, an engaging personality, self-confidence, quick-wittedness, and physical attractiveness, or ascribed characteristics, such as the most powerful gender or ethnic group, influence cultural

Even the sports one plays—such as polo or stickball—are greatly influenced by social class and convey different kinds of social and cultural capital. Polo clearly requires a good deal of economic capital in order to play, whereas stickball requires only a ball and a straight stick.

and social capital. Interactions with meso-level organizations help shape the influence of these individual traits.

Meso-Level Access to Resources

Many of the resources we use come from institutions at the meso level: family, education, religion, economic and political institutions, and health care. We first learn our social status and the roles associated with it through our interactions with family members. The socialization we undergo in our families influences how we see ourselves, how others perceive us, and our access to resources, such as education and jobs. For example, we learn grammar and manners from our families; that, in turn, affects how our teachers and peers view and judge us. Educational organizations treat children differently according to their social status, revealed through such symbols as language (e.g., if we speak standard English) and manners (e.g., not interrupting, saying please and thank you when appropriate, and addressing adults by their proper titles). Our education can result in differential access to prestigious jobs and affect our social status in society—and therefore our position in the social stratification hierarchy.

Macro-Level Factors Influencing Stratification

The global economic position of a nation affects the opportunities available to individuals in that nation, illustrating that macro-level factors also influence placement in the stratification system (see Figure 7.2). Haiti provides a powerful illustration of this fact. Located on the island of Hispaniola in the Caribbean, Haiti is the poorest country in the Western Hemisphere and one of the poorest countries in the world, with little technology, few resources, ineffective government, a very weak educational system, and an occupational structure based largely on subsistence farming. Even its forest resources are essentially gone due to desperately poor people cutting down the last trees for firewood and shelters, leaving the land to erode (J. Diamond 2005; World Bank 2015).

The 2010 earthquake and floods added to Haitians' economic woes and misery. Residents were driven from what meager shelters they had and then faced a cholera epidemic from contaminated water. Haitians now have very few opportunities to get ahead and be successful. This is but one example of macro-level factors (failing

FIGURE 7.2   Gross National Income per Capita in 2014

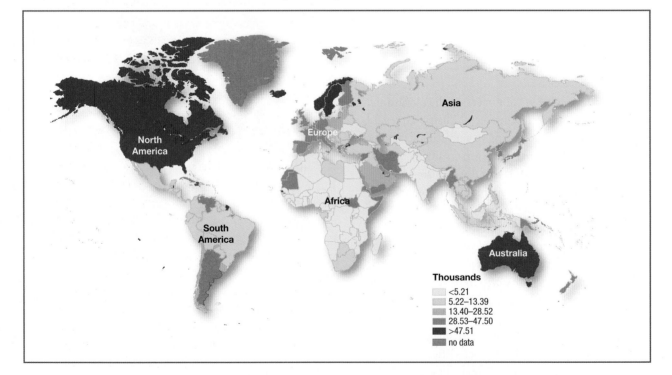

Source: World Bank (2016a).

economy; eroded land; lack of infrastructure, such as schools and health facilities; and lack of opportunity to participate in the global economy) affecting the opportunities available to people in the country. A major influx of international money has allowed for some public projects, but progress is slow as political tensions and instability increase ("Haiti" 2015).

Almost all societies stratify members, and societies themselves are stratified in the world system, so that each individual or nation experiences the world in unique ways related to its position. Stratification is one of the most powerful forces that we experience, but we are seldom conscious of how it works or how pervasive it is in our lives. This is the driving question sociologists ask when developing theories of stratification: How does it work?

● Thinking Sociologically

Place yourself in the center of the social world model. Working outward from micro-level interactions toward the meso-level institutions and the macro-level global stratification system, indicate what has influenced where you fall in the stratification system.

THEORETICAL EXPLANATIONS OF STRATIFICATION

As we traverse the world, we see continuous examples of rich and poor—those who have more resources than they need and those who do not have enough to survive. Why is the distribution of resources so uneven? Is the unequal distribution inevitable, healthy, or harmful for society?

Sociologists have developed theories to explain social stratification based on the lens through which they view society. These explanations range from individual micro-level to national and global macro-level theories (e.g., symbolic interaction, rational choice, structural-functional, and conflict theories).

Micro-Level Theory

Our now familiar theories that relate to the micro level help us again, this time, to understand differences among individuals in the stratification hierarchy.

Symbolic Interaction Theory. Have you ever been to a party where almost everyone came from a social class that had either much more or much less money than you? Even if you have not, you can probably imagine what it would be like. Awkward! Each social group has norms that members learn through the socialization process. These norms are recognized within that group and can make clueless outsiders feel very uncomfortable.

People learn what is expected in their groups—family, peer group, or social class—through interaction with others. For instance, children are rewarded or punished for behaviors appropriate or inappropriate to their social position. The socialization process transmits and perpetuates our positions in the social stratification system. Learning our position means learning values, speech patterns, consumption habits, appropriate group memberships (including political, economic, and religious affiliations), and even our self-concept. This knowledge provides us with the cultural capital necessary to interact effectively with people who share our social position.

Children start to learn cultural knowledge at home; they then bring that with them to school. Some home environments teach children to obey rules and authority and to develop hands-on skills, such as repairing houses and cars. Other families teach children by expanding vocabularies; developing good grammar; experiencing concerts, art, and theater; visiting historical sites; providing reading materials; and modeling engagement with reading. The higher-class parents tend to stress thinking and questioning skills, as opposed to primarily obeying authority figures. The result of this learning at home is that all children attain cultural capital that helps them interact with others at their social class level. The class difference in the types of cultural capital, though, means that children from the middle and upper classes or higher castes are more likely to get the best education, setting them up to be future leaders with better life chances. Schools place children into courses and academic groups, influenced, in part, by the labels children receive due to their cultural capital. In this way, children's home experiences and education help reproduce the social class systems and perpetuate the family's social class position in society (Ballantine, Hammack, and Stuber 2017).

Like language, other symbols can also represent social positions. Clothing, for example, sets up some people as special and privileged. In the 1960s, wearing blue jeans was a radical act by college students to reject status differences—showing solidarity with and support for the working class. Today, many young people wear expensive designer jeans that low-income people cannot afford.

Look at all those forks and knives. Some people know what to do with each of them! Knowing which fork or knife to use for each course of a meal is a sign of cultural capital that can influence your chances of acceptance into elite society or success on a job interview.

In India, many people must bathe in public in whatever water supply they can find. Even many people with homes do not have their own water supply. Privacy for one's grooming is a symbol of privilege for the affluent.

Drinking wine that most people do not have the means to buy, driving a Jaguar rather than a less expensive car, and living in a home that has six or eight bedrooms and is 5,000-plus square feet is an expression of *conspicuous consumption*—displaying goods in a way that others will notice and that will presumably earn the owner respect (Veblen 1902). Thus, purchased products become symbols

intended to define the person as someone of high status in the stratification hierarchy.

Privacy can also symbolize affluence. For example, in most of the Global North, one symbol of middle-class "decency" is the right to bathe and do one's grooming in private. Indeed, many young people in the United States have their own bedrooms and expect no interruptions when sprucing up for the day. Homeless people in the United States do not have this luxury, and in India, bathing on the streets is not uncommon. Privacy requires money.

Rational Choice Theory. As you know, rational choice theorists focus on individuals and the way they make decisions regarding their own self-interest. From this view, people make decisions influenced by their perception of costs and benefits. Some people evaluate potential benefits with a view to the long term. They are willing to endure short-term expense or "pain" if the long-term gains are substantial. In order to take this view, one needs a sense of delayed gratification—delaying rewards or benefits until a later time. People who are willing or in a position to do this—living austerely now in order to experience prosperity later—may be more likely to have upward mobility and to experience greater affluence at a later time. Whereas your friend from high school may have a job and drive a nicer car than you can afford, you may be building debts and attending college in hopes of a better future. Thus, rational choice theorists would focus on how personal choices influence one's place in the social system. The idea is that one's socioeconomic position is shaped largely by individual decisions. What, though, influences those individual decisions?

In high school, many college prep students make "rational" decisions to become involved in athletic programs, student council, the Spanish Club, leadership roles in the National Honor Society, or community service because they want to list those involvements on college applications. They commit effort now—sometimes in activities that they care little about—in hopes of having a payoff in admission or scholarships to the college of their choice. Those same students become discouraged with classmates who will not help with student council activities or with building the junior class float. However, for young people whose parents did not go to college and whose past experiences do not lead them to believe that they, themselves, could ever attain a college degree, spending time decorating a float makes no sense. It is not seen as a "rational" choice. Thus, past experiences and social position can influence the way one evaluates costs and benefits.

These micro-level theories help us to understand how our daily interactions and decisions can impact our social positions (and vice versa) within society's stratification hierarchy. We now look at theories that examine the larger social structures, processes, and forces that affect stratification and inequality: structural-functional theory and various forms of conflict theory.

Meso- and Macro-Level Theories

Structural-Functional Theory. Structural-functionalists view stratification within societies as an inevitable—and generally necessary—part of the social world. The stratification system provides individuals a place or position in the social world and motivates them to carry out their roles. Societies survive by having an organized system into which each individual is born and raised and contributes to the maintenance of the society.

The basic elements of the structural-functional theory of stratification were explained by Kingsley Davis and Wilbert Moore (1945), and their work still provides the main ideas of the theory today. Focusing on stratification by considering the rewards given to people in various occupations, they argue the following:

1. *Value of positions*: Some positions are more important to society than others. For example, society needs people to fill occupations that require specialized training and long hours, such as physicians and CEOs. Societies must motivate talented individuals to prepare for and occupy the most important and difficult positions.

2. *Preparation requires talent, time, and money*: To motivate talented individuals to make the sacrifices necessary to prepare for difficult positions, such as a physician or CEO, differential rewards of income, prestige, power, or other valued goods must be offered. Thus, a doctor and a CEO receive high income, prestige, and power as incentives.

3. *Unequal distribution of rewards*: The differences in rewards, such as pay for the most-valued positions, in turn, lead to the unequal distribution of resources—or inequality—for occupations in society. The result is that stratification is inevitable.

Look at the example of poverty. Some sociologists argue that poverty serves certain *functions* for society, thus making it difficult to eliminate (Gans 1971, 1995). Some people may actually benefit from having poor people kept poor. Consider the following points:

1. *Poverty provides us with a convenient scapegoat*—someone to blame for individual and societal problems. We can put the blame for poverty on the poor individuals themselves. That way we can ignore the meso- and macro-level causes of poverty—like economic and political systems—and maintain the present way those institutions operate for the benefit of those now in positions of power.

2. *Having poor people creates many jobs for those who are not poor*, especially in the "helping" professions, such as social workers, and law enforcement jobs, such as police, judges, and prison workers.

3. *The poor provide an easily available group of surplus laborers* to do undesirable jobs when needed.

4. *The poor reinforce and legitimate our own lives and institutions*. Their existence allows the rest of us to feel superior to someone, enhancing our self-esteem.

5. *Their violation of mainstream values helps reaffirm the values among the affluent* (Gans 1971, 1995).

In the mid-20th century, structural-functional theory was the dominant theory used to explain stratification. However, it has been criticized for its inability to explain why some people in society who do not provide vital services for society (e.g., professional basketball players and hedge fund managers) receive great rewards. It also does not explain why CEOs now make so much more money compared with the typical worker than they once did. For example, in 1965, CEOs made, on average, 18 times the average worker's salary. In 2013, the average pay of CEOs at the top 350 U.S. firms was almost 300 times the pay of the average nonsupervisory worker in their field (A. Davis and Mishel 2014). Functionalist explanations of stratification have also been critiqued for an inability to fully explain the conflict that societies experience. This is the primary focus of conflict theory.

Conflict Theory. Conflict theorists see stratification as the outcome of struggles for dominance and scarce resources, with some individuals in society taking advantage of others. Individuals and groups act in their own self-interest by trying to exploit others, leading inevitably to a struggle between those who have advantages and want to keep them and those who want a larger share of the pie.

Conflict theorist Karl Marx (1818–1883) described four possible ways to distribute wealth, according to (1) what each person needs, (2) what each person wants, (3) what each person earns, or (4) what each person can take. It was this fourth way, Marx believed, that was dominant in competitive capitalist societies (Cuzzort and King 2002; Marx and Engels 1955).

Marx viewed the stratification structure as composed of two major economically based social classes: the *haves* and the *have-nots*. The *haves* consist of the owners (capitalist bourgeoisie), whereas the *have-nots* are the working class (proletariat). Individuals in the same social class have similar lifestyles, share ideologies, and hold common outlooks

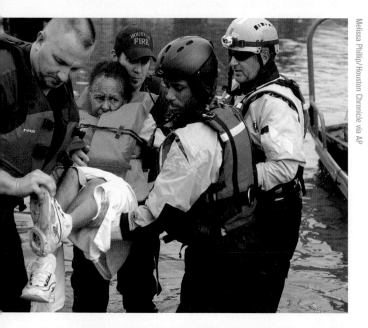

Who do you think makes more money, Leonardo DiCaprio (here at the Oscars) or these emergency personnel? What does this imply about the structural-functionalist argument that societies motivate (through higher salaries) individuals to prepare for and occupy the most critically important and challenging positions?

on social life. The struggle over resources between the haves and have-nots is a cause of conflict (Hurst 2013).

The *haves* control what Marx called the *means of production*—property, machinery, and cash owned by capitalists—the valued resources in society (Marx [1844] 1964). The haves dominate because the lower-class have-nots cannot accumulate enough money and power to change their positions. The norms and values of the haves dominate the society because of their power and ability to make the distribution of resources seem "fair" and justified. Laws, religious beliefs, and educational systems spread ideas that support the domination of the haves. This keeps the *have-nots* from understanding their own self-interests and is why working-class people often support politicians whose policies really favor the wealthiest 1%. The haves' control of political structures, policies, and police and military forces ensures their continued dominance in society.

The unorganized lower-class *have-nots* cannot overcome their exploitation until they develop a *class consciousness*—a shared awareness that they, as a class, have interests that differ from those of the haves. They need to understand that what is good for the *haves* is bad for the *have-nots*. Marx contended that with the help of enlightened intellectuals (like him), the working class would develop a class consciousness, rise up, and overthrow the haves, culminating in a classless society in which wealth would be more equally shared (Marx and Engels 1955).

Unlike the structural-functionalists, then, conflict theorists maintain that money and other rewards are not necessarily given to those in the most important positions in the society. Can we argue that a rock star or baseball player is more necessary for the survival of society than a teacher or police officer? Yet the pay differential is tremendous. It takes most teachers (even those with a master's degree) an entire career to earn as much as many celebrities earn in a matter of months.

As you can see, not all of Marx's predictions have come true. Whereas many nations have labor laws that require owners to pay workers a minimum wage and provide safe working conditions and that prevent them from discriminating on the basis of race, gender, or religion, inequality still exists throughout the world. Even societies that claim to be classless, such as China, have privileged classes and poor peasants. In recent years, the Chinese government has allowed more private ownership of shops, businesses, and other entrepreneurial efforts, motivating many Chinese citizens to work long hours at their private businesses to "get ahead." The only classless societies are a few small hunter-gatherer groups that have no extra resources that would allow some members to accumulate wealth.

Some theorists criticize Marx for his focus on only the economic system, pointing out that noneconomic factors enter into the stratification struggle as well. Max Weber (1864–1920), another influential theorist, agreed with Marx that group conflict is inevitable, that economics is one of the key factors in stratification systems, and that those in power try to perpetuate their positions. However, he added two other influential factors that he argued determine stratification: power and prestige. Sometimes, these are identified as the "three *P*s"—property, power, and prestige. Depending on the type of economic and political era, one *P* tends to be more important than the others (prestige in feudal times, property in the industrial era, and power in the postindustrial time period), but usually, having one *P* gives a person access to the other two as well.

Recent theorists suggest that using the three *P*s, we can identify five classes—capitalists, managers, small-business owners or the petty bourgeoisie, workers, and the underclass—rather than just the *haves* and *have-nots*. *Capitalists* own the means of production, and they purchase and control the labor of others. *Managers* sell their labor to capitalists and manage the labor of others for the capitalists. The *petty bourgeoisie*, such as small-business owners, own some means of production but control little of the labor of others; they have modest prestige, power, and property (Sernau 2010). *Workers* sell their labor to capitalists and are low in all three *P*s. Finally, the *underclass* has virtually no property, power, or prestige.

The distribution of wealth and income in the United States is more uneven today than at any time since before the Great Depression hit in 1929. **Income** *is money received from work or investments* while **wealth** *is the worth of a person based on his or her financial holdings (stocks, bank accounts, and investment income) and property (homes, cars, etc.) minus debt*. Today, the richest 1% of U.S. households own more wealth than *all* of the bottom 90% combined (Saez 2012) and 40% of the nation's total wealth (Archer 2013). In the world, the richest 1% own more than the other 99% of the combined world's population (Byanyima 2015).

Workers have also become more anxious about declining wages and job insecurity. Since the 1990s, companies have begun to outsource more and more jobs. Fewer people now work for one company in a stable position, with benefits and some sense of job security, and more now work in temporary positions as consultants (without benefits and job security). Some economists refer to this as the *Uberization* of the job market, referring to the fast-growing ride-sharing company, Uber, that directly employs only 4,000 of the 160,000 people who work for the company in the United

Uber, the online transportation company, employs 160,000 drivers in the U.S. alone. Only 2.5% of them are full-time employees with secure work hours and benefits.

States. Hiring people as consultants allows employers greater flexibility. They can hire and fire as needed and do not have to worry much about employees organizing together to demand higher compensation or better benefits. This is great for employers but not so great for most workers, who must wonder for how long they can count on getting a paycheck, how many hours of work they might get each week, and how much their next work "gig" might pay. Approximately 1 out of every 4 Americans worries about facing reduced pay or work hours (Scheiber 2015).

Thinking Sociologically

How would conflict theorists explain the fact that on average, the top 350 CEOs make nearly 300 times the pay of the average worker and that the richest 1% in the world own more than the combined wealth of the other 99%? Does their argument make sense? Why, or why not?

The Evolutionary Theory of Stratification: A Synthesis

Evolutionary theory, developed by Gerhard Lenski, borrows assumptions from both structural-functional and conflict theories in an attempt to determine how scarce resources are distributed and how that distribution results in stratification (Lenski 1966; P. Nolan and Lenski 2014). The basic ideas are that (a) to survive, people must cooperate; (b) despite this, conflicts of interest occur over important decisions that benefit one individual or group over another; (c) valued items, such as money and status, are always in demand and in short supply; (d) there is likely to be a struggle over these scarce goods; and (e) customs or traditions in a society often prevail over rational criteria in determining distribution of scarce resources. After the minimum survival needs of both individuals and the society are met, power determines who gets the surplus: prestige, luxury living, the best health care, and so forth. Lenski believes that privileges (including wealth) flow from having power, and prestige usually results from having access to both power and privilege (Hurst 2013).

Lenski tested his theory by studying societies at different levels of technological development, ranging from simple to complex. He found that the degree of inequality increases with technology until it reaches the advanced industrial stage. For instance, in subsistence-level hunter-gatherer societies, little surplus is available, and everyone's needs are met to the extent possible. As surplus accumulates in agrarian societies, those who acquire surpluses also control power, and they use this to benefit their friends and relations. However, they must share at least some of the wealth or fear being overthrown.

When societies finally reach the advanced industrial stage, there should be less inequality. Industrialization brings surplus wealth, a division of labor, advanced technology, and interdependence among members of a society. No longer can one individual control all of the important knowledge, skills, or capital resources. The surplus can be spread to more people without diminishing that received by those who have the most. Therefore, this should eliminate the extreme gaps between haves and have-nots because resources would normally be more evenly distributed. Also, at this point in history, societies tend to have constitutions and recognize the rights of citizens, making it harder to exploit them.

Evolutionary theory takes into consideration an idea shared by the structural-functionalists and rational choice theorists: that talented individuals need to be motivated to make sacrifices. This produces motivated, competent, and well-educated people in the most important social statuses. The theory also recognizes exploitation leading to inequality, a factor that conflict theorists find in systems of stratification.

Whereas some inequality may be useful in highly complex societies, as functionalists have argued, evolutionary theorists note that extraordinary amounts of inequality may undermine motivation and productivity. The most talented people will not even try to attain the most demanding and important jobs if upward mobility seems impossible. Therefore, high levels of inequality do not make sense for a healthy industrial or postindustrial society (P. Nolan and Lenski 2014).

Each of the theories already discussed—symbolic interaction, rational choice, structural-functional, conflict, and evolutionary theory—provides a different explanation for understanding stratification in modern societies. These theories provide the basis for micro- to macro-level discussions of stratification. Our next topic looks at some factors that influence an individual's position in a stratification system and the ability to change that position.

Thinking Sociologically

Why is the income gap between the rich and the poor currently increasing in the United States? Which theory seems most helpful in explaining this pattern? What are some possible ramifications of this widening income gap?

INDIVIDUALS' SOCIAL STATUS: THE MICRO LEVEL

You are among the world's elite. Less than 7% of the world's population has a college degree (Erickson and Vonk 2012). Being able to afford the time and money for college is a luxury beyond the financial or personal resources of almost 93% of people in the world. However, the global number of college students is expanding rapidly as countries such as China provide more higher education opportunities to support their growing economies.

In fact, enrollment of Chinese students in higher education surpassed the percentage enrolled in the United States in 2011. Because the demand for a college education far exceeds the opportunity in China, many Chinese college students are studying abroad, adding to their opportunities and enhancing China's knowledge of the world. Chinese students make up the largest number of international students studying in the United States—accounting for more than one third of all international students (Frost 2014).

In the United States, access to higher education is greater than in many other countries because there are more levels of entry—including technical colleges, community colleges, state universities, and private 4-year colleges. However, with limited government help, most students must have enough financial resources to cover tuition and the cost of living.

The prestige of the college that students choose can also make a difference in their future opportunities. Students born into wealth can afford private preparatory schools and tutors to increase SAT and ACT test scores that increase their chances of gaining acceptance to prestigious colleges. Such colleges offer social networking and other opportunities not available to those attending the typical state university or nonelite college (Jaschik 2013; Persell 2005). For men, attending an elite college makes a significant difference in future earnings, but for women, entering a field that pays well makes more of an impact on future earnings than the college they attend (Ma and Savas 2014). Women tend to enter fields that pay less than those in which men predominate.

For a variety of reasons, ascribed characteristics, such as gender, can affect one's chances for success in life. Gender socialization and embedded gender stratification systems may make it difficult for women to rise in the occupational hierarchy. Many Japanese women, for example, earn college degrees but leave employment after getting married and having children because of both gender socialization and gender discrimination in the workforce (Globe Women 2013). We examine gender stratification in more depth in Chapter 9, but note that it intersects with socioeconomic status and must be viewed as part of a larger pattern resulting in inequality in the social world.

Individual Life Chances

Life chances refer to one's opportunities, depending on both achieved and ascribed statuses in society. That you are in college, probably have health insurance and access to health care, and are likely to live into your late 70s or 80s are factors directly related to your life chances. Let us consider several examples of how placement in organizations at the meso level affects individual experiences and has global ramifications.

Education. Although education is valued by most individuals, the cost of books, clothing, shoes, transportation, child care, and time taken from income-producing work may be insurmountable barriers to school attendance for many people. One's level of education affects many aspects of life, including economic, political, religious, and family attitudes and behavior. Generally speaking, the higher the education level, the more active individuals are in political life; the more mainstream or conventional their religious affiliation; and the more likely they are to marry, remain married, and have good health.

Health, Social Conditions, and Life Expectancy. If you have a sore throat for an extended period of time, you will probably go see a doctor. Yet many people in the world will never see a doctor. Access to health care requires doctors and medical facilities, money for transportation and treatment, access to childcare, and released time from other tasks. Often, the poor do not have these luxuries. In contrast, the affluent eat better food; are less exposed to polluted water and unhygienic conditions; and are able to pay for health insurance, medical care, and drugs when they do have ailing health. As a result, they tend to live much longer than poorer people.

Examining causes of death among different classes illustrates some of the deadly results of the differences in access to health care among people at different places in the stratification hierarchy. For example, in the poor Global South, shorter life expectancies and deaths, especially among children, are due to controllable infectious diseases, such as cholera, malaria, AIDS, typhoid, tuberculosis, and other respiratory ailments. In contrast, in affluent countries, heart disease, stroke, and lung cancer are the most common causes of death, and most deaths are of people above the age of 65. With improvements in immunizations, mosquito nets to prevent malaria, better sanitation and water quality, access to medicines, better nutrition, and female literacy, life expectancy rises. Yet the chance to live a long and healthy life is a privilege available primarily to those living in wealthy countries. Indeed, despite medical advances, the gap in life spans between the wealthy and those with low incomes has been widening since 1970 (Tavernise 2016).

By studying Table 7.1 in the next "Engaging Sociology" feature, you can compare life expectancy with two other measures of life quality for the poorest and richest countries: the gross national product (GNP) per capita income—the average amount of money each person has per year—and the infant mortality rates (death rates for babies). Note that life expectancy in poor countries is as low as 49 years in Chad and 50 in Guinea-Bissau, Africa (many of the people in these countries are subsistence farmers), and as high as 89.6 years in the wealthy country of Monaco and 85 in Japan and Singapore. In the United States, life expectancy is 79.7 (*World Factbook* 2016c). Average annual income is as low as $400 in Somalia and as high as $102,900 in Liechtenstein and $145,000 in Qatar. The average U.S. income is $56,300 a year (*World Factbook* 2016a). Infant mortality is as high as 115.1 deaths per 1,000 births in Afghanistan (more than 1 in 10) and as low as 2.1 in Iceland and 1.81 in Monaco. In the United States, the estimated 2015 rate is 5.9 deaths per 1,000 births (*World Factbook* 2016b).

ENGAGING SOCIOLOGY

Life Expectancy, Infant Mortality, and Per Capita Income

Analyzing the meaning of data can provide an understanding of the health and well-being of citizens around the world. A country's basic statistics, including life expectancy, per capita gross national product, and infant mortality, tell researchers a great deal about its economic health and vitality.

1. What questions do the data in Table 7.1 raise regarding differences in mortality and life expectancy rates around the world?

2. Considering what you know from this and previous chapters and from Table 7.1, what do you think are some differences in the lives of citizens in the richest and poorest countries?

Table 7.1 Life Expectancy, Infant Mortality, and Per Capita Income for Selected Poor and Rich Countries

Poor Countries	Life Expectancy (in Years) (2015 est.)	Infant Mortality (Deaths per 1,000 Births)	Per Capita GDP ($)	Rich Countries	Life Expectancy (in Years) (2015 est.)	Infant Mortality (Deaths per 1,000 Births)	Per Capita GDP ($)
Chad	49.8	88.7	2,800	Iceland	83.0	2.1	46,100
Guinea-Bissau	50.2	89.2	1,500	Japan	84.7	2.1	38,200
Afghanistan	50.9	115.1	2,000	Singapore	84.7	2.5	85,700
Somalia	52.0	98.4	400	Hong Kong	82.9	2.7	57,000
Zambia	52.2	64.7	4,300	Switzerland	82.5	3.7	59,300
Central African Republic	51.8	90.6	600	Sweden	82.0	2.6	48,000
Nigeria	53.0	72.7	6,400	Canada*	81.8	4.7	45,900
Uganda	55.0	59.2	2,100	France	81.8	3.3	41,400
Niger	55.0	84.6	1,100	Australia	81.4	4.4	65,400
Mali	55.3	102.2	1,800	United States**	79.7	5.9	56,300

Note: Infant mortality is per 1,000 live births. Most figures are 2015 estimates.

*Canada is 18th in life expectancy and 46th in infant mortality rates.

**United States is 43rd in life expectancy and 58th in infant mortality rates.

Source: World Factbook 2016b and 2016c for infant mortality and life expectancy; *World Factbook* 2016a for per capita income.

 Thinking Sociologically

Explain how some specific factors at the micro, meso, and macro levels affect your life expectancy and that of your family members.

One does not have to look beyond the borders of the United States, though, to see the relationship between health and wealth. The United States has much larger gaps between rich and poor people than most other wealthy nations, and that has led to a corresponding gap in health and life expectancy among social classes, much wider than that in other highly developed nations. As the video *In Sickness and In Wealth: Health in America* (2008) reveals, there is "a health–wealth gradient" in the United States, in "which every descending rung of the socioeconomic ladder corresponds to worse health." The result is that 41 other nations have higher life expectancy rates than the United States (E. Meyer 2012; *World Factbook* 2016c). Most other postindustrial countries also have universal health care.

Individual life chances are determined, in part, by the per capita income of individuals. If people are poor, they have little disposable income. This means a life of poverty and less access to education, health, and other social conditions that determine life chances and lifestyle, discussed next.

Individual Lifestyles

Your individual **lifestyle** includes *your attitudes, values, beliefs, behavior patterns, and other aspects of your place in the world, as shaped by socialization.* As individuals grow up, the behaviors and attitudes consistent with their culture and their family's status in society become internalized through the process of socialization. Lifestyle is not simply a matter of having money. Acquiring money—say, by winning a lottery—cannot buy a completely new lifestyle (Bourdieu and Passeron 1977). This is because values and behaviors are ingrained in our self-concept from childhood. A person may gain material possessions, but that does not mean she has the lifestyle of the upper-class rich and famous. Remember the awkward party when you were around people of a different social class? Even if you suddenly made the same amount of money as those at an elegant party, you would not know the norms associated with that social class. Some examples of factors related to your individual lifestyle that tend to differ among social classes include attitudes toward achievement, family life and child-rearing patterns, religious membership, and political involvement.

Attitudes Toward Achievement. Attitudes toward achievement differ by social status and are generally closely correlated with life chances. As noted previously, motivation to get ahead and beliefs about what we can achieve are, in part, products of our upbringing and the opportunities we see as available to us. These attitudes differ greatly depending on the opportunity structure around us, including what our families and friends see as possible and desirable. For example, the primary concern of poor families in poor nations may be to put food on the family's table. They may view education as a luxury not appropriate for people of their

social class. In Global North countries, opportunity is available for most children to attend school at least through high school and often beyond. However, some students do not learn to value achievement in school due to lack of support from their primary socializing agents: family, peers, and teachers (Ballantine, Hammack, and Stuber 2017).

Family Life and Child-Rearing Patterns. Attitudes toward achievement are not the only things that differ among socioeconomic groups. Child-rearing patterns also vary and serve to reinforce one's attitude toward achievement and social position in society. When you were growing up, were your after-school hours, weekends, and summers filled with adult-organized activities (e.g., formal lessons, youth sports, camps), or were you pretty much free to play on your own, watch TV, or hang out with friends or extended family? A family's social class location shapes the daily rhythms of family life (Lareau 2003).

Differences in parenting behavior can lead to the "transmission of differential advantages to children" (Lareau 2003:5). Through their socialization by their parents, middle-class children are better able to navigate the educational and, later, professional occupational worlds than working-class children. This, in turn, influences the social class destinies of each group (Lashbrook 2009).

Religious Membership. Religious affiliation also correlates with the social status variables of education, occupation, and income. For instance, in the United States, upper-class citizens are found disproportionately in Episcopalian, Unitarian, and Jewish religious groups, whereas lower-class citizens tend to be attracted to Nazarene, Southern Baptist, Jehovah's Witness, and other holiness and fundamentalist sects. Although there are exceptions, such as Catholicism, most religious groups attract members predominantly from one social class (Roberts and Yamane 2016).

Political Involvement. Political party identification and general ideological beliefs affect voting, and they are, in turn, affected by social factors, such as race, religion, region of the country, social class, gender, marital status, and age (Interuniversity Consortium for Political and Social Research 2011). Throughout the world, the lower the social class, the more likely people are to vote for parties that support greater distribution of wealth, and the higher the social status, the more likely people are to be conservative on economic issues—consistent with protecting their wealth (Domhoff 2014; Kerbo 2008). However, those with lower levels of education and income tend to vote conservatively on many social issues relating to minorities and civil liberties (e.g., rights for lesbians, gays, bisexuals, and transgender people; access to birth control and abortions; and voter registration laws) (Gilbert 2011; Kerbo 2008).

Money also influences who can run successful campaigns. For example, during the 2012 congressional elections, the average candidate running for a position in the House of Representatives or the Senate spent, respectively, $660,540 and $2,738,385. During the presidential campaign of 2012, President Obama and Mitt Romney (along with their allies) raised approximately a billion dollars each. This contributes to the fact that those with more money, who can help support such campaigns, also have more influence in elections (Center for Responsive Politics 2012a, 2012b, 2015; King 2012).

Status Inconsistency. Some people experience high status on one trait, especially a trait achieved through education and hard work, but may experience low standing in another area. For example, a professor may have high prestige but low income. Max Weber called this unevenness in one's social standing *status inconsistency*. In societies with high levels of racism and sexism, racial minorities and women in high-status positions experience status inconsistency. If their lowest ascribed status is treated as most important, they are likely to experience discontent with the current system and become more liberal in political views (Weber 1946).

Life experiences such as hunger, the unnecessary early death of family members, or the pain of seeing one's child denied opportunities are all experienced at the micro level, but their causes are usually rooted in events and actions at other levels of the social world. This brings us to our next question: Can an individual move up or down in a stratification system?

Thinking Sociologically

Describe your own lifestyle and life chances. How do these relate to your socialization experience and your family's position in the stratification system? What difference do they make in your life today and for what you think you will accomplish in the future? What can you do to improve your life chances?

SOCIAL MOBILITY: THE MICRO–MESO CONNECTION

The LeBron Jameses and Peyton Mannings of the world make millions of dollars—at least for the duration of their playing careers. For professionals in the world of sport, each hoop, goal, or touchdown throw is worth thousands of dollars. These riches give hope to those in rags that if they "play hard," they too may be on the field or court making millions. The problem is that the chances of making it big are so small that such hopes are some of the cruelest hoaxes perpetrated on poor young African Americans and others in the lower or working class today. It is a false promise to think of sports as the road to wealth when chances of success are extremely limited (Dufur and Feinberg 2007; Edwards 2000; Hattery and Smith 2012).

Those few minority athletes who do "make it big" and become models for young people tend to experience *stacking*, holding certain limited positions in a sport. Moreover, those young players who make it into the major leagues may have done so by going in right after high school or leaving college after a single year. This thwarts their post-athletic career opportunities. When retired from playing, few Black athletes rise in the administrative hierarchy in the sports of football and baseball. (Basketball has a better record of hiring Black coaches and managers.) If young people put all of their hopes and energies into developing their muscles and physical skills, they may lose the possibility of moving up in the social class system, which requires developing their minds and technical skills.

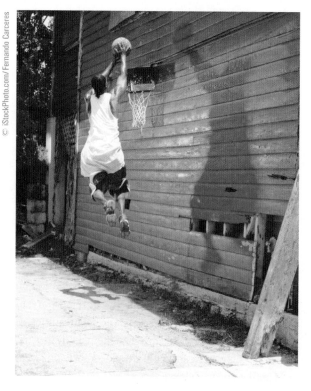

© iStockPhoto.com/Fernando Carceres

This young street basketball player has dreams of glory on the courts. Despite many grand hoop dreams, few experience dramatic social mobility through sports.

Social mobility refers to *the extent of individual movement up or down in the class system, changing one's social position in society—especially relative to one's parents* (Gilbert 2011). What is the likelihood that your status will be different from that of your parents over your lifetime? Will you start a successful business? Marry into wealth? Win the lottery? Experience downward mobility due to loss of a job, illness, or inability to complete your education? What factors at different levels of analysis might influence your chances of mobility? These are some of the questions addressed in this section and the next.

The four issues that dominate the analysis of mobility are (1) types of social mobility, (2) methods of measuring social mobility, (3) factors that affect social mobility, and (4) whether there is a "land of opportunity" for those wishing to improve their lot in life.

Types of Social Mobility

Mobility can be up, down, or sideways. *Intergenerational mobility* refers to change in social class status compared with one's parents, usually resulting from education and occupational attainment. If you are the first to go to college in your family and you become an engineer, this represents intergenerational upward mobility. The amount of intergenerational mobility—that is, the number of children who move up or down in the social structure compared with where their parents are—measures the degree to which a society has an *open class system*. The more movement there is between classes, the more open the class system.

You can change positions at the same level in the stratification system. For example, you could move from your job as a postal worker and become a firefighter. This type of mobility is called *horizontal mobility*. You have changed your position, but your income, power, and social prestige remain essentially the same.

Intragenerational mobility (not to be confused with *inter*generational mobility) refers to a change in position within a single individual's life. For instance, if you begin your career as a teacher's aide and end it as a school superintendent, that is upward intragenerational mobility. However, mobility is not always up. *Vertical mobility* refers to movement up *or* down in the hierarchy and sometimes involves changing social classes. You may start your career as a waitress, go to college part-time, get a degree in computer science, and get a more prestigious and higher-paying job, resulting in upward mobility. Alternatively, you could lose a job and take one at a lower status and pay. In recent years, people at all levels of the occupational structure have experienced downward intragenerational

mobility after being laid off from one job and having difficulty finding another at the same level and pay grade.

How Much Mobility Is There? Measures of Social Mobility

One traditional method of measuring mobility is to compare fathers with sons and, in more recent research, with daughters. Determining the mobility of women is more difficult because they often have lower-level positions, and their mothers may not have worked full-time, but a conclusion that can be drawn is that both women's and men's occupational attainment is powerfully influenced by class origins. As Figure 7.3 indicates, the level of social mobility in the United States is lower than in most other Global North nations (E. Gould 2012). This figure shows correlations, and a lower number in this case means the more likely it is that sons will end up in the same (or higher) social class as their fathers.

Factors Affecting an Individual's Mobility

Why are some people successful at moving up the ladder, whereas others lag behind? Mobility is driven by many factors, from your family's background to global economic variables. One's chances to move up depend on micro-level factors (e.g., cultural capital, socialization, personal characteristics, and education)—and meso- and macro-level factors (e.g., the occupational structure and economic status of regions and countries; population changes in the number of births, deaths, or people migrating; the numbers of people vying for similar positions; discrimination based on gender, race, or ethnicity; and the global economic situation).

Studying mobility can be a complicated process because these key variables are interrelated. Macro-level forces (such as the occupational structure and economic status in a country) are related to meso-level factors (such as access to education and type of economy) and micro-level factors (such as socialization, family background, and education level) (Blau and Duncan 1967).

Researchers from Harvard and Berkeley recently conducted the largest study on inequality in the United States to date (Chetty et al. 2014). Their research revealed large regional variations in mobility (as seen in Figure 7.4). For example, they found that "the probability of a child born into the poorest fifth of the population in San Jose, California making it to the top fifth is 12.9%.... In

FIGURE 7.3   Social Mobility: Correlations Between Earnings of Fathers and Sons

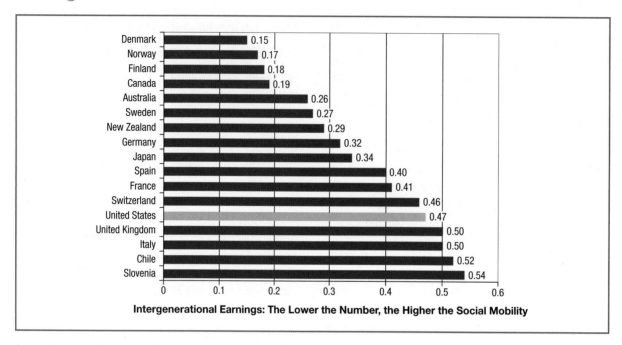

Intergenerational Earnings: The Lower the Number, the Higher the Social Mobility

Source: Figure 3H in *The State of Working America,* 12th Edition, an Economic Policy Institute book. Reprinted with permission.

Charlotte, North Carolina, [however,] it is 4.4%, far lower than anywhere else in the rich world" ("Mobility, Measured" 2014).

The researchers noted five factors that help explain the level of mobility in different areas of the United States: "residential segregation (whether by income or race); the quality of schooling; family structure (e.g., how many children live with only one parent); 'social capital' (such as taking part in community groups); and inequality (particularly income gaps among those outside the top 1%)." They point out that "social mobility is higher in integrated places with good schools, strong families, lots of community spirit and smaller income gaps within the broad middle class" ("Mobility, Measured" 2014). We now look in more detail at a few of the variables that can make a difference in your chances for mobility.

Family Background, Socialization, Marriage, and Education. Whether you marry and whom you marry can move you up or down the social class ladder. As men's wages have fallen over the past few decades and more women have joined the workforce, household incomes (rather than just male incomes) play more of a role in people's social class positions. As people increasingly tend to marry those of similar income levels, marriage makes even more of an impact on family income. Two high-income

earners make much more than two low-income earners (and *much* more than one low-income or even middle-income worker) (Haskins, Isaacs, and Sawhill 2008; Pew Charitable Trusts 2012).

As we have noted throughout this chapter, our family background has a major influence on our chances for upward mobility on the social class ladder. For example, recent research discusses the continuing social class *word gap* between children from different classes. Disparities in vocabulary are noticeable as early as 18 months (National Public Radio [NPR] 2013). Children from higher social classes learn nuances in language, whereas lower-class children learn primarily commands and short directive sentences. Professional parents use 3 times as many different words at home as parents in low-income families. By the time the children of professional families are 3 years old, they have a vocabulary of about 1,100 words and typically use 297 different words per hour. Children in working-class families have a 700-word vocabulary and use 217 words per hour while children from low-income families have 500 words and use 149 per hour. These numbers represent a gap in the range of words they hear at home and illustrate the difference family background and socialization can make in education and future opportunities. A University of Chicago study recommends a three *T*s approach—tune

FIGURE 7.4 Location and Social Mobility for a Child in the Bottom Fifth of Income in the United States

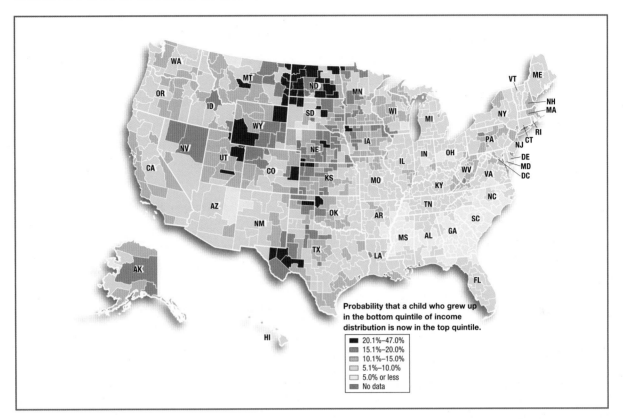

Note: Commuting zones are geographic areas that help define local economies and labor markets—where people live and work, independent of political boundaries.

Source: Chetty, R., Hendren, N., Kline, P., & Saez, E. (2014). "Intergenerational Mobility Statistics by Commuting Zone." *The Equality of Opportunity Project.* http://www.equality-of-opportunity.org/index.php/data

in, talk more, and take turns—to increase vocabulary (Hart and Risley 2003; NPR 2013). Because language usage at home impacts school success, that, in turn, plays a role in a child's chances of getting into college and climbing the stratification ladder.

Thinking Sociologically

How might your vocabulary affect your success in school? How might an expanded vocabulary affect your opportunities in life (for example, impressing a potential employer)? What can you do to increase your vocabulary?

A college degree potentially helps those at the bottom of the stratification system move up and helps those in the middle and upper classes to remain in those higher positions. This positive impact on social class position relates to the fact that, as Figure 7.5 reveals, employment rates and earnings tend to go up dramatically with a college degree. For example, in 2014, the unemployment rate for adults over 25 years old was 6% for those with a high school degree, but just 3.5% for those with a degree from a 4-year college. The median weekly earnings were $1,101 for those with a four-year degree but just $668 for those with only a high school diploma (U.S. Bureau of Labor Statistics 2015).

However, as Figure 7.6 indicates, there is a huge difference in access to higher education. In 2014, among all bachelor's degrees awarded by age 24, 54% went to children from families in the top quartile of income earning, as opposed to 10% of the bottom quartile (Cahalan et al. 2016). Further, this is not just a matter of more capable

FIGURE 7.5   Earnings and Employment Rates by Educational Attainment

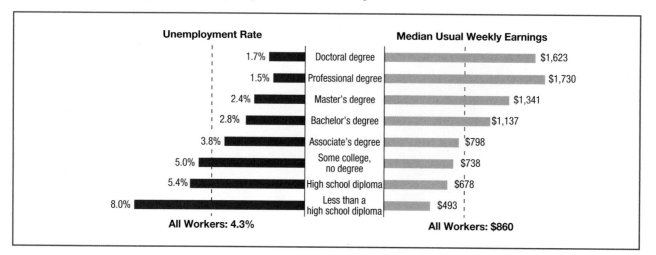

Source: U.S. Bureau of Labor Statistics (2015).

FIGURE 7.6   Differences in Bachelor's Degree (by age 24) by Family Income

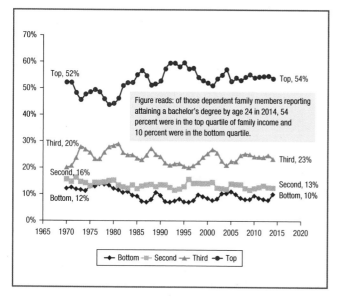

Figure reads: of those dependent family members reporting attaining a bachelor's degree by age 24 in 2014, 54 percent were in the top quartile of family income and 10 percent were in the bottom quartile.

Source: Cahalan et al. (2016).

students succeeding in college. As Figure 7.7 demonstrates, a high-income student with just mediocre math scores has the same chances of earning a BA as a low-income student with the highest test scores. If U.S. society were truly a **meritocracy**, *positions would be allocated in a social group or organization according to individuals' abilities and credentials*. One would expect cognitive ability to be the most important variable (Gilbert 2011).

Even when a young person from a low-income background is admitted to a college or university, she or he may be at a disadvantage in the classroom and feel alienated from past social ties. The culture of 4-year colleges, particularly elite ones, is typically the culture of the well-educated upper middle class and may be different and uncomfortable for those from other class backgrounds (Dews and Law 1995; Foster 2015). The alienation many first-generation poor and working-class students experience at 4-year colleges is explored in more detail in the next "Engaging Sociology."

FIGURE 7.7   Advantage of Wealth in College Success

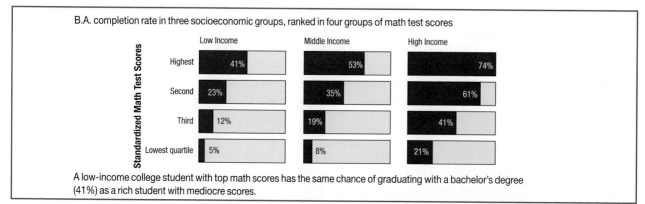

B.A. completion rate in three socioeconomic groups, ranked in four groups of math test scores

A low-income college student with top math scores has the same chance of graduating with a bachelor's degree (41%) as a rich student with mediocre scores.

Sources: Dynarski (2015); National Center for Educational Statistics (2015).

ENGAGING SOCIOLOGY

First-Generation College Students: Issues of Cultural and Social Capital

Socioeconomic classes develop subcultures that can be quite different from one another, and when one changes subcultures, it can be confusing and alienating. College campuses provide an example because they are dominated by middle-class cultures. First-generation college students often find themselves in a world as alien as visiting another country. Students whose parents went to college are more likely to have cultural and social capital that helps them understand their professors, who are generally part of the middle-class culture. Answer the following survey questions. How might your own cultural and social capital cause you to feel at home or alienated, privileged or disprivileged, in a college environment?

A. Which of the following experiences were part of your childhood?

☐ Had a library of books (at least 50 adult books) in your childhood home

☐ Had parents who read a newspaper on a daily basis

☐ Had parents who subscribed to news magazines (e.g., *Time*, *The Economist*)

☐ Listened to music as a family, including classical or instrumental music such as harp or flute

☐ Traveled to at least 20 other states or to at least five other countries

☐ Took regular trips to the library

☐ Took regular trips to museums

☐ Attended plays (theater productions) and concerts

☐ Played a musical instrument

☐ Took dance lessons

☐ Listened to National Public Radio (NPR)

☐ Watched PBS (Public Broadcasting Service) on television

B. Which of the following *relationships* were part of your childhood?

☐ My parents knew at least two influential people in my community on a first-name basis—such as the mayor, members of the city council, the superintendent of schools, the governor, and the district's representative to Congress.

☐ The regional leader of my religious group—church, temple, or mosque—knew and respected my family.

☐ My parents knew, on a first-name basis, at least three CEOs of corporations.

☐ When I entered new situations in high school, it was likely that my parents were known by the coaches, music directors, summer camp directors, or others "running the show."

☐ When I came to college, one or more professors and administrators at the college knew my parents, a sibling, or another family member.

☐ I have often interacted directly and effectively (in a nonadversarial way) with authority figures.

* * * * * * *

Engaging With Sociology

1. If you experienced many of the items under A at home, you had fairly high cultural capital. If you marked most of the items under B, you had a lot of social capital. If you did not, you may find the culture of a 4-year college campus to be alien and even confusing. How well does your background match up with the cultural capital of a college?

2. Which of the following aspects of a college campus do you think might make a first-generation college student feel most alienated at your college: *economic* capital (money), *social* capital (networks with those who have resources), or *cultural* capital (knowledge of important aspects of the culture)? Why?

Source: Survey constructed, in part, using ideas from J. Morris and Grimes (1997).

Economic Vitality and Population Trends. The economic health of a nation and population trends can also influence individuals' chances for social mobility. As noted earlier, the economic vitality of a country affects the chances for individual mobility because there will be fewer positions at the top if the economy is stagnant. Macro-level factors such as a country's economy and its place in the global system shape the employment chances of individuals.

The *fertility rates*, or number of children born at a given time, influence the number of people looking for jobs and their chance of moving up in society. For example, the U.S. nationwide baby boom following World War II resulted in a flood of job applicants and downward inter-generational mobility for the many who could not find work comparable with their social class at birth. In contrast, the smaller group following the baby boomer generation had fewer competitors for entry-level jobs. Baby boomers hold many of the executive and leadership positions today, so promotion has been hard for the next cohort. As baby boomers retire, opportunities will open up, and mobility should increase.

Gender, Race, Ethnicity, and Earnings. Many women and racial and ethnic minority groups, locked in a cycle of poverty, dependence, and debt, have little chance of changing their status. For example, African Americans tend to remain poor or fall from the middle-class more often than members of other ethnic groups (Pew Charitable Trusts 2012). Likewise, whereas women have made some gains, women in the U.S. workforce are more likely than men to be in dead-end clerical and service positions with no opportunity for advancement. Overall, women also still make less money than men (U.S. Department of Labor 2011). Figure 7.8 shows the median annual earnings for population groups by race or ethnicity and gender.

Women, on average, earn less money than men, but they now have more degrees than men. Women are 33% more likely than men (33% compared to 24%) to earn a

FIGURE 7.8 Median Annual Earnings by Race, Ethnicity, and Gender

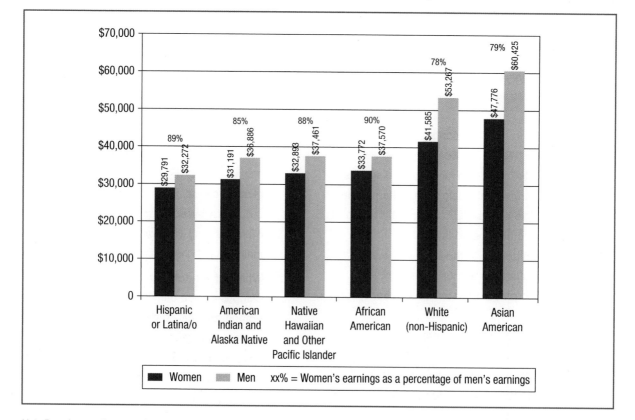

Note: Based on median annual earnings of full-time, year-round workers, ages 16 and older.

Source: Adapted from Infoplease (2016), from U.S. Census Bureau, based on data from Institute for Women's Policy Research.

bachelor's degree by the time they are 27 (A. Meyer 2014). Whereas women are still woefully underrepresented in upper-level management positions—only 4%, or 20, CEOs of Fortune 500 companies are women—their increasing edge in education should, eventually, lead to more women in high-level positions in the workforce (Catalyst 2016).

The Interdependent Global Market. All members of an economy are vulnerable to international events and the swings in the global marketplace. If the Chinese or Japanese stock markets hiccup, it sends ripples through world markets. If high-tech industries in Japan or Europe falter, North American companies in Silicon Valley, California, may go out of business, costing many professionals their lucrative positions. In ways such as these, the interdependent global economies affect national and local economies, and that, in turn, affects individual families.

Whether individuals move from "rags to riches" is not determined solely by their personal ambition and work ethic. As the information in this chapter indicates, mobility for the individual, a micro-level event, is linked to a variety of events at other levels of the social world. What we see and hear in the media, though, may have us believe otherwise.

Thinking Sociologically

Think of family members or friends who have recently lost or acquired jobs. Using your sociological imagination, how can you connect those individual experiences to the national and global economy? How do you think the national and global economies will impact your experience in the marketplace after you earn your college degree?

Is There a "Land of Opportunity"? Cross-Cultural Mobility

Television shows bombard us with images of rich bachelors and the desirability of marrying a millionaire to improve our status in life. By playing a game of trivia or being challenged on an island on a TV show, we too might "strike it rich." Another possibility is that we might win the lottery by buying a ticket at our local convenience store. In reality, these quick fixes and easy get-rich-fast plans are seldom realized, and the chances of us profiting are slim indeed.

The question for this section concerns your realistic chances for mobility and whether you have a better chance to improve your status by moving to some other country. The answer is not simple. Countless immigrants have sought better opportunities in new locations. Their economic future depended on the historical period, the economic conditions, attitudes toward immigrants, their job skills, and their ability to blend into the new society.

During economic growth periods, many immigrants have found great opportunities for mobility in the United States and Europe. However, opportunities for upward mobility have changed significantly with globalization. Multinational corporations look for the cheapest sources of labor in the Global South, with low taxes, few labor unions and workplace safety regulations, and many workers needing jobs. This has drained away low-skilled manufacturing jobs from Global North countries, making it even more essential to have advanced educational credentials (such as a bachelor's or master's degree).

Most jobs in the United States today focus on providing services. These service-sector jobs tend to require either a great deal of education (e.g., lawyers, computer engineers, or doctors) or minimal training (e.g., retail sales, nurse's aides, fast-food workers, or security guards). The low-skill jobs do not pay well, and labor unions, with declining memberships and political clout, have increasingly limited influence on the wages and working conditions of workers. The result is a shrinking middle class in the United States, as is shown in Figure 7.9 (Parlapiano, Gebeloff, and Carter 2015).

FIGURE 7.9 The Shrinking American Middle Class

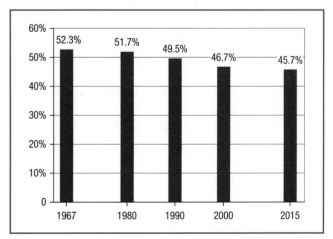

Note: Middle income is defined here as $35,000 to $100,000 per year.

Source: Adapted from U.S. Census Bureau 2016, Historical Income Tables: Households, Table H-3.

This inequality trend exists throughout the world. Although the new factories for multinational industries springing up in Global South countries such as Malaysia, Mexico, and the Philippines provide opportunities for mobility to those of modest origins, much of the upward mobility in the world is taking place among those who come from small, highly educated families with individualistic achievement-oriented values (Featherman and Hauser 1978; Gratton 2012; Rothman 2005). They tend to be positioned to take advantage of the changing occupational structure and high-tech jobs. Their education and social and cultural capital allows them to work effectively in multiple nations (Gratton 2012). As the gap between rich and poor individuals widens, education becomes more important.

Thinking Sociologically

What social factors in your society limit or enhance the likelihood of upward social mobility for you and other members of your generation? Explain.

MAJOR STRATIFICATION SYSTEMS: MACRO-LEVEL ANALYSIS

Mansa works on a plantation in Mozambique. He tries in vain to pay off his debt. Like his parents, however hard he and his wife and children work, they will always be in debt because they cannot pay the total amount due for their hut or food from the owner's store. Basically, they are slaves—they do not have control over their own labor. They were born into this status, and there they will stay.

Imagine being born into a society in which you have no choices or options in life because of your family background, age, sex, and ethnic group. You cannot select an occupation that interests you and cannot live in the part of town you prefer. You see wealthy aristocrats parading their advantages and realize that this will never be possible for you. You can never own land or receive the education of your choice.

This situation is reality for millions of people in the world—they are born this way and will spend their lives this way. In **ascribed stratification systems**, *characteristics beyond the control of individuals—such as family background, age, sex, and race—determine their position in society*. In contrast, **achieved stratification systems** *allow individuals to earn positions through their ability, efforts, and choices*. In an open class system, it is possible

to achieve a higher ranking by obtaining education, working hard, and choosing an occupation that pays well.

Ascribed Status: Caste and Estate Systems

Caste systems are *the most rigid ascribed stratification systems. Individuals are born into a status, which they retain throughout life.* That status is deeply embedded in religious, political, and economic norms and institutions. Individuals born into caste systems have predetermined occupational positions, marriage partners, residences, social associations, and prestige levels. A person's caste is easily recognized through clothing, speech patterns, family name and identity, skin color, or other distinguishing characteristics. From their earliest years, individuals learn their place in society through the process of socialization. To behave counter to caste prescriptions would be to go against religion and social custom and to risk not fitting into society. That can be a death sentence in some societies.

In caste-based societies, the institution of religion works together with the family, education, the economy, and political institutions to shape both expectations and aspirations and to keep people in their prescribed places in caste systems. For example, Hindu ideas dictate that violating the caste prescriptions can put one's next *reincarnation* (or rebirth in the Hindu tradition) in jeopardy. Stability in Hindu societies is maintained, in part, by the belief that people can be reborn into a higher status in the next life if they fulfill expectations in their ascribed position in this life.

The clearest example of a caste system is found in India, a predominantly Hindu society. The Hindu religion holds that individuals are born into one of four *varnas*, broad caste positions, or into a fifth group below the caste system, the *outcaste* group. The first and highest varna, called *Brahmans*, originally was made up of priests and scholars but now includes many leaders in society. The second varna, *Kshatriyas* or *Rajputs*, includes the original prince and warrior varna and now embraces much of the army and civil service. The *Vaishyas*, or merchants, are the third varna. The fourth varna, the *Sudras*, includes peasants, farmers, artisans, and laborers. The final layer, below the caste system, encompasses profoundly oppressed people—"a people put aside"—referred to as untouchables, outcastes, *Chandalas* (a Hindu term), and *Dalits* (the name preferred by many "untouchables" themselves). Although the Indian Constitution of 1950 granted full social status to these citizens, and a law passed in 1955 made discrimination against them punishable, deeply rooted traditions can be difficult to change. Caste distinctions are still very prevalent, especially in rural areas.

Estate systems are *characterized by the concentration of economic and political power in the hands of a small minority of political-military elite, with the peasantry tied to the land* (Rothman 2005). They existed in ancient Egypt, the Incan and Mayan civilizations, Europe, China, and Japan. In estate systems, an individual's rank and legal rights are clearly spelled out, and arranged marriages and religion bolster the system. In Europe, during the Middle Ages, knights defended the realms and the religion of the nobles. Behind every knight in shining armor were peasants, sweating in the fields and paying for the knights' food, armor, and campaigns. For farming the land owned by the nobility, peasants received protection against invading armies and enough of the produce to survive. Their lives were often miserable. If the yield of crops was poor, they ate little. In a good year, they might save enough to buy a small parcel of land. A very few were able to become independent in this fashion. Today, similar systems exist in some Central and South American, Asian, and African countries on large banana, coffee, cacao, and sugar plantations.

Thinking Sociologically

What might be some advantages, for both the society and the individuals living in it, of a society where status was ascribed rather than achieved? Do you think you would enjoy living in such a society? Why, or why not?

Achieved Status: Social Class in the United States

In contrast to ascribed status systems, *achieved stratification systems* maintain that everyone is born with common legal status and equality before the law. In principle, all individuals can own property and choose their own occupations. However, in practice, most achieved status systems, like the class system found in the United States, pass privilege or poverty from one generation to the next. Individual upward or downward mobility is more difficult than the ideology invites people to believe.

Social class refers to *the wealth, power, and prestige rankings that individuals hold in society*. Members of the same social class have similar income, wealth, and economic position, lifestyles, levels of education, cultural beliefs, and patterns of social interaction. Our families, rich or poor and educated or unskilled, provide us with an initial social ranking and socialization experience. We tend to feel a kinship and sense of belonging with those in the same social class and tend to live, attend school, and work with people from our social class. We think alike, share interests, and probably look up to the same people as a reference group.

Our social class position is based on the three main factors in the stratification system: (1) property, (2) prestige, and (3) power. This is the trio—the three *Ps*—that, according to Max Weber, determines where individuals rank in relation to each other (Weber 1946, 1947). By *property* (wealth), Weber refers to owning or controlling the means of production. *Power*, the ability to control others, includes not only the means of production but also the position one holds. *Prestige* involves the esteem and recognition one receives, based on wealth, position, or accomplishments. Chances of being granted high prestige improve if one's patterns of behavior, occupation, and lifestyle match those valued in the society (e.g., in U.S. society today that would include scientists, physicians, military officers, lawyers, and college professors).

Although these three dimensions of stratification are often found together, this is not always so. Recall the idea of *status inconsistency*: an individual can have a great deal of prestige yet not command much wealth (Weber 1946). Consider winners of the prestigious Nobel Peace Prize such as Wangari Maathai, a Kenyan environmentalist who won the prize for starting a movement to plant trees and for her political activism, or Betty Williams and Mairead Corrigan of Northern Ireland, founders of the Community of Peace People, who won for their efforts to find a peaceful end to their country's conflicts. None of them was rich, but each made contributions to the world that gained them universal prestige. Likewise, some people gain enormous wealth through crime or gambling, but this wealth may not be accompanied by respect or prestige.

Some theorists see power as the key element in systems of stratification. Conflict theorists maintain that those who hold power control the economic capital and the means of production in society (Ashley and Orenstein 2009). Consistent with Marx, many recent conflict theorists argue that a **power elite** composed of *top leaders in corporations, politics, and the military* rules society (Domhoff 2014).

These interlocking groups of elites grow up together, attending the same private schools and belonging to the same private clubs. There is an unspoken agreement to protect each other's positions and ensure that their power is not threatened. Those not in this interlocking elite group do not hold real power and have little chance of breaking into the inner circles (Domhoff 2014; Dye 2002, 2014; C. Mills 1956).

Pluralist **power theorists**, on the other hand, argue that *power is not held exclusively by an elite group but is shared among many power centers, each of which has its own self-interests to protect* (Ritzer and Goodman 2004). Well-financed special interest groups (e.g., insurance industry, dairy and cattle farmers, or truckers' trade unions) and professional associations (e.g., the American Medical Association or American Bar Association) have considerable power through collective action. From the pluralist perspective, officials who hold political power are vulnerable to pressure from influential interest groups, and each interest group competes for power with others. Creating and maintaining this power through networks and pressure on legislators is the job of lobbyists. For example, in the intense U.S. debate over health care legislation, interest groups from the medical community, insurance lobbies, and citizens' groups wielded their power to influence the outcome, but because these major interests conflict, and no one group has the most power, no one group attained all it wanted. Some groups wanted to nationalize health care, and others wanted to completely privatize it; the Affordable Care Act did neither. The core idea of pluralist theorists, then, is that many centers of power create at least some checks and balances on those in elite positions.

Examples of Social Classes in the United States

Imagine that you are a politician. The public is clamoring for more help for the middle class. Flash back to the most recent U.S. presidential campaign. All the candidates were talking about the middle class. Did you ever hear the politicians define what they meant? You probably did not because the broader and more inclusive the definition, the more useful it is to politicians who are trying to appeal to a range of voters.

When given a choice among lower, middle, and upper class, almost all Americans will say they are middle class. When given a choice that includes working class, however, 45% say middle class, and another 45% define themselves as working class (Gilbert 2011). Sociologists have different ways of measuring social class. You can see sociologist Dennis Gilbert's social class model in Figure 7.10.

Most social scientists measure social class by looking at the income, education, and profession of respondents. Sometimes, social scientists break down members of the middle class into two groups: the white-collar middle class and the working class. Most white-collar workers have a college education, have professions with salaries (rather

FIGURE 7.10 Gilbert's Model of Social Class

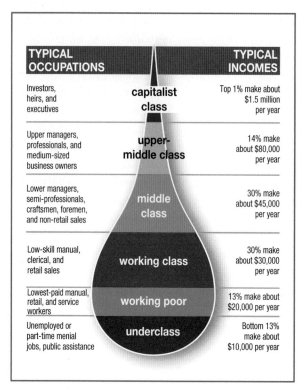

Source: Gilbert (2011).

than jobs where they are paid by the hour), work in an office setting, and earn within a specified range around the median income. Members of the working class work for hourly wages, do manual labor, and do not usually have a college degree.

● Thinking Sociologically

How does today's popular culture on TV and in films, magazines, and popular music reflect interests of different social classes? How are rich and poor people depicted? Who appears responsible for their wealth or poverty—the individuals, the society, or some other combination? Do any of these depictions question the U.S. class system?

POVERTY AND SOCIAL POLICY

Nothing describes poverty more vividly than hunger. Stories about hunger and famine in Global South countries fill the newspapers. Chronic hunger has declined by

130 million people since 1990 (World Food Programme 2013; World Hunger Education Service 2013). Yet around the world, nearly 870 million people, or roughly 1 in every 8 people on Earth, still go to bed hungry every night. Figure 7.11 shows where hunger is most severe.

One hardly expects to see hunger in rich countries, yet in the United States, over 50 million people, or 1 in 7 in the U.S. population and 1 in 5 children, are hungry some of the time (Feeding America 2015; Sauter and Hess 2013). States most severely affected by food insecurity (lack of consistent access to food) include Mississippi, Arkansas, Texas, Alabama, North Carolina, Georgia, Missouri, Nevada, Tennessee, and Ohio. These states also have among the highest obesity rates due to poor diets (Coleman-Jensen, Gregory, and Singh 2014). Households led by single women are especially likely to be food insecure, with 34.4% lacking sufficient food. Race also influences the likelihood of food insecurity. One out of four Black (26.1%) and Hispanic (23.7%) households are food insecure (Coleman-Jensen et al. 2014).

Most people living in poverty have no property-based income and no permanent or stable work, only casual or intermittent earnings in the labor market. They often depend on help from government agencies or private organizations to survive. In short, they have personal troubles in large part because they have been unable to establish linkages and networks in the meso- and macro-level organizations of our social world. The reality is that most of the gap is due to structural issues, with the wealth gaps becoming so extreme that in 2016, just 62 individuals owned more wealth than 3.5 billion people—half of the world's population (Cohen 2016; Oxfam 2016).

Thinking Sociologically

Explain how your family's ability to provide food for its members at the micro level is largely dependent on its connectedness to the meso and macro levels of society.

Sociologists recognize two basic types of poverty: (1) absolute poverty and (2) relative poverty. **Absolute poverty**, *not having resources to meet basic needs*, means no prestige, very little access to power, no accumulated

FIGURE 7.11 Global Hunger Index

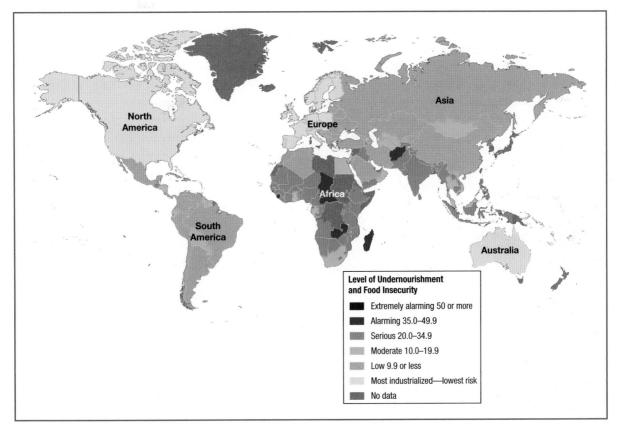

Source: von Grebmer et al. (2015). Used with permission from the International Food Policy Research Institute.

wealth, and insufficient means to survive. Some die of easily cured diseases because the bodies of those in absolute poverty are weakened by chronic and persistent hunger and almost total lack of medical attention.

Relative poverty occurs *when one's income falls below the poverty line, resulting in an inadequate standard of living relative to others in the individual's country*. In the United States, relative poverty means shortened life expectancy, higher infant mortality, and poorer health. Whereas few people starve on the street and suffer from the easily cured diseases more common among the poor in Global South nations, food insecurity and the stress and hardships of relative poverty lead to more health problems and earlier deaths for the poor in the United States and other Global North nations with high levels of inequality.

The *feminization of poverty* refers to the trend in which single females with children make up a growing proportion of those in poverty. In 2013, 11.8% of males and 15.3% of females aged 18 to 64 in the United States lived in poverty, and Table 7.2 shows how much income would remove one from the poverty line. One in five children (20% of girls and 19.8% of boys) were in poverty (DeNavas-Walt and Proctor 2014). If you are raised by a single mother, you have a greater chance of experiencing poverty. Almost 1 out of 3 (30.6%) families with a female head of household were in poverty in 2013 (DeNavas-Walt and Proctor 2014). Some of those in poverty find themselves without a home. As of January 2014, there were an estimated 578,424 homeless people in the United States (U.S. Department of Housing and Urban Development 2014). Among them, 69% were in transitional or emergency

shelters, and 31% were unsheltered. Almost 1 out of 4 of the homeless (23%) were children under the age of 18. Families now make up over one third (37%) of the homeless population.

The Obama administration made a concerted effort to combat homelessness and used social scientific research to do so. Studies have shown that "mainstream housing, health, education, and human service programs must be fully engaged and coordinated to prevent and end homelessness" (Sullivan 2013). Research also reveals that providing a wide range of services for the homeless actually saves taxpayers money in the long run "by interrupting a costly cycle of emergency room visits, detoxes, and even jail terms" (Sullivan 2013). Thanks to strategies based on these finding, the number of homeless has declined by 11% since 2007 (despite the impact of the Great Recession and rising levels of inequality) (U.S. Department of Housing and Urban Development 2014).

How can we effectively address inequality? First, we must become aware of the problem. As this chapter has described, almost every society has some system of stratification. We do not all have the same chances of "making it." Most of us, though, do not fully realize the extent of the inequality in the society we call home. For example, in a recent study, a nationally representative sample of U.S. citizens was shown three charts that displayed different distributions of wealth, ranging from somewhat equal to very unequal. When asked which of the three charts illustrated how wealth was distributed in the United States, most respondents chose the chart that actually described wealth distribution in Sweden, the nation with the *lowest level* of economic inequality in the world. The chart most often picked by respondents as an "ideal" distribution of wealth illustrated an even *more equitable* distribution of wealth than that found in Sweden (Norton and Ariely 2011). Figure 7.12 shows the actual U.S. wealth distribution plotted against the estimated and ideal distributions across all respondents. Note that the ideal distribution is closest to the results of the survey described. Responses varied a bit by age, income, and political party, but there was overall agreement that America would be better off with a smaller wealth gap (Weissmann 2014).

Thinking Sociologically

What distribution of wealth and income would you favor for your nation, and why? What changes would you make to approach your favored distribution?

TABLE 7.2 Poverty Thresholds for 2014 by Size of Family

Size of Family Unit	Weighted Average Thresholds
One person	$12,071
Two people	$15,379
Three people	$18,850
Four people	$24,230
Five people	$28,695
Six people	$32,473

Source: U.S. Census Bureau (2015a).

FIGURE 7.12 Wealth Inequality in the United States: Actual, Estimated, and Perceived Ideal Percentage of Wealth Owned

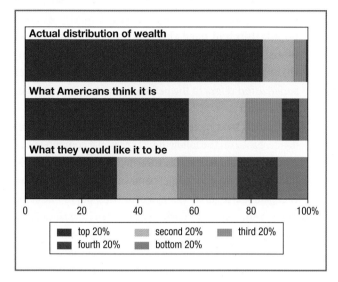

Actual distribution of wealth

What Americans think it is

What they would like it to be

| 0 | 20 | 40 | 60 | 80 | 100% |

top 20%   second 20%   third 20%
fourth 20%   bottom 20%

Note: The actual U.S. wealth distribution plotted against the estimated and ideal distributions across all respondents. Because of their small percentage share of total wealth, both the "fourth 20%" value (0.2%) and the "bottom 20%" value (0.1%) are not visible in the "Actual" distribution.

The bar labeled "What Americans think it is" represents the *actual* distribution of wealth in Sweden.

Source: Norton and Ariely (2011).

After reading this chapter, you understand that the United States has higher levels of inequality and poverty and less class mobility than most other wealthy nations. Once we understand the extent of inequality and poverty, we can start to develop ways to address these issues. We can also critique poverty reduction programs now under way in different nations and help to create more effective ones, if needed.

NATIONAL AND GLOBAL DIGITAL DIVIDE: MACRO-LEVEL STRATIFICATION

Mamadou from Niger and Eric from Ghana answer their iPhones to the sound of chimes from London's Big Ben clock tower and a Bob Marley song. In addition to English, one speaks in Kanuri and French and the other in Twi to friends and family thousands of miles away. They are the future generation of elites from the Global South, fluent in the languages of several countries, adept in computer software, and at the forefront of their countries in digital technology. Many of their

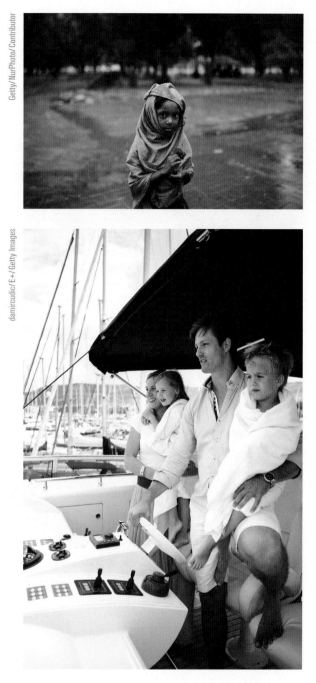

This homeless girl walks in the rain in Dhaka, Bangladesh. The child's family has little power to improve its situation or her life chances. Compare her circumstances to those of the boy and girl in their parents' arms on a yacht.

fellow citizens in Niger and Ghana in Africa are not so fortunate. With insufficient education to participate in the changing economy and new technologies, they have little contact with the digital world swirling overhead through satellite connections.

Global economic and political institutions increasingly produce and transmit information through digital technology. Few tools are more important than computers,

In Laos, where many people live in grass houses such as this one (*top*), most families do not have access to electronic devices or the Internet. Their homes and their life chances stand in stark contrast to those of the children seen here working on computers—seen as necessary equipment.

smartphones, and the Internet. In nearly every salaried and professional position, computer knowledge and the ability to navigate the Internet are critical employment skills. The *digital divide* refers to the gap between those with knowledge and access to information technology and those without it. The lines of the divide are drawn by the position of the country in the world, socioeconomic status of citizens, and urban-versus-rural residence (World Economic Forum 2015).

Many individuals in Global South countries have insufficient technology and education to participate in this new economy. Approximately 90% of residents of low-income nations have never gone online (World Economic Forum 2015). Still, the number of Internet users in the world is increasing rapidly. In 2000, just 250 million people (around 1%) could access the Internet, but by June 2014, 42.3% of the world's population had used the Internet (Internet World Statistics 2016; Renick 2011). As Table 7.3 makes clear, this varies greatly by region of the world. *Internet penetration* refers to the percentage of Internet users in each country.

Researchers have laid out three tiers in the digital divide, based on the following: (1) personal computers per 100 in the population, (2) Internet users per 100 in the population, and (3) Internet bandwidth per person. Using these standards, all developed countries, plus some additional countries in the Caribbean, Eastern Europe, and the Middle East, are Tier 1—the places with the most access. The second tier includes Brazil, Russia, China, and some smaller countries in South America. African nations account for the majority of members in the lowest tier, reflecting the disadvantage of the continent in terms of lack of computers, computer use, and bandwidth ("International Digital Divide" 2011). However, undersea fiber optic cables are being laid around Africa to provide faster and more reliable Internet access ("African Undersea Cables" 2013).

As Internet technology expands, it brings the world to remote villages, opening new horizons and options and changing lifestyles. Some poor countries are transitioning into the electronic age and making policies that facilitate rapid modernization. They are passing over developmental stages that rich Global North countries went through. As an illustration, consider the telephone. Most telephones in the world are cell phones, many using satellite connections. Some countries never did get wired for landlines and have skipped that step in development. With the satellite technology now in place, some computer and Internet options are available to them without landlines (World Economic Forum 2015). Use of cell phones in poor countries has boomed, giving people access to health care and other services. By 2014, the number of mobile phones in the world was over 7 billion (enough for 96% of the world's population), with 77% of growth from smartphones (Cisco 2014). Africa had the lowest number of subscribers, at 63% (Pramis 2013; Whitney 2012).

The growing use of cell phones has helped shrink the digital divide more than anything else. For example,

TABLE 7.3 World Internet Usage by Region

World Regions	Internet Penetration (% Population)	% of Total Global Internet Users
Africa	28.6	9.8
Asia	40.2	48.2
Europe	73.5	18.0
Middle East	52.2	3.7
North America	87.9	9.3
Latin America/ Caribbean	55.9	10.2
Oceania/ Australia	73.2	0.8
WORLD TOTAL	**46.4**	**100.0**

Source: Internet World Statistics (2016).

around the world people can buy and sell goods and send money through their cell phones. The influence is felt from the micro to the macro level, as it improves the lives of individuals, increases business in the area in which they live, and helps connect them to the global economy by allowing individuals to save and invest money in the local and global economies (Langfitt 2011).

Haiti, one of the poorest nations in the world, also provides a great example of the potential positive power of Internet technology. Whereas only 10% of Haitians have bank accounts, 80% have cell phones. Aid agencies, after the earthquake of 2010, have been able to make use of this technology, distributing aid to far-flung refugees via their cell phones (Beaubien 2011; Partners in Prepaid 2012).

Using the Internet to promote saving and investment is one powerful means, just now being tapped, of addressing global poverty and inequality. Digital technology is an example of one important force changing the micro- to macro-level global stratification system—a spectrum of people and countries from the rich and elite to the poor and desperate.

We leave this discussion of stratification systems, including class systems, with a partial answer to the question posed at the beginning of this chapter: Why are some people rich and others poor? In the next two chapters, we expand the discussion to include other variables in stratification systems—race, ethnicity, and gender.

By the end of these chapters, the answer to the opening question—why some have riches and some have only rags—should be even clearer. Socioeconomic status is important as a measure in any society, but it is not the sole basis for stratification. In the next chapter, we look at the role of race and ethnicity in social inequality.

WHAT HAVE WE LEARNED?

The issue of social stratification calls into question the widely held belief in the fairness of our economic system. By studying this issue, we better understand why some individuals are able to experience prestige (respect) and to control power and wealth at the micro, meso, and macro levels of the social system, whereas others have little access to those resources. Few social forces affect your personal life at the micro level as much as stratification. That includes the decisions you make about what you wish to do with your life or whom you might marry. Indeed, stratification played a role in why you are reading this book.

- *Stratification*—the layering or ranking of people within society—is one of the most important factors shaping the life chances of individuals. This ranking is influenced by micro, meso, and macro forces and resources.

- Depending on the theoretical perspective, stratification can be viewed as either functional or harmful for society and its members.

- The United States has less social mobility and higher levels of inequality and poverty than most other Global North nations.

- For individuals, where they stand in the system of stratification is highly personal, but it is influenced by the way the social system works at the meso and macro level—due to access to education; the problems created by gender, racial, and ethnic discrimination; and the vitality of regions and the global economy.

- People without much social capital have fewer connections to the meso and macro levels and are less likely to attain power, wealth, and prestige.

- Some macro systems stress ascribed status (assigned to one, often at birth, without consideration of one's individual choices, talents, or intelligence). Other systems purport to be open and based on achieved status (depending on one's contributions to the society and one's personal abilities and decisions).

- Poverty can be costly to a society as a whole. Various solutions at the micro, meso, and macro levels have had mixed results, partly because as conflict theorists note, it is in the interests of those with privilege to have an underclass to do the unpleasant jobs.

- Technology is both a contributor to and a possible remedy for inequality, in that the digital divide creates problems for the poor, but electronic innovations also create new job opportunities and opportunities for networking and making connections to the meso and macro levels—even for those in the Global South, the poorer regions of the world.

DISCUSSION QUESTIONS

1. Were you surprised to learn that among rich nations, life expectancy in the United States is among the lowest? Explain. What sociological theory best explains this fact? Support your answer.

2. How has the social class of your parents and your upbringing influenced your success in school and your professional aspirations?

3. What is the social class of most of the people with whom you hang out? Why do you think you tend to associate with people from this social class?

4. Describe factors at the (a) micro, (b) meso, and (c) macro levels that impact your ability to move up the social class ladder.

5. How do the forces that have led to the shrinking of the middle class impact your chance of becoming (or remaining) a member of the (a) middle, (b) upper middle, or (c) upper class after you graduate from college?

6. How can bridging the global digital divide lead to a decrease in inequality across the world? How does your ready access (or lack of access) to a computer and the Internet impact *your* life chances?

KEY TERMS

CONTRIBUTING TO OUR SOCIAL WORLD: WHAT CAN WE DO?

At the Local (Micro) Level

- *Volunteer to serve a meal* at an area soup kitchen. Your campus activities office should be able to help you find one in your area and even connect you with a group on campus that regularly volunteers at one.

- *Tip service people in cash.* Housekeepers in hotels and motels, maids, meal servers at restaurants, and food delivery employees may depend on tips to survive. In order to make it more likely that they receive the tips intended for them, be sure to tip in cash, rather than using a credit card.

At the Organizational/Institutional (Meso) Level

- *Habitat for Humanity* pairs volunteers with current and prospective homeowners in repairing or constructing housing for little or no cost. Habitat projects are under way or planned for many communities in the United States and around the world. See the organization's website at www.habitat.org for more details and to see if you can volunteer for a project in your area.

- Founded in the early 1990s, AmeriCorps: Corporation for National and Community Service (US), includes a variety of programs from intensive residential programs to part-time volunteer opportunities in communities across the United States.

For more information, go to the organization's website at https://www.nationalservice.gov/programs/americorps.

At the National/Global (Macro) Levels

- *The Peace Corps* involves a serious, long-term (two-year) commitment, but most who have done it agree that it is well worth the time and energy. The Peace Corps is an independent agency of the U.S. government, founded in 1961. Volunteers work in foreign countries throughout the world, helping local people improve their economic conditions, health, and education. The Peace Corps website (www.peacecorps.gov) provides information on the history of the organization, volunteer opportunities, and reports of former and present volunteers.

- *Grameen Bank* (www.grameenfoundation.org), a microcredit organization, was started in Bangladesh by Professor Muhammad Yunus, winner of the 2006 Nobel Peace Prize. It makes small business loans to people who live in impoverished regions of the world and who have no collateral for a loan. Consider doing a local fundraiser with friends for the Grameen Bank or other microcredit organizations, such as FINCA (www.Finca.org), KIVA (www.kiva.org), and Care International (www.care-international.org).

- *WE Charity* is a youth-focused organization whose international programs help free people across the globe from the cycle of poverty by providing clean water, schools, health care, and sanitation. You can learn more about this organization and how you can join its efforts at we.org.

⑤SAGE edge™

Get the edge on your studies. **edge.sagepub.com/ballantinecondensed5e**

- Take a quiz to find out what you've learned.
- Review key terms with eFlashcards.
- Watch videos that enhance chapter content.

8 Race and Ethnic Group Stratification

Beyond "Us" and "Them"

As human beings, we are all part of "us," but there is a tendency to define those who look or behave differently as "them." Those labeled as "them" are often separated from "us" and even dehumanized and mistreated by "us."

ME (AND MY MINORITY FRIENDS)

LOCAL ORGANIZATIONS AND COMMUNITY
Locally, members of ethnic groups may experience exclusion and prejudice.

NATIONAL ORGANIZATIONS, INSTITUTIONS, AND ETHNIC SUBCULTURES
Policies in large organizations may discriminate— intentionally or unintentionally.

SOCIETY
National laws or court rulings often set policies that relate to discrimination.

GLOBAL COMMUNITY
Racial and ethnic hostilities around the world may result in wars, genocide, and "ethnic cleansing."

WHAT YOU WILL LEARN IN THIS CHAPTER

This chapter will help you do the following:

8.1 Distinguish between racial and ethnic groups.

8.2 Describe the difference between prejudice and discrimination.

8.3 Provide examples of dominant and minority group contact in the world today.

8.4 Outline effects of prejudice, racism, and discrimination on minority and dominant groups.

8.5 Describe efforts to reduce racial and ethnic inequality at the micro, meso, and macro levels of analysis.

◑ THINK ABOUT IT

Micro: Local community	Why do people in the local community categorize "others" into racial or ethnic groups?
Meso: National institutions, complex organizations, and ethnic groups	How might your education, religion, politics, economics, and health experiences differ depending on your ethnicity?
Macro: National and global systems	Why are minority group members in most countries economically poorer than dominant group members? In what ways might ethnicity or race shape international negotiations and global problem solving?

DeBrun was a well-liked African American college student, actively involved in extracurricular activities. Like many college students, he enjoyed both alcohol consumption on weekends and the outrageous things that happened when people were inebriated. However, DeBrun's anger, normally kept in check, tended to surface when he was drunk. One weekend, some racial slurs were thrown around at a party, and when one of the perpetrators pushed DeBrun too far—including a sucker punch—DeBrun exploded in a fury of violence. No one died, but there were some serious injuries—the worst inflicted by the muscular DeBrun—and at one point, a knife was pulled. DeBrun was expelled from the university, and felony charges were leveled against him. Because there had been a weapon—one that did not belong to DeBrun but at one point ended up in his hand—the university president would not consider readmission. The local White prosecutor, who saw a powerfully built young Black man with tattoos and dreadlocks, assumed that this campus leader was a "thug" and insisted on the most severe felony charges and penalties.

DeBrun, who had no previous encounters with law enforcement, ended up with a felony record and 2 years in prison. Because of both state and federal laws, the felony charges meant that he no longer qualified for federal financial aid. As his family had very few resources, his hopes for a college degree were crushed. As a convicted felon, he would not be able to vote in many states for the rest of his life, his future employment prospects were greatly diminished, and his family's hopes that he would be their first college graduate were crushed. The president of the college was not a bigot, but the professors who knew DeBrun well were convinced that neither his expulsion, nor his arrest, nor his conviction as a serious felon would have occurred had he been White.

This recent incident represents a way that African American males can experience a different United States of America than middle-class White males. The cause is not necessarily personal bigotry by people in power. Differential treatment and harmful actions against minorities can sometimes occur at individual and small-group levels but are particularly problematic at the meso or institutional level. In any case, life in the United States can be very different for people whose skin tone is dark.

In a recent study, sociologists interviewed Black and White schoolchildren, whose ages ranged from 11 to 14, and asked them, "What would happen if an alien entered your room at night and turned you into a Black [or White] child?" The majority (65%) of the White children and an overwhelming majority (93%) of the Black children thought their lives would be different if their race changed (Risman and Banerjee 2013).

What do you think? Would your life change if your race changed? Imagine that you were given the opportunity to choose your own racial and ethnic background. What would you do? Why? How do you think your life would be different if you chose a different racial and ethnic background? In this chapter, we explore racial and ethnic stratification. In doing so, we look at related issues, such as the social construction of race, prejudice, racism, and discrimination. Some are micro-level issues, whereas others are best addressed at the meso and macro levels.

WHAT CHARACTERIZES RACIAL AND ETHNIC GROUPS?

In this section, we consider the characteristics of racial and ethnic groups and their positions within the stratification system. **Minority groups** *differ from other groups in some characteristics and are subject to less power, fewer privileges, and discrimination.* Like all minority groups, racial and ethnic minority groups have less power than the dominant group in society.

Minority Groups

Several factors characterize minority groups and their relations with dominant groups in society (Dworkin and Dworkin 1999). Minority groups

1. can be distinguished from the group that holds power by physical appearance, dress, language, or religion;

2. are excluded from or denied full participation at the meso level of society in economic, political, educational, religious, health, and recreational institutions;

3. have less access to power and resources within the nation and are evaluated less favorably, based on their characteristics as minority group members;

4. are stereotyped, ridiculed, condemned, or otherwise defamed, allowing dominant group members to justify and not feel guilty about unequal and poor treatment; and

5. develop collective identities to insulate themselves from the unaccepting world; this, in turn, perpetuates their group identity by creating ethnic or racial enclaves, intragroup marriages, and segregated group institutions, such as religious congregations.

⬤ Thinking Sociologically

Based on the preceding list of minority group characteristics, explain how membership in dominant or minority groups influences people's interactions at the micro (family and friends), the meso (institutional), and macro levels of society.

Minority and majority status can change over time and among societies. For example, throughout England's history, wars and assassinations changed the ruling group from Catholic to Protestant and back several times. Today, in Iraq, Shiite Muslims are dominant, but they were a minority group, and Sunni Muslims were the dominant group when Saddam Hussein ruled Iraq.

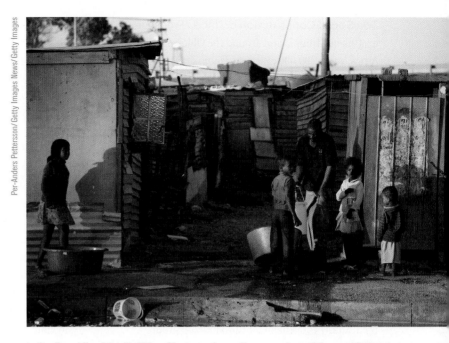

Per-Anders Pettersson/Getty Images News/Getty Images

In the Republic of South Africa, Blacks make up three quarters of the population, but they are still considered a minority group because they face racial discrimination and have far less access to economic power and privilege than the "majority" of White South Africans, who comprise 9% of the population. Residents fetch water at a community tap near Cape Town.

As in the case of Iraq under Saddam Hussein, dominant groups are not always the numerical majority. In the case of South Africa, possession of advanced European weapons placed the native African Bantu population under the rule of a relatively small number of White British and Dutch descendants in what became a complex system of planned discrimination called *apartheid*. From 1948 to 1994, each major racial group in South Africa—White, "Indian" (meaning Asian), "Coloured" (meaning mixed race), and Black—had its own living area, and members carried identification cards showing the "race" to which they belonged. Racial classification and privilege were defined by the laws of the dominant group.

The Concept of Race

Race is *a socially created concept that identifies a group as "different," usually on the basis of ancestry or certain physical characteristics*. This allows members of the groups to be singled out for dissimilar treatment. Most attempts at racial classifications have been based on combinations of appearance, such as skin color and shade, stature, facial features, hair color and texture, head form, nose shape, eye color and shape, height, and blood or gene type. As you will see, though, racial categories are social constructions that vary over time and place.

The Social Construction of Race. From our earliest origins in Ethiopia and around the Olduvai Gorge in East Africa, about 200,000 years ago, *Homo sapiens* slowly spread around the globe, south through Africa, north to Europe, and across Asia. Original migration patterns of early humans over thousands of years are shown in Figure 8.1. As the map shows, most theorists believe that humans crossed Asia and the Bering Strait to North America around 20,000 BCE and continued to populate North and South America (Diamond 1999, 2005). However, continuing archaeological research indicates that indigenous human populations may have reached South America well before the map indicates (Mann 2005). The point is that mixing of peoples over the centuries has left few, if any, genetically isolated people, only gradations in appearance as one moves around the world. Thus, the way societies choose to define race has come about largely through what is culturally convenient for the dominant group.

Throughout history, political and religious leaders, philosophers, and even scientists have struggled with the meaning and significance of race. The first systematic classification of all living phenomena was published in 1735 by Carl von Linné (Linnaeus). His hierarchy of species was actually quite complex—including monkeys, elephants, and angels—and suggested four human types: Americanus (Native Americans), Asiaticus, Africanus, and Europeanus (Cashmore and Troyna 1990). Johann Blumenbach was the first to use the word *race* in his 1775 classification system: Caucasian, Mongolian, Ethiopian, American, and Malay.

By the 19th century, many began to use pseudoscientific rankings of racial groups to justify slavery and colonialism. Comte de Gobineau (1816–1882) argued that each race has specific characteristics, and he attributed the demise of societies to the mixing of the White race with other (inferior) races. His book *Essay on Inequality of the Human Races*, published in 1853–1855, earned him the title "father of modern racism." In 1899, the Brit-turned-German Houston Stewart Chamberlain ([1899]1911) published an aristocratic, anti-Semitic work in which he argued that northern and western European populations, Teutonic in particular, were superior. He argued for racial purity, a theme the Nazis of the 1930s and 1940s adopted.

Looking through history, one can see many more examples of how racial categorizations have been misused across

FIGURE 8.1   The Spread of Humans Around the World

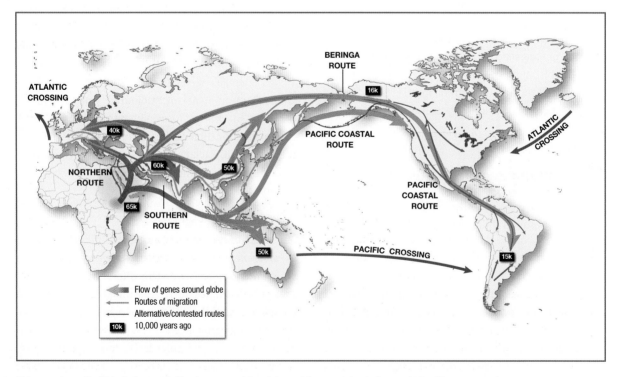

This map shows the historical spread of humans around the globe and the approximate time periods of the movements.

Source: Phys.org (2009).

time and societies. For example, in the United States, Irish and Italians were once seen as distinct races that were clearly inferior to the White race. Clearly, racial categories are social, rather than biological, constructions.

In 1978, the United Nations, concerned about racial conflicts and discrimination based on scientifically inaccurate beliefs, issued a Declaration on Race and Race Prejudice prepared by a group of eminent scientists from around the world. This declaration and similar statements by scientific groups pointed out the harmful effects of racist arguments, doctrines, and policies. The conclusion of their document upheld that (a) all people are born free and equal both in dignity and in rights, (b) racial prejudice impedes personal development, (c) conflicts (based on race) cost nations money and resources, and (d) racism foments international conflict. Racist doctrines lack any scientific basis, in that all people belong to the same species and have descended from the same origin. In summary, problems arising from race relations are social, not biological, in origin. Differential treatments of groups based on "race" falsely claim a scientific basis for classifying humans.

Thinking Sociologically

How would you describe the other people in your sociology class? Do you use racial terms for everyone? Why, or why not? How does your own racial background influence how much you notice the racial characteristics of others? Why?

Symbolic Interactionist Analysis of the Social Construction of Race. Why are sociologists concerned about a concept that has little scientific accuracy and is ill defined? The answer is its *social significance*. The social reality is that people's group membership can influence how they are treated by others and how they view themselves. Remember the *looking-glass self* concept—we see ourselves based on how we think others perceive us. Our self-concept can be greatly affected by whether we see ourselves as members of a dominant or minority racial group.

Strangely, we might be seen as part of a dominant group in one society and a minority group in another. For example, imagine it is 1970, and you have White parents, three White grandparents, and one Black grandparent. Imagine, too, that no one would guess by your appearance that you had an ancestor who was not White. In South Africa, you would be treated as "Coloured" (in between Black and White); in many U.S. states, you would be defined as Black; and in Brazil, you would be perceived as White (Kottak 2014).

In 1977, the U.S. Office of Management and Budget issued a directive to ensure consistent ethnic and racial categories for both statistical and administrative goals. Federal programs directed toward specific racial and ethnic groups and the U.S. Census use these categories. Many very different groups have been combined under these five racial and ethnic categories: (1) American Indian or Alaska Native, (2) Asian or Pacific Islander, (3) Black, (4) Hispanic, and (5) White. (Hispanic/Latino Americans are an ethnic group and can be of any race.) For example, in North America, those racially classified as Native American or Alaska Native use 600 independent tribal nation names to identify themselves, including the Ojibwa (Chippewa), the Dineh (Navajo), the Lakota (Sioux), and many others. Most consider themselves very different from other "Native American" groups. Some even fought against one another in past wars. Likewise, people of Korean, Filipino, Chinese, Japanese, and Malaysian descent are all identified as *Asian Americans*, but they come from very different cultures (including some that were once mortal enemies). In addition, people from (or who have ancestors from) Mexico, Bolivia, Cuba, and many other nations are grouped together in an ethnic category called *Hispanics* or *Latinos*, even though they do not think of themselves as being alike.

When government aid is tied to such categories, people must identify as such in order to receive funds. When federal funds for social services were made available to Asian Americans or American Indians, these diverse people began to think of themselves as part of a larger grouping for political purposes (Esperitu 1992). The federal government essentially created a racial group by naming and providing funding to that group. If people wanted services (health care, legal rights, and so forth), they had to become a part of a particular group—such as "Asian Americans."

Before civil rights laws were passed in the United States in the 1960s, a number of states had laws that spelled out differential treatment for racial groups. These were commonly referred to as Jim Crow laws. States in the South passed laws defining who was Black and subject to these discriminatory laws. In many cases, it was difficult to determine to which category an individual belonged. For instance, Blacks in Georgia were defined as people with any ascertainable trace of "Negro" blood in their veins. In Missouri, one-eighth or more "Negro" blood was the standard, whereas in Louisiana, 1/32 "Negro" blood defined one as Black. In Texas, the father's race determined the race of the child. Even the U.S. Census Bureau finds categories that indicate race or ethnicity to be very confusing and complex. Over the history of the United States, the racial classifications on the Census have changed many times.

Thinking Sociologically

Go to www.census.gov/population/race/data/MREAD_ 1790_2010.html where you will find a timeline of U.S. Census racial and ethnic categories. List at least two changes among the many throughout the history of the United States, and then, describe some social forces behind those changes. How does this timeline provide evidence that racial categories are social constructions?

The Continuing Significance of Race. The civil rights legislation of the 1960s that prohibited racial discrimination in voting, housing, and employment has helped diminish discrimination. Unfortunately, though, racial discrimination still exists, and the combination of the impact of past and present discrimination has led to disparities in wealth and income among Black, Hispanic, and White Americans. As Tables 8.1 and 8.2 make clear, income levels for Blacks, Hispanics, and Whites, even when controlling for education level, are still quite disparate.

A clear racial economic hierarchy exists, with White Americans on the top and other racial groups below.

Not only do race and ethnicity impact income, regardless of educational level, but Black Americans are more likely than Whites to be unemployed at every level of educational achievement. Table 8.3 displays the differences.

Differences in *wealth* (one's income, property, and total assets) by race are even more stark. As Figure 8.2 indicates, in the United States, Whites have 13 times the wealth of Blacks and 10 times the wealth of Hispanics. In 2013, the median White family had $142,000 in wealth, compared with $11,000 for the median Black family (Kochhar and Fry 2014).

This hierarchy is due to current as well as past discrimination. For example, in one well-known study, Black, White, and Hispanic applicants (of similar age, similar physical appearance, and the same level of educational attainment and qualifications) responded to help wanted ads for jobs in the low-wage sector in New York City. The results showed that Whites received a callback about the position or job offer 31% of the time compared with 25.2% for Hispanics and 15.2% for Blacks. Other studies reveal that among equally qualified job candidates, those with

Table 8.1 Race or Ethnicity and Family Income

	Asian	White	Black	Hispanic
Median family annual income	$74,297	$60,256	$35,398	$42,491
Percentage under $15,000	8.7	10.4	22.4	14.6
Percentage above $100,000	19.1	28.0	12.8	14.7

Source: DeNavas-Walt and Proctor (2015).

Table 8.2 Mean Annual Earnings by Educational Level and Race/Ethnicity

Education	White Annual	Black Annual	Hispanic Annual
Not a high school graduate	$25,636	$22,880	$24,232
High school graduate	$36,192	$30,108	$30,940
Some college, no degree	$41,132	$33,124	$35,828
College graduate	$50,180	$46,540	$48,724
Advanced degree	$72,280	$59,748	$64,220

Source: U.S. Bureau of Labor Statistics (2015).

lighter skin tones are more likely to be selected than those with darker skin (Harrison 2010; Harrison and Thomas 2009).

Being Black also exposes one to a string of humiliating, frustrating, and sometimes dangerous situations. For example, the chances of being pulled over by the police are 5 times higher for Blacks than Whites in cities as diverse as Torrington, Connecticut, and Chicago, Illinois. Moreover, despite the overwhelming evidence that Whites are more likely to have drugs or illegal materials in their cars, Blacks have their cars searched for drugs or contraband far more often (LaFraniere and Lehren 2015).

Table 8.3 Unemployment Rates for Blacks and Whites by Educational Level

Education	White	Black
Less than a high school diploma	9.7%	20.5%
High school graduate	6.6%	12.6%
Some college or associate degree	5.6%	9.8%
Bachelor's degree or higher	3.5%	5.7%

Source: Irwin, Miller, and Sanger Katz (2014).

After the recent highly publicized shootings of Black men by police, including Michael Brown in Ferguson, Missouri, people of all races have gloomier outlooks on race relations in the United States. In 2008, two thirds of all those surveyed thought race relations in the United States were good and improving (Sack and Thee-Brenan 2015). By 2015, however, a *New York Times*/CBS News Poll indicated that a substantial majority of both Whites and Blacks thought race relations were bad, and 40% thought they were getting worse. Only 20% thought the racial situation in the United States was improving.

Thinking Sociologically

Were you aware of the race-based disparities in income and wealth? Why do you think income among races differs, even when controlling for education?

Ethnic Groups

Ethnic groups are *based on cultural factors: language; religion; dress; foods; customs; beliefs; values; norms; a shared group identity or feeling; and sometimes loyalty to a homeland, monarch, or religious leader*. Members are grouped together because they share a common cultural heritage, often connected with a national or geographical identity. There can be many ethnic groups under one racial category (e.g., Black Americans include African immigrants, West Indian immigrants, and African Americans). Visits to ethnic enclaves in large cities in the United States give a picture of

FIGURE 8.2 Wealth Gaps Based on Race Have Grown Since the Great Recession

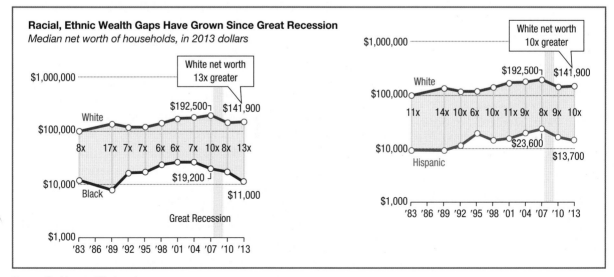

Source: Kochhar and Fry (2014).

Hill Street Studios/Blend Images/Getty Images

One constant frustration for Blacks is being pulled over for DWB—driving while Black. Blacks are many times more likely to be stopped, humiliated, and even endangered than are Whites.

ethnicity. Indian, Chinese, and Dominican neighborhoods may have non-English street signs and newspapers, ethnic restaurants, culture-specific houses of worship, and clothing styles that reflect the ethnic subculture.

Census 2010 data show the ethnic ancestry of millions of Americans and their distribution across the United States. Those with German ancestry make up the largest group at almost 50 million, followed by African Americans at 41 million, Irish at 36 million, Mexican at 32 million, and English at 30 million. Twenty million claim "American" as their ancestry. American Indians and Alaska Natives, the original Americans, make up about 5 million people (O'Connor, Lubin, and Spector 2013).

Figure 8.3 shows where each ethnic group, by county, has the largest concentration, though this does not necessarily mean the group makes up more than 50% of the population of that county.

Multiracial Populations: Immigration, Intermarriage, and Personal Identification

"Push" factors drive people from some countries, and "pull" factors draw them to other countries. The most common push-pull factors today are job opportunities, the desire for security, individual liberties, and availability of medical and educational opportunities. The target countries of migrants are most often in North America, Australia, or Western Europe, and the highest emigration rates are from Africa, Eastern Europe, Central Asia, and South and Central America.

Immigration into the United States from every continent has led to a very diverse population, with 13% of the current U.S. population born elsewhere (Grieco et al. 2012). As Figure 8.4 reveals, among the Black population, the foreign born have tripled in number since 1980. Today, almost 1 out of 10 (8.7%) are foreign born. About half are from the Caribbean (Monica Anderson 2015).

With new immigration, increasing rates of intermarriage, and many more individuals claiming multiracial identification, color lines are changing (DaCosta 2007; J. Lee and Bean 2004, 2007). In 2012, almost 1 in 5 Americans under 18 were identified with two or more racial groups (Alpert 2013). Figure 8.5 illustrates the current ethnic group distribution and projections for the future for the United States.

Some scholars, such as Eduardo Bonilla-Silva, say that the United States is moving from a Black–White racial hierarchy to a three-tiered racial hierarchy, with the top positions held by "*Whites* 'traditional' Whites; new 'White' immigrants; and, in the near future, assimilated Latinos, some multiracials [light-skinned ones], and individual members of other groups [some Asian Americans, etc.]" (Bonilla-Silva and Embrick 2005:33). Next will come a middle group consisting of "*honorary Whites* (most light-skinned Latino Americans, Japanese Americans, Korean Americans, Asian Indian [Americans], Chinese Americans, the bulk of multiracials . . . and most Middle Eastern Americans" (Bonilla-Silva and Embrick 2005:33). The bottom group, the "*collective Black*," will contain Black Americans, dark-skinned Latino Americans, Vietnamese Americans, Cambodian Americans, Laotian Americans, and maybe Filipino Americans. The lines are shifting, but the racial hierarchy remains (Bonilla-Silva 2009; Bonilla-Silva and Embrick 2005).

FIGURE 8.3 Ancestry With Largest Population in Each County, 2010

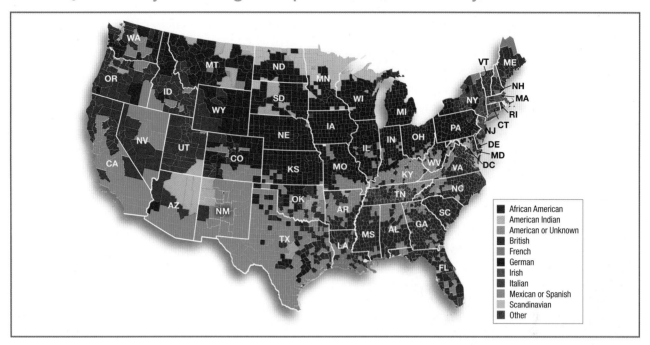

Source: Lombard (2014).

FIGURE 8.4 Immigrants as Part of the Black U.S. Population

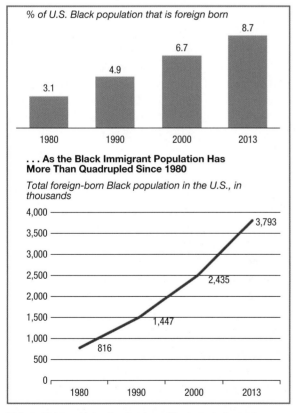

Note: In 2000 and later, foreign-born Blacks include single-race Blacks and mixed-race Blacks, regardless of Hispanic origin. Prior to 2000, Blacks include only single-race Blacks, regardless of Hispanic origin, since a mixed-race option was not available.

Source: Monica Anderson (2015).

FIGURE 8.5 Percentage of the Population, by Race and Hispanic Origin, 1980–2060

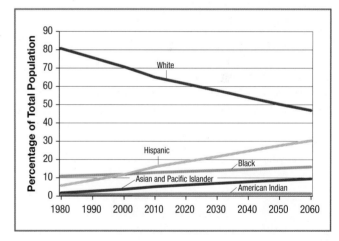

Source: U.S. Census Bureau (2014).

Thinking Sociologically

Identify one dominant and one minority group in your community or on campus. Where does each group fit into the stratification system in the United States? How are the life chances of individuals in these groups influenced by factors beyond their control?

PREJUDICE: MICRO-LEVEL ANALYSIS

Have you ever found yourself in a situation in which you were viewed as different, strange, or undesirable? Perhaps you have felt the sting of rejection, not based on judgment of you as a person but solely because of the ethnic or racial group into which you were born. Then again, you may have been insulated from this type of rejection if you grew up in a homogeneous community or in a privileged group. Where and when we are born can determine how we are treated, our life chances, and many of our experiences and attitudes.

Prejudice influences dominant–minority group relations. **Prejudice** refers to *attitudes or prejudgment about a group, usually negative and not based on facts.* Prejudiced individuals lump together people with certain characteristics without considering individual differences. In this section we also look at *stereotyping*, when prejudiced individuals use distorted, oversimplified, or exaggerated ideas to categorize a group of people and attribute personal qualities to them. Whereas prejudice and stereotypes can be stimulated by events such as conflicts at the institutional level and war at the societal level, attitudes are held by individuals and can be best understood as a micro-level phenomenon.

Prejudice refers to attitudes rather than actions. **Discrimination**, on the other hand, is *differential treatment and harmful actions against minorities.* These actions at the micro level might include refusal to sell someone a house because of the religion, race, or ethnicity of the buyer or not hiring someone because of her or his minority status (Feagin and Feagin 2010). Discrimination in the legal system, such as laws that deny opportunities or resources to members of a particular group, operates largely at the meso or macro level, discussed later in this chapter.

The Nature of Prejudice

Prejudice is an understandable response of humans to their social environment. To survive, every social group or unit—a sorority, sports team, civic club, or nation—needs to mobilize the loyalty of its members. Each organization needs to convince people to voluntarily commit energy, skills, time, and resources so the organization can meet its needs. As people commit themselves to a group, they invest a portion of themselves and feel loyalty to the group. This loyalty leads to a preference for the group and attempts to distinguish it from others. It is important to recognize prejudice, though, and how it can foster discriminatory actions.

In wartime, the enemy may be depicted in films or other media as villains. During World War II, American films often showed negative stereotypes of Japanese and German people. These negative images helped lead to the decision to intern more than 110,000 Japanese Americans, the majority of whom were U.S. citizens, in detention camps following the bombing of Pearl Harbor.

Similar issues and stereotypes have arisen for Muslim Americans in recent years. For example, hate crimes against Muslims spiked after the attacks on the New York World Trade Center on September 11, 2001, and the Boston Marathon bombing on April 15, 2013 (Potok 2013b). Sociologist Saher Selod explains,

> The September 11, 2001, attacks claimed the lives of close to 3,000 Americans. The terrorists were Muslims from Saudi Arabia, United Arabs Emirates, and Egypt. These horrific events changed the lives of all Americans, including Muslim Americans and immigrants. Muslims have [since] become targets for anti-terrorist laws and policies that were a part of a government-led campaign known as the "War on Terror" (Cainkar, 2009). According to a Gallup report, 43% of Americans admitted to feeling some

After Japan bombed Pearl Harbor on December 7, 1941, more than 110,000 Japanese Americans, including those pictured here, were forcibly removed from many western states and sent to relocation camps.

prejudice towards Muslims and 31% of Americans view Islam unfavorably (Gallup 2010). These rising anti-Muslim sentiments have had a direct impact on the everyday life of the Muslim population. (Selod 2018)

Explaining Racial Discrimination at the Micro Level. Why do individuals commit acts of racial discrimination? Why would people be so angry at racial minorities that they would act to harm them? The following is one theory that has attempted to explain acts of racial discrimination.

Frustration-Aggression Theory. On June 17, 2015, Dylann Roof "entered the church, asked for the pastor, and sat next to him during Bible study before opening fire. 'I have to do it,' he said, according to [reports]. 'You rape our women and you're taking over our country. You have to go'" (Horowitz, Dewan, and Oppel 2015). He has been charged with killing nine people in an historic African American church in South Carolina. According to *frustration-aggression theory*, many of those who carry out acts of racial discrimination feel angry and frustrated because they cannot achieve their work or other goals. Frustration-aggression theory focuses largely on poorly adjusted people who express their frustration through aggressive attacks on others. From all accounts, Dylann Roof, a 21-year-old high school dropout with a history of heavy drug use and scrapes with the law, was a poorly adjusted young man with racist beliefs (Horowitz et al. 2015; Robles, Horowitz, and Dewan 2015).

When people cannot take out their aggression on its source and turn it on innocent victims, they are *scapegoating*. The word *scapegoat* comes from the Bible (see Leviticus 16:5–22). Once a year, a goat (which was obviously innocent) was laden with parchments on which people had written their sins. The goat was then sent out to the desert to die. This was part of a ritual of purification, and the creature took the blame for the sins committed by the people. Scapegoating occurs when a minority group is blamed for the failures of others. It is often difficult to look at oneself to seek reasons for failure but easy to transfer the blame for one's failure to others. Individuals who feel they are failures in their jobs or other aspects of their lives may turn the blame toward minority groups. From within such a prejudiced mindset, violence toward the out-group may seem acceptable. Hate groups evolve when people with such mindsets unite. As Figure 8.6 reveals, there are active hate groups in every state, but some states have more than others.

The shooting of Blacks in the United States has shaken the country and spawned the Black Lives Matter Movement. Pallbearers release doves over the casket of one of the nine people killed in the shooting at Emanuel AME Church in Charleston, South Carolina, in 2015. They were engaged in a Bible study when attacked.

The Color-Blind Ideology and Racism Evasiveness

A bigot is someone who blindly insists that certain other people are so different that they are inferior—even, perhaps, less than human. Hate groups in the United States, Europe, and many other countries justify themselves on the basis of bigoted thinking. They loudly proclaim that those outside their racial or ethnic group deserve to face discrimination.

Many other people are not bigoted but simply oblivious to racial inequality and the hidden privileges that Whites experience in U.S. society. They do not want to hear about the realities of racial inequality. In fact, they maintain that race no longer matters. A racial ideology that grew out of opposition to affirmative action programs in the 1980s, the *color-blind ideology* is now the dominant racial ideology in the United States (Bonilla-Silva 2009; Brunsma 2006; K. Korgen and Brunsma 2012). Promoters of the color-blind ideology maintain that we should all act as though we are "color-blind" when it comes to race and avoid the topic in personal interactions. However, for many people of color, their blackness or brownness is so integral to their identity that to say one is "color-blind" is to fail to see the whole person. They feel they are being made invisible and forced to be part of the mainstream culture—to be assimilated (Dalton 2012; Dyer 2012; Feagin 2012).

FIGURE 8.6   Active Hate Groups in 2015

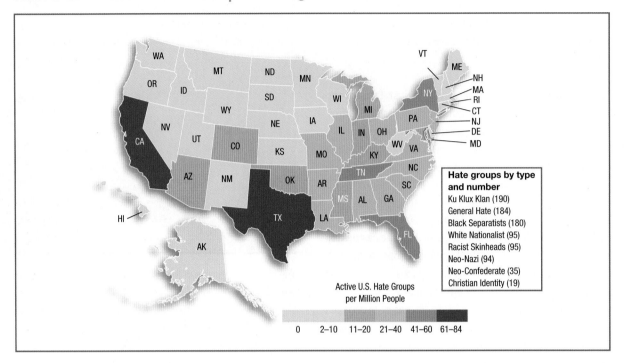

Hate groups by type and number
Ku Klux Klan (190)
General Hate (184)
Black Separatists (180)
White Nationalist (95)
Racist Skinheads (95)
Neo-Nazi (94)
Neo-Confederate (35)
Christian Identity (19)

Active U.S. Hate Groups per Million People

0   2–10   11–20   21–40   41–60   61–84

Source: Reprinted by permission of the Southern Poverty Law Center (2016).

Those who have a color-blind perspective on race do not notice the *invisible privileges* of Whites in U.S. society. (Rothenberg 2015). Consider the following privileges that most people who are part of the dominant group take for granted (McIntosh 2002:97–101):

- I can avoid spending time with people who mistrust people of my color.
- I can protect my children most of the time from people who might not like them.
- I can criticize our government and talk about how I fear its policies and behavior without being seen as a cultural "outsider" or not patriotic.
- I can easily buy posters, postcards, picture books, greeting cards, dolls, toys, and children's magazines featuring people of my race.
- I can arrange my activities so that I will never have to experience feelings of rejection owing to my race.

Thinking Sociologically

What is your reaction to this list? How does your own racial and ethnic background influence your reaction?

The color-blind ideology leads people to practice *racism evasiveness*. For indeed, "what people are ultimately avoiding

when they say they do not see color, when they overlook differences in power, or avoid 'race words' is racism" (Beeman 2015:131). Therefore, the color-blind perspective on race allows discrimination hidden within the society's institutions to remain in place. Advocates of the color-blind racial ideology reject blatant bigotry as crude and ignorant, but fail to recognize that their own actions may perpetuate inequalities at the institutional or meso level.

DISCRIMINATION: MESO-LEVEL ANALYSIS

Dear Teacher,

I would like to introduce you to my son, Wind-Wolf. He is probably what you would consider a typical Indian kid. He was born and raised on the reservation. He has black hair, dark brown eyes, and an olive complexion, and, like so many Indian children his age, he is shy and quiet in the classroom. He is 5 years old, in kindergarten, and I can't understand why you have already labeled him a "slow learner." He has already been through quite an education compared with his peers in Western society. He was bonded to his mother and to the Mother Earth in a traditional native childbirth ceremony. And he has been continuously cared for by his mother, father, sisters, cousins, aunts, uncles, grandparents, and extended tribal family since this ceremony. . . .

Wind-Wolf was strapped (in his baby basket like a turtle shell) snugly with a deliberate restriction on his arms and legs. Although Western society may argue this hinders motor-skill development and abstract reasoning, we believe it forces the child to first develop his intuitive faculties, rational intellect, symbolic thinking, and five senses. Wind-Wolf was with his mother constantly, closely bonded physically, as she carried him on her back or held him while breast-feeding. She carried him everywhere she went, and every night he slept with both parents. Because of this, Wind-Wolf's educational setting was not only a "secure" environment, but it was also very colorful, complicated, sensitive, and diverse.

As he grew older, Wind-Wolf began to crawl out of the baby basket, develop his motor skills, and explore the world around him. When frightened or sleepy, he could always return to the basket, as a turtle withdraws into its shell. Such an inward journey allows one to reflect in privacy on what he has learned and to carry the new knowledge deeply into the unconscious and the soul. Shapes, sizes, colors, texture, sound, smell, feeling, taste, and the learning process are therefore functionally integrated—the physical and spiritual, matter and energy, and conscious and unconscious, individual and social.

It takes a long time to absorb and reflect on these kinds of experiences, so maybe that is why you think my Indian child is a slow learner. His aunts and grandmothers taught him to count and to know his numbers while they sorted materials for making abstract designs in native baskets. And he was taught to learn mathematics by counting the sticks we use in our traditional native hand game. So he may be slow in grasping the methods and tools you use in your classroom, ones quite familiar to his White peers, but I hope you will be patient with him. It takes time to adjust to a new cultural system and learn new things. He is not culturally "disadvantaged," but he is culturally different. (R. Lake 1990:48–53)

This letter expresses the frustration of a father who sees his son being labeled and discriminated against by the school system without being given a chance.

Discrimination, introduced earlier in this chapter, refers to differential treatment and harmful actions taken against members of a minority group. It can occur at individual and small-group levels but is particularly problematic at the organizational and institutional levels—the meso level of analysis.

Thinking Sociologically

How might schools unintentionally misunderstand Wind-Wolf and other minority children in ways that have negative consequences for children's success?

Institutional racial discrimination is *any meso-level institutional arrangement that favors one racial group over another; this favoritism may result in intentional or unintentional consequences for minority groups* (Farley 2011). This form of discrimination results from the normal or routine part of the way an organization operates that systematically disadvantages members of one group. It can include intentional actions, such as laws restricting minorities, as well as unintentional actions, that have consequences restricting minorities. Jim Crow laws, passed in the late 1800s in the United States, and laws that barred Jews in Germany from living, working, or investing in certain places are examples of intentional discrimination embedded in organizations.

Often, though, institutional racial discrimination is done quite unintentionally. For example, in some states, local funding of schools leads to schools with racial minorities receiving fewer funds than most predominantly White schools. This type of funding policy can be supported by nonracists who simply want local control over schools. Whether intended or not, though, such a policy benefits a particular race at the expense of others. As you can see, racial discrimination does not have to be the result of a nasty or mean-spirited person bullying others; it often operates independently of prejudice (Bonilla-Silva 2003; Rothenberg 2015).

Side-effect discrimination and past-in-present discrimination are two other types of unintentional institutional discrimination (Feagin and Feagin 1986; Rydgren 2004). **Side-effect discrimination** *refers to practices in one institutional area that have a negative impact because they are linked to practices in another institutional area; because institutions are interdependent, discrimination in one results in unintentional discrimination in others*. Figure 8.7 illustrates this idea. Each institution uses information from the other institutions to make decisions. So discrimination in one can lead to discrimination in others.

FIGURE 8.7   Side-Effect Discrimination

Family   Education

Religion   Health

Economics   Political System

Note: Each circle represents a different institution—family, education, religion, health, political-legal system, and economics. These meso-level systems are interdependent, using information or resources from the others. If discrimination occurs in one institution, the second institution may unintentionally borrow information or practices that result in discrimination. In this way, discrimination occurs at the meso level without awareness by individuals at the micro level.

Side-effect discrimination occurs when discrimination in the criminal justice system leads to discrimination in the employment sector. For example, in an interview conducted by one of the authors, a probation officer in a moderate-sized city in Ohio said that he had never seen an African American in his county get a not-guilty verdict and that he was not sure it was possible. He had known of cases in which minorities had pled guilty to a lesser charge even though they were innocent because they did not think they could receive a fair verdict in that city. When people apply for jobs, however, they are usually required to report the conviction on the application form. Employers discriminate against applicants with a criminal record, whether or not the applicant was guilty of the crime. Side-effect discrimination is *unintentional discrimination*; the criminal justice system has reached an unjust verdict, and the potential employer is swayed unfairly.

A second example of side-effect discrimination shows that the Internet also plays a role in institutionalized discrimination and privilege. For example, in Alaska, 15.2% of the population is Native, but Natives hold only 5% of state jobs, and 27.3% of Native men and 16% of Native women are unemployed (AAANativeArts 2011; U.S. Census Bureau 2011). Consider that the State of Alaska uses the Internet as its primary means of advertising and accepting applications for state jobs. In the early 2000s, Internet access was unavailable in the 164 predominantly Native villages in Alaska—a state so large and spread out that it is 2.2 times the size of Texas and has only 1.2 people per square mile (Denali Commission 2001; Hudson 2011). Although efforts have been made in recent years to expand Internet access, as of 2015, 81% of Alaskans still did not have access to broadband Internet (Federal Communications Commission 2015).

Other options for application for state jobs include requesting applications by mail, but a person must first know about the opening. Moreover, the usefulness of this process is limited by the reliability and speed of mail service to remote villages and the often short application periods for state jobs. State officials may not intentionally try to prevent Aleuts, Inupiats, Athabaskans, or other Alaska Natives from gaining access to state jobs, but the effect can be institutionalized discrimination. Here, Internet access plays a role in the participation of minorities in the social

In this residential area of the rural Tlingit village of Hoonah, Alaska, finding jobs through the internet is not an option.

John Greim/LightRocket/Getty Images

world. The privileged members may not purposely disadvantage others and may not be prejudiced, but the playing field is not level. The discrimination may be completely unintentional (Rothenberg 2015).

Thinking Sociologically

Imagine you run a business that is hiring people. You routinely do a criminal background check on applicants and discard the applications of those with a criminal record. You have just read this chapter and realize that some of that information may be a source of unintended side-effect discrimination for a minority group member. What will you do now? Why?

Past-in-present discrimination refers to *practices from the past that may no longer be allowed but that continue to have consequences for people in the present* (Feagin and Feagin 1986; Verbeek and Penninx 2009). Examples of this abound if you dig deep enough. For example, in Mississippi, during the 1950s, state expenditures to educate a White child averaged $147 per pupil, whereas the average was $34 per Black pupil in segregated schools (Luhman and Gilman 1980). Such blatant segregation and inequality in use of tax dollars is no longer legal, and this may seem like ancient history. Yet some African Americans who were in school in the 1950s and 1960s are receiving low Social Security checks because their earning power was diminished due to their poor schooling. One result is that they cannot help pay for their grandchildren to go to college. This is not ancient history to them; it affects their opportunities and those of their children and grandchildren today.

As you can see, then, the great disparity in wealth between White and Black Americans described earlier relates to the legal discrimination many generations of Black Americans experienced in the past. Another reason for the great racial disparity in wealth lies in racially discriminatory housing practices common before the Fair Housing Act of 1968 and that continue to exist in more subtler forms today (e.g., steering Black people toward low-income minority neighborhoods, not showing them as many housing options as Whites home seekers, and offering them subprime loans even when they qualify for better, conventional loans). These practices allowed more Whites than Blacks to buy homes and to pass down the wealth invested in their homes to their children. It also made it (and continues to make it) more likely for Whites than Blacks to invest in homes that will appreciate in value, as those in stable, middle-class neighborhoods tend to do ("Ending the Cycle" 2015; Leonhardt 2015). Even

This sign was posted directly opposite the Sojourner Truth homes, a U.S. federal housing project constructed in Detroit, Michigan, after World War II. A riot was caused by White neighbors' attempts to prevent Black tenants from moving in. Note the use of flags as a symbol indicating that only Whites are real Americans—African Americans do not belong.

today, Blacks with middle-class incomes are more likely than middle-class Whites and Asian Americans to live in low-income neighborhoods, and those homes do not grow in value over time, so net worth does not grow (Reardon, Fox, and Townsend 2015). In order to gain a good, affordable (not a subprime) loan for a house, you need to have accumulated enough wealth for a down payment. Research on one community in New Jersey has demonstrated that there are huge benefits to Whites, Blacks, and the entire community when desegregation is implemented ("Ending the Cycle" 2015; Massey et al. 2013).

Children who live in low-income neighborhoods tend to have relatively few life chances. Those raised in low-income neighborhoods with poor schools, high crime rates, and fewer two-parent families have less chance of moving up in social class in their lifetimes than other children (Chetty and Hendren 2015). Therefore, it is past-in-present *and* contemporary discrimination that leads to relatively high percentages of middle-income Black families raising their children in low-income neighborhoods and perpetuates racial inequality (Leonhardt 2015).

With a sociological eye, it is easy to see how events from the past continue to echo into our current times, creating barriers for some citizens and clear paths for others. The next "Engaging Sociology" feature explores how discrimination can occur at different levels and in intentional or unintentional ways.

ENGAGING SOCIOLOGY

Using and Relating Key Concepts

Figure 8.8 indicates the levels at which discrimination can operate and how such acts can be intended or unintended.

FIGURE 8.8   Understanding Key Concepts

	Micro Level	Meso and Macro Level
Conscious and intended	Prejudice and individual acts of direct discrimination	Direct institutional discrimination
Unconscious and unintended	Color-blind perspective	Indirect institutional discrimination Side-effect discrimination Past-in-present discrimination

Engaging With Sociology

1. Define and give an example of the term(s) or concept(s) in each of the preceding boxes.

2. Identify ways that each of these elements of intergroup conflict might foster the others.

3. Describe how you might take steps to counter each of the various types of discrimination.

In the United States, we had a president who had both a Black and a White parent. It is also true, though, as Table 8.4 indicates, that today, only two senators (out of 100) are Black.

We have also seen in Table 8.2 on page 218 that African Americans with some college but no degree earn $8,000 per year less than Whites with similar levels of education. The gap for Whites and Blacks specifically with a professional degree (e.g., law or medicine) is even greater. The racial earnings disparity between Whites and Blacks with an advanced degree (such as a master's degree or a doctorate) is $12,500 per year, and it is even higher in some categories. The U.S. Census Bureau reported in 2012 that on average, Whites with a professional degree earned $128,000 per year—$25,000 per year more than Blacks with the same degree (U.S. Census Bureau 2012). This means that over a 40-year career, Whites could earn $1 million more than Blacks with the same degree credentials. As long as these and other examples of discrimination exist—such as differences in unemployment even with the same amount of education (see Table 8.3 on page 219)—we must acknowledge and take steps to address racial inequality.

Table 8.4   Representation in the U.S. Congress, 2015–2016

	Native American	Asian	Black	Hispanic
Senate	0	1 (1%)	2 (2%)	4 (4%)
House	2 (0.5%)	13 (2.9%)	46 (10.5%)	34 (7.8%)
Percentage of Population	0.9%	4.8%	12.6%	16.3%

Source: Manning (2015).

Thinking Sociologically

How do the different types of discrimination, as discussed previously, help us understand world conflicts, such as the intense hostility between Palestinians and Jews in the Middle East?

DOMINANT AND MINORITY GROUP CONTACT: MACRO-LEVEL ANALYSIS

Meso-level analysis is essential to understanding the primary issues of racism in contemporary Global North countries, but ultimately, the tone for interracial relationships is set at the macro level. The first question is how those in power decide to structure relationships between racial and ethnic groups.

Dominant-Group Policies to Manage Racial and Ethnic Relations

Dominant–minority relations depend on the time, place, and circumstances. However, dominant groups tend to structure or manage the dominant and minority relationships with one of five policies, indicated in Figure 8.9.

Genocide is *the systematic effort of one group, usually the dominant group, to destroy a minority group by killing them*. Examples of race- and ethnicity-based genocide exist throughout history. In the 13th century, Mongols under Temüjin Genghis Khan destroyed entire nations in their path. Germany's Adolf Hitler sent Jews and other non-Aryan groups into concentration camps to be gassed in the 1930s and 1940s. In Rwanda, in the mid-1990s, members of the Hutu tribe committed mass murders of people from the Tutsi tribe. As recently as 2015, the terrorist group ISIS tried to wipe out the Yazidis, a religious minority group, in Iraq. Genocide has existed at

One of the most horrific results of discriminatory racial or ethnic policies was the Holocaust, the murder of 11 million people, including 6 million Jews, by the Nazi government in Germany under Adolf Hitler. This photo is difficult to view, but this is the consequence of bigotry that leads to genocide.

many points in history, and it still exists today. These examples illustrate the lethal consequences of racism—one group at the meso level systematically killing off another, often a minority, to gain control and power.

Subjugation refers to *the subordination of one group to another that holds power and authority*. Haiti and the Dominican Republic are two countries sharing the island of Hispaniola in the Caribbean. Because many Haitians are poor, they are lured by promises of jobs in the sugarcane fields of the Dominican Republic. However, many are forced to work long hours for little pay and not allowed to leave until they have paid for housing and food, which may be impossible to do on their low wages.

FIGURE 8.9   Types of Dominant–Minority Group Relations

Most Hostile to "Others" ←→				**Most Accepting of "Others"**
Genocide	**Subjugation**	**Population Transfer**	**Assimilation**	**Pluralism**
Extermination of minorities	Oppression, slavery	Removal to new location	Cultural blending of groups	Groups share in legitimacy and power

Slavery is one form of subjugation that has existed throughout history. When the Roman Empire defeated other lands, the captives became slaves. This included ancient Greeks, who also kept slaves at various times in their history. African tribes enslaved members of neighboring tribes, sometimes selling them to slave traders, and slavery has existed in Middle Eastern countries such as Saudi Arabia. As we saw in Chapter 7, slavery is flourishing in many parts of the world today and even exists in the United States (Bales 2000, 2007, 2012).

Segregation, a specific form of subjugation, separates minorities from the dominant group and deprives them of access to the dominant institutions. Jim Crow laws, instituted in the southern United States after the end of Reconstruction after the Civil War, legislated separation between racial groups—separate facilities, schools, and neighborhoods (Alexander 2010; Feagin and Feagin 2010; Massey and Denton 1998).

Population transfer refers to *the removal, often forced, of a minority group from a region or country*. Generally, the dominant group wants land or resources. For example, Native Americans in the United States were removed to reservations. The Cherokee people were forced to walk from Georgia and North Carolina to new lands west of the Mississippi—a "Trail of Tears" along which 40% of the people perished so that Whites in these states could have access to Cherokee land. As noted earlier, during World War II, Japanese Americans were forcibly moved to "relocation centers" and had their land and property confiscated. In 1972, Idi Amin, dictator of Uganda, gave Asian Ugandans 36 hours to pack their bags and leave—even though it had been the homeland for many of them from birth—because they had great economic resources that he argued should belong to native Ugandans.

Assimilation refers to *the social and cultural merging of minority and dominant groups*. It is often a voluntary process, during which members of a minority group choose to adopt the values, norms, and institutions of the dominant group. Assimilation is more likely to occur when the minority group is similar in culture and appearance to the dominant group. For instance, in the United States, the closer a group is to being White and English speaking, the faster its members will be assimilated into the dominant group, adopting the culture and blending in further through intermarriage. Whereas some assimilation happens naturally when different groups interact in housing, schooling, employment, political circles, family groups, friendship, and social relationships, other assimilation policies in certain times and places have forced ethnic minorities to change their cultural attributes (e.g., language, religions, style of eating, etc.) in order to avoid ridicule or even death (Marger 2012).

Forced assimilation occurs when members of a minority group are compelled to suppress their cultural identity. For example, in the late 1800s and early 1900s, Native American children were forced to leave their families and go to White-run boarding schools. There, they had to cut their hair, attend Christian religious services, dress as Whites did, and speak only in English.

Pluralism occurs *when each ethnic or racial group in a country maintains its own culture and separate set of institutions but has recognized equality in the society*. For example, Switzerland has four dominant cultural language groups: French, German, Italian, and Romansh (or Rumantsch). The government and schools use and teach all of these official languages. Each group respects the rights of the other groups to maintain a distinctive language and way of life. In Malaysia, three groups share power: Malays, Chinese, and Indians. Although the balance is not completely stable because Chinese and Indians have higher levels of education and hold more political and economic power than the native Malays, most Malaysians want to maintain a pluralistic society. Although tensions do exist in both nations, both Switzerland and Malaysia represent examples of pluralist societies. Legal protection of smaller or less powerful groups is often necessary to have pluralism. In the United States, religious pluralism (at least among religions practiced by White Americans), as a policy, was embraced by the nation's first president, George Washington, as explained in the photo of Touro Synagogue on the next page.

Thinking Sociologically

Think of examples from current news stories of positive and harmful intercultural contact. Where do your examples fit on the continuum from genocide to pluralism? What is your reaction to each? How do your experiences of intercultural context influence your reaction to these examples?

Minority Reactions to Prejudice, Discrimination, and Racism

How have minority groups dealt with their status? Five reactions are common: assimilation, acceptance, avoidance, aggression, and change-oriented actions directed at the social structure. The first four are micro-level responses; they do not address the meso- and macro-level issues.

This picture of a U.S. McDonald's helps illustrate that the U.S. is a pluralistic society. The *McDonald's* on this sign is in the Hmong language. This pluralism is very long-standing in the United States. After George Washington was elected president of the new nation, he received a letter from a Jewish congregation in Newport, Rhode Island (*bottom*), asking about his policies of pluralism or multiculturalism (though those words had not been coined yet). In response in 1790, Touro Synagogue—the oldest synagogue in the U.S.—received a handwritten letter signed by President Washington (now proudly on display at the synagogue) embracing an open and "liberal" policy toward all American citizens, regardless of origins or religious affiliation.

Micro-Level Coping Strategies. *Passing* is a means of avoiding the prejudice and discrimination associated with minority group membership. Some minority group members, if their appearance allows them to do so, attempt to *pass* as members of the dominant group. This strategy usually involves abandoning their own culture and turning their back on family roots and community ties, a costly strategy in terms of self-esteem and sense of identity. People who select this coping strategy must deny their minority background and live with the fear that it will be exposed. They often live in constant anxiety, feeling as though they must hide something about themselves. Passing—which is a form of assimilation—also cuts people off from their family members, ancestors, and communities. This often severs them from a part of their identity, so the personal cost of assimilation can be high.

Acceptance is another reaction to minority status. Some members of minority groups have learned to live with their minority status and do not challenge the system. They may or may not hold deep-seated hostility, but they ultimately conclude that change in the society is not very likely, and acceptance may be the rational means to survive within the existing system.

There are many possible explanations for this seeming indifference. For example, religious beliefs allow poor Hindus in India to believe that if they accept their lot in life, they will be reincarnated in a higher life-form. If they rebel, they can expect to be reincarnated into a lower life-form. Their religion is a form of social control. In other cases, members of minority groups believe that they are, in fact, inferior and, therefore, should be treated that way. Socialized in a society that treats them as second-class citizens, they begin to accept this image of themselves. Others may simply fear the negative consequences of refusing to accept their minority status.

Avoidance entails coping with minority group status through shunning all contact with the dominant group. This can involve an active and organized attempt to leave the culture or live separately as some political exiles have done. For example, in the United States, Marcus Garvey organized a Back-to-Africa movement in the 1920s, encouraging Blacks to give up on any hope of justice in American society and to return to Africa. Today, some Native Americans on reservations avoid contact with other Americans and do all they can to live as their ancestors once did—before the intrusion of White people onto their land. For example, among some groups of isolated Apaches (or Dine—pronounced *din-eh*) in New Mexico and Arizona, nearly half of the older population speaks no English and has no need or desire to learn it. They live according to traditional cultural ways in rather isolated desert climates. They have simply withdrawn from contact with the larger society (Farrer 2011).

Aggression resulting from anger and resentment over minority status and from subjugation may lead to retaliation or violence. Direct confrontation can be very costly to those lacking political or economic power. So aggression often takes one of two forms, indirect aggression or displaced aggression. Indirect aggression includes biting assertiveness in the arts—literature, art, racial and ethnic humor, and music—and in job-related actions such as inefficiency and slowdowns by workers. The arts can represent indirect aggression or efforts toward social change, as shown in the following photo. Displaced aggression, on the other hand, involves hostilities directed toward individuals or groups other than the dominant group, such as happens when youth gangs attack other ethnic or racial gangs in nearby neighborhoods. They substitute aggression against the dominant group by acting out against other minority groups.

The four responses discussed thus far address the angst and humiliation that individual minorities feel. Each strategy allows an individual to try to cope, but none addresses the structural causes of discrimination. The final strategy is *change-oriented action*.

Meso- and Macro-Level Efforts to Bring Change: Resistance. Passing, acceptance, and avoidance are forms of adaptation to the existing structures. Aggression,

© Keith Roberts

The Penumbra Theatre in St. Paul, Minnesota, uses the performing arts to promote social change. It fosters laughter at socially absurd norms and ideas, often a form of biting commentary. As the theater company tells the story of African Americans in the United States, the performers carry out their mission to use theater to "teach, criticize, comment, and model."

if not used strategically, can also work to support the status quo by creating opposition to changes that would help the minority group. Yet rather than accepting the current system and adapting to it, minority groups may choose strategic resistance. Resistance to the White framing of what life is like in the United States can take place through offering positive definitions of one's racial or ethnic group and preserving pride in one's culture (Feagin 2012). This was at work in the "Black is beautiful" theme that emerged early in the civil rights movement. That movement led to more books and films that relate the stories of courage, stamina, and contribution by minority groups. These media images and those of the more recent Black Lives Matter campaign provide a challenge and an alternative to those developed through the White perceptions of minority groups and U.S history.

Efforts to change cultural attitudes toward minority groups have been complemented by work within the legal system to challenge unjust laws. The National Association for the Advancement of Colored People (NAACP) sought to bring about legal changes through lawsuits that created new legal precedents supporting racial equality. Often, these lawsuits addressed side-effect discrimination—a meso-level problem. Many other associations for minorities—including the Anti-Defamation League (founded by Jews) and La Raza Unida (a Mexican American organization)—also seek to address problems both within organizations and institutions (meso level) and in the nation as a whole (macro level).

One of the most important efforts to bring change in the United States has been nonviolent resistance. The model for nonviolent resistance by minority groups comes from Mahatma Gandhi who, from 1915 to 1947, led the struggle for India's independence from Britain. Although Britain clearly had superior weapons and armies, Indian boycotts, sit-ins, and other forms of resistance eventually led to British withdrawal as the ruling colonial power. This strategy has been used by workers and students to bring about change in many parts of the world.

In the United States, Martin Luther King Jr. followed in the nonviolent resistance tradition of Gandhi, who sought to change India's laws so that minorities could have equal opportunities within the society. King's strategy involved nonviolent popular protests, economic boycotts, and other challenges to racially discriminatory norms of society. His nonviolent disruptive efforts brought attention to the plight of Black people in the United States and created the political pressure needed to pass the civil rights legislation of the 1960s.

Martin Luther King Jr. (who majored in sociology in college) and many other public sociologists (e.g., W. E. B.

Du Bois) have used their training to address issues of discrimination through empowerment and change. Their efforts to strategically counter the power of the dominant group have helped create a more equitable society for all residents of the United States.

Football players at the University of Missouri carried out a nonviolent action against racism in November 2015. Angered by the university president's lack of support for students of color who had reported racist incidents, 30 Black players organized themselves, gained the support of their head coach, and said they would not play in the upcoming game unless the president of the university resigned. The forfeiture of the game would have cost the university more than a million dollars. Facing intense pressure, the university president did resign, and the University of Missouri began actions to address the concerns of minority students (Pearson and Sutton 2015; Svrluga 2015). Such action represents systematic organizing, though change rarely happens so fast.

Mahatma Gandhi used nonviolent strategies to lead a successful revolt against the British colonization of India. He used demonstrations of cloth weaving, as seen in this picture, to stress the dignity of the manual labor undertaken by many Indians.

Thinking Sociologically

The preceding discussion presents five types of responses by minorities to the experience of discrimination and rejection. Four of these are at the micro level, and one is at the meso and macro levels. Why do you think most of the coping strategies of minorities are at the micro level?

Theoretical Explanations of Dominant–Minority Group Relations

Given that dominant–minority group relations take place on the micro, meso, and macro levels, we must use a wide variety of theoretical perspectives in order to fully understand these types of group interactions. For example, psychological and social-psychological theories are most relevant when examining prejudice in individuals and small groups. To understand discrimination embedded in institutions, studying meso-level organizations is helpful, and to understand the pervasive nature of prejudice and stereotypes over time in various societies, cultural explanations are useful. Finally, we must turn to macro-level theories to understand national and global group relations.

Structural-Functional Theory. Some functionalists point out that prejudice, discrimination, and institutional racism are dysfunctional for society, resulting in the loss of human resources, costs to societies due to poverty and crime, hostilities between groups, and disrespect for those in power. For example, Durkheim divided social

inequalities into *internal* (based on people's natural abilities) and *external* (those forced upon people). He argued that the existence of *external inequality* in an industrial society indicates that its institutions are not functioning properly. Because an industrial society needs all of its members doing what they do best in order for it to function most effectively, external inequality—like racial discrimination—that prevents some people from fulfilling their innate talents damages all of society (Durkheim [1893] 1997). Prejudice, discrimination, and institutional racism, then, are dysfunctional for society, resulting in the loss of human resources, costs to societies due to poverty and crime, hostilities between groups, and disrespect for those in power (Schaefer 2012).

However, other functionalists note that maintaining a cheap pool of laborers (e.g., members of a minority group) who are in and out of work serves several purposes for society. Not only does this minority group function to provide a ready labor force for dirty work or menial unskilled jobs, but these laborers also serve other functions for society. Having minority groups makes possible occupations that service the poor, such as social work, public health, criminology, and the justice and legal systems. The oppressed buy goods others do not want—day-old bread, old fruits and vegetables, and secondhand clothes (Gans 1971, 1994). In short, having a supply of people in desperate need at the bottom of the social structure, according to some analysts, has some useful functional aspects, and this makes change more difficult.

Conflict Theory. Conflict theorists argue that creating a less powerful group protects the dominant group's advantages. Because privileges and resources are usually limited, those who have them want to keep them. One strategy used by privileged people, according to conflict theory, is to perpetrate prejudice and discrimination against minority group members. For example, in the 1840s, as the United States set out to build a transcontinental railroad, large numbers of laborers emigrated from China to do the hard manual work. When the railroad was completed and competition for jobs became stiff, the once-welcomed Chinese became targets of bitter prejudice, discrimination, and sometimes violence. Members of this minority group banded together in towns or cities for protection, founding the Chinatowns we know today (Kitano, Aqbayani, and de Anda 2005). Non-Chinese Asian groups suffered discrimination as well because the bigoted generalizations were applied to all Asians (Winders 2004).

Karl Marx argued that exploitation of the lower classes is built into capitalism because it benefits the ruling class. Unemployment creates a ready pool of labor to fill the marginal jobs, with the pool often made up of identifiable minority groups. This pool allows people to remain in their higher-level positions and prevents others from moving up in the stratification system and threatening their jobs.

Three critical factors contribute to animosity between groups, according to one conflict theorist: First, if two groups of people can each be identified by their appearance, clothing, or language, then us-versus-them thinking and ethnocentrism may develop (Noel 1968). However, this, by itself, does not mean there will be long-term hostility between the groups. Second, if the two groups compete for scarce resources that both want, hostilities are very likely to arise. The resources might be the best land or cattle, the highest-paying jobs, access to the best schools for one's children, energy resources such as oil, or positions of prestige and power. If the third element is added to the mix—one group having much more power than the other—then intense dislike between the two groups and misrepresentation of each group by the other is fairly certain to occur.

The group with more power uses that power to ensure that its members (and their offspring) get the most valued resources. However, because they do not want to see themselves as unfair and brutish people, they develop stereotypes and derogatory characterizations of "those other people" so that it seems reasonable and justified not to give "them" access to the valued resources. Discrimination

(often at the macro level) comes first, and bigoted ideology comes later to justify the discrimination (Noel 1968). Thus, macro- and meso-level conflicts can lead to micro-level attitudes.

Split labor market theory, a branch of conflict theory, characterizes the labor market as having two main types of jobs. The primary market involves clean jobs, largely in supervisory roles, and provides high salaries and good advancement possibilities, whereas the secondary market involves undesirable, hard, and dirty work, compensated with low hourly wages and few benefits or career opportunities. Competition for lesser jobs pits minorities against each other and low-income Whites. By encouraging division and focusing antagonism between worker groups, employers reduce threats to their dominance and get cheaper labor in the process. Workers do not organize against employers who use this dual system because they are distracted by the antagonisms that build up among themselves—hence, the *split labor market* (Bonacich 1972, 1976; Martinez 2008). This theory maintains that competition, prejudice, and ethnic animosity serve the interests of the powerful owners of capital because that atmosphere keeps the laboring classes from uniting.

Conflict theory has taught us a great deal about racial and ethnic stratification. However, conflict theorists often focus on people with power quite intentionally oppressing others to protect their own self-interests. They often depict the dominant group as made up of nasty, power-hungry people. As we have seen in the meso-level discussion of side-effect and past-in-present discrimination, racial discrimination is often subtle and unconscious and can continue even without conscious ill will among those in the dominant group.

Thinking Sociologically

Do you think the split labor market perspective is useful when examining the racial and ethnic hierarchy in the United States? Why, or why not? Can you see any evidence on your campus or in your local community to support the split labor theorists' view of racial and ethnic stratification?

POLICIES GOVERNING MINORITY AND DOMINANT GROUP RELATIONS

The dominant ethnic group in northern Sudan is Arabs—led by President Omar al-Bashir and his armies. In South

Sudan, a newly formed country, the citizens are dark-skinned Africans who have a very different culture. Until a tenuous peace was brokered by the United Nations, the southern Sudanese people were tortured and killed and their villages burned by the more powerful northern Sudanese. Two issues at stake are (1) cultural and ethnic differences and (2) oil reserves. Conflict over oil, primarily located near the border between the two countries, has made the peace plan tenuous. Whereas the hope was that the new border would separate warring factions, skirmishes continue to threaten the peace. In this case, macro-level policies from the United Nations and world powers intervened to stop the atrocities, but this has not eliminated the meso-level causes of conflict: cultural differences and resources such as land and oil. Remember that conflict over resources is usually the cause of animosity between groups.

War, famine, and economic dislocation force families to seek new locations where they can survive and perhaps improve their circumstances. Refugees may end up in a new country, perhaps on a new continent. The degree of acceptance children and their families find in their newly adopted countries varies depending on the government's policies, the group's background, economic conditions in the host country, and whether the refugee group poses a threat to residents (Rumbaut and Portes 2001). Some formerly refugee-friendly countries are closing their doors to immigration because of the strain on their economy and fear of terrorism. In this section, we consider the policies that emerge when dominant and minority groups come into contact and interact.

Policies to Reduce Prejudice, Racism, and Discrimination

In the preceding pages, we considered some of the costs to individuals, groups, societies, and the global community inflicted by discriminatory behavior and policies.

Discrimination's influence is widespread, from slavery and subjugation to unequal opportunities in education, work and political arenas, and every other part of the social world. If one accepts the premise that discrimination is destructive to both individuals and societies, then ways must be found to address the root problems effectively.

From our social world perspective, we know that no problem can be solved by working at only one level of analysis. A successful strategy must bring about change at every level of the social world: individual attitudes, organizational discrimination, cultural stereotypes, societal stratification systems, and national and international structures. However, most current strategies focus on only one level of analysis. Table 8.5 shows some of the programs enacted to combat prejudice, racism, and discrimination at the individual, group, societal, and global levels.

Thinking Sociologically

Do you think walls such as the one pictured on the next page create more positive or negative repercussions? Why, and for whom?

Individual or Small-Group Solutions. Programs to address prejudice and stereotypes through human relations workshops and group encounters can achieve goals at the micro level. Two groups with strong multicultural education programs are the Anti-Defamation League and the Southern Poverty Law Center's Teaching Tolerance program. Both groups provide schools and community organizations with literature, videos, and other materials aimed at combating intolerance and discrimination toward others. Schools can also create interracial friendship opportunities with racially integrated classrooms where students of different racial and ethnic backgrounds interact regularly (S. Cheng and Xie 2013; Ellison and Powers 1994).

Table 8.5   Problems and Solutions

Types of Problems at Each Level	Types of Solutions or Programs at Each Level
Individual level: stereotypes and prejudice	Therapy, tolerance-education programs
Group level: negative group interaction	Positive contact, awareness by majority of their many privileges
Societal level: institutionalized discrimination	Education, media, legal-system revisions
Global level: deprivation of human rights	Human rights movements, international political pressures

The photo above shows a section of the wall built to keep undocumented immigrants from crossing the U.S.–Mexican border and entering the United States. Some believe that walls of this sort foster us-versus-them thinking.

Group Contact. Some social scientists advocate organized group contact between dominant and minority group members to improve relations and break down stereotypes and fears. Although not all contact reduces prejudice, many studies have shown the benefits of structured contact. Some essential conditions for success are equal status of the participants, noncompetitive and nonthreatening contact, and projects or goals on which to cooperate (Farley 2011).

In a classic study of group contact, social psychologists Muzafer Sherif and Carolyn Sherif and their colleagues ran summer camps for 11- and 12-year-old boys and studied how they interacted with one another under different circumstances. On arrival, the boys were divided into two groups that competed periodically. The more fierce the competition, the more hostile the two cabins of boys became toward each other. The experimenters tried several methods to resolve the conflicts and tensions:

1. Appealing to higher values (be nice to your neighbors): This proved of limited value.
2. Talking with the natural leaders of the groups (compromises between group leaders): The group leaders agreed, but their followers did not go along.
3. Bringing the groups together in a pleasant situation (a mutually rewarding situation): This did not reduce competition; if anything, it increased it.
4. *Introducing a superordinate goal that could be achieved only if everyone cooperated:* This technique worked. The boys were presented with a dilemma: The water system had broken, or a fire needed to be put out, and all were needed to solve the problem. The groups not only worked together, but their established stereotypes eventually began to fade away. Such a situation in a community might arise from efforts to get a candidate elected, a bill passed, or a neighborhood improved. At the global macro level, representatives from hostile countries could sit together to solve issues that threatened all nations (Sherif and Sherif 1953).

College students can be actively engaged in this level of change by confronting and challenging bigotry and stereotypes, as is illustrated in the next "Sociologists in Action."

SOCIOLOGISTS IN ACTION
ANNA MISLEH

Challenging Bigotry Toward the Roma

In the spring of 2013, a group of students from St. John's University in Queens, New York, were involved in a study abroad program in Rome, Italy, and performed weekly service work in a Roma (Gypsy) population to better understand an ethnic group that experienced discrimination. In the process we, as college students, learned we could raise awareness of the discrimination against the Roma and its impact. We worked one on one with Roma children living in Monachina, a settlement camp of Roma that is not officially recognized but is tolerated by the Italian government. Through our work at the camp, interviewing Italians knowledgeable about the Roma and interacting closely with one of the families at Monachina, my peers and I were able to better understand the Roma lifestyle and the discrimination they face in Rome.

To deepen our understanding of the Roma population in Rome, we interviewed two Italian women involved in a *doposcuola* (after-school) program at Monachina. These women had been visiting Monachina for several years and understood the culture at the camp and the views of Italians toward the Roma. We also read and researched all we could about the Roma to supplement the information given to us by the women involved in the doposcuola program. The Roma who reside in Rome and other European cities have come from dozens of different countries. Most have fled political unrest in their home countries. The Roma at the Monachina camp, for example, migrated to Rome in the early 1990s when the country of Yugoslavia dissolved, and ethnic wars broke out across the area.

Italians were not pleased by the arrival of the Roma. Generally, Italians stereotype them as an inferior ethnic group that is lazy, dirty, uncooperative, and unwilling to assimilate into Italian culture. This has led to a self-fulfilling prophecy. The discrimination the Roma face prevents them from obtaining reputable jobs, owning property, receiving a good education, and generally integrating into Italian society.

Our response to this discrimination against the Roma, which we saw evidenced in the Monachina community, was to raise awareness. We invited students from several U.S. universities to visit Monachina with us and meet the Roma. Through this experience, they gained a deeper understanding of the Roma and how they are an oppressed minority group in Italian society. They were able to see that the stereotype of all Roma being lazy pickpockets was far from the truth. We also took time to discuss with them how this discrimination negatively impacts Italian society, as well as all other European countries that host these Roma populations and see them through the eyes of negative stereotypes. Being seen only as a societal nuisance hurts both the life chances of the Roma and their ability to fully contribute to the societies in which they live.

After experiencing the plight of the Roma population firsthand, my peers and I were able to use our sociological imagination to relate what we saw to the social issue of racial and ethnic discrimination. Sociology has taught me that a well-functioning society has institutions that support and respect the rights and dignity of all its members. Seeing the discrimination against the Roma at the Monachina camp in Rome has brought this truth home to me in a very real way and made me more committed than ever to teach others that racial and ethnic discrimination hurts everyone in a society—not just those who are its direct victims.

• •

Anna Misleh graduated from St. John's University in Queens, New York, with a major in sociology. She now works for the Center of Concern, a Catholic social justice organization in Washington, DC.

Positive group contact experiences can be effective in improving relations in groups at a micro level by breaking down stereotypes, but to solidify the positive gains, we must also address institutionalized inequalities.

Institutional and Societal Strategies to Improve Group Relations. Sociologists contend that institutional and societal approaches to reduce discrimination get closer to the core of the problems and affect larger numbers of people than do micro-level strategies. Changes at the macro level that can impact racial and ethnic stratification include legislation and government programs that enforce laws mandating racial and ethnic equality. For example, laws requiring equal treatment of minorities, such as the Civil Rights Act of 1964 that prohibited discrimination on the basis of race, religion, sex, or nation of origin, have resulted in increased tolerance and opened doors once closed to minorities. The U.S. Civil Rights Commission and the Equal Employment Opportunity Commission are government organizations that protect rights and work toward equality for all citizens.

In the United States, executive action to end discrimination has been taken by a number of presidents. In 1948, Harry Truman moved to successfully end military segregation, and subsequent presidents have urged the passage of civil rights legislation and equal employment opportunity legislation. Affirmative action laws, first implemented during Lyndon Johnson's administration, have been used to fight pervasive institutional racism (Crosby 2004; Farley 2011). The following discussion addresses the goals and forms of policies under the umbrella of *affirmative action*.

Affirmative Action. As a societal policy for change, affirmative action actually involves three different policies: *Strict affirmative action*, its simplest and original form, involves taking affirmative or positive steps to make sure that unintentional discrimination does not occur. It mandates, for example, that an employer who receives federal monies advertise a position widely and not just through internal or friendship networks. If the job requires an employee with a college education, then by federal law, employers must recruit through minority and women's colleges, as well as state and private colleges in the region. If employers are hiring in the suburbs, they are obliged to contact unemployment agencies in poor and minority communities, as well as those in their affluent neighborhoods.

After taking these required extra steps, employers are expected to hire the most qualified candidate who applies, regardless of race, ethnicity, sex, religion, or other external characteristics. The focus is on providing opportunities for the best-qualified people. For many people, this is the meaning of affirmative action, and it is inconceivable that this could be characterized as "reverse discrimination," for members of the dominant group will be hired if they are, in fact, the most qualified. These policies do not overcome the problem that qualified people who have been marginalized may be competent but do not have the traditional paper credentials that document their qualifications (Gallagher 2004).

A *quota system*, the second policy, is a requirement that employers *must* hire a certain percentage of minorities. For the most part, quotas are now unconstitutional. They apply only in cases where a court has found a company to have a substantial and sustained history of discrimination against minorities.

Preference policies are the third form, the one that has created the most controversy among opponents of corrective action. Preference policies are based on the concept of equity, the belief that sometimes people must be treated differently in order to be treated fairly. This policy was enacted to level the playing field, which was not rewarding highly competent people because of institutional racism. To overcome these inequalities and achieve certain objectives (e.g., a diverse workforce to serve a diverse population), employers and educational institutions take account of race or sex by making special efforts to hire and retain workers or accept students from groups that have been underrepresented. In many cases, these individuals bring qualifications others do not possess. Consider the following examples.

A goal of the medical community is to provide access to medical care for underserved populations. There is an extreme shortage of physicians on the Navajo reservation. Thus, a Navajo applicant for medical school might be accepted, even if her scores are slightly lower than those of another candidate's, because she speaks Navajo and understands the culture. One could argue that she is more qualified to be a physician on the reservation than someone who knows nothing about Navajo society but has a slightly higher grade point average or test score. Some argue that tests should not be the only measure to determine the merit of applicants.

Likewise, an African American police officer may have more credibility in an African American neighborhood and may be able to defuse a delicate conflict more effectively than a White officer who scored slightly higher on a paper-and-pencil placement test. Thus, being a member of a particular racial or ethnic group can actually make one more qualified for a position.

Many colleges and universities admit students because they need an outstanding point guard on the basketball team, an extraordinary soprano for the college choir, or a student from a distant state for geographic diversity. These students are shown preference by being admitted with lower test scores than some other applicants because they are *differently qualified*. Many colleges also give preference to children of former graduates—called legacies. In order to achieve gender balance, at some schools, male students are given preference, even if more qualified females apply. Giving racial minority students preference follows this same reasoning.

A landmark case filed in a Detroit district court in 1997 alleged that the University of Michigan gave unlawful preference to minorities in undergraduate admissions and in law school admissions. In this controversial case, the court ruled that these undergraduate admissions were discriminatory because numbers rather than individualized judgments were used to make the admission determination (University of Michigan Documents Center 2003). Consider the next "Engaging Sociology" feature and decide whether you think the policy was fair and whether only race and ethnicity should have been deleted from the automatic preferences allowed.

ENGAGING SOCIOLOGY

Preference Policies at the University of Michigan

To enhance diversity on the campus—a practice that many argue makes a university a better learning environment and enhances the academic reputation of the school—many colleges have preference policies in admissions. However, the University of Michigan was sued by applicants who felt they were not admitted because others replaced them on the roster due to their racial or ethnic background.

The University of Michigan is a huge university where a numbering system is needed to handle the volume (tens of thousands) of applicants; the admissions staff cannot make a decision based on personal knowledge of each candidate. Thus, they give points for each quality they deem desirable in the student body. A maximum of 150 points is possible, and a score of 100 would pretty much ensure admission. The university feels that any combination of points accumulated according to the following formula will result in a highly qualified and diverse student body.

For academics, up to 110 points are possible:

- 80 points for grades (a particular grade point average in high school results in a set number

of points; e.g., a 4.0 result in 80 points, and a 2.8 results in 56 points)
- 12 points for standardized test scores (ACT or SAT)
- 10 points for the academic rigor of high school (so all students who go to tougher high schools earn points)
- 8 points for the difficulty of the curriculum (e.g., points for honors curriculum versus keyboarding courses)

For especially desired qualities, including diversity, up to 40 points are possible for any combination of the following (but no more than 40 in this "desired qualities" category):

- Geographical distribution (10 for Michigan resident, an additional 6 for underrepresented Michigan county)
- Legacy—a direct relative has attended Michigan (4 points for a parent, 1 point for a grandparent or sibling)
- Quality of submitted essay (3 points)
- Personal achievement—a special accomplishment that was noteworthy (up to 5 points)

(Continued)

(Continued)

- Leadership and service (5 points each)
- Miscellaneous (only one of these can be used):
  - __ Socioeconomic disadvantage (20 points)
  - __ Underrepresented racial or ethnic minority (Black, Hispanic, or Native American) (20 points; disallowed by the court ruling)
  - __ Men in nursing (5 points)
  - __ Scholarship athlete (20 points)
  - __ Provost's discretion (20 points; usually the son or daughter of a large financial donor or of a politician)

In addition to race or ethnicity, athleticism, socioeconomic disadvantage, having a relative who is an alum, and being the child of someone who is noteworthy to the university are also considered. Some schools also give points for being a military veteran. The legal challenge to this admissions system was based only on the points given for race or ethnic background, not on the other reasons for which some students are given preference.

* * * * * * *

Engaging With Sociology

1. Does this process seem reasonable as a way to get a diverse and highly talented incoming class of students? Why, or why not?

2. Does it significantly advantage or disadvantage some students? Explain.

3. Should there be preferences for predominantly White students—such as "legacy" students, whose family members attended the university? Why, or why not?

4. How would you design a fair system of admissions, and what other factors would you consider?

In 2013 and again in 2016, the Supreme Court, in the case of *Fisher v. University of Texas*, ruled that affirmative action was permissible in order to achieve the goal of a diverse student body. The Court has also warned that not all such programs will pass constitutional muster—that universities must verify that they are unable to achieve sufficient diversity without using racial considerations (Liptak 2013, 2016). In April 2014, the Supreme Court went further, upholding a ban on affirmative action for racial or ethnic groups that was approved by 58% of Michigan voters, arguing that a lower court did not have the authority to overturn the referendum. Thus, publicly funded colleges in Michigan cannot grant preferential treatment on the basis of race, sex, color, ethnicity, or national origin (Mears 2014). So now all such policies are illegal in Michigan, as well as in public universities in California, Washington, Nebraska, Arizona, Oklahoma, New Hampshire, and Florida (Century Foundation 2014).

The question remains: Should preferences be given to accomplish diversity? Some people feel that programs involving any sort of preference for minorities are unfair and should not be allowed. Others believe that such programs do much more good than harm. They have encouraged employers, educational institutions, and government to look carefully at hiring policies and minority candidates, and many more competent minority group members are working in the public sector as a result of these policies. What is the most equitable thing to do?

Global Movements for Human Rights

The rights granted to citizens of any nation used to be considered the business of each sovereign nation, but after the Nazi Holocaust, German officers were tried at the Nuremberg Trials, and the United Nations passed the Universal Declaration of Human Rights. Since that time, many international organizations have been established, often under the auspices of the United Nations, to deal with health issues, world poverty and debt, trade, security, and many other issues affecting world citizens—the World Health Organization, the World Bank, the World Trade Organization, and numerous regional trade and security organizations.

The United Nations and privately funded advocacy groups speak up for international human rights as a principle that transcends national boundaries. The most widely recognized private group is Amnesty International, a watchdog group that lobbies on behalf of human rights and supports political prisoners. When Amnesty International was awarded the Nobel Peace Prize in 1997, the group's visibility dramatically increased. Some activist sociologists have formed groups such as Sociologists Without Borders, or SSF (*Sociólogos Sin Fronteras*; www .sociologistswithoutborders.org), a transnational organization committed to the idea that "all people have equal rights to political and legal protections, to socioeconomic security, to self-determination, and to their personality."

Everyone can make a positive difference in the world, and one place to start is in our own communities (see "Contributing to Our Social World"). We can counter prejudice, discrimination, and socially embedded racism in our own groups by teaching children to see beyond "us" and "them" and by speaking out for fairness and against stereotypes and discrimination.

Some human rights movements focus on international justice issues in countries around the world. Amnesty International is one such movement, with chapters throughout the United States and the world. This Moroccan protester wears a blindfold that reads in Arabic, "Stop torture." This is part of an Amnesty International demonstration on United Nations' International Day in Support of Victims of Torture, in 2014.

Socioeconomic inequality and racial and ethnic stratification create many problems for a society. However, a full understanding of inequality also requires insights into discrimination based on gender. We turn to issues of gender inequality in Chapter 9.

WHAT HAVE WE LEARNED?

If there is competition over resources in a society, groups tend to form. Groups with the most power become dominant, and those with less power become minority groups. Those with the most power stratify their society in a way that ensures that their group has more access to power, money, and status. Racial and ethnic prejudice and discrimination at the micro, meso, and macro levels work to uphold dominant–minority group relations.

- Race is a social construction.

- Racial and ethnic stratification are common throughout the world. Racial and ethnic minority groups have less power and less access to resources than dominant groups.

- Prejudice operates at the micro level of society while discrimination can occur at the micro, meso, and macro levels.

- The racial ideology of color blindness does not acknowledge the reality of racial discrimination and leads to racism evasiveness.

- At the meso level, institutionalized discrimination operates through two processes: side effect and past in present. These forms of discrimination are unintended and unconscious—operating quite separately from any prejudice of individuals in the society.

- The policies of the dominant group may include genocide, subjugation, population transfer, assimilation, or pluralism.

- The costs to society from racial discrimination are high, including loss of human talent and resources.

- The coping devices used by minorities include five main strategies: assimilation, acceptance,

avoidance, aggression, and organizing for societal change. Only the last of these addresses the meso- and macro-level causes.

- Policies to address problems of prejudice and discrimination range from individual and small-group efforts at the micro level to institutional, societal, and even global social movements.

- Affirmative action includes three different sets of policies that are quite distinct and have different outcomes.

DISCUSSION QUESTIONS

1. Have you ever experienced being stereotyped because of your race or ethnicity? Why, or why not? How can racial stereotypes harm societies, as well as groups and individuals?

2. What is the difference between the color-blind perspective on race and blatant bigotry? How does the color-blind ideology lead to racism evasiveness? Why is it often so difficult to recognize and address racial discrimination in the United States today?

3. Give two examples, respectively, of both side-effect discrimination and past-in-present discrimination. How have they impacted you and your life chances? Why?

4. We know that efforts to reduce prejudice, racism, and discrimination must take place at all levels

(micro, meso, and macro). Most organizations, though, must choose one level on which to focus their particular efforts. If you were going to start an organization to decrease racial or ethnic prejudice, would you focus on the micro, meso, or macro level? Why? Explain what your organization would do.

5. Do you agree with preferences for college applicants at the University of Michigan who were scholarship athletes or the sons or daughters of a large donor or a politician but not for racial or ethnic minorities? Why, or why not? Was the Supreme Court correct in ruling that a referendum passed by voters in Michigan should trump concerns about diversity? Why?

KEY TERMS

assimilation   230

discrimination   222

ethnic group   219

genocide   229

institutional racial
   discrimination   225

minority groups   214

past-in-present
   discrimination   227

pluralism   230

population transfer   230

prejudice   222

race   215

side-effect discrimination   225

subjugation   229

CONTRIBUTING TO OUR SOCIAL WORLD: WHAT CAN WE DO?

At the Local (Micro) Level

- *African American, Arab American, and Native American student associations* are examples of student organizations dedicated to fighting bigotry and promoting understanding and the rights of racial and ethnic minorities. Identify one of these groups on your campus and arrange to attend a meeting. If appropriate, volunteer to help with its work.

At the Organizational/Institutional (Meso) Level

- *The Leadership Conference on Civil and Human Rights* is a national coalition dedicated to combating racism and its effects. It maintains a website that includes a directory of its membership of more than 200 organizations (www.civilrights.org). On its website, you can find a "take action" link that will help you to explore ways in which you can participate in its efforts.

- *Teaching Tolerance* (www.splcenter.org/center/tt/teach.jsp), a program of the Southern Poverty Law Center, has curriculum materials for teaching about diversity and a program for enhancing cross-ethnic cooperation and dialogue in schools. Check into internship opportunities in local primary and secondary schools, and explore ways in which the Teaching Tolerance approach can be incorporated into the curricula in your school district with local teachers and administrators.

At the National/Global (Macro) Levels

- The *Anti-Defamation League* (www.adl.org) acts to "stop the defamation of the Jewish people and to secure justice and fair treatment to all." Members of this organization develop and implement educational programs on interfaith/intergroup understanding, scrutinize and call attention to hate groups, monitor hate speech on the Internet, and mobilize communities to stand up to bigotry throughout the United States and abroad. Job listings, summer internships, and opportunities in Israel and other locations are listed on the ADL website.

- *National Relief Charities* strives "to help Native American people improve the quality of their lives by providing opportunities for them to bring about positive changes in their communities." To do so, it partners with tribal and other groups on the ground in the tribal regions of the Plains and Midwest. You can find out how to support the work of this group and its partners by going to www.nrcprograms.org/site/PageNavigator/index.

- *Cultural Survival* and the *UN Permanent Forum on Indigenous Issues* (www.cs.org and www.un.org/esa/socdev/unpfii) provide opportunities for combating racism globally.

- Consider purchasing only fair-trade-certified (packages are clearly marked as such) coffee and chocolate and encouraging your school to sell fair-trade products. You can learn more about fair-trade products and issues by reading this article—www.nytimes.com/2012/09/28/business/media/green-mountain-coffee-begins-fair-trade-campaign-advertising.html—and looking at educational materials provided by the Fair Trade Resource Network at www.fairtraderesource.org.

- *Amnesty International* campaigns against abuses of human rights. It relies heavily on volunteers organized into chapters, many of them campus based. You can join the organization and learn how to participate in its actions through its website at www.amnesty.org. Consider joining or starting one on your campus.

$SAGE edge™

9 Gender Stratification

She/He—Who Goes First?

Social inequality is pervasive in gender relations, and although in some societies, women are treated with deference, they are rarely given first access to positions of significant power or financial reward. The men often "go first."

ME (AND MY GENDER)

LOCAL ORGANIZATIONS AND COMMUNITY
Peers, neighbors, teachers, and religious congregations socialize us into gendered expectations.

NATIONAL ORGANIZATIONS, INSTITUTIONS, AND ETHNIC SUBCULTURES
Organizations and institutions limit access to many positions based on gender.

SOCIETY
National policies provide sex-based privileges.

GLOBAL COMMUNITY
Gender status is determined by laws and power structures; the United Nations champions equal rights for women.

WHAT YOU WILL LEARN IN THIS CHAPTER

This chapter will help you do the following:

9.1 Describe the difference between sex and gender.

9.2 Identify agents of gender socialization.

9.3 Give examples of meso- and macro-level gender stratification.

9.4 Illustrate the relationship between minority status and gender and sexual orientation.

9.5 Discuss costs and consequences of gender stratification.

9.6 Explain social policies that could decrease gender stratification.

THINK ABOUT IT

Micro: Local community	How does being female or male affect your thoughts, behaviors, and opportunities? Why do some people face violence in their homes and communities because of their gender or sexual orientation?
Meso: National institutions, complex organizations, and ethnic groups	What can be done in our organizations and institutions to make men and women more equal in pay and promotions?
Macro: National and global systems	Why do women have second-class status in many societies?

As women around the world wake up to International Women's Day, each woman, no matter where she lives, holds the same basic goals: a trusting and happy relationship; the option of having healthy, educated children with a fair chance in life; enough food on the table; self-respect; access to health care; and whatever individual desires are relevant in her society. Consider the following example from a Global North country that illustrates the problems some women face in meeting basic goals.

Jocelyn, who lives in the United States, is now retired and having trouble making ends meet. After training in nursing, including a master's degree, she married and dropped her career to raise her family. The marriage did not work out, and 15 years after college, she found herself with no credit, two children, little job experience, and mounting expenses. She was a conscientious and hard worker, but with two children and meager child support from their father, she could not put much away for retirement. Nursing did not pay well in her town in the Midwest, but there had been few other career options for females in the early 1960s, when she was getting her education.

Moreover, two decades does not build a very large retirement annuity, and she had never been able to buy an adequate home on her income. If she had been a typical male with a master's degree, her lifetime earnings would have been $1 million more in cumulative income (Catalyst 2014; Julian and Kominski 2011). Her life chances were clearly affected by the fact that she was a female.

Due to changes in gender roles and opportunities over the past 50 years, Jocelyn's granddaughter, Emma, will have a range of opportunities that were beyond consideration for her grandma. Ideas about sex, gender, and appropriate roles for women and men not only transform over time, but they also vary a great deal from one society to the next. Some practices of your own society may seem very

strange to women and men in another society. Gender identities and roles are not stagnant; they change over time, reflecting the economic, political, and social realities of one's society. For instance, women in today's India, with the exception of some rural areas, seldom commit *sati* (suicide) on their husband's funeral pyre (Greenan 2013; Ziel 2013); however, before the practice of *sati* was outlawed, it was a common way to deal with widows who no longer had a social role or means of support (Ahmad 2009).

In this chapter, we explore the concepts of sex, gender, and sexuality. When we combine gender issues with race and class, we get a better understanding of the stratification system and why people hold the positions they do in society. Although gender refers to a range of social behaviors, we place more emphasis on women's status and roles than on men's because this is generally more relevant to our concern about stratification and minorities. At the micro level, we consider gender socialization or how girls and boys learn to be gendered individuals in their respective societies. At the meso and macro levels we consider gender stratification, or the placement of individuals in society's stratification system. A discussion of the costs and consequences of gender stratification, plus policy implications, ends this chapter.

SEX, GENDER, AND THE STRATIFICATION SYSTEM

You name it, and some society has probably done it! Gender relations are no exception. Variations around the world show that most roles and identities are not biological but rather socially constructed. In Chapter 7, we discussed factors that stratify individuals into social groups (castes and classes), and in Chapter 8, we discussed the roles that race and ethnicity play in stratification. Add the concepts of sex and gender, and we have a more complex and complete picture of how class, race, ethnicity, and gender together influence the experiences that make us who we are and our positions in society. Consider the following examples from societies that illustrate some interesting human social constructions based on sex and gender. These examples show that gender roles are created by humans to meet the needs of their societies. We then move to more familiar societies.

The Wodaabe, a subgroup of the Fulani ethnic group, are herders and traders in the Sahel region of Africa (especially Niger and Nigeria); they would be defined as effeminate by most Western standards. Men are like birds, showing their colorful feathers to attract females. They take great care in doing their hair, applying makeup, and dressing to attract women. They also gossip with each other while sipping their tea. Meanwhile, the women are cooking meals, caring for the children, cleaning, tending to the animals, planting small gardens, and preparing for the next move of this nomadic group (Beckwith 1993; Human Planet 2012; Saharan Vibe 2007). These patterns have developed over time and carry on as traditions. The point is that groups have developed cultural norms over time, often independently of other groups, that cause gender behaviors to differ widely.

Under ISIS in some Middle Eastern countries and Taliban rule in Afghanistan, women cannot be seen in public without a total body covering that meets strict requirements (Human Rights Watch 2016). Those not obeying can be stoned to death. Women cannot hold public positions or work outside their homes. If they become ill, women cannot be examined by a physician because all doctors are male. Instead, they have to describe their symptoms to a doctor through a screen (Makhmalbaf 2003; Trust in Education 2013).

Certain tasks must be carried out by individuals and organizations in each society for members to survive. Responsibilities include raising children, providing people with the basic necessities (such as food, clothing, and shelter), having leaders, defending the society, and solving conflicts. One's sex and age are often used to determine who holds what positions and who carries out what tasks. Each society develops its own way to meet its expectations and its own interpretations of right and wrong gender role behaviors. This results in gender role variations from one society to the next. If the genders are identified as fundamentally different, distinguishing symbols such as dress, head coverings, hairstyles, and, of course, roles become important for each gender's identity.

Liba Taylor/Alamy Stock Photo

Wodaabe men in Niger, Africa, appear to reverse some gender norms typically associated with males and females. They go to great pains with makeup, hair, and jewelry to ensure that they are highly attractive.

©AP Photo/Hasan Jamali

Muslim girls in some parts of the world cover their faces when in public. The display of skin, even in a classroom, would be immoral to many Muslims. However, in other Muslim countries, such coverings would be unusual.

Thinking Sociologically

Why do you think societies in different corners of the globe develop such radically different ways of organizing their gender roles?

Sex and Sexuality

At birth, when doctors say, "It's a . . .!" they are referring to the distinguishing primary characteristics that determine sex—that is, the penis or vagina. Sex is *a biological term referring to ascribed genetic, anatomical, and hormonal differences between males and females*. This is actually only partially true. *Sex* is also a term that categorizes people using "socially agreed upon biological criteria for classifying persons as females or males" (West and Zimmerman 1987:127). In other words, occasionally, this binary male–female categorization by biological criteria is not clear. Approximately 1 in 1,500 babies are born with ambiguous genitalia, not fitting the typical definitions of male or female (the *intersexed*) (Fausto-Sterling 2000).

In Global North countries, most of these babies undergo surgeries to clarify their gender, with hormonal treatments and possible further surgery at adolescence (Chase 2000). However, governments in some Global North countries have begun to discourage surgeries in favor of more acceptance of intersexed individuals. A new law in Germany, for example, allows the category of *indeterminate gender* on birth certificates, recognizing *intersex* as a third indeterminate gender option, with surgery seen as unnecessary. Australian laws also acknowledge the intersex status (Agius 2013).

Where medical interventions are not possible or desired, people with sex anomalies may have special status and roles in societies, such as the transgendered Hijras (or Aravanis) in India. These unique people are called on for special religious observances and other ceremonial occasions (Gannon 2009). Whether male, female, or intersexed, anatomical differences at birth and chromosomal typing before birth result in attempts by people in various cultures to clearly categorize people based on their sex. The word *sex*, when applied to a person, refers largely to elements of one's anatomy.

The struggles that some individuals have with their sexual identity are especially compelling in studies of transgender—when intersexed individuals do not fit clearly into female or male sex classifications (Kinsey Institute for Research in Sex, Gender, and Reproduction 2012; Leeder 2004). Transgender(ed) *describes someone who is challenging, questioning, or changing gender from that assigned at birth to a chosen gender—male to female, female to male, transitioning between genders, or genderqueer* (Lorber and Moore 2011:6). Transgendered individuals have especially interested sociologists because of how they challenge gender norms.

The reason many societies go to great lengths to assign a sex to an infant is that sex constitutes a major organizing principle. Surgeries to clarify the sex of an infant are done mainly because of the stigma attached to those who do not fit socially approved categories. Despite emphasis on

achieved status in modern societies, society's expectations guiding roles and statuses are largely ascribed—determined by a person's sex.

Our attraction to others is expressed by our sexuality and our sexual identity (e.g., heterosexual—attracted to the other sex, homosexual—attracted to the same sex, or bisexual—attracted to both sexes). In most societies, our sexual identities follow the prevailing belief that a "normal" girl or boy will be sexually attracted to and eventually have sex with someone of the other sex (Lorber and Moore 2011). However, as we have seen, sex is not always a straightforward distinction and is as social as it is biological.

Sexuality *refers to culturally shaped meanings both of sexual acts and of how we experience our own bodies—especially in relation to the bodies of others*. Strange as it may seem, sexuality is socially constructed. A sex act is a *social enterprise*, with cultural norms defining what is normal and acceptable in each society, how we should feel, and hidden assumptions about what the act means (Steele 2005). Even what we find attractive is culturally defined. For a period in China, men found tiny feet a sexual turn-on—hence, some women bound their feet to be attractive to men. In some cultures, legs are the attraction, and in others, men are fascinated by breasts. Likewise, the ideal male body, as depicted in popular magazines in contemporary Western cultures, is "over 6 feet tall, 180 to 200 pounds, muscular, agile, with straight white teeth, a washboard stomach, six-pack abs, long legs, a full head of hair, a large penis (discreetly shown by a bulge), broad shoulders and chest, strong muscular back, clean shaven, healthy, and slightly tanned if White, or a lightish brown if Black or Hispanic" (Lorber and Moore 2011:89–90). We grow up learning what is appealing.

As individuals mature, they are expected to adopt the behaviors appropriate to their anatomical features as defined by their society. In addition to the physical sex differences between males and females, a few other physical conditions are commonly believed to be sex linked, such as a prevalence of color blindness, baldness, learning disabilities, autism, and hemophilia. Yet some traits that members of society commonly link to sex are actually learned through socialization. There is little evidence, for instance, that emotions, personality traits, or ability to fulfill most social statuses are determined by inborn physical sex differences. However, the social messages urging people to conform to expectations for their sex category are strong. What is defined as normal behavior for a male, a female, or an intersexed person in one society could get one killed in another.

Gender

Gender refers to *a society's notions of masculinity and femininity—socially constructed meanings associated with being male or female—and how individuals construct their identity in terms of gender within these constraints.* Gender identity, then, is how individuals form their identity using the categories of sex and gender and negotiate the constraints they entail. The examples at the beginning of this section illustrate some differences in how cultures are structured around gender.

Statuses are positions within the structures of society, and roles are expected behaviors within those statuses (Rothenberg 2014). **Gender roles**, then, are those *commonly assigned tasks or expected behaviors linked to an individual's sex-determined statuses* (Lips 2010, 2013). Members of each society learn the structural guidelines and positions expected of males and females (West and Zimmerman 1987). Our positions, which affect access to power and resources, are embedded in institutions at the meso level, with culture defining what is right and wrong. There is not some global absolute truth governing gender or gender roles. Whereas both vary across cultures, gender is a learned cultural idea, and gender roles are part of the structural system of roles and statuses in a society.

Although the terms *sex*, *sexuality*, and *gender* are often used interchangeably, they do have distinct meanings. Individuals who negotiate the meanings attached to gender and sexuality are *doing gender*, a process discussed later in this chapter (Schoepflin 2011; West and Zimmerman 1987).

Sex, Gender, and Sexuality: The Micro Level

"It's a boy!" brings varying cultural responses. In many Western countries, that exclamation results in blue blankets, toys associated with boys (e.g., footballs, soccer balls, and trucks), roughhousing, and gender socialization messages. In some Asian societies, boys are sources for great rejoicing, whereas girls may be seen as a burden. Abortion rates in some countries are much higher when ultrasound tests show that the fetus is female ("Gendercide" 2010). In China and India, *female infanticide* (killing of newborn girl babies) is sometimes practiced in rural areas, in part because of the cost to poor families of raising a girl and paying the dowry to get the daughter married, all diminishing the value of girls. In China, the male preference system has been exacerbated by the government's edict that most couples may have only one child, although this law has recently been relaxed (T. Phillips 2015). As a result of government policy and female infanticide and abortion, a sex imbalance developed and is causing other consequences, such as a shortage of brides.

At the micro level, we can trace stages in an individual's life as a female or male: early childhood socialization, school and community activities and experiences, adult statuses and roles of females and males, and so on through the life cycle. At each stage, messages reinforce appropriate gender behavior. Cultural traditions learned from birth guide individuals into proper gender roles. These gender expectations are inculcated into children by parents, siblings, grandparents, neighbors, peers, and even day care providers. If we fail to respond to the expectations of these significant people in our lives, we may experience negative sanctions: teasing, isolation and exclusion, harsh words, and stigma. Therefore, children usually learn to conform, at least in their public behavior.

The lifelong process of gender socialization continues once we reach *school age* and we become more involved in activities separate from our parents. Other people in the community—teachers, religious leaders, coaches, and peers—influence us. We are grouped by sex in many of these social settings: boys versus girls, us versus them. Even if our parents are not highly traditional in their gender expectations, we still experience many expectations to conform from peers, school, and other sources. Yet schools and colleges today are faced with challenges such as transgendered students and how to deal with

Two students place a new sticker on the door at the ceremonial opening of a gender-neutral bathroom at Nathan Hale High School in Seattle. Since 2012, Seattle has mandated that transgender students be able to use the bathrooms and locker rooms of their choice; one high school has had a transgender bathroom for 20 years. The issue has been highly controversial in other parts of the country.

sex-differentiated classes such as physical education and sex-designated bathrooms (Scelfo 2015).

With adulthood, the differential treatment and stratification of the sexes take new forms. Men traditionally have more networks and statuses, as well as greater access to resources outside the home. This has resulted in many women around the world having less power because they depend more on husbands or fathers for resources. The subtitle of this chapter asks, "Who goes first?" When it comes to the question of who walks through a door first, the answer is that in many Western societies, *she* does—or at least formal etiquette would suggest this is proper. The strong man steps back and defers to the weaker female, graciously holding the door for her, and women are served first at restaurants. This seems little compensation for the fact that doors are often closed to women at the meso and macro levels of society.

Language can be powerful in shaping the behavior and perceptions of people, as discussed in Chapter 3. Have you ever been in a classroom or meeting when a woman makes a point that is barely acknowledged, but when a man says pretty much the same thing, he is applauded for his fine idea? The dilemma for women is to speak up loudly and be considered aggressive or hostile or to speak softly, say less, appear weak—and be largely ignored (Sandberg and Grant 2015). In addition, women adopt speech patterns to avoid appearing aggressive, often ending sentences with tag questions; that is, ending a declarative statement with a short tag that turns it into a question: "That was a good idea, don't you think?" This pattern may cause male business colleagues to think women are insecure or uncertain about themselves, preventing a woman from getting the job or the promotion. The women themselves may view it as an invitation to collaboration and dialogue. On the flip side, when women stop using these "softening" devices, they may be perceived as strident, harsh, or "bitchy" (Sandberg 2013; J. Wood and Reich 2006). Women also tend to use more words related to psychological and social processes, whereas men prefer more discussion of objects and impersonal topics (M. Newman et al. 2008).

The same adverb or adjective, when preceded by a male or female pronoun, can take on very different meanings. When one says, "He's easy," or, "He's loose," it does not generally mean the same thing as when someone says, "She's easy," or, "She's loose." Likewise, there are words such as *slut* or *bitch* for women with no equivalents for men. The word *spinster* is supposed to be the female synonym for *bachelor*, yet it has very different connotations. Even the more newly coined *bachelorette* is not usually used to describe a highly appealing, perhaps lifelong role. What might be the implications of these differences?

Those who invoke the biological argument that women's options to participate in public affairs and politics are limited by pregnancy, childbirth, or breastfeeding ignore the fact that in most societies, these biological roles are time limited, and women play a variety of social roles in addition to keeping the home and hearth. They also ignore those societies in which males are deeply involved in non-aggressive and nurturing activities such as child-rearing.

Thinking Sociologically

Until recently, words like *mankind* and phrases like "all men are created equal" were commonly used. Today, some people always write *he* first when writing "he and she." Others put *she* first. How do these examples—and others you can think of—reveal how language is used and relates to gender roles?

Sex, Gender, and Sexuality: The Meso Level

By whatever age is defined as being an *adult* in a society, members are expected to assume leadership roles and responsibilities in the institutions of family, education, religion, government, economics, health care, and the military. Our roles in these institutions often differ depending on our sex, which determines our placements and many of our experiences in the social world (Brettell and Sargent 2012). This makes it difficult—but not impossible—for women to attain the most powerful and financially rewarding positions in a society. For example, two women in the United States recently completed the most challenging military training to be U.S. Army Rangers, yet following training, they were not permitted to carry out the same missions as their male counterparts. Israel is one of the few countries to have female conscription, though women are restricted from some jobs. Many countries do not consider the military the proper place for women.

In most societies, sex and age stipulate when and how we experience *rites of passage*—rituals and ceremonies in institutions that mark a change of status in the family and community—the meso levels of society. These rites include any ceremonies or recognitions that admit one to adult duties and privileges (Brettell and Sargent 2012). Rites of passage are institutionalized in various ways: religious rituals, such as the Jewish male bar mitzvah or the female bat mitzvah ceremonies; education celebrations, such as graduation ceremonies, which often involve caps and gowns of gender-specific colors or place females on one side of the room and males on the other; and different ages at which men and women are permitted to marry.

Other institutions also segregate members by sex. For example, in very traditional Greek Orthodox Christian churches and Orthodox Jewish synagogues, men sit on one side of the sanctuary and women on the other. In mosques, women are often put in separate and removed spaces for prayer.

Empowerment of Women. Thirty village women gather regularly to discuss issues of health, crops, their herds, the predicted rains, goals for their children, and how to make ends meet. They are from a subsistence farming village in southern Niger on the edge of the Sahara desert. Recently, the women established a microcredit organization with a small grant of $1,500 with donations from abroad. With training from CARE International, an international nongovernmental organization (NGO), the women selected a board of directors to oversee the loans. Groups of five or six women joined together to explain their projects to the board and request small loans. Each woman is responsible for paying back a small amount on the loan each week once the project is established and bringing in money. Typical microcredit participants are women with several children, living at or below poverty, and sharing shelter with other families. With loans, women can make and sell items and build businesses to feed, clothe, and educate children (Foundation for Women 2012). A loan of between $20 and $50 from the microcredit organization is a tremendous sum to launch a career in some Global South countries. Strong social norms are instituted to encourage repayment. Participation in the program encourages women and grants them economic and social capital (more status in the community and family) otherwise unavailable to them.

With the new possibilities for their lives, these women have big plans: For instance, one group bought a press to make peanut oil, a staple for cooking in the region. Currently, people pay a great deal for oil imported from Nigeria. Another group bought baby lambs, fattened them, and sold them at a great profit for festivals. Yet another group set up a small bakery. Women are also discussing the possibility of making local craft products to sell to foreign fair-trade organizations, such as Ten Thousand Villages (a fair-trade organization that markets products made by villagers and returns the profits back to the villagers).

Some economists and social policymakers claim that grassroots organizations, such as microcreditors, may be the way out of poverty for millions of poor families and that women are motivated to be small-business entrepreneurs to help support their families and buy education and health care for their children. Muhammad Yunus, the founder of Grameen Bank—a microcredit lender for the very poor—received the Nobel Prize for Peace in 2006 for his work setting up co-ops, primarily for women.

Critics suggest such organizations work on a micro level but fail to address macro-level national and international problems of inequality (Mayoux 2008). For better or worse, microloans also may shift relations between husbands and wives, leaving men in a less powerful position within marriages and changing gender dynamics. Whereas this has led to more respect for women in some areas, this shift of power has also left some women vulnerable to criticism, harassment, violence, and isolation (*Business Insider* 2012). Most economists agree that microlending works best alongside macro-level initiatives seeking to address national economic problems.

Thinking Sociologically

How might the lack of women in positions of authority in organizations and institutions—the meso level of society—influence females' roles at the micro level? How might it influence women's involvement at the macro level?

Sex, Sexuality, and Gender: The Macro Level

People around the world go to school, drive cars, and work, but in some parts of the world, school, driving, and work are forbidden for women. Fourteen-year-old Malala Yousafzai, a girl from northwest Pakistan, was shot and

Catarina lives in Guatemala. She started a weaving business—and turned her life around—with the help of a microfinance loan from FINCA.

© Keith Roberts

In 2016, 22 women served as the head of their nations, including Angela Merkel (*top*), the chancellor of Germany, and Ellen Johnson Sirleaf (*bottom*), the president of Liberia and the first elected female head of state in Africa.

severely wounded by a Taliban gunman for both going to school and speaking out for other girls to have educational opportunities (Mehsud 2012). The Taliban, a regional organization that extends beyond the local boundaries, is opposed to girls going to school due to the organization's beliefs about proper gender roles. Malala gained worldwide fame and, since her recovery, has spoken out about the right for education for all children. In recognition of her work and worldwide impact, the Nobel Peace Prize committee honored her in 2014. Malala is the youngest person ever to win the prestigious award.

When we turn to the national and global level, we witness inequality between the sexes quite separate from any form of personal prejudice or animosity toward women. Patterns of social action embedded in the entire social system may influence women and men, providing unrecognized institutionalized privilege or disprivilege.

Over the past decade, the number of women in governing roles has increased in many parts of the globe. Also, voting is a universal right for most women. In 2015, women finally gained the right to vote in Saudi Arabia and the United Arab Emirates (Townsend 2015). In the United States, women have voted in federal elections for more than 90 years, following the passage of the Nineteenth Amendment in 1920 prohibiting voter discrimination on the basis of sex. Yet in the entire history of the United States Senate, only 2% (46) have been women, and just 297 have been elected to the House of Representatives ("Every Woman Who Has Served" 2015). The first woman was elected to Congress in 1917. As of 2016, 20 of 100 senators and 108 of 435 representatives in the House were women, an all-time high (Desilver 2015). So today, women compose a mere 20% of all national representatives in the U.S. Congress (Desilver 2015).

The nation with the highest percentage of women (63.8%) in the national parliament or congress is Rwanda (sub-Saharan Africa)—one of only two countries (Bolivia being the other) to reach or surpass 50%. Canada is 64th among nations, and the United States, between Kenya and Kyrgyzstan, ranks 97th—well below Global North countries like Sweden (#5), Norway (#14), Spain (#18), and Germany (#26) and trailing Global South countries like Afghanistan (#52), Iraq (#61), and even Saudi Arabia (#93) (Inter-Parliamentary Union 2016). Nations like Rwanda, with political systems that stress proportional representation and gender quotas for government positions, have more women in political offices (Yoon 2011a, 2011b). Without such systems and quotas, democratization of governmental systems is sometimes linked to a *decrease* in representation by women, a sad reality for those committed to establishing democracy around the world (Yoon 2005). Globally, women's access to power and prestige is highly variable, with some African and northern European countries having a position of leadership when it comes to gender equity in government (see Table 9.1). As you study Table 9.1, note that researchers find the needs and

Table 9.1   Women in National Parliaments (Governments) (Selected Countries), 2016

Rank	Country	Lower Chamber (House of Representatives) or Single Chamber	Upper Chamber (Senate)
1	Rwanda	63.8	38.5
2	Bolivia	53.1	47.2
3	Cuba	48.9	—
4	Seychelles	43.8	—
5	Sweden	43.6	—
6	Senegal	42.7	—
7	Mexico	42.4	33.6
8	South Africa	42.0	35.2
9	Ecuador	41.6	—
10	Finland	41.5	—
11	Iceland	41.3	—
11	Namibia	41.3	23.8
11	Nicaragua	41.3	—
14	Spain	40.0	—
15	Norway	39.6	—
15	Mozambique	39.6	—
26	Germany	36.5	40.6
39	New Zealand	31.4	—
48	United Kingdom	29.4	24.6
50	Afghanistan	27.7	26.5
54	Australia	26.7	38.2
56	Iraq	26.5	—
60	Canada	26.0	37.3
91	Saudi Arabia	19.9	—
95	United States	19.4	20.0

Note: To examine the involvement of women in other countries or to see even more recent figures, go to www.ipu.org/wmn-e/classif.htm.

Source: Inter-Parliamentary Union (2016). Reprinted with permission of the Inter-Parliamentary Union.

interests of women are not fully represented unless a critical mass of female representatives is reached, and that critical mass is usually about 35% (Yoon 2011b).

Thinking Sociologically

What factors might explain why the United States and Canada have low rankings in representation of women in their governments?

Cross-cultural analyses confirm that gender roles, having evolved over centuries, can be transformed by sweeping government reforms, economic upheaval, or wars. In many societies, though, gender roles are passed down from one generation to the next. The fact that women in China generally work outside the home, whereas women in some Muslim societies hardly venture from their homes, is due to differences in cultural norms about proper gender roles dictated by traditions, religious beliefs, and governments and learned through the socialization process. Consider the example of Japan where the birth rate is one of the lowest in the world and will result in sharp population decline. Women, even highly educated ones, have traditionally left their jobs when a child was born because of norms favoring the stay-at-home mom and the difficulty of juggling work and family. However, with Japan's shrinking population resulting in fewer workers to support the aging population, the prime minister (head of the government) is advocating more state-funded childcare and other supports so that more women can have children *and* stay in the labor force. It may take some time to overcome traditions, but government intervention in the economy may help Japan deal with its economic problems (Soble 2015).

GENDER SOCIALIZATION: MICRO- TO MESO-LEVEL ANALYSES

"Sugar and spice and everything nice—that's what little girls are made of. Snips and snails and puppy dog tails—that's what little boys are made of." As this verse implies, different views of little girls and little boys start at birth, based on gender and stereotypes about what is biologically natural. Behavioral expectations stem from cultural beliefs about the nature of men and women, and these expectations can guide socialization from the earliest ages and in intimate primary-group settings.

Gender role socialization is the process by which people learn the cultural norms, attitudes, and behaviors appropriate to their gender. That is, they learn how to think and act as boys or girls, women or men. Socialization reinforces the "proper" gender behaviors and punishes the improper behaviors. This process, in turn, reinforces gender stereotypes. In many societies, traits of gentleness, passivity, and dependence are associated with femininity, whereas boldness, aggression, strength, and independence are identified with masculinity. For instance, in most Western societies, aggression in women is considered unfeminine, if not inappropriate or disturbing (Sandberg and Grant 2015). Likewise, the gentle, unassertive male is often looked on with scorn or pity, stigmatized as a "wimp." Gender stereotypes in the United States are less rigid than in the past, but they are still a big part of popular culture and provide guidelines for parents and especially for boys' behavior. Girls' norms of acceptable female behavior have expanded more than norms of masculinity, and more girls have aspirations for formerly male-dominated professions, such as engineering, law, and medicine, than boys have for nursing. Girls have more flexibility in sports they choose and in toys they can play with ("Gender Stereotypes" 2011).

Stages in Gender Socialization

Bounce that rough-and-tumble baby boy and cuddle that precious, delicate little girl. Thus begins gender socialization, starting at birth and taking place through a series of life stages, discussed in Chapter 4 on socialization. Examples from infancy and childhood show how socialization into gender roles takes place.

© iStockPhoto.com/MattoMatteo

Children, like the girl in this picture, begin to conform to gender expectations once they are old enough to understand that their sex is permanent.

Infancy. Learning how to carry out gender roles begins at birth. Parents in the United States describe their newborn daughters as soft, delicate, fine featured, little, pretty, cute, awkward, and resembling their mothers. They depict their sons as strong, firm, alert, and well coordinated—and treat them as such (Lindsey 2015). Although gender stereotypes have declined in recent years, they continue to affect the way we handle and treat male and female infants.

Clothing, room decor, and toys also reflect notions of gender. An interesting fact is that only a century ago pink was considered the "manly" color, and self-respecting men were steered away from the very soft feminine color: blue. A trade publication, *Earnshaw's Infants' Department*, published an article in June 1918 that advised parents, "The generally accepted rule is pink for the boys, and blue for the girls. The reason is that pink, being a more decided and stronger color, is more suitable for the boy, while blue, which is more delicate and dainty, is prettier for the girl." In 1927, *Time* magazine printed a chart showing sex-appropriate colors for children: pink is for boys—blue for girls (Maglaty 2011). Moreover, prior to the 20th century, both boys and girls in the United States were dressed mostly in frilly dresses until they were about 6 (Maglaty 2011).

Childhood. Once they are out of infancy, boys receive more encouragement than girls to be independent and exploratory. More pressure is put on boys to behave in "gender-appropriate" ways, with an emphasis on achievement, autonomy, and aggression (Kramer and Beutel 2014). Boys are socialized into this "boy code" that provides rigid guidelines for their behavior.

Girls, on the other hand, are trained to express aggression in subtler ways: through gossip, rumors, name-calling, backbiting, and excluding other girls from social activities (Beran 2012). Friendship and needing to belong are the weapons—rather than the "sticks and stones" used by boys. This form of bullying is subtle and hard to detect, but it can have long-lasting effects on girls (Beran 2012; Girls Health 2009; Simmons 2002).

Names for children also reflect stereotypes about gender. Boys are more often given strong, hard names, often ending in consonants. The top 10 names given to boys in 2016 were Liam, Noah, Ethan, Lucas, Mason, Oliver, Aiden, Elijah, James, and Benjamin. Girls are more likely to be given soft, pretty names with vowel endings, such as most of the 2016 top 10: Emma, Olivia, Ava, Sophia, Isabella, Mia, Charlotte, Harper, Amelia, and Abigail (BabyCenter 2016).

Alternatively, girls may be given feminized versions of boys' names—Roberta, Jessica, Josephine, Nicole, Michelle, Donna, Charlotte, Georgia, or Antonia. Sometimes traditional boys' names are given to girls without first feminizing them. Names such as Lynn, Stacey, Tracey, Faye, Dana, Jody, Lindsay, Robin, Carmen, Kelly, Kim, Beverly, Ashley, Carol, Shannon, and Leslie used to be exclusively for men, but within a decade or two after they were applied to girls, parents stopped using them for boys (Kean 2007). So a common name for males may, for a time, be given to either sex, but then, it is given primarily to girls. The pattern rarely goes in the other direction. Once feminized, the names seem to have become tainted and unacceptable for boys (Lieberson, Dumais, and Bauman 2000).

As children are rewarded for performing proper gender roles, these roles are reinforced, setting the stage for gender-related interactions, behaviors, and choices in later life. We now turn to meso-level agents of gender socialization.

Meso-Level Agents of Gender Socialization

Clues to proper gender roles surround children in materials produced by corporations (e.g., books, toys, and games), in technology and mass-media images, in educational settings, and in religious organizations and beliefs. In Chapter 4, we learned about agents of socialization. Those agents play a major role in teaching children proper gender roles. The following examples demonstrate how organizations and institutions in societies teach and reinforce gender assumptions and roles.

Corporations. Corporations create many materials that help socialize children into conduct socially approved for their gender. Publishers, for example, produce books that present images of expected gender behavior. The language and pictures in preschool picture books, elementary children's books, stories for teenagers, and school textbooks are steeped in gender role messages, reflecting society's expectations and stereotypes. In a recent study of children's books published in the United States during the 20th century, researchers found males more frequently represented than females throughout the entire time period (McCabe et al. 2011). Studies on more recent books have found some change in this pattern—even an overcorrection in some cases—but many children's books still show stereotyped images of females, especially those with animal or other types of nonhuman characters (D. A. Anderson and Hamilton 2005; Diekman and

Murmen 2004; Houlis 2011). Recent lists of books that defy gender stereotypes have been created for parents who wish to present gender-neutral images to their children, but most parents are not aware of these options (Krueger 2015).

Producers of toys and games also contribute to traditional messages about gender. Wall posters and store-bought toys fill rooms in homes of children in the Western world, and it is usually quite clear which are boys' rooms and which are girls' rooms. Each toy or game prepares children for future gender roles. Choices ranging from college major to occupational choice appear to be affected by these early choices and childhood learning experiences (Deerwester 2013).

Boys' rooms are filled with sports equipment, army toys, building and technical toys, and cars and trucks. Girls' rooms have fewer toys, and most are related to dolls and domestic roles. Boys have more experience manipulating blocks, Tinkertoys, LEGO bricks, and Erector Sets—toys paralleling masculinized activities outside the home in the public domain, from constructing and building trades to military roles and sports. Girls prepare for domestic roles with toys related to domestic activities and play with Barbie dolls that stress physical appearance, consumerism, and glamour. Toy stores are generally divided into distinct boys' and girls' sections, shaping parents' and children's choices and girls' and boys' future skills and interests (Abadi 2013; C. Williams 2006). Each toy or game prepares children through anticipatory socialization for future gender roles. The bottom line is that gender portrayals are unequal, and the females presented in books, video games, and toys tend to be in stereotypical roles—supporting, needing rescue, or sexually alluring.

Mass Media. Mass media comes in many forms—magazines, ads, films, music videos, and Internet sites—and is a major agent of socialization into gender roles. We can see its influence all around us, even during a typical weekend evening for many boys. It is Friday night, and a group of adolescent males gather to play games. Their two favorites are the card game *Magic: The Gathering* (MTG or *Magic*) and the online game *World of Warcraft* (WoW). WoW is played with many online players, and the individual players can sit in front of their computers alone, interacting only online.

In the United States, most teens are wired. Ninety-one percent use the Internet on a mobile device. Snapchat (72%), Facebook (68%), Instagram (66%), and Twitter (36%) are the most often used platforms (Statistica 2016b), with girls the primary users of visually oriented social media platforms. Seventy-one percent of all teens play video

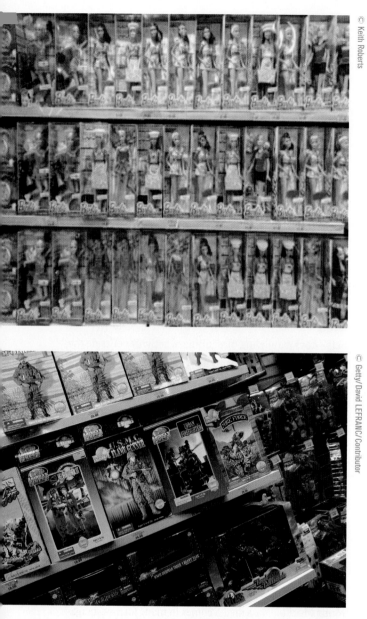

Mattel's Barbie dolls and other girls' toys have been criticized for their extremely traditional and highly sexualized images of young women. The second photo is of a boys' toy department; note the difference in images and colors. What is communicated?

However, girls are generally peripheral to the action. Notice the next time you are around people playing video games that the fighting characters are typically male and often in armor. When fighting women do appear, they are usually clad in skin-revealing bikini-style attire—odd clothing in which to do battle!

Thinking Sociologically

Why are video and role-playing games primarily a "boy social thing"? How do you see girls using social media? What effect might girls' and boys' different technology activities have on their futures?

Some recent action films include adventurous and competent girls and women, helping to counter images of sexy and helpless females. *The Hunger Games* heroine, Katniss Everdeen, has become a brave idol for teenage girls; Mattel has even made a Barbie version of the heroine. *The Girl With the Dragon Tattoo* and other films in that series present an extremely clever and unique heroine in Lisbeth Salander. More recently, strong women characters appear in films such as *Sisters, Kidnap, Americanah, The Intern, Star Wars: The Force Awakens,* and *Don't Mess With Texas.* These new examples of women in strong leadership roles may help change images, although highly competent females are still seen less frequently than men in the media. In addition, in 2015, there were only seven (of roughly a hundred) major commercial films directed by women (Dockterman 2015).

Young men and women, desiring to fit in, can be influenced in harmful ways by messages from the media. For instance, the epidemic of steroid use or hormones among boys to stimulate muscle growth results from a desire to be successful in sports and have an appealing body image. Professional athletes set an example, and the dark side of steroids, especially for teen boys, is often overlooked: acne, mood swings, depression, elevated suicide attempts, aggressive behavior, high blood pressure, heightened sex characteristics, and liver damage (Global Sports Development 2013). Adolescent girls are more prone to dieting, bingeing, and purging (Stephen et al. 2014). Dieting among girls, driven in part by ads, is a health concern in the United States and some other countries (Taub and McLorg 2010). Studies show that from 40% to 60% of children ages 6 to 12 are worried about their weight. Eighty percent of 10-year-olds have dieted. Over half (53%) of 13-year-old girls and more than 3 out of 4 (78%) 17-year-old girls have issues with their bodies (Hepworth 2010; C. Roberts 2012).

Television is another part of the media that works as a powerful socializing agent. Seventy percent of children

games, with 83% of teen boys and 59% of teen girls involved (Pew Research Center 2015c). For teen boys, video games become key elements in friendships, helping them establish and maintain friendships either in the same room or over the Internet (Lenhart 2015). Teen girls love to play many different games too, often role-playing games. Whereas video games are social for boys, more girls play them alone without a mic to chat (Marcotte 2015). Media makes the connection to others for many teens, especially boys.

Adolescents identify with characters in video games and often view them as role models (Mou and Peng 2009).

Like most U.S. glamour stars, Kate Bosworth (*left*) must conform to the image of very thin, shapely femininity. By contrast, an older, not particularly thin actor, Dame Judi Dench (*right*) stars in many BBC productions and played a leading role in *The Second Best Exotic Marigold Hotel*—a movie largely about old people.

ages 8 to 18 have TVs in their bedrooms, and many of these have access to cable or satellite TV (Uzoma 2015). Children ages 2 to 11 watch, on average, over 100 hours of TV each month; add to that time with other devices, and the figure increases by 50% (Nielsen 2014). Television presents a simple, stereotyped view of life, from advertisements to situation comedies to soap operas. Women in soap operas and ads, especially those working outside the home, are often depicted as having problems in carrying out their role responsibilities.

Films and television series in the United States seldom feature average-size or older women. Most U.S. films feature stars who are attractive and thin, presenting an often unattainable model for young women (Taub and McLorg 2010). In U.S. television, overweight women are almost entirely depicted as comic figures. By comparison, a much greater variety of ages and body types is seen in British productions (such as the films *The Best Exotic Marigold Hotel* and *Philomena*).

Educational Systems. Girls and boys often have very different experiences in school. As noted in the upcoming examples, educational systems socialize children through classroom, lunchroom, and playground activities; students' popularity and recognition; sports and Title IX programs; and teachers' attitudes and expectations. In academics, girls achieve at a higher level than boys overall. According to a recent study, girls have better social and behavioral skills than boys and are more likely to study, whereas boys have lower engagement in school and weaker preparation (DiPrete and Buchmann 2013). However, in subjects that lead to high-paying jobs such as high-level physics and math courses, girls lag. Recent concerns over the number of scientists and engineers needed and the lack of students pursuing these careers points to the subtle and blatant biases against women, especially women of color, but also raises questions about boys' education.

Past debates about the causes for women's lower performance in math and fewer women entering math-related fields were intense: Was this difference due to boys having more natural math ability or due to gender bias and lower expectations for girls (Porter 2015)? Several interpretations of the differences have dominated the current discussion: differences between boys and girls in values and attitudes toward math and its usefulness; variations between the sexes in spatial and problem-solving abilities (skills that can be taught); and the consequence of teacher stereotypes about math and gender. Today, these differences in the United States are small, and many social scientists agree that the differences are accentuated by socialization and stereotypes. In societies where math is considered gender neutral, achievement of girls is on a par with their male classmates (Ganley and Lubienski 2016). In the international PISA test taken by 15-year-olds around the world, however, boys outscored girls in math in 63 countries; girls scored higher in only two countries (Organisation for Economic Co-operation and Development 2014b). In addition, in a study of Israeli and European elementary classrooms, girls were judged less able in math than boys by their teachers, though anonymous tests showed girls performed as well as or better than boys. Thus, even classroom teachers can influence the math and science trajectory of young girls (Lavy and Sand 2015).

Despite the higher scores for boys in math, boys' educational attainment has—with the exception of math and science—fallen behind girls' (Porter 2015). Women score higher in reading in all countries, and 34% receive a college degree compared with 30% of men. Studies find that more boys than girls have poor performance, low motivation, disengagement with school, and lack of ambition—not a recipe for succeeding in the job market.

Broad suggestions about what to do to remedy the disparities include programs to increase girls' self-confidence in math and science and efforts to engage boys in schooling. As early as elementary school, girls may be subtly discouraged from pursuing math and science courses that lead to careers in STEM (science, technology, engineering, and math) fields. (Only 12% of college computer science degrees are earned by women.) Girls lack role models, teachers may unwittingly discourage young girls from math and science, and even girls' activities and toys at young ages do not generally encourage the pursuit of science. Four patterns emerge in research on women in the sciences: (1) Women have to provide more evidence that they are competent in STEM fields; (2) women fear appearing too masculine if they excel in science and technology; (3) public perceptions depict women as losing their commitment and competence after they have children; and (4) gender bias too often pits women against one another (Gender Bias Against Women of Color in Science 2015).

Research also indicates, however, that in communities where women are employed in STEM fields and girls have models for pursuing STEM courses, girls are equally represented with boys in physics classes. Thus, girls may excel in physics and other STEM courses in communities where traditional gendered status is interrupted (Riegle-Crumb & Moore 2013). Pursuing a STEM career does not necessarily require stellar math scores, but some girls are socialized to believe they are not good in math and therefore do not take higher-level courses or expect to do well on tests in STEM fields (Wade 2013b).

In sports, boys are encouraged to join competitive team sports and girls to support them. Some argue that this simulates hierarchical adult roles of boss/secretary and physician/nurse. Many girls and boys have separate experiences in grade school and middle school that reinforce boundaries of "us" and "them" in classroom seating and activities, in the lunchroom, and in playground activities; girls and boys are seated, lined up, and given assignments by sex (Sadker and Zittleman 2013). Those who go outside the boundaries, especially boys, are ridiculed by peers and sometimes teachers, reinforcing stereotypes and separate gender role socialization (Sadker and Zittleman 2013; Thorne 1993).

Part of the issue of male–female inequality in schools is tied to the issue of *popularity*, which seems to have less to do with being liked than with being known and visible. If

Getty/Win McNamee / Staff

Sara Seager, professor of planetary science and physics at the Massachusetts Institute of Technology, speaks at a press conference on potentially habitable worlds elsewhere in the universe. She is a researcher in the forefront of what really is *rocket science*.

everyone knows a person's name, she or he is popular. At the middle school level, there are more ways by which boys than girls can become known. In sports, even when there are both boys' and girls' basketball teams, many spectators come to the boys' contests and very few to the girls' games. Thus, few people know the female athletes by name. In fact, a far more visible position is cheerleader—standing on the sidelines cheering for the boys teams and sometimes for girls' teams—because those girls are at least seen. One effort is to redefine cheerleading as a legitimate sport in its own right. The American Medical Association now argues that the risks and rigors of cheerleading require trained coaches and more safety measures, thus qualifying it as a varsity sport (Tanner 2014). The bottom line is that there are far more visible positions for the boys than for girls in middle and high school, allowing them to be recognized and become leaders.

Title IX of the U.S. Education Amendments of 1972 was a major legislative attempt to level the educational and sports playing field. Passed in order to bar gender discrimination in schools receiving federal funds, this legislation mandates equal opportunity for participation in school-sponsored programs (Lindsey 2015). The law has reduced or eliminated blatant discrimination in areas ranging from admissions and health care to counseling and housing, sex-segregated programs, financial aid, dress codes, and other areas of concern. However, the biggest impact of Title IX legislation has been in athletics.

Women's athletic programs and scholarship opportunities have grown but still lag behind those for men. Since passage of Title IX in 1972, the number of women competing in college sports had climbed from 30,000 to almost 3.3 million; about 2 in 5 high school girls participate in varsity sports (A. Wong 2015). However, there are still 1.3 million fewer opportunities for girls to play high school sports compared with boys, and NCAA colleges receive only 44% of athletic dollars for women's sports (Dusenbery and Lee 2012). Advocates for Title IX argue that there is still work to be done to level the playing field (Title IX 2015). Participation in athletics, especially team sports, is important because sports can foster skills in teamwork, strategic thinking, and anticipating counteractions by a competitor, useful skills in business and government.

Thinking Sociologically

Explain why you think there is a gap between men and women playing sports at high school and college levels: limited opportunity, lack of interest among girls, or other factors such as profits from sports? What, if anything, should be done about the gap?

Religious Organizations. Religious organizations serve as agents of gender socialization by defining, reinforcing, and perpetuating gender roles and cultural beliefs. Religious teachings provide explanations of proper male and female roles. Although the specific teachings vary, the three major monotheistic religions that affirm only one God—Christianity, Islam, and Judaism—are traditionally patriarchal, stressing separate female and male spheres (Kramer and Beutel 2014).

Some interpretations of the Adam and Eve creation story in the Hebrew Bible (the Old Testament in the Christian Bible) state that man was created first and that men are, therefore, superior. Because Eve, created from the rib of man, was the enticer to the first sin, she has kept women forever in an inferior, second-class position. For these and other reasons, in some branches of these religions, women are restricted in their roles within the family and religious organizations. They cannot be priests in Catholic churches and cannot vote on business matters in some religious organizations. However, recent work by feminist scholars challenges the notion of patriarchy in Judaic and Christian history, pointing out that women may have played a much broader role in religious development than currently recognized (Hunter College Women's Studies Collective 2005). Even *Yahweh*—the name for God in the Hebrew Bible—had both male and female connotations, and when God was referred to as a source of wisdom in the "Wisdom Literature" (Psalms, Proverbs, and so forth), feminine pronouns and references were used (Borg 2001). Increasingly, denominations are granting women greater roles in the religious hierarchies, ministries, and priesthood.

Women in Judaism lived for 4,000 years in a patriarchal system where men read, taught, and legislated while women followed (Lindsey 2015). Today, 3 of the 5 main branches of Judaism allow women equal participation, illustrating that religious practices do change over time. However, Hasidic and Orthodox Jews have a division of labor between men and women following old laws, with designated gender roles for the home and religious life.

Some Christian teachings have treated women as second-class citizens, even in the eyes of God. For this reason, some Christian denominations have excluded women from a variety of leadership roles and told them they must be subservient to their husbands. Other Christians point to the admonition by Saint Paul that, theologically speaking, the distinction between men and women is not relevant and that women and men are not spiritually different.

Traditional Hindu religion painted women as seductresses, strongly erotic, and a threat to male spirituality and asceticism. To protect men from this threat, women were kept totally covered in thick garments and veils and seen only by men in their immediate families. Today, Hinduism comes in many forms, most of which honor the woman's domestic sphere of life—as mothers, wives, and homemakers—while also accepting women in public roles (Lindsey 2015).

Traditional Islamic beliefs also portrayed female sexuality as dangerous to men, although many women in Islamic societies today are full participants in the public and private sphere. The Quran (also spelled Qur'an or Koran), the Muslim sacred scripture, has a few passages that seem to favor men, but most of the text actually supports women's rights (Aslan 2011). Still, aspects of traditional Sharia law, strict Islamic law, have carried over in several countries and among some groups. It has been used to punish women accused of violating rules about gender behavior (Mydans 2002; Proudman 2012).

Women in strict literalist Muslim societies such as Algeria, Iran, Syria, and Saudi Arabia are separated from men (except for fathers, brothers, and husbands) in work and worship. They generally remain covered. *Purdah*, which means curtain, refers to practices of seclusion and separate worlds for women and men in Islamic cultures. Screens in households and veils in public enforce female modesty and prevent men from seeing women where this is dictated (Ward and Edelstein 2014). In the days of Muhammad, only his wives wore such veils for privacy, and there were no commandments in the Quran instructing women to be covered, so these patterns are more cultural and national than Islamic religious requirements. In any case, today, some women argue that the veil they wear is for modesty, for cosmetic purposes, or to protect them from the stares of men.

Meso-level religious systems influence how different societies interpret proper gender roles and how sometimes these belief systems change with new interpretations of scriptures. (Further discussion of the complex relationship between religion and gender appears in Chapter 12.) From family and education to media and religion, meso-level agents of socialization teach and reinforce "appropriate" gender roles in each society.

Thinking Sociologically

What are some of the books, toys, games, television shows, school experiences, religious teachings, and peer interactions that have influenced your gender role socialization? In what ways did they do so?

GENDER STRATIFICATION: MESO- AND MACRO-LEVEL PROCESSES

The phrase glass ceiling refers to *processes that limit the progress of women and other minorities from the highest job or status positions because of invisible barriers that limit or bar promotion within an organization*. Although they may have superior skills or experience, they are passed over (Berrey 2013). "The glass ceiling keeps women from reaching the highest levels of corporate and public responsibility, and the 'sticky floor' keeps the vast majority of the world's women stuck in low-paid jobs" (Hunter College Women's Studies Collective 2005:393). This discrimination results in a loss of talent and lower salaries for women, who make up almost half of the workforce in the United States and are the main or equal breadwinners in 4 out of 10 families. Although there are high-profile women serving as CEOs and in government leadership positions in the United States, they occupy only 4.6% of both the Fortune 500 and the Fortune 1000 CEO positions (Catalyst 2014). Women now represent 52.2% of PhDs (Council of Graduate Schools 2014) and 67% of college graduates, but they earn only about 79 cents for every dollar earned by men (depending on what variables are used to calculate the gap), a 21% wage gap. This holds across occupations (AAUW 2016; Hegewisch et al. 2014; Matson 2013). In 2015 the gender wage gap even widened a bit, mostly because the highest earning positions, fields like law and engineering, dominated by men, had larger pay increases than other jobs (Zarya 2015).

Figure 9.1 compares pay for women as a ratio of what men earn. For example, women who are health care practitioners or work in technical occupations earn 78.3% of what men in those occupations earn, and women in legal occupations earn 56.3% of what men earn. The pattern of unequal pay is true in a number of Global North countries (World Economic Forum 2016).

Men, on the other hand, often ride the *glass escalator*, especially in traditionally female occupations. Even if they do not seek to climb in the organizational hierarchy, occupational social forces push them up the job ladder to the higher echelons (C. Williams 2013). The next "Engaging Sociology" provides an exercise to think about how our ideas may subtly maintain the glass ceiling and the glass escalator by defining leadership the same way we define masculinity.

FIGURE 9.1   Ratio of Women's to Men's Earnings for Selected Occupations, U.S., 2014

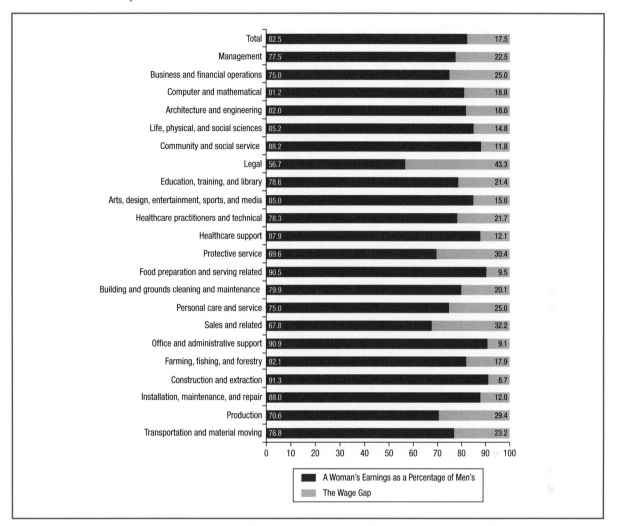

Note: Based on median annual earnings of full-time, wage, and salary workers, 16 years old and over.

Source: U.S. Department of Labor (2014).

Women and Men at Work: Gendered Organizations

"How can I do it all—marriage, children, education, career, social life?" This is a question many college students ask. They already anticipate a delicate balancing act. Work has been central to the definition of masculinity in U.S. society, yet for 6 decades women ages 25 to 54 have seen increased participation in the U.S. labor force (Kramer and Beutel 2014). Participation of women climbed to a high of 74% in 1999; today, it has fallen to 69%, in part because of lack of support for working mothers of young children and also because young women plan "career pauses" for family (C. Miller 2015).

In many other Global North countries, the percentage of women in the labor force is growing, with family-supportive policies making this possible (C. Miller and Alderman 2014).

Among countries of the Global North, Sweden has the highest percentage of working women, with 72% working (compared with 76% of men) (Organisation for Economic Co-operation and Development 2015a). Yet even in Sweden, with its parental leave and other family-friendly policies, women and men feel pressures of work and family responsibilities (Eshleman and Bulcroft 2010). Dual-career marriages raise questions about child-rearing, power relations, and other factors in juggling work and family.

ENGAGING SOCIOLOGY

Masculinity and Femininity in Our Social World

1. Mark each characteristic with an *M* or an *F* depending on whether you think it is generally defined by society as a masculine or feminine characteristic.

    __ achiever

    __ aggressive

    __ analytical

    __ caring

    __ confident

    __ deferential (defers to others; yields with courtesy)

    __ devious

    __ dynamic

    __ intuitive

    __ loving

    __ manipulative

    __ nurturing

    __ organized

    __ passive

    __ a planner

    __ powerful

    __ relationship oriented (makes decisions based on how others will *feel*)

    __ rule oriented (makes decisions based on abstract procedural rules rather than feelings)

    __ sensitive

    __ strong

2. Next, mark an *X* just to the right of 10 characteristics you think are essential qualities for a leadership position in a complex organization (e.g., business or government). You might want to ask 20 of your acquaintances to do this, and then, add up the scores for *masculinity*, *femininity*, and *leadership trait*.

3. Do you (and your acquaintances) tend to view leadership as having the same traits as those marked "masculine" or "feminine"? What are the implications of your findings for the glass ceiling or glass escalator?

4. How might correlations between the traits of leadership and gender notions help to explain the data on income in Table 9.2?

Table 9.2   U.S. Income by Educational Level and Sex—Full-Time Workers

Education	Men	Women
Not a high school graduate	$21,701	$12,364
High school graduate	$32,080	$19,208
College graduate (bachelor's)	$60,933	$40,033
Master's degree	$76,386	$50,255
Doctorate	$91,770	$62,388
Professional degree	$107,050	$63,353

Source: U.S. Census Bureau (2015a).

Around the world, workplaces have gendered relationships: ratios of female to male workers; gender reflected in subordinate–supervisor positions; and distribution of positions between men and women. This, in turn, affects our experiences in the workplace. Consider the example of mothers breastfeeding their babies. Must they quit their jobs or alter their family schedules if the workplace does not provide a space for breastfeeding? Some workplaces accommodate family needs, but many do not.

Using data from the OECD (Organisation for Economic Co-operation and Development), *The Economist* constructed a "glass ceiling index" using five indicators: the number of men and women, respectively, with college educations; female labor force participation; the gender wage gap; the proportion of women in senior positions in corporations and professions; and net childcare costs compared with incomes. Cross-national comparisons indicate that Finland, Norway, Sweden, Poland, France, Hungary, and Denmark have the best conditions for working women. Nations that scored least women friendly in employment were Turkey, Japan, and South Korea, where few women obtain top jobs. Among the 26 nations studied, Canada ranked 11th and the United States ranked 17th for women's employment conditions ("The Glass-Ceiling Index" 2015). The results of the ranking appear in Figure 9.2.

Thinking Sociologically

If corporate structures were reversed so that women organized the workplace, how might the workplace environment change? How might these changes impact women, men, and their families?

FIGURE 9.2 Glass Ceiling Index

Source: "The Glass Ceiling Index." *The Economist.* March 5, 2015. Copyright © The Economist Newspaper Limited, London 2015. Reprinted with permission.

Institutionalized Gender Discrimination

Gender stratification at the meso level—like race and ethnic stratification—can occur independently of any overt prejudice or ill will by others. It becomes part of the social system, and we are not even conscious of it. *Discrimination* is often built into organizations and cultural expectations and includes both intentional actions and unintentional actions or structures that have consequences harmful to minorities. It is embedded in institutions.

You will recall from the previous chapter that side-effect discrimination involves practices in one institutional area that have a negative impact because they are linked to practices in another institutional area. Institutions are interdependent, so discrimination in one can result in unintentional discrimination in others. For example, when roles of women in family life are determined by rigid gender expectations, women find it more difficult to devote themselves to gaining job promotions. In addition, as long as little girls learn through socialization to use their voices and to hold their bodies and to gesture in ways that communicate deference, employers assume a lack of the self-confidence necessary for major leadership roles. If women are paid less than men, despite the same levels of education (see Table 9.2), they are less likely to have access to the best health care or to be able to afford a $40,000 down payment for a house, unless they are married. This makes women dependent on men in a way that most men are not dependent on women.

A factor affecting differences in incomes is the type of academic degrees that men and women receive, as discussed earlier (e.g., engineering rather than education). However, even when these differences are factored in, men still make considerably more, on average, than women with identical levels of experience and training.

Past-in-present discrimination, discussed in Chapter 8, refers to *practices from the past that may no longer be allowed but that continue to affect people today*. For example, in a Midwest appliance industry investigated by one of the authors, there is a sequence of jobs one must hold to be promoted up the line to floor supervisor. This requirement ensures that the floor supervisor understands the many aspects of production at the plant. One of the jobs involves working in a room with heavy equipment that cuts through and bends metal sheets. The machine is extremely powerful and could easily cut off a leg or hand if the operator is not careful. Because of the danger, the engineers designed the equipment so it would not operate unless three levers were activated at the same time. One lever was triggered by stepping on a pedal on the floor. The other two required reaching out with one's hands so that one's body was extended. When one was spread-eagled to activate all three levers, there was no way one could possibly have a part of one's body near the blades.

This little girl looks cute but not very powerful or confident. When women tilt their heads—either forward or to one side—they also look like they lack confidence, and this hurts their chances of promotion in the corporate world.

It was brilliant engineering, but there was one unanticipated problem: The hand-activated levers were 5 feet, 10 inches off the ground and 5 feet apart. Few women had the height and arm span to run this machine, and therefore, no women had yet made it through the sequence of positions to the higher-paying position of floor supervisor. The equipment cost millions of dollars, so it was not likely to be replaced. Neither the engineers who designed the machine nor the upper-level managers who established the sequence of jobs to become floor supervisor had deliberately tried to exclude women. Indeed, the managers were perplexed when they looked at their employee figures and saw so few women moving up through the ranks. The cause of women's disadvantage was not mean-spirited men but features of the system that had unintended consequences resulting in past-in-present discrimination. A machine built in the past to service workers at that time is still in use and now disqualifies women for an important job. The barriers women face, then, are not just matters of socialization or other micro-level social processes. The nature of sexism is often subtle yet pervasive in society, operating at the meso and macro levels as institutional discrimination.

Another example of how prejudices and discrimination in the past can still affect us in the present can be seen in children's books, discussed earlier. Although recent books show expansion in the roles of males and females, the tens of thousands of older, classic books in public and school libraries mean that a parent or child picking a book off of the shelf is still likely to select a book that has old stereotypical views of boys and girls.

Men often get defensive and angry when people talk about sexism in society because they feel they are being attacked or asked to correct past injustices. However, the empirical reality is that the playing field is not level for men and women. Most men do not do anything to intentionally harm women, and they may not feel prejudiced toward women, but sexism operates so that men are given privileges they never asked for and may not even recognize.

Gender Differences in Internet Use

Internet-related gender stratification exhibits itself not just in terms of *whether* a person uses the Internet but also in terms of *how* a person uses the Internet. In the United States, women tend to use social networking sites 12% more than men (women 74%, men 62%), with the intent of keeping up with family and friends (Pew Research Center Internet and American Life Project 2014b). Women's use focuses on personal growth, maintaining a social group, and getting information about products and brands. Globally, women account for 47.9% of visitors to social networking sites and spend 30% more time on social networking sites than men (ComScore 2010; Morrison 2010).

Men tend to use the Internet to gather information and to exchange ideas, gain job skills, and form and maintain professional networks. Thus, women use social media more than men for their private lives, and men are more likely to use the Internet for engaging in the public sphere. The difference also reflects dissimilarities in the professional positions men and women tend to hold. Men's greater use of the Internet to enhance their careers relates to the preponderance of men in upper-level management positions (Madden and Zickuhr 2011).

Thinking Sociologically

Ask several people from different generations and different genders how they use computer technology and the Internet and how they learned these skills. What do you conclude from their responses about the impact of gender on Internet use? Explain how your findings compare with those discussed in this book.

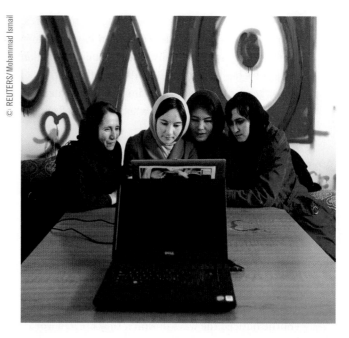

In some countries, there is a huge gender digital divide, and research shows that women and men tend to use computers in different ways. These women in Afghanistan are learning computer skills, narrowing that divide.

GENDER STRATIFICATION: MICRO- TO MACRO-LEVEL THEORIES

Recent research by some biologists and psychologists has considered whether there are innate differences in the makeup of women and men. For instance, males produce more testosterone, a hormone found to be correlated with aggression. Research shows that in many situations, males tend to be more aggressive and concerned with dominance, whether the behavior is biologically programmed, learned, or both. Other traits, such as nurturance, empathy, and altruism, show no clear gender difference (Fausto-Sterling 1992; Sapolsky 2014).

Although biological and psychological factors make up part of the difference between females and males, our focus here is on the major contribution that

social factors make in the social statuses of males and females in human society (DiPrete and Buchmann 2013). This section explores social theories that explain gender differences.

Symbolic Interaction Theory: Micro-Level Analysis

Traditional notions of gender are hard to change. Confusion over proper masculine and feminine roles creates anxiety and even anomie in a society. People want behavioral guidelines. Thus, many believe it is best to adhere to traditional notions of gender that are reinforced by religious or political dogmas, making those ideas appear sacred, absolute, and beyond human interference. Others believe the male prerogatives and privileges of the past were established by men to protect their rights and should be challenged. Change in concepts of gender can be hard to bring about precisely because they are rooted in the meaning system and status and power structures present in the social world.

Symbolic interactionists look at gender as socially constructed. Sex is the biological reality of different "plumbing" in our bodies, and interactionists are interested in how those physical differences come to be symbols, resulting in different social rights and rewards. The meaning assigned to one's sex is connected to notions of masculinity and femininity. The symbolic interaction perspective has been forceful in insisting that notions of proper gender behavior are not intrinsically related to a person's sex. Rather, gender is a socially created or constructed idea.

More than any other theory, symbolic interaction stresses the idea of *human agency*—the notion that humans not only are influenced by the society in which they live but also actively help create it (Charon 2010; Hewitt and Shulman 2011). In a classic study of elementary children in classrooms and on playgrounds, Barrie Thorne found that whereas teachers influenced the children, the children themselves were active participants in creating the student culture that guided their play (Thorne 1993). As children played with one another, Thorne noticed the ways in which they created words, nicknames, distinctions between one another, and new forms of interaction. This is a very important point: Humans do not just passively adopt cultural notions about gender; they *do gender*. They create it as they behave and interact with others in ways that define "normal" male or female conduct (West and Zimmerman 1987). *Doing gender* is an everyday, recurring, and routine occurrence. It is a constant ongoing process that defines each situation and takes place in organizations and between individuals. Understanding the process of *doing gender* helps us understand why we think and act as we do.

When children are in an ambiguous situation, they may spontaneously define their sex as the most relevant trait about themselves or others. Indeed, when children act as if gender matters, they are helping make it a reality for those around them. As the next child adopts the "definition of reality" from the first, acting as if sex is more important than hair color or eye color, it makes gender the most prominent characteristic in the mind of the next child. Yet each child, in a sense, could choose to ignore gender and decide that something else is more important. This is part of *human agency*—the freedom to define reality differently from others. The same principle applies to adults. When a person "chooses" to recognize gender as a critical distinction between two individuals or two groups, that person is "doing gender." We *do gender* all the time, every day. In fact, we cannot avoid it! It is present in our interactions, and we are conscious that we will be judged by others on how well we follow our gender roles. That judgment could be harsh if we go outside accepted boundaries of gender behavior (Cahill, Sandstrom, and Froyum 2013; Hewitt and Shulman 2011; Schoepflin 2011).

Through interaction, people do gender, and although this process begins at a micro level, it has implications all the way to the global level. The next section explores meso- and macro-level forces that shape gender and stratification based on sex.

Thinking Sociologically

How do you do gender*? How did you learn these patterns of behavior? How do you think people would react if you did not follow the expected behavior patterns assigned to your gender in your social setting? How comfortable would you feel when violating those gender norms? Why?*

Structural-Functional and Conflict Theories: Meso- and Macro-Level Analyses

Meso- and macro-level theories provide the big picture related to gender issues. When the government passes laws that affect women (or men), like abortion or birth control laws, they affect individual women at the micro level. Likewise, laws related to child custody, payment of child support, and other laws related to marriage and divorce are made by state and national governmental offices and enforced by courts. In the following sections, we visit our familiar theories as they relate to gender issues.

Structural-Functional Theory. From the structural-functional perspective, each sex has a role to play in the interdependent groups and institutions of society. Some early theorists argued that men and women carry out different roles and are, of necessity, unequal because of the needs of societies and practices that have developed since early human history. Social relationships and practices that have proven successful in the survival of a group are likely to continue and to be reinforced by society's norms, laws, and religious beliefs. Thus, relationships between women and men believed to support survival are maintained. In traditional hunter-gatherer, horticultural, and pastoral societies, for instance, the division of labor and social roles are based on sex and age. The females often take on the primary tasks of childcare, gardening, food preparation, and other duties near the home. Men do tasks that require movements farther from home, such as hunting, fishing, and herding.

As societies industrialize, roles and relationships change due to structural changes in society. Émile Durkheim described a gradual move from traditional societies held together by *mechanical solidarity* (the glue based on shared beliefs, values, and traditions) to modern societies united through *organic solidarity* (social coherence based on division of labor, with each member playing a highly specialized role) (Durkheim [1893] 1947). According to early functionalists, gender-based division of labor exists in modern societies because it is efficient and useful to have different but complementary male and female roles. They believed this helps members of society to accomplish essential tasks and maintains societal stability (Lindsey 2015).

In the structural-functionalist view of the traditional Global North family in the 20th century, the father worked, the mother stayed at home, and they had two children. The female played the expressive role through childbearing, nursing, and caring for family members in the home. The male carried out the instrumental role by working outside the home to support the family (Dilon 2009; Parsons and Bales 1953). Although this pattern was relevant for White, middle-class, and wealthier families during the Industrial Revolution and for some decades before and after World War II, when men returned to take jobs women had held during the war, it characterizes relatively few families in the United States now.

Today, more children are being raised by single moms than married couples, and the turnover in partners has created complex families not seen before (Aulette 2010; Coontz 2011). Fewer people are marrying, and those who do tend to be older than in previous decades. Increasing numbers of women do not have children (about 20% now, compared with just 10% in the 1970s) (Angier 2013). In addition, a growing number of families today have two adult partners of the same sex.

Conflict Theory. Conflict theorists view gender relations through the lens of power. Men are the *haves*—controlling the majority of power positions and most wealth—and women are the *have-nots*. By keeping women in subordinate roles, males control the means of production and protect their privileged status.

A classical conflict explanation of gender stratification is found in the writings of Karl Marx's colleague,

Friedrich Engels ([1884] 1942). In traditional societies, where size and strength were essential for survival, men were often dominant, but women's roles were respected as important and necessary to the survival of the group. Men hunted, engaged in warfare, and protected women. Over time, male physical control was transformed into control by ideology—by the dominant belief system itself. Capitalism and inheritance traditions strengthened male dominance by making more wealth available to men and their sons. Women became dependent on men, and their roles were transformed into "taking care of the home" (Engels [1884] 1942).

Ideologies based on traditional beliefs and values have continued to be used to justify the social structure of male domination and subjugation of women. It is in the interest of the dominant group—in this case, men—to maintain a position of privilege. Conflict theorists believe it unlikely that those in power by virtue of sex, race, class, or political or religious ideology will voluntarily give up their positions as long as they are benefiting from them. By keeping women in traditional gender roles, men maintain control over institutions and resources (R. Collins 1971).

Other Theoretical Perspectives

Some theories cross over the micro and macro levels of analysis so regularly that they need separate treatment. Yet these approaches add much to our understanding of gender.

Feminist Theory. Feminist theorists agree with Marx and Engels that gender stratification is based on power struggles, not biology. On the other hand, some feminist theorists argue that Marx and Engels failed to consider fully a key variable in women's oppression: patriarchy. Patriarchy involves a few men dominating and holding authority over all others, including women, children, and less powerful men (Arrighi 2000; Lindsey 2015). According to feminist theory, no matter what the economic or political system, women will continue to be oppressed by men until patriarchy is eliminated. There is a range of feminist theories. However, all feminist theories argue for bringing about a new and equal ordering of gender relationships to eliminate the patriarchy and sexism of current gender stratification systems (Kramer and Beutel 2014).

Feminist theorists try to understand the causes of women's lower status and seek ways to change the systems to provide more opportunities, to improve the standard of living, and to give women control over their bodies and reproduction. Feminist theorists also feel that little change will occur until group consciousness is raised so that women understand the system that limits their options and do not blame themselves for their situations (Sapiro 2003).

As societies become technologically advanced and need an educated workforce, women of all social classes and ethnic groups around the world are likely to gain more equal roles. Women are entering institutions of higher education in record numbers, and evidence indicates they are needed in the world economic system and the changing labor force of most countries. The economies of countries in which women are not integrated into the economic system generally lag behind other countries. Feminist theorists examine these global and national patterns, but they also note the role of patriarchy in micro-level interpersonal situations—such as domestic violence.

Violence against women perpetuates gender stratification, as is evident in the intimate environment of many homes. Because men have more power in the larger society, they often have more resources within the household as well (an example of side-effect discrimination). Women are often dependent on the man of the house for his resources, meaning they must yield on many decisions. Power differences in the meso- and macro-level

social systems also contribute to power differentials and vulnerability of women in micro-level settings. In addition, women have fewer options when considering whether to leave an abusive relationship. Although there are risks of staying in an abusive relationship, many factors enter into a woman's decision to stay or leave; rational choice theory has been used by some researchers to evaluate the gains and losses from staying versus leaving (Copp et al. 2013; Estrellado and Loh 2013).

Feminist analysis finds gender patterns embedded in social institutions of family, education, religion, politics, economics, and health care. If the societal system is patriarchal, ruled by men, the interdependent institutions are likely to reflect and support this system. Feminist theory helps us understand how patriarchy at the meso and macro level can influence patriarchy at the micro level and vice versa.

Thinking Sociologically

Imagine you were asked to reduce domestic violence in your society. How would you address it differently if you looked at it as a social issue, rather than just as a problem for the individuals directly affected by it?

Interaction of Class, Race, and Gender. Some feminist theorists look at the ways in which discrimination related to class, race, and gender intersects in society (Margaret Anderson and Collins 2016). In the process, some groups of people face multiple forms of oppression that reinforce one another.

Zouina was born in France to parents who emigrated from Algeria. She lived with them in a poor immigrant suburb of Paris until she was forced by them to go to Algeria for an arranged marriage to a man who already had one wife. That marriage ended, and she returned to France. Since she returned to France, Zouina has been employed wherever she can find work. The high unemployment rate and social and ethnic discrimination, especially against people from North African backgrounds, makes life difficult.

The situation is complex. Muslim women from Tunisia, Morocco, and Algeria living in crowded slum communities outside Paris face discrimination in the workplace and their communities (Lazaridis 2011). Expected to be both good Muslim women and good family coproviders—which necessitates working in French society—they face ridicule when they wear their *hijabs* (coverings) to school or to work. However, they encounter derision in their community if they do not wear them. They are caught between

Men—like these in Amman, Jordan—are much more likely than women to play cards, games, or sports together and to develop networks that enhance their power and their ability to "close deals." When women are not part of the same networks, they are denied the same insider privileges.

mediacolor's/Alamy Stock Photo

two cultures and may be the scapegoats for frustrated young men who cannot find work.

Because of high unemployment in immigrant communities, many youth roam the streets. Gang rapes by North African youth against young women have been on the rise in France and elsewhere abroad. The victims of these rapes often face rejection and disdain in their immigrant communities (Killian 2006).

Women of color in the United States also face multiple barriers on their "unlevel playing field." In the more than 15 million households headed by women, their wages are necessary for families to survive. Yet they are faced with a gender-based wage gap across industries, occupations, and education levels. "Women in the United States who work full time, year round are paid $10,876 less annually than men who work full time, year round" (National Partnership for Women and Families 2015:1). Table 9.3 shows the median weekly earnings of workers in the United States by race, ethnicity, and sex and helps illustrate how racism and sexism can reinforce one another and lead to the *double marginalization* of women of color.

These examples illustrate that race, class, and gender have crosscutting lines that may affect one's status in the society. Women of color can face the triple status determinants of being poor (class), women (gender), and of color (race or ethnicity). Lesbians and women identifying as bisexual or transgender face yet another form of oppression that intersects with the other three.

Age, nationality, and other factors also have the effect of either diminishing or increasing minority status of specific women, and theorists are paying increasing attention to these intersections (Rothenberg 2014). Chapter 8 discussed the fact that race and class lines may be either crosscutting or parallel. In the case of gender, there are always crosscutting lines with race and social class. However, gender always affects one's prestige and privilege within that class or ethnic group. Thus, to get a full picture, these three variables—race, class, and gender—need to be considered simultaneously.

Thinking Sociologically

How have race, class, and gender intersected in your life and impacted your life chances? Do you think your experience is common among other members of your local community? Why, or why not?

Gender, Sexual Orientation and Minority Status

We have already learned that sex, gender, and sexuality are complex concepts. **Heterosexism** is *an assumption that every person is heterosexual, legitimizing heterosexuality as the only normal lifestyle and marginalizing persons who do not identify as heterosexual* (Gender Equity Resource Center 2013). Heterosexism operates at all levels of society: micro, meso, and macro (Swank, Fahs, and Frost 2013).

Homophobia—*intense fear and hatred of homosexuality and homosexuals, whether male or female*—is highly correlated with and perhaps a cause of people holding traditional notions of gender and gender roles (S. Shaw and Lee 2005). This concept, which operates on the micro level, was coined by a psychologist who noted that intense hatred of LGBTQ people is due to a personality disorder or illness (Weinberg 1972). LGBTQ stands for lesbian, gay, bisexual, transgender, and queer or questioning. Various acronyms are used such as LGBT or GLBTQ, but we will be consistent in using LGBTQ.

Despite some fear and hostility, homosexual and transgendered people have always existed. They have been accepted and even required for certain positions at some times and places and rejected or outlawed in others. In some societies, homosexuals and transgendered individuals have been placed in a separate sexual category with special roles. For example, the *Hijras* in India and some other areas in South Asia are usually physiological males who have feminine gender identity. Many live in Hijra communities and have designated roles in Indian festivals and celebrations.

Some societies ignore the existence of LGBTQ members of the community. Some consider them to have psychological illnesses or forms of depraved immorality. Some societies even consider these forms of sexuality a

Table 9.3 Median Weekly Earnings of Workers by Race, Sex, and Percentage of Men's Earnings by Women, 2016

Race and Ethnicity	Male	Female	Women's Percentage of Men's Earnings
Asian American	$1,151	$902	78
White	942	766	81
Black or African American	718	641	89
Hispanic or Latino	663	586	88

Source: U.S. Bureau of Labor Statistics (2017).

crime (as in 38 out of 54 African nations today and in most states in the United States during much of the 20th century). In at least 10 countries in Africa and the Middle East (Iran, Iraq, Yemen, Mauritania, Qatar, Saudi Arabia, Sudan, Somalia, Nigeria, and United Arab Emirates), many of them following Sharia law, to be accused of homosexuality can result in the death penalty (Nossiter 2014; Rupar 2014). In each case around the world, the government or dominant religious group determines the status of LGBTQ members of society. The reality is that deviation from a society's gender norms, such as attraction to a member of the same sex, may cause one to experience minority status. (See Figure 9.3.)

Some members of the LGBTQ community deviate from traditional notions of masculinity and femininity and therefore from significant norms of many societies. This may result in hostile reactions and stigma from the dominant group. Indeed, homosexual epithets are often used to reinforce gender conformity, particularly among men, and to intimidate anyone who would dare to be different from the norm. Because, in many societies, women are economically dependent on men, their status in society is typically based on their relationship with men. Therefore, lesbians—women who are attracted to other women—are, in some instances, perceived as a threat to men's power (Burn 2011; Ward and Edelstein 2014).

The mass media have begun to include LGBTQ characters in films such as *Behind the Candelabra* (2013), *Dallas*

© REUTERS/Rafiqur Rahman

A transsexual (Hijra) dances at a gathering in Bangladesh, where a group met in the capital to demand government action to provide legal protection from persecution. Hijras are treated as social outcasts but assigned a special status. They typically earn a living by singing, dancing, and other performances.

FIGURE 9.3 Lesbian and Gay Laws Around the World, 2015

Russia
"Propaganda law" restricting freedom of expression and association

ASIA

EUROPE

USA
Marriage equality now across the United States

NORTH AMERICA

AFRICA

Iraq
Persecution by organized non-state agents

SOUTH AMERICA

AUSTRALIA

PERSECUTION
■ Death penalty
■ Imprisonment

RECOGNITION
■ Marriage
■ Equal (almost equal) substitute to marriage
■ Clearly inferior substitute to marriage

■ No specific legislation

Source: International Lesbian, Gay, Bisexual, Trans and Intersex Association (2015).

Buyers Club (2013), *In Bloom* (2013), *Beginners* (2010), *A Single Man* (2009), *Milk* (2008), *Shelter* (2007), and *Brokeback Mountain* (2005). In 2015 alone, almost 50 films featured gay themes (IMDb 2015). Television shows with positive images of lesbians and gays—such as *Ellen*, *Will & Grace*, *Pretty Little Liars*, *Glee*, *Modern Family*, *Grey's Anatomy*, *Chicago Fire*, and *The Good Wife*—have also become popular. Seventeen television shows had positive images of gay characters in 2015. In addition, there are many well-known lesbians and gay news commentators and show hosts, reflecting an increased level of acceptance of LGBTQ people in many nations.

National polls in the United States indicate shifting attitudes about same-sex relationships. In 2001, 35% of U.S. citizens supported same-sex marriage, and 57% opposed it; in 2015, 55% supported and 39% opposed it. Attitudes do change over time (Pew Research Center 2015a). Citizens born between 1928 and 1945 are least supportive of same-sex marriage, at 39%, whereas the millennial generation, born in 1981 and later, are most supportive, at 70%. Religion is also a factor, with White evangelical Protestants at 24% in favor and those unaffiliated at 92%. Mainline Protestants favor same-sex marriage by 62%. Political party affiliation shows 66% of Democrats, 61% of independents, and 32% of Republicans support marriage equality.

In June 2015, the United States Supreme Court ruled that all states must honor same-sex marriages. Although attitudes are changing, many still oppose granting LGBTQ people equal rights. Legally backed discrimination still remains in many places across the United States. Despite indications of greater openness in attitudes, in most states in the United States, it is still legal to fire people because of their sexual orientation or their gender identity (Edelson 2014). Campaigns to change such laws have started to gain traction, however.

Macro-level cultural notions about gender and sexuality are influencing meso-level institutions, such as family, politics, economics, and religion. Note further how meso-level institutions, such as government and religion, control personal relationships. In sexuality and love, as in everything else, the micro, meso, and macro levels are connected in complex ways.

Thinking Sociologically

What are some societal changes that have influenced the dramatic changes over the past decade in attitudes toward same-sex marriage? Have they impacted your perspective or your friends' on this issue? Why, or why not?

COSTS AND CONSEQUENCES OF GENDER STRATIFICATION

The consequences of gender stratification affect every level of society. They impact life chances for individuals and how institutions, nations, and the global society function. As illustrated in the following examples, sex- and gender-based stratification limit individual development and cause problems in education, health, work, and other parts of the social world.

Psychological and Social Consequences: Micro-Level Implications

For both women and men, rigid gender stereotypes can be very constraining. Individuals who hold highly sex-typed attitudes feel compelled to behave in stereotypical ways—ways that are consistent with the pictures they have in their heads of proper gender behavior (Kramer and Beutel 2014). However, individuals who do not identify rigidly with masculine or feminine gender types tend to have a broader repertoire of acceptable behaviors and know how to cope with changing situations (C. Cheng 2005). They are more flexible in thoughts and behavior, score higher on intelligence tests, have greater spatial ability, and have higher levels of creativity. Because they allow themselves a wider range of behaviors, they have more varied abilities and experiences and become more tolerant of others' behaviors.

According to a recent study by Centers for Disease Control and University of Georgia, high masculinity in males sets up rigid standards for male behavior and has been correlated with anxiety, guilt, neuroses, and poor health outcomes, whereas less rigid masculine expectations are associated with emotional stability, sensitivity, warmth, and enthusiasm. Rigid stereotypes and resulting sexism can limit our activities, behaviors, and perspectives (Adams 2016).

Results of Gender Role Expectations. Women in many societies are expected to be beautiful, youthful, and sexually interesting and interested while, at the same time, preparing the food, caring for the children, keeping a clean and orderly home, bringing in money to help support the family, and being competent and successful in their careers. Multiple, sometimes contradictory, expectations for women can cause stress and even serious psychological problems.

The resulting strain contributes to depression and certain health problems, such as headaches, nervousness, and insomnia, and thus, up to 40% more women than men develop mental health conditions. Women are more likely to report problems such as depression and anxiety, whereas men may turn to substance abuse or anger (Ball 2013; Slaughter 2012).

Gender expectations also affect women's self-concepts and body images. As noted earlier, beautiful images jump out at us from billboards, magazine covers, and TV and movie screens. Only 5% of women possess the body type shown in advertising; thus, these images are unattainable for most women. In ads, the images have been created through surgeries, eating disorders, and the use of air-brushing on photographs. Disorders, including anorexia and bulimia nervosa, relate to societal expectations of the ideal woman's appearance (Taub and McLorg 2010). In the United States, close to 30 million people suffer from eating disorders, with 85% to 90% of those being females. Women are more likely to have eating disorders and often receive help, but men are less likely to seek help when they do have a problem, resulting in serious health problems, including death (ANAD 2015; James 2013).

Thinking Sociologically

How much time, energy, and money do you spend on your physical appearance? Why? From what social-izing agents did you learn how to judge your physi-cal appearance? Overall, how have those socializing agents impacted how you view yourself?

Men die earlier than women, in part due to environ-mental, psychological, and social factors. Problems in Global North countries such as heart disease, stroke, cir-rhosis, cancers, accidents, and suicides are linked, in part, to the role expectations that males should appear tough, objective, ambitious, unsentimental, and unemotional—traits that require men to assume great responsibility and suppress their feelings (Tull 2012). So gender expectations can have a substantial cost for men, as well as for women.

Societal Costs: Meso- and Macro-Level Implications

Gender stratification creates costs for societies around the world in a number of ways. *Poor educational achievement* of female children leads to the loss of human talents and resources, a serious cost for societies. *Social divisive-ness*—us-versus-them thinking based on sex—can create alienation, if not hostility, and this can result in physical or emotional aggression, discrimination, and violence against women.

Human capital—the resources of the human popula-tion—is central to social prosperity in societal systems. Yet resistance to expanding women's public sphere and professional roles is often strong. For example, 62.5% of Japanese women participate in the labor force, compared with 80.6% of men. If women's participation matched that of men's, the country's working population would grow by 7 million people, raising output. However, many women are reluctant to take on additional responsibilities because of family commitments and lack of childcare and other resources for working parents.

As an aging population, Japan is losing workers, and the economy is showing the strain (Covert 2014). Working conditions in Japan and Korea tend to favor men. They have among the highest gender wage gaps in the world at 26.6% and 36.6% respectively, and the largest wage gaps among Global North countries (Organisation for Economic Co-operation and Development 2015b). *The Global Gender Gap Report* ranked Japan 104 out of 142 countries in terms of gender disparities at work (Gilman 2015). Although Japanese women score higher in science than men and are almost half of university graduates, few can break through the glass ceiling they face in the job market (Hewlett 2013).

Inequality based on class, race, ethnicity, and gender takes place at all levels of analysis and is often entrenched at the meso level within the institutions found in every society—family, education, religion, government, economics, and health care. Complex societies incorporate other institutions as well, including science and technology, sports, and the military. We turn, in the next chapter, to a discussion of institutions in our social world.

WHAT HAVE WE LEARNED?

At the beginning of this chapter, we asked how being born female or male affects our lives. Because sex is a primary variable on which societies are structured and stratified, our sex affects our public and private-sphere activities, our health, our ability to practice religion or participate in political life, our opportunities for education, and just about everything we do.

- Whereas sex is biological, notions of gender identity and gender roles are socially constructed and learned and vary across cultures.

- Notions of gender are first taught in micro settings—in the intimacy of the home—but reinforced at the meso and macro levels.

- Whereas *she* may go first in micro-level social encounters (served first in a restaurant or the first to enter a doorway), *he* goes first in meso and macro settings—with the doors open wider for men to enter leadership positions in organizations and institutions.

- Greater access to resources at the meso level makes it easier to have entrée to macro-level positions, but it also influences the respect one receives in micro settings.

- Much of the gender stratification today is unconscious and unintended—not caused by angry or bigoted men who purposefully oppress women. Gender inequality is rooted in institutionalized privilege and disprivilege.

- Various social theories shed different light on the issues of inequality in gender roles assigned to various sexes.

- For modern postindustrial societies, there is a high cost for treating women like a minority group—individually for the people who experience it and collectively for the society, which loses many potential contributions from women.

DISCUSSION QUESTIONS

1. Describe some of the ways socializing agents (e.g., family, peers, the media, religion, and schools) encouraged you to conform to traditional gender norms. Do you think you will encourage (or have you encouraged) your own children to conform to traditional gender norms? Why, or why not?

2. Give two examples of side-effect gender discrimination that lead to economic inequality between men and women.

3. How does gender socialization influence who runs for office and for whom we vote? How are female politicians treated by the media, compared with male politicians? How has that impacted your own perception of female politicians?

4. How does gender discrimination harm society? What could be done on your campus to improve the status of women or men? How might you join these efforts?

5. Why do many boys perform poorly in school, and what impact does this have on their lives? What can be done to correct this problem?

6. What are your career goals? Do they follow traditional gender roles? Why or why not? How has your gender socialization impacted your career plans?

7. More women than men are now in college. How do you think this fact will impact gender roles on campus and in the larger society?

KEY TERMS

gender   251

gender roles   251

glass ceiling   262

heterosexism   271

homophobia   271

sex   250

sexuality   250

transgender   250

CONTRIBUTING TO OUR SOCIAL WORLD: WHAT CAN WE DO?

At the Local (Micro) Level

- Schedule an interview with the director or other staff members of the human resources or affirmative action offices on your campus to learn about your school's policies regarding gender discrimination. What procedures exist for hiring? Do women and men receive the same salaries, wages, and benefits for equal work? Explore the possibility of working as a volunteer or an intern in the office, specifically in the area of gender equity.

At the Organizational /Institutional (Meso) Levels

- *The National Organization for Women (NOW)* is the world's leading advocate for gender equity. It deals with issues such as reproductive rights, legislative outreach, economic justice, ending sex discrimination, and promoting diversity. The organization's website, www.now.org, lists contact information, state and regional affiliates, and NOW jobs and internships (now.org/about/job-and-internships).

- *Sociologists for Women in Society (SWS)*, an organization that "works to improve women's lives through advancing and supporting feminist sociological research, activism and scholars," provides many resources for students. SWS provides students with scholarships, opportunities to be mentored, and an award to recognize students who improve the lives of women through activism. Visit the SWS website at www.socwomen.org.

- *The NEW Leadership National Network at the Center for American Women and Politics* is an annual 6-day residential summer program that "educates college women about the important role that politics plays in their lives and encourages them to become effective leaders in the political arena." To learn more about NEW Leadership and to find out how to apply to the program go to www.cawp.rutgers.edu/education_training/NEW_Leadership/overview.

At the National/Global (Macro) Level

- *MADRE*, an international women's rights organization, works primarily in less developed countries. You can find numerous opportunities for working on issues of justice, human rights, education, and health on its website at www.madre.org.

- *Equality Now*, an international nongovernmental organization, provides many venues for those interested in promoting equality for women and curbing gender violence and discrimination. You can find more about this organization at www.equalitynow.org.

- *The United Nations Inter-Agency Network on Women and Gender Equality* works on global issues, including violence against women and women's working conditions. Its WomenWatch website, at www.un.org/womenwatch, contains news, information, and ideas for contributing to the worldwide campaign for women's rights.

$SAGE edge™

Get the edge on your studies. **edge.sagepub.com/ballantinecondensed5e**

- Take a quiz to find out what you've learned.
- Review key terms with eFlashcards.
- Watch videos that enhance chapter content.

PART IV

Institutions

Picture a house, a *structure* in which you live. Within that house are the actions and activities that bring the house alive—the *processes*. Flip a switch, and the lights go on because the house is well wired. Adjust the thermostat, and the room becomes more comfortable as the structural features of furnace or air-conditioning systems operate. If the structural components of the plumbing and water-heating systems work, you can take a hot shower when you turn the knob. These actions taken within the structure make the house livable. If something breaks down, you need to get it fixed so that everything works smoothly.

Institutions, too, provide a *structure* for society, a framework that promotes stability. *Processes* are the action dimension within institutions—the activities that take place. They include the interactions between people; socialization in families, schools, and religious institutions; decision making in organizations and political institutions; and other actions in each society and the world. These processes are often dynamic and can lead to significant change within the structure—like a decision about whether new homeowners should remodel their kitchen. Institutions are meso-level structures because they are larger in scope than the face-to-face social interactions of the micro level, and yet, they are smaller than the nation or the global system. However, each institution includes processes at all levels of analysis, micro to macro, as we shall see from the examples in the following chapters.

Institutions such as family, education, religion, politics, economics, and health care include certain necessary actions, patterns, and expectations that differ in each society. They are interdependent and mutually supportive, just as the plumbing, heating system, and electricity in a house work together to make a home functional. However, a breakdown in one institution or conflict over limited resources between institutions affects the whole society, just as a malfunction in the electrical system may shut the furnace off and cool down the water heater.

IMPORTANCE OF INSTITUTIONS

Institutions are not anything concrete that you can see, hear, touch, or smell. The concept of *institutions* is a way of describing and understanding how society works. For example, the institution of family meets certain needs found in almost all societies. Family, as an institution, refers to the behavior of thousands of people, which—taken as a whole—forms a social structure. Think of your own family. It has unique ways of interacting and raising children, but it is part of a community with many families. Those many families, in turn, are part of a national set of patterned behaviors we call the family. This pattern meets the basic needs of the society for producing and socializing new members and providing an emotionally supportive environment. In this way, family processes occur at each level of analysis. Table IV.1 illustrates the impact of social institutions in society at each level of analysis.

Institutions do not dictate exactly how you will carry out the roles within your individual family. However, they do specify certain needs families will meet and statuses (e.g., spouse/partner, parent, or child) that relate to each other in certain mutually caring ways and fill certain semi-negotiable roles. An institution provides a blueprint (much like a local builder needs a blueprint to build a house), and in your local version of the institution, you may make a few modifications to the plans to meet your individual micro-level needs. Still, through this society-encompassing structure and interlocking set of statuses, the basic needs for individuals at the micro level and for society at the macro level are met.

Institutions, then, are *organized, patterned, and enduring sets of social structures that provide guidelines for behavior and help each society meet its basic survival needs*. Whereas institutions operate mostly at the meso level, they also act to integrate micro and macro levels of society. Let us look more deeply at this definition.

1. *Organized, patterned, and enduring sets of social structures* means that institutions are not brick-and-mortar buildings but refer to a complex set of groups or organizations, statuses within those groups, and norms of conduct that guide people's behavior. These structures ensure socialization of children, education of the young, a sense of meaning in life, companionship, and production and distribution of needed goods (e.g., food, clothing, automobiles, cell phones, and computers) for the members of the society. If this patterned behavior were missing, these needs might not be addressed. At the local level, we may go to a neighborhood school, or we may attend worship at a congregation we favor. These are local organizations—*franchises*, if you will—of a much more encompassing structure (education and religion) that provides guidelines for education or addresses issues of meaning of life for an enormous number of people. The Catholic church in your town, for example, is a local franchise of an organization transnational in scope and global in its concerns.

2. *Guidelines for behavior* help people know how to conduct themselves and obtain basic needs in their society. Individuals and local organizations actually carry out the institutional guidelines in each culture, but the exact ways they do so vary by locality. In local franchises of the political system, people know how to govern and how to solve problems at the local level because of larger norms and patterns provided by the political institution. Individual men and women operate a local hospital or clinic (a local franchise of the medical institution) that follows a national blueprint of how to provide health care. The specific activities of a local school, likewise, abide by the guidelines and purposes of the larger goals of "formal education" in a given nation.

3. *Meeting basic survival needs* is a core component of institutions because societies must meet needs of their members; otherwise, the members die, or the society collapses. Institutions, then, are the structures that support social life in a large, bureaucratized society. Common to all industrialized societies are family, education, health care, economics, politics, and religion. The first five of these institutions are discussed in the following chapters.

4. *Integrating micro and macro levels of society* is also critical because one of the collective needs of society is coherence and stability—including some integration between the various levels of society. Institutions help provide that integration for the entire social system. They do this by meeting needs at the local franchise level (e.g., food at the grocery store, education at the local school, and health care at the local clinic) while, at the same time, coordinating national and global organizations and patterns.

Table IV.1   The Impact of Institutions at Each Level of Analysis

	Family	Education	Economic Systems	Political Systems	Religion	Medicine
Micro (local "franchises" of institutions)	Your family; local parenting group; local Parents Without Partners; county family counseling clinic	Your teacher; local neighborhood school; local school board	Local businesses; local chamber of commerce; local labor union chapter	Neighborhood crime watch program; local city or county council	Your local religious study group or congregation	Your doctor and nurse; local clinic; local hospital
Meso (institutions, complex organizations, ethnic subcultures, state/provincial systems)	The middle class family; the Hispanic family; the Jewish family	State/provincial department of education; American Federation of Teachers*	State/provincial offices of economic development; United Auto Workers*	State/provincial governments; national political parties; each state or province's supreme court	National denominations/movements (e.g., United Methodist Church or American Reform Judaism)	HMOs; Minnesota Nurses Association; American Medical Association
Macro (national and global social systems and trends)	Kinship and marriage structures, such as monogamy versus polygamy; global trends in family, such as choice of partners rather than arranged marriages	National education system; United Nations Girls' Education Initiative	Spread of capitalism around the world; World Bank; International Monetary Fund; World Trade Organization	National government; United Nations; World Court; G-7 (most powerful seven nations in the world)	Global faith-based movements and structures; National Council of Churches; World Council of Churches; World Islamic Council; World Jewish Congress	National health care system; World Health Organization; transnational pandemics

*These organizations are national in scope and membership, but they are considered meso level here because they are complex organizations *within* the nation.

Again, if all this sounds terribly abstract, that is because institutions *are* abstractions. You cannot touch institutions, yet they are as real as air, love, or happiness. In fact, in the modern world, institutions are as necessary to life as is air, and they help provide love and happiness that make life worth living.

THE DEVELOPMENT OF MODERN INSTITUTIONS

If we go all the way back to early hunting and gathering societies, there were no meso or macro levels to their social experience. People lived their lives in one or two villages, and whereas a spouse might come from another village or one might move to a spouse's clan, there was no national or state governance and certainly no awareness of a global social system. In those earlier times, family and community provided whatever education was needed, produced and distributed goods, paid homage to a god or gods, and solved conflicts and disputes through a system of familial (often patriarchal) power distribution. One social unit, such as the family, served multiple functions, from education to religion to health care and an economic base.

As societies have become more complex and differentiated, multiple levels of the social system and various new institutions have emerged. Sociology textbooks in the 1950s identified only "five basic institutions": family, economic systems, political systems, religion, and education (with compulsory formal education not established in every state until the 20th century). These five institutions were believed to be the core structures that met the essential needs of individuals and societies in an orderly way.

Soon thereafter, *medicine* moved from the family and small-town doctors and became another institution. Medicine has become bureaucratized in hospitals, medical labs, professional organizations, and other complex structures that provide health care. *Science* is also now something more than flying kites in thunderstorms in one's backyard, as Ben Franklin did. It is a complex system that provides training, funding, research institutes, peer review, and professional associations to support empirical research. New information is the lifeblood of an information-based or postindustrial society. Science, discussed in Chapter 16, is now an essential institution. Although it is arguable whether sports are an essential component for social viability, sports have clearly become highly structured in the past 50 years, and many sociologists consider sports an institution. The mass media and military also fall into the category of institutions in more advanced countries. There are gray areas as to whether something is considered an institution, but the questions to ask are (a) whether the structure meets basic needs of the society for survival, (b) whether it has become a complex organization providing routinized structures and guidelines for society, and (c) whether it is national or even global in its scope while also having pervasive local (micro) impact.

Thinking Sociologically

Using Table IV.1, try placing other modern-day institutions (e.g., mass media, science, sports, and the military) in the framework. Where do organizations you belong to fit into the institutional structure?

THE CONNECTIONS AMONG INSTITUTIONS

The Great Recession of 2007–2009 illustrates how institutions can impact one another. Many individuals in the United States became unemployed as credit dried up and companies reduced their payrolls. Their families then also faced various stresses that come with an unemployed breadwinner. In turn, the government faced pressure because citizens expected political leaders to intervene and find ways to bring the nation out of an economic recession. At the same time, religious congregations experienced increased demands at their food banks and soup kitchens *and* declining contributions from religious congregants who lost their jobs. Funding for schools also suffered during the Great Recession, as tax revenues fell. Today, the United States is still recovering from the recession, and it has taken its toll on high-paying jobs.

Connections among meso-level institutions are a common refrain in this book. As you read these chapters, notice that change in one institution affects others. Sociologists studying the legal system, mass media, medicine, science, sports, or the military as institutions would raise questions similar to those raised in the institutions discussed in the following three chapters. We begin our examination of institutions with the family and education. In Chapter 10, we diverge from our model of discussing the micro, meso, and macro levels and focus primarily on the micro-to-meso connection. These institutions also have an important macro-level function, but family and education are institutions that play a particularly significant role in socialization at the micro level. Chapter 11 (health care) examines all three levels. Chapter 12 (political and economic institutions) focuses more on the meso-to-macro connection.

10 Family and Education

Institutionalizing Socialization

Through the institutions of the family and education, we are socialized and learn to participate in the larger world. The whole society benefits when these two institutions work in tandem.

MICRO

ME (AND MY FAMILY AND SCHOOLS)

LOCAL ORGANIZATIONS AND COMMUNITY

Family is the basic unit of action within a community. Schools and classrooms provide education for family members.

MESO

NATIONAL ORGANIZATIONS, INSTITUTIONS, AND ETHNIC SUBCULTURES

Families socialize children into social roles so they can function in society. State or provincial funding, regulations, and learning standards affect local schools.

MACRO

SOCIETY

Governments develop family and educational policies.

GLOBAL COMMUNITY

International organizations support families and children and create international standards for education.

WHAT YOU WILL LEARN IN THIS CHAPTER

This chapter will help you do the following:

10.1 Discuss how definitions of families are socially constructed and change over time.

10.2 Illustrate different patterns of mate selection.

10.3 Provide examples of how families interact with other institutions.

10.4 Describe controversial topics facing the family today.

10.5 Give examples of micro-level interactions in schools.

10.6 Explain the formal and informal structures of schools.

10.7 Present evidence that schools contribute to the reproduction of social class.

THINK ABOUT IT

Micro: Local community	What did you learn—both formally and informally—from your family and school experiences that make you who you are today?
Meso: National institutions, complex organizations, and ethnic groups	How does the institution of state or national government influence family and education?
Macro: National and global systems	How do family and education influence the nation and vice versa? Why and in what ways are these institutions becoming globalized?

Baby Tambara could be any one of us. Baby Tambara is born into a family in some community and country in the world. What will be her fate? Will she be rich, well fed, loved, educated, and successful, or will she be one of the billions of world citizens living in poverty, hungry, with little chance for education or success? The two institutions introduced in this chapter shed light on how Baby Tambara is introduced into her social world. Macro-level factors like whether her country is in the Global North or South and what her opportunities in her country are will affect her future life. Her state or province and her ethnic background—factors at the meso level—also influence her life chances. In this chapter, we focus primarily on the micro level and how that shapes Baby Tambara's socialization experiences, launches her into contact with the organizations in her life, and helps her become a productive member of her society.

Family is where socialization starts. It provides Baby Tambara with her initial grounding in the world, meeting her basic needs for food, clothing, shelter, and social interaction. She would not survive long without these necessities. It is in the family that she will also begin to learn language, survival skills, and the values and beliefs that are needed in her social world.

If Baby Tambara is fortunate, she will start her education sometime between ages 3 and 6. Here, she will learn her ABCs and 1-2-3s, enabling her to function in a literate society and eventually develop the skills necessary to make a living in her society. Our personal interactions with these institutions—our family and our schools—are involved from birth and early childhood through adulthood to the end of life.

Once again, you will be asked to apply the theories with which you are now familiar to the discussion of these institutions. Briefly, *structural-functional theory* focuses on the purposes each institution serves for society. *Conflict theory* considers the tensions between different institutions and the way people with power use institutions to

protect their interests and their privileges. *Symbolic interaction theory* considers the socialization process and interactions that result from individuals learning proper behaviors and expectations in their social worlds. *Rational choice theory* studies how individuals weigh the costs and benefits of their options when making decisions. *Feminist theory* advocates for seeing the woman's point of view when doing research.

This chapter focuses primarily on micro-level socialization experiences, as it provides an overview of how the institutions of family and education contribute to our learning to be a member of society. We now follow Baby Tambara through her early socialization process.

FAMILY

HOW DO WE MAKE PEOPLE?

Let us assume that Baby Tambara has been born into a family in Niger, Africa, one of the poorest countries on earth. Baby Tambara will have many relatives to watch over her and teach her the ways and beliefs of the group. However, she may not have access to school, as education has little to do with her immediate needs and family's expectations. Each of the children in her large family has chores appropriate for his or her age and gender. The older girls help their mother with the youngest children, the household chores, preparing meals, fetching water, and caring for the animals. Most likely, they—and eventually Baby Tambara—will be married at a young age to a man who has several wives. They will then care for his herds and many children.

However, let us imagine another scenario: Baby Aina has been born into a Swedish family, one of two children. When she is a few months old, she will spend part of her day in a day care center while her parents work and her brother attends school. She will spend most of her years to adulthood in some type of schooling, learning the knowledge and skills she needs to enter the workforce and be successful in this Global North country—and she will have opportunities to pursue her choice of a career.

What a difference! Families come in many shapes, sizes, and color combinations. We begin our exploration of the institution of family with a discussion of what family is.

WHAT IS A FAMILY?

Who defines what constitutes a family: individuals, the government, or religious groups? Is a family just Ma, Pa, and the kids? Let us consider several definitions. The U.S. Census Bureau defines *family* as "a group of two or more people (one of whom is the householder) related by birth, marriage, or adoption and residing in the same housing unit; all such people (including related subfamily members) are considered as members of one family" (Pemberton 2015). Thus, a family in the United States might be composed of siblings, cousins, a grandparent and grandchild, or other groupings. Some sociologists define family more broadly, such as "two or more individuals who maintain an intimate relationship that they expect will last indefinitely—or in the case of parent and child, until the child reaches adulthood—and who usually live under the same roof and pool their incomes and household labor"

(Cherlin 2010:14). Some religious groups and governments define family as a mother, father, and their children, whereas others include several spouses, multiple generations, or several siblings living under the same roof.

The definition and the typical composition of family are changing as societies and social norms change (Angier 2013). The traditional composition of married parents with a mother who tends to the household, a father who brings in

REUTERS/Joan Castro

In recent decades, the definition of family has broadened in many areas of the world to include families with parents of the same sex, like these two families.

FIGURE 10.1 Living Arrangements of Children Under 18, 1960–2015

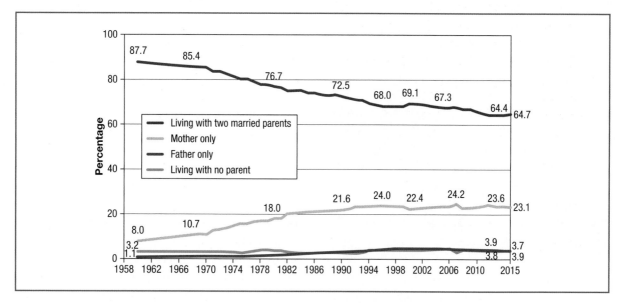

Source: Child Trends Data Bank (2015). Reprinted with permission conveyed through Copyright Clearance Center, Inc.

most of the income, and biological children living in an intact family compose 64% of U.S. families today, with 24% of children living with a single mother. Figure 10.1 illustrates the change in family structures from 1970 to 2015.

As noted earlier, the family is often referred to as the most basic institution of any society. First, it is the place where we learn many of the norms for functioning in the larger society. Second, most of us spend our lives in the security of a family. People are born and raised in families, and many will die in a family setting. Through good and bad, sickness and health, most families provide for our needs, both physical and psychological. Therefore, families meet our primary, most basic needs. Third, major life events—marriages, births, graduations, promotions, anniversaries, religious ceremonies, holidays, and funerals—take place within the family context and are celebrated with family members. In short, family is where we invest the most emotional energy and spend much of our leisure time.

The family is capable of satisfying a range of social needs: sexual regulation; reproduction and replacement of members of society as children are born; socialization of children into society, religion, and other institutions; emotional support, protection, and sense of belonging; economic support; and so forth. The family carries out functions necessary for individual and societal survival (Benokraitis 2015).

Types of Families and Marriages

In Global North societies, most individuals are born and raised in the **family of orientation**, *the family into which we are born*. This family consists of parent(s) and possibly grandparents and sibling(s). Individuals receive early socialization and learn the language, norms, core values, attitudes, and behaviors of the community and society. A **family of procreation** *is the family we create ourselves*. We find a life mate and/or have children. The transmission of values, beliefs, and attitudes from our family of orientation to our family of procreation generally preserves and stabilizes the family system. We *make people* in families—not just biologically but socially. In the family, we take an organism that has the potential to be fully human, and we mold this tiny bit of humanity into a caring, compassionate, productive person—at least, that is the ideal plan. Yet, the Ma-Pa-and-kids monogamous model familiar in many industrialized parts of the world is not as typical as it appears. From a worldwide perspective, it is only one of several structural models of family.

Extended families include *two or more adult generations that share tasks and living quarters*. This may include brothers, sisters, aunts, uncles, cousins, and grandparents. In most extended family systems, the eldest male is the authority figure. This is a common pattern around the world, especially in agricultural societies. Some ethnic groups in the United States, such as Mexican Americans and some Asian Americans, live in extended monogamous families, with several generations under one roof. This is financially practical and helps group members maintain their traditions and identity.

As societies become more industrialized and fewer individuals and families engage in agriculture, the **nuclear family**, consisting of *two parents and their children—or any two of the three*—becomes more common. A worldwide movement toward more nuclear families is under way because of urbanization, fewer arranged marriages, and growing equality between men and women (Burn 2011; W. Goode 1970).

No matter what form the family takes in a society, the family, like all of the other major institutions, is interdependent at the meso level with each of the other institutions. For example, if the health care institution is unaffordable or not functioning well, families may not get the care they need to prevent serious illness.

If the economy goes into a recession and jobs are not available, families experience stress, abuse rates increase, and marriages are more likely to become unstable. In worst-case scenarios, families who lose their incomes may become homeless.

Kristian Buus/Corbis Historical/Getty Images

Living in the mountains of Nepal, the Chepang family lives a simple life, but the children learn many survival skills, and their most basic needs, physical and psychological, are met.

FAMILY DYNAMICS: MICRO-LEVEL PROCESSES

The process of finding a mate is not random. Your partner was or will not be randomly selected from the entire global population. What factors enter into your mate selection?

Mate Selection: How Do New Families Start?

At the most micro level, two people get together to begin a new family unit. In early 2016, the world population passed 7.3 billion people, but your partner was or will not be randomly selected from the entire global population (U.S. Census Bureau 2016). Even in Global North societies, where we think individuals have free choice of marriage partners, mate selection is not an entirely individual choice. Indeed, mate selection is highly limited by geographical proximity, ethnicity, age, social class, and a host of other variables. As we shall see, micro- and macro-level forces influence each other even in a process as personal as mate selection.

Choice of Marriage Partners. Monogamy and polygamy are the main forms of marriage found around the world. Monogamy *refers to marriage of two individuals and is the most familiar form of marriage in industrial and postindustrial societies*. Polygamy, *marriage of one person to more than one partner at the same time*, is most often found in agricultural societies where multiple spouses and children mean more help with the farmwork.

A number of cultural rules—meso- and macro-level expectations—govern the choice of a mate in any society. Most are unwritten cultural norms. They vary from culture to culture, but in every society, we learn the cultural norms from an early age. One of the cultural norms is exogamy, *norms governing the choice of a mate that requires individuals to marry outside of their own immediate group.* The most universal form of exogamy is the *incest taboo*, including restrictions against father–daughter, mother–son, and brother–sister marriages. Some countries and about half the U.S. states also forbid first cousins to marry (see Table 3.3 on page 70). Others, such as some African groups and many Syrian villages, encourage first-cousin marriages to solidify family ties and property holdings.

Exogamy also alleviates sexual jealousy within groups. For example, if father and son became jealous about who was sleeping with the wife, mother, or sister, relationships

Families vary a great deal from one culture to another; this polygynous family (one husband and several wives) from Tibet illustrates one variation, a man with several wives. If the members of a family work well together, they provide support, a sense of identity, and feelings of belonging and caring.

would be destroyed and parental authority sabotaged. Likewise, if the father were always going to the daughter for sexual satisfaction, the mother–daughter bond would be severely threatened (Williams, Sawyer, and Wahlstrom 2013). No society can allow this to happen to its family system. Any society that failed to have an incest taboo self-destructed long ago.

On the other hand, norms of endogamy *require individuals to marry inside certain human boundaries,* whatever the societal members see as protecting the homogeneity of the group. The purpose is to encourage group bonding and solidarity and to help minority groups survive in societies with different cultures. Endogamous norms may require individuals to select mates of the same race, religion, social class, ethnic background, or clan (Williams et al. 2013). Examples of strictly endogamous religious groups include the Armenian Iranians, Orthodox Jews, Old Order Amish, Jehovah's Witnesses, and the Parsis of India. Such practices result in less biologically diversified groups but protect the minority identity (Belding 2004).

Most people also choose a mate with similar social characteristics—age, race, place of residence, educational background, political philosophy, moral values, and psychological traits—a practice called *homogamy*. Going outside the expected and accepted group in mate selection can make things tough for newlyweds who need family and community support. Few take this risk. For instance, in the United States, close to 90% marry people with similar religious values (Williams et al. 2013). So cultural norms of societies limit individual decisions in a way that most individuals do not consciously recognize. Yet today, some of these norms are weakening as the rapidly rising number of interracial marriages in the United States reveals. Still, the question remains: How do we settle on a life partner?

Finding a Mate. In most societies, mate selection takes place through arranged marriages, free-choice unions, or some combination of the two. Whether marriages are arranged or entered into freely, both endogamy and exogamy limit the number of possible mates. In either case, micro-level mate selection is shaped by meso- and macro-level cultural rules of the society.

Arranged marriages *involve a pattern of mate selection in which someone other than the couple—elder males, parents, or a matchmaker—selects the marital partners.* This method of mate selection is most common in traditional, often patriarchal, societies. For many girls in traditional Muslim societies, marriage is a matter of necessity, for their support comes from the family system. Marriages create and strengthen economic arrangements and political alliances between family groups. Daughters are highly valuable in securing ties between families (Burn 2011). Beauty, youth, talent, and pleasant disposition bring a high bride price and a good match. Should the young people like each other, it is icing on the cake. Daughters must trust that their families will make the best possible matches for them. Most often, the men hold the power in this vital decision.

Kako and Hiroshi of Japan met for the first time for tea after a matchmaker had worked with each one's family to find a suitable mate. If they get along and do not object to the match, the wedding will be planned. Today, about 30% of marriages in Japan are still arranged this way, the rest being called "love marriages" ("Getting Married in Japan" 2014). Abdul's father has arranged a marriage for him with a girl from a nearby village. This marriage will solidify bonds between the families and the villages, reducing the chance of future conflict. Love has nothing to do with such arranged marriages, but political and economic factors matter big time! Some marriages are based on individual choice and love, and some are based on what is good for the family and community group.

Where arranged marriages are the norm, love has a special meaning. The man and woman may never have set eyes on each other before the wedding day, but respect and affection generally grow over time as the husband and wife live together. People from societies with arranged marriages are assured a mate and have difficulty comprehending marriage systems based on love, romance, and courtship—factors believed to be insufficient grounds for a lifelong relationship. They wonder why anyone would want to place themselves in a marriage market, with all the uncertainty and rejection. Such whimsical and unsystematic methods would not work in many societies, where the structure of life is built around family systems.

Free-choice marriage is *a pattern of mate selection in which the partners select each other based primarily on romance and love.* The idea that each person has the right to choose a partner with minimal interference from others has become increasingly prevalent as societies around the world become more Westernized, women gain more rights and freedoms, and families exert less control over their children's choice of mates (Eshleman and Bulcroft 2010). Sonnets, symphonies, rock songs, poems, and plays have been written to honor romantic love and the psychological and

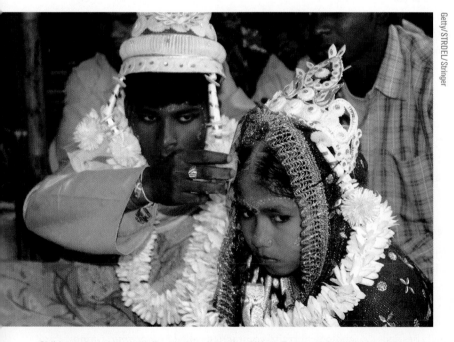

Getty/STRDEL/Stringer

Child marriage is especially common in parts of West, East, and Central Africa; the Middle East; and South Asia. In some countries, as many as 1 out of every 10 girls is married by the time she is 15 years old, some as young as 10, and nearly half are married by age 18. An Indian groom in this photo puts vermilion, the holy mark of Hindu marriage, on the forehead of his underage bride.

physiological pain and pleasure that the mating game brings. However impractical romance may seem, in industrial and postindustrial societies, people generally value love and individualism and tend to have high marriage rates, low fertility rates, and high divorce rates.

Starting with the assumption that eligible people are most likely to meet and be attracted to others who have similar values and backgrounds, sociologists have developed various mate selection theories, several of which view dating as a three-stage process—a series of sequential decisions (see Figure 10.2).

1. *Stimulus:* We meet someone to whom we are attracted by appearance, voice, dress, similar ethnic background, sense of humor, or other factors. Something serves as a stimulus that makes us take notice. Of course, sometimes the stimulus is simply knowing the other person is interested in us.
2. *Value comparison:* We are more likely to find someone compatible if she or he affirms our own beliefs and values toward life, politics, religion, and roles of men and women in society and marriage. If our values are not compatible, the person does not pass through our filter. We look elsewhere.
3. *Roles and needs stage:* Another filter comes when the couple explores roles of companion, parent, housekeeper, and lover. This might involve looking for common needs, interests, and favored activities. If the roles and needs are not complementary, desire for a permanent relationship wanes.

Thinking Sociologically

Conduct a small survey of dating and married couples you know. Ask them about how they became involved in their relationship and their process of deciding to get together or marry. How do their comments mesh with the three-stage process described here?

Who Holds the Power?

Power relations in individual families, another micro-level issue shaped by cultural norms at the macro level, affect the interactions and decision making in individual families. Two areas that have received particular sociological attention are decision making in marriage and work roles.

Decision Making in Marriage. Cultural traditions establish the power base in society and family: patriarchy, matriarchy, or egalitarianism. The most typical authority pattern in the world is patriarchy, or male authority. Matriarchy, female authority, is rare. Even where the

FIGURE 10.2 Mate Selection "Filtering"

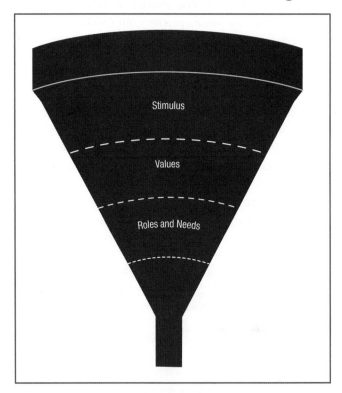

The notion of mate selection described previously is sometime referred to as a filter theory. It is as though you were filtering specks of gold, and the first filter holds out the large stones, the second filter holds back pebbles, and the third filter stops sand, but the flakes of gold come through. Each stage in the mate selection process involves filtering some people out of the process. For you there may be other filter factors as well—such as religious similarities or common ethnicity.

lineage is traced through the mother's line, males usually dominate decision making.

Egalitarian family patterns—in which power, authority, and decision making are shared between the spouses and perhaps with the children—are emerging, but they are not yet a reality in most households. For example, research indicates that in many U.S. families, decisions concerning vacation plans, car purchases, and housing are reached democratically, but males generally have a disproportionate say in major decisions, such as whether to move to a new city or buy a new home (Lindsey 2015). Social scientists find no evidence that there are any inherent intellectual or personality foundations for male authority, as opposed to female authority (Kramer and Beutel 2014; Ward and Edelstein 2014).

Sociologists using *resource theory* to explain why men tend to have more power than women in families look at connections between resources outside the family and power inside the family. They argue that the spouse with more resources—education, occupational prestige, and income—has more power within the family. If only one spouse brings home a paycheck, the other is usually less powerful (Jory and Yodanis 2014).

In families where the wife is a professional, however, other factors in addition to outside resources may enter into the power dynamic (Jory and Yodanis 2014; Lindsey 2015). As noted in Chapter 9, regardless of who has greater resources, men in two-earner couples tend to have more say in financial matters and less responsibility for children and household tasks.

Who Does the Housework? The second shift, a term coined by Arlie Hochschild, refers to the housework and

child care that employed women do after their "first-shift" jobs (Hochschild 1989). While the differential in house-work done by men and women has diminished in recent decades, it still exists. The gap in household chores is a lit-tle over 4 hours per day for women, versus two and a half for men, and on an average day, 83% of women, compared with 65% of men, spend some time doing household activ-ities (Organisation for Economic Co-operation and Development 2016; U.S. Bureau of Labor Statistics 2015). Further, men spend just 7% of their time doing childcare activities, whereas women spend 14% of their day caring for children (Parker and Wang 2013). The next "Engaging Sociology" shows the breakdown in hours spent by men and women at various household activities.

ENGAGING SOCIOLOGY

Household Tasks by Gender

In many families, household tasks are highly gen-dered. As recently as the 1980s, wives and daugh-ters spent 2 or 3 times as much time as fathers and sons in household tasks, such as cleaning, laundry, and yard work. However, the tides have been shift-ing, and while they are not entirely equal, they are more balanced.

Engaging With Sociology

1. What is the division of labor (by gender) for household maintenance in your family?

2. How did it evolve?

3. Is it considered fair by all participants?

4. How does it compare with the data in Figure 10.3?

FIGURE 10.3   Percentage of Men and Women Who Engage in Some Type of Household Tasks Each Day

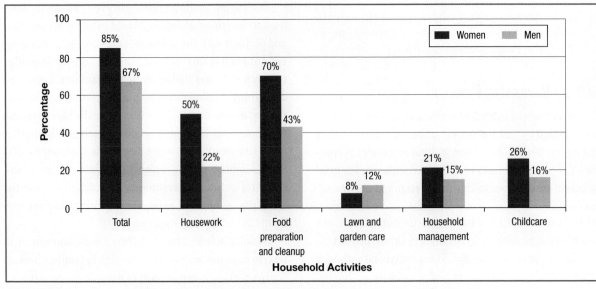

Source: U.S. Bureau of Labor Statistics (2016).

Although recent research clearly shows a narrowing of the gap in time spent by men and women on household tasks, such factors as the ages of children, how many years the mother has worked outside the home, and socioeconomic status of the family influence how involved men are and how much real "free time" each experiences. When women do have free time, it is much more likely to be interrupted than men's free time (Kan, Sullivan, and Gershuny 2011).

A positive relationship exists between equity in households and successful marriages. Husbands who do an equitable share of the household chores actually report higher levels of satisfaction with the marriage, and such couples are less likely to divorce (Dockterman 2014; Lorillard 2011). The success or failure of a marriage depends in large part on patterns that develop early in the marriage for dealing with the everyday situations, including power relationships and division of labor.

FAMILY AS AN INSTITUTION: MESO-LEVEL ANALYSIS

We experience family life at a very personal level, but the sum total of hundreds of thousands of families interacting in recognizable patterns results in *family as an institution* at the meso level. In this section, we look at the structure and parts of family as an institution and the family and its relationship to other institutions. Some of the changes in the family have resulted from—or caused—changes in other institutions.

Family and Economics: Who Supports the Family?

The answer to this question of who supports the family has been changing in many countries as women have joined the paid workforce. The following discussion outlines two types of family support patterns: dual-career families and families who must rely on government support for survival.

Dual-Worker Families. In dual-worker families, both adults work outside the home to bring in income. In many Global North societies, government and industry support dual-career families with various family-friendly policies: readily available childcare facilities, parenting leaves for childbirth and illness, and flexible work hours or telecommuting (working from one's home). These policies allow families to combine both work and family lives, with some time for leisure thrown in.

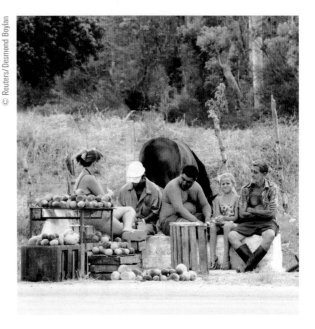

In many societies, the family is still the primary unit of economic production. This family of farmers selling mangoes waits for customers at the side of a road on the outskirts of Havana, Cuba.

The United States has been slower than many other Global North countries to adopt family-friendly policies. The U.S. government passed the Family and Medical Leave Act in 1993, which requires employers with 50 or more employees to grant 12 weeks of unpaid leave to workers who request it in order to care for the birth of a baby or a newborn, foster care or adoption, serious health issues in the immediate family, or serious medical conditions (U.S. Department of Labor 2013). However, many corporations in the United States have been slow to respond to dual-career family needs. A few businesses are experimenting with family-friendly policies, such as flextime (allowing individuals to schedule their own work hours within certain time frames) and job sharing (allowing individuals to split a job, perhaps with one family member working in the morning and the other in the afternoon). In comparison with other countries, the government in the United States does little to ensure that women can take time off to have a baby and not lose their jobs. Figure 10.4 indicates the legal requirements of maternal leave in several countries.

Thinking Sociologically

What are the challenges facing dual-career families? What social policies might relieve some of the stress on families with two working parents?

FIGURE 10.4   Total Duration of Paid Leave After Childbirth: Selected Countries

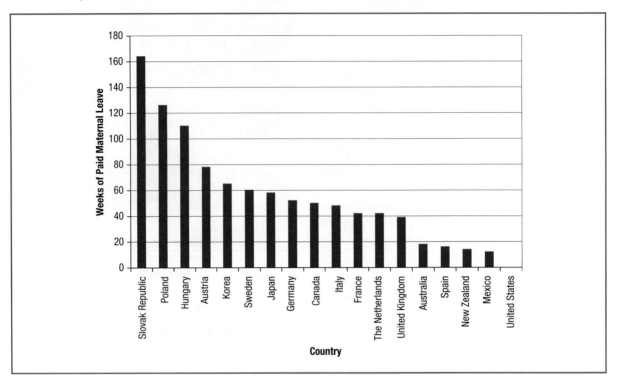

Source: Organisation for Economic Co-operation and Development (2014a).

Poverty and Families in the United States. The poverty threshold for a family of four in the United States was $24,250 in 2015, and for a single person, it was $11,770 (U.S. Department of Health and Human Services 2015a). The 2014 poverty rate, the most recent available, was 14.8%, at 46.7 million people. However, for children under 18, the poverty rate was higher: 21.1% in 2014. The poverty rate in the United States was 2.3% higher than in 2007, reflecting the recession's continuing effect on some families (U.S. Census Bureau 2015b). Table 10.1 shows the percentage of individuals and families in poverty.

The *feminization of poverty*, discussed in earlier chapters, is a global problem. It occurs where single motherhood is widespread and where there are few policies to reduce poverty, especially for this group (B. Williams et al. 2013). Single mothers, whether in capitalist or socialist countries, have some common experiences, including dual roles as workers and mothers, lower earnings than men, irregular paternal support payments, and underrepresentation in policy-making bodies. What differs around the world are governmental policies that help mothers with child support, childcare, health care, maternity leave, and family allowances. Single mothers are as prevalent in Sweden as in the United States, but U.S. single mothers are many times more likely to be poor because of fewer support systems from the state (Casey and Maldonado 2012). For single teens, early motherhood, lack of education, and insufficient

Table 10.1   Families in Poverty by Type of Family: 2013

Poverty Status and Family Type	Total Percentage Below Poverty Level
Total (all) families	11.6% (9.5 million)
Married-couple families	6.2% (3.7 million)
Single female householder	30.6% (4.8 million)
Single male householder	15.7% (1.0 million)

Source: DeNavas-Walt and Proctor (2015).

income lead to a multiproblem family pattern. Table 10.2 shows the change over 3 decades in births to unmarried women.

Socioeconomic Status and Parenting. Poverty is not the only way the economic system affects families. Complex societies develop significant inequalities, especially under capitalism. The inequalities are passed on to the next generation through social capital (important contacts and networks) and cultural capital (knowledge about the culture that enhances social mobility). In Chapter 7 ("Stratification") we discussed the fact that what one learns from one's family, including the way one approaches life, can enhance or restrain social mobility. The way parents in different classes parent their children has important implications for the children's economic circumstances.

Upper- and middle-class parents engage in the *concerted cultivation* of their kids. They schedule their children in multiple activities, engage in more elaborate verbal communication with them, and intervene on their behalf with teachers and other authority figures. Working-class parents, other than providing daily essentials, tend to be more hands-off, an approach that

This young woman sits at the wheel of her car with all of her possessions inside and her children in the backseat. These conditions do not make for effective parenting.

researcher Annette Lareau labeled the "accomplishment of natural growth" (Lareau 2003: 238). Their kids engage in more casual, unstructured play; have fewer opportunities to hear and use extended vocabularies; and are left to fend for themselves in dealings with adults. Their parents tell them what to do with orders, rather than reasoning with them, as many middle- and upper-class parents do with their children. Their parents also tend to use more physical punishment than middle-class parents, who use guilt, reasoning, time-outs, and other nonphysical sanctions to control children's behavior. These differences help shape children's assumptions about how authority is exercised and whether it is acceptable to challenge authority figures.

Thus, social class factors influence parenting, and parenting, in turn, influences one's prospects for social mobility and affluence within the system. The economic system and family system are linked and interrelated.

Table 10.2 Percentage of Births to Unmarried and Married U.S. Women

Year	Births to Unmarried Women (%)	Births to Married Women (%)
2013	40.6	59.4
2010	40.8	59.2
2005	36.9	63.1
2000	33.2	66.8
1995	32.2	67.8
1990	28.0	72.0
1985	22.0	78.0
1980	18.4	81.6

Source: Centers for Disease Control and Prevention (2015a); ChildStats.gov (2013); DeParle and Tavernise (2012).

FAMILY ISSUES: DIVORCE AND SAME-SEX MARRIAGE

Because family is the basic institution in which all of us get our start and most have a lifelong relationship, it is no wonder certain issues gain attention from the micro to macro levels. Here, we discuss two of these issues that crosscut levels of analysis: divorce and same-sex marriage.

Divorce: Contract Breaking

Although most cultures extol the virtues of family life, the reality is that not all partnerships work. There is lack of support, trust is violated, abuse is present, and relationships deteriorate. So we cannot discuss family life without also recognizing the often painful side of family life that results in contract breaking.

Some commentators view divorce rates, declining marriage rates, and problems created by divorce as evidence that the family is losing importance. There are costs to adults, who suffer guilt and failure; to children from divided homes; and to the society that does not have the stabilizing force of intact lifelong partnerships. Many children around the world, including in the United States, grow up in homes without both natural parents present (ChildStats.gov 2015). Nearly half of all U.S. children today have lived at least part of their lives in single-parent families (Kreider and Ellis 2011). Some scholars and policy analysts view this as dysfunctional instability.

Others argue that marriage is not so much breaking down as adapting to a different kind of social system. Indeed, more people today express satisfaction with marriage than at any previous time period, and 6% of married couples reach their 50th wedding anniversary, 35% reach their 25th, and 50% reach their 15th anniversary (U.S. Department of Commerce 2011). As recently as the late 19th century, the average length of a marriage was only 13 years—mostly because life expectancy was relatively short. "'Til death do us part" was not as long a time then as it is today, when average life expectancy in Global North countries reaches into the 80s (Coontz 2016).

Divorce rates for most groups in the United States have been dropping since the early 1980s. The divorce rate has fallen from 5.9 per 1,000 citizens in 1979 to 4 per 1,000 in 2000 and 3.4 per 1,000 in 2012 (Centers for Disease Control and Prevention 2013; Reich 2013). Figure 10.5 shows that divorce rates today are almost as low as they were in 1970. There is also variation by region of the country. Figure 10.6, indicates where in the United States the divorce rates are the highest. You may be surprised at which states have especially high or low divorce rates. Why do you think there would be so much variation by state?

● Thinking Sociologically

Micro-level issues of divorce are often rooted in the personalities and relationships of the individuals involved. Talk with friends and family members who have divorced about micro-level factors that contributed to the dissolution of their marriages. Now, based on information from this chapter, make a list of meso-level factors (e.g., religious, economic, legal, and educational) that contribute to or reduce divorce rates. What connections do you see between the micro and meso factors?

Many find the emotional aspects of divorce most difficult. Divorce is often experienced as a failure, rejection, or even punishment. Moreover, a divorce often involves splitting with more than just a spouse. It often entails separating from some family and friends, a religious community, and other social contexts where one's identity is tied to one's marriage (Amato 2000). No wonder divorce is so wrenching. Unlike simple societies, most modern ones have no ready mechanism for absorbing people back into stable social units such as clans.

Adjustment to divorced status varies by gender: Men typically have a harder time emotionally adjusting to singlehood or divorce than women. Divorced men must often leave not only their wives but also their children, and whereas many women have support networks, fewer men have developed or sustained deep supportive relationships outside marriage. Finances, on the other hand, are a bigger problem for divorced women and

FIGURE 10.5   Divorce Rate in the United States From 1970 to 2015 (number per 1,000 married women)

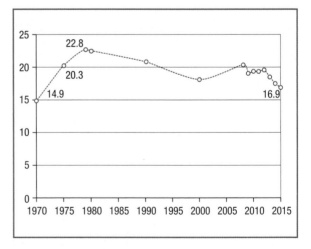

Source: 1970–2000 National Center for Health Statistics. Retrieved from National Center for Family & Marriage Research. 2015. "Divorce Rate in the U.S.: Geographic Variation, 2015." (http://www.bgsu.edu/content/dam/BGSU/college-of-arts-and-sciences/NCFMR/documents/FP/anderson-divorce-rate-us-geo-2016-fp-16-21.pdf).

FIGURE 10.6 U.S. States With Highest and Lowest Divorce Rates

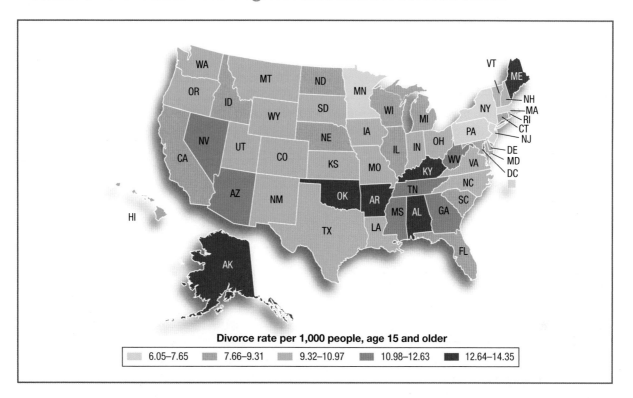

Divorce rate per 1,000 people, age 15 and older

6.05–7.65	7.66–9.31	9.32–10.97	10.98–12.63	12.64–14.35

Source: Reich (2013).

their children than for men. Women are more likely to be living in poverty than men across all racial and ethnic groups in the United States (Reason 2011). Single mothers are twice as likely to be in poverty as single fathers, and over 35% experience food insecurity (not enough food) (Gray 2012). Support from the noncustodial parent can help relieve poverty, yet 29% of custodial parents receive no help at all, and 30% receive only some of what is owed. Only 41% receive full child support (Child Trends 2013). Many children move to new houses and locations, leave one parent and friends, and must make adjustments to new schools and to reduced resources. Adjustment depends on the age of the children and the manner in which the parents handle the divorce. Further, children in families with high levels of marital conflict may be better off in the long term if their parents divorce (Conley 2014; Rhoades 2008; Yu et al. 2010).

Overall, children have an easier time with divorce if they can remain in their home and in their familiar school, keep both parents in their lives, and maintain their

Divorce often results in major feelings of failure, rejection, and isolation.

friendship networks. Grandparents, too, can provide stability during these traumatic times.

As we have seen, family is a diverse and complex social institution. Families prepare the next generation. They talk—and many pray—together about what happens after death. They provide care for disabled, infirm, or sick members. As a basic institution, the family plays a role in the vitality of the entire nation.

Same-Sex Marriage

As same-sex relationships have become more widely acknowledged and accepted in the Global North, increasing numbers of gay and lesbian couples live together openly as families. Denmark was the first country to recognize same-sex unions, granting legal rights to such couples in 1989. In 2001, the Netherlands was the first country to allow same-sex marriages. The U.S. Supreme Court declared same-sex marriages legal in all 50 states on June 26, 2015. As of October 2015, 22 countries allow same-sex couples to marry (see Figure 10.7) (McCarthy 2015). Some countries, however, punish openly gay and lesbian individuals. Uganda almost passed a bill authorizing the death penalty for homosexuals,

FIGURE 10.7   Countries Where Same-Sex Marriage Is Legal

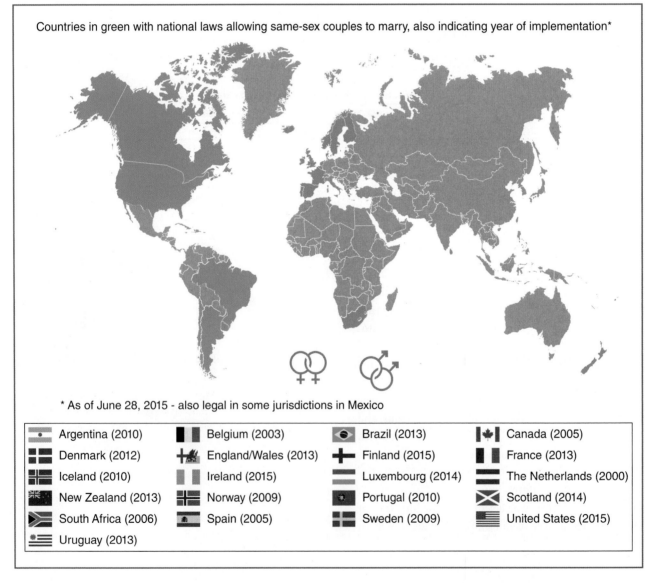

Countries in green with national laws allowing same-sex couples to marry, also indicating year of implementation*

* As of June 28, 2015 - also legal in some jurisdictions in Mexico

Argentina (2010)	Belgium (2003)	Brazil (2013)	Canada (2005)
Denmark (2012)	England/Wales (2013)	Finland (2015)	France (2013)
Iceland (2010)	Ireland (2015)	Luxembourg (2014)	The Netherlands (2000)
New Zealand (2013)	Norway (2009)	Portugal (2010)	Scotland (2014)
South Africa (2006)	Spain (2005)	Sweden (2009)	United States (2015)
Uruguay (2013)			

Source: McCarthy (2015).

but it was deterred by international condemnation. Nigeria has passed a bill outlawing homosexuality, and mobs have attacked LGBTQ people in that nation (Goodstein 2012).

In the United States, support for same-sex marriage has rapidly increased, and the number of married couples is now estimated to be between 170,000 (according to the Pew Research Center) and 390,000 (according to a Gallup poll). There are also an estimated 1.2 million U.S. adults living in same-sex domestic partnerships (Cohn 2015; Schwartz 2015). Most scholars acknowledge that this is probably an underreporting because of continuing stigma in reporting that one is gay or lesbian.

One reason many people in the LGBTQ community had been so intent on the legalization of same-sex marriage is that same-sex partnerships were *insufficiently institutionalized*, making them somewhat less stable and creating ambiguity about their roles and rights (Cherlin 1978; Stewart 2007). LGBTQ advocates argue that if we actually believe that stable relationships and families make for a healthier and more stable society, then families with same-sex adults need public recognition.

Opponents of same-sex marriage argue that marriage has been a function of the church, temple, and mosque for centuries. Marriage was historically governed in Europe by the church or temple until Martin Luther insisted that the government play a role. Gradually, after that time, marriage came to be monitored and recorded by governments. Still, that did not happen in England until as recently as 1837, so religious groups have defined marriage for most of Western history (England Church Records 2014). None of the religious traditions has historically recognized same-sex relationships as legitimate (although a number are doing so now). Some opponents appeal to biology with the assertion that marriage is a legitimate way to propagate the species. Because same-sex unions do not serve this purpose, they do not serve the society, according to these opponents of same-sex marriage. However, many same-sex couples are providing loving, supportive homes for children, their own or adopted.

The controversy about same-sex marriage has been a passionate one precisely because the family is so very important to society and to people's lives. Social and legal legitimacy helps to stabilize those important relationships, which, in turn, helps to bring stability to the society.

It is a deeply personal social tie, but it has implications for the larger society.

EDUCATION

WHAT ARE WE LEARNING?

Schooling—learning skills such as reading and math via systematic instruction by a trained professional—is a universal means of socialization; yet it is a luxury some children will never know. In most urban areas around the world and in all areas of affluent countries, formal education has become a necessity. **Formal education** is *schooling that takes place in a formal setting with the goal of teaching a predetermined curriculum.* Education of the masses in a school setting is actually a modern concept that developed when literacy and math skills became essential for societies with democratic forms of government and for many jobs (even if just to read instructions for operating machinery). In this part, we focus on micro-level interactions in educational organizations, what happens in schools after the school bell rings, and whether education is the road to opportunity.

THE INS AND OUTS OF LOCAL SCHOOLS: MICRO-LEVEL INTERACTIONS

The process of education takes place at the micro level in the classrooms and corridors and on the playgrounds of local schools, with players who enact the everyday drama of teaching and learning. At the micro level, much sociological analysis has focused on interpersonal exchanges within the classroom and in the school as a social setting within a community. Sociologists look at roles and statuses in educational settings and the informal norms and interaction patterns that evolve in those settings. We begin by reviewing two micro-level theories and how they make sense of some common in-school interactions.

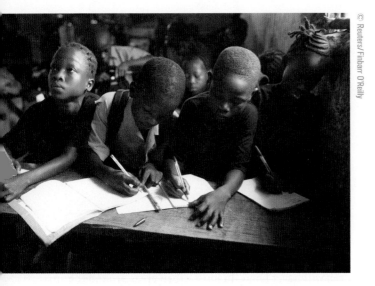

Overcrowding in classrooms is not uncommon in Global South countries, such as Sierra Leone, where these schoolchildren work to gain the skills they will need to "make" it in our global economy. Some countries have as many as 45 children per classroom.

Statuses and Roles in the Education System

Students, teachers, staff, and administrators hold statuses, or positions, in educational systems. These statuses are part of the larger school organization at the meso level, and individuals hold them only during their tenure in the organization. The roles associated with each status in educational organizations bring both obligations and challenges. When those in each status agree on expected behaviors (role expectations), schools function smoothly. When they do not agree, conflicts can arise.

Students and the Peer Culture of Schools. In a private Rwandan secondary school, students crowd onto benches. They are quiet, respectful, and very hardworking. They know that they are in a privileged position, and many students are lined up to take their place on the bench should they not carry out their roles, work hard, and succeed. Although they have no written texts, students write down the lectures in their notebooks and memorize the material. In some countries, such as Rwanda, going to high school is a privilege. In others, such as the United States, it is a necessary part of life that many students resist.

Schools exist to serve students and to expand their skills and knowledge. Still, there are many dynamics within a school that may undermine that primary objective. The role expectations of anyone in the status of student can be complicated by variables such as race, ethnicity, gender, sexual orientation, and socioeconomic standing. Thus, the experience of being a student can be quite different for different students. Consider a child whose family has recently immigrated to the United States and does not yet understand English. She may feel that her entire culture is being denigrated because her language and ethnic history are ignored or even scorned. This would not be an environment in which she would feel safe or respected, both of which are needed for learning to occur.

There are many dynamics within a school that may undermine students' capacity to learn. In addition to race, class, and gender, health status can also impact students' ability to receive a good education. Sick children tend to miss more days of school than healthy children. Children with more highly educated and affluent parents tend to be healthier than those with less educated parents and those who live in poverty (Bloom, Jones, and Freeman 2013).

In turn, education levels impact health. Those with higher levels of education are less likely to have heart attacks, strokes, hypertension, high cholesterol, emphysema, diabetes, asthma, and ulcers. They also miss fewer days of work, just as healthier students tend to be absent from school less often than sick children (Picker, 2014).

Gender issues make schooling complex. Research for several decades showed that boys were favored by teachers and given more privileges and scored higher in many academic areas than girls. However, researchers point out the incredible gains in recent years made by females, who tend to study more and be more compliant in school than boys. In Global South countries, the picture is not rosy. For example, for every 100 boys, there are 66 girls in primary and secondary school in Afghanistan; 69 in the Central African Republic, and 68 in Chad (World Bank 2013a). Studies show, though, that schooling has a very positive influence on the life chances of women, their children, and the whole society.

Some of the benefits of educating girls in poorer countries include higher wages, increased agricultural productivity, accelerated economic growth, and better health in the society overall (Sperling 2006). More educated girls and women

- have lower fertility rates,
- are less likely to die in childbirth,

- are less likely to have their infants die,
- are less likely to contract HIV/AIDS,
- have increased labor force participation and earnings,
- provide better health care and education to their children,
- lift households out of poverty, and
- pass these benefits on to the next generation (World Bank 2012).

One indicator of girls' success in education in the United States is the *feminization* of higher education. Since 1980, more women in the United States have gone to and graduated from college than men. In 2014, 71% of women entered college right after high school versus 61% of men. This gender pattern held true for all U.S. racial groups: Whites (72% vs. 62%), Blacks (69% vs. 57%), Hispanics (76% vs. 62%), and Asians (86% vs. 83%) (Lopez and Gonzalez-Barrera 2014b).

An estimated 18% of youth between the ages of 16 and 24—mostly ethnic and racial minorities—are without postsecondary education and are neither in school nor employed. High dropout rates are part of a phenomenon that the Children's Defense Fund calls the *cradle-to-prison pipeline*, with 1 of every 3 African American boys expected to eventually be imprisoned (Children's Defense Fund 2013). College attendance rates also vary markedly by race and ethnicity, as shown in Table 10.3 (Lopez and Gonzalez-Barrera 2014a).

Teachers: The Front Line. Teachers in the classroom occupy the front line in implementing the goals of the school, the community, and the society. Teachers

Table 10.3 College Attendance Rates (percent of each group attending college)

Race	College Attendance Rate
Asian	66.9
White	44.9
Black	35.6
Hispanic	34.3

Source: Pew Research Center (2015b).

Schoolgirls in Kenya wait for classes to begin. Children like this, whose parents can afford to send them to school, will have more life chances than those who cannot attain an education. Conflict theorists point out that inequality is deeply embedded in the institution of education.

serve as gatekeepers, controlling the flow of students, activities, resources, and privileges. One scholar estimated that teachers have more than a thousand interactions a day in their roles as classroom managers (P. Jackson 1968).

As primary socializers and role models for students, teachers are expected to support and encourage students and, at the same time, judge their performance—giving grades and recommendations. This creates role strain, which can interfere with the task of teaching and contribute to teacher burnout. U.S. teachers are held accountable for students' progress, as measured on standardized tests. Although teachers play a role in how students do on these tests, other factors, such as the influence of students' families and peers, also influence test scores. This can cause stress for teachers and an overemphasis on teaching only material that will help students earn high scores on standardized tests (Dworkin and Tobe 2012).

In some other nations of the world, like Japan, teachers are treated with great respect and honor. They receive salaries and respect commensurate with those in industry and professions such as law and medicine (Ballantine, Hammack, and Stuber 2017). In Europe, many high schools are organized like universities. Teachers think of themselves as akin to professors. In contrast, studies in

Australia and the United States show teachers feel they are unappreciated and not treated with much respect (Saha and Dworkin 2006). In the United States, high school teachers think of themselves as more like middle school teachers than like university professors (Legters 2001). Raising the respect for teaching requires better recruiting and training and upgrading the status and pay of teachers (Ingersoll and Merrill 2015). For example, we may learn something from Finland, which tops other OECD nations in test scores. Finland has very competitive teaching programs, and all teachers, even in primary schools, must have a master's degree. Teachers have higher-than-average salaries, freedom to create their own curriculum, and high status in their society ("How Finnish Schools Shine" 2012).

Thinking Sociologically

Who should create curricula for public schools? Who should enforce high teacher standards: the federal, state, and local government or teacher unions? Explain your answers, and describe how to carry out what you envision.

Administrators: The Managers of the School System. Key administrators—superintendents, assistant superintendents, principals and assistant principals, and head teachers—hold the top positions in the educational hierarchy of local schools. They are responsible for a long list of tasks: issuing budget reports; engaging in staff negotiations; hiring, firing, and training staff members; meeting with parents; carrying out routine approval of projects; managing public relations; preparing reports for boards of directors, local education councils, legislative bodies, and national agencies; keeping up with new regulations; and many other tasks.

The Informal System: What Really Happens Inside a School?

It is the first day of high school, and the teacher asks a question. Should you respond or let someone else answer? If you respond, the teacher might be impressed, but the other students might think you are showing off or trying to become a teacher's favorite. What if you answer incorrectly and sound foolish? Does that scenario sound familiar to you?

The informal system of schooling includes the unspoken, unwritten, and implicit norms of behavior that we learn in school. These norms may be created or enforced by teachers or by the student peer culture. The informal system does not appear in written goal statements or course syllabi but nevertheless influences our experience in school in important ways. Dimensions of the informal system include the hidden curriculum, the educational climate, the value climate, power dynamics, and coping strategies in the classroom.

The **hidden curriculum** *refers to the implicit "rules of the game" that students learn in school* (Ballantine, Hammack, and Stuber 2017; Snyder 1971). It includes everything not explicitly taught, such as unstated social and academic norms. Students have to learn and respond to these rules to be socially accepted and succeed in the education system (Snyder 1971).

In many societies, children attend preschool and kindergarten, which provide the basis for schooling in the society (Neuman 2005). During these early school years, teachers teach children to follow rules, to cooperate with each other, and to accept the teacher as the boss who gives orders and controls how time is spent (Gracey 1967). Sometimes, students learn that being tardy has a bigger impact on grades than whether one has actually learned the material. Teachers instill such lessons in students even though they are not part of the formal curriculum of reading, writing, and arithmetic. These less formal messages form an alternative set of "three Rs"—rules, routines, and regulations.

According to functional theorists, it is through the hidden curriculum that students learn the expectations, behaviors, and values necessary to succeed in school and society. For conflict theorists, the hidden curriculum is a social and economic agenda that maintains class differences. Many working-class schools stress order and discipline, teaching students to obey rules and accept their lot as responsible, punctual workers (Willis 1979). More is expected of elites, and in higher-income schools, students have greater responsibility and opportunities for problem solving that result in higher achievement (Brookover and Erickson 1975).

Thinking Sociologically

What are some examples of the hidden curriculum you learned in your K–12 education? How has this training impacted how you act now in college?

STRUCTURE AND FUNCTION OF EDUCATION: MESO-LEVEL ANALYSIS

Schools can be like mazes, with passages to negotiate, hallways lined with lockers, and classrooms that set the scene for the education process. Schools are mazes in a much larger sense as well. They involve complex, interwoven social systems at the meso level—the state agencies above the local community that affect a school's operations. At this level, we encounter the formal organization of the school system in a more bureaucratized form.

Organizational requirements of education systems at a meso level can influence the personal student–teacher relationship at the micro level. Bureaucratic systems provide a way to document and process masses of students coming from different backgrounds in an efficient and cost-effective way. Yet the very structure that facilitates mass education may put constraints on individual classrooms and students with different learning styles and problems.

Bureaucratic School Structure

Recall Weber's bureaucratic model of groups and organizations, discussed in Chapter 5. The points below show how bureaucracy applies to schools.

1. Schools have a division of labor among administrators, teachers, students, and support personnel. The roles associated with the statuses are part of the school structure. Individual teachers or students hold these roles for a limited time and are replaced by others coming into the system.
2. The administrative hierarchy incorporates a chain of command and channels of communication.
3. Specific rules and procedures in a school cover everything from course content to discipline in the classroom and use of the schoolyard.
4. Personal relationships are downplayed in favor of formalized relations among members of the system, such as placement on the basis of tests and grades.
5. Rationality governs the operations of the organization; people are hired and fired on the basis of their qualifications and how well they do their jobs (unless or until they attain tenure) (Weber 1947).

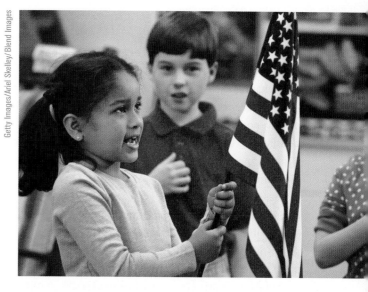

Getty Images/Ariel Skelley/Blend Images

Four-year-old preschoolers recite the Pledge of Allegiance. Developing patriotism is part of the implicit and informal curriculum of schools—and sometimes part of the formal curriculum.

One result of bureaucracy is that some children's special needs—such as personal problems or learning difficulties—are not always met (Kozol 2006; Sizer 1984; Waters 2012). Impersonal rules can lock people into rigid behavior patterns, leading to apathy and alienation. In schools, these feelings cause passivity or acting out among students, which, in turn, frustrates teachers. These children view school not as a privilege but as a requirement imposed by an adult world. Caught between the demands of an impersonal bureaucracy and individual goals for their students, teachers cannot always give every child the personal help she or he needs. Thus, we see how organizational requirements of education systems at a meso level can influence the personal student–teacher relationship at the micro level.

Functions of Education. Formal education in schools serves certain crucial purposes in society, especially as societies modernize. The functions of education as a social institution are outlined in Table 10.4. Note that some functions are planned and formalized (*manifest functions*), whereas others are unintended and unorganized—the informal results of the educational process (*latent functions*). Latent functions of schooling are often just as important to the society as manifest functions. For example, imagine what would happen to productivity if schools did not give parents release time from childcare responsibilities so that they could perform other roles.

The means of carrying out the manifest functions do not go unchallenged, especially when decisions about what should be taught and how are discussed. Consider conflicts that occur routinely in many local communities over what to teach in sex education and science courses, as well as over content thought to contain obscenity, sex, nudity, political or economic bias, profanity, slang or nonstandard English, racism or racial hatred, and antireligious or presumed anti-American sentiment. For example, Family Friendly Libraries, an online grassroots interest group that started in Virginia argues that the popular *Harry Potter* books should be banned from school libraries. The members of this group believe the series promotes the religion of witchcraft (DeMitchell and Carney 2005). Each year the American Library Association studies the most frequently challenged books. In 2013, they included *Captain Underpants* (Dav Pikey), *The Bluest Eye* (Toni Morrison), *The Absolutely True Diary of a Part-Time Indian* (Sherman Alexie), *Fifty Shades of Grey* (E. L. James), *The Hunger Games* (Suzanne Collins), *A Bad Boy Can Be Good for a Girl* (Tanya Lee Stone), *Looking for Alaska* (John Green), *The Perks of Being a Wallflower* (Stephen Chbosky), *Bless Me Ultima* (Rudolfo Anaya), and *Bone* (Jeff Smith). (To see the most recent list and the reasons they were banned, go to www.ala.org/bbooks/frequentlychallengedbooks/top10.)

These battles over curriculum are so fierce because the vast majority of U.S. schoolchildren attend public schools, one institution where differences of opinion are played out because parents can have a say about the curriculum. We now turn to how both public and private schools can produce and reproduce inequality from one generation to the next.

Education and the Family

The social institutions of family and education impact each other in many ways, some of which we have already mentioned. When children enter kindergarten or primary school, they bring their prior experience, including socialization experiences and cultural capital from a parent or parents, brothers, sisters, and other relatives (Jaeger 2011). Family background, according to many sociologists, is the single most important influence on children's school achievement. Children succeed, in large part, because of what their parent(s) do to support them in their education (Jaeger 2011).

Most families stress the importance of education, but they do so in different ways. Often, teachers' perceptions of their students and behavior toward them are influenced by their interactions with parents. Middle- and upper-class parents are more likely to ask about their children's progress, consult with teachers on strategies to help them learn better at home and in the classroom, and make it clear that they want teachers to focus on their children. Parents from lower-socioeconomic-status families tend to be less involved in their children's schooling, with less time to help with homework and fewer interactions with teachers. Language barriers (for new immigrants), lack of time (for single parents and those working many hours per week), and views toward

Table 10.4 Key Functions of Formal Education (Schools)

Manifest Functions (intended; formalized)
• Teach students the skills necessary to become educated, effective participants of society.
• Socialize children to be productive members of society.
• Select individuals for key positions in society.
• Promote social participation, change, and innovation.
• Enhance personal independence and social development.
Latent Functions (unintended; informal)
• Confine and supervise underage citizens.
• Weaken parental controls over youths.
• Provide opportunities for peer cultures to develop.
• Provide contexts for the development of friendships and mate selection.

teachers (as authority figures who should be left alone to do their job) are some of the reasons many lower-income parents do not play an active role in their children's schooling (Cheung and Pomerantz 2012). Children who must make educational decisions on their own have a greater likelihood of doing poorly or dropping out of school (Jaeger 2011).

Wealthier students also tend to be healthier students—another advantage in the educational institution. Healthier children do better academically. Children from low-income families tend to have less access to nutritious food and safe areas to play. Providing a variety of healthy food choices at school and devising ways to make exercise fun and available for all students can impact the health gap between poor and wealthier students as well as educational inequality. Recognizing the connection between health and educational achievement, as well as the obesity epidemic, the Obama administration established higher nutritional standards for school lunches, working to ensure that low-income students who rely on free or reduced-price lunches have healthy meals to eat (Nixon 2012).

When children are hungry, they are not likely to concentrate on learning. Thus, provision of quality nutrition for low-income children has become an issue in educational programs. The federal government has stepped in to provide support and standards for nutrition in schools.

Thinking Sociologically

Provide some examples of links between academic success in schools and at least two other social institutions.

EDUCATION ISSUES: THE ROAD TO OPPORTUNITY?

Elite preparatory (prep) schools in England, Japan, the United States, and many other countries traditionally have been the training ground for the sons and daughters of the elite. Because elite schools are very expensive and highly selective, affluent members of society have the most access to them and thereby learn class privilege and advantage (Howard and Gaztambide-Fernandez 2010; Persell and Cookson 1985; Wade 2012). Only about 8% of U.S. students attended private K–12 schools in 2011 (Ewert 2013). Elite schools perpetuate elevated prestige and "reproduce social class."

When elites of society protect their educational advantages, the result is **reproduction of class**—*the socioeconomic positions of one generation passing on to the next.* This process takes place, in part, through the socialization of young people into adult work roles and compliance with the modern economic and political institutions and their needs. Schools teach students from lower socioeconomic positions to obey authority and accept the dominant ideology that justifies social inequality. If citizens believe that those with the best educations and jobs in their society personally earned them, they are not motivated to change the system. By promoting the legitimacy of the system, schools serve the interests of the privileged (Bowles and Gintis 2002; R. Collins 2004).

Critics of the increasing efforts to promote school choice and more charter schools (publicly funded independent schools) fear that public schools might be left with the least capable students and teachers, further stratifying an already troubled system. Students often gain entrance into charter schools through a lottery for which some—but not all—parents register. This can result in a "creaming process" that leaves traditional public schools with students whose parents are less involved in their educational process. This leads us to our next issue: Can schools bring about equality in societies?

Thinking Sociologically

Consider the community in which you went to high school. Do you think the education there enhances upward social mobility and serves all students and the community, or does it serve the affluent, reproducing social class and training people to fulfill positions at the same level as their parents, or is it some combination of the two? Explain.

Can Schools Bring About Equality in Societies?

Equal opportunity exists when all people have an equal chance of achieving high socioeconomic status in society regardless of their class, ethnicity, race, or gender (Riordan 2004). James Coleman describes the meaning and goals of equal opportunity:

- To provide a common curriculum for all children regardless of background
- To allow children from diverse backgrounds to attend the same school
- To provide equality within a given locality (Coleman 1968, 1975, 1990)

Equal educational opportunity *means that children are provided with equal facilities, financing, and access to school programs.* Schools in poor neighborhoods or in rural villages around the world, however, often lack the basics: safe buildings, school supplies and books, and funds to operate. Students who live in these areas fall disproportionately to the bottom of the educational hierarchy. Many children face what seem to be insurmountable barriers to educational success, such as poverty, lack of health care, homelessness, hunger, and pressure to drop

Does it matter how one gets to school? These children who live near Inle Lake in Myanmar (Burma) take a gondola school bus—the only option for them. For a photo essay and further exploration about transportation to and from school, visit www.SAGE.com/ballantineOSWc5e.

out to help the family (Kozol 2012; Noguera 2011). These conditions at home and in neighborhoods affect children's achievement in school and on standardized test scores (Boger and Orfield 2009; J. S. Coleman 1990).

Who Gets Ahead and Why? The Role of Education in Stratification

Any school or educational institution is supposed to be a *meritocracy*, a social group or organization in which people are allocated to positions according to their abilities and credentials, as in level of education attained. This, of course, is consistent with the principles of a meritocratic social system, where the most qualified person is promoted, and decisions are impersonal and based on "credentials" (Charles, Roscigno, and Torres 2007). Still, in societies around the world, we see evidence that middle-class and elite children receive more and better education than equally qualified poor children. Children do not attend school on an equal footing, and in many cases, meritocracy does not exist at all.

Three practices that tend to lead to inequality in schools—testing, tracking, and funding—illustrate how schools perpetuate and reproduce social class and social stratification systems. They also give clues as to what might be done to mitigate inequality in education.

Assessing Student Achievement: Testing. Testing is one means of placing students in schools according to their achievement and merit and of determining academic progress. Yet many scholars, including sociologists of education, argue that standardized test questions, the vocabulary employed, and testing situations disadvantage lower-class, minority, and immigrant students. These disadvantages often result in lower scores among these groups, relegating these students to lower tracks in the education system (Gardner 1987, 1999; M. Smith 2008).

Moreover, higher-income parents have the means to seek educational opportunities outside of school that give their children a further edge over other students on standardized tests. Families with more economic resources can provide more chances to learn through travel, going to museums, and mixing with members of the elite. They can also provide **shadow education**—*learning opportunities outside of school, such as tutoring, test prep, and summer programs* (Buchmann, Condron, and Roscigno 2010). Table 10.5, in the next "Engaging Sociology," shows differences in ACT and SAT scores depending on sex, race, and ethnic group. Answer the questions posed as you engage with the following sociological data.

ENGAGING SOCIOLOGY

Test Score Variations by Gender and Race or Ethnicity, 2015

Evaluate your testing experiences and compare them with those of other groups.

Table 10.5   ACT and SAT Scores by Gender and Race or Ethnicity

ACT Scores	Average	SAT Scores	Average
Composite, total scores	21.0	SAT Writing, all students	484
Male*	21.2	Male*	482
Female*	20.9	Female*	493
White	22.4	White	513
Black/African American	17.1	Black/African American	418
American Indian/Alaska Native	17.9	American Indian/Alaska Native	460
Hispanic	18.9	Hispanic	439
Asian American	23.9	Asian American	531
SAT Scores	**Average**	**SAT Scores**	**Average**
SAT Critical Reading, all students	495	SAT Math, all students	514
Male*	496	Male*	531
Female*	494	Female*	499
White	529	White	534
Black/African American	431	Black/African American	428
Hispanic	449	Hispanic	457
Asian American	525	Asian American	598
American Indian/Alaska Native	481	American Indian/Alaska Native	482

*No male/female scores listed for 2015; scores reflect 2013 data.

Source: ACT (2013); College Board (2013); Jaschik (2016a, 2016b).

* * * * * * *

Engaging With Sociology

1. Do you think your scores were an accurate measure of your ability or achievement? Why, or why not?

2. Do you think your race or ethnicity, social class, or gender affected your scores? Why, or why not?

3. Have your scores affected your life chances? Are there ways in which you have been privileged or disprivileged in the testing process?

4. What might be some causes of the variation in test scores between groups or categories of students?

Student Tracking. Judgments by school administrators, counselors, and teachers affect children for a lifetime. There are several forms of separating students by ability in schools. *Ability grouping places students into different-level groups within classes.* This is often done by tracking or streaming. *Tracking* separates students into different-level classes within a school. *Streaming*, practiced in Europe and Asia but not in the United States, separates students into different secondary schools. All of these practices have the goal of allowing educators to more effectively address the needs of students of different abilities.

Many sociologists of education have argued against tracking, pointing out that it contributes to the stratification process that perpetuates inequality. Research finds that levels at which students are tracked correlate with factors such as the child's background and ethnic group, language skills, appearance, and other socioeconomic variables (Loveless 2013; Rosenbaum 1999; A. Wells and Oakes 1996). Students from lower social classes and minority groups tend to be clustered in the lower tracks and complete fewer years of school (Lucas and Berends 2002; Oakes et al. 1997). In other words, track placement is not always a measure of a student's ability. It can be arbitrary, based on teachers' impressions or questionable test results. Even language differences between teachers and students can affect placement.

On the other hand, tracking provides many benefits for teachers and students. In tracked classes, teachers do not have to slow down to help some students catch up while trying to make sure that their more advanced students are not bored. Students tend to make more progress when working in groups with similar academic aptitudes.

Thinking Sociologically

Were you tracked in any subjects? What effect, if any, did this have on you? What effect did tracking have on friends of yours? How might tracking shape friendship networks?

School Funding. The amount of money available to fund schools affects the types of programs they can offer, an important issue for nations that must compete in the global social and economic system. Money for education, in some societies, comes from central governments and, in others, from a combination of federal, state, and local government and private sources, such as tuition, religious denominations, and philanthropies. In the United States, public school spending comes from local property taxes, as well as state and federal funds. On average, local governments provide 44% of education funding for elementary and secondary school budgets from income taxes, corporate taxes, sales taxes, and fees. States provide about 43%, mostly from property taxes. About 12% of education funding comes from the federal government (New America Foundation 2014).

The Elementary and Secondary Education Act, first passed by Congress in 1965, requires equitable state and local funding for high-poverty and low-income schools. States must send more money to low-income districts that have less money coming in from the local community than high-income districts. Many states were slow to respond to this requirement, and controversies over equitable school funding in the United States have reached the courtroom in a number of states. Most states, however, now contribute more state money to poor areas, so funding is distributed more evenly across districts within states than it once was (Education Law Center 2013). Federal money has also helped narrow the gap in funding (Brown 2015).

Getty/RJ Sangosti/Contributor

Funding is a serious issue in many school districts, and rather than raise taxes, some school systems, such as this one in Colorado, have decided to sell advertising on the sides of school buses. Having a particular product being apparently "endorsed" by the school and exposed daily to children raises some concerns for some citizens.

The family and education are two of the first institutions that a child encounters and that follow her or him throughout life. Both institutions have a primary concern with the process of socialization.

Another supportive and essential institution is one that addresses health and illness, and the next chapter examines the role of medicine in our society and our lives.

WHAT HAVE WE LEARNED?

Our happiest and saddest experiences are integrally intertwined with family. Family provides the foundation through which individuals' needs are met and helps prepare children for the demands of society. Societies depend on families as the unit through which to funnel services. They provide the base from which other institutions—education, religion, politics, economics, and health care—carry out their functions.

The educational institution has a vested interest in stability but is also viewed as a means to reduce inequality by training children for upward mobility in society. Schools foster patriotism and loyalty toward political systems. It should not be surprising, therefore, that most schools do more to enhance stability than to create change that might threaten those who have power, privilege, and influence. Still, many families put faith in schools providing their children with the means to succeed in society. Schools work largely with young minds in the socialization process—carrying out what powerful policy makers feel is important.

- Families are diverse entities at the micro level, having many forms in different societies; they help carry out needs for societies to replace and train members.

- The family is sometimes called the most basic unit of society, providing the core unit for pairing into groups (partner taking), for making and socializing new members of society (people making), and sometimes for contract breaking.

- The process of partner taking involves rules of exogamy, endogamy, free choice or arranged marriage, and polygamy or monogamy.

- Power within a partnership—distribution of tasks and decision making—is determined within each family, guided by societal norms.

- The structure of the family has changed in recent years, with more single-parent families, more couples cohabitating outside of marriage, and the legalization of same-sex marriages in a majority of states in the United States

- Education is one of the primary institutions of society, focusing on the socialization of children and adults into their cultures so that they become contributing members.

- At the micro level, various statuses and roles interact within a school, and classrooms develop their own cultures that may or may not enhance learning.

- What we learn in schools goes far beyond the formal curriculum. We also learn a *hidden curriculum* in school that helps socialize us into our roles in society.

- At the micro level, social theory is attentive to interaction in classrooms and local schools, using concepts of symbolic interaction or cost–benefit analysis to understand the climate of learning.

- At the meso level, education can be understood as a formal organization that works toward certain goals (bureaucracy) but that has many of the dysfunctions of other bureaucracies.

DISCUSSION QUESTIONS

1. Does (or did) your family expect you to marry someone of a particular (a) race or ethnicity, (b) social class, (c) educational background, or (d) religion? Why, or why not? How do you think endogamous norms impact (a) individual marriages and (b) society?

2. What are arguments for and against monogamy versus polygamy as a form of marriage? Which might be more stable, and why?

3. A majority of Americans and a strong majority of young Americans (those below 30) now support same-sex marriages. What are some cultural and structural changes that have led to this increase in support for marriage equality over the past decade?

4. What are examples of the *hidden curriculum* in schools? Describe your own school experience with the formal and informal systems.

5. Do you think there should be tracking in schools? Why, or why not? How has tracking (or an absence of tracking) in your school impacted your education and sense of yourself as a student? How does tracking in schools impact society?

6. How do schools "reproduce and perpetuate social stratification"? If you had the power and desire to use the school system to reduce inequality, what policies would you implement? What do you think the chances are of your policies actually being put into place? Why?

KEY TERMS

ability grouping   308
arranged marriages   290
endogamy   289
equal educational
    opportunity   306
exogamy   289

extended families   288
family of orientation   288
family of procreation   288
formal education   299
free-choice marriage   290
hidden curriculum   302

institutions   280
monogamy   289
nuclear family   288
polygamy   289
reproduction of class   305
shadow education   306

CONTRIBUTING TO OUR SOCIAL WORLD: WHAT CAN WE DO?

At the Local Level

• *Support groups for married or partnered students* respond to the needs of an ever-increasing number of undergraduate students living on or near campus with spouses, partners, and children. If your campus has a support group, arrange to attend a meeting, and work with members to help them meet the challenges associated with their family situation. If such a group does not exist, consider forming one.

• Is there *day care available on your campus*? Day care on campus can be invaluable for parents. If

there is, look at the cost and availability of care for the children of faculty, staff, and students. If there is no day care, look at the possibilities of creating, funding, and staffing one. How might it benefit the college or university, as well as the families it will serve?

• Some colleges and universities have established programs called *FIGs (First-Year Interest Groups)* to assist first-year students as they adjust to college and help them form a community with other students. Learn more about FIGs at schools such as the University of Wisconsin (http://figs.wisc.edu). If your school does not have this program, try to initiate one.

At the Organizational or Institutional Level

- *House builders* have begun to change how they design some houses in order to meet the needs of multigeneration households. Contact your local *Habitat for Humanity* chapter (www.habitat.org), and ask if you can help the organization create more homes suitable for such households. You can find some ideas for such homes at http://articles.chicagotribune.com/2012-09-10/special/chi-primetime-multigen-091412_1_bedroom-floor-plan-designs.

- Most primary schools welcome *reading and math tutors*, volunteers and service-learning students who can read to young students and tutor them in reading and math. Contact a faculty member on your campus who specializes in early childhood education, and investigate the opportunities for such volunteer work.

- *Volunteers of America* (www.voa.org) chapters organize to provide low-income and homeless children with school supplies and backpacks every year through Operation Backpack. You can learn more about the program and how to locate your local VOA chapter at the VOA website or by Googling "VOA" and "Operation Backpack" and the name of your state.

At the National and Global Levels

- *Voices* is a multi-issue advocacy group for children, with member organizations across the nation. The organization strives to improve the lives of children and their families, particularly those most at risk. You can learn about the issues on which this group is working and join its efforts, if you would like to do so, by going to its website at www.voices.org.

- *Teach for America* (www.teachforamerica.org), a national organization, modeled along the lines of AmeriCorps and Peace Corps, places recent college graduates in short-term (approximately 2-year) assignments teaching in economically disadvantaged neighborhood schools. "Teach for America is the national corps of outstanding recent college graduates and professionals of all academic majors and career interests who commit 2 years to teach in urban and rural public schools and become leaders in the effort to expand educational opportunity. . . . [Its] mission is to build the movement to eliminate educational inequity by enlisting our nation's most promising future leaders in the effort."

- *Teaching abroad* provides an opportunity to make a difference in the lives of children. Consider teaching English abroad through one of many organizations that sponsor teachers. Visit www.globaltesol.com, www.teachabroad.com, www.jetprogramme.org, and related websites.

$SAGE edge™

Get the edge on your studies. **edge.sagepub.com/ballantinecondensed5e**

- Take a quiz to find out what you've learned.
- Review key terms with eFlashcards.
- Watch videos that enhance chapter content.

iStock/laflor

11

Health Care

An Anatomy of Health and Illness

Health and illness are social matters, influenced by social interactions, affected by complex organizations intended to provide health care, and shaped by social policies at national and global levels. Sociological analyses look deeply into these processes.

ME (AND MY TEACHERS AND CLASSMATES)

LOCAL ORGANIZATIONS AND COMMUNITY
Neighborhood schools and classrooms within those schools affect our everyday lives.

NATIONAL ORGANIZATIONS, INSTITUTIONS, AND ETHNIC SUBCULTURES
State or provincial funding, regulations, and learning standards affect local schools.

SOCIETY
National policies are also developed to improve schools.

GLOBAL COMMUNITY
United Nations programs try to improve education in poor countries.

WHAT YOU WILL LEARN IN THIS CHAPTER

This chapter will help you do the following:

11.1 Provide examples of health at the societal level. Illustrate how health issues impact us at the micro, meso, and macro levels.

11.2 Use the symbolic interaction perspective to show that illness is a social construction.

11.3 Describe the role of the sick person.

11.4 Explain modern hospitals as complex organizations with bureaucratic features.

11.5 Describe how globalization influences health care issues at micro, meso, and macro levels.

◑ THINK ABOUT IT

Micro: Local community	What does it mean for you to be sick or healthy? Why is being sick a social status and not just an individual concern? How does the health or illness of family and community members affect the functioning of you and your local community?
Meso: National institutions, complex organizations, and ethnic groups	What type of health care system keeps people healthiest? Why?
Macro: National and global system	What are costs to the nation of having a national health care system, and what are the costs of not having one? How do health care systems vary around the world?

In late 2015, Angela traveled to visit her family in Puerto Rico. Three months pregnant, she faced a threat she had never imagined. The Zika virus was spreading across the island and posed a particular threat to pregnant women. The World Health Organization and the U.S. Centers for Disease Control and Prevention issued travel warnings (Centers for Disease Control and Prevention 2016a). The dilemma for pregnant women is that if they contract the mosquito-borne virus, their pregnancies may result in a child with microcephaly or other neurological disorders.

Two tragic cases—each involving brain-dead, pregnant women on life support—show that health care is not just an individual matter. It can necessitate decisions by family, medical practitioners, and even politicians. In the case of

Piergiorgio Welby, an Italian poet and artist, suffered from advanced muscular dystrophy and was confined to a bed, attached to a respirator. He was lucid and spoke via a computer that interpreted his eye movements. He petitioned the Italian government to let him commit medically assisted suicide and "find peace for my tortured and shattered body." The government finally granted his wish, but the church denied him a Catholic burial.

© AP Photo/Associazione Luca Coscioni

brain-dead Marlise Munoz from Texas, her husband and family wanted her taken off of life support, as she had expressed to them that she would never want to be kept alive that way. The hospital where she was admitted refused to do so, however, because Texas state law prohibited taking life support away from a pregnant woman, even though Munoz was only 14 weeks pregnant, and the fetus was not viable. After nearly two months, Munoz's husband sued the hospital, and she was taken off of life support by order of the district court in Tarrant County, Texas (CBS News 2014). In the case of brain-dead Robyn Benson from Victoria, British Columbia (Canada), 22 weeks pregnant, her family and doctors decided to keep her alive with feeding tubes and ventilators. The baby was successfully delivered by C-section 16 days later (Payne 2014). Who has the right to decide what to do in situations like this, when a patient cannot communicate?

Another end-of-life situation involved Debbie, a 20-year-old woman in Portland, Oregon, lying in pain and dying from ovarian cancer. She had not eaten or slept for 2 days and was struggling for air. She said to the young medical resident (doctor, in training) on duty, "Let's get this over with." The resident then gave her an injection of morphine, causing her to die 4 minutes later (Standler 2012). These cases and others like them raise great controversy in medical, legal, and religious communities. End-of-life legislation that determines if patients have the legal right to decide when to die is the topic of vociferous debates and varies across the United States and among nations throughout the world.

Today, anyone in the United States can sign a living will or right to die or do not resuscitate form, requesting that no extraordinary efforts be made to help keep the person alive when death would naturally occur (passive euthanasia). However, just six U.S. states (California, Colorado, Montana, Oregon, Vermont, and Washington) and the District of

Columbia give competent, terminally ill adults the legal right to commit medically assisted suicide. In Montana, the state supreme court ruled in 2009 that the state's Rights of the Terminally Ill Act includes the right to assisted suicide. Montana has yet, however, to pass legislation on assisted suicide that establishes rules on how it must be carried out (Death with Dignity 2017; FindLaw 2015).

Since Brittany Maynard's widely publicized medically assisted suicide in 2014, calls for legalization have increased throughout the United States. Similar legislation has been proposed and is now being debated in more than half the states in the nation (Monir 2015). Belgium, the Netherlands, and Switzerland have permitted physician-assisted suicide since 1942, even for nonterminal patients ("Assisted Suicide" 2012).

Under Death with Dignity laws in the United States, patients themselves, not doctors, administer the drugs. Those who wish to obtain a prescription for drugs to euthanize themselves under the California, Oregon, Washington, or Vermont laws must

- prove residency in one of the four states;
- be at least 18 years old;
- be able to make and communicate health care decisions for themselves;
- be diagnosed with a terminal illness, expected to lead to death within the next 6 months;
- have two physicians determine they have met the criteria above; and
- make two written requests for the prescription from the physician, witnessed by two people who are not family members or primary care givers.

The physician filling out the prescription must share with the patient all other possible options (e.g., hospice and pain management) and attest that the patient is mentally competent (Death with Dignity 2017). A scenario like the one with Debbie and the medical resident would be considered illegal under the Death with Dignity laws.

Those who favor euthanasia argue that (a) physicians should be able to create comfortable environments for death to occur, (b) terminally ill individuals have a right—without interference by the state—to determine how they die and to make the decision to die, (c) legal safeguards are available to prevent abuse of physician-assisted suicide, (d) high rates of self-induced suicide already exist among terminally ill patients, (e) a majority of the public favors legalization of physician-assisted suicides, and (f) extending life with no hope of recovery is costly to families, as well as to the medical care system.

Those opposed to euthanasia argue that (a) physicians are obligated to sustain life; (b) medical measures are available to relieve pain, so few have to suffer; (c) religious beliefs affirm the sanctity of life, which means supporting life at every turn; (d) terminally ill individuals who request to die often act out of depression, or they may feel pressured to accept a facilitated death to save the family's resources; and (e) a terminally ill patient's acceptance of active euthanasia may make suicide a more acceptable option for those people who are depressed, disabled, elderly, or mentally disabled (G. Weiss and Lonnquist 2015).

Relatively few people have chosen to use the Death with Dignity laws to arrange their own deaths. For example, in Oregon, since assisted suicide was legalized in 2007 until 2014, 1,327 were prescribed lethal medication, and 859 died by using it. Similarly low numbers of assisted-suicide deaths occur in the European nations that allow them ("Assisted Suicide" 2012; Monir 2015).

The cost of dying differs tremendously, from nothing in many poor Global South countries with no health care for the dying to many thousands of dollars per person in the United States. **Medicare** is *a government-run health insurance system for those 65 and older in the United States* but as the population ages, it faces great pressure to cover expenses. More than 1 out of every 4 Medicare dollars (or approximately $170 billion) was spent on patients' final 6 months of life (that's $42,500 per person) (Daucher 2015; Pasternak 2013). At the current rate and with projections on size of the elder population in the future, the Medicare system will deplete its funds by 2026 (Social Security and Medicare Boards of Trustees 2013).

Policy analysts point out that costs for elder care could be reduced and quality of care improved by providing more in-home services to allow people to die at home or in a hospice setting, rather than in an intensive-care unit of a hospital. Efforts to encourage this have yielded some positive results. The percentage of people dying at home or in hospice increased, respectively, from 23% to 27% and from 21.6% to 42.2% from 2000 to 2009. Today, about half of all older Americans spend some time in hospice before they die (Jaslow 2013; Whoriskey and Keating 2015).

How we die, where we die, who is with us when we die, and whether we have a choice about when to die are decisions bound in cultural values, beliefs, and laws. Death and its various issues are but one aspect of the interrelationship between our physical condition and our social system. In this chapter, we consider why health is a social issue and examine theoretical perspectives on health and illness, the status and roles of sick people, modern health care systems, and health care policy issues at the national and global levels.

WHY IS HEALTH A SOCIAL ISSUE?

One of the responsibilities of governments is to protect citizens. Therefore, one of the duties of governments is to keep diseases at bay. In parts of Nigeria, however, vaccination campaigns were suspended for several years. Muslim religious and political leaders in the northern part of the African country refused to allow international medical teams to immunize children against polio, a disease that had almost been eradicated elsewhere. The leaders had little trust in the motives of Western medical teams, as rumors circulated that immunization efforts were a plot to sterilize Muslims. As a result, two-year-old Abubarkar Al Hassan is just one of the children who can no longer run around with his friends. Stricken with polio, he must now be carried everywhere. The government now mandates such vaccines and, thanks to a nationwide vaccination program carried out with UNICEF, cases in Nigeria have declined (Cooke 2012; Otieno 2013).

Outbreaks of illness and death also occur within countries due to food poisoning; environmental problems, such as leaks of toxic chemicals; and contamination of medicines. In the United States, the government has set up several organizations, such as the Occupational Safety and Health Administration (OSHA), the Food and Drug Administration (FDA), and the Environmental Protection Agency (EPA), to protect workers and consumers from such threats. The powers of these agencies are limited (and adequate funding is always an issue), however, and examples of lack of adequate safeguards are easy to find. One example is Blue Bell Creameries recalling all of its products in April of 2015 due to a listeria contamination. Documents released by the FDA shortly after the recall indicate that the company had been aware of the listeria problem since 2013. At least three deaths have been linked to the listeria contamination (Abrams 2015). The point is that an important role of governments is to protect people's health, whether through food inspections, immunizations, or other means. Obviously, they are not always successful in doing so.

We now turn to some of the other factors that affect health, illness, and death in the world. **Health** is *a state of physical, mental, and social well-being or the absence of disease.* **Illness**, or *lack of health*, affects the way we perform our individual responsibilities in the social world. Like any social institution, *health care*—our efforts to foster health and treat illness—affects how individuals and groups carry out their lives at the micro, meso, and macro levels.

Health at the Micro Level

Sociologists examine how our state of health affects our ability to carry out social responsibilities. Our everyday lives are shaped by our own state of health or illness and those of our loved ones and close associates. If a roommate, significant other, or child is ill, it affects our lives in a number of ways. It alters our schedules, causes us to worry, and costs us time and (usually) money. If a parent injures her back or a child has leukemia, our lives are influenced in profound and disruptive ways.

Health at the Meso Level

The health of individual citizens can impact how a society functions. The institution of health care provides for the physical, mental, and social well-being of citizens. For example, one sick child can lead to a serious outbreak of influenza in the public schools, a meso-level institution. This could cause repercussions in workplaces throughout the community as parents struggle to deal with childcare issues and visits to the doctor. No doubt, if the outbreak spread dramatically, citizens would demand that their government act to address it. Thus, health status affects other institutions in the society, such as the government, the family, the educational system, and the workplace.

To illustrate how health care connects to the major social institutions in society, consider the following examples:

- *Economy*. Economically successful nations have more money to devote to health care.
- *Education*. Well-educated citizens are more likely to develop health-enhancing lifestyles.
- *Family*. Families often have responsibility to care for the sick.
- *Political systems*. Governments often determine standards for health care and regulate medical drugs.
- *Religion*. Religious organizations establish support systems and health services, sometimes offer faith-healing alternatives to supplement the established medical system, and offer solace in times of illness and death.

These examples help reveal the interconnections between health and other institutions at the meso level.

Health at the Macro Level

Each society has a vested interest in the health of its citizenry because the general state of health affects the quality of life of the people and the state of the economy. Imagine a society in which citizens had "permission" to be sick frequently. How would that society continue to function? Cultural beliefs about illness and how to treat the sick vary by society.

Consider the case of the former, now dissolved, Soviet Union. After the Soviet victory over Czarist Russia in 1917, the new revolutionary government was faced with an underdeveloped nation that still produced its food with human-powered plows and simple hoes. The task of leading the country out of the 16th century and into the 20th was formidable. It called for a total effort from the nation's workforce. The new government determined that absenteeism at work, regardless of excuse, had to be kept very low. Accordingly, the government instituted rules that required workers who were ill to obtain a certificate allowing them to be absent from work because of illness (G. Weiss and Lonnquist 2015). These certificates could be obtained only from government clinics, and each clinic could issue only a limited number of permits. In some cases, the government encouraged physicians to compete with one another to see how few certificates they could issue. Thus, absence due to illness was controlled, and the human resources needed for rebuilding the nation were augmented. The macro-level needs were met at the expense of individuals.

Global health focuses on several issues, including possible pandemics of highly contagious diseases, which have become worldwide threats as global travel increases. A *pandemic* is a disease prevalent throughout an entire country that may infect a continent or reach around the world. Major efforts by international organizations and Global North countries contained the Ebola outbreak in West Africa beginning in March 2014, and efforts are under way to control the Zika virus that is fast spreading in countries around the world. Figure 11.1 illustrates the global nature of the HIV/AIDS pandemic. As of June 2015, 36.9 million people around the world were living with HIV, and 66% of new cases occur in sub-Saharan Africa. Only 15.8 million were receiving treatment. Since 2000, 25.3 million people have died of AIDS-related illness (Centers for Disease Control and Prevention 2016b).

Controlling such diseases requires cooperation across national boundaries by organizations such as the United Nations. Smallpox, for example, remained a serious global threat from the Middle Ages until the World Health Organization of the United Nations eliminated the disease completely in the 1960s. Likewise, river blindness once afflicted thousands of West Africans but has been eradicated

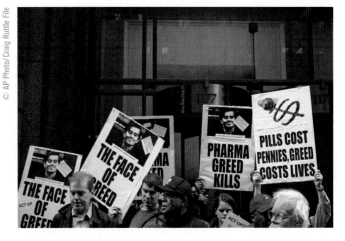

© AP Photo/Craig Ruttle File

Pharmaceutical chief Martin Shkreli bought out the company that invented a life-saving drug called Daraprim. He then promptly raised the price about 5,000 percent—from $13.50 to $750 per pill. The public response was outrage, and he was called to testify to Congress. One role of governments is to protect the public's health.

due to international cooperation. Funding by organizations such as the Bill and Melinda Gates Foundation supports research, treatment, and eradication of killer diseases such as malaria, AIDS, and tuberculosis.

When you are sick, illness may seem like an individual problem, but as shown in the previous examples, it is far more than that. It is also a national and global issue. This chapter examines health care at each level of analysis, from individual behaviors and decisions, to religious, political, and economic aspects, to the effect of stratification and ethnic status on the quality of health care one receives. Keep the social world model in mind as you read about health, illness, and health care.

Thinking Sociologically

Why might diseases that affect a local community require international attention and solutions? What is a recent example?

THEORETICAL PERSPECTIVES ON HEALTH AND ILLNESS

In the analysis of institutions, each major paradigm or perspective in sociology offers a lens for understanding different aspects of the institution. Let us consider how the major theoretical perspectives help us understand health and illness.

FIGURE 11.1 Adult HIV Prevalence Rate, 2014

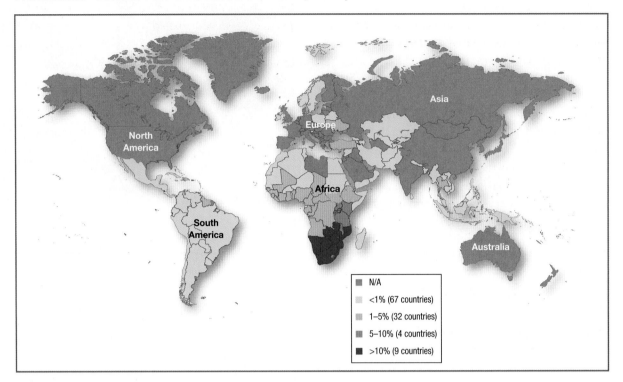

N/A

<1% (67 countries)

1–5% (32 countries)

5–10% (4 countries)

>10% (9 countries)

Notes: Data are estimates. Prevalence rates include adults ages 15 -49.

Source: Kaiser Family Foundation (2015a).

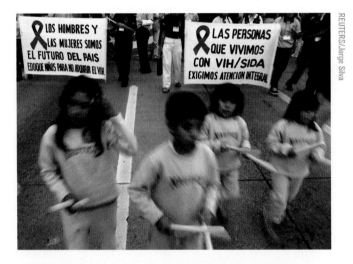

These Guatemalan children infected with HIV march outside the site of an AIDS conference in Guatemala City. Hundreds of people from different countries marched to bring attention to the lack of government aid and medical assistance for those infected with the virus that causes AIDS.

REUTERS/Jorge Silva

Micro-Level Theoretical Perspectives

Whereas once unruly schoolchildren faced punishments for being "bad," many now receive medications. New understandings of medical disorders have led to the diagnosis of millions of children with medical labels such as attention deficit, autism spectrum, and other disorders. Advances in medical science have also led to diagnosis and treatment of learning disabilities such as dyslexia, a disorder that makes it harder for some children to achieve academic success. The changes in the labeling of such conditions result in changes in social stigma and different policies to deal with disorders.

Symbolic Interaction Perspective and Labeling Theory. Symbolic interactionists point out that definitions of illness vary over time and from society to society. In recent years, the definition of illness in many Global North societies has expanded to encompass substance abuse and some forms of deviant behavior, giving physicians more power and authority over broad areas of social life. As noted earlier, many behaviors once seen as criminal or "bad" are now viewed as symptoms of medical disorders.

Medicalization and Labeling. Medicalization *refers to handling some forms of deviance, as well as some normal human functions (such as pregnancy and childbirth), in the health care system rather than the family, legal, or religious arenas.* In some cases, the shift is away from individual self-control and toward medical diagnosis and treatment.

Consider addictive behaviors such as alcoholism and drug abuse. How we define alcoholism influences our understanding of the problem, whether we hold the patient to blame, and the course of treatment we pursue (Cockerham 2015). If we see alcoholism as a personal failing, we view the alcoholic as a moral degenerate who needs to start abiding by the norms of society. On the other hand, if we define alcoholism as a disease, we see the alcoholic as a sick person in need of medical care (Conrad 2007). The next "Engaging Sociology" explores social policy toward alcoholism.

ENGAGING SOCIOLOGY

Alcoholism, Medicalization, and Policy

Perhaps you know someone who struggles with an alcohol problem. The American Medical Association (AMA) officially designated alcoholism as an illness in 1956 (Jellinek 1960). Alcoholism is a dependency on alcohol (alcohol addiction), a chronic disease that includes strong craving, continued use of alcohol despite physical and social problems, and inability to limit drinking (CDC 2016b). The disease is often progressive and fatal. By labeling alcoholism as a disease, the medical profession gains more power and influence as an agent of social control (Conrad 2007).

Some health care professionals, however, argue that the disease concept is the wrong approach—that what is really at stake is "heavy drinking" as a way of life. Rather than treating a "disease," they feel that professionals should be concerned with approaches that will change the way in which individuals organize their behaviors. These researchers and practitioners argue that heavy drinkers can become nondrinkers or moderate drinkers who can control their drinking.

Whereas the Alcoholics Anonymous approach to alcoholism treatment involves lay people in groups helping each other stay away from alcohol in a spiritually oriented manner, the *medicalization of alcoholism* calls for treatment by professionals—psychiatrists, psychologists, hospitals, and clinics. Some people see these approaches as complementary, but others think they are incompatible and conflict with one another (Conrad 2007; Roisen 2012).

There may be truth in both models based on individual differences. Treatment programs can be

The label alcoholic has a number of implications, including the fact that the stigma associated with the term may prevent some people from seeking help. Alcoholics Anonymous and other alcohol treatment centers have recast alcoholism as a disease, hoping that the redefinition will remove stigma. These people discuss their alcoholism at an AA meeting.

found based on both of these models, and the debate about the best approach continues.

* * * * *

Engaging With Sociology

1. Many of us have a friend or relative who struggles with alcohol or drug problems. What labels do others place on that person?

2. Do you think alcohol or drug problems come from a lack of self-discipline or a physical illness requiring medical treatment? What might you do to help the person?

3. How can you approach this person to help prevent future disease or chronic problems?

As societal norms change, so do perceptions of behavior once considered signs of mental or physical disorders. For example, until 1986, homosexuality appeared in the American Psychiatric Association's (APA) *Diagnostic and Statistical Manual of Mental Disorders*. Since that time, it has lost the label of a mental disorder. The increasing acceptance of gay people in the United States has led, in this case, to demedicalization. We turn now to how forces at the meso and macro levels in our social world shape the experience of illness or health at the micro level.

Meso- and Macro-Level Theoretical Perspectives

Different cultures have different perspectives on illness. Some Hispanic cultures practice a unique, ancient, and complex system of healing known as *curanderismo*. The origins can be found in traditional herbal medicine, precolonial religious belief systems, witchcraft, and Spanish Catholicism. Members of these subcultures view good health and a strong body as God's blessing for the faithful. Illness comes either when one has sinned or as a message from God to help the person learn to be good. The relationship between the *curandero*, or healer, and the patient is close, relying on psychological and spiritual, as well as physical, treatments. Many Hispanics combine Western medicine and *curanderismo*. For "non-Hispanic illnesses," the physician is the healer of choice. However, for culture-specific conditions, such as *susto* (characterized by extreme fright), the *curandero* may be consulted

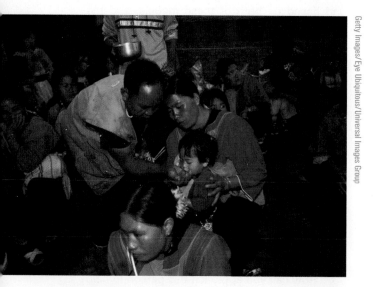

Doi Lan, a Lisu shaman in Thailand, gives an infant a liquid as part of a healing ceremony. Others wait for their turn to receive the healing powers of the respected shaman.

because many believe that such conditions are impervious to even the highest technology of the scientific physician (G. Weiss and Lonnquist 2015). The role of the *curandero* combines elements of a psychologist and a healer.

Consider how people perceive, experience, and react to pain (Addictionblog.org 2011; Galanti 2008). For example, Asian patients rarely ask for pain medication, but patients from Mediterranean cultures readily ask for help to relieve the slightest pain. Why is there a difference? In a classic U.S. hospital-based study of reactions to pain, researchers observed that patients' responses fell into two main categories: stoic and emotive. Patients with Jewish and Italian cultural backgrounds tended to respond to pain emotionally, whereas patients of English background were usually stoic and tried to bravely endure pain. Those of Irish descent often denied pain altogether. Although the Jewish American and Italian American patients exhibited similar reactions to pain, their reasons for these reactions were different. The Jewish American patients took a long-term view toward pain. They were concerned about its meaning for their future, and their reactions did not subside when pain-relieving drugs were administered. The Italian American patients, on the other hand, were mainly concerned with the pain itself, and drugs both relieved the pain and their complaints (Lasch 2002; Thomas and Rose 1991; Zborowski 1952).

Other studies of culturally learned differences related to health have linked expressive, emotive responses to Hispanic, Middle Eastern, and Mediterranean patients, whereas stoic patients were more often from northern European and Asian backgrounds (Azize et al. 2013; D'Arcy 2009; Galanti 2008). Even young children show cultural differences in reacting to pain (Azize et al. 2013). Sociological theories and cross-cultural knowledge help us to understand these and other cultural differences in approaches to health care.

Functionalist Perspective. Functional theorists focus primarily on the macro level of the health care system. Studies of suicide, carried out by French sociologist Émile Durkheim (discussed in Chapter 5), illustrate that social conditions and events in the larger society and people's group affiliations affect inclinations to commit suicide. Other studies have linked illnesses such as heart disease, kidney failure, stroke, mental illness, and infant mortality to macro-level processes and trends in societies. For example, economic recessions cause social stress and disruption in lifestyles, which, in turn, can result in health problems.

According to functionalists, the purpose of the health care system in society is to maintain the social structure and a harmonious balance between individuals and institutions in society. Illness is potentially disruptive to the balanced social world because it "robs" the society of normal role functioning; if too many people claim the sick role at the same time, the tasks necessary to maintain the society cannot be performed. The primary task, or function, of the medical profession is to control illness and ensure that individuals can perform their social roles.

Functionalists like Talcott Parsons see positive value in the hierarchical structure of the medical profession and in the power of the physician over the patient (Parsons 1971). Parsons believed that having "experts" in charge led to better care for patients. That view, however, is not shared by all, as we will see shortly. We now turn to conflict theory for a different perspective on the health care system.

Conflict Perspective. Poverty, unemployment, low wages, malnutrition, and a host of other economic conditions affect people's access to and ability to compete for health care and medicine in many countries. Differential access is a key theme in conflict theorists' approach to health issues. Consider the case of Nkosi, a 4-year-old boy in a rural Ghanaian village. He came down with an infection due to polluted water, causing diarrhea and vomiting. Nkosi was already weakened by malnutrition and parasites, and by the time his family got medical help, he was so dehydrated that he died. Why was health care for this easily treatable condition not available in time?

Nkosi had less access to medical treatment, immunizations, antibiotics, vitamins, and a balanced diet than children in the Global North countries or even in urban areas of the Global South. Many children in poor countries around the world suffer from malnutrition and chronic disease before succumbing to pneumonia or other infections, diseases for which treatment is normally available.

Relatively new emerging infectious diseases such as AIDS, Brazilian purpuric fever, new strains of Ebola, and various insect-transported diseases such as Zika and swine flu (H1N1) add to the problems faced by health care workers in the Global South. Efforts by medical activists such as Dr. Paul Farmer, a U.S. infectious disease specialist and anthropologist, help poor countries. He set up an organization, Partners in Health, with the goal of conquering diseases among the world's poor (D. Alexander 2015; Kidder 2004). With life expectancy (average length of life) as low as 46 years in some drought-ridden and war-torn countries, the challenge is formidable.

Conflict theorists point out that individuals suffer different illnesses depending on the level of development of their society and their position in it. As mentioned in

Chapter 7, many low-income residents in Global North nations live in *food deserts*, areas that lack grocery stores and other means of access to affordable, healthy food. The residents in these food deserts tend to consume highly processed foods full of artificially cheap, corn-based ingredients, sugar-laden soft drinks, and other addictive foods that spark cravings for more such food. The 2004 movie *Super Size Me* illustrates this well.

At the global level, many multinational companies that build factories in the poor Global South provide examples of the profit motive's influence on health conditions. Businesses seeking large profit margins and cost-cutting opportunities may move operations to countries with lower health and safety standards than those in the Global North, which has more stringent health regulations. Global North multinational companies pressure manufacturers to produce cheap goods, and corrupt government officials fail to enforce regulations designed to provide safe buildings and to control the treatment and dispersal of factory waste, resulting in unsafe practices and poor health conditions (Yardley 2013).

Conflict theorists also point out that most physicians work in affluent, urban areas and go into specialties that pay more than primary (general, family care) doctors receive. The most lucrative positions with the most prestige are generally located in major global urban areas and at well-known clinics, where people can pay for private care. As a result, a severe shortage of

Abdur Rahman holds a family photo of his wife Cahyna Akhter, a garment worker who died when the Rana Plaza building collapsed, killing more than 1,000 people. Bangladeshi factory workers face risks from both unsafe working conditions and pollution created by the factories. Conflict theorists argue that self-interest of the affluent to increase profits results in unsafe conditions.

primary-care doctors exists in rural areas of the world, including the rural United States (Snyderman and Sottile 2013). Conflict theorists emphasize that poverty and inequality—whether in the Global North or the Global South—have a major impact on quality of life and health care. The next "Engaging Sociology" illustrates the impact a lack of health care can have on individuals in the United States.

ENGAGING SOCIOLOGY

Health Care During a Financial Crisis

Look at the following list of basic needs. Most of us provide these for our families through our jobs. Now imagine that you and your family are faced with a major financial crisis, and you simply cannot meet all of your needs.

- Health care and health insurance
- A car or other reliable transportation
- Food for the family
- Clothing—appropriate for the weather and your occupation
- Housing in a safe neighborhood
- Access to good schools for your children
- Other essentials . . .

* * * * * * *

Engaging with Sociology

1. Which of these items would you give up? If that was still not sufficient to make ends meet, what decisions would you make to balance the budget?

2. Many people choose to postpone or sacrifice health insurance or doctors' visits. How might poor health care affect your income *and* at least three of the items previously listed?

    a. _____

    b. _____

    c. _____

3. Now consider items you chose to eliminate in Question 1. How might those decisions have a long-term impact on other aspects of your quality of life—*including* the health of family members?

    a. _____

    b. _____

    c. _____

Feminist Theory

Feminist theorists examine the impact of gender on health, illness, and health care, among other topics. They argue that the patriarchal control of women carries over to health care systems and reinforces the dependence and submission of women.

Some of the procedures practiced on women are unnecessary, according to feminists in medical professions. For example, many doctors recommend that women deliver their babies via cesarean section surgery rather than vaginally. The percentage of cesarean births has risen dramatically from 5% in 1970 to approximately 33% today. Some of them are necessary, but others may be for convenience or to avoid lawsuits (Centers for Disease Control and Prevention 2015a; N. Lake 2012; R. Weiss 2010). According to feminist theorists, controlling women's reproductive health and defining women's normal biological experiences as medical problems reflect and support a patriarchal (male-dominated) society.

To regain control of women's health, some feminists have formed health organizations concerned with reproductive health. Such organizations may provide midwifery and natural childbirth services and help women deal with issues related to menopause. With increasing numbers of women physicians, attitudes toward women's health and communication practices between women and physicians have also started to change. Thanks to these changes, more doctors recognize the importance of listening to and working *with* patients on their health issues.

Gender also plays a role in doctors' specialty positions. Women now account for almost half of all those in medical school but, more than men, tend to opt for medical specialty areas with less prestige and less money but with more family-friendly emphases and hours. Women, for example, compose about one-third of all physicians in the United States but make up over half of all pediatricians and primary-care doctors (American Medical Association 2015; Dotinga 2011).

There is greater risk of sexually transmitted diseases for young women, due to widespread sexual violence against women. Also, many girls in Global South countries face pressure to marry at a young age, which can lead to major health problems. The risk of dying during childbirth increases the lower the age of the mother, yet 7.3 million girls under 18 in the Global South give birth each year, 2 million of them 14 and under (Vinograd 2013).

As you can see, each theory illuminates different issues in health, illness, and health care at the meso and macro levels. We now examine health and illness at a micro level. In doing so, we focus on the status and roles of the sick person.

STATUS AND ROLES OF THE SICK PERSON: MICRO-LEVEL ANALYSIS

How do you know if you are sick? How you answer this question depends on your culture, as well as your physical symptoms (G. Weiss and Lonnquist 2015). A poor Central American woman illustrated this point. When asked if she was sick, she replied that she wished she knew what it meant to be sick. Sometimes she felt so bad she thought she could curl up and die, but she kept going because the kids needed her, and she lacked money to spend on a doctor. She did not have time to be sick. She asks, "How does one know when someone is sick?" Some of us can go to bed almost any time with any illness, but many of the world's people cannot be sick, not even when they need to be (Koos 1954).

To this woman, being sick was not just a physical condition or how she felt or any physical symptoms she displayed. So who defines this poor woman as sick? She herself? Her friends and family? Her employer? A health care professional? The answer is ambiguous. Illness, then, is, in part, socially constructed. Health care providers, schools, and workplaces acknowledge illness only if certain society-defined conditions are present.

Both individual (micro) and structural (meso or macro) factors influence health care decisions and treatment. The political and economic environment, access to medical services, and the predisposition by an individual to seek medical care all enter into health care decisions.

Thinking Sociologically

How do you determine whether you are sick? How do your obligations influence your perceptions of your health? Was it easier for you to be sick as a child than it is now? Why, or why not?

The Sick Role

Think of all the social relationships, engagements, and responsibilities affected when you are sick. You miss class and work and have to avoid your friends so that you do not infect them with your germs. Most people are sympathetic for a few days, but then, they expect you to get back to your usual routines and responsibilities. Unless those around you perceive you as *very* ill, you probably cannot play the *sick role* for a long period of time without facing negative sanctions.

Ill people occupy a special status in society that requires them to perform a certain role. The **sick role** is *a special position in society in which one is temporarily relieved of responsibilities and accepts a position of dependence.* This role allows one to deviate from usual role expectations, and other people must pick up those responsibilities. Unlike other acts of deviance, however, the sick role is not punished—as long as the sick individual cooperates and acts to overcome illness, returning as soon as possible to fulfill his or her usual social roles. That can be difficult for people facing chronic illness, as seen in the following model (Varul 2010).

In an early contribution to the sociology of health, Parsons (1951) presented a functional theoretical model of the sick role, outlining four interrelated behavioral expectations—two rights and two obligations.

Right 1. The sick person has the right to be excused from normal social responsibility, as needed, to be restored to normal functioning in the society. For example, sick students expect to receive permission to miss class or to make up a missed exam.

Right 2. The sickness is not the individual's fault. The sick person did not mean to deviate from normal social expectations and cannot become well by self-decision or by willing it so.

Obligation 1. The sick person should define being sick as undesirable. To avoid the accusation of laziness or malingering, the sick person must not prolong illness unnecessarily to avoid social obligations.

Obligation 2. Those in the sick status should seek technically competent help and cooperate in getting well. In Western countries, the help most often comes from a medical doctor.

Parsons describes the physicians' roles as complementing the sick role—to restore routine behavior and "orderliness" in patients. The model presented by Parsons clearly relates to functionalist thought. Functionalists focus on integrating all aspects of medical care into a working social system (Parsons 1951).

Some individuals, however, might like being excused from tasks and allowed to deviate from social responsibility (such as taking tests or doing an arduous task). Certainly, being sick requires a less demanding lifestyle than going to work or school or taking care of a family. The sick role can

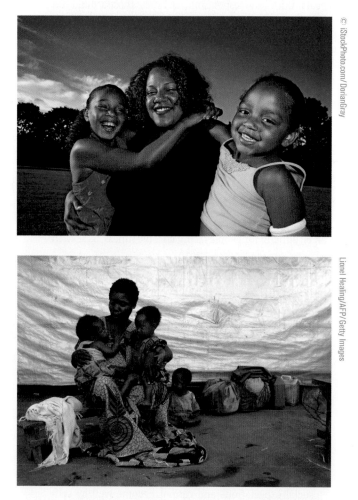

These two women are of similar age, both in their 30s. Health facilities make an enormous difference in one's life chances, one's health, and how one ages. The woman on the top lives in North America; the woman on the bottom raises a family in Senegal, West Africa.

also legitimize failure by providing a ready excuse for poor performance at some task. People who believe they are permanently unable to fulfill their normal social roles may be motivated to define themselves as sick. Yet an excess of sick people could be disruptive to the social fabric, so it is necessary to develop means to control who enters the sick status and to guard against misuse of illness as an excuse for avoiding social responsibility. In most societies today, possible negative sanctions, ranging from colleagues' raised eyebrows to being fired, discourage many people from pretending to be sick to get out of work.

Thinking Sociologically

Are you able to be sick? Why, or why not?

Individuals can also earn negative sanctions for engaging in unhealthy behavior that results in not carrying out one's expected roles. For example, if you smoke, there is a very good chance that someone has chastised you for doing so. Your decisions about what you eat and drink, your use of alcohol and other drugs, and your sexual behavior affect your health. Any of these, taken to extremes, can result in illness.

Attitudes toward health, illness, and death vary from society to society. In countries with high infant mortality rates and low life expectancy, illness and death are all too familiar. In Global South nations, parents may have many children because they expect some to die before reaching adulthood.

Social Factors and Attitudes Toward Health, Illness, and Death. An American Peace Corps volunteer in a South American village could not understand the passive attitude of the mother, Mónica, as she held her dying baby. He offered to help Mónica get the baby to the clinic 15 miles away, but she seemed resigned to its death. The expectations that shaped Mónica's behavior were learned in her cultural setting. Three of her seven children had died already. In this rural Global South setting, as many as half of the babies born will die in infancy because of poor sanitation, lack of clean water, and lack of health care and medicine, often from curable illnesses. People come to accept infant deaths, often easily preventable, as part of life. Many parents do not even name their children until they have displayed indications of good health for several weeks after birth.

Social Predictors in Individual Health and Illness. Individual micro-level variables such as age, gender, ethnicity, economic factors, social status, and urban or rural residence help determine patterns of health and illness. For example, *age* affects health in several ways. Those 65 years or older tend to have more health issues than younger people. Two out of three U.S. residents 65 or over have at least one chronic illness (CDC 2013), and one-quarter of Medicare spending is for services in the last year of life (Kaiser Family Foundation 2015b).

Gender patterns are clear, too: In Global North cultures, women are more inclined to go to the doctor than men, and they receive more preventive and reproductive care. In contrast, men tend to go to the doctor less and receive less preventative care. As a result, they tend to use emergency services more than women (G. Weiss and Lonnquist 2015).

Ethnic groups socialize individuals into lifestyles that help or harm their health. Ethnicity also influences people's perceptions of health, the medical interventions they seek, and their response to medical treatment. Recall the cases of Hispanic *curanderismo* and the different experiences of pain discussed earlier. Socialization into possible health care options ranges from modern medical practitioners to alternative medical practitioners (from traditional folk healers to modern chiropractors), nonmedical professions (e.g., social workers and clergy), lay advisers, and self-care (Pescosolido 1992). In the United States, African Americans, Hispanics, and Native Americans are less likely to have regular health care providers and more likely to use hospital emergency rooms and health clinics than White Americans. In addition, racial and ethnic minority residents tend to live in poor and rural areas, where there is less available health care.

On average, most women of color receive less prenatal care than White women, and the infant-mortality gap (i.e., the number of live-born infants who die in their first year per 1,000 births) reflects this disparity, as shown in Table 11.1. The relatively high infant-mortality rate in the United States, compared with rates in other affluent countries, stems largely from the lack of adequate health care available to low-income Americans and racial and ethnic minorities (DeSantis 2013). Infant mortality also varies widely within the United States due to health care variations; Figure 11.2 illustrates this well.

Wealthier individuals tend to seek professional help earlier for physical or psychological distress because they can better afford the cost and time for such treatment. Despite this fact, people in the lowest income group have more contact with physicians (7.6 doctor visits per year, compared with an average of 6 for the entire population) (G. Weiss and Lonnquist 2015). This is one powerful indicator that lower-income people are less healthy.

Table 11.1 Infant Deaths per 1,000 Live Births by Race of Mother (in the United States)

Race or Ethnic Origin	Number per 1,000
All racial/ethnic groups	6.0
Black	11.1
American Indian/Alaska Native	7.6
Hispanic	5.9
White	5.1
Asian American	4.1

Source: Mathews, MacDorman, and Thoma (2015).

Lower-income citizens in many states still do not have access to medical insurance, despite the existence of **Medicaid**, *the government-run insurance plan for low-income families*. More than 4 million "working-poor" citizens who make too much to qualify for Medicaid (because they live in a state that refused to expand Medicaid under the Affordable Care Act) but do not receive it through work and do not make enough money to qualify for subsidized health care under the Affordable Care Act must do without health care (Garfield et al. 2015). Since people began being insured through the ACA in 2013, the percentage of people uninsured in the United States has dropped from 20.3% to 13.2% in 2015, but more must be done to ensure universal coverage, such as more states expanding Medicaid (U.S. Department of Health and Human Services 2015b; G. Weiss and Lonnquist 2015). Without universal access to health care, income affects health status. Differences in access to health care also relate to meso and macro levels of the social system, as discussed in the next sections.

MODERN HEALTH CARE SYSTEMS: MESO-LEVEL ANALYSIS

At one time, health care was largely an issue addressed in homes by families. Today, in wealthy countries, health care has become institutionalized. Much of the treatment of diseases depends on research funded by governments or foundations, and bureaucratized corporations deliver care. This section explores the institution of medicine: the organization of health care systems, hospitals as complex organizations, and changes of professional status for physicians.

FIGURE 11.2   Infant Mortality Rates by State in the United States: 2013

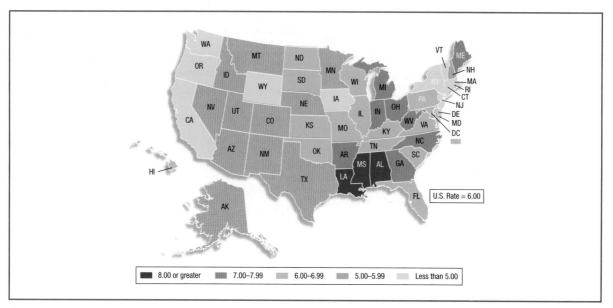

Note: Number per thousand.

Source: Kaiser Family Foundation (2016).

Availability of health resources is an important structural factor in health. This primary health care center in rural India does not have a pharmacist. A filing clerk makes decisions about who gets what drugs.

Organization of Health Care Systems

Citizens' access to health care depends on the cultural values concerning the government's role in providing health care—whether health care is seen as a human right for all citizens or a privilege for those who can pay for it—and the type of health care available. Societies around the world struggle with issues of cost, quality and access to care, and

medical technology. In the Global North, these struggles result from aging populations with more health needs and smaller numbers of citizens in the tax-paying working population as the aging populations grow. Nations in the Global South struggle with problems that result in high death rates from curable diseases and epidemics. Nations develop health care philosophies and systems based on population needs and their ability to address them.

Types of National Health Care Systems. The two most common national models for providing health care—socialized medicine and decentralized national health care programs—are based on the philosophy of health care as a human right. The United States moved closer to the health-care-for-all philosophy with the passage of the Affordable Care Act, or Obamacare, signed into law in 2010. Figure 11.3 shows the countries of the world that have universal health care as of 2015.

Socialized medicine *provides a government-supported consumer service that assures equal access to health care for all citizens of a country* (Cockerham 2015). The political system controls the organization and financing of health services and owns most facilities, pays providers directly, and allows private care for an extra fee. Global North countries that have different forms of socialized-medicine systems include Canada, Great Britain, Israel, Norway, Sweden, and several other European countries.

Countries with decentralized national health programs have many of the same characteristics, but the

FIGURE 11.3   Countries With Universal Health Care

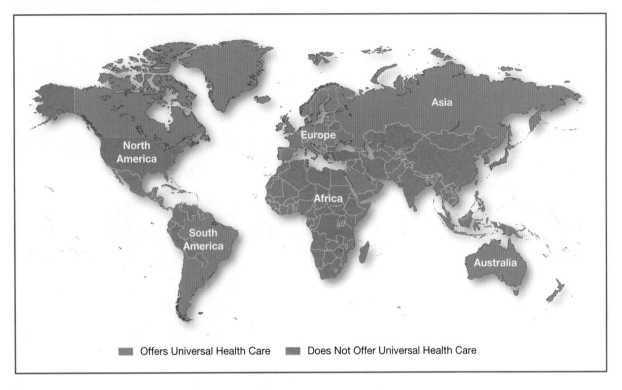

Offers Universal Health Care ▪▪▪ Does Not Offer Universal Health Care

Source: From Wikimedia Commons.

government's role is different. The government has less direct control over health care and acts to regulate the system but not operate it (Cockerham 2015). Countries with decentralized systems include France, Germany, Japan, and the Netherlands.

The United States, unique among Global North countries, has a mix of socialized (Medicaid for poor and Medicare for elderly) and private health care programs (for which some qualified people may receive a government subsidy under the Affordable Care Act). Both types of programs tend to rely on *fee-for-service health care*, in which doctors and hospitals are paid for each service they perform and decide the prices charged for every service. They typically can order as many tests as they feel necessary and decide the price for each. The fee-for-service aspect has led to doctors and hospitals charging enormous (and varying) fees for every conceivable thing used (e.g., ibuprofen and sponges) and exceedingly high health care costs (Brill 2013).

Thinking Sociologically

What kind of access do you have to health care? Are you able to see a physician without worrying about the cost? Why, or why not?

Most governments in Europe decided to support health care as a human right for all citizens and put their universal health care systems into place beginning in the late 1800s (in Germany) through the mid-1900s. Their motivations were to develop healthier populations, strengthen their military forces and economic systems, and reduce the possibility of revolution.

Canada is an interesting case, with two principles underlying the health care system: All Canadians should have the right to health care, and financial barriers to care should be eliminated. After World War II, the Canadian government established a group of health insurance plans (*socialized insurance*) that provided universal health insurance to improve the health of all Canadians. Most of the costs are shared by federal and provincial governments, with 70% paid by public funds and 30% by copayments, insurance, and other funding. The government, in consultation with medical professionals, sets prices for services (Canadian Health Care 2010).

Infant mortality and life expectancy rates, two key measures of a country's health status, reveal that Canada has lower infant mortality than the United States (4.6 deaths per 1,000 live births in Canada versus 5.8 in the United States) (*World Factbook* 2017a) and higher life expectancy—81.9

years (12th in the world), compared with 79.8 years (53rd in the world) in the United States (*World Factbook* 2017b). Taxes in Canada are 10% to 15% higher than those in the United States, but total cost per capita (per person) is 33% less for health care. In other words, the overall cost to consumers means higher taxes but lower costs overall—and much lower cost for health care. The Commonwealth Fund ranks the United States 11th out of 11 in overall health care in wealthy countries (Commonwealth Fund 2015b). Table 11.2 shows health care spending and life expectancy for the most affluent countries.

Comparing Canada and the United States with 16 developed countries shows that the United States spent the most per capita ($9,086 on health care in 2013); Canada is only about half as expensive at $4,567. (See Table 11.2.) In addition, controls by insurance companies result in hospital stays in the United States that are 20% to 40% shorter than in most other countries for similar procedures.

Thinking Sociologically

Based on the discussion of health care in Canada compared with the United States, what do you conclude about the pros and cons of these two approaches to health care?

Table 11.2   Health Care Spending

Country	Total Health Care Spending per Capita ($)	Average Life Expectancy (Years)
Australia	4,115	82.8
Canada	4,569	82.8
Denmark	4,847	80.6
France	4,361	82.4
Germany	4,920	81.0
Japan	3,713	83.7
Netherlands	5,131	81.9
New Zealand	3,855	81.6
Norway	6,170	81.8
Sweden	5,153	82.4
Switzerland	6,325	83.4
United Kingdom	3,364	81.2
United States	9,086	79.3

Source: Commonwealth Fund (2015a); Index Mundi (2014).

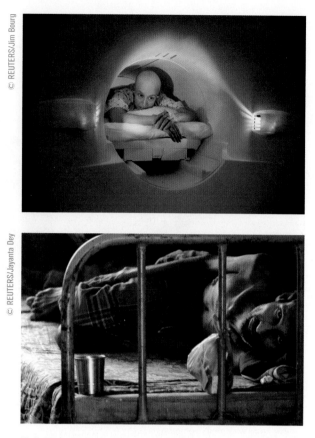

© REUTERS/Jim Bourg

© REUTERS/Jayanta Dey

High-tech medical equipment (top) is expensive, but in places such as Ethiopia (bottom), hospitals have few resources, and physicians must use whatever limited technology is available.

Hospitals as Complex Organizations. *Hospitals* are organizations that provide care and treatment for the sick and injured, providing centralized medical knowledge and technology for treatment of illnesses and accidents. Rational, systematic approaches to health care replaced individual folk remedies in the late colonial period in North America. The first colonial hospital opened in 1752, and the first medical school began accepting students in 1765. The focus of these early hospitals was on segregating the destitute and terminally ill, who might be contagious and were likely to die. At this time, most hospitals were still small, but improvements in medical knowledge and competency began to change both these institutions and the entire medical profession. In the late 1800s, the number of hospitals, many of which were sponsored by religious organizations, grew very rapidly.

The status of the hospital shifted dramatically in the early 1900s due to advances in medical science. Trained staff, sterile conditions, and more advanced techniques and technology changed hospitals from being the last resort of the urban poor and the dying to places of healing for all classes. Small community hospitals became an essential element of town life.

The post–World War II period produced huge growth in health care facilities and the number of employees in the U.S. health care system. Medicines and vaccines controlled many infectious diseases that had formerly killed and disabled individuals. This period also saw the growth of medical schools and large medical facilities that provided not only patient care but also education and research. Thus began the dominance of the hospital in providing medical care. Today, many hospitals are centers of medical knowledge and technology, housing not only patients and surgical units but also laboratories and diagnostic centers, specialty clinics, and rehabilitation centers (Pescosolido et al. 2011).

Although medical health systems differ across societies, hospitals generally exhibit many characteristics similar to other large, bureaucratic organizations: hierarchical structures, rules and regulations, statuses (e.g., doctors and nurses) based on competency and training, hiring and promotion based on merit, and contracts for work performed. Primary-care physicians and other gatekeepers control client access to hospitals. Historically, U.S. hospitals were designed for the convenience of physicians. However, today, two rather independent bureaucracies function within modern large-scale hospital organizations. Physicians dominate the medical operations, whereas lay administrators control the other areas of the hospital (e.g., finance, human resources, and support services).

Health care systems act as major employers in most affluent nations. In the United States, for instance, hospitals directly employ 5.6 million people and support a total of 16 million jobs (American Hospital Association 2015). People in hospitals hold jobs as nurses, hospital administrators, pharmacists, physical therapists, physician's assistants, imaging specialists (those who work with X-rays, MRIs, and the like), aides, and custodial staff—and the number of employees continues to grow. Nurses compose the largest group of health care workers, with licensed registered nurses (2,711,500) and licensed practical and vocational nurses (738,400) accounting for nearly six nurses per physician in the United States (U.S. Bureau of Labor Statistics 2014b). In a hospital, the nurse manages the patient care team under the authority of the physician, who is the prime decision maker. Under the nurse's authority in this hierarchical structure come increasing numbers of ancillary personnel.

As more for-profit corporations own and operate hospitals and other medical facilities in the United States, the power of the professional or medical line is giving way to

corporate management—the lay or administrative line. Physicians have become the customers of the hospital, buying space and time to carry out their functions. Sometimes, the cost-saving goals of administrators and medical decisions of physicians come into conflict.

Thinking Sociologically

Who controls the medical facilities in your community? What structure do they have, and what roles predominate? Do you see evidence of a conflict between the cost-saving goals of administrators and medical decisions of physicians? How are the hospitals in your community regarded by the community? Why?

Changing Professional Status of Employees in the Health Care System

Some of you may be planning careers in the health care system. If you are taking the MCAT exams for medical school, you will find questions on social sciences, including sociology. These questions focus on understanding social structures (including the health care system); demographic characteristics and processes (such as migration, fertility, and mortality); social stratification (e.g., differences in health care depending on one's status in society); and social inequality (e.g., inequality in access to health care) (Edward Kain 2012; Olsen 2016). In this section, you will read about these topics, some of which you have already reviewed, but now in the health care context.

Special features distinguish the hospital from other large-scale organizations or bureaucracies. The division of labor in the hospital is extensive and more highly specialized than in other formal organizations. The hospital has a hierarchical structure based on prestige and power, and hospitals depend on the cooperation of highly skilled people who must coordinate their work. Hospital employees rigidly follow patterns of authority and wear clothing and symbols indicating particular positions in the hospital hierarchy. At the top of the stratification ladder, physicians exercise the most power and receive the highest financial and prestige rewards. Signs of their superior status include wearing long white coats or not wearing special uniforms at all.

Physicians rank among the most respected professionals in most societies. The widespread acceptance of physician authority is relatively recent, however. The status of physicians began to climb after medical discoveries in the 1800s led to greater success rates in treatment and more specialized training for physicians (Pescosolido and Boyer

2010). The transformation of physicians to a position of professional recognition gained great traction in the United States when some 250 physicians meeting in Philadelphia in May 1847 established the American Medical Association (AMA). This umbrella organization became the means to gain legitimacy and power over health care practice (Cockerham 2015). The powerful new AMA delegitimized predominantly female health care areas such as midwifery and other holistic approaches, such as osteopathy, chiropractic medicine, and homeopathy. Only one approach was granted credibility: *allopathy*, medical treatment supported by the American Medical Association and most Western medical organizations, involving remedies based on directly countering a patient's symptoms with drugs or surgery.

Included in the professionalization of doctors was the relationship with patients. Parsons presented a model of the doctor role that had rights and obligations, just as patients had. Among the expectations were that doctors would have a high degree of skill and knowledge, act for the patient and community welfare, be objective and emotionally detached, and be professional. These expectations are still valid in today's changing system (Parsons 1951).

Deprofessionalization is *the process through which a professional occupation loses autonomy, respect, and service orientation because the professionals come to be controlled by nonprofessionals and outside forces, such as financial concerns, government regulation, technological changes, and administrators or management*. Whereas their position as a physician entails a very high status in society, physicians have lost some control over health care

to insurance companies and hospital administrators. Many physicians now work for managed care systems, by whose established guidelines for medical care they must abide, reducing their autonomy (Pescosolido and Boyer 2010).

We have explored issues of health care at the micro level (the role of sick people) and at the meso level (organization of health care and hospitals as complex organizations). We now move on to macro-level policy issues at the national and global level.

● Thinking Sociologically

What meso and macro level forces lead to some people in the world having more access to health care than others? At the micro level, what does this mean for the health and productivity of individuals and their ability to support their families? What might it mean for societies as a whole?

HEALTH CARE ISSUES AT THE NATIONAL AND GLOBAL LEVEL: MACRO-LEVEL ANALYSIS

Health Care System in the United States

The United States has the best—and the worst—health care system among Global North countries in terms of quality medical care, trained practitioners, facilities, and advanced medical technology. People from around the world seek training and care in the United States. It is also the worst system, with the highest cost per capita in the world, unequal access, inefficiencies, and competing interests. The Affordable Care Act (Obamacare) was designed to address some of these issues, but it is unclear how or if the health care system under the Trump administration will do so.

Medical emergencies occur across the United States for the more than 13% of people who lack medical insurance (U.S. Department of Health and Human Services 2015b). Some critics claim that the U.S. health care system is, itself, a social problem. It developed without specific direction and responded to demands piecemeal, allowing practitioners, medical facilities, and insurance and drug companies to establish themselves and then protect their self-interests, sometimes at the expense of patients.

Health Care Advances. Medical research into gene therapy, understanding the human genome, and new drug

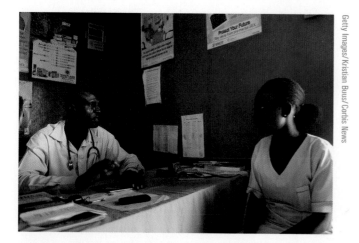

Getty Images/Kristian Buus/Corbis News

The clothing worn by health care workers is significant. It communicates status, authority, and rights to certain prerogatives within the hospital or clinic. What sort of attire do nurses, technicians, and aides wear in your local hospital?

and technological therapies make research one of the most rapidly advancing medical fields. New therapies will help people live longer, more comfortable, and productive lives—*if* they can afford and have access to the care. As science moves rapidly, ethical questions about the use of fetal tissue in experiments and treatments, cloning, prolonging life, and other issues challenge ethicists and lawmakers.

In addition to advances in medical science, there have been other positive steps taken to increase the health of the population. *Public health* refers to efforts to fight disease, promote health, and raise life expectancy rates. Recent public-health accomplishments include improved motor vehicle safety, safer workplaces, control of more infectious diseases, greater access to family planning and prenatal care, and education of citizens about the dangers of tobacco and other unhealthy substances.

Problems in the U.S. Health Care System. Although the United States is the country of choice for many types of surgeries, and the health care is exceptional for those with plenty of money, issues like life expectancy are alarming, as Figure 11.4 indicates. The bar in the middle labeled OECD is the average for countries in the Organisation for Economic Co-operation and Development, all of which are Global North countries. The United States is below the average. It loses 3 times as many years of life to infectious diseases and 2 times as many to metabolic diseases as the average OECD nation (Kliff 2014). Much of this is because the health care is so unevenly distributed in the United States.

Maldistribution of Health Care. In addition to a lack of doctors in rural and poor areas, inequality in U.S. health care also relates to the unequal distribution of doctors by state. Some states have higher ratios of physicians per residents than other states. Massachusetts has the most "active patient care doctors" per 100,000 residents with 432.4; Mississippi has the fewest with 184.7. Look at Figure 11.5 to see the variation.

Thinking Sociologically

Given the previous discussion, how might where you live affect your health care?

Health Care Cost and Funding. One of the most serious problems for health care systems and consumers in the United States, however, is the cost of health care. Now at 174% of the gross national product, the United States spends twice as much per year on health care as most other Global North countries (Centers for Medicare and Medicaid Services 2014). The cost of drugs is also higher than in most

FIGURE 11.4 Life Expectancy at Birth

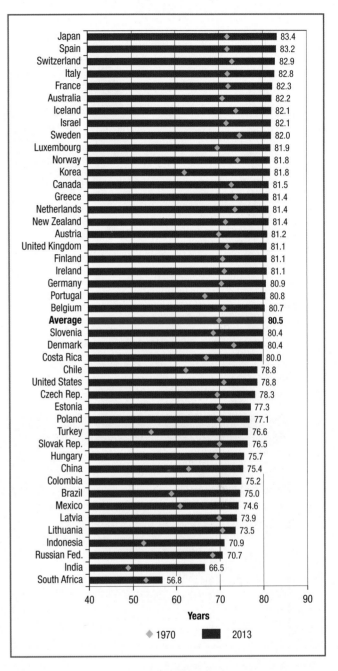

Source: Organization for Economic Co-operation and Development (2015b). Reprinted with permission conveyed through Copyright Clearance Center, Inc.

other countries. In order to find affordable medicine, some U.S. citizens are mail-ordering drugs from foreign pharmacies, a practice that critics say lacks quality controls and could be dangerous (Rosenthal 2013). Table 11.3 shows the increases in health care costs over time in the United States.

Out-of-pocket expenses (the costs of insurance plus deductibles) have doubled over the past 10 years and are now almost 10% of the median income (Schoen, Radley,

FIGURE 11.5 Active Patient Care Physicians per 100,000 Population by State, 2014

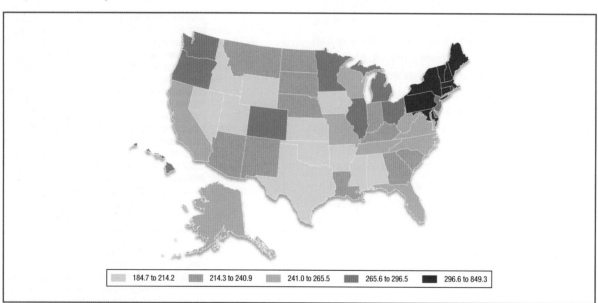

| | 184.7 to 214.2 | | 214.3 to 240.9 | | 241.0 to 265.5 | | 265.6 to 296.5 | | 296.6 to 849.3 |

Source: American Association of Medical Colleges (2015). Copyright © 2015 Association of American Medical Colleges. Reprinted with permission.

Table 11.3 National Health Expenditures: United States

Year	Trillions of Dollars	Percentage of Gross Domestic Product
1960	.027	5.0%
1970	.075	7.0
1980	.255	8.9
1990	.724	12.1
2000	1.378	13.4
2010	2.604	17.4
2013	2.919	17.4

Source: CDC (2015c); Centers for Medical and Medicaid Services (2014).

and Collins 2015). The Affordable Care Act offers some hope. For example, it encourages health providers to move away from the fee-for-service model.

Before the passage of the Affordable Care Act, the greatest criticism of the U.S. system was the inaccessibility of health care insurance for many. For people who do not have access to health insurance through their employer, lose a job that did provide it, or have a preexisting condition, health care was unattainable. More than 1 out of 4 Americans, or from 48 to 50 million people, below 65 years of age were uninsured at

some point in 2011, in part due to job loss (Morgan 2012). Just half that number are now uninsured.

The United States, however, still remains the only Global North nation without a national health insurance program providing health care coverage for *all* legal residents. Although the Supreme Court upheld most of the Affordable Care Act, it also ruled that states cannot be forced to expand Medicaid programs (government insurance for low-income residents primarily funded by the federal and state governments). Initially, almost half of the states refused to do so, even though the federal government will pay for almost all of the extended coverage. The expansion of Medicaid was a key part of the law, and the Supreme Court ruling (and the decision of some states) means that many poor citizens will remain without health insurance and that access to health care will become even more disparate among states. As seen in Figure 11.6, 32 states and the District of Columbia have adopted the Medicaid expansion while 19 states have not.

Provisions of the Affordable Care Act declared constitutional by the Supreme Court include the following (National Conference of State Legislatures 2011):

- Requiring employers to provide health coverage for their workers or pay penalties, with exceptions for employers with under 50 employees
- Requiring individuals to have insurance (with some exceptions and with tax credits to help lower-income people pay for it)
- Requiring insurance companies to cover young adults until age 26 on parents' health insurance plan
- Prohibiting lifetime caps and limiting the use of annual caps on insurance coverage
- Prohibiting the exclusion of people with preexisting conditions from private (as well as public) insurance plans (individual health insurance plans—bought by individuals, not through an employer—are grandfathered and can refuse to cover someone because of a preexisting condition)
- Establishing a limit on the percentage of insurance payments used for nonmedical payments (e.g., salaries and other administrative costs)

REUTERS/Jonathan Ernst (left); REUTERS/Joshua Roberts (right)

Supporters (*left*) and opponents (*right*) of the Affordable Care Act rally on the sidewalk at the Supreme Court in Washington, DC, illustrating the controversy over national health care policy.

Health Care Around the Globe

During a yearlong sabbatical in England, the Ballantine family signed up with a local surgeon, as the British call family physicians. Their sore throats, upset tummies, and bruised feet were taken to the doctor at no direct cost. The school referred their daughter to the hospital eye clinic for glasses at no cost. Their son was diagnosed and treated for "glandular fever" (mononucleosis), again at no cost. In Great Britain, all citizens have access to treatment by family physicians and dentists, to the dispensing of prescribed drugs, to eye care, and to community nursing and health visitor services. Taxes fund universal health care coverage at an expense much less than the U.S. cost for health care, and the administrative costs are low.

FIGURE 11.6   Medicaid Expansion by State

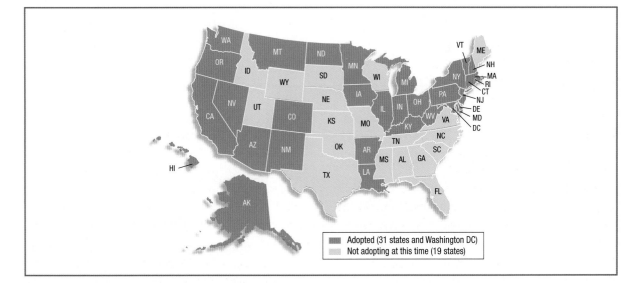

Adopted (31 states and Washington DC)
Not adopting at this time (19 states)

Source: Henry J. Kaiser Foundation (2016).

The demographic makeup, value system, and financial status of each country have an effect on how health care is delivered. Global North societies, with a high proportion of elderly and a low proportion of young people, have very different needs from those of Global South societies with many dependent children. In societies with many elders, special care for chronic illness is more necessary, whereas societies with many children must deal with more childhood illnesses.

The maldistribution of physicians is a global, as well as a U.S., issue. As illustrated in Figure 11.7 in the next "Engaging Sociology," the countries with the most doctors—the highest number of physicians per 1,000 people—are Greece (6.2), Belarus (5.2), Austria (4.9), Georgia (4.8), Norway (4.2), and Switzerland (4.1). The United States has 2.4 doctors per 1,000 people, and Canada has 2.0. The lowest numbers are found in Global South countries such as Colombia, Ghana, and Mauritania, with 0.1 physicians per 1,000 people, and Afghanistan and Cambodia, with 0.2 physicians per 1,000 people (NationMaster 2014). Most of these physicians are found in urban areas. The World Health Organization recommends at least 1 physician for every 600 citizens. In some Global South countries, local rural residents are trained both in emergency medicine and to recognize illnesses. In Rwanda, Africa, health care workers make house calls to inquire about diseases and provide the required treatment, referring those with serious illnesses to regional hospitals.

ENGAGING SOCIOLOGY

Access to Health Care for Rich and Poor

FIGURE 11.7 Number of Physicians per 1,000 People

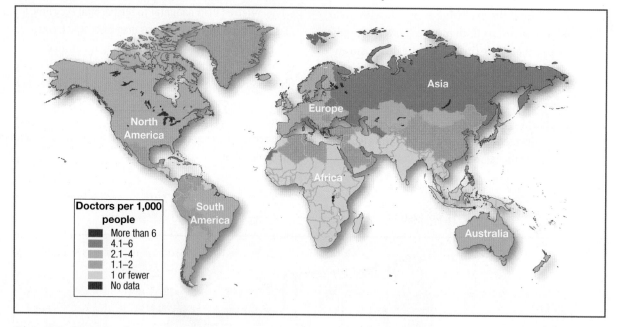

Source: NationMaster (2014).

Engaging With Sociology

Study the map in Figure 11.7. Then, answer the following questions:

1. How do you think the scarcity of physicians in the Global South and rural areas affects the health care of individuals and the functioning of communities and society?

2. How might a surplus of physicians influence health care?

3. How could a nation increase the number of qualified medical workers and people who have access to health care?

4. How might health care differ depending on where one lives in the United States?

Each society organizes its health care system in ways congruous with its culture. All nations search for ways to contain costs; provide accessible, high-quality, and effective care; manage care for disabilities and chronic illnesses; and find treatments for infectious diseases (Pescosolido and Boyer 2010). Western scientific medicine has spread throughout the world but some of the ideas from other parts of the world now influence Western approaches to health and illness, as the following example from China illustrates.

One result of the spread of medical ideas around the world is the complementary and alternative medicines (CAM) movement in the United States and other Global North countries. CAM includes health care systems, practices, and products used to complement conventional medicine or as alternative medicine used in place of conventional medicine. CAM therapies include acupuncture and chiropractic, natural products, special diets, and megavitamin therapy, and nearly 40% of U.S. citizens use one or more of these approaches (GoodTherapy.org 2012; National Center for Complementary and Alternative Medicine 2013). Although acupuncture has been practiced for more than 5,000 years in China, only in the 1970s, when relations with China improved, did this treatment become known and practiced in the West. Many doctors in the Global North reject the practice as unscientific and ineffective, and some regulating agencies have put limits on its practice. However, many patients seek out those who can practice it. Some insurance companies cover the costs of acupuncture, and the World Health Organization recognizes more than 40 conditions that acupuncture can treat effectively (G. Weiss and Lonnquist 2015).

Health care systems around the world illustrate the impact of national and global political and economic factors on the health care available to citizens. The political and economic systems of countries and the health of their economies influence their philosophy toward health care and the money each country puts into it. International events, such as wars and the spread of refugees, influence availability of health care within countries. International organizations, such as the World Health Organization, play a key role in addressing epidemics and pandemics throughout the world.

Thinking Sociologically

What can countries learn by studying other health care systems? Give examples.

An unemployed man, Dwi Waryono, holds a placard advertising his kidney for sale in Jakarta in 2013. The placard reads, "I was a blood donor. I will donate my kidney to pay for the cost of my children's schooling." For people in severe poverty, selling a body organ is a way to care for one's family, for it can raise several thousand dollars.

Globalization of Medical Problems. The international sale of body parts reveals how health care relates to social stratification and crosses national borders. In some countries, people at the bottom of the stratification system are so desperately poor that they sell parts of their body to help their families survive. For example, mothers and fathers in some poor slums of Mumbai and other cities in India and Pakistan sell their kidneys to those who plan to resell them to patients (primarily in Global North nations) in need of a new kidney and with the money to buy one. The individuals who sell their body parts tend to do so for money to pay for housing, food, education for their children, and dowries for their daughters to marry. In the process, their health can suffer due to complications during or after the surgery to remove their organ, and when the money is gone, life is even more difficult. Although laws were passed in India in 1994 banning the sale of human organs, few violators face capture and punishment ("Body Parts for Sale" 2008, Scheper-Hughes 2014). At last report, the only nation where the sale of body organs was legal was Iran, which permits the sale of blood, breast milk, hair, eggs, sperm, and even the womb ("Body Parts for Sale" 2008; Kasperkevic 2014).

Three crimes are common in the organ trade: deceiving victims into giving up an organ, not paying an agreed price for removal of an organ, and treating persons for an ailment that may or may not exist and taking organs in

FIGURE 11.8 Top 10 Causes of Death in Low-Income Countries, 2012

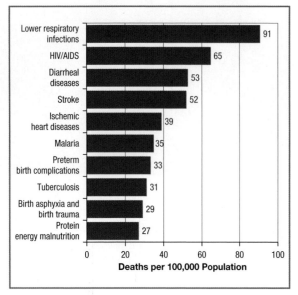

Deaths per 100,000 Population

Source: World Health Organization (2014b).

FIGURE 11.9 Top 10 Causes of Death in High-Income Countries, 2012

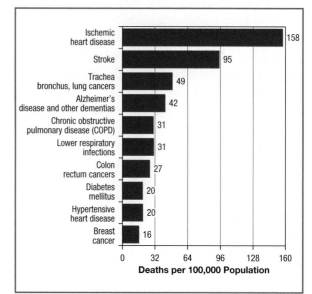

Deaths per 100,000 Population

Source: World Health Organization (2014b).

the process. The most commonly trafficked are kidneys, the liver, and any other organ that can be removed (United Nations Office on Drugs and Crime 2017). Recently, sales of skin, bones, tissue, and dental implants from fresh corpses have grown, with a center of such activity in the Ukraine. The United States is the biggest market, with 2 million such products bought each year. These body parts allow those willing and wealthy enough to buy them to see with cornea transplants, walk with recycled tendons, and replace a dying kidney with a healthy one (K. Wilson et al. 2012).

The global stratification of health care can also be seen in the different causes of death in affluent/Global North versus poor/Global South countries for the 55 million people who die worldwide every year (World Health Organization 2014b). Relatively few people in the Global North die of infectious diseases. Yet infectious diseases still cause the majority of deaths in the Global South, reducing life expectancy in some poor countries to 50 years or less. Figures 11.8 and 11.9 show the leading causes of death in low- and high-income countries.

Thinking Sociologically

What are some factors that account for the differences in causes of death between high- and low-income countries? What might be done to tackle these disparities?

Globalization and the Mobility of Disease. Traveling humans throughout history have provided passage to pathogens on their bodies and in their luggage—great plagues, smallpox, syphilis, and others. Today, influenza, Ebola, SARS, polio, and other diseases thought to be under control many years ago are resurfacing (Ostroff 2013). Because far more people travel around the globe today than in the past, diseases can spread more widely and quickly.

Consider measles in the United States, which has reemerged in several areas. Measles, a vaccine-preventable disease, has ranged from 37 U.S. cases in 2004 to 220 in 2011, 187 in 2013, and over 600 cases in 2014. Why? One source of the disease is travelers returning from trips to foreign countries where the disease is still common. For example, U.S. residents who visited the Philippines in 2014 brought back the disease and infected others (CDC 2015b, 2015d; Iannelli 2014). Also, measles can spread if it reaches a community where many people are not vaccinated (such as parts of California where the movement to "opt out" of vaccinations has been high). This is one reason why California passed a law in 2015 making it mandatory for all public and private school children to be vaccinated against measles and other diseases (unless they cannot for medical reasons) (Perkins 2015).

The density and urbanization of the world's population (discussed in Chapter 15) also affects human health. For example, use of land and space determines the number of rodents and insects, the water supplies, and the direct contact people have with one another. Currently, about half of the world's people live in urban areas, many in slums surrounding major cities. Problems such as open sewers, inadequate sanitation, lack of electricity, and polluted water pervade these slums. Overcrowding, combined with these problems, causes infectious diseases to spread more rapidly. Growing numbers of locations with shared circulated air (airplanes, domed stadiums, and air-conditioned office buildings and hotels) also spread disease. Even climate change and antimicrobial resistance affect the spread of diseases (World Health Organization 2013).

The growing threat of pandemics is one cause for global concern, but the global disparity in the handling of treatable diseases remains an even more pressing issue. The uneven distribution of health care, doctors, and medicines around the world and resistance of some religious groups to inoculating their children has led to many preventable and curable diseases going untreated. In spite of increasingly sophisticated medical technology, as long as there is inequality in countries of our social world, adequate health care will not reach all people and all countries equally.

Getty Images/CARL DE SOUZA/AFP

A health care worker, wearing a protective suit, feeds an Ebola-infected child at a medical facility in Kailahun, the epicenter of the world's Ebola outbreak in 2014.

Thinking Sociologically

We live in a global world, yet our most immediate experiences are local. How might you and your family benefit if international agencies resolve health problems in Africa, Asia, and South America?

In the next chapter we explore two more institutions: politics and economics. Democracy comes in many forms and structures. If you want to live in a society where you have a voice, get involved in the political system and stay well informed about the policies your government is considering or has recently enacted. Political systems need diverse voices and critics—regardless of what party is currently in power—to create vibrant societies that represent the citizens.

WHAT HAVE WE LEARNED?

Sickness and the roles of sick people are social constructions that vary across societies. Although health is a private, personal concern, it is also a public concern, delivered through organizations dispensing health care and government practices determining access and funding of health care. Distant from your daily life but important to your well-being are the global health organizations that concern themselves with global epidemics. In addition, whether you can afford or have access to medical care depends, in part, on the economic conditions in society and the global marketplace of health care delivery.

- Sociology examines the social implications of health and illness—from the micro level of individuals coping with illness to the meso level of institutional interactions and complex organizations that manage health and illness to the global issues of controlling the spread of diseases around the world.

- Whether looking at the medicalization of social problems through labeling or examining functions and socioeconomic conflicts regarding health care in society, various social theories offer alternative lenses through which to view health care systems.

- At the micro level, we can look at issues such as the sick role; how social and cultural factors affect our responses to pain and ill health; and how our age, gender, and other personal aspects of identity relate to our responses to health and illness.

- Hospitals and other elements of organizational complexity, the issues of professionalism and of deprofessionalization of medical personnel, and the linkages between institutions such as the economy, politics, education, and family are all aspects of health care at the meso level.

- Health care is a national issue that relates to the nation's resources, security of its citizens, and types of health care delivery.

- Globally, diseases spread around the planet much faster in our age of rapid travel and migrations. Different forms of health care have also spread throughout the world and influence the approaches we each choose in our own local communities.

- The disparity in health care within and among nations remains the most pressing health care issue facing societies today.

DISCUSSION QUESTIONS

1. Imagine that your state has a law on the ballot that would legalize assisted suicide, following the model of Oregon's law. Would you vote for or against the ballot question? Why? Would the conditions necessary for the legality of assisted suicide described in Oregon's law influence your vote? Why, or why not? Why do you think most of those who participated in the Death with Dignity program in Oregon were Whites with college degrees?

2. Think of the last time you or someone close to you was seriously ill. What were the repercussions of the illness on the micro level? How did these repercussions relate to health care issues on the meso and macro levels?

3. What are three ways social class impacts health? Describe how social class has impacted your health and the health of your family members.

4. Do you think health care is a human right? Why, or why not? How can equality or inequality in health care impact a society?

5. If you were a policy maker, how might you try to curb binge drinking or smoking among college students?

6. Do you think vaccinations should be mandatory for schoolchildren? Why, or why not?

KEY TERMS

deprofessionalization   330
health   316
illness   316

Medicaid   325
medicalization   318
Medicare   315

sick role   323
socialized medicine   326

CONTRIBUTING TO OUR SOCIAL WORLD: *WHAT CAN WE DO?*

At the Local (Micro) Level

- The *Endocrine Society* (http://endocrinefacts.org/ health-conditions/obesity) provides information on a wide range of resources related to studies on eating behavior, many of which are directly applicable to problems faced by students. Plan a support group for those facing weight issues.

- Can you find *healthy food on campus*? If your school does not offer enough healthy options, start a petition, and present it to your campus administrators, asking them to address this issue. Articles that describe some schools' attempts to go healthy can be found at www.hercampus.com/health/10-healthiest-college-dining-halls-america?page=2 and http://greatist.com/health/healthiest-colleges.

At the Organizational/Institutional (Meso) Level

- *Free or low-cost clinics.* Most communities provide health screening and other services to uninsured individuals and families. The U.S. Department of Health and Human Services has a locator website at findahealthcenter.hrsa.gov/Search_HCC.aspx that searches for free clinics by state and city. Most have volunteer and internship opportunities that afford interesting and valuable experiences, especially if you are considering a career in a health care field.

At the National/Global (Macro) Level

- *The Joint United Nations Program on HIV/AIDS* (www.unaids.org/en) works throughout the world to fight the pandemic. If you are interested in learning more about and possibly raising funds for this effort, go to www.unaids.org/en.

- *World Vision* (www.worldvision.org) helps children, their families, and their communities in an effort to combat malnutrition, AIDS, and other health- and poverty-related problems across the world. The organization's Hope Child program lists several suggestions for getting involved, including sponsorship of a child.

- *AVERT*, an international AIDS charity, provides material to educate yourself and your classmates about AIDS on the organization's website at www.avert.org/worldaid.htm.

⑤SAGE edge™

Get the edge on your studies. **edge.sagepub.com/ballantinecondensed5e**

- Take a quiz to find out what you've learned.
- Review key terms with eFlashcards.
- Watch videos that enhance chapter content.

12 Politics and Economics

Probing Power, Dissecting Distribution

Power probes every aspect of our lives with intimidating force, even as economic distribution cuts across the social fabric. Sociology helps us probe and dissect the sources and consequences of political and economic power.

MICRO

ME (AND MY FAMILY)

LOCAL ORGANIZATIONS AND COMMUNITY
Power struggles and finances influence how well a local fraternity or a women's civic club functions.

MESO

NATIONAL ORGANIZATIONS, INSTITUTIONS, AND ETHNIC SUBCULTURES
State or provincial governments, political parties, and corporations within the state affect quality of life.

MACRO

SOCIETY
National governments and court systems set rules that resolve conflicts and establish standards for conducting business.

GLOBAL COMMUNITY
Cross-national organizations such as the United Nations and the World Court and global human rights movements like Amnesty International set standards for nations.

WHAT YOU WILL LEARN IN THIS CHAPTER

This chapter will help you do the following:

12.1 Describe the sociological definition of power.

12.2 Discuss the importance of power and privilege in societies.

12.3 Compare the key points of the pluralist and elite theories of power.

12.4 Explain why some people participate in political systems and others do not.

12.5 Describe the major types of governmental systems in operation today.

12.6 Provide examples of the threats political systems can face from internal and external groups vying for power.

● THINK ABOUT IT

Micro: Small groups and local community	How do people in your local community use power in constructive or destructive ways?
Meso: National institutions, complex organizations, and ethnic groups	How does the political institution interact with the economic institution? How are different racial and ethnic groups affected by power and privilege?
Macro: National and global systems	How does economic instability threaten a national government? Why do struggles over power and privilege often evolve into war and terrorism?

Imagine that a nuclear disaster has occurred. The mortality rate is stunning. The survivors gather for human support and collectively attempt to meet their basic survival needs. They come from varying backgrounds and have diverse skills. Before the disaster, some—the stockbroker and the business executive, for instance—earned more money and held higher social status than the others, but that is in the past. Faced with the new and unfamiliar situation, different skills are more immediately important for survival.

Where should this group begin? Think about the options. Some sort of organization seems essential, a structure that will help the group meet its needs. Food, shelter, and medical care are paramount. Those with experience in agriculture, building trades, and health care are likely to take leadership roles to provide these initial necessities. As time goes on, the need for clear norms and rules emerges. These survivors decide that all members must work—must contribute their share of effort to the collective survival. At first, these norms are unwritten, but gradually, some norms and rules are declared more important than others and are recorded, with sanctions (penalties) attached for noncompliance. Survivors form committees to deal with group concerns, and a semblance of a judicial system emerges. One person is appointed to coordinate work shifts and others to oversee emerging aspects of this small society's life. This scenario could play out in many ways.

What is happening? A social structure is evolving. Not everyone in the group will agree with the structure, and some people will propose alternatives. Whose ideas will be adopted? Leadership roles may fall to the physically strongest, or perhaps the most persuasive, or those with the most skills and knowledge for survival. Those most competent at organizing may become the leaders, but that outcome is by no means assured.

In our world of power and privilege, a war, an invading power, or a revolutionary overthrow of an unstable government can change the form of a political system overnight, necessitating rapid reorganization. The daily news brings stories of governments overthrown by military leaders in coups, with new governments emerging to fill the gap, as has been happening in various parts of the Middle East and Africa. The opening scenario and the political activity in our modern society share a common element: power. The concept of power is critical to understanding many aspects of our social world.

In this chapter, we focus primarily on the political and economic dimensions of society because both political and economic systems enforce the distribution of power and resources in a society. Political systems involve the power relationships between individuals and larger social institutions. Economic systems produce and distribute goods and services. Not everyone gets an equal share, thus giving some citizens privileges that others do not have.

We consider the nature of power, politics, and economics at each level in our social world: theoretical perspectives on power and privilege; individuals and power; political systems and the distribution of power and privilege through political and economic institutions; and national and global systems of governance, including international conflicts, war, and terrorism. Because the topic of economics has been explored in many chapters of this book, we put more emphasis on political systems and their relation to economic systems.

● Thinking Sociologically

Imagine that global climate change has caused massive flooding on your island nation. Only a few people have survived. How would you construct a new social system? What are the issues you would need to resolve to build a new society?

WHAT IS POWER?

Power is an age-old theme in many great scholarly discussions. Social philosophers since Plato, Aristotle, and

Socrates have addressed the issue of political systems and power. Machiavelli, an early 16th-century Italian political philosopher, is perhaps best known for his observation that "the ends justify the means." His understanding of how power was exercised in the 15th, 16th, and 17th centuries significantly influenced how monarchs used the powers of the state (the means) to obtain wealth, new territories, and trade dominance (the ends) (Machiavelli [1532] 2010).

The most common definition of power used in social sciences today comes from Max Weber, who saw **power** as *the ability of a person or group to realize its own will in group action, even against resistance of others who disagree* (Weber 1947). Building on Weber's idea of power, we can identify various power arenas. Two key arenas of power are the nation-state and the economic system. The leaders of a national government attempt to control the behavior of individuals through (a) *physical force and the threat of violence* (through a police force), (b) *symbolic control*, such as the manipulation of people (through control of the media), and (c) *rules of conduct* that channel behavior toward desired patterns (through laws). For example, the dictator and military in Syria have used torture, rape, and death to intimidate dissidents and their families and used the media to present the opposition as terrorists. The opposition has also used force and social media but does not have the same degree of power.

Control of the economy is another important source of power. Conflict theorists argue that those with power over the economy can control government officials (who are dependent on campaign contributions from the wealthy) and can convince the public that what is good for the wealthy is good for everyone. The members of the middle and working classes become convinced via the media that further tax breaks and advantages to the wealthy are—in the long run—in their own self-interest. In the United States, the media is largely controlled by wealthy owners of large corporations. Five companies—Time Warner, Disney, News Corporation, Bertelsmann, and Viacom (formerly CBS)—control 90% of television, radio, and newspaper outlets, and they protect the interests of wealthy owners in the way news is presented (Lutz 2012; Scheiber and Cohen 2015; Sommer 2014).

POWER AND PRIVILEGE IN OUR SOCIAL WORLD

Power can be found at even micro levels of interaction, from individuals to family groups. In family life, relations often involve negotiation and sometimes conflict over how to run

Former secretary of state and senator Hillary Clinton (*top*) and billionaire business man and former reality TV star Donald Trump campaign during the 2016 presidential campaign. The outcome of the election led to Republicans gaining control of the executive branch of the U.S. government, as well as the House and the Senate.

a household and spend money. Interactions between parents and children also involve power issues, as parents socialize their children. Indeed, the controversy over whether spanking is an effective discipline or an abusive imposition of pain is a question of how parents use their power to teach their children and control their behavior.

At the meso level, power operates in cities, counties, and states or provinces. Governments make decisions about which corporations receive tax breaks to locate their plants within the region. They pass laws that regulate everything from how long one's grass can grow before a fine is imposed to how public schools will be funded. Therefore, people have an interest in influencing governments by contributing to political campaigns and helping elect the people who support their views. Interest

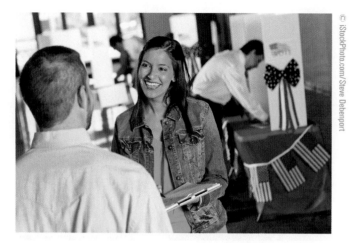

Individual campaign workers in local communities try to influence voters at the micro level to determine who will wield power in meso and macro systems.

groups, such as environmental advocacy, flat tax, and gay rights organizations, also wield power and try to influence the political process at the meso level.

Power processes pervade and cut across micro, meso, and macro levels. Locally organized groups can force change that influences politics at the local, state or provincial, national, or global level. Provincial or state laws shape what can and cannot be done at the local level. These laws may either limit or enhance the ability of citizens to protest or express their views by determining where and when protests can occur. At the macro level, laws at the national and global levels influence state, provincial, and county politics and policies. Global treaties, for example, affect national autonomy. Reluctance to yield national autonomy is the main reason the United States and a few other countries have refused to ratify seemingly very benign global treaties, such as the Convention on the Rights of the Child (UNICEF 2005).

Power can also be understood in terms of the allocation of economic resources in a society and what factors influence patterns of resource distribution. Both economic and political systems are important in sociologists' consideration of power distribution in any society. Let us first consider the theoretical lenses that help us understand power and politics.

Thinking Sociologically

Weber's definition of power involves control over group action from micro to macro levels. At what level do you have the most power? Why? Be sure to give examples.

THEORETICAL PERSPECTIVES ON POWER AND PRIVILEGE

Do you and I have any real decision-making power? Can our voices or votes make a difference, or do leaders hold all of the power? Many sociologists and political scientists have studied these questions and found several answers to who holds power and the relationship between the rulers and the ruled.

Micro- and Meso-Level Perspectives: Legitimacy of Power

Symbolic interactionists look at how loyalty to the power of the state is created—a loyalty so strong that citizens are willing to die for the state in a war. In the early years of the United States, citizens' loyalty tended to be mostly to individual states. Even as late as the Civil War, Northern battalions fought under the flag of their own state rather than that of the United States.

Most people in the United States now tend to think of themselves as U.S. citizens more than Virginians, Pennsylvanians, or Oregonians, and they are willing to defend the whole country. National symbols such as anthems and flags help create loyalty to nations. The treatment of flags illustrates the social construction of meaning around national symbols. The next "Engaging Sociology" explores this issue.

Socialization of individuals at the micro level generally instills a strong sense of the legitimacy and authority of the reigning government in a particular society. This includes loyalty to a flag or other symbol that represents the nation. Individuals learn their political and economic attitudes, values, and behaviors—their political socialization—from family, schools, the media, and their nation. For example, national leaders provide much of the information for newspapers and other media and can spin that information to suit their needs and manage the perceptions of the public. Governments also play a role in what is taught in schools, which shapes attitudes of the citizenry regarding democracy, capitalism, socialism, and other political and economic systems (Glasberg and Shannon 2011).

ENGAGING SOCIOLOGY

The Flag, Symbolism, and Patriotism

Flags have become pervasive symbols of nations, helping to create a national identity (Billig 1995). National loyalty becomes sacred, and that sacredness is embedded in the flag as a symbol of patriotism.

Care of the U.S. flag is an interesting example of symbolism and respect for that symbol. Flag etiquette instructions make it clear that flying a flag that is faded, soiled, or dirty is considered an offense to the flag.

Other aspects of the U.S. Flag Code, which specifies what is considered official respect for or desecration of the flag, are interesting precisely because many people violate this code while they believe themselves to be displaying their patriotism (Sons of Union Veterans of the Civil War 2010).

1. The flag should never be used in any form of advertising. It should not be embroidered on cushions, handkerchiefs, or scarves or reproduced on paper napkins, carry-out bags, wrappers, or anything else that will soon be discarded.

2. No part of the flag—depictions of stars and stripes that are in any form other than that approved for the flag itself—should ever be used as a costume, a clothing item, or an athletic uniform.

3. Displaying a flag after dark should not be done unless it is illuminated, and it should not be left out when it is raining.

4. The flag should never be represented flat or horizontally (as many marching bands do). It should always be aloft and free.

5. The flag should under no circumstances be used as a ceiling covering. (U.S. Flag Code 2008)

According to the standards established by U.S. military representatives and congressional action, any of these forms of display may be considered a desecration of the flag, yet the meaning that most citizens give to these acts may be quite different. Symbolic interactionists are interested in the meaning people give to actions and how symbols themselves inform behavior.

* * * * *

Engaging With Sociology

1. Do you think wearing a shirt or sweater with the U.S. stars and stripes in some sort of artistic design is an act of desecration of the flag or a statement of patriotism? Why?

2. Is it disrespectful to use a flag in advertising, to put stars and stripes on disposable napkins, or to have a flag flat, covering a football field? Why might the military personnel who developed the flag code think that it is disrespectful?

© iStockphoto.com/&#169 MelissaAnneGalleries

This man no doubt feels he is expressing his patriotism, yet technically, he is violating the U.S. Flag Code and "desecrating" the American flag. During the Vietnam War, protesters risked being attacked for dressing this way and "disrespecting" the flag and the country.

Social Constructions of Politics: Legitimacy, Authority, and Power.

Max Weber distinguished between legitimate and illegitimate power. *Power that people consider legitimate and that is recognized as rightful by those subject to it* is authority (Weber 1947). Governments are given legitimate power when citizens acknowledge that the government has the right to exercise power over them. They adhere to a judge's rulings because they recognize that court decrees are legitimate. In contrast, illegitimate power, or coercion, includes living under force of a military regime or being kidnapped or imprisoned without charge. These distinctions between legitimate and illegitimate power are important to our understanding of how leaders or political institutions establish the right to lead. To Weber, illegitimate power is sustained by brute force or coercion (see Figure 12.1). Authority, on the other hand, is granted by the people subject to the power. They believe in the legitimacy of the authority, so they willingly obey (Weber 1946).

How Do Leaders Gain Legitimate Power?

Generally, leaders with legitimate power gained their positions in one of three ways.

1. *Traditional authority* is passed on through the generations, usually within a family line, so that positions are inherited. Tribal leaders in African societies pass their titles and power to their sons. Japanese and many European royal lines pass from generation to generation. Usually called a monarchy, this has been a very common form of leadership throughout history. Authority is seen as "normal" for a family or a person because of tradition. It has always been done that way, so no one challenges it. When authority is granted based on tradition, authority rests with the position rather than the person. The authority is easily transferred to another heir of that status.

2. *Charismatic authority* is power based on a claim of extraordinary, even divine, personal characteristics. Charismatic leaders often emerge at times of change, when strong, new leadership is needed.

FIGURE 12.1 Weber's Formula Regarding Power

Force + Consent = Power

Force < Consent = Legitimate Power (authority)

Force > Consent = Illegitimate Power (e.g., dictatorship)

REUTERS/Itsuo Inouye/Pool

Japan's Emperor Akihito (*right*) and Empress Michiko leave after praying at the altar of the late prince Tomohito. Japan has the only monarch in the world with the title *emperor*, a position that is inherited through the family line. This is an example of traditional authority.

For charismatic leaders, unlike traditional-authority leaders, the right to lead rests with the person, not the position. Followers believe power is rooted in the personality of a dynamic individual. This is an inherently change-oriented and unstable form of leadership because authority resides in a single person. The most common pattern is that as stability reemerges, power will become institutionalized—rooted in stable routine patterns of the organization. Charismatic leaders are effective during transitional periods but often replaced by rational-legal leaders once affairs of state become stable.

Some examples of charismatic religious leaders include Jesus, Muhammad, Ann Lee (founder of the Shakers in the United States), and Joseph Smith (founder of the Mormon Church). Charismatic political leaders include Mao Zedong in China and Mahatma Gandhi in India. Both men led their countries to independence and had respect from citizens that bordered on awe. One charismatic leader today is Aung San Suu Kyi, a pro-democracy activist and Nobel Prize winner who was imprisoned for many years by the military leadership in Myanmar (formerly known as Burma).

3. *Rational-legal authority* is the most typical type of legitimate power in modern nation-states. Authority is given not to a particular person but to the position the person holds. Such authority is often found in political and economic bureaucracies in the modern states. For example, the president of the United States has authority due to the office he

Aung San Suu Kyi, Nobel Prize winner and opposition leader in Myanmar (Burma), spent 15 years under house arrest after an authoritarian military junta took over the government. Released from house arrest to participate in the changing political situation in Burma, she and her party recently won 40 of 45 elected seats in the government. She is now the state counselor, a position superior to the presidency, and she has authority to direct many of the country's affairs.

holds, just as the CEO of a corporation does. Individuals are granted authority because they have proper training or have proven their merit.

Each of these three types of authority is a "legitimate" exercise of power because the people being governed give their consent, at least implicitly, to the leaders (Weber 1947, [1904–1905] 1958). However, on occasion, leaders overstep their legitimate bounds and rule by force. Some of these rulers, such as Muammar Gaddafi in Libya and Hosni Mubarak of Egypt, are challenged and overthrown.

Self-Interest as a Path to Legitimacy. In contemporary democratic politics, politicians and political commentators often explicitly refer to the self-interests of voters. This reflects the *rational choice perspective* that humans tend to vote for their own benefit, regardless of whether the actions of government would be fair to all citizens.

Both U.S. Republican and Democratic parties try to convince the public and donors that their policies will serve their self-interests. Democrats tend to argue that their government policies benefit citizens directly, with government programs for the middle and working classes, such as government support for preschool and higher education. Republicans, on the other hand, often stress that less government and lower taxes create a greater stimulus to the economy than anything the government can do. Again, the appeal is to self-interests. Members of both political parties promise to help those who support and vote for them once they are put in positions of power.

Many voters do not understand the issues at play in elections and vote for people who support policies that would actually harm them. To make it even more complex, some people vote based on values—right to life, support for the needy, or protection of the environment, for example—because they think it is the right thing to do. The policy may not be in the person's economic self-interests—unless the person is considering the interest of his or her children and grandchildren or long-term noneconomic interests, such as a desire to build a society pleasing to God.

Macro-Level Perspectives: Who Rules?

Pluralist Model of Power. As noted in previous chapters, the pluralist model holds that power is distributed among various groups so that no one group has complete power. According to pluralists, it is primarily through interest groups that you and I influence decision-making processes. Groups such as unions or environmental organizations represent our interests and act to keep power from being concentrated in the hands of an elite few (Dahl 1961; Dye and Zeigler 1983).

One recent example of an interest group in the United States is the Tea Party movement. The Tea Party began as a small group of disaffected individuals opposed to government expansion but became a major influence on Republican Party politics (Skocpol and Williamson 2012). Citizens join such a movement because of a common core of concerns—for example, concern over the size of the national debt; a desire for lower taxes; and a deep distrust of the federal government and power in a centralized location (Tea Party 2016; U.S. Debt Clock 2016; U.S. Government Accountability Office 2015). The group has elected a substantial number of its members to the U.S. Congress and now has a very strong influence over the direction of the Republican-led House of Representatives (Martin and Meckler 2012; Skocpol and Williamson 2012).

Interest groups can influence laws and policies by mobilizing large numbers of voters or political donors. Examples include efforts to influence health care reform in the United States; combat global climate change; and reform government, business, and banking industry practices. Greenpeace; Common Cause; Earth First!; Bread for the World; Focus on the Family; the Family Research Council; the Service Employees International Union; American Enterprise Institute; and other consumer, environmental, religious, and political action groups have had impacts on policy decisions. According to pluralists, shared power is found in each person's ability to join groups and influence policy decisions and outcomes.

National or international nongovernmental organizations (NGOs or INGOs) can have a major impact on global issues and policy making, as exemplified by Save the Children, Doctors Without Borders, Islamic Relief International, and microcredit organizations like the Grameen Bank that work in the field of international development (Briner 2015; Global Journal 2013). NGOs exert influence on power holders because of the numbers they represent, the money they control, the issues they address, and the effectiveness of their spokespeople or lobbyists. Sometimes, they form coalitions around issues of concern, such as the environment, human rights, health care, or women's and children's issues. The efforts of religious, business, and labor unions for immigration reform provide an example of such a coalition. Each of these groups, with its own set of constituents, believes that immigration reform is in its best interest.

According to pluralists, multiple power centers offer the best chance to maintain democratic forms of government because no one group dominates and many citizens are involved. Although an interest group may dominate decision making on a specific issue, no one group dictates all policy. On the other hand, some theorists maintain that only a small group of elite people really have much power.

Elite Model of Power. The power elite model asserts that it is inevitable that a small group of elite will rule societies. As we discussed in earlier chapters, they argue that this is the nature of individuals and society and that pluralists are imagining a world that does not exist. Individuals have limited power through interest groups, but real power is held by the power elite (Domhoff 2008, 2014; Dye 2002; C. Mills 1956). They wield power through their institutional roles and make decisions about war, peace, the economy, wages, taxes, justice, education, welfare, and health issues—all of which have a serious impact on citizens. These powerful elites attempt to maintain, perpetuate, and even strengthen their rule. Indeed, they are seen as playing central roles in both Republican and Democratic political parties in the United States.

Robert Michels, a well-known political philosopher, believed that elite rule is inevitable. He described this pattern of domination as the *iron law of oligarchy*. In democratic and totalitarian societies alike, leaders have influence over who succeeds them and to whom they give political favors. This influence eventually leads those in elite positions to abuse their power (Michels [1911] 1967).

Social philosopher Vilfredo Pareto expanded on this idea of abuse of power, pointing out that abuse would cause a counter group to challenge the elite for power. Eventually, as the latter group gains power, its members would become corrupt as well, and the cycle—a *circulation of elites*—would continue (Pareto [1911] 1955). Corruption in many countries illustrates this pattern, as can be seen in current headlines from such various nations as Greece, Guatemala, Zimbabwe, and Bangladesh.

C. Wright Mills also argued that there is an invisible but interlocking power elite in U.S. society, consisting of leaders in military, business, and political spheres, wielding their power from behind the scenes. They make the key political, economic, and social decisions for the nation and manipulate what the public hears (C. Mills 1956). A few wealthy citizens of the United States form a cohesive economic-political power structure that represents their interests. Many of those who hold top positions on corporate boards or in the foreign-policy-making agencies of national government attended the same private preparatory schools and Ivy League colleges—Brown, Columbia, Cornell, Dartmouth, Harvard, University of Pennsylvania, Princeton, and Yale—and created lasting connections (Domhoff 2008, 2014; Howard 2007; Persell and Cookson 1985).

Elite theorists believe that government seldom regulates business. Instead, business co-opts politicians to support its interests by providing the financial support needed to run political election campaigns (Domhoff 2014).

Pluralists, however, believe that a powerful government serves as a balance to the enormous power of the corporate world. Big business and big government are safety checks against tyranny—and each is convinced that the other is too big.

● Thinking Sociologically

Do you think your national society is controlled by pluralist interest groups or a power elite? Can an individual outside of a power elite help to influence policies in your nation? What makes you think so?

INDIVIDUALS, POWER, AND PARTICIPATION: MICRO-LEVEL ANALYSIS

Whether you have health insurance or are subject to a military draft depends, in part, on the political and economic decisions made by the government in power. Political systems influence our personal lives in myriad ways, some of which are readily apparent: health and safety regulations, taxation, a military draft, and regulations on the food and the drugs we buy. In this section, we explore the impact individuals have on the government and the variables that influence participation in political and economic policy-making processes. At the micro level, individuals decide to vote or otherwise participate in the political system. This private decision is, in turn, affected by where those individuals fall in the stratification system of society, not just by personal choices.

Participation in Democratic Processes

Citizens in democratic countries have the right to free and fair elections. Many social scientists, including sociologists, have tried to understand what influences citizens' decisions on whether and how to vote. Political sociologists want to know how participation affects (and is affected by) an individual's perception of his or her power in relationship to the state. They look at how such trends as growth in Hispanic and Asian groups, shifts of the population to different regions of the country and from rural to urban areas, changing family structures and shifting women's roles, the aging of baby boomers, and increasing resentment of the political status quo by many less educated citizens influence the electorate and elections (Teixeira and Halpin 2012). These factors combine with ideology and attitudes about government to influence participation in elections.

Levels of Participation in Politics. As mentioned in previous chapters, wealthier people are more likely to vote. For example, they tend to

- have been socialized to believe they can make an impact on the political process,
- benefit from an educational background that allows them to understand the issues at hand and how their own self-interests are at stake,

Two woman in Afghanistan cast their ballots during the 2014 presidential elections. In many parts of the world, voting is not just a treasured privilege, it is an act of courage.

- have the time to follow the news and political issues, and
- experience a more flexible schedule that allows them the time to vote.

Those with little money, on the other hand, tend to feel that politics has little relevance for them (apathy) or that they cannot affect the process and are disaffected by the scandals or corruption in politics (alienation from a system that does not value them). Participation in elections in the United States is the second lowest of the Global North democracies, as indicated in Table 12.1.

Structural factors also influence voting. The debates over voter registration in the United States are a case in point, with some states combing their voter lists for ineligible voters or making registration and voting difficult for some citizens, usually the elderly, minorities, and people in poverty who may have problems obtaining acceptable ID. By contrast, in 28 countries, voting is compulsory, a legal obligation of citizenship, and voter turnout tends to be close to 90%. For example, 10 countries that enforce voting are Argentina, Australia, Brazil, the Democratic Republic of the Congo, Ecuador, Luxembourg, Nauru, Peru, Singapore, and Uruguay; it is a violation of the law not to vote (Desilver 2015; Frankal 2011; *World Factbook* 2016b). Fines, community service, and even jail time are penalties for not voting. Elections are held over many days to ensure that people can get to the polls. Some other countries also make sure that ethnic minorities and women have a voice by structuring elections to ensure broad representation. Even inmates in

Table 12.1   Average Voter Participation (1950–2012) and Most Recent Election Participation

Country	Voter Participation (All Elections From 1950 to 2012)*	Most Recent Parliamentary or Congressional Election**
Italy	92.5%	75.2% (2013)
Iceland	89.5%	81.4% (2013)
New Zealand	86.2%	77.0% (2014)
South Africa	85.5%	73.5% (2014)
Austria	85.1%	74.9% (2013)
Netherlands	84.8%	74.6% (2012)
Australia	84.4%	93.2% (2013)
Denmark	83.6%	85.9% (2015)
Sweden	83.3%	85.8% (2014)
Germany	80.6%	71.3% (2013)
United Kingdom	74.9%	66.1% (2015)
Argentina	70.6%	81.1% (2015)
Japan	69.0%	52.7% (2014)
Canada	68.4%	68.3% (2015)
France	67.3%	55.4% (2012)
Bolivia	61.4%	87.5% (2014)
United States	48.3%	42.5% (2014)
Mexico	48.1%	47.7% (2015)

Note: The figures are averages of voter participation for all elections since 1945. Note that enfranchisement of women and various ethnic minorities changed in some countries during that time, so these should be viewed as very crude overall indicators of voting patterns. To see the voting participation figures for 172 countries in the world, go to www.idea.int/vt.

Sources: *International Institute for Democracy and Electoral Assistance (2012). **International Institute for Democracy and Electoral Assistance (2016).

prison are expected to vote in some countries. As we learned in Chapter 9, a war-torn African country—Rwanda—now has the highest percentage of women in government of any nation in the world (see Table 9.1 on page 255) (Inter-Parliamentary Union 2016; McCrummen 2008; Paxton and Hughes 2007).

A higher percentage than normal of eligible U.S. voters turned out in the 2012 and 2016 presidential elections: 58.7% and 59.7% respectively, but that means more people abstained from voting than voted for either of the top-two candidates (41.6% not voting in 2016) (Ingraham 2016; United States Elections Project 2016). Still, the numbers have generally been higher in the 21st century than in the 3 decades from 1970 to 2000 (Lederman 2012). There is also considerable range in voter participation by state, with a high of 74.2% in Minnesotans' voting to a low in the mid-40% range in Hawaii and Utah (United States Elections Project 2016b).

In off-year elections—when many senators, congressional representatives, and state governors are elected—the turnout hovers in the low 40s or even below. If 40% of the eligible population votes, and it is a very close election, only slightly more than 20% of the citizenry may have elected the new officeholder. So voter turnout is an important issue for a society that purports to be a democracy. In 2014, a non-presidential election year, the overall national turnout was only 33.9%, and Indiana had the lowest turnout at 28.7% (Alter 2014; United States Elections Project 2016b). Figure 12.2 indicates U.S. voter turnout since 1990.

POWER AND RESOURCE DISTRIBUTION: MESO-LEVEL ANALYSIS

In southern Africa, Bantu tribal groups provide for heirs to take on leadership when a leader dies. When there is no male heir to the position, a female from the same lineage is appointed. This woman must assume the legal and social roles of a male husband, father, and chief by acting as a male and taking a "wife." The wife is assigned male sexual partners, who become the biological fathers of her children. This provides heirs for the lineage, but the female chief is their social father because she has socially become a male. This pattern has been common practice in many southern Bantu societies and among

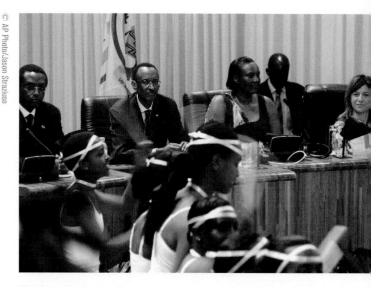

The Rwandan government has a higher percentage of women in its legislature than any government in the world.

many other populations in four separate geographic areas of Africa. Anthropologists interpret this as a means of maintaining public positions of dominance and power in the hands of males in a particular family and community (D. O'Brien 1977). Ruling groups in society—in this

FIGURE 12.2 Voter Turnout in the United States, 1990–2014 (Percentage of Eligible Voters)

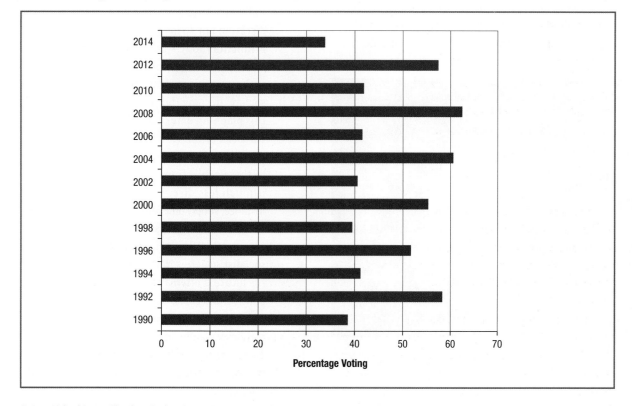

Source: United States Elections Project, "Voter Turnout Data" (http://www.electproject.org/home/voter-turnout/voter-turnout-data).

case, a meso-level tribal society under the jurisdiction of a nation-state—have mechanisms for ensuring a smooth transition of power to keep the controlling structure functioning.

Meso-level political institutions include state or provincial governments, national political parties, and large formal organizations within the nation. Those political institutions also influence and are influenced by other meso-level institutions: family, education, religion, health care, and economics.

Purposes of Political and Economic Institutions

We have learned in earlier chapters that each institution has purposes or functions in society. Just as family, education, health care, and religion meet certain societal needs, so do the political and economic institutions. The following six activities are typical societal purposes (functions) of meso-level political and economic institutions. They set the stage for power and privilege carried out at the macro level in national and international arenas.

1. *To maintain social control.* We expect to live in safety, to live according to certain "rules," to be employed in meaningful work, and to participate in other activities prescribed or protected by law. Ideally, governments help clarify expectations and customs and implement laws that express societal values.

One function of governments is to provide protection from external threats—the role of the military establishment. These soldiers are in training for that role.

2. *To serve as an arbiter in disputes.* When disputes arise over property or the actions of another individual or group, a judicial branch of government can intervene. In some systems, such as the tribal groups mentioned before, a council of elders or powerful individuals performs judicial functions. In other cases, elected or appointed judges have the right to hear disputes, make judgments, and carry out punishment for infractions.

3. *To protect citizens.* Governments are responsible for protecting citizens from takeover by external powers or disruption from internal sources.

4. *To represent the group in relations with other groups or societies.* Individuals cannot negotiate agreements with foreign neighbors. Official representatives deal with other officials to negotiate arms and trade agreements, establish and maintain a nation's airways, determine fishing rights, and establish military bases in foreign lands, among other agreements.

The four functions listed thus far are rather clearly political in nature; the two that follow are areas of contention between political and economic realms.

5. *To make plans for the future of the group.* As individuals, we have little direct impact on the direction our society takes, but the official governmental body—be it elected, appointed, or imposed through force—shares responsibility with economic institutions for planning in the society. In some (but not all) socialist societies, this planning determines how many engineers, teachers, or nurses are needed. The appropriate numbers of people are then trained according to these projections. In other societies, power is much less direct. In capitalist systems, for instance, supply and demand are assumed to regulate the economic system, and there is less governmental planning in economic matters than in socialist societies. The question of who plans for the future is often a source of stress between the political and economic institutions: Are the planners elected politicians and public servants or private entrepreneurs?

6. *To provide for the needs of its citizens.* Governments differ greatly in the degree to which they attempt to meet the material needs of citizens.

Some provide for most of the health and welfare needs of citizens, defined as *positive human rights*—to life, health, education, a healthy environment, and survival of one's culture (Frezzo 2015). Other governments tend to leave these largely to individuals, families, local community agencies, and other institutions, such as faith communities. Not everyone agrees that providing for needs is an inherent responsibility of the state. Some people believe that the economy will produce jobs, goods, and services for the population if the government gets out of the way and lets individuals make decisions based on their self-interests. Those who take this position define human rights in "negative" terms—that is, what governments can *not* do to people: abuse, humiliation, exploitation, exclusion, and interference with individual freedom (Frezzo 2015). The debates over health care and welfare systems in the United States point to conflicts over who should be responsible: the state or private individuals. Should such services be coordinated by the government or left to "the invisible hand" of market forces?

Clearly the role of political legislators is complex. Not only are they supposed to protect the self-interests of their constituents—those who elected them—but they are to make decisions about governmental policy that are in the best interest of the society as a whole. *Policy* (a course of action adopted and pursued by a government, ruler, or political party) is complex precisely because there are always unanticipated consequences, sometimes shocking to the advocates of that policy. One role of public sociologists—such as Lindsay Owens, described in the next "Sociologists in Action" feature—is to advise legislators.

The ways in which governments and economic institutions carry out the six functions of government are largely determined by society's dominant philosophies of power and political structures. Political and economic institutions, like family and religious institutions, come in many forms. In essence, these variations in political institutions reflect variations in human ideas of power.

Thinking Sociologically

In an era of terrorist threats, how do you think the "protecting the safety of the citizens" function has affected the ability of governments to perform other functions?

Meso- and Macro-Level Systems of Power and Distribution

Whereas *politics* refers to the social institution that determines and exercises power relations in society, *economics* is the social institution that deals with the production and distribution of goods and services. Both politics and economics focus on questions related directly to the concept of power and power relationships among and between individuals, organizations, nation-states, and societies. Economic and political systems overlap, in part, because those who have power also have access to resources. How goods are distributed to the members of society—a major function of economics—is often determined by who has political power.

Successful political campaigns, except at the most local level, require significant financial resources, so attaining political positions involves cultivating relationships with leaders in the economic system. Thus, there is a reciprocal relationship between economics and politics. In many countries, the government is the largest employer, purchaser of goods, controller of exports and imports, and regulator of industry and of interest rates. In the United States, many government regulatory agencies, such as the Food and Drug Administration, Consumer Financial Protection Bureau, Department of Agriculture, and Justice Department, attempt to watch over the economic sector to protect consumers.

Government officials have a vested interest in the well-being of the economy, for should the economy fail, the state would be likely to fail as well. Recessions, depressions, and high rates of inflation put severe strains on governments that need stable economies to run properly. When problems occur, government officials are inclined to increase their roles in the economic sector. Witness the measures, such as bailouts of financially unstable banks and corporations, taken by governments to stabilize their economies when they are in jeopardy.

On September 29, 2008, the Dow Jones Industrial Average dropped an unprecedented 777 points and fell another 782 points a week later. President Bush and Congress immediately began to look for "stimulus packages" to keep the economy from going into a deep recession. When Barack Obama became president in 2009, turning the economy around became one of the key challenges of his presidency.

A dramatic drop in financial markets indicates a loss of the population's confidence in the economy and a mass reluctance to invest in it. Lending institutions cannot

SOCIOLOGISTS IN ACTION
LINDSAY OWENS

Using Sociological Training in Government Policy Work

I work as a policy adviser for a senator in the United States Congress. Certain aspects of my job appear, at first, to be wildly incompatible with my sociological training. For one, I am tasked with being an expert on hundreds of topics—from how payroll taxes are allocated between the two Social Security trust funds, to whether a big parent company has legal obligations to the employees in one of its franchises, to how securities regulation differs for fixed and variable annuities. In academia, I would not be considered an expert on any of these topics. I have not written a peer-reviewed article on them, given a colloquium talk on them, or covered them in a course lecture.

Senate offices, however, particularly the offices of relatively new members, are small. As a result, each policy expert covers an enormous range of topics. When an issue in one of the areas I am responsible for bubbles to the surface—because there is legislation on the floor, a committee hearing, or a constituent matter back in our home state—I have to get up to speed immediately. I do not have 3 months to dive into the academic literature. Instead, I rely on my sociological training to find information fast. I have to figure out quickly where I can get trustworthy information. I talk to experts— sometimes academics, sometimes Senate committee staff, and sometimes the Congressional Research Service—and then I read as much as I can as rapidly as I can and recommend a course of action. Although this was initially nerve-racking, I now find the intellectual challenge stimulating and rewarding.

The legislative process, by design, is slow and incremental, and the details of a legislative proposal— how much it costs, how it will be implemented, and how it interacts with current laws—can quickly overshadow larger policy aims. I find that my ability as a sociologist to step back and look at the big picture can be critically important.

My sociological training also leads me to ask certain key questions: What are the potential unintended consequences of this policy? Will the intended effect of the policy be stymied by firmly entrenched structural constraints? Will the effects of this policy differ for men or women, for people of color, or for people at different income levels? Sociologists bring a unique perspective to policymaking—a perspective that complements the extraordinary political and legal expertise of my colleagues.

I am not sure how long I will stay on the Hill, but I know that this experience will make me a more insightful scholar and teacher, and I know that my sociological training has made me a more effective policymaker. Above all, it is humbling and gratifying to be able to help a member of the U.S. Senate make a tangible difference in the lives of Americans.

• •

Lindsay Owens is currently an economic policy adviser in the U.S. Senate for Senator Elizabeth Warren (D-Mass.). She received her PhD from Stanford in 2014.

loan money easily, business stagnates, unemployment rates skyrocket, and the entire government may be held responsible for a lack of economic vitality. When a country goes into a recession, the party in power is often held responsible and will not likely be reelected if the recovery takes too long. Economic recessions can destroy the careers of politicians but can also create such dissatisfaction that the entire government may be at risk of a citizen uprising. Indeed, in 2009, Dennis Blair, the U.S. director of national intelligence, declared the global economic crisis the most serious national security issue facing the nation, calling it a "bigger threat than Al Qaeda terrorists" (Haniffa 2009). Recession in one country also influences other countries around the world because of trade and international markets.

Types of Governments. The major systems of government in the world range from fascist totalitarianism to democracy. However, each culture puts its own imprint on the system it uses, making for tremendous variation in actual practice.

Authoritarian Governments. In **authoritarian governments**, *power is concentrated in the hands of one absolute monarch, dictator, or small group not accountable to the people.* They often have the backing of the military to keep them in power. Authoritarian regimes are common forms of government. Some are helpful to citizens—benevolent dictators—but almost all exert tremendous power and discourage dissent. The Castro brothers—Fidel and more recently Raúl—have maintained effective political control of Cuba since 1959. Although they are despised by many Cuban immigrants in the United States, they are admired by many Cubans (especially older Cubans) as ruling in the best interests of the people, even if autocratically (Clement 2015). For example, the literacy rate in Cuba has gone from 17% when the Castros took power to 99.8% in 2015, and older people have accepted some loss of individual freedoms in exchange for universal education and health care (*World Factbook* 2016a).

Totalitarian Governments. A **totalitarian government** *is any form of government that almost totally controls people's lives.* It differs from authoritarian governments in that the political leaders also control the social and economic institutions. Totalitarian states are often based on a specific political ideology and run by a single ruling group or party, referred to as an *oligarchy*. Russia under Joseph Stalin, Germany under Adolf Hitler, Libya under Muammar Gaddafi, and North Korea under Kim Jong-un are examples. The state typically controls the workplace, education, the media, and other aspects of life. All actions revolve around state-established objectives. Dissent and opposition are discouraged or forcefully eliminated, with violent crackdowns

A stable economic system is essential to political stability, and extreme fluctuations in the economy threaten those in power. Indeed, market fluctuations in one country can influence financial stability in other countries because of global trade and international markets. This man is analyzing the stock market at a brokerage house in Hangzhou City, China.

on demonstrators. Interrogation by secret police, imprisonment, and torture are used to quiet dissenters. Terror is used as a tactic to deal with both internal and external dissent, but when it is used by the state to control the citizenry or to terrorize those of another nation, it is called *state terrorism.*

During the totalitarian Khmer Rouge regime in Cambodia from 1975 to 1979, approximately 1.7 million people (21% of the population) were slaughtered for minor offenses. The term *killing fields* is used to describe the execution sites (Cambodian Genocide Program 2015). The Cambodian government today, while not carrying out nationwide purges like the Khmer Rouge, is widely perceived as authoritarian, violent, and corrupt (Cuddy 2015; Loy 2012).

Throughout history, most people have lived under authoritarian or totalitarian systems. Under certain conditions, totalitarian regimes can turn into democratic ones, and of course, democratically elected leaders can change or ignore laws to retain their positions of power, as was the case for a number of elected leaders who changed the constitutions to allow for them to run again (Venezuela, Zimbabwe, and Russia are examples).

Democratic Systems of Government. In contrast to totalitarian regimes, **democratic governments** *are characterized by accountability of the government to citizens and a large degree of control by individuals over their own lives.* Democracies always have at least two political parties that compete in elections for power and that generally

These skulls are the remains of people massacred by the Khmer Rouge in the killing fields of Cambodia.

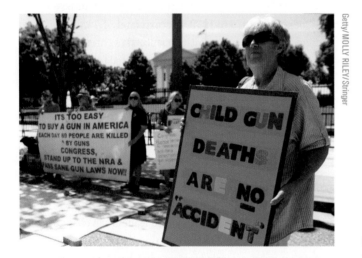

People gather to protest gun violence and call for sensible gun laws outside the White House in 2016. Protests are one way citizens try to keep a government accountable and influence policy.

accept the outcome of elections. Mechanisms for the smooth transfer of power are laid out in a constitution or another legal document. Ideal-type democracies share the following characteristics, although few democracies fit this description exactly.

1. *Citizens participate in selecting the government.* There are free elections with anonymous ballots cast, widespread suffrage (voting rights), and competition between members of different parties running for offices. Those who govern do so by the consent of the majority, but political minorities have rights, representation, and responsibilities.

2. *Civil liberties are guaranteed.* These usually include freedom of association, freedom of the press, freedom of speech, and freedom of religion. Such individual rights ensure dissent, and dissent creates more ideas about how to solve problems. These freedoms are therefore essential for a democracy to thrive.

3. *Government powers are limited by a constitution.* The government can intrude only into certain areas of individuals' lives. Criminal procedures and police power are clearly defined, thus prohibiting harassment or terrorism by police. The judicial system helps maintain a balance of power.

4. *Governmental structure and process are spelled out.* Generally, some officials are elected whereas others are appointed, but all are accountable to citizens. Representatives are given authority to pass laws, approve budgets, and hold the executive officer accountable for activities. The two main forms of democratic constitutional government are the parliamentary and presidential systems. In typical parliamentary governments, the head of government is a prime minister, chancellor, or premier, and there is also a president or monarch, with less power. Countries with this model include Belgium, Canada, Denmark, the United Kingdom, Japan, Sweden, Ireland, India, Israel, Pakistan, and Turkey. Examples of presidential governments include France, Italy, the United States, Germany, Argentina, Brazil, Kenya, and the Philippines.

Proportional representation means that each party is given a number of seats corresponding to the percentage of votes it received in the election. In winner-takes-all systems, the individual with more than 50% of the votes gets the seat. In the United States, the winner-takes-all presidential electoral system has come under attack because the winner of the nationwide presidential popular vote can lose the election. This actually happened in five presidential elections in the United States: 1824, 1876, 1888, 2000, and 2016 (FactCheck 2016). In the most recent two instances—both in recent memory—Al Gore and Hillary Clinton, respectively, received the most votes for president. Due to the system for electing the Electoral College, however, George W. Bush and Donald Trump gained the majority of Electoral College votes and won the presidency. In 2016, Hillary Clinton won the total popular vote with 2.8 million more votes, 48.2% compared to 46.1% for Donald Trump (Cook Political Report 2016; United States Elections Project 2016b). Defenders of this system of choosing the president argue that this protects the voice of each state, even if each individual voice is not given the same weight.

Constitutional governments may include representatives from two to a dozen or more parties, as has been the case in Switzerland. Most have four or five viable parties. In European countries, typical parties include Social Democrats, Christian Democrats, Communists, Liberals, and other parties tied to specific local or state issues, such as Green parties.

Modern electronic technology has a complex relationship with democracy, enhancing it in some ways and undermining it in others. Electronic technology—the Internet and other "smart" telecommunications technologies—can enhance democracy, providing an opportunity for people around the world to be informed citizens, or be a burden that hinders thoughtful debate and civic engagement in ideas, these being essential ingredients of a functioning democracy (Barber 2006).

Cell phones and other telecommunications devices have been major instruments for indigenous people, linking them to the outside world and combating oppressive governments.

As one political scientist put it,

Recent events confirm that social media is playing a significant role in modern political protests. For example, social media has helped maintain news coverage of events going on inside Syria since the civil war began there in 2011. After the Syrian government attempted to restrict non-state reporters following the outbreak of protests, members of the rebel groups and bystanders tweeted and uploaded YouTube videos of government-led violence going on there (Mackey 2011). These videos helped bolster support for the rebels both inside Syria and in some parts of the broader international community. (Castle 2016)

In representative democracies a key contribution that these technologies bring is helping citizens stay in touch with their elected representatives. On the other hand, news shows and online opinion outlets are often known more for sound bites and polemical attacks on opponents than for reasoned debates in which opposing sides express views in search of a better solution than either side originally had.

Thinking Sociologically

How can technology be problematic for representative democracy? How can it be beneficial? What are some ways technology has impacted elections in your country?

Types of Economic Systems. As societies become industrialized, one of two basic economic systems evolves: a planned system or a market system. Planned or centralized systems involve state-based planning and control of property, whereas market systems stress individual planning and private ownership of property, with much less governmental coordination or oversight. These basic types vary, depending on the peculiarities of the country and its economy. For instance, China has a highly centralized planned economy with government control, yet some private property and incentive plans exist, and these are expanding. The United States is a market system, yet the government puts many limitations on business enterprises and regulates the flow and value of money. Distinctions between the two major types rest on the degree of centralized planning and the ownership of property. In each type of system, decisions must be made concerning which goods to produce (and in what quantity), what to do in the event of shortages or surpluses, and how to distribute goods. Who has the power to make these decisions helps determine what type of system it is.

Market or Capitalist Economic Systems. **Market or capitalist economic systems** *are driven by the balance of supply and demand, allowing free competition to reward the efficient and the innovators with profits.* They stress individual planning and private ownership of property. As noted earlier, the goal of capitalism is profit, made through free competition between competitors for the available markets. Proponents of pure capitalism assume that the laws of supply and demand will allow some to profit while others fail. Needed goods will be made, and the best product for the price will win out over the others. No planning by an oversight group is necessary because the invisible hand of the market will ensure sufficient quality control, production, and distribution of goods. This system also rewards innovative entrepreneurs who take risks and solve problems in new ways, resulting in potential growth and prosperity.

Capitalist manufacturers try to bring in more money than they pay out to produce goods and services. As Karl

Marx described, because workers are a production cost, getting the maximum labor output for the smallest wage benefits capitalists. Therefore, multinational corporations look throughout the world for the cheapest sources of labor with the fewest restrictions on employment and operations. The potential for (and practice of) labor exploitation leads most governments to exercise some control over manufacturing and the market, although the degree of control varies widely (Marx [1844] 1963).

Capitalism was closest to its pure form during the Industrial Revolution, when some entrepreneurs gained control of large amounts of capital and resources, and legislation to control owners and protect workers did not yet exist. Using available labor and mechanical innovations, these entrepreneurs built industries and, soon, monopolies (exclusive control over supplying certain goods). Craftspeople such as cobblers could not compete with the efficiency of the new machine-run shops, and many were forced to become laborers in new industries to survive.

As we noted in earlier chapters, Marx predicted that capitalism would cause citizens to split into two main classes: the *bourgeoisie*, capitalists who own the means of production (the "haves"), and the *proletariat*, those who sell their labor to capitalists (the "have-nots"). He argued that institutions such as education, politics, law, and religion work to preserve the privileges of the elite.

Religious ideology often stresses hard work and deference to authority, allowing entrepreneurs to increase profits that benefit the owners. Furthermore, members of the economic and political elite usually encourage patriotism to distract the less privileged from their conflicts with the elite. According to Marx, the elite want the masses to draw the line between "us" and "them" based on national loyalty, not based on lines of economic self-interests (Gellner and Breuilly 2009). So in Marxist thought, even patriotism is a tool of the elite to control the workers. However, Marx believed that ultimately, the workers would realize their plight, develop a class consciousness, and rebel against their conditions. They would overthrow the "haves" and bring about a new and more egalitarian society.

The revolutions that Marx predicted have not occurred in most countries. Labor unions have protected workers from the severe exploitation that Marx witnessed in the early stages of industrialization in England, and capitalist governments have created and expanded a wide array of measures to protect citizens, including antimonopoly legislation, social security systems, unemployment compensation, disability programs, welfare systems, and health care systems. Therefore, most workers have not been discontent to the point of trying to overthrow their

governments. Marx's vision of a small group of owners controlling the economy has borne out, however. For example, today, among all transnational companies, just 1% controls 40% of all of the world's collective wealth (Coghlan and MacKenzie 2011). Among individuals, the wealthiest 0.2% of the world's population now owns 41% of the world's wealth and is expected to own close to half (49%) by 2019 (Matthews 2015).

One of the major criticisms of pure capitalism is that profit is the only value that drives the system. Human dignity and well-being, environmental protection, rights of ethnic groups, and other social issues are important only as they affect profits. This leaves some people deeply dissatisfied with capitalism.

Planned Economic Systems. In **planned (or centralized) economic systems,** *the government or another centralized group oversees production and distribution.* They deemphasize private control of property and economic autonomy and have the government do economic planning. Matters of production and labor are, in theory, governed with the "communal" good in mind. There is deep suspicion of the exploitation that can occur when individuals all pursue their own self-interests. Those who hold this philosophy believe that the market system also results in oligarchy—a system run by the financial elite in the pursuit of their own self-interests. Therefore, they believe the state needs to oversee the total economy. Roughly two dozen nations in Africa, Asia, and Latin America have planned economies with industry controlled by the state—Cuba and Zimbabwe being examples (Noesselt 2014; Reference.com 2016).

In reality, however, no system is totally planned, with the complete elimination of private property or differences in privilege. China, based on a planned, government-controlled system, made rapid progress in tackling hunger, illiteracy, drug addiction, and other problems by using its strong central government to establish 5-year economic development plans. Today, however, charges of corruption among those who control state-run companies and a desire for increased economic growth have led it to experiment with new economic plans, including limited private entrepreneurship, more imported goods, and trade and development agreements with other countries. China is now the largest trading nation and the world's largest economy (IMF 2014; Organisation for Economic Co-operation and Development 2013).

One key criticism of planned systems is that placing both economic and political power in the hands of the same people can lead to control by a few leaders, resulting in tyranny. Multiple power centers in government, the business world, and the military can balance each other and help protect against dictatorships and tyranny (Heilbroner and Milberg 2007).

Mixed Economies. Some systems are mixed economies, sometimes called democratic socialism, because they try to balance societal needs and individual freedoms. **Democratic socialism** refers to *collective or group planning of the development of the society but within a democratic political system*. Private profit is less important than in capitalism, and the good of the whole is paramount. Planning may include goals of protecting the environment, wealth redistribution through progressive taxation, universal health care, or supporting families through government-subsidized health care and family leave legislation, but individuals' rights to pursue their own self-interests are also allowed within certain parameters. Mixed economies seek checks and balances so that both political and economic decision makers are accountable to the public.

Several countries, including Sweden, the United Kingdom, Norway, Austria, Canada, France, and Australia, have incorporated some democratic socialist ideas into their governmental policies, especially in public services. Many Western European democracies redistribute income through progressive tax plans that tax according to people's ability to pay. The government uses these revenues to nationalize education, health plans and medical care, pensions, maternity leaves, and sometimes housing for its citizens (Heberlein 2016). Although much of the industry is privately run, the government regulates business and assesses high taxes to pay for government programs. Typically, public-service industries such as transportation, communications, and power companies are government controlled.

When U.S. president Obama was first elected, he was faced with a major economic crisis caused by the deregulation of banks and the system of loans for home mortgages and businesses. He—as his Republican predecessor, George W. Bush, did before him—pushed a massive ($787 billion) stimulus plan through Congress (Espo 2009). The problem was lack of regulation of the economy, and the solution was massive support for corporations and businesses, actions that some called socialistic.

Other programs and policies in the United States that follow the structure of democratic socialism include Social Security, Medicaid, Medicare, farm subsidies, federal unemployment insurance, the national parks system, public schools, environmental policies, and thousands of

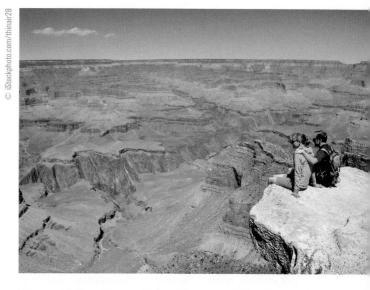

Hikers enjoy Grand Canyon National Park, one of 58 national parks and hundreds of national monuments publicly accessible because they are controlled by the federal government. This is one form of socialism that is very popular in the United States.

other programs that support and protect U.S. citizens. So despite hostility to the term *socialism*, any government program that protects consumers or the environment is part of a mixed economy that includes some socialist policies. Note that both Republicans and Democratic administrations have supported such policies, and the policies have usually been very popular. The popularity of Bernie Sanders—an ardent supporter of democratic socialism—in the 2016 U.S. presidential primaries is also an indication of the appeal of this approach with some Americans.

Just 2 centuries ago, it was widely believed, perhaps rightly at that time, that democracy could not work. The notion of self-governance by the citizenry was discredited as a pipe dream. Yet this experiment in self-governance is continuing, despite some flaws and problems. In a speech to the British House of Commons in 1947, then–prime minister Winston Churchill said that "democracy is the worst form of government, except for all those other forms that have been tried" (Churchill 2009). Some economists and social philosophers have argued that if the people can plan for self-governance, they certainly should be able to plan for economic development in a way that does not put economic power solely in the hands of a political elite.

The institutions of politics and economics cannot be separated. In the 21st century, new political and economic relationships will emerge as each institution influences the other. Both institutions ultimately have close connections to power and privilege.

NATIONAL AND GLOBAL SYSTEMS: MACRO-LEVEL ANALYSIS

Each nation-state develops its own systems of power and privilege in unique ways, depending on its history, leaders, needs, and relations with other nations. A macro-level analysis of national and global systems of governance and power includes both individual nation-states and international organizations, including terrorist groups that cross borders.

Power and the Nation-State

A *nation-state* is a political, geographical, and cultural unit with recognizable boundaries and a system of government. These boundaries change as disputes over territory are resolved by force or negotiation. For example, the boundaries of Israel have changed multiple times since the establishment of the nation in 1948.

There are officially 195 nation-states in the world today that are recognized by each other's governments in the United Nations, and 6 more with partial recognition, making 201 nation-states (Political Geography Now 2015). The Vatican, Taiwan, Palestine, and Kosovo do not have UN representation, but the Vatican and Palestine now have UN *observer status* (Political Geography Now 2015; Rosenberg 2015). The number of nations increases as new independent nation-states continue to develop in Europe, Asia, Africa, and other parts of the world. One of the newest countries is South Sudan, which broke away from Sudan in 2011.

Leaders of the Zapatista movement in southern Mexico (Chiapas) hold a Mexican flag as they attend a mass rally in Mexico City. They have fought for indigenous rights, including clean water and schooling through sixth grade for their children. Their struggle with the Mexican government helps to illustrate power dynamics within nations.

Within each nation-state, systems of power govern people through leaders, laws, courts, the tax structure, the military, and the economic system. Different forms of power dominate at different times in history and in different geographical settings.

The notions of the nation-state and of nationalism are so accepted that we rarely stop to think of them as social constructions of reality, created by people to meet group needs. In historical terms, though, nationalism is a rather recent or modern concept, emerging only after the nation-state (Gellner 1983, 1993; Gellner and Breuilly 2009). Medieval Europe, for example, knew no nation-states. One scholar writes that

> throughout the Middle Ages, the mass of inhabitants living in what is now known as France or England did not think of themselves as "French" or "English." They had little conception of a territorial nation (a "country") to which they owed an allegiance stronger than life itself. (Billig 1995:21)

Some argue that nation-states have "no precedent in history" prior to the 16th century. Nation-states did not become widely acknowledged until they formed throughout Europe in the 19th century (Giddens 1986:166). This raises an interesting question: Why did nation-states emerge in Europe and then spread throughout the rest of the world? The answer to this puzzle of modern history has to do with the change to rational organizational structures (Billig 1995).

It is noteworthy that in the modern world, every square foot of the Earth's land space is thought to be under the ownership of a nation-state. Yet even today, a sense of nationalism or patriotism linking one's personal identity to the welfare of a nation is a foreign idea in many areas of the world. For example, people in Kenya, Pakistan, and Afghanistan have loyalty to their region, their ethnic or tribal group, their religious group, or their local community, but a sense of being Pakistani, Kenyan, or Afghani is weak at best. Yet in places such as the United States, having a passionate sense of national loyalty for which one would die is so taken for granted that anyone lacking this loyalty is suspect or deviant. Note the earlier discussion of the role of the flag. The nation is largely an imagined reality, something that exists because we choose to believe that it exists, but it can exert tremendous influence over us (B. Anderson 2006; McCrone 1998). Indeed, for some people, belonging to the nation has become a substitute for religious faith or belonging to local ethnic groups (Theroux 2012).

Revolutions and Rebellions

From the 1980s to the present, significant social and political changes have taken place throughout the world. The Berlin Wall was dismantled, leading to the reunification of East and West Germany. The government of South Africa that supported apartheid fell. The Baltic states of Estonia, Latvia, and Lithuania became independent. In Eastern Europe, political and social orders established since World War II underwent radical change. When the Soviet Union and Yugoslavia broke apart, national boundaries were redrawn. Internal strife resulted from ethnic divisions formerly kept under check by the strong centralized governments in these areas. In addition, the Arab Spring of 2011–2012 led a number of dictators in the Middle East to fall from power.

Were these changes around the world revolutions? **Revolution** refers to *social and political transformations of a nation that result when states fail to fulfill their expected responsibilities* (Skocpol 1979). Revolutions can be violent and generally result in altered distributions of power. Revolutions typically occur when the government does not respond to citizens' needs and when leadership emerges to challenge the existing regime. News reports from around the world frequently announce that nation-states have been challenged by opposition groups attempting to overthrow the regimes. This is the case in Syria and some other Middle Eastern nations today.

The Meso-to-Macro Political Connection

State or provincial governments and national political parties are both meso-level organizations that operate beyond the local community but with less widespread influence than national or federal governments or global systems. Still, decisions at the state or provincial government level can have a major impact on political processes at the national level. Here, we look at recent controversies about how to nominate and elect a president within the United States. Although the focus is on the U.S. political system, this discussion should be seen as illustrative of the tensions and peculiarities of the meso–macro link in any complex political system.

In some U.S. states, only members of the respective political parties (e.g., Democrat and Republican) can vote in their election of candidates for office. In other states, registered independents can vote in either primary election and help select either party's candidate in a primary election; these are called semiclosed primaries. In other

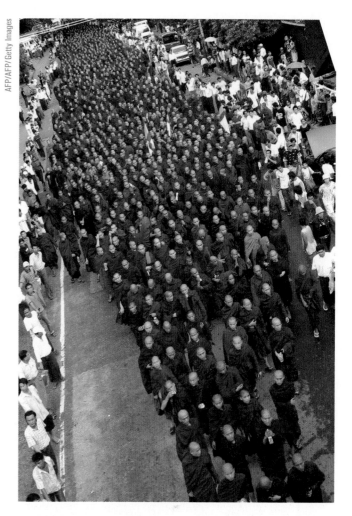

AFP/AFP/Getty Images

Revolutions can involve a violent attack on governments or nonviolent events such as this protest march by Burmese monks whom the government in Myanmar (Burma) brutally suppressed.

states, Democrats and Republicans can cross over and vote in the primary for the other party, called open primaries (Kamarck 2016; Real Clear Politics 2016).

In some U.S. states, each political party runs its own caucuses (face-to-face meetings of voters in homes, schools, and other buildings) to discuss policy and to carry out public votes. Each political party funds the process and sets the rules. In contrast, other states have primary elections, usually run by the state government. (See Table 12.2 for caucus and primary states.) However, even states that use a primary are not all the same. In most states, delegates to the convention are selected based on the proportion of the vote won by a candidate in that state. If a candidate wins 42% of the vote, she or he wins approximately 40% of the delegates. However, in 16 states on the Republican side, the delegate selection process is a winner-takes-all system. In such elections, if one candidate wins by a mere hundred votes, she or he wins all of the delegates for that state. This is true even if the winner of that primary only captures 35% of the vote. In short, there is no uniformity. In addition, one state, New Hampshire, has in its state laws a mandate to the secretary of state that the state *must* have the first presidential primary, and this means the state has more influence on winnowing down the presidential candidates than other states (Kamarck 2016). (To see the processes for various states—whether winner-takes-all or proportional—go to www.realclearpolitics.com/epolls/2016/president/republican_delegate_count.html.)

 Thinking Sociologically

Some states never get any say in the nomination of candidates because the process is completed before they vote. One state has written into its legal code a requirement directing the state's secretary of state

that it must have the first primary election. Should these decisions be made at the state or the national level? Who has the authority to tell a state it cannot put into its constitution a regulation that it must have the first presidential primary?

Some state governments decide when primaries will be held, whereas elsewhere, the political parties control the process of selecting nominees. Can a political party—a meso-level political entity—tell a state—another meso-level political entity—when to have its primary elections? On the other hand, can a state legislature tell a major national political party how to run its nomination process? The answers to these questions are not clear and they have sometimes resulted in conflict, yet they can have profound effects on who becomes the president of the most powerful nation on earth (Kamarck 2016).

Table 12.2 Meso-Level Presidential Nomination Variations in the United States

Open Allowing citizens to cross over to vote in the other party's primary	Semiclosed Allowing Independents to vote in a party's primary	Closed Only party members may vote	States With Caucuses Rather Than Primaries Controlled by the political parties
AL AR GA IL IN MI MO MS MT SC TN TX VA VT WI	NH	AZ CT DE FL LA MD NM NY OR PA	Open: MN Closed: CO KS ME NV WY
Open in the Democratic but closed in the Republican processes: ND*	Semiclosed in Democratic but closed in Republican: CA OK SD UT**	Closed Democratic primary; closed Republican caucus: KY	Semiclosed in Democratic; closed in Republican: AK HI IA ＊＊＊＊＊
Open in Republican but semiclosed in Democratic: MA NC OH RI WV		Closed Republican caucus; closed Democratic caucus: ID NE	Caucus for Republican but not Democratic: ND KY UT
Open in Republican but closed in Democratic: NJ		Closed Republican primary; open Democratic caucus: WA	Caucus for Democratic but not Republican: ID NE WA

*North Dakota has an open primary for Democrats and a closed caucus for Republicans.

**Utah has a semiclosed primary for Democrats and closed caucus for Republicans.

Sources: Kamarck (2016); Real Clear Politics (2016).

In several states, the Republican primary is a "beauty contest" with no binding outcome. The results are purely advisory, and the delegates from that state are free to ignore the outcome of the election. The delegates are selected by party leaders in that state, not by the voters. The Democratic Party has no nonbinding elections, and all states distribute delegates based on the proportion of the vote won in that state, but it has more than 700 *superdelegates*—party leaders who have not been elected by the populace and who may commit their votes to anyone they please (Kamarck 2016). So both parties allow delegates not representing any constituency to help choose the presidential nominee. What are the implications for a democracy when there are such irregularities?

Even selection of the Electoral College, which truly decides who will be president after the general election, is not uniform in policy across the states. Two states—Nebraska and Maine—have proportional distribution of electors, and all the others have winner-takes-all. Should there be consistency among the states in the way the Electoral College is selected? Should state elections all be proportional or winner-takes-all? Should the president and vice president be elected by popular vote rather than the Electoral College? These are important issues for how a democracy operates.

Because the Constitution grants considerable autonomy to states to make these decisions, how does the nation ever get consistency? At the state (meso) level, legislatures are very protective of their right to make their own decisions. Yet governance of the nation and the nation's relationships with the global community may be at stake. As you can see, meso-level political power can shape power at the macro level, which then influences policies relevant to individual lives. The three levels are intimately linked. The next "Engaging Sociology" raises questions about where authority for decisions resides at each level in the social system.

ENGAGING SOCIOLOGY

Political Decisions: Social Processes at the Micro, Meso, and Macro Levels

Imagine that your state legislature is considering a change in the presidential election process. Your state representatives in the Electoral College would be selected according to the percentage of the popular vote in your state going to each candidate (Republican, Democratic, Libertarian, and Green Party). (*Note*: Currently, most—but not all—states distribute their electors on a winner-takes-all basis.)

* * * * * * *

Engaging With Sociology

1. Identify two possible micro-level consequences of this policy change. (For example, how might it affect an individual's decision to vote?)

2. Identify three consequences at the macro level. (For example, how might the change

affect how presidential candidates spend their resources and time? How might Congress respond to such an initiative?)

3. How does this proposed change illustrate the influence of meso-level organizations on micro and macro levels of the social system? For example, is it a problem for a *national* democracy when the delegate selection system is so variable at the meso level, or does this make elections even more democratic because states can make their own autonomous decisions? Explain your answer.

4. Which system—winner-takes-all or percentage of the popular vote—would produce the fairest outcome? Why?

Global Interdependencies: Cooperation and Conflicts

The most affluent countries in the Global North are democracies, but a democratic system of government may not be functional in poor countries with different cultural values and systems (Etounga-Manguelle 2000). Despite the movement toward political liberalization, democracy, and market-oriented reforms in countries such as Chile, Mexico, Nigeria, Poland, Senegal, Thailand, and Turkey, not all of these societies are ready, willing, or able to adopt democratic forms of governance (L. Diamond 1992, 2009).

Foreign powers can do little to alter the social structure and cultural traditions of other societies, and as indicated, these structures are key to the successful development of democracy. If one tries to impose a system that is incompatible with the society's level of development and other institutional structures, authoritarian dictatorship rather than democracy may emerge as the traditional authority structure breaks down. We can see signs of this in Afghanistan and Iraq, two nations in which the United States tried to establish democratic forms of government. Certain preconditions tend to be necessary for the successful emergence of democracy:

- High levels of economic well-being
- The absence of extreme inequalities in wealth and income
- Social pluralism, including a particularly strong and autonomous middle class
- A market-oriented economy
- Influence in the world system of democratic states
- A culture relatively tolerant of diversity and that can accommodate compromise
- A functioning and impartial media that will hold the government accountable
- A literate population (80% or more) informed about issues
- A written constitution with guarantees of free speech and freedom of assembly (Bottomore 1979; Inglehart 1997)

Thinking Sociologically

Why might some analysts believe that Iraq or Afghanistan—where the United States has attempted to set up democracies—may not be ready for a successful democratic government? Can you describe societies with which you are familiar that are—or are not—ready for democratic government? If you are not able to answer these questions, discuss why it is important for you, as a citizen of your own society, to be knowledgeable about other nations (and what you will do to become better informed).

An outside power like the United States can help establish the structures necessary to support democracy but can seldom successfully impose those structures. If countries in the Global North want more democracies around the world, a more successful strategy would focus on supporting economic development in less affluent countries. Again, politics and economics are intertwined.

Some Global South countries see discussions of democracy as a ploy—a cover-up used by dominant affluent nations for advancing their wealth. For example, the Global North nations have combined to form a coalition of nations calling itself the Group of Seven (or the G7—the United States, Japan, Germany, Canada, France, Great Britain, and Italy). Russia was in what was called the G8 but was asked to leave because of political disputes over the country of Ukraine. The G7 uses its collective power to regulate global economic policies to ensure stability (and thereby ensure that its members' interests are secure). The G7 has the power to control world markets through the World Trade Organization, the World Bank, and the International Monetary Fund (Brecher, Costello, and Smith 2012; Council on Foreign Relations 2016). Global South nations have responded to the G7 with an organization of poor countries that they call the G77 to create collective unity and gain enough power to determine their own destinies (Brecher et al. 2012; Eitzen and Zinn 2012; Hearn 2012). Figure 12.3 shows the location of G7 and G77 nations.

Political systems can face threats from internal sources, such as disaffected citizens, the military, and interest groups vying for power, or they can be challenged by external sources, such as other nations wanting land or resources or by coalitions of nations demanding change. This is the situation for North Korea and Iran, where coalitions of nations have demanded that they drop their nuclear enrichment programs. Sometimes these power struggles erupt into violence. The following section discusses how war, terrorism, and rebellion challenge existing systems.

Violence on the Global Level. Although some wars were brutal and entire populations were slaughtered (Genghis Khan's ruthless campaigns are one example), it is also true that in the Middle Ages, gallant knights in shining armor went forth to battle with good-luck tokens from their ladies and the cause of their religion or their

FIGURE 12.3   Countries of the G7 and of the G77

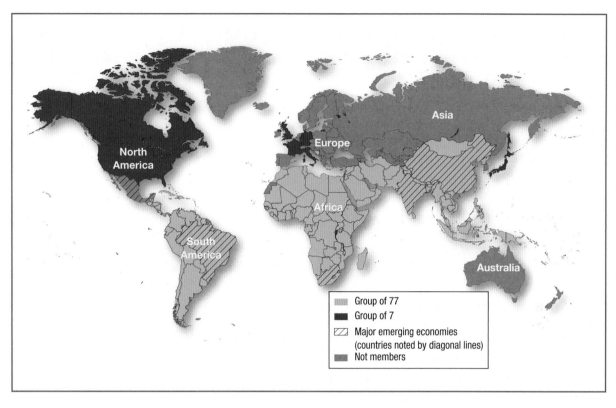

Source: www.g77.org. Map by Anna Versluis.

monarch to spur them on. They seldom died in these battles, and the daily life of the society went on as usual.
Likewise, battles between First Nations in North America
often resulted in four or five deaths. In contrast, since the
invention of modern weaponry and chemical and nuclear
weapons, no one has been safe from death and destruction
in war. Weapons can destroy whole civilizations. A mal-
functioning computer, a miscalculation, a deranged person, a misunderstanding between hostile factions, or a
terrorist attack could kill millions of people.

War is *armed conflict occurring within, between, or
among societies or groups*. It is sometimes called *organized mass violence* (Danielsson and Jacob 2017; C. Nolan
2002). War is a frequent but not inevitable condition of
human existence. Many countries are now engaged in wars
detrimental to their economies and morale. Some of these
wars (between India and Pakistan, between the Palestinian
Territories and Israel, and between rival factions in the
Congo) have lasted many years. Others have been short
and decisive, such as Operation Desert Storm, the war
against Iraq under the first president Bush. Table 12.3 lists
ongoing world conflicts as of 2015.

Why Do Nations Go to War? Leaders use moral, religious, or political ideology to legitimize war, although the
cause may be conflicts over economic resources or ethnic
tensions. Wars have been waged to support religions
through crusades and jihads; to liberate a country from
domination by a foreign power; to protect borders,
resources, and cultural customs; and to capture resources,
including slaves, land, and oil. War can also distract citizens
from other problems in their country and may therefore be
used by politicians intent on staying in power. The United
States has been involved in numerous wars spanning from
the colonial wars (1620–1774) to the war on terrorism
(2001–present). The United States has been at war 193 out of
the 241 years since the colonies declared independence.
Indeed, during the entire 20th century, there were only 6
years when the United States was not engaged in some sort
of military action around the world (Brandon 2005; Noguera
and Cohen 2006). On the other hand, in some cultures, war
is virtually unknown. These groups, often isolated, live in
peace and cooperation, with little competition for land and
resources. War is not inevitable but a product of societies
and their leaders, created by societies and learned in

Table 12.3   Significant Ongoing Armed Conflicts, 2015

Main Warring Parties	Year Conflict Began
Middle East	
Syria vs. Free Syrian Army and other militants	2011
Iraq vs. Islamic State of Iraq and Syria (ISIS)	2003
Israel vs. Palestine	1948
Yemen: government forces vs. the rebel group Shabab al-Moumineen and other militants	2004
Turkey: government forces vs. the Kurdistan Workers' Party (PKK) and Kurdistan Freedom Falcons (TAK)	2003
Libya: fighting between militia groups	2012
Asia	
Afghanistan: U.S., UK, and coalition forces vs. al-Qaeda and Taliban	1978
Burma (Myanmar) vs. Kachin Independence Army (Kachin and Rakhine states)	1988
India vs. Kashmir Harkat-ul-Ansar, Northeast United People's Democratic Front, Maoist insurgents (and other splinter groups)	1947
Philippines vs. the Mindanaoan separatists (MILF/ASG), the Bransamoro Islamic Freedom Fighters (BIFF), the National Democratic Front (NDF), and New People's Army (NPA)	1969
Thailand vs. antigovernment insurgents	2004
Africa	
Algeria vs. al-Qaeda in the Islamic Maghreb	1992
Chad vs. Chadian Popular Front for Recovery (FPR)	1965
Democratic Republic of Congo vs. March 23 Movement (M23)	1990
Central African Republic vs. Christian vigilantes and ex-Séléka (rebel) soldiers	2014
Ethiopia vs. Ogaden National Liberation Front (ONLF)	2007
Kenya vs. Somali Islamists	1991
Nigeria vs. Boko Haram	1990
South Sudan vs. Sudan People's Liberation Army (SPLA) and Darfur	1983
Europe	
Russia vs. Chechen separatists in Chechnya	1999
Russian-backed separatists vs. Ukraine	2014
Latin America	
Colombia vs. Revolutionary Armed Forces of Colombia (FARC)	1964

Note: Where multiple parties and long-standing but sporadic conflict are concerned, date of first combat deaths is given.

Source: Project Ploughshares (2015). http://ploughshares.ca/pl_armedconflict/central-african-republic-update-of-status-2014 societies. Note, however, that many businesses profit from wars because their manufacturing power is put to full use. In fact, more money is spent on war than on prevention of disease, illiteracy, and hunger.

A concern of conflict theorists is that those with power have the most control over decisions to go to war, but citizens from the lower classes and racial minorities join the military, fight, and die in disproportionate numbers. Those with less privilege are more likely to join the military as an avenue to employment and job training. They join as enlistees who serve on the front lines and are more at risk.

All sociological theorists agree that war is not a natural or biological necessity but a social construction (Stoessinger 1993). Likewise, societies create ways to resolve and avoid war.

How Might Nations Avoid War? What can nations do to avoid war? Powerful nations have employed two primary methods: deterrence and negotiation. *Deterrence* is a theory of conflict management and a strategy aimed at preventing undesirable behavior by another group or country. Any parties contemplating action against others are deterred because the costs to them, should they strike, exceed any possible gains (Lebow 1981). This rational cost–benefit calculus is similar to rational choice theory, with which you are familiar. This approach was paramount during the Cold War between the United States and the Soviet Union, and many argue it worked because no nuclear war ensued. Today, those who advocate building defense capability as a deterrent against nuclear attacks or war align themselves with this theory.

Many, however, argue that deterrence will not work against the growing threat of terrorists, who tend to be irrational, difficult to locate, and willing to incur loss of lives to achieve goals (Kroenig and Pavel 2012; U.S. Department of Defense 2012). Moreover, continual buildup of weapons increases mistrust and raises the potential for misunderstandings, mistakes, and disaster.

The world spent $1.78 trillion on defense in 2014, with only 15 countries accounting for 80% of global defense spending. The United States accounted for more than one third of world military spending, an estimated $609.9 billion. China was second, with a budget of $190.9 billion. Russia was third, spending $84.5 billion, and Saudi Arabia was fourth, having spent $80.8 billion on its military (Stockholm International Peace Research Institute 2016). Military spending usually comes at the expense of social programs, such as education and health care, simply because there is not usually enough money to fund all of these programs when the military consumes so much

(Hinton 2010). Still, many people feel that protection of the citizenry is the government's most essential responsibility and that deterrence is the way to achieve security.

Negotiation is the second approach to avoiding war and involves resolving conflicts by discussions to reach agreement. For example, diplomacy and treaties have set limits on nuclear weapons and their use. President Obama has pointed out that, as well as increasing the threat of nuclear war, maintaining Cold War weapons systems is expensive and can drain weakened economies. He negotiated a treaty with Russia in 2010 that led to a reduction in deployed, long-range nuclear warheads by 30% (Sheridan and Branigin 2010; Zeleny 2009).

Many nongovernmental peace groups carry out efforts to prevent war, including protest marches, educational programs, and museum displays. The horrors depicted in the Hiroshima Peace Memorial Museum in Japan; the Killing Fields Museum in Cambodia; the Holocaust Memorial Museum in Washington, DC; the Anne Frank Museum in Amsterdam, Netherlands; the Kigali Genocide Memorial in Rwanda; and the Korean War and Vietnam Veterans Memorials in Washington, DC, all help sensitize the public and politicians to the effects of war. Interestingly, most war memorials in the United States glorify the wars and lionize the heroes who fought in them. In Europe, many memorials stress the pathos and agony of war. The Vietnam Veterans Memorial in Washington, DC, also sends a message about the sorrows of war. Peace advocates and veterans of the war have stood and wept together in front of that memorial.

Scholars draw several conclusions from studies of war in the past century: (a) No nation that began a major war in the 20th century emerged a clear winner; (b) in the nuclear age, war between nuclear powers could be suicidal; and (c) a victor's peace plan seldom lasts. Peace settlements negotiated on the basis of equality tend to be much more permanent and durable. Economic issues, such as an inequitable distribution of resources, can incite a war. Therefore, a lasting peace requires attention to at least semiequitable distribution of resources.

As long as conflict over resources, discrimination, hunger, and poverty exist, the roots of violence are present. The world is a complex interdependent system. When the linkages between peoples are based on ideologies that stress us-versus-them polarities and power differentials that alienate people, then war, terrorism, and violence will not disappear from the globe.

Terrorism. "Got Him: Vengeance at Last! US Nails the Bastard" was the *New York Post's* headline (Ortutay and

The Vietnam Veterans Memorial in Washington, DC—like many European war memorials do—expresses and elicits a sense of the anguish and suffering of war. This man mourns the loss of a close friend and comrade.

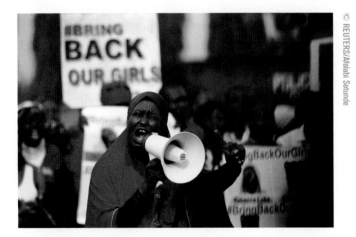

A protester addresses the "Bring Back Our Girls" protest group as they march to the presidential villa to deliver a protest letter to Nigeria's president Goodluck Jonathan in Abuja. The letter calls for the release of the Nigerian schoolgirls kidnapped by the Islamist militant group Boko Haram on May 22, 2014.

Zongker 2011). For the 10 years following September 11, 2001, the search had been on. That was when three commercial airplanes became the missiles of terrorists, two crashing into the Twin Towers of the World Trade Center in New York City and one into the Pentagon in Washington, DC. Another crashed into the fields of Pennsylvania after the passengers heroically attacked the terrorists piloting the plane. Altogether more than 3,025 people from 68 nations died, and countless others were injured. This was an act of terrorism. Why did bin Laden and his followers do it?

Terrorism refers to the planned use of random, unlawful (or illegal) violence or threat of violence against civilians to create (or raise) fear and intimidate citizens in order to advance the terrorist group's political or ideological goals (U.S. Department of Defense 2012). Terrorism usually refers to acts of violence by private nonstate groups to advance revolutionary political goals, but state terrorism—government use of terror to control people—also proliferates. Terrorists are found at all points on the political continuum: anarchists, nationalists, religious fundamentalists, and members of ethnic advocacy groups. Worldwide, terrorist attacks rose by 80% from 2013 to 2014, killing 32,685 globally. Most of these terrorist activities took place outside the United States. More than 3 out of 4 of these deaths by terrorism occurred in only five nations: Afghanistan, Iraq, Nigeria, Pakistan, and Syria (Institute for Economics & Peace 2015).

What makes terrorism effective? Terrorists strike randomly and change tactics so that governments have no clear or effective way of dealing with them. This unpredictability causes public confidence in the ability of government to protect citizens to waver. Private terrorist groups tend to be most successful when attacking democratic governments. They seldom attack targets in oligarchic or dictatorial societies because these countries ignore their demands despite the risk to innocent civilians and hostages' lives (Frey 2004).

Why do terrorists commit hostile acts? In our anger against terrorists, we sometimes fail to look at why they commit these atrocities. Who are the terrorists, and what have they to gain? Without understanding the underlying causes of terrorism, we can do little to prevent it.

Few terrorists act completely alone. They tend to be members of or connected in some way (even if only through the Internet) to groups highly committed to an ideology or a cause—religious, political, or both. Class, ethnic, racial, or religious alienation often lies at the roots of terrorism. The ideology of terrorist groups stresses us-versus-them perceptions of the world, viewing "them" as evil. Those committing terrorist acts often feel victimized by more powerful forces, and they sometimes see their lives as the only weapon they have to fight back. Many believe they have nothing to lose by committing terrorist acts, even suicidal terrorist acts. One person's terrorist may be someone else's freedom fighter—it is in *the eye of the beholder*.

Ahmad is a 20-year-old terrorist. All of his life, his family has been on the move, forced to work for others for barely a living wage and controlled by rules made up by other people—ones he feels are hostile to his group. When he was very young, his family's home was taken away, and the residents of his town scattered to other locations. He began to resent those who he thought had dislocated his family, put neighbors in jail, and separated him from friends and relatives. Ahmad sees little future for himself or his people and little hope for education or a career of his choosing. He feels he has nothing to lose by joining a resistance organization to fight for what he sees as justice. Its members keep their identities secret. They are not powerful enough to mount an army to fight, so they rely on terrorist tactics against those they see as oppressors.

Ahmad puts the "greater good" of his religious and political beliefs and his group above his individual well-being. When he agrees to commit a terrorist act, he truly believes it is right and is the only way he can retaliate and bring attention to the suffering of his people. If killed, he knows he will be praised and become a martyr within his group. His family may even receive compensation for his death.

Political and religious beliefs are usually at the root of what leads terrorists to commit violent acts. Timothy McVeigh and Terry Nichols, convicted of bombing the Alfred P. Murrah Federal Building in Oklahoma City, Oklahoma, in 1995, had connections to paramilitary antigovernment militia groups, many of which opposed government intervention in the private lives of U.S. residents. These groups are White supremacist and antigovernment (despite their fanatic pro-Americanism). Most such paramilitary groups consider themselves to be devoutly Christian, and they believe that their religion and "good intentions" justify their acts. Figure 8.6 on page 224 shows how such groups are scattered throughout the United States.

Structural explanations help predict when conditions are ripe for terrorism. Again, terrorism and war tend to be sparked by conflict and strife within and between societal systems. Ahmad learned his attitudes, hatreds, and stereotypes from his family, his friends, charismatic leaders, and media such as the Internet. These beliefs were reinforced by his religious beliefs, schools, and political leaders. However, their origin was anger and economic despair.

Conflict theory explanations of terrorism lie in the unequal distribution of world resources and the oppression of minority groups. Countries such as Germany, China, and the United States and multinational corporations control immense resources and capital and have considerable economic and cultural influence and power over peripheral nations. This inequity results in feelings of alienation and hostility—and sometimes terrorism.

Terrorism, then, is a means by which those with less power can gain attention to their cause and some power in the global system, even if it involves hijackings, bombings, suicides, kidnappings, and political assassinations. Terrorists feel they are justified in their actions. The victims of these acts are understandably outraged.

Democracy comes in many forms and structures. If you want to live in a society where you have a voice, get involved in the political system, and stay well informed about the policies your government is considering or has recently enacted. Political systems need diverse voices and critics—regardless of what party is currently in power—to create vibrant societies that represent the citizens. What follows is the beginning of Part V on "Social Dynamics," and the next chapter focuses on population and urbanization.

WHAT HAVE WE LEARNED?

Political and economic systems are both sources of power and are highly interlinked. Those who have high status in one institution tend to also have high status in the other. However, some political and economic systems do a better job of producing and distributing resources, ensuring accountability of power so it is less probing, and providing checks on abuses of power.

- Power involves the ability to realize one's will, despite resistance.

- Power and economics impact our intimate (micro-level) lives, our (meso-level) organizations and institutions, and our (macro-level) national and global structures and policies.

- Leadership facilitates getting things done in any social group. It can be accomplished through raw power (coercion) or through authority (granted by the populace). Different types of leadership invest authority in the person, the position, or both.

- Various theories illuminate different aspects of political power and view the U.S. policymaking processes very differently—as dominated by the power elite or as distributed among various groups so that no one group has complete power (pluralism).

- At the micro level of a political institution, individuals decide whether to vote or participate in politics. These decisions are not just individual choices but are shaped by the culture and structures of society.

- At the meso level, the political institution (when it functions well) works to resolve conflicts and to address social needs within the political system. This may be done with authoritarian or democratic structures. Within nations, meso-level policies can also have major implications for national power distribution.

- The economic system ensures production and distribution of goods in society, and the type of economy in a society determines who has the power to plan for the future and who has access to resources.

- At the macro level, nation-states have emerged only in the past few centuries as part of modernity.

- At the global level, issues of power, access to resources, alienation, and ideology shape economic policies, war, terrorism, and the prospects for lives of peace and prosperity for citizens around the planet.

DISCUSSION QUESTIONS

1. As you were growing up, did your parents encourage you to try to influence your local community or society? Why, or why not? Was their perspective on power more like the pluralist or elite theoretical perspective? Explain. How have their views about power influenced your own?

2. Is your family of origin part of the *power elite*? What makes you think so? Are you a member of the power elite? Why, or why not? If you are not, what do you think your chances are of becoming a member of the power elite? Why?

3. Do you think that large corporations have undue influence over the U.S. government? Why, or why not?

4. If you had the choice, would you rather live in a society with a planned, centralized economic system or market capitalist economic system? Why?

5. How do conflict theorists explain terrorism? Do you agree? Why, or why not? How would you suggest the U.S. government try to stem terrorism? What theoretical perspective do you think is most helpful in terms of understanding and dealing with terrorism? Why?

KEY TERMS

authoritarian governments   355
authority   346
democratic governments   355
democratic socialism   359

market or capitalist economic
    systems   357
planned (or centralized)
    economic systems   358

power   343
revolution   361
totalitarian government   355
war   365

CONTRIBUTING TO OUR SOCIAL WORLD: *WHAT CAN WE DO?*

At the Local (Micro) Level

- Consider getting involved in the *student government* on your campus. Most students do not know the power they have on their own campus. Organized students can have a major impact. If you would like to see something changed on your campus, establish relationships with key administrators, and organize other students. Consider running for a leadership position in a student club or the student government association. Doing so will help you learn how to gain and use power and to better understand the basic principles of the democratic process.

- *Model Legislature or Model U.N. programs* may be found on most campuses and are usually administered through the department of political science. Consider joining yours, and gain valuable knowledge and skills in debating and governing.

- *Arrange a campus visit by a local political candidate or officeholder.* If this can be done through a sociology club, it would be especially appropriate to have the visitor discuss the political system as a social institution.

At the Organizational/Institutional (Meso) Level

- *Government internships.* Consider doing an internship in your *state or provincial legislature* (www.ncsl.org/legislative-staff.aspx?tabs=856,33,816) or in *Congress* (www.senate.gov/reference/Index/Employment.htm and www.house.gov/content/educate/internships.php) with a state or provincial legislator, the governor's office (Google "governor's office," "internship," and the name of your state), or with a court judge (Google "court judge," with the name of your district, and "internship").

- *Special-interest parties.* Become involved in a special interest political group, such as the Green Party (www.gp.org), the Libertarian Party (www.lp.org), the Socialist Party (www.socialistparty-usa.net), the Tea Party (www.teaparty.org), Bread for the World (www.bread.org), People for the Ethical Treatment of Animals (www.peta.org), or any number of others.

At the National/Global (Macro) Levels

- *Internships at the White House or one of the executive offices, such as the Departments of State, Agriculture, or Commerce,* can be a great learning experience. You can learn about the White House internship program and how to apply for one at www.whitehouse.gov/about/internships. Google the name of a cabinet office to obtain contact information for the other executive offices.

- Several agencies of the *United Nations* hire interns. The general contact for relevant information is www.un.org/Depts/OHRM/sds/internsh.

$SAGE edge™

Get the edge on your studies. **edge.sagepub.com/ballantinecondensed5e**

- Take a quiz to find out what you've learned.
- Review key terms with eFlashcards.
- Watch videos that enhance chapter content.

YASUYOSHI CHIBA/AFP/Getty Images

PART V

Social Dynamics

Social structures such as institutions tend to resist change. Nonetheless, this entire book demonstrates that societies are dynamic and changing. Institutions and organizations come alive with processes that are fluid and vibrant. Globalization, a major theme in this book, is a process bringing transformation to our social world, as shown by the very different world inhabited by our grandparents. The macro- and meso-level dimensions of society have become increasingly powerful, which is exactly why we need a sociological imagination to understand how the events in our own micro worlds are influenced by the larger society.

This section looks at some of those dynamic, fluid, and vibrant processes: population changes, urbanization, expansion of technology, social movements, and more. In periods of rapid change, understanding how and why that change occurs can help us to influence the direction those changes take in our society. From global climate change to terrorism and from new digital technologies to immigrants in our communities, we need to understand causes and consequences in order to respond constructively. To do so, we must grasp the micro-, meso-, and macro-level dimensions of change in our lives and the linkages between parts of our social world. We turn first to population dynamics and urbanization.

MUNIR UZ ZAMAN/AFP/Getty Images

13 Population and Urbanization

Living on Planet Earth

Humans are confined to this one moderate-sized planet on which we depend for survival. The challenges of controlling population size, migration patterns, the spread of disease, and climate change add to the need for global cooperation.

MICRO

ME (AND MY NEIGHBORS)

LOCAL ORGANIZATIONS AND COMMUNITY
Local schools and community organizations serve the local population.

MESO

NATIONAL ORGANIZATIONS, INSTITUTIONS, AND ETHNIC SUBCULTURES
Population trends influence institutions such as politics, economics, and education.

MACRO

SOCIETY
National governments set policies that influence birth incentives, birth control, and immigration.

GLOBAL COMMUNITY
Cross-national migration patterns can spread epidemics or meet pressing needs for labor.

WHAT YOU WILL LEARN IN THIS CHAPTER

This chapter will help you do the following:

13.1 Illustrate the pattern of the world's population growth over time.

13.2 Give examples of institutional influences on fertility, mortality, and migration.

13.3 Describe individual decisions that affect population patterns.

13.4 Discuss national and global urbanization trends.

13.5 Explain why moving from rural to urban settings can lead to anomie.

13.6 Compare industrial and postindustrial cities.

13.7 Explain three major social problems facing urban areas in the Global South.

THINK ABOUT IT

Micro: Local community	What is the population profile of your hometown: economic status of residents, ethnic and racial composition, and recent immigrant groups? Where do you fit into that population profile?
Meso: National institutions, complex organizations, and ethnic groups	Why do people move from rural areas to urban areas? What problems might this pattern of movement create?
Macro: National and global systems	How do global issues relating to demographic changes, urbanization, and the environment affect your family and your local community?

When Sally Ride, the first U.S. woman in space, looked down at Earth, she, like other astronauts who have the opportunity to see the planet from far above, experienced the *overview effect*. This occurs when Earth is viewed from a new angle, from the perspective of space. Ride described the impact it had on her.

Mountain ranges, volcanoes, and river deltas appeared in salt-and-flour relief, all leading me to assume the role of a novice geologist. In such moments, it was easy to imagine the dynamic upheavals that created jutting mountain ranges and the internal wrenching that created rifts and seas. I also became an instant believer in plate tectonics; India really is crashing into Asia, and Saudi Arabia and Egypt really are pulling apart, making the Red Sea wider. Even though their respective motion is really no more than mere inches a year, the view from overhead makes theory come alive. (Quoted in Beaver 2012)

Ride's perspective changed, and thus, her ability to recognize and understand the world also changed. Ride saw and noticed things she had not seen or noticed before because of this new view of the world. In this chapter, you will learn to observe changes in the world's population from a sociological perspective and, in the process, see and notice patterns you may not have paid attention to before.

Since the emergence of *Homo sapiens* in East Africa almost 200,000 years ago, human populations have grown in uneven surges and declines due to births, deaths, and migrations. The World Population Clock (see Table 13.1) illustrates the current state of the human population. As you can see, there are now more than 7 billion people on Earth, and the number is increasing rapidly.

The world's human population grew sporadically over the millennia, but the explosion of human beings on the planet in the past 2.5 centuries is stunning. If we collapsed all human history into one 24-hour day, the time period since 1750 would consume 1 minute. Yet 25% of all humans have lived during this 1-minute time period. In the 200 years from 1750 to 1950, the world's population

Table 13.1 Population Clock, 2015

	World	Global South	Global North
Population	7,336,435,000	6,082,235,000	1,254,199,000
Births per day	399,926	362,226	37,700
Births per year	145,973,000	132,213,000	13,760,000
Deaths per day	156,306	122,654	33,652
Deaths per year	57,052,000	44,769,000	12,283,000
Infant deaths per day	14,660	14,459	201
Natural annual increase	88,921,000	87,444,000	1,477,000

Source: Population Reference Bureau (2015).

mushroomed from 800 million to 2.5 billion. On October 12, 1999, the global population reached 6 billion. It has now expanded to over 7.3 billion, with almost all of the latest growth in the Global South (U.S. Census Bureau 2016).

Let us start by focusing on one area of our world: East Africa. We begin here partly because East Africa is believed to be home to Earth's earliest human inhabitants, remains of Homo sapiens. Scientists believe that a jawbone found in the Afar region of Ethiopia dates back 2.8 million years ago, predating Lucy in the Olduvai Gorge between Kenya and Tanzania by half a century (Shreeve 2015).

Here, we focus on Kenya in East Africa because it is making human history for another reason. With a population of 45 million people and a growth rate of 2.11% annually, Kenya has one of the most rapidly growing populations on Earth (*World Factbook* 2014d). Kenya is made up of many tribal groups. With different religions and value systems, the tribes have clashed in power struggles in recent years. Still, there are several themes that pervade most Kenyan subcultures, as illustrated by the following example.

Wengari, like Kenyan girls of most tribal affiliations, married in her teens. She has been socialized to believe that her main purpose in life is to bear children, to help with the farming, and to care for parents in their old age. Children are seen as an asset in Kenya. Religious beliefs and cultural value systems encourage large families. However, due to high birth rates and high death rates caused by AIDS, the working-age population has declined and cannot continue to feed the growing population. Almost half (44.8%) of the Kenyan population consists of *dependents*: people under 15 or over 65 years of age who rely on working-age citizens to support them (*World Factbook* 2014d). Almost all of the dependent population consists of children under 15, rather than adults over 65 (42.1%, compared with 2.7% of the population). Adding to Kenya's problems are severe droughts that kill animal herds and destroy crops. These facts, however, have little impact on the behavior of young women like Wengari, who, socialized to conform to the female role within her society, plans on having many children.

By contrast, far to the north, in many of the industrialized, urbanized countries of Europe, birth rates are below population replacement levels, meaning population size has begun to drop. The population growth rate in Germany is 0.18%; in France, 0.45%; and in the United Kingdom, 0.54%. Russia, Hungary, Latvia, the Czech Republic, and many other countries in Eastern Europe are also losing population (*World Factbook* 2015d, 2015e, 2015f). Germany, the most prosperous nation in Europe,

USAID

Changes in the environment and in the global economy compel many families like this one to join the worldwide urbanization trend and move to the nearest city in search of work. Much of the socialization they received in villages will not be relevant to their new urban lives.

does not have enough working-age people to support the pensions of older Germans. Much of Europe faces this problem (Daley and Kulish 2013). This may have influenced the decision to welcome Syrian refugees.

Whereas Asia's share of world population is likely to hover around 60% through the next century, Europe's portion has declined sharply and will likely drop even more during the rest of the 21st century. Countries outside of Europe growing by less than 1% annually include Albania, Brazil, China, and Russia. Africa and Latin America each will gain part of Europe's portion. By 2100, Africa is expected to capture the greatest share (World Bank 2016a).

As societies develop, birth rates tend to go down. For example, typical European young people often wait until their late 20s or even 30s to start a family, postponing children until their education is complete and a job is in hand. Moreover, they have access to effective birth control options, widely used throughout their societies. Unlike many children in the Global South, most children born in Europe will survive to old age. Parents do not feel as though they must have many children in order to see some grow to maturity. **Life expectancy**, the *number of years a person in a particular society can expect to live*, is 63.5 years in Kenya (*World Factbook* 2014d). In Japan and some European countries, it is more than 82 years.

China, the country with the largest population in the world (1.35 billion people), had the greatest drop in population growth in the late 20th century, due to strict governmental family-planning practices (*World Factbook* 2014a). India, the second-largest country, has a current *population growth rate* (increase in a country's population during a specified period of time) of 1.25% a year, just over replacement level (*World Factbook* 2014c).

Although some countries have birth rates below population replacement levels, the world's population continues to grow because of the skyrocketing growth rate in other countries and because of *population momentum* caused by the large number of individuals of childbearing age having children. After a baby boom, even though birth rates per couple may drop, the number of girls who grow to childbearing age 16 years later becomes very high, resulting in continued growth in population size. Most of the countries with the highest growth rates are in the Global South, where societies value large families and have less access to birth control but fewer resources to support the additional population.

Thinking Sociologically

Do you have a choice in how many children you have or will have? Explain. If you do, what factors go into your decision? How might your decision differ if you lived in a different country? Should global patterns—which include food shortages and climate change—be a consideration in the size of your family and your neighbors' families? Why, or why not?

We know the previous information thanks to research gained through **demography**, *the study of human populations*. When demographers speak of **populations**, they mean *all permanent societies, states, communities, adherents of a common religious faith, racial or ethnic groups, kinship or clan groups, professions, and other identifiable categories of people*. Demographers examine various aspects of a population, including the size, location, movement, concentration in certain geographical areas, and changing characteristics. For example, the next "Engaging Sociology" asks you to imagine that the entire world population is only 100 people and look at how it would be composed given the current world distribution of certain characteristics.

With few jobs to support populations in rural areas (areas outside of cities and their surrounding suburbs), many people move to cities in hopes of finding employment. This *pattern of movement from rural areas to cities* is called **urbanization**. The second half of this chapter considers the evolution, growth, and development of populated areas, including movements from rural areas to cities, the organization of micro-level urban life, the relationship between individuals and the city, and some problems facing cities. The previous chapters have moved from micro- to macro-level analysis, but in this chapter, because of the nature of the material and the need to explain certain issues before the micro issues make sense, we discuss macro-level patterns in world population growth first. We then describe meso-level institutional influences on population and finally micro-level factors affecting population patterns.

MACRO-LEVEL PATTERNS IN WORLD POPULATION GROWTH

Earlier we noted that Global North societies tend to see reduced population growth as they continue to develop.

The overcrowding in some cities means that governments have a difficult time providing the infrastructure and services needed for the growing urban population. Rio de Janeiro, Brazil, is one example.

Mario Tama/Getty Images

ENGAGING SOCIOLOGY

If the World Were 100 People

Geography

First Language

Religion

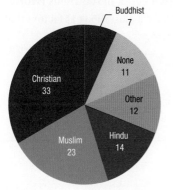

Literacy	83 would be able to read and write
	12% of males would not be able to read and write
	21% of females would not be able to read and write
Education	7 would have a college degree
Urban/Rural	51 would be urban dwellers; 49 would be rural dwellers
Water	87 would have access to safe drinking water; 13 would not
Food	15 would be undernourished and 1 starving; 21 would be overweight
Poverty	48 would live on less than 2 U.S. dollars per day; half of the children would live in poverty
Electricity	78 would have electricity; 22 would not
Technology	30 would be active Internet users; 75 would be cell phone users

* * * * * * *

Engaging With Sociology

1. Did any of these facts surprise you? If so, which ones? Why? If not, where did you learn these facts?

2. In which ways are you highly privileged compared to most others in the world?

3. Which of the factors in this list cause the most suffering?

4. If you were a public sociologist and wanted to address two of these factors that affect world populations, which ones would you focus on? Why?

What happens before this, though? Why did the world's population grow so slowly and then, recently, so rapidly? Sociologists look for patterns in population growth over time to answer these demographic questions.

Patterns of Population Growth Over Time

Members of the small band of early *Homo sapiens* who inhabited the Olduvai Gorge moved gradually, haltingly, from this habitat into what are now other parts of Africa, Asia, and Europe. The process took thousands of years. At times, births outnumbered deaths and populations grew, but at other times, plagues, famines, droughts, and wars decimated populations. From the beginning of human existence, estimated at over 1 million years ago, until modern times, the number of births and deaths balanced each other over the centuries (J. Diamond 2005). The large population we see today resulted from three phases of population evolution.

1. Humans, because of their thinking ability, competed satisfactorily in the animal kingdom to obtain the basic necessities for survival of the species.

2. With the agricultural revolution that occurred about 10,000 years ago and the resulting food surplus, mortality rates declined, and the population grew as more infants survived, and people lived longer.

3. The biggest increase in population came with the Industrial Revolution, beginning about 300 years ago. Improved medical knowledge and sanitation helped bring the death rate down.

Industrialization not only brought about the social and economic changes in societies discussed in Chapter 3 (e.g., machines replacing human labor and mass production using resources in new ways), but it also led to the rapid growth of populations. The population explosion began with industrialization in Europe and spread to widely scattered areas of the globe. Figures 13.1 and 13.2 show population growth throughout history. The worldwide *rate* of population growth reached its peak in the 1960s (Worldometers 2014). We now take a closer look at factors that impact population growth.

FIGURE 13.1   Exponential World Population Growth From About 8000 BCE to 21st Century

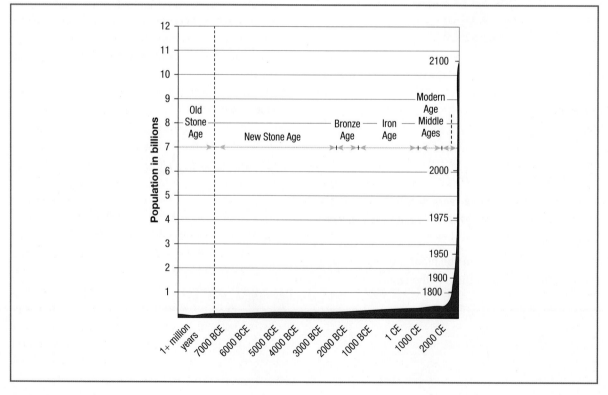

Source: Abu-Lughod (2001:50).

FIGURE 13.2   World Population Growth Rate, 1950–2050

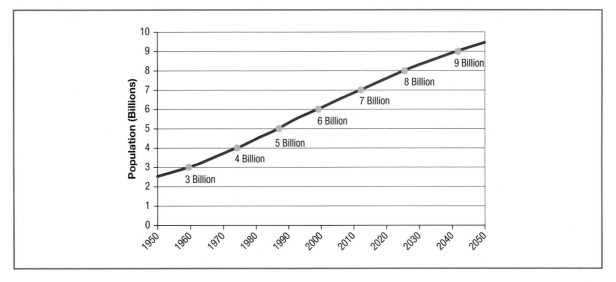

Source: U.S. Census Bureau (2015b).

Predictors of Population Growth

Think for a moment about the impact that your age and sex have on your position in society and your activities. Are you of childbearing age? Are you dependent on others for most of your needs, or are you supporting others? Your status is largely due to your age and sex and what they mean in your society. These demographic variables greatly influence your behavior and the behavior of others like you, and collectively, they shape the population patterns of an entire society. In analyzing the impact of age and sex on human behavior, three concepts can be very useful: youth and age dependency ratios, sex ratios, and age–sex population pyramids.

The *youth dependency ratio* is the number of children under age 15 divided by the number from 15 to 64. The number of those older than 64 divided by those age 15 to 64 is called the *age dependency ratio*. Although many of the world's young people under 15 help support themselves and their families, and many over 64 are likewise economically independent, these figures have been taken as the general ages when individuals are not contributing to the labor force. They represent the economic burden (especially in wealthy countries) of people in the population who must be supported by the working-age population. The **dependency ratio**, then, is *the ratio of those in both the young and aged groups compared with the number of people in the productive age groups from 15 to 64 years old* (Sengupta 2014).

In several resource-poor countries, nearly half of the population is under 15 years of age. These include Kenya (42.1%, as mentioned), Niger (49.8%), Uganda (48.7%), the Democratic Republic of the Congo (43.1%), and Afghanistan (42%) (*World Factbook* 2014b, 2014d, 2014f, 2014g, 2015a). Working adults in less developed countries have a tremendous burden in supporting the dependent population, especially if a high percentage of the population is urban and not able to support itself through farming.

Similarly, most Global North countries have high percentages of older dependent people over 64. In the European countries of Norway, Sweden, Denmark, Germany, and the United Kingdom, between 15% and 20% of the population is 65 or older. These countries have low death rates, resulting in the average life expectancy at birth being as high as 82.8 in Switzerland, followed by Japan, Italy, and Spain at 82.7 years (UPI 2014).

Consider the case of Japan, which faces the problem of its "graying" or aging population. In 2014, 24.8% of its population was 65 or older, and the average life expectancy had reached 83 years (*World Factbook* 2014e). The death rate is higher than the birth rate, and the population is shrinking in size. Only 13.2% of the population is under 15 years old. With a declining population and almost no influx of immigrants, there are not enough replacement workers to support the aging population. The result is a strange pattern; with the older population (between 60 and 85) being larger than any age group under 50 and tapering down to younger generations, Japan may provide a glimpse into the future for other rapidly aging societies, including Germany, the United States, and China. These different societies, however, vary in their approach to immigration and population control policies, which will impact both the demographic challenges they face and how they handle them.

The *sex ratio* refers to the ratio of males to females in the population. For instance, the more females there are, especially in their fertile years, the more potential there is for population growth. The sex ratio also determines the supply of eligible spouses. Other factors that influence marriage patterns include economic cycles, wars in which the proportion of males to females may decrease, sex-selective abortions favoring males, and migrations that generally take males from one area and add them to another.

Population pyramids *are pyramid-shaped diagrams that illustrate sex ratios and dependency ratios (see*

Figure 13.3). The graphic presentation of the age and sex distribution of a population tells us a great deal about that population. The structures are called pyramids because that is the shape they took until several decades ago. By looking up and down the pyramid, we can see the proportion of population at each age level. Looking to the right and left of the centerline tells us the balance of males to females at each age. The bottom line shows us the total population at each age.

The first pyramid shows the population of Germany with low birth rates and death rates. This is typical of Global North countries. The second pyramid—Uganda—is typical of Global South countries and illustrates populations with high birth rates and large dependent youth populations. As these images show, the world population has been getting both younger (the Global South) *and* older (the Global North), resulting in large numbers of

FIGURE 13.3   Population Pyramids in Global North (Germany) and Global South (Uganda) Countries in 2014

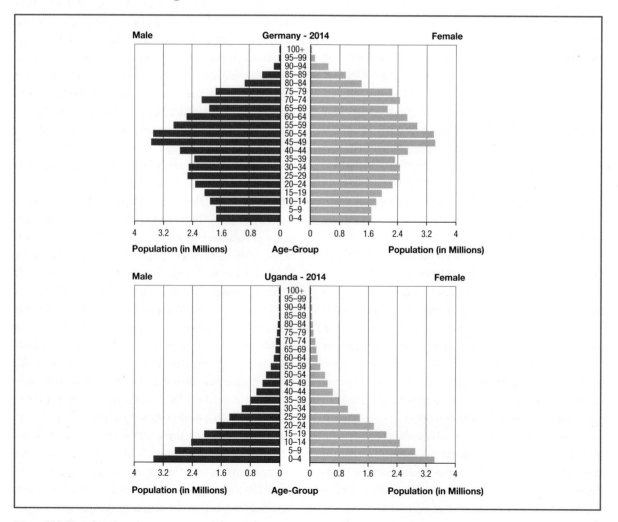

people dependent on the working-age population, from 15 to 65 years of age. As Global South nations have more and more children, they create more potential parents in later years, adding momentum to the world's population growth. Fewer deaths of infants and children, due to immunizations and disease control, result in lower mortality rates, younger populations, and higher potential numbers of births in the future.

Thinking Sociologically

Consider your own country's population pyramid. You can find it at www.census.gov/population/international. What can you tell about your country's age and sex ratios and level of development by studying the population pyramid? How might societies differ if they have a young versus an old population?

Population Patterns: Theoretical Explanations

The earliest historical writings reveal that interest in population size is nothing new. Scriptures written many centuries ago, such as the Quran and the Bible, encourage population growth to increase the ranks of the faithful. Of course, population expansion made sense at the time these holy tracts were written, and populations grew slowly. Government leaders throughout the ages have adopted various philosophies about the best size of populations. The ancient Greek philosopher Plato argued that the ideal city-state should have 5,040 citizens and that measures should be taken to increase or decrease the population to bring it in line with this figure (Plato [350 BCE] 1960). However, the first significant scholarly analysis that addressed global population issues came from Thomas Malthus (1766–1834), an English clergyman and social philosopher.

Malthus's Theory of Population. In his "Essay on the Principle of Population," Malthus argued that humans are driven to reproduce and will multiply excessively without checks imposed to slow population growth (Malthus [1798] 1926). He noted that an unchecked population increases geometrically: 2 parents could have 4 children, 16 grandchildren, 64 great-grandchildren, and so forth—just with a continuous average family size of 4 children. Meanwhile, the means of subsistence (food) increases at best only arithmetically or lineally (5, 10, 15, 20, 25). Therefore, population growth must be controlled. Malthus described two types of checks that control population growth: (1) positive checks that lead to higher death rates (e.g., wars, disease, epidemics, and food shortages leading to famine) and (2) preventative checks that result in lower birth rates (e.g., delaying marriage and practicing abstinence). Hoping to avoid the positive checks, Malthus advocated for implementing the preventative checks. He did not approve of contraception, viewing it as immoral.

Contemporary neo-Malthusians, like Paul and Anne Ehrlich, favor contraception rather than simple reliance on the moral restraint that Malthus proposed. They also add to the formula of "too many people and too little food" the additional problem of a "dying planet" caused by environmental damage. They argue that "the human predicament is driven by overpopulation, overconsumption of natural resources and the use of environmentally damaging technologies and socio-economic-political arrangements to service Homo Sapiens' aggregate consumption." Successfully addressing these threats and avoiding the "collapse" of global society will require dramatic cultural and political shifts across the world (Ehrlich and Ehrlich 1990:1).

Looking at the world today, we see examples of the "positive" population checks described by Malthus. War decimated the populations of several countries during the world wars and has taken its toll on other countries in Central and Eastern Europe, Africa, and the Middle East since then. Waterborne diseases, such as cholera and typhus, strike after floods, and the floods themselves are often caused by large populations clearing and using almost all of the trees in their environment for fuel and building materials. Every year, famines strike parts of Africa and cause immense suffering. For example, in 2016, 50,000 children faced starvation due to famine in Somalia (World Famine Timeline 2016).

Disease has also taken a toll on the world's population. In some villages in sub-Saharan and East African countries, AIDS has wiped out large percentages of the population, and many children must fend for themselves. Orphaned children take care of their younger siblings. PEPFAR (President's Emergency Plan for AIDS Relief), begun under President George W. Bush and continued under President Barack Obama, distributes generic forms of antiviral drugs to those with AIDS and has helped bring the death toll down. Without this relief effort, the loss of life would be even more staggering in this region of the world (Aguirre 2012). However, population control needed to keep the population growth rate in check still needs to be addressed.

Whereas Malthus's work raised many issues still discussed today, his pessimistic vision of the future has not come to pass. He overemphasized *environmental determinism*, the idea that we can do little about the environment because it controls our lives. Malthus and neo-Malthusians were not able to anticipate the advances in agriculture that have increased the food supply tremendously. Nor did they foresee the importance of vaccines in controlling diseases. However, they have raised important issues that have helped government leaders in many parts of the world become aware of the need to plan for and take steps to control population growth (M. Bell 2012).

Thinking Sociologically

What are contemporary examples of what Malthus described as positive checks on population growth—war, disease, famine? Are family planning and contraception (a) suitable and (b) sufficient means to solve the problem of global overpopulation by humans? Can you think of other alternatives?

Demographic Transition: Explaining Population Growth and Expansion. Why should a change in the economic structure, such as industrialization and movement from rural agricultural areas to cities, have an impact on population size? The **demographic transition theory**, *which links trends in birth rates and death rates with patterns of economic and technological development*, offers one explanation.

This theory identifies four clear stages of development and posits that a fifth one is in process.

Stage 1. Populations have *high birth rates and death rates that tend to balance each other* over time. Births may outpace deaths until some disaster diminishes the increase. This has been the pattern for most of human history.

Stage 2. Populations still have high birth rates, but death rates decline (i.e., more people live longer) because of improvements in health care and sanitation, the establishment of public-health programs, disease control and immunizations, and food availability and distribution. This imbalance between the continuing high number of births and the declining number of deaths means that the *population growth rate is very high.*

Stage 3. Populations begin to level off due to access to contraception, wage increases, urbanization, increases in education levels and the status of women, and other changes. Most industrial societies are in this stage.

Stage 4. Birth rates and death rates are both low. Birth rates in some Global North countries drop below replacement level, resulting in declining population. Death rates remain fairly constant and low, though lifestyle diseases caused by smoking, obesity, and lack of exercise may increase death rates in some areas.

Stage 5. This stage is emerging in some Global North societies but has not yet come into full existence. Many demographers predict it will. As death rates remain stable and birth rates decline, the total population will begin to decrease for the first time. Japan and Germany are in the beginning of Stage 5.

These stages are illustrated in Figure 13.4.

FIGURE 13.4   Stages of Demographic Transition

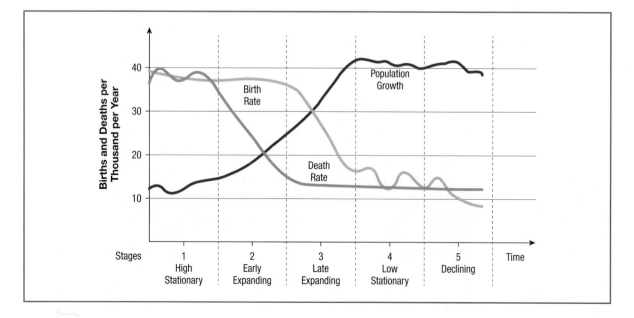

Demographic transition theory helps explain the developmental stages and population trends in countries around the world, but it does not consider some important factors that affect the size of populations.

1. People's age at marriage determines how many childbearing years they have. (Late marriage means fewer years until menopause.)
2. Contraceptive availability determines whether families can control their number of children.
3. A country's resources and land may determine how much population it can support.
4. The economic structure, religious beliefs, and political philosophies of a country affect attitudes toward birth control and family size.
5. Economic expansion rates influence a country's need for labor and its ability to create jobs.

The *wealth flow theory* suggests that two possible strategies operate in couples' personal decisions about family size. When wealth flows from children to parents—that is, when children are an asset working on the family farm or laboring—parents have larger families. When wealth flows from parents to children—that is, when parents must support the children—families tend to have fewer children (Caldwell 1982). To raise a child born in 2013 to 18 years in the United States, for instance, costs an average of more than $245,000 (using 2013 dollars), *not including college expenses* (Lino 2014).

Elements of both the demographic transition and wealth flow theories describe why families in poor nations tend to have more children than those in wealthier nations. Consider the following:

1. Many poor societies are agricultural societies where more children equals more people to work the farm.
2. Poor societies have higher rates of child mortality, leading parents to have more children because they know some are likely to die at a young age.
3. Girls in poor societies tend to leave school early (if they attend at all) and to marry at a young age, leading to early and more childbearing.
4. Artificial contraception tends to be less available in poor nations.

With these facts in mind, Jeffrey Sachs, an economist and leading expert on world poverty, advocates (along with many other social scientists) "a quality education for every

© REUTERS/ Mike Hutchings

Overpopulation presents a challenge to food and water resources, and large populations damage the environment and provide little ecological recovery time. This photo shows the smog from fires, factories, and automobiles—called *brown haze*—that routinely hovers over Cape Town, South Africa, in the morning.

child" and improved health care and access to contraceptives in poor nations (Sachs 2011, 2015).

Conflict Theorists' Explanations of Population Growth.

Karl Marx did not agree with Malthus's idea that high fertility rates and population growth that outstrips food and resources produce poverty (Marx [1844] 2009). He believed that social and structural factors built into the economic system—inequitable distribution and control of resources—cause poverty. Capitalist structures lead to wealth for the owners and create overpopulation and poverty for workers. Workers are expendable, kept in competition for low wages, used when needed, and let go when unprofitable to capitalists.

Socialist societies, Marx argued, could absorb the growth in population so the problem of overpopulation would not exist. In a classless society, all would be able to find jobs, and the system would expand to include everyone (Magnus 2009). Marx's writing partner, Friedrich Engels, asserted that population growth in socialist societies could be controlled by the central government, as was done by the Chinese government when it imposed a one-child-per-family policy in 1979 (Marx and Engels 1975). (The policy in China has gone through several revisions since that time.)

Conflict theorists also point out the impact that capitalism has on the health of people living in poor areas, as exemplified by the dumping of toxic waste from industries into predominantly poor areas with high percentages of people of color. Environmental racism, *when environmental pollution disproportionately affects racial and ethnic minorities*,

In a dump in Accra, the capital of Ghana, teenage boys can be seen smashing old computers and other electronic devices so that they can sell the metals inside to local businesses.

In an urban area in Cambodia (Kampuchea), residents crowd onto this truck, a common form of transportation. With a high fertility rate and migration from rural to urban areas, crowded transportation is common.

relates directly to the social status differences of groups in society. For example, in Dickson, Tennessee, a well where the African American Holt-Orsted family got their drinking water was being polluted with toxic chemicals that leaked from a nearby landfill. They continued to use this well, unaware of any problems, for 9 years. Although some of the neighbors—those who were White—were notified within 48 hours after local waste treatment agencies learned of the danger (in 1993), the Holt-Orsted family was not informed and, in fact, was told by county officials that things were fine (Holt 2007; Huang 2011). By the time Sheila Holt-Orsted was finally informed (in 2002) that the water the family had been using for showers, cooking, and beverages was contaminated with cancer-causing agents, Sheila had breast cancer, and her father had terminal prostate cancer. Four additional Holt-Orsted family members suffered from various other illnesses believed to be caused by the spills into the water supply. The family finally won their court case in 2011, but by then, several family members had died from cancer (Holt 2007; Huang 2011).

In the United States, people of color are 2 to 3 times more likely than Whites to live in communities with hazardous-waste problems and are exposed to 38% more toxins that cause cancer than are Whites (M. Bell 2012; Clark, Millet, and Marshall 2014). The Environmental Protection Agency now has an interactive environmental map that shows where U.S. low-income minority communities face the most environmental pollution (see www2.epa.gov/ejscreen). Activists and researchers involved in the *environmental justice movement* work to address such problems.

One classic study in Chicago focused on the impact of efforts to make Chicago a more eco-friendly or "green" city by encouraging more recycling. However, there were substantial problems of pollution, disease risk, and other costs

to the low-income, minority neighborhoods where the recycling plants were located (Pellow 2002). In a similar vein, if you sent your old computer to a recycling center, there is a good chance it ended up in a West African dump. To save money, many electronic recycling centers in Global North nations illegally send what they take in to Global South nations like Ghana, where governments are unable or unwilling, if they are being paid, to stop dumps from taking in e-waste.

In a dump in Accra, the capital of Ghana, teenage boys can be seen smashing old computers and other electronic devices so that they can sell the metals inside to local businesses. Exposed to the chemicals that leach out of the abandoned computers, they are being poisoned and injuring their health. It is sobering to realize that environmentally friendly policies (recycling or donating—rather than throwing away—electronic devices) aimed at prolonging the health of Earth and the human population have often been implemented in ways that hurt those who have the fewest resources—people living in poverty and minorities (Hugo 2010; J. Korgen and Gallagher 2013).

MESO-LEVEL INSTITUTIONAL INFLUENCES ON POPULATION CHANGE

Meso-level analysis focuses on institutions and ethnic subcultures within a country. In this section, we examine how institutions influence birth rates and other population patterns. Populations change in three main ways: (1) *size* (overall number of people), (2) *composition* (the makeup of the population, including sex ratio, age distribution, and religious or ethnic representation in the population), and (3) *distribution* (density or concentration in various portions of the land).

The key *demographic processes* that cause population changes are **fertility** (*the birth rate*), **mortality** (*the death rate*), and **migration** (*movement of people from one place to another*). Populations change when births and deaths are not evenly balanced or when significant numbers of people move from one area to another. Migration does not change the size or composition of the world as a whole but can affect size or makeup in a micro- (family), meso- (institution or ethnic subculture), or macro-level (national) population. Fertility is the most easily controllable factor impacting population change.

Institutions and Population Patterns

Demographers consider micro-, meso-, and macro-level factors in attempting to understand fertility rates around the world. In the United States, about half of all pregnancies are unplanned (Kost 2015). Lack of access to contraception and laws affecting individuals' fertility decisions contribute to unexpected pregnancies in the United States and elsewhere (Tavernise 2015). Couples' decisions to use or not use contraception, their ideas about the acceptability of abortion, and whether they want to have children (and how many) can also have an impact on national and global rates of population change. So choices at the micro level make a difference at the macro level. Consider the following meso-level institutional factors affecting the size of the population.

Economic Factors and Population Patterns. Fertility fluctuates with actions in meso-level institutions, such as the economy and the government. During economic depressions, for example, the rate of fertility tends to drop due to lack of family resources. Also, government policies to encourage or discourage births and access to health care influence decisions within families about fertility. For example, in the state of Colorado, the rate of teenagers giving birth dropped 40% and the abortion rate among teenagers fell 42% after Colorado (through a private grant) provided free intrauterine devices and implants to poor women and teenagers (Tavernise 2015).

The economic prosperity of nations also influences population growth. Figure 13.5 compares population trends in affluent Global North regions of the world—like Europe and North America—with the less affluent Global South regions—like Africa, Latin America, and Oceania, where poverty is widespread (Roser 2016).

● Thinking Sociologically

What does Figure 13.5 tell you about the lives of individuals in these different regions of the world?

Political Systems and Population Patterns. Some governments provide incentives to parents to have more children through *pronatalist policies* (those that encourage fertility), whereas others discourage high fertility with *antinatalist policies* (those that discourage fertility). Thus, meso-level social policies established by the political system can shape decisions of families at the micro level. Government policies can take several forms: (a) manipulating contraceptive availability; (b) promoting change in factors that affect fertility such as the status of women, education, availability of abortion, and degree of economic development; (c) using propaganda for or against having children; (d) creating incentives (parental leaves, benefits such as medical care and housing, and tax breaks) or penalties (such as fines) for having children; and (e) passing laws governing age of marriage, size of family, contraception, and abortion.

Antinatalist policies arise out of concern over available resources and differences in birth rates among population subgroups. Singapore, a small island country in Asia, consists of one main island and many smaller islands. It is one of the most crowded places on Earth, with 7,405 people per square kilometer (compared with 351 in Japan, 34 in the United States, and 4 in Canada) (World Bank 2013b). The entire population of Singapore is urban, and 90% live in the capital city. The country has little unemployment and one of the highest per capita incomes in Asia. However, it depends on imports from other countries for most of its raw materials and food.

Some years ago, the central government in Singapore started an aggressive antinatalist plan. It made birth control widely available, and residents of Singapore who had more than two children were penalized with less health care, smaller housing, and higher costs for services such as education. As a result of these policies, Singapore now claims one of the lowest natural increase rates (the birthrate minus the death rate) in Southeast Asia, at 0.6% a year (Population Reference Bureau 2013a).

As noted earlier, China instituted its current antinatalist policy, which included the "one child" rule, in 1979. The government has discouraged traditional preferences

FIGURE 13.5   Population Growth by World Regions: 1950 to 2050

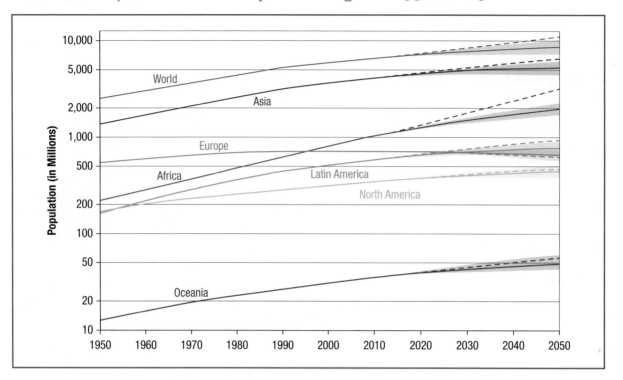

Note: Based on United Nations population projections. Nearly all future population growth will be in the Global South, though in Asia and Latin America it is leveling off. The dotted lines and shaded areas indicate speculation for trends that could vary depending on possible changes in key variables.

Source: Roser (2016).

for early marriage, large families, and many sons by using fines, group pressure, privileges for small families, and easy availability of birth control and abortion. The government has reduced the fertility rate to 1.55 children per family (*World Factbook* 2015c).

Some of the results of the Chinese antinatalist policies were unanticipated, however. For a variety of reasons (including a lack of government support for the elderly), male babies tend to be preferred more than female babies. Faced with a limit of one child, many people decided to have abortions rather than girls. As a result of the policy, China now faces a rapidly aging population in which many men will have difficulty finding a woman to marry. In 2014, the government began to allow parents to have a second child, if the mother or father was an only child (McKenzie 2015).

Examples of pronatalist government policies can be seen in Eastern Europe, where governments are worried about the drop in birth rates. There are fewer young people to pay taxes and to do jobs needed in the society. Pronatalist policies established to raise birthrates include giving workers a day off to "have sex," free summer camps for young couples (without condoms), cars and monetary gifts for new parents, and additional benefits for parents

and their children. Abortions and even birth control have been restricted in some Eastern European countries to curb dropping population numbers (Stracansky 2013).

In the United States, it is sometimes hard to pin a simple label of antinatalist or pronatalist on the administration in power. Presidents Ronald Reagan, George H. W. Bush, and George W. Bush each implemented a "gag rule" (requiring parental notification) that limited the availability of birth control for teens in the United States. Presidents Bill Clinton and Barack Obama each eliminated the gag policy. President Clinton also signed the Family and Medical Leave Act, which allows employees (in organizations with 50 or more employees) to take up to 12 weeks of (unpaid) leave to take care of a family member, without risk of losing their job.

Whereas family-planning programs and contraceptive use have increased in much of the world, many people in sub-Saharan Africa still do not have access to birth control devices. The percentage of married or in-union women in sub-Saharan Africa using contraceptives tripled between 1990 and 2012 but still remains relatively low (34%) (Kantorová, Biddlecom, and Newby 2014). The vast majority of the 16 million girls ages 15 to 19 who give birth each year live in Global South countries (WHO 2014a).

Thinking Sociologically

Do you think it is appropriate for governments to use enticements or penalties to encourage or discourage fertility decisions by couples? Why, or why not? Identify several possible positive and negative repercussions of either pronatalist or antinatalist policies.

Religion and Population Patterns. Religion is a primary shaper of norms and values in most societies, including those related to fertility. In some societies, children born out of wedlock are accepted into the mother's family. In other societies, a woman can be stoned to death for having a child or even sex out of wedlock.

Some religious groups oppose any intervention, such as birth control or abortion, in the natural processes of conception and birth. Roman Catholicism, for example, teaches that large families are a blessing from God and that artificial birth control is a sin. The Roman Catholic Church officially advocates natural family planning (NFP) to regulate conception, a less reliable method than artificial birth control, using medication, or physical barriers. Many Catholics, however, do use artificial birth control methods, and the recent outbreak of the Zika virus presents a challenge to the ban on contraceptives. In the United States, only 2% of Catholics rely on NFP, whereas almost 70% rely on the birth control pill, an IUD (intrauterine device), or sterilization to control their family size (Guttmacher Institute 2013).

A religious officer canes an Acehnese youth onstage as punishment for dating outside of marriage, which is against Sharia law, outside a mosque in Banda Aceh on August 1, 2016. The strictly Muslim province, Aceh, has become increasingly conservative in recent years and is the only one in Indonesia implementing Sharia law.

Education and Population. If a country wants to control population growth, providing better access to schools and raising the education level of women is a key to success. The higher women's status in society—as measured by education level and job opportunities—the lower their fertility (Population Reference Bureau 2013b; Pradhan 2015; Testa 2014). Figure 13.6 shows the relationship between education and family size in five Global South

FIGURE 13.6 Women's Education and Family Size—Selected Countries

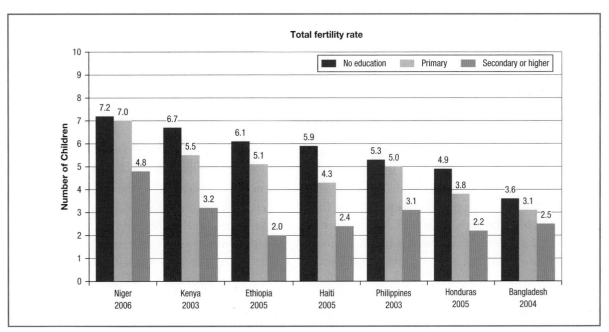

Total fertility rate

Legend: No education | Primary | Secondary or higher

Country/Year	No education	Primary	Secondary or higher
Niger 2006	7.2	7.0	4.8
Kenya 2003	6.7	5.5	3.2
Ethiopia 2005	6.1	5.1	2.0
Haiti 2005	5.9	4.3	2.4
Philippines 2003	5.3	5.0	3.1
Honduras 2005	4.9	3.8	2.2
Bangladesh 2004	3.6	3.1	2.5

(y-axis: Number of Children)

Source: Population Reference Bureau (2016).

A sick and displaced Chadian woman watches as her malnourished infant sleeps at a health clinic run by Doctors Without Borders. This mother knows that life expectancy for her child is less than 50 years, and many children die in infancy.

© REUTERS/ Finbarr O'Reilly

countries (Population Reference Bureau 2016). Note that the higher the education level, the lower the fertility rate and population growth.

Lower population growth means less pressure on governments to provide emergency services, such as food and water rations for booming populations and more attention to services such as schools, health care, and jobs. Most population experts encourage governments and other meso-level institutions in fast-growing countries to act aggressively to control population size. Consequences of population fluctuations affect affluent parts of the world as well as poor parts.

Factors Affecting Mortality Rates

Recall that life expectancy refers to the average number of years a person in a particular society can expect to live. It indicates the overall health conditions in a country. Imagine living in Chad, Africa, where the life expectancy at birth is 49.44 years. In this low-income, largely agricultural society, families tend to have many children (4.68, on average, or 37.3 per 1,000 members of the population). Of every 1,000 babies born alive, 90.3 will die within the first year. Over 72% of men and women live in rural areas, where most are subsistence farmers, working small plots that may not provide enough food to keep their families from starving (*World Factbook* 2015b). When one plot is overfarmed and the soil depleted so that plants will no longer grow, the family moves to another and clears the land, depleting more arable land and cutting down trees resulting in erosion of rich soil. This scenario repeats itself, leading to little arable land, shortages of food, malnutrition, and a population susceptible to illnesses and disease. The limited medical care that exists is mostly available in urban areas.

Some other African countries face similar situations, with life expectancy in South Africa at 49.56, Somalia at 51.58, and Zimbabwe at 55.68. Average life expectancy for sub-Saharan Africa as a whole is about 56 years (World Bank 2014).

Why are these societies so dramatically different from Global North countries, many of which have average life expectancies into the 80s? The low life expectancy stems from lack of medical care, epidemics such as Ebola and AIDS, wars and civil strife, corrupt governments, droughts and famine, malnutrition, resulting susceptibility to diseases, and high infant mortality. Table 13.2 shows the number of children who die before the age of 1 (per 1,000 live births) for various regions of the world. This is another key indicator of a country's overall well-being.

Even within Global North nations, mortality rates can vary according to social class, geography, and social policies. In the United States, the life expectancy of the richest continues to rise—and pull away from that of the poor. The gap in life expectancy between the top 1% and bottom 1% in income in the United States has increased since 2001 (2.3% for men and 2.9% for women) and is now 14.6 years for men and 10.1 years for women. The good news is that new studies show that social policies can influence life expectancy for poor people. Those who live in areas with higher government expenditures and more positive health behaviors (such as lower smoking rates) have much higher life expectancy rates than those who live in other areas of the nation (Chetty et al. 2016).

Migration and Mobility: Where People Move and Why

Most of us have moved one or more times in our lives, a process called migration. Perhaps we have moved to a larger house down the block, maybe to another area for a job opportunity or school, or even to another country altogether. The process of changing one's place of residence is called *geographic mobility*. Over the history of the human race, people have migrated to the far reaches of the globe. Because of adaptability to climatic and

Table 13.2 Infant Mortality Rates Around the World (per 1,000 live births)

Region	Infant Mortality Rate (per 1,000 live births)
World	37
More affluent (Global North) countries	5
Less affluent (Global South) countries	40
Least affluent (the very poor Global South)	62
Africa	59
Sub-Saharan Africa	64
North America	6
Latin America and the Caribbean	17
Central America	14
South America	18
Asia	33
Europe	6
Western Europe	3
Northern Europe	4
Eastern Europe	8

Source: Population Reference Bureau (2015).

geographic barriers, humans have dispersed to more areas of the world than any other species. Even inhospitable locations, such as the Arctic North and the South Pole, have human settlements.

As noted in previous chapters, the *push–pull* model points out that some people are pushed from their original locations by wars, plagues, famine, political or religious conflicts, economic crises, or other factors and pulled to new locations by economic opportunities or political and religious tolerance. Most people do not leave a location unless they have been forced out, or they have a viable alternative in the new location. They weigh the benefits of moving versus the costs (Weeks 2012).

Migration is often initiated at the micro level: a lucrative job offer in another location requires a move, the family dwelling becomes too small, a relative needs help, or a family member's health requires a different climate. However, if the risks are high, if the information about migration is scarce, or if the move involves negative factors such as leaving family, individuals may decide to stay put. For rational choice theorists, assessment of costs and benefits by individuals impacts migration patterns.

Although the decision to move is often a micro-level personal or family one, the macro-level sociocultural environment also influences it. Examples of large groups of people leaving an area because of aspirations to improve their life chances; hopes of retaining a way of life; or expulsion by political, economic, or religious forces have existed throughout history. Chinese railroad workers came to the United States for economic reasons. Amish and Mennonite settlers from Europe sought religious freedom and preservation of their way of life. The Amish, a group originating in Germany, left Germany *en masse*, and members of this group now live entirely in North America. Italian immigration to the United States took place in a collective manner. When a family left Italy, they would usually move to a U.S. city where a relative, friend, or acquaintance lived. Thus, residents of entire apartment buildings in the North End of Boston were from the same extended family, and entire city blocks of people came from the same town or region of southern Italy (Gans 1962). Many European countries are multicultural environments today because of immigrants from former colonies.

Those living at the receiving end have not always been welcoming and, in fact, have often tried to isolate the newcomers in ghettos, preventing them from moving into other neighborhoods. Especially in difficult economic times, when competition for jobs is greatest, newcomers may find few employment opportunities (Foner 2005). Immigration laws in the United States reflect the nation's attitudes toward immigrants at different time periods. The United States tended to welcome immigrants during boom economic times and tried to repel them during recessions and depressions. Exclusionary acts include the Chinese Exclusion Act of 1882, which ended Chinese immigration; the Gentlemen's Agreement of 1907, which halted Japanese immigration; and the National Origins Act of 1924, which heavily restricted immigration from Southern and Eastern Europe and excluded non-Whites.

The Immigration and Nationality Act of 1965 abolished the policies that excluded Asians, Africans, and Latin

Humans are able to live and have dispersed to some very inhospitable places, like Antarctica, where there is no sunshine at all for 5 to 6 months of the year, and temperatures at the South Pole have dropped as low as −135.8 degrees Fahrenheit. Antarctic communities are mostly research stations.

Americans and based immigration policy on family relationships and skills. Current debates in the U.S. Congress over immigration reform, however, reveal the persistent contentious nature of policies related to immigration, including undocumented migration from Latin America.

After the Great Recession began in 2008, immigration to the United States slowed. In Mexico, an economic rebound and successful efforts to lower the birth rate have led to fewer people looking for jobs in the United States. Those factors, in combination with the economic recession, anti-immigrant environment, and tighter U.S. border controls, have led to fewer Mexicans making the trip to the United States and more returning to Mexico. Since 2013, most new immigrants have been from Asia rather than Latin America (Barrera 2013).

Immigrants seeking a better life often struggle in their new locations. Consider Mohammed from Senegal who traverses the streets of Verona, Italy, trying to make a living selling children's books and hoping he might have some money left to send back to his family. Mohammed speaks five languages and has a high school education, but opportunities in his homeland are limited, and he is an undocumented immigrant in Italy. European countries, especially those with former colonies, have large populations of immigrants from North Africa and the Middle East. These immigrants often face great peril in

their attempts to gain entry into more prosperous nations; and once they arrive, many find themselves in crowded, unsanitary housing with little economic opportunity.

Social scientists study the impact of immigration, pointing out that immigration tends to yield significant economic gains for receiving countries. Scholars who study migration—especially long-distance migration that involves crossing into another society—point out that migrants are usually among the most hardworking, ambitious, optimistic, healthy, and well-adjusted people, for it takes considerable courage and motivation to undertake a migration to a new land. Isabel Wilkerson summarizes,

> Any migration takes some measure of energy, planning, and forethought. It requires not only the desire for something better but the willingness to act on that desire to achieve it. Thus, the people who undertake such a journey are more likely to be either among the more educated in their homes of origin or those most motivated. (Wilkerson 2010:261)

A recent study of immigrants to the United States shows people born elsewhere who later acquire U.S. citizenship are more likely than their native-born neighbors to marry, less likely to divorce, and more likely to avoid poverty. In the 10 poorest U.S. states, native-born citizens earn just $0.84 to every $1 earned by naturalized citizens. In the richest states, the ratio is $0.97 to $1. One reason for this difference in earnings comes from the fact that foreign-born naturalized citizens tend to bring with them the tools and attitudes they need to be successful. They had to have the wherewithal to leave their home country, find sponsors in the United States, navigate visa and green card requirements, and fulfill the requirements for U.S. citizenship. Those who can do all that tend to be self-reliant and willing to take risks and have an entrepreneurial spirit (Giridharadas 2014).

International Migration. More than 3.1% of the world's population is "on the go" each year. That is 232 million international migrants, or 1 out of every 33 persons in the world. Half are women. These migrants change the size and characteristics of populations around the world, expanding some areas and emptying out others (Swing 2015).

Many people have taken great risks to enter Global North nations illegally in search of work. Luis is one such undocumented immigrant. His story, in the next "Engaging Sociology," illustrates the hardships that many migrants must endure as they seek a better life for themselves and their families. To these migrants, a better life awaits *if* they can reach it.

ENGAGING SOCIOLOGY

From South to North of the U.S. Border
by Nancy Diggs

When Luis and the group of 60 undocumented immigrants made the journey across the Arizona desert, it was March; temperatures ranged as high as the 90s during the day to freezing at night. The group was told that they would be walking in the desert for about 6 hours and to bring food and water for that time. To travel quickly, they were told to carry nothing else. Their guide claimed that in order to avoid the Immigration and Naturalization Service (U.S. Citizenship and Immigration Services) they would have to change plans and march through more of the desert—a hellish two-and-a-half days, most of it without food or water. It was so hot that when they chanced upon water tanks for animals, most of them rushed to gulp down the green, slimy water. Along the path, the travelers passed the remains of one man who had not made it. Having nothing but the clothes on their backs, they were unable to bury him.

At night in the desert cold, without extra clothing or blankets, Luis and his companions huddled together for warmth. In order not to be spotted, they wore dark clothes. Smoking and whistling were also forbidden. At last, they came to a highway to be crossed, where they would wait until late at night when there was no traffic. When a car stopped on the road, the guide warned everyone not to move and to keep their eyes closed so the light wouldn't reflect off the whites of their eyes.

When all was dark and quiet, the guide called another coyote (a person who helps undocumented immigrants into the United States in exchange for money), who arrived with two vans. The sound of a helicopter caused everyone to push and shove in a vain attempt to squeeze 60 people into the two vehicles.

At the next step of the journey, the immigrants were loaded onto a truck trailer that was "incredibly hot," with no water. After traveling some 400 miles, the group eventually arrived in Los Angeles, where they were able to buy food and drinks. After spending the night in a safe house, Luis and his group met their new U.S. coyote, who sent them off in different directions. Luis took a bus to Las Vegas, where his uncle lived (Diggs 2011).

* * * * *

Engaging With Sociology

1. What do you think may have led Luis to risk what he did to enter the U.S.? What circumstances might lead you to try to cross a national border without documents, as Luis did?

2. Over the past few years, hundreds of thousands of unaccompanied minors have tried to cross the U.S.–Mexico border to escape from gang-related violence in their hometowns (see www.pbs.org/newshour/updates/country-lost-kids). Their parents often encourage them to go because they believe they will be killed if they remain. Do you think the United States should let them enter and remain in the United States? Why, or why not?

3. As a public sociologist, what advice would you give to government policymakers trying to deal with the undocumented migration of minors to the United States?

International migration is especially common where political turmoil, wars, famines, or natural disasters ravage a country. More than 50 million migrants are *refugees*, those who flee in search of refuge in times of war, political oppression, natural disaster, or religious persecution. Today, there are more refugees in the world than at any time since World War II.

The ongoing crisis in Syria has added significantly to the number of refugees. By July 2015, almost 4 million Syrians had registered as refugees with the United Nations. The tiny nations of Jordan and Lebanon have taken in well over 600,000 and 1 million refugees respectively. Ten percent of the Jordanian population now consists of refugees, and that number increases daily (United Nations High Commissioner for Refugees 2015).

Thinking Sociologically

Think about your grandparents or great grandparents. How long have your ancestors occupied the same house or lived in the same community? Do they go back more than one generation on the same property? If they have been mobile, what factors were critical in their decision to move? How has their mobility or stability influenced your family's experiences? How were they received in their new home?

Internal Migration in the United States. The rate of internal migration in the United States is high compared with that in most places in the world. Patterns of migration have primarily involved individual "pull" to economic opportunities and better housing. According to the U.S. Census, about 40% of people who move cite a housing reason, including a new or better home or apartment, a better neighborhood,

After crossing the Aegean Sea from Turkey on an inflatable boat in 2015, Syrian refugees arrive on the Greek island of Lesbos. Despite horrible weather and rough seas, migrants and refugees are risking their lives—and those of their children—in search of a better life within the European Union.

Getty Images/Matej Divizna/Getty Images News

cheaper housing, owning rather than renting, or establishing their own household (Demographics Livability 2014).

During different historical periods, movement directions have varied. During the 20th century, until the 1960s, people moved out of the southern states and into northern states. This included the Great Migration of 6 million Black Americans who left the rural South for northern cities. Then, the pattern reversed, and the flow started going south and west. Movement starting in the 1960s and increasing in the 1970s has been toward the Sunbelt, especially to California, Arizona, Texas, and Florida. Movement to the Pacific Coast and even Alaska has also increased, due to economic opportunities in these locations.

MICRO-LEVEL POPULATION PATTERNS

Understanding demography can be extremely important for comprehending social processes in your everyday life. Although most Global North countries do not have massive famines or population explosions, population fluctuations influence them in many ways. Consider the life choice decisions you will make regarding education, employment, and retirement.

Keith, one of the coauthors of this book, lived in Boston, and his wife taught in a suburban school system there at a time when the fertility rate was falling. The elementary school where she taught had four first-grade classrooms, with 28 children per room—112 first graders in the school. By the next year, the school felt the decline in the fertility rate 6 years earlier, and the number of first graders declined. Within 4 years, there were only 40 first graders in her school, with two classrooms and only 20 students per class. Some school systems lost half of their student population in a few years. One year, first-grade teachers were losing their jobs or having to move to another grade, and the next year, it was second-grade teachers who were scrambling. The third year, third-grade teachers were in oversupply and so forth. With low demand, these were not times for college students to be pursuing teaching careers. A personal decision was being influenced by population trends—and this pattern continues.

We have already mentioned the impact of the baby boom (the high fertility rates from 1946 to about 1963) and the following baby bust (the drop in fertility for more than a decade following the baby boom). The population pyramid of the United States reveals the impact on the population (see Figures 13.7 and 13.8). As we can see, the U.S. population no longer looks anything like a pyramid. From these figures, we can tell a great deal about job prospects, retirement security, career decisions, and other outcomes of demographic

FIGURE 13.7   United States, 2014

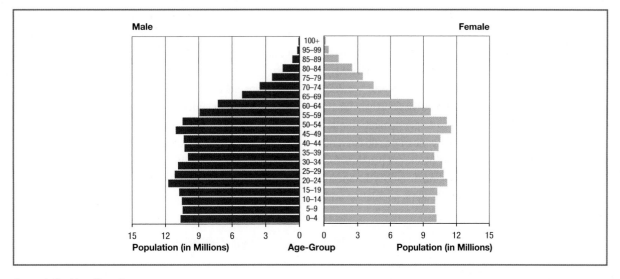

Source: Index Mundi (2015).

FIGURE 13.8   United States, 2050

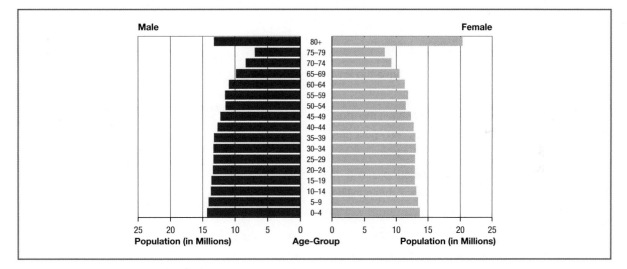

Source: NationMaster (2011).

changes. As that bulge for the baby boomer group moves into the senior citizens' category, society will have new challenges.

Thinking Sociologically

Why do population experts predict the population pyramid will look like Figure 13.8 by 2050? What factors in society might lead to this? What kinds of problems do you think this sort of configuration might cause?

Retirement is another topic for which population patterns are critical. When Social Security was established in the United States in the 1930s, life expectancy from birth was 58 for men and 62 for women (Social Security Administration 2013). The number of people in the age-dependent categories of under 15 and over 65 was low. For each person who received Social Security in 1945, 42 workers paid Social Security taxes. Forty people, each paying $255 a year, could easily support a retired person, receiving $10,000 per year. However, the average life expectancy has shifted, and the age-dependent population has increased. Currently, in the United States, nearly 14% of the population is over the age of 65, as opposed to 4% in the 1930s (*World Factbook* 2017b). Moreover, predictions are that by 2035, 20% of the population will be over 65. In 2013, there were just 2.8 workers contributing Social Security taxes for each person covered by Social Security (Social Security Administration 2014). When commentators and politicians say Social Security is in trouble, they refer to problems created by changes in the composition of the U.S. population.

In the 1980s, the U.S. administration and Congress saw the problem coming and for the first time began to save funds in a Social Security account for the baby boomers. They also passed laws requiring baby boomers to work longer before they qualify for Social Security. The fact that there are so many baby boomers—and that an extremely high percentage of citizens over the age of 65 vote—makes it unlikely that the government will cut back on benefits to this group. Still, members of the younger generation may not receive as much Social Security income as do current retirees. Meanwhile, Medicare, the insurance program for retired adults, has less money on hand than does the Social Security system. It appears that the aging population and need for funds may have a profound influence on your own family budget and retirement.

As noted in Chapter 6, population patterns also influence rates of deviance and juvenile delinquency. Most deviant acts are committed by young people in their mid-teens to early 20s. Thus, when the baby boom generation was in their teens and early 20s, in the 1960s and 1970s, the overall rates of deviance climbed higher. When the birth dearth group was in their teens, overall rates of crime dropped because there were fewer teenagers. Thus, private and personal decisions by thousands of couples (micro level) may result in the crime rates for the entire country rising or falling 15 years later.

ENGAGING SOCIOLOGY

Population Pyramids and Predicting Community Needs and Services

Study these three population pyramids. Based on what you see, answer the following questions:

1. Which community would likely have the lowest crime rate? Explain.

2. Which community would likely have the most cultural amenities (theaters, art galleries, concert halls, and so forth)? Explain.

3. Imagine you were an entrepreneur planning on starting a business in one of these communities.

a. Name three businesses that you think would succeed in each community. Explain.

b. Name one business that you think would not succeed in each community. Explain.

Naples, Florida

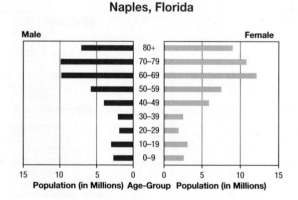

(Hint: Naples is a major retirement community.)

Bloomington, Indiana

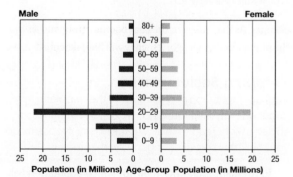

(Hint: Bloomington, a smallish city, is the home of Indiana University.)

Norfolk, Virginia

(Hint: Norfolk is home to one of the nation's largest navy bases.)

Because population trends shape your life, understanding those trends can help you use that knowledge to your advantage. To illustrate the power of demographic trends on individual decisions, the "Engaging Sociology" on the previous page provides an exercise in problem solving using information from population pyramids of U.S. cities.

URBANIZATION: MOVEMENT FROM RURAL TO URBAN AREAS

Tokyo-Yokohama, Japan; Jakarta, Indonesia; Delhi, India; Seoul-Incheon, South Korea; Manila, Philippines; Mumbai (Bombay), India; Karachi, Pakistan; Shanghai, China; and New York, U.S., are *megacities* (cities and their surrounding metropolitan areas with more than 10 million people) (Cox 2016). They are characterized by traffic congestion and people rushing to their destinations. Carts, bicycles, and taxis weave in and out of traffic jams. The local spices and other aromas scent the air. Sidewalk merchants display vegetables and fruits unique to the country. Beggars and the homeless, often migrants from rural areas, dot the sidewalks while merchants sell colorful wares. Cities provide a kaleidoscope of humanity as more of the world's population becomes urban.

Today, more than half of all people in the world live in urban areas, and projections indicate that 7 out of 10 people will do so by 2050 (WHO 2013). The U.S. Census breaks down the geographic regions of the nation into urbanized areas (of 50,000 or more), urban clusters (2,500–50,000), and rural areas (all nonurban areas). In 1900, 60.4% of Americans lived in nonurban, or rural, areas, and in 1960, 36% did so. By 2010, just 19.3% of the population lived in rural parts of the country while 80.2% resided in urban areas.

The move from rural to urban areas has always stemmed from the increased opportunities for employment and investment that come with living around more people. Globalization has made this more important than ever, as markets and job opportunities have become transnational. Population growth often spurs job growth. For example, in the United States, all but one of the 10 urban areas with the most population growth between 2000 and 2010 also increased its number of jobs. The exception was Atlanta, which had a slight decline. While the growth in these urban areas in the United States focuses primarily in the low-density, suburban areas surrounding the cities, in other parts of the world, poor migrants to urban areas live in crowded slums. In many parts of the Global South, the rural poor, who come to cities to find opportunities, often

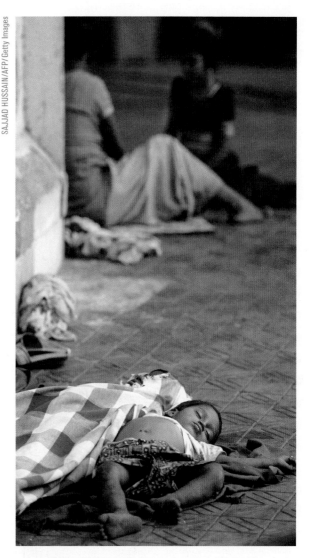

SAJJAD HUSSAIN/AFP/Getty Images

In Mumbai (Bombay) many children have no choice but to sleep on the streets each night.

live with no running water, electricity, or sewage disposal and lack basic services, including health care and education (Kotkin 2013; Kotkin and Cox 2011; World Bank 2013a).

Megacities around the world are part of a global trend that has gained momentum over several centuries: urbanization. The next "Engaging Sociology" feature invites you to explore some consequences of major urbanization trends in the world (Brunn, Hays-Mitchell, and Ziegler 2011).

Theories of Urban Development

Some of the first U.S. sociologists studied problems in the city of Chicago. These members of the *Chicago School*, as they were collectively known, focused on the patterns of land use and residential distribution of people in the city.

ENGAGING SOCIOLOGY

World Urbanization Trends

World Urbanization Prospects are reports published by the United Nations Population Division. They provide valuable data on past, present, and future urbanization trends in regions and subregions of the world. They also provide data on individual cities and urban areas. Consider the impact of major migration trends on the environment, friends and relatives left behind, dual-worker families, maintaining one's culture, new cultural ideas spreading, and more. The major findings of the most recent *World Urbanization Prospects* follow in Figures 13.9 and 13.10.

FIGURE 13.9 Percentage of Population Residing in Urban Areas

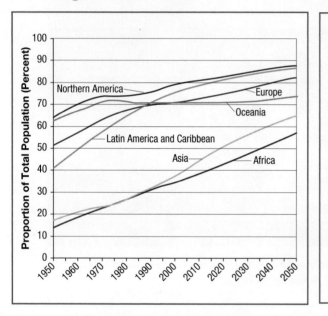

FIGURE 13.10 Urban and Rural Population of the World, 1950–2050

Engaging With Sociology: Figure 13.9

1. What do you learn from these graphs about world urbanization trends? Which continents seem to be urbanizing most rapidly?

2. How might these trends affect people moving to urban areas?

3. What might be some effects on global climate change, the possibility of globally transmitted diseases, political stability or instability, or the global economy?

4. How might the global trend toward urbanization affect your own life?

Engaging With Sociology: Figure 13.10

1. When the size of the rural population declines, how might it affect the culture of a nation?

2. Identify two positive and two negative consequences of this urbanization trend for a nation.

• •

Source: United Nations, Department of Economic and Social Affairs, Population Division (2014). *World Urbanization Prospects: The 2014 Revision, Highlights.* Reprinted with the permission of the United Nations.

They pictured the city's growth pattern as a series of circles. Moving out from the center, each circle was dominated by a particular type of activity and residential pattern, from central city ghettoes and rooming houses to working-class apartments and bungalows, to middle-class housing, to upper-class suburbs (Park, Burgess, and McKenzie [1925] 1967). See Figure 13.11 for an illustration of this pattern.

Urban ecologists further refined the Chicago School's original ideas by exploring social, economic, political, and technological systems of cities' spatial patterns (Abu-Lughod 1991). Several processes constantly take place in urban areas: residential segregation; invasion by a new ethnic, religious, or socioeconomic group; and successive movement by that group. These processes are part of dynamic city life (Berry and Kasarda 1977).

Robert Park's work influenced our understanding of urban life, but we now know it was tainted by his belief that Blacks were biologically and culturally inferior to Whites and not capable of civilized urban life (A. Morris 2015). Decades before Park and the Chicago School published their work on urban life, W. E. B. Du Bois completed *The Philadelphia Negro*, the first empirical study of urban Black people (Du Bois [1899] 1996). It revealed how rural Blacks who migrated to cities adjusted to urban life while dealing with past and present racial discrimination. In doing so, he showed that Blacks were confronted and stymied by socially constructed obstacles generated by a racist society rather than innate or cultural inferiority. Largely ignored or dismissed by White social scientists of the time, *The Philadelphia Negro* and other works by Du Bois have only recently been acknowledged as groundbreaking studies. Indeed, Du Bois may have been the first completely empirical sociologist in the United States.

Racial discrimination is a continuing and troubling issue in many urban areas of the United States. Despite some reductions in racism in the nation, American cities—especially northern cities—have high levels of residential segregation.

FIGURE 13.11 Burgess's Theory of City Growth

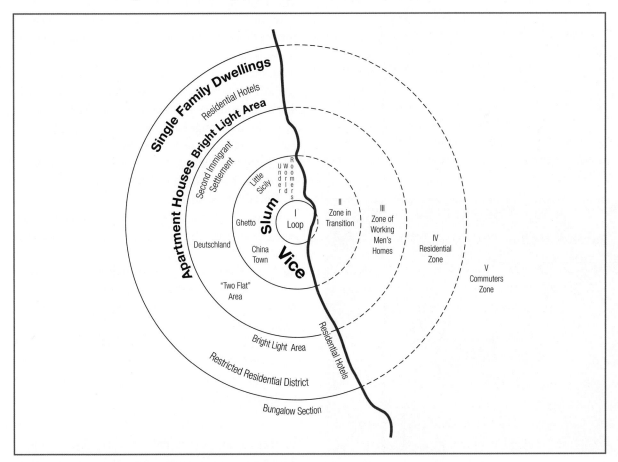

Note: The Chicago School envisioned urban growth as a series of concentric circles, with ethnicity, class, residential patterns, and types of activity evolving with each ring removed from the central city.

Source: Park et al. ([1925] 1967:55).

This segregation affects individual networking, school composition, and access to community resources.

Thinking Sociologically

Go to www.censusscope.org/segregation.html, and enter your city or a city near you to see the level of diversity members of each racial and ethnic group experience in that city. Which groups experience the most segregation in the city you investigated? What might be some consequences of living in racially homogeneous neighborhoods? Which group might experience more negative consequences because of the isolation? Why?

THE URBAN ENVIRONMENT AND SOCIAL POLICY: MACRO-LEVEL PERSPECTIVES

The mountains rise from the sea, dotted with pastel-colored shanties. On the drive from the port city of La Guaira up into the mountains to the capital city of Caracas, Venezuela, one sees settlements nestled into the hillsides. The poor, who have come from the country to find opportunities in the capital, make shelters in the hills surrounding Caracas, often living with no running water, electricity, or sewage disposal. The laundry list of urban problems facing Venezuela's government, as well as other governments in similar situations, is overwhelming: excessive size and overcrowding; shortages of services, education, and health care; slums and squatters; traffic congestion; unemployment; and effects of global restructuring, including loss of agricultural land, environmental degradation, and resettlement of immigrants and refugees (Brunn, Williams, and Zeigler 2003). This section considers several of the many problems mentioned earlier in the chapter and now facing urban areas such as Caracas.

Rural Migrants and Overcrowding

In Cairo, Egypt, a huge sprawling graveyard full of large mausoleums, called the City of the Dead, has become home to thousands of families transplanted from rural areas. Cities in India such as Chennai (the former colonial name was Madras), Mumbai (Bombay), and Kolkata (Calcutta) have thousands of homeless migrants living on the sidewalks, on highway medians, and in river channels that flood during the rainy season.

Overcrowding exists in cities throughout the world but causes special problems in the Global South. Indeed, the pattern of change is remarkable when we look at the world's urban population by region, as Figure 13.12 illustrates. Between 1950 and 2014, the percentage of the population that is urban rather than rural has tripled. Poor migrants set up shacks of any material available—tin, cardboard, leaves, mud, and sticks—in settlements known as *barriadas* in Spanish, *shantytowns* in English, *bidonvilles* in French, *favelas* in Portuguese-speaking Brazil, and *bustees* in India. The majority of migrants to the city are young. They are pulled to the city in hopes of finding jobs and often have been pushed from the rural areas because of limited land on which to farm and too many mouths to feed.

Most Global South countries have little time or money to prepare infrastructures and provide services for the rapidly increasing numbers of urban residents. Technological development, job opportunities, and basic services have not kept up with the large migrations of would-be laborers. Lack of basic services has become a major problem, resulting in contagious diseases that can cause deadly epidemics due to lack of services and poor sanitary conditions. Recent outbreaks of Ebola and Zika viruses are examples. For fear of a worldwide pandemic, Global North countries contributed medical aid, doctors, and research funds to help curb the epidemics.

Urban Planning for Structures That Meet Human Needs

Ideal city planning is quite a task. City planners must meet citizens' needs for housing, sanitation, education, food

© Khalil Hamra/AP

With few places to live, rural migrants to Egypt's largest city, Cairo, find shelter in the large ancient mausoleums in the burial grounds of the City of the Dead.

FIGURE 13.12   Changing Urban and Rural Population as Proportion of Total Population, by Continent, 1950–2050

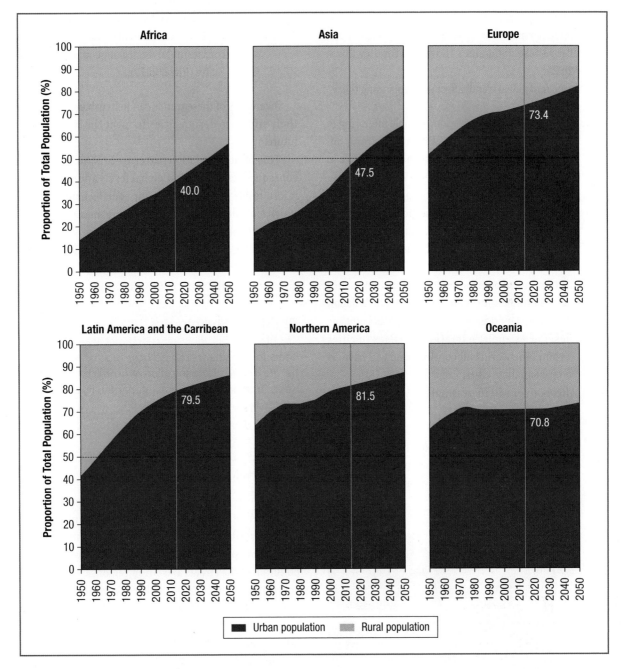

Note: Urban percentage at blue line is for 2014.

Source: United Nations Department of Economic and Social Affairs (2014).

distribution, jobs, family life, and recreation. The problem is that most urban planners do not have the luxury of starting from scratch. They must work with decaying areas, being cognizant of meaningful landmarks and treasured sites. Planners may also have to undo mistaken or inadequate planning by previous administrations. Leaders in some U.S. cities have begun to take more active roles on issues related to demographic and economic changes. For example, New York City has invested in diversifying the city's economy by recruiting a top-level university (Cornell) to develop a new high-tech graduate school. It is also creating an applied-science district that will bring in new companies, new jobs, and tax revenues for the city. Building on its expertise in high tech and sustainability, Portland, Oregon, has created a "We Build Green Cities" marketing campaign to promote its clean tech companies and created partnerships in other nations to expand the market for these companies (Katz and Bradley 2013; Lieber 2015).

A number of global trends affect urban planning today.

1. The process of urbanization—people migrating to cities—will continue, exacerbating the already difficult situation of providing services for people in the world's crowded urban areas.

2. Information and transportation technologies allow people in any part of the globe to be in contact. However, this may also reduce the feeling of belonging to a specific place, thus reducing commitment to work on city problems.

3. International boundaries diminish in importance as the flow of information, goods, services, labor, and capital increasingly ignores national boundaries. For example, migration of Asians to cities around the world will continue and will have an impact on these cities.

4. Economies will increasingly rely on brain work, including invention of new technologies and high-tech manufacturing. Thus, the gap between the haves and have-nots is likely to continue.

5. Conflicts between cultural and political groups, including religious and political extremists (as described in previous chapters), will impact urban life.

6. *McDonaldization*—the creation of a consumer world dominated by American food, music, fashion, and entertainment—will continue, even as we see an increasing diversity of people within the United States (Ritzer 2013).

Awareness of these trends can help urban planners in their efforts to design cities to meet the needs of the future.

This basic population pattern—urbanization—has consequences at the most global levels and at the most micro levels of human life. Our social world model—which looks at the connections of micro, meso, and macro levels of the social system—makes us aware of the consequences of decisions made by millions of individuals and families. It also makes us mindful of the consequences of global trends and forces for individuals and for cities.

Thinking Sociologically

Try planning an ideal city. First, list everything you need to consider, such as how big the city should be. Now think of organization: Who will handle what? Keep in mind services, maintenance, financing, and leadership.

Intersection of Demographics and Environmental Policy

Traffic congestion and pollution are chronic problems, so intense in some cities that the slow movement of people and goods reduces productivity, jobs, health, and vital services. Increasing automobile use around the world adds to pollution of the streets and air. In regions of China, parents confine their children to their homes in order to keep them from breathing the outside air. In Beijing and other Chinese cities, the air has 40 times the pollutants deemed safe to breathe (E. Wong 2013). Parents of students at the International School in Beijing demanded that the school build an enclosed playground with filtered air, so their children will not have to breathe the polluted outside air while they play (Doane 2013).

In Global North countries, concern for these problems has brought some action and relief, but in impoverished countries where survival issues are pressing, environmental contamination is a low priority. Thus, the worst air pollution is now found in major cities in the Global South, such as Mexico City, São Paulo, and several Chinese cities, including Beijing.

Getty/Kevin Frayer/Stringer

A Chinese woman wears a mask and filter as she walks to work during heavy pollution in Beijing, China. Levels of PM 2.5, considered the most hazardous pollution, surpassed 400, nearly 40 times the acceptable standard set by the World Health Organization. In some cities, entrepreneurs sell cans of fresh air for people to breathe.

In order to improve the Earth's ecosystems, we must rebalance consumption between Global North and Global South countries; stabilize population growth, especially in Global South countries; continue efforts to bring those in extreme poverty (those who live on $1.25 or less per day) out of this condition; develop plans for urban growth; provide access to reproductive health and family planning; and adopt plans to reduce overall human consumption (Royal Society 2012).

Many factors, including population dynamics and urbanization, create change in a society. Some factors contributing to social dynamics push for innovation and change in a particular direction; other factors can retard change. The next chapter examines the larger picture of social transformation and change in our complex and multileveled social world.

WHAT HAVE WE LEARNED?

Population trends, including migration resulting in urbanization, provide a dynamic force for change in societies. Whether one is interested in understanding social problems, social policy, or factors that may affect one's own career, it is helpful to understand demographic processes. We ignore them at our peril—as individuals and as a society. If we overlook demographic patterns, family businesses can be destroyed, retirement plans obliterated, and the health of our communities sabotaged. Awareness of such patterns can enhance planning that leads to prosperity and enjoyment of our communities. Urban living creates problems, but it can have enormous benefits as well.

- Population analysis (called demography) looks at the composition, distribution, and size of a population and how variables of fertility, mortality, and migration impact society.

- The population of the world has increased dramatically since industrialization. Its implications for society can be viewed in population pyramids.

- Various theories explain the causes and repercussions of rapid population growth.

- Many institutions affect and are affected by fertility and mortality rates at the meso level—government, religion, the economy, education, and health care.

- Migration is also an important issue for society—whether the migration is international or internal—for it can change the size, distribution, and composition of a nation's citizenry.

- Population patterns can also affect individual decisions at the micro level, from career choices to business decisions to retirement plans.

- A major element of population migration has been urbanization. As populations become more densely concentrated, this creates a series of opportunities and problems for meeting human needs.

- At the macro level, urban environments must be understood as ecosystems that have dense poverty and homelessness, major pollution issues, and higher crime rates but also the potential to reduce environmentally harmful energy use. These are the focus of urban planners, who try to use sociological knowledge to plan for a better future.

DISCUSSION QUESTIONS

1. Why is it important for policymakers, including urban planners, to understand demographic trends in their communities and nation? Why should *you* be interested in such knowledge?

How might it impact your understanding of and positions on issues related to (a) immigration, (b) education, (c) health care, and (d) Social Security legislation?

2. How many children (if any) do you think you would ideally like to have? Why? What might make this ideal number change?

3. What are some examples of (a) pronatalist and (b) antinatalist policies? Do you approve of such policies? Why, or why not? How might your perspective differ depending on the demographics of your particular nation?

4. How is the social status of girls and women related to a society's ability to control population growth? If you were a male leader in the government of an overcrowded nation, why and how might you use this information to promote gender equality in your country? How might your ideas be perceived differently, depending on your sex?

5. What are some of the major reasons people leave their country of origin and move to another? Have you ever done so? Why? If not, under what circumstances would you be willing to leave the country in which you were born and move to another?

KEY TERMS

demographic transition
    theory 384
demography 378
dependency ratio 381

environmental racism 385
fertility 387
life expectancy 377
migration 387

mortality 387
population pyramids 382
populations 378
urbanization 378

CONTRIBUTING TO OUR SOCIAL WORLD: WHAT CAN WE DO?

At the Local (Micro) Level

• The *U.S. Census Bureau* is always at work collecting, analyzing, and disseminating demographic information. It is a great source of data, ranging from information on your block to the whole nation. Invite a representative to your campus to discuss the bureau's activities. You can check internship and job opportunities with the Census Bureau at www.census.gov/about/census-careers/opportunities/programs/student.html.

• Check out your *local department of urban planning, urban and regional development, or community development* by Googling those terms and the name of your town, county, or province. Invite a representative to your campus, or visit the department's offices. Discuss how population information is used in planning and service delivery contexts. Consider an internship with one of the organizations you find in your area.

At the Organizational/Institutional (Meso) Level

• *The Population Association of America* (PAA) "is a non-profit, scientific, professional organization that promotes research on population issues," according to its website. At www.populationassociation.org, you can find information on demographic issues and ways to get involved in efforts to address them.

At the National/Global (Macro) Levels

• The *Population Reference Bureau* (www.prb.org/About.aspx) "informs people around the world about population, health, and the environment, and empowers them to use that information to advance the well-being of current and future generations." The organization offers fellowships for recent college graduates with a B.A. or a B.S.

• *Planned Parenthood* (www.plannedparenthood.org) promotes family-planning education and outreach programs throughout the United States. The International Planned Parenthood Federation (www.ippf.org) works in 180 nations. The organizations use volunteers and interns, as well as provide long-term employment opportunities.

- *World Vision* (www.worldvision.org/?open&lpos=facebook-sponsor_bot_Home) is "a Christian humanitarian organization, dedicated to working with children, families, and their communities worldwide to reach their full potential by tackling the causes of injustice and poverty." The organization provides many ways you can get involved in efforts to alleviate poverty and promote justice around the world.

- *The Population Council* (www.popcouncil.org) promotes family planning in order to reduce poverty, create healthier populations and communities, empower women, and improve lives across the globe. You can find fact sheets and other information at their website. You can also look for possible job and internship opportunities at www.popcouncil.org/employment/index.asp.

$SAGE edge™

14 Process of Change

We Can Make a Difference!

Individuals are profoundly influenced by changes in the macro structures around them, but people are also capable of creating change, especially if they band together with others in an organized way.

MICRO

ME (AND MY FAMILY)

LOCAL ORGANIZATIONS AND COMMUNITY
Individuals and local groups can work together to organize and mobilize others and create social change.

MESO

NATIONAL ORGANIZATIONS, INSTITUTIONS, AND ETHNIC SUBCULTURES
The environmental movement has put pressure on governments to address global climate change.

MACRO

SOCIETY
National government policies about trade, war, or immigration may cause change in families, the economy, or international relationships.

GLOBAL COMMUNITY
World Bank loans or United Nations poverty programs may result in change for poor nations and stimulate international trade.

WHAT YOU WILL LEARN IN THIS CHAPTER

This chapter will help you do the following:

14.1 Give examples of how change takes place at each level of analysis.

14.2 Explain how stresses and strains can lead to organizational change.

14.3 Explain the six factors necessary for collective behavior to occur.

14.4 Provide examples of the difference between planned and unplanned change.

14.5 Illustrate the stages of social movements.

14.6 Describe how the development of technology brings about change in societies and their environments.

◑ THINK ABOUT IT

Micro: Local community	What do you think needs to change in your community?
Meso: National institutions, complex organizations, and ethnic groups	How can complex organizations or social movements create, hamper, or shape change?
Macro: National and global community	How can national governments affect the process of change in your country and in the world through training and supporting technological innovation?

Islands are disappearing due to rising ocean levels, glaciers are melting, extreme weather events and wildfires are increasing, and species are dying off due to extreme weather changes. Our planet is in peril from the Arctic to the Antarctic (Environmental Protection Agency [EPS] 2016). Seven hundred and seventy-two scientists from around the world have signed on to the statement that "the world is not ready for the impacts of climate change, including more extreme weather and the likelihood that populated parts of the planet could be rendered uninhabitable" (Intergovernmental Panel on Climate Change [IPCC] 2014). Although there are still some climate change deniers, evidence presented by climate scientists and the IPCC indicates a dire future with extreme weather events and other disastrous results. One approach by climate scientists to convince the public of the dangers to come is to analyze the history of climate change (Gillis 2015). Other scientists use current data to make their case. Most U.S. citizens, including most Democrats and almost 50% of Republicans, support government efforts to curb global warming (Davenport and Connelly 2015). With 2016 the hottest year in the 137 years of record keeping and the third year in a row to be the hottest, major mainstream corporations like Johnson and Johnson, Proctor and Gamble, Starbucks, and Walmart are using renewable energy sources as a response to the climate crisis (Gillis and St Fleur 2015; Andrea Thompson 2017).

A major factor in climate change is the waste humans create. Wet, dry, smelly, and sometimes recyclable—garbage is a problem, and we are running out of space to dispose of our refuse. We dump it in the ocean and see garbage surfacing on beaches and killing fish and birds (Heyes 2012; "Trash-Mapping Expedition" 2015). We bury it in landfills, and the surrounding land becomes toxic. Recycling and waste reduction efforts are relatively new movements in response to the urgent pleas from environmentalists.

Recycling, salvaging items that can be reused, is part of this social reform movement: the environmental movement. However, few issues have simple solutions. The dumping and recycling have to take place somewhere. As noted in Chapter 13, many of the recycling plants and trash dumps are located in areas where poor people and racial and ethnic minorities live—part of a practice referred to as *environmental racism* because racial and ethnic minorities usually face the greatest environmental dangers from proximity to environmental hazards such as toxic waste and almost always experience the brunt of illnesses caused by the pollutants from recycling (M. Bell 2012).

At the micro level, individuals can help save the planet through responsible personal actions. At the meso level, the environmental movement can encourage local and regional governments to enact policies and plans to reduce waste and pollution and address environmental racism. At the macro level, world leaders need to hold all nations accountable for and find ways to adapt to and lessen global climate change. Our social world is, indeed, complex and interdependent.

Turn on the morning or evening news, and information about other aspects of our changing social world abounds. We see headlines about medical advances and cures for disease; biological breakthroughs in cloning and the DNA code; terrorist bombings in Afghanistan, Israel, Pakistan, and other parts of the world; streams of migrants attempting to escape dangerous situations in their home countries; disasters such as droughts, earthquakes, hurricanes, tsunamis, and floods; and social activists calling for boycotts of chocolate, coffee, oil companies, Walmart, or other multinational corporations. Some events seem far away and hard to imagine: thousands killed by a tidal wave in India or a massive oil spill in the Gulf of Mexico. Others may impact you directly—having affordable access to health insurance, living in an area suffering from the results of a local recession, or accessing financial aid for increasing college costs. Whether the result of natural events or human actions, they may create dissatisfaction with current social arrangements.

Social change refers to *variations or alterations over time in the structure, culture (including norms and* *values), and behavior patterns of a society*. Some change is controllable, and some is out of our hands, but change is inevitable and ubiquitous. Change can be rapid, caused by some disruption to the existing system, or it can be gradual and evolutionary. Often, change at one level in the social world occurs because of change at another level. Micro, meso, and macro levels of society often interconnect in the change process but are sometimes out of sync.

In this chapter, we explore the process of change, the causes of change, and some strategies for bringing about desired change. We consider the complexity of change in our social world, explanations and theories of social change, the role of collective behavior in bringing about change, planned change in organizations, macro-level social movements, technology, and environmental actions as they affect and are affected by change.

Our social world model is based on the assumption that change, whether evolutionary or revolutionary, is inevitable and ever present in the social world. The impetus for change may begin at the micro, meso, or macro level of analysis. Studies of the change process are not complete, however, until the level under study is understood in relation to other levels in the model, for each level affects the others in multiple ways.

● Thinking Sociologically

How do your activities impact the environment? Have you taken steps to address climate change? If so, what socializing agents prompted you to do so? If not, why do you think you have not?

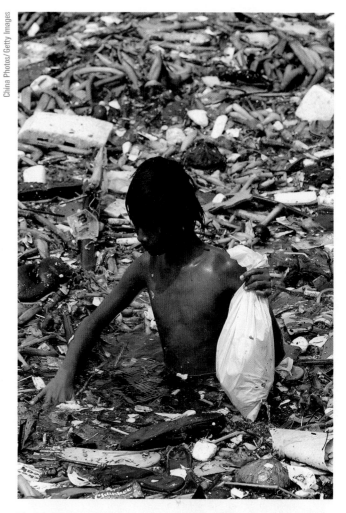

China Photos/Getty Images

The oceans have become garbage dumps, and this is creating a major pollution hazard. This boy picks out plastic waste that he hopes to recycle from floating rubbish along Manila Bay in the Philippines.

COMPLEXITY OF CHANGE IN OUR SOCIAL WORLD

The Yir Yoront, a group of Australian aborigines, long believed that if their own ancestors did not do something, then they must not do it. It would be wrong and might cause evil to befall the group (Sharp 1990). However, contact with European cultures and missionaries brought new tools such as the steel ax, changing the role of men whose job it was to make stone axes. Gradually other European ways were introduced, changing the culture dramatically so that old ways were obsolete. The group's original culture disintegrated as it adopted others' ways, but a major contributor was the introduction of new technological ideas, especially the steel ax. In the 1940s, missionaries gave steel axes to the Yir Yoront women, and the hunting and gathering economy changed due to changing roles of women and men. Men, who used to control the stone axes, lost their high status in the community when they had to borrow axes and other tools from women, and thus, the power structure of the community changed (BushTV 2010; Hotchkiss 2014).

Obviously, the Yir Yoront are not a people who favored change or innovation. In contrast, *progress* is a positive word in much of Australia and in many other countries where change is seen as normal, even desirable. The traditions, cultural beliefs, and internal and external pressures all affect the degree and rate of change in society (B. Berman 2011).

Change at the Individual Level: Micro-Level Analysis

One of the top U.S. entrepreneurs, Microsoft's founder Bill Gates, combines intelligence, business acumen, and philanthropy, qualities that appeal to American individualism. Gates has the power to influence others because of his fame, wealth, and personal organizational skills. Although now retired from Microsoft, he is able to bring about change in organizations through his ability to motivate people and set wheels in motion. Some people have persuasive power to influence decision making, based on expertise, wealth, privileged position, access to information, or the ability to use coercive force. Any of us, if we feel strongly about an issue, can rally others and bring about

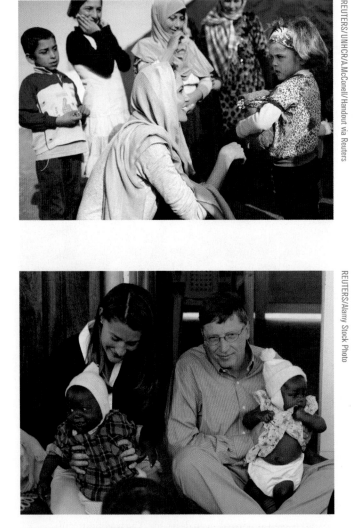

REUTERS/UNHCR/A.McConell/Handout via Reuters

REUTERS/Alamy Stock Photo

Angelina Jolie (*top*) has used her fame as an Academy Award– winning actress to bring attention to problems of refugees, serving as a special envoy and goodwill ambassador for the United Nations High Commissioner for Refugees. Bill and Melinda Gates (*bottom*) hold babies receiving a trial malaria vaccine at a medical research center in Mozambique. Gates announced a grant of $168 million to fight malaria, a disease that kills more than 1 million people a year, 90% of them children. Sometimes, social change occurs because of individual initiatives.

change in society. Each individual in society has the potential to be a change agent.

Individuals are active agents, and they can either stimulate or resist change. Sometimes they prod organizations to change, insisting on more family-supportive policies (like an on-site day care center), better safety precautions for employees, or more environmentally friendly buildings and programs. For example, at the urging of students and others, colleges may develop more recycling programs, more energy-efficient buildings or transportation systems, and more degree programs that involve study of the environment.

Sometimes, individuals are not eager to change. They must be enticed or manipulated into change by organizations. When this does occur, most organizations—schools, businesses, and volunteer associations—use one or more of the following strategies to persuade individuals to accept change: They appeal to individuals' values, use persuasion by presenting hard data and logic, convince individuals that the existing benefits of change outweigh the costs, remove uncooperative individuals from the organization, provide rewards or sanctions for acceptance of change to alter the cost–benefit ratio, or compel individuals to change by an order from authority figures. In any case, individuals are critically important parts of any understanding of social change.

Change at the Institutional Level: Meso-Level Analysis

Global climate change, an issue connected to pollution and use of Earth's natural resources, affects people at all levels in the social system. Many meso-level organizations have developed policies and practices to reduce emission of pollutants and change the way they use resources. For example, many religious denominations have developed programs to be more "green" or "Earth friendly." The United Church of Christ is one such group, passing a resolution in July 2009 encouraging local churches to become "Earthwise Congregations." Mayflower United Church of Christ in Minneapolis was one of the first to seek the designation. The church has an action team that works on ways to help members have more energy-efficient homes, but it also brought a resolution to the congregation that by 2030, the church would be entirely carbon neutral. The resolution was approved, and fund-raising began to change the heating system to solar energy. The roof of the church is now covered with 240 solar panels. Within 18 months, the church reported a reduction of carbon emissions of almost 50% (Mayflower Church 2016; R. Riley 2014). Members of the congregation have also begun lobbying the state legislature to have more public transit and especially more transportation that runs on electricity rather than oil-based fuels. Other United Church of Christ congregations are also taking actions, as are other communities of faith—inspired by denominational resolutions at the meso level.

Another example of meso-level change takes place at universities. Under pressure from college students, many have changed their policies about production of clothing with campus logos. Multinational corporations like Gap and Nike, seeking higher profits, fostered the growth of sweatshops in the Global South. Many professors, students, and concerned citizens in the United States and other Global North nations began to insist that these companies establish acceptable labor and human rights conditions in their factories in the Global South. Their efforts gradually grew into an antisweatshop movement with strong labor and religious support and tens of thousands of active participants. College students on hundreds of campuses in the United States have taken up the antisweatshop cause, holding sit-ins on many campuses to force their college bookstores to ban the use of college logos on products not produced under acceptable labor conditions (Brecher, Costello, and Smith 2012; Wang and Currier 2015). In doing so, they have helped shape the conditions for production of clothing on other continents.

Change at the National and Global Levels: Macro-Level Analysis

Change also may begin at the national level in response to some concern, or it may be stimulated by a global organization (like the United Nations or the World Bank) or by a global issue, like climate change. In this section we discuss national and then global forces that can bring about change.

Societal-Level Change. Take a look at the impact of national policies and trends on the global environment and the constant change we bring to our planet. To illustrate the increasingly complex and biologically interdependent social world, consider that pollution of the environment by any one country now threatens other countries. Carcinogens, acid rain, and other airborne chemicals carry across national boundaries

A part of its "Earthwise" mission to protect the environment; this church in Minneapolis installed 240 solar panels in a commitment to be carbon neutral by 2030.

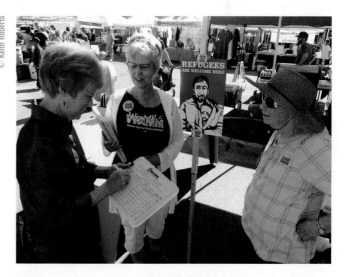

People at the local level often try to influence policies at the meso level. At this farmer's market in Minneapolis, people lobby their neighbors and seek signatures for a petition about state legislation that would be welcoming to immigrants and protect refugees in the state.

(Brecher et al. 2012). Heat-trapping gases have risen dramatically in the past several years, causing pessimism about reversing the environmental effects (Borenstein 2013). People in the United States compose about 4.5% of the world's population but emit almost a fourth of the heat-trapping gases ("Global Warming and Climate Change" 2013). In 2015, however, China topped the United States as the top contributor to global climate change (Doyle 2015).

According to scientists, Earth's surface has warmed by 1.5 degrees in the past century. That does not sound like much until one considers that during the last ice age, Earth's surface was only 7 degrees cooler than it is today. Small variations can make a huge difference, and those consequences are likely to be dire if the Earth's surface temperature increases by another 2 or 3 degrees. Currently, massive blocks of sea ice are melting each year at a rate that equals the size of Maryland and Delaware combined ("Global Warming and Climate Change" 2013). In the Northern Hemisphere, Greenland is home to many glaciers, such as the huge Petermann Glacier. Warming recently caused the Petermann Glacier to calve (break off)

an iceberg twice the size of Manhattan ("Iceberg Breaks Off" 2012; "Petermann Glacier" 2015). One study by scientists using computer modeling found that the oceans are rising at a rate faster than at any time in the past 28 centuries (Gillis 2016).

In a warmer world, there is less snowfall, resulting in smaller mountain icecaps and, thus, a smaller spring runoff of crucial freshwater. In fact, one fifth of the world's people, 1.2 billion, live in areas with water scarcity. Another quarter of the world's population, 1.6 billion people, face shortages from lack of infrastructure to provide water from sources (United Nations Water 2015). The sad truth is that every minute a child dies of a water-related disease because 1 in 9 people lack access to safe water (Water.org 2015).

Whereas some of the environmental change may be rooted in natural causes, the preponderance of evidence suggests that human activity—and the way we live our lives—is the primary cause (Gore 2012; Intergovernmental Panel on Climate Change 2013). So national policies and cultural attitudes within a country can have consequences at many levels of our social world. Human actions and decisions are of primary interest to sociologists.

Thinking Sociologically

What do you think happens when people do not have enough water in their current location to survive? What happens when they try to move into someone else's territory to gain access to needed resources such as land and water?

This global issue requires nations to work together for change, yet some nations resist change because they feel climate control efforts will impede economic progress. The Kyoto Protocol on global warming requires commitment by nations to curb carbon dioxide and other emissions, but U.S. president Bush rejected it, saying it "does not make economic sense" (Lindsay 2006:310–311). As of February 2014, 192 countries and the European Union had approved the treaty. The exceptions are the United States, Afghanistan, the Vatican, Canada (which signed and then withdrew), and the newly formed country of South Sudan (United Nations Framework Convention on Climate Change 2015).

The Kyoto Protocol, which took effect in 2005, has had some success: The countries that signed on to the protocol had reduced emissions by 22.6% in 2012, well above the commitment of 5% reduction. A new commitment was signed by the signatory countries in 2012 (United Nations Framework Convention on Climate Change 2015). In 2015, 195 nations, including the

Petermann Glacier, 5 August 2009

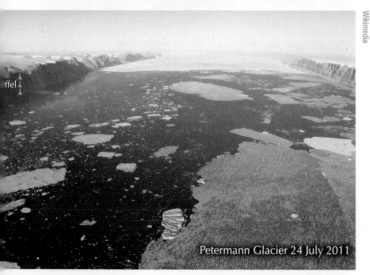

Petermann Glacier 24 July 2011

These before and after shots of the Petermann Glacier in Greenland show a massive loss of glacier in just one calving (breaking off of chunks of ice at the edge of a glacier). For many parts of the world, glaciers are a major source of fresh water, but they are melting because of global climate change.

United States, signed the Paris Agreement on Climate Change, the first universal legally binding agreement to combat global climate change. All governments pledged to reduce their emissions and Global North nations promised to provide aid to Global South nations facing disproportionate threats from climate change (European Commission 2016).

Currently, impoverished countries bear most of the costs and consequences of pollution. It is becoming increasingly clear, though, that rich nations will also pay a price. Not only will they have to face pollution, increasingly severe weather and intense storms, and contaminated food supplies from around the world, but if Global South countries cannot support their populations, affluent nations will also face increasing pressure from immigration (legal or not).

Yet fixing the environmental issues will be expensive for nations and may add to economic woes by temporarily hindering economic growth. Because slow-growth economies and recessions can lead to an unhappy public and political unrest, making changes to address climate change is not easy. However, such action is crucial because nations are still the most powerful units for allocating resources and for setting policy.

Global Systems and Change. As the world becomes more interconnected and interdependent, impetus for change increasingly comes from global organizations, international and transnational government agencies, and multinational corporations. As discussed in other chapters, nongovernmental organizations (NGOs) work on such efforts as eradicating polio or controlling AIDS, Ebola, and malaria. Some promote human rights, and others support local social movements for clean water, environmental protection, and access to health care. One NGO, *Sociologists Without Borders*, works transnationally to develop globally inclusive sociology curricula, advance human rights, and support the needs of vulnerable groups.

New and shifting alliances among international organizations and countries link together nations, form international liaisons, and create changing economic and political systems. The following international alliances among countries, for example, are based primarily on economic ties:

- SADC: Southern African Development Community
- NAFTA: North American Free Trade Agreement
- CAFTA-DR: Dominican Republic–Central America Free Trade Agreement

- WIPO: World Intellectual Property Organization
- G7: Group of Seven—the most affluent and most powerful countries in the world
- OPEC: Organization of the Petroleum Exporting Countries
- APEC: Asia-Pacific Economic Cooperation
- EU: European Union
- AU: African Union

Consider NAFTA, which is approaching its 25th anniversary. It was initiated in 1993 to establish a free-trade area between Canada, the United States, and Mexico in order to facilitate trade in the region. Promoters, including many global corporations, promised that the agreement would create thousands of new high-wage jobs, raise living standards in each of the countries, improve environmental conditions, and transform Mexico from a poor developing country into a booming new market. Opponents (including labor unions, environmental organizations, consumer groups, and religious communities) argued the opposite—that NAFTA would reduce wages; destroy jobs, especially in the United States; undermine democratic policy making in North America by giving corporations a free rein; and threaten health, the environment, and food safety (U.S. Trade Representative 2012).

Analyses of NAFTA show mixed results. It has helped boost intraregional trade among Canada, Mexico, and the United States but has fallen short of generating the jobs and deeper regional economic integration its advocates promised decades ago (Council on Foreign Relations 2014). Trade has increased significantly, from $290 billion in 1993 to more than $1.1 trillion in 2012. There is some indication that tariffs are down, and U.S. exports have increased (U.S. Trade Representative 2012; Zahniser, Angadjivand, and Hertz 2015). NAFTA has been more effective in increasing trade in agricultural commodities than nonagricultural products. Some analysts argue that there is improvement in the areas of environmental protection and labor rights, but many others argue that these areas have declined (Zahniser et al. 2015). The truth is hard to determine, but there are probably both gains and losses.

In the previous discussion of changes at different levels of analysis, one principle carries through all: Change at one level leads to change in other levels, as it has done in the global cases of climate change and NAFTA. Changes at the macro level affect individuals, just as changes at the micro level have repercussions at the meso and macro levels. Most of the gains have been to the Global North and most losses to poorer regions of the world (Witness for Peace 2016).

SOCIAL CHANGE: PROCESS AND THEORIES

Process of Social Change

Something always triggers a social change. The impetus may come from within an organization or a society, a source of change known as *strain*. Sometimes, it comes from outside an organization, what sociologists call *stress*. Let us consider two examples of *strain*: (1) conflicting goals and (2) contrasting belief systems within an organization.

Conflicting goals are seen in the case of the platinum mining industry and its union workers. In the Lonmin South African platinum mines (providing materials for catalytic converters and jewelry), 44 workers died and 78

Getty Images/ Ethan Miller/ Getty Images News

Natural disasters—floods, droughts, hurricanes, tornadoes, earthquakes, and volcanic eruptions—can be the cause of major social changes in a community. California and places like this—Lake Mead National Recreation Area in Nevada—can find the entire economy is turned on its head by a severe drought.

were injured in August 2012, and 2 more died in May 2014 during strikes against the company. In a report on the deaths at the mine, police, company managers, and union officers were blamed for letting the strike escalate to violent confrontation (St. Claire and Smith 2015). Two feuding unions both demanded pay hikes, and in an ugly confrontation, police opened fire on an unruly crowd. Individual miners work in difficult, dangerous conditions to try to meet their basic needs for food and shelter for their families. Sometimes, they must live at the mines, away from their families for many months, but when jobs are scarce, one does what one must. Company goals focus on the bottom line: being profitable in a competitive environment. The company argues that it cannot afford to raise wages and still be competitive, yet its profit margin has dropped as a result of the strikes (Herskovitz 2012; "Lonmin Profit Plunges" 2014). This conflict and others like it demonstrate how the needs of the workers can be at odds with those of the company, creating *internal strain*.

Contrasting belief systems (political, religious, economic, and social) within a society can also have a major effect on the type and rate of change. For example, some religious groups oppose stem cell research, which often uses the cells of fetuses created in test tubes. Yet other members of those same religious groups may believe this research will alleviate the suffering of loved ones and save lives. Although both sides in the organization believe they are pro-life, the internal conflicts can be disruptive and cause internal strain (Religious Tolerance 2014).

Stresses, those pressures for change that come from the organization's external environment, can be traced to several sources: the natural environment and natural disasters, population dynamics, actions of leaders, new technologies, changes in other institutions, and major historical events. For example, the natural environment can bring about either slow or dramatic change in a society, as seen in the effects of droughts in many parts of the world. In California, households are cutting their water usage, recycling wastewater, and changing from grass lawns to desert landscapes requiring little water (Cameron 2015).

Natural disasters such as floods, hurricanes, tsunamis, heavy snows, earthquakes, volcanic eruptions, mudslides, tornadoes, and other sudden events are not planned occurrences, but they can have dramatic consequences. Disease epidemics are often unpredictable, such as the 2010–2013 cholera epidemic in Haiti and the Ebola epidemic in several African countries (UNICEF 2014). Natural disasters and diseases are important as a dramatic change agent, and the sociology of disasters has become a specialty field within the discipline.

Population dynamics—birth rates and death rates, size of populations, age distribution, and migration patterns—can be important contributors to external stress on organizations. Where populations are growing at extremely rapid rates, government systems may be unable to meet the basic needs of the people. Immigration due to political upheavals or motivated by anticipated economic opportunities can also create stress on the societies that receive the newcomers as they attempt to meet the immigrants' needs. For example, many refugees from the conflict in Syria fled to camps in the nearby countries of Turkey and Jordan and are now making their way to European countries to start new lives. Figure 14.1 shows the global hot spots for refugees entering other countries in 2015.

Leaders influence change through their policy decisions or the social movements they help generate. India's Mohandas (Mahatma) K. Gandhi taught the modern world nonviolent methods of bringing about change in political systems. The policies of Charles Taylor, former military dictator of Liberia, created long-term war that resulted in thousands of deaths. President Robert Mugabe of Zimbabwe locked his country in a downward spiral of economic turmoil and disease, killing thousands. These leaders' actions created internal strains in their own countries and external stressors, resulting in discussions and sometimes change in the international community.

Technology also influences societal change. William F. Ogburn compiled a list of 150 social changes in the United States that resulted from the invention of the radio, such as instant access to information (Ogburn 1933). Other lists could be compiled for cell phones, automobiles, television, computers, and new technologies such as smartphones. Some of these changes give rise to secondary changes. For example, automobile use led to paved highways, complex systems of traffic patterns and rules, and the development of suburbs. The next "Engaging Sociology" explores several issues involving the automobile and change.

The diffusion or spread of technology throughout the world is likely to be uneven, especially in the early stages of the new technology. For example, computer technology has advanced rapidly, but those advances began in corporate boardrooms, military bases, and university laboratories. Policies of governing bodies—such as funding for school computers—determine the rate of public access.

FIGURE 14.1 Countries Receiving the Most Refugees in 2015 (per 1,000 Inhabitants)

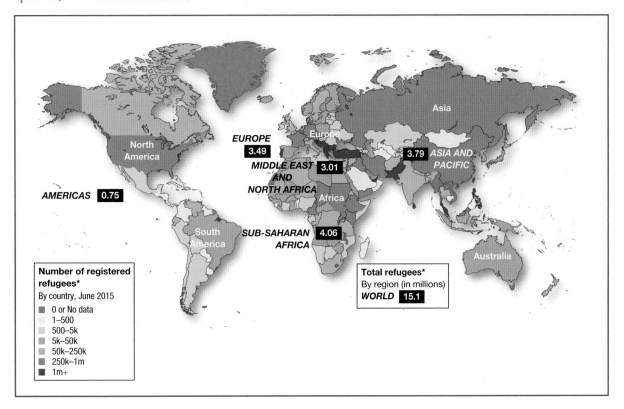

*Or people in a refugee-like situation.

Source: "Looking for a Home." *The Economist,* May 28, 2016. Copyright © The Economist Newspaper Limited, London 2016. Reprinted with permission.

ENGAGING SOCIOLOGY

Technology and Change: The Automobile

At the turn of the 20th century, the "horseless carriage" was often referred to in rural areas as the "devil wagon." In the 1890s and early 1900s, some cities and counties had rules forbidding motorized vehicles. In Vermont, a walking escort had to precede the car by an eighth of a mile with a red warning flag, and in Iowa, motorists were required to telephone ahead to a town they planned to drive through to warn the community, lest their horses be alarmed (M. Berger 1979; Clymer 1953; Glasscock 1937; L. Morris 1949). In most rural areas, motorists were expected to pull their cars to a stop or even to shut down the motor when a horse-drawn buggy came near. "Pig and chicken legal clauses" meant the automobile driver was liable for any injury that occurred when passing an animal near the road, even if the injury was due to the animal running away (Scott-Montagu 1904).

Roughly 85,000 motored vehicles were in use in America in 1911. By 1930, the number was nearly 10 million, and in 2011, the estimated number of registered passenger vehicles was 253 million (M. Berger 1979; Statistica 2014). Forms of entertainment began to change when people were able to be more mobile, and entertainment became available virtually any night of the week (M. Berger 1979; McKelvie 1926). Thus, dependence on family was lessened, possibly weakening familial bonds and oversight (M. Berger 1979). Even courting was substantially changed because individuals could go farther afield to find a possible life partner, couples could go more places on dates, and two people could find more privacy. School attendance rates of rural children also increased substantially with motorized buses (U.S. Department of Interior Office of Education 1930).

As people could live in less congested areas but still get to work in a reasonable amount of time via an automobile, the suburbs began to develop around major cities. A dispersed population needs to use more gasoline, thereby creating pollution. As the wealthy moved to expensive suburbs and paid higher taxes to support outstanding schools, socioeconomic and ethnic stratification between communities increased. These are some of the *unintended consequences* of the spread of the automobile. It sometimes takes decades before we can identify the consequences of the technologies we adopt.

* * * * * * *

Engaging With Sociology

1. What might be some long-term social consequences for our individual lives and societies of the widespread use of smartphones, microwave ovens, and computer games?

2. How might the introduction of smart cars that can navigate themselves and warn us of hazards change our lives?

Thus, only gradually are computers reaching the world's citizenry through schools, libraries, and eventually private homes. Clearly, internal strains and external stressors give impetus to the processes of change. The question is how do these processes take place?

Theories of Social Change

Social scientists seek to explain the causes and consequences of social change, sometimes in the hope that change can be controlled or guided. Theories of change often reflect the events and belief systems of particular historical time periods. For example, conflict theory developed during periods of change in Europe. It gained adherents in the United States during the 1960s, when intense conflict over issues of race and ethnic relations, the morality of the Vietnam War, and changes in social values peaked. Theories such as structural functionalism that focused on social harmony were of little help.

The major social change theories can be categorized as micro-level (symbolic interaction and rational choice theories) or meso- and macro-level (evolutionary, functional, conflict, and world systems theories). As we review these theories, many of them will be familiar to you from previous chapters. Here, we relate them to the process of change.

Micro-Level Theories of Change

Symbolic Interaction. According to symbolic interaction theory, human beings are always trying to make sense of the things they experience, figure out what an event or interaction means, and determine what action is required of them. Humans construct meanings that agree with or diverge from what others around them think. This capacity to define one's situation, such as concluding that one is oppressed, even though others have accepted the circumstances as normal, can be a powerful impetus to change. It can be the starting point of social movements, cultural changes, and revolutions.

Some sociologists believe that individuals are always at the core of any social trends or movements, even if those movements are national or global (Blumer 1986; Giddens 1986; Simmel [1902–1917] 1950). After all, it is individuals who act, make decisions, and take action. There are a number of leaders, for example, who have changed the world—for better (Mahatma Gandhi) or worse (Adolf Hitler). Neither corporations nor bureaucracies nor nations make decisions—people do. The way in which an individual defines the reality he or she is experiencing makes a huge difference in how she or he will respond to it.

Social institutions and structures are always subject to maverick individuals "thinking outside the box" and changing how others see things. Individual actions can stimulate riots, social movements, planned change in organizations, and a host of other outcomes that have the potential to transform society. That people may construct reality in new ways can be a serious threat to the status quo, and those who want to protect the status quo try to ensure that people will see the world the same way they do. If change feels threatening to some members who have a vested interest in the current arrangements, those individuals who advocate change may face resistance. Consider the current state of the world, in which some nations are making rapid technological advances and others are resisting modernization as a threat to their traditional political and religious way of life. In either case it has to do with how individuals make sense and define the meaning of their situation, a core emphasis of symbolic action theory.

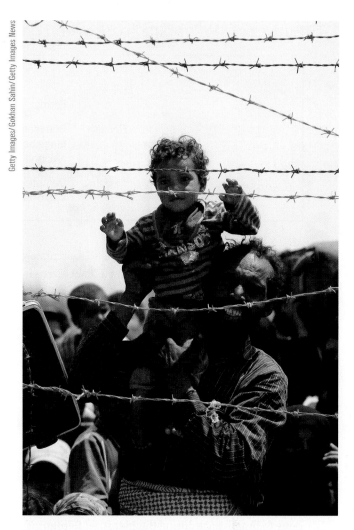

Getty Images/Gokhan Sahin/Getty Images News

Syrian refugees wait on the Syrian side of the border to cross into Turkey. Thousands of Syrians cut through a border fence to flee intense fighting in northern Syria between Kurdish fighters and jihadis. According to Turkish security officials, 10,000 people crossed the border in just two days in June 2015. Immigration to avoid persecution and war can stimulate massive change for people and for countries.

Rational Choice. To rational choice theorists, behaviors are largely driven by individuals seeking rewards and reduced costs. They maintain that most individuals engage in those activities that bring positive rewards and try to avoid actions that can have negative outcomes. A group seeking change can attempt to set up a situation in which the desired behavior is rewarded. The typology presented in Figure 14.2 shows the relationship between behaviors and sanctions.

Bringing about change may not, however, require a change in costs or rewards. It may be sufficient simply to change people's perception of the advantages and disadvantages of certain actions. Sometimes, people are not

FIGURE 14.2   Relationship Between Behaviors and Sanctions

		Sanction	
		Formal	Informal
Behavior	Positive	Bonuses, advances, fringe benefits, recognition	Praise, smile, pat on the back
	Negative	Demotion, loss of salary	Ridicule, exclusion, talk behind back

aware of all of the rewards, or they have failed to accurately assess the costs of an action. For example, few citizens in the United States realize all of the financial, health, and legal benefits of marriage. To change the marriage rates, we may not need more benefits to encourage marriage. We may do just as well to change the population's appraisal of the benefits already available.

Meso- and Macro-Level Theories of Change

Social Evolutionary Theories. Social evolutionary theories at the macro level assume that societies change slowly from simple to more complex forms. Early unilinear theories maintained that all societies moved through the same steps and that advancement or progress was desirable and would lead to a better society. These theories came to prominence during the Industrial Revolution, when European social scientists sought to interpret the differences between their own societies and the "primitive societies" of other continents. Europe was being stimulated by travel, exposure to new cultures, and a spawning of new philosophies, a period called the Enlightenment. Europeans witnessed the development of mines, railroads, ships, weaponry, cities, educational systems, and industries, which they defined as "progress" or "civilization." World travelers reported that other peoples and societies did not seem to have these developments. These reports provided the empirical evidence that early sociologist Auguste Comte used in proposing his theory of unilinear development from simple to complex societies. Unilinear theories came to legitimate colonial expansion and exploitation of other people and lands seen as less developed and "inferior."

In a more recent version of evolutionary theory, Patrick Nolan and Gerhard Lenski discuss five stages through which most societies progress: hunter-gatherer, horticultural, agrarian, industrial, and postindustrial

(P. Nolan and Lenski 2014; see also Chapter 3). This does not mean that some stages are "better" than others. It simply means that this is the typical pattern of change to greater social complexity resulting from new technologies and more efficient harnessing of energy. Contemporary evolutionary theories acknowledge that change takes place in multiple ways and not just in a straight line. The rapid spread of ideas and technologies means that societies today may move quickly from simple to complex, creating modern states. They skip steps or are selective about what aspects of technology they wish to adopt. For example, countries such as India and China are largely agricultural but are importing and developing the latest technology that allows them to skip over developmental steps. As noted in Chapter 7, many countries will not see landlines for phones but instead will have cell phones even in the more remote areas.

Some scholars disapprove of the term *developing countries* because it might imply that all societies are moving toward the type of social system characterized by the affluent or "developed" societies. As we have noted in earlier chapters, many now use the term *Global South* because poor countries are disproportionately located south of the 20th parallel north, whereas affluent nations are typically situated north of that latitude. Note that the term is a metaphor for all poor countries, meant to avoid an assumption of inevitable evolution toward Western cultures.

Functionalist Theories. Functional theorists assume that societies are basically stable systems held together by the shared norms and values of their members. The interdependent parts work together to make the society function smoothly. A change in one part of the society affects all the other parts, each changing in turn until the system resumes a state of equilibrium. Change can come from external or internal sources, from stresses in contact with other societies or from strains within.

Slow, nondisruptive change occurs as societies become more complex, and this may be a very functional adaptation. Functional theorists, however, often see rapid change as dysfunctional or disruptive to stability. Because functionalists often view major change with suspicion, many sociologists have turned to conflict theories to help explain change, especially rapid or violent change.

Conflict Theories. Conflict theorists assume that societies are dynamic and that change and conflict are inevitable. According to Karl Marx, socioeconomic class conflict is the major source of tension leading to change in any society. Marx and Friedrich Engels predicted that the antagonistic relationship they saw developing between the workers (proletariat) and the owners of the production systems (bourgeoisie) in 19th-century England would lead to social revolution. From this, they believed a new world order would emerge in which the workers themselves would own the means of production. Thus, conflict between the owners and the workers would be the central factor driving social change (Marx and Engels [1848] 1969).

Other conflict theorists study variables such as gender, religion, politics, and ethnic or interest group problems in their analyses, feeling that these factors can also be the grounds for oppression and us-versus-them differences (Dahrendorf 1959). Some see conflict as useful for society because it forces societies to adapt to new conditions and leads to healthy change (Coser 1956). Conflicts over slavery and over gender inequality are examples of problems that cause stresses and strains, often resulting in an improved society.

World Systems Theory of Global Change. World systems theorists are conflict theorists who take into account how world history has influenced the status of individual countries today. Capitalist economies first appeared in about 1500. Since then, except for a few isolated tribal groupings, almost all societies have been at least indirectly influenced by dominant capitalist world economic and political systems (Wallerstein 1974).

This theory divides the world system into three main parts: the core, semiperipheral, and peripheral areas (see Figure 14.3). *Core countries* include most Western European states, Australia and New Zealand, Japan, Canada, the United States, and a few others (Wallerstein 1974). Historically, they have controlled

The modes of transportation for goods and people vary around the world, often reflecting the level of development of the region or country. Sometimes, technological progress has high costs, including pollution.

global decision making; received the largest share of the profits from the world economic system; and dominated the peripheral areas politically, economically, and culturally by controlling the flow of technology and capital into and out of those countries. *Peripheral countries*, most of which are in Africa, Asia, and South America, provide cheap labor and raw materials for the core countries' needs.

The *semiperipheral countries* hold an intermediate position, trading with both the core and the peripheral countries. Brazil, Argentina, South Africa, India, the Philippines, Iran, Mexico, and the Baltic region of Eastern Europe are among the semiperipheral areas. Because most semiperipheral countries are industrializing, they serve as areas to which core-country businesses and multinational corporations can move for continued growth, often in partnerships, because semiperipheral states aspire to join the core countries. The core and semiperipheral countries process raw materials, often taken from peripheral countries for little in return, and may sell the final products back to the peripheral countries. The semiperipheral countries and the peripheral countries need the trade and the resources of the core countries, but they are also at a severe disadvantage in competition and are exploited by those at the core, resulting in an uneasy relationship.

Core countries have been a major force in the development of global institutions, such as the International Monetary Fund (IMF), that facilitate and attempt to control international capital flow. By creating the frameworks for debt restructuring for peripheral countries and some

FIGURE 14.3   World Systems Theory

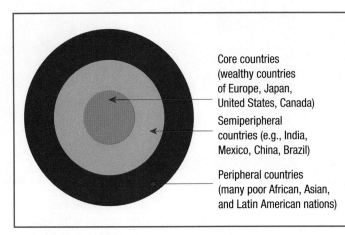

Core countries
(wealthy countries
of Europe, Japan,
United States, Canada)

Semiperipheral
countries (e.g., India,
Mexico, China, Brazil)

Peripheral countries
(many poor African, Asian,
and Latin American nations)

semiperipheral countries, the IMF attempts to restore sustainability and growth to countries that default on their loans. At least 95 countries have restructured their debt under IMF guidelines since the 1950s. A recent example is Greece, which has struggled to keep its economy from defaulting on its loan payments (Bergthaler et al. 2015; Das, Papaioannou, and Trebesch 2012). However, the IMF leaves countries little economic autonomy. The restructuring plans control what countries do even within their own national boundaries, creating debt dependencies on core countries that most poorer countries can never overcome and often resent (Dollars and Sense Collective 2012; Rothkopf 2012; Stiglitz 2012).

World systems theorists note that some groups of noncore countries have increased their collective power by forming alliances such as OPEC (Organization of the Petroleum Exporting Countries), OAS (Organization of African States), and SEATO (Southeast Asia Treaty Organization). These alliances present challenges to the historically core countries of the world system because of their combined economic and political power. For example, the price we pay at the gas pump reflects, in part, the power of OPEC to set prices.

When we understand international treaties and alliances as part of larger issues of conflict over resources and economic self-interests, the animosity of noncore countries toward core countries such as the United States begins to make sense. Likewise, the threat felt by the United States from countries that seem to be getting jobs once found in the United States is not entirely unfounded. The problem is an extraordinarily complex system that tends to leave the most vulnerable more at risk and the wealthiest even richer (Gibler 2012; McBride 2015; Stiglitz 2012).

The climate crisis illustrates the world systems theory and rift between rich and poor nations. For example, tiny Pacific islands such as Nauru soon will be underwater due to global warming and water rising. Human activity, mostly from development in Global North countries, is causing what some groups of countries call *climate injustice*, and Global South nations harmed by climate change now demand compensation for damages. This world systems outlook assumes that developed Global North countries are most to blame for climate change problems and therefore should be held accountable. However, nations like India and China, in the midst of phenomenal economic growth, are now major contributors to increasing global carbon emissions. The causes of climate change are complex and not solely due to the actions of Global North countries (Myers and Kulish 2013).

We have discussed examples of planned change, but sometimes, behavior that results in change is unplanned, even spontaneous, as described in the following section.

Thinking Sociologically

Where is your clothing made? Did a multinational corporation have it assembled in the Global South? What steps can you take to ensure that the workers who made your clothes receive tolerable working conditions and a fair wage?

COLLECTIVE BEHAVIOR: MICRO- TO MESO-LEVEL CHANGE

Individuals in local communities often come together over some issue that irritates or even enrages them, and these gatherings can evolve into mobs, riots, panics, or other forms of collective reaction to events. It is often at the micro or local level that change movements get started. These can evolve into large statewide, national, or even global movements with implications for the larger society, but since they begin with individuals in local communities deciding to take some sort of common action, we discuss it as a micro- to meso-level event. Political demonstrations and stock market sell-offs are all forms of collective behavior that can stimulate change. In this section, we introduce a form of change that typically has uncertain outcomes.

Collective behavior *is spontaneous, unstructured, and disorganized action that may violate norms; this behavior arises when people are trying to cope with stressful situations under unclear or uncertain conditions* (E. Goode 1992; Smelser 1963, 1988). Collective behavior falls into two main types: crowd behavior and mass behavior. It often starts as a response to an event or a stimulus. It could begin with a shooting or beating, a speech, a sports event, or a rumor. The key is that as individuals try to make sense of the situations they are in and respond based on their perceptions, collective social actions emerge.

Crowd behaviors—mobs, panics, riots, and demonstrations—are forms of collective behavior in which a crowd acts, at least temporarily, as a unified group (LeBon [1895] 1960). Crowds are often made up of individuals who see themselves as supporting a just cause. Because the protesters are anonymous in such a large group, they may not feel bound by normal social controls—either internal (normal moral standards) or external (fear of police sanctions).

Mass behavior occurs when individual people communicate or respond in a similar manner to ambiguous or uncertain situations, often based on common information from word-of-mouth rumors, websites, social networking, and television. Examples include fashions and fads, such as the ALS (Lou Gehrig's disease) "Ice Bucket Challenge." Unlike social movements, these forms of collective behavior generally lack a hierarchy of authority and clear leadership, a division of labor, and a sense of group action.

Collective Behavior: Middle-Range Theories

Several explanations of individual involvement dominate the collective behavior literature. These theories are middle-range theories that seek to explain specific social behaviors or patterns. Social scientists studying group and crowd dynamics find that most members of crowds are respectable, law-abiding citizens, but faced with specific situations, they act out (Berk 1974; R. Turner and Killian 1993).

Based on principles of rational choice theory, the *minimax strategy* suggests that individuals try to minimize their losses or costs and maximize their benefits (Berk 1974). People are more likely to engage in behavior if they feel the rewards outweigh the costs. Individuals may become involved in a riot if they feel the outcome—drawing attention to their plight, the possibility of improving conditions, solidarity with neighbors and friends, or looting goods—will be more rewarding than the status quo or the possible negative sanctions.

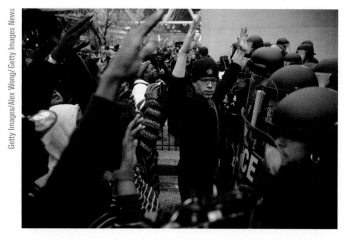

Getty Images/Alex Wong/Getty Images News

Crowds can stimulate change in a society, but they can also become unruly and unpredictable, so governments spend a good deal of money and time equipping and training officers to control crowds. Here, protesters hold up their hands as they stand off with police during a march in honor of Freddie Gray, a young Black man who died from a severe spinal cord injury he received while in police custody for possession of a switchblade knife.

Emergent norm theory points out that individuals have different emotions and attitudes guiding their behaviors in crowds than when they act alone (R. Turner and Killian 1993). The theory addresses the unusual situations involving the breakdown of norms, in which most collective behavior takes place. Unusual situations may call for the development of new norms and even new definitions of acceptable behavior. The implication of this theory is that in ambiguous situations, people look to others for clues about what is happening or what is acceptable, and norms emerge in ambiguous contexts that may be considered inappropriate in other contexts. This is the most widely used approach to understanding collective behavior (R. Turner and Killian 1993).

Imagine you are at an athletic event. Someone in the crowd with a very loud voice begins to taunt a player from the visiting team. Initially some people around you laugh, but as the initiator begins to chant an insult, your friends and others around you begin to join in. Chances are good that in the camaraderie of the moment, you follow suit and start chanting the insult, too—even if it is very disrespectful. Normally, you would not make such an insulting remark to someone's face, but in this situation where you are anonymous, the pattern of behavior emerged, and you felt compelled to follow the crowd. This would be an example of an emergent norm affecting an entire crowd.

Value-added theory (sometimes called structural-strain theory) describes the conditions for crowd behavior and social movements. Key elements are necessary for collective behavior, with each new variable adding to the total situation until conditions are sufficient for individuals to begin to act in common. At this point, collective behavior emerges (Smelser 1963). These are the six factors identified that can result in collective behavior:

1. *Structural conduciveness.* Existing problems create a climate ripe for change. Consider the example of the independent country of Ukraine, caught between Russia and Western Europe. The (now-deposed) president of Ukraine stated that he planned to align Ukraine with the West, but under pressure and promises from Russia, he changed his mind. This change angered many Ukrainians.

2. *Structural strain.* The social structure is not meeting the needs and expectations of the citizens, which creates widespread dissatisfaction with the status quo—the current arrangements. Ukrainians who felt the country would fare better if aligned with Western Europe demonstrated in the capital of Kiev.

3. *Spread of a generalized belief.* Common beliefs about the cause, effect, and solution of the problem evolve, develop, and spread. Charges spread that the pro-Russian president was corrupt, lived opulently, and had stolen money belonging to the Ukrainian people to support his lifestyle.

4. *Precipitating factor.* A dramatic event or incident occurs to incite people to action. The Ukrainian

president left Kiev in fear after the guards defending him left their posts. President Putin of Russia amassed Russian troops on the Ukrainian border, charging that the president of Ukraine had been rightfully elected and that Crimea should be part of Russia. Russian troops then entered Crimea, and Russia officially annexed it (declared it part of Russia).

5. *Mobilization for action.* Leaders emerge and set out a path of action, or an emergent norm develops that stimulates common action. Ukrainian leaders emerged to defend Ukraine against what they saw as Russian aggression. A newly elected Ukrainian president sent troops to eastern Ukraine to defend it against Russians who want to align it with Russia.

6. *Social controls are weak.* If the police, the military, or political or religious leaders are unable to counter the mobilization, a social movement or other crowd behavior may form. Ukraine's new president, parliament, and army resisted the efforts of the pro-Russian groups (assisted by Russian troops) in eastern Ukraine to establish a separate (pro-Russian) state, but Ukrainian forces and resources are much less than Russia's. As we write these words, the outcome remains unclear.

When all six of these factors are present, some sort of collective behavior will emerge. Those interested in controlling volatile crowds must intervene and take control when one or more of these conditions exists (Flynn 2014; Smelser 1963).

Thinking Sociologically
Think of an example of a crowd behavior or social movement. Which of the previous theories best explains this act, and why?

Types of Collective Behavior
Collective behavior ranges from spontaneous violent mobs to temporary fads and fashions. Figure 14.4 shows the range of actions.

Mobs are emotional crowds that engage in violence against a specific target. Examples include lynchings, killings, and hate crimes. Near the end of the U.S. Civil War, self-appointed vigilante groups roamed the countryside in the South looking for army deserters, torturing and killing both those who harbored deserters and the deserters themselves. There were no courts and no laws, just

All six social factors that contribute to collective behavior were present in 2014 in Kiev, Ukraine, and the results were riots in the streets, the overthrow of the Ukrainian president, and the annexation of Crimea by Russia.

© AP Photo/Sergei Grits

FIGURE 14.4   Types of Collective Behavior

Spontaneous and often violent					Less spontaneous and seldom violent
	Crowd behavior			**Mass behavior**	
Mob	Riot	Panic	Rumor	Fad	Fashion

"justice" in the eyes of the vigilantes. The members of these groups constituted mobs. The film *Cold Mountain* depicts these scenes vividly. Unless deterred, mobs often damage or destroy their target.

Riots—an outbreak of illegal violence against random or shifting targets committed by crowds expressing frustration or anger against people, property, or groups in power—begin when certain conditions occur. Often, a sense of frustration or deprivation sets the stage for a riot—hunger, poverty, poor housing, lack of jobs, discrimination, poor education, or an unresponsive or unfair judicial system. If the conditions for collective behavior are present, many types of incidents can be the precipitating factor setting off a riot. For example, in the summer of 2014, residents of Ferguson, Missouri, became outraged when a police officer shot and killed Michael Brown, an unarmed Black 18-year-old. Whereas some residents peacefully protested, others looted stores and threw rocks at police officers. The difference between riots and mobs is illustrated in Figure 14.5.

Panic occurs when a large number of individuals become fearful or try to flee threatening situations beyond their control, sometimes putting their lives in danger. Panic can occur in a crowd situation, such as a restaurant or theater in which someone yells, "Fire!" Or it can occur following rumors or information spread by the media. Panic started by rumors set off the run on the stock market in October 1929. A large number of actions by individuals caused the stock market crash in the United States, with repercussions around the world. In 2008, the collapse of the global investment banking and securities trader Bear, Stearns & Co. resulted in turmoil in the financial markets. Only radical intervention by the federal government abated the immediate panic. Panics can result in the collapse of an organization, destruction of communities, or the death of innocent people.

Rumors are forms of mass behavior in which unsupported or unproven reports about a problem, issue, or

FIGURE 14.5   **The Difference Between Riots and Mobs**

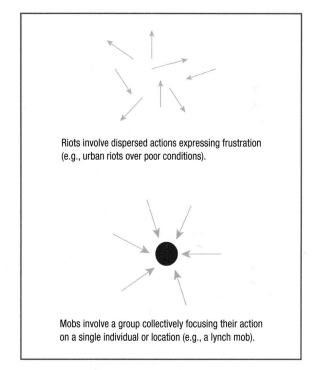

Riots involve dispersed actions expressing frustration (e.g., urban riots over poor conditions).

Mobs involve a group collectively focusing their action on a single individual or location (e.g., a lynch mob).

concern circulate widely throughout the public. Rumors may spread only in a local area, but with electronic means available, rumors spread more widely and rapidly. Without authoritative information, ambiguous situations can produce faulty information on which decisions are made and actions are based. *Urban legends*, one example of widely spread but unverified messages, are unsubstantiated stories that sound plausible and become widely circulated. The people telling these stories usually believe them (Mikkelson and Mikkelson 2012). The next "Engaging Sociology" provides an example. (Go to www.snopes.com/college/college/asp for some additional entertaining urban legends about professors, exam scams, embarrassments, and other college pranks.)

ENGAGING SOCIOLOGY

Exam Stories: Testing the Truth

College exams are quickly approaching, so it is a good time to take a look at the latest chapter in the tome of teacher–student legend and rumors.

The first one was reported from Calgary, Alberta, by a civil engineering student at the University of Manitoba. This tale says a professor announced an open-book final examination in which the students could "use anything they are able to carry into the exam room." One innovative undergraduate, it is reported, carried in a graduate student who wrote his exam for him.

Another legend came from North Carolina. Supposedly, on the day before the final exam, the professor left his office unattended, with the door open and the examinations sitting on his desk. A student who came by to ask a question found the room empty and quickly left with one of the exams. However, the professor had printed the exact number of exams that he needed, and the next morning, he counted them again before going to the classroom. Discovering that he was one short, he suspected that it had been stolen, so he trimmed a half-inch from the bottom of the remaining exams. When the exam papers were turned in, the student whose paper was longer than the others' received a failing grade.

Finally, two guys were taking introductory chemistry, and they had done so well on all the quizzes that by the last week of class, they each had a solid A. These friends were so confident going into the final that on the weekend before the exam, they partied. However, with hangovers on Monday, they overslept

and missed the exam. They found the professor and told him they missed the final because they had been away, had had a flat tire on the way back to campus, and were without a spare. The professor thought this over and agreed that they could make up the final. The two studied intensely that night and went in the next day for the exam. The professor placed them in separate rooms and handed each of them a test booklet and told them to begin. The first problem was simple and was worth 5 points. They were both relieved. They did the first problem and then turned the page. The next question was, "Which tire? (95 points)."

Campus legends such as these help reduce the strain of college life and spread the reputations of legendary professors. Furthermore, they keep alive hopes of someday outfoxing the professors—or the students, depending on which side you are on.

* * * * * * *

Engaging With Sociology

1. Can you think of examples to add to this list? How do you know whether they are true or not?

2. How did you hear about the urban legends with which you are familiar? How did you learn they were not, in fact, true?

3. In what ways do such stories illustrate *collective behavior*?

Source: www.snopes.com.

Fads are temporary behaviors, activities, or material objects that spread rapidly and are copied enthusiastically by large numbers of people. Body modification, especially tattooing, appeals mostly to young people of all social classes. Tattoo artists emblazon IDs, secret-society and organization emblems, fraternity symbols, and decorations on all parts of

customers' bodies. Body modification has taken place for centuries, but it goes through fads (University of Pennsylvania 2010). Sometimes, fads become institutionalized—that is, they gain a permanent place in the culture. Other fads die out, replaced by the next hot item. In 2015, one fund-raising fad was the Ice Bucket Challenge, a gimmick to support research on ALS (also known as Lou Gehrig's disease), and it raised $115 million in just 6 weeks (Kristof 2015).

Fashions refer to a style of appearance and behavior temporarily favored by a large number of people. Examples include clothing styles, music genres, color schemes in home decor, types of automobiles, and architectural designs. Fashions typically last longer than fads but sometimes survive only a season, as can be seen in the clothing industry. Music styles such as dark bass, progressive heavy electro rock, air pop, glitch soulazz, country dance music, and space trap were popular among some groups as this book was being written (Maniac Agenda 2016). These styles will probably be passé by the time you read this, replaced by new, emerging fads.

Each of these forms of collective behavior involves micro-level individual actions that cumulatively become collective responses to certain circumstances. Insofar as these various types of collective activity upset the standard routines of society and the accepted norms, they can unsettle the entire social system and cause lasting change. When we move to meso- and macro-level analyses, the established structures and processes of society become increasingly important. Much of the change at these levels is planned change.

PLANNED CHANGE IN ORGANIZATIONS: MESO-LEVEL CHANGE

The board of trustees of a small liberal arts college has witnessed recent drops in student enrollments that could cause the college to go out of business, but the college has a long tradition of fine education and devoted alumni. How does the college continue to serve future students and current alumni? The problem is how to plan change to keep the college solvent.

A company manufactures silicon chips for computers. Recently, the market has been flooded with inexpensive chips, primarily from Asia, where they are made more cheaply than this North American firm can possibly make them. Does the company succumb to the competition, figure out ways to meet it, or diversify its products? What steps should be taken to facilitate the change? Many companies in the Silicon Valley of California have faced exactly this challenge.

A Native American nation within the United States faces unemployment among its people due, in large

Supermodel Heidi Klum pours an ice bucket onto Project Runway host Tim Gunn during the "Ice Bucket Challenge" fad—a fundraiser for combating Lou Gehrig's disease, a neurodegenerative ailment that often results in death within five years. The money raised went to support medical research for this illness.

measure, to discrimination by Anglos in the local community. Should the elders focus their energies and resources on electing sympathetic politicians, boycotting racist businesses, filing lawsuits, becoming entrepreneurs as a nation so they can hire their own people, or beginning a local radio station so they will have a communication network for a social movement? What is the best strategy to help this proud nation recover from centuries of disadvantage?

All of these are real problems faced by real organizations. Anywhere we turn, organizations face questions involving change, questions that arise because of internal strains and external stresses. How organizational leaders deal with change will determine the survival and well-being of the organizations.

How Organizations Plan for Change

When working for an organization, we engage in the process of planning for change. Some organizations spend time and money writing long-range strategic plans and doing self-studies to determine areas for ongoing change. Sometimes, change is desired, and sometimes, it is forced on the organization by *stresses* from society and more powerful organizations or *strains* from individuals and groups within organizations pushing for new ideas. Moreover, a problem solved in one area can create unanticipated problems someplace else.

Organizational leaders must be prepared to guide their organization through planned and unplanned changes. Planned change involves strategic planning: deliberate, structured attempts, guided by stated goals, to alter the status quo of the social unit (Bennis, Benne, and Chin 1985; Ferhansyed 2008). The relationship between leaders and recipients of change is key to successful change, and employee commitment to change is necessary for that success (Hughes 2015; van der Voet 2015).

Several important questions should be considered before undertaking planned change: How can we identify what needs to be changed? How can we plan or manage the change process successfully? What kind of systems adapt well to change? Here, we outline three of the many approaches to planned change. Keep in mind the levels of analysis as you read about change models.

Models for Planning Organizational Change. Change models fall into two main categories: (1) closed-system models, which deal with the internal dynamics of the organization, and (2) open-system models (such as our social world model), which consider the organization and its environment. *Closed-system models*, often called classical or mechanistic models, focus on the internal dynamics of the organization. The goal of change using closed models is to move the organization closer to the ideal of bureaucratic efficiency and effectiveness. An example is time and motion studies, which analyze how much time it takes a worker to do a certain task and how it can be accomplished more efficiently. Each step in McDonald's process of getting a hamburger to the customer has been planned and timed for the greatest efficiency (Ritzer 2015).

In some closed-system models, top executives legislate change, and it filters down to the workers. Other organizations follow a closed-system change model with an organizational-development approach. They involve participants in the organization in decision making leading to change. The leadership is more democratic and supportive of workers, and the atmosphere is transparent—open, honest, and accountable to workers and investors. This model emphasizes that change comes about through adjusting workers' values, beliefs, and attitudes regarding new demands on the organization. Many variations on this theme have evolved, with current efforts including team building and change of the organizational culture to improve worker morale. Closed-system models tend to focus on change from within the organization.

Open-system models combine both internal processes and the external environment. The latter provides the organization with inputs (workers and raw materials) and feedback (acceptability of the product or result). In turn, the organization has outputs (products) that affect the larger society. There are three implications of this model: (1) Change is an ever-present and ongoing process, (2) all parts of the organization and its immediate environment are linked, and (3) change in one part has an effect on the other parts. Change can be initiated from within or from outside of the organization. The model in Figure 14.6 illustrates the open system.

Thinking Sociologically

Using the model in Figure 14.6 below, fill in the parts as they relate to your college or university. For example, inputs might include students, federal student aid grants, new knowledge, and technology.

Process of Planned Change. A huge issue in the Global South is the availability of clean drinking water. For example, in parts of Africa, women must spend as much as 6 hours a day carrying water to their homes. Because older daughters care for the younger siblings while the mother is away, many girls cannot attend school. Sometimes, the water found is not clean, leading to water-related diseases and more lost school days. This, in turn, has implications for the continuation of poverty (WaterAid 2012). Scientists and public-policy NGOs work to plan changes and address such problems. Consider the following example.

With global climate change, the glaciers on top of mountains such as Mount Kenya are melting. Although that mountain peak has been snow covered for more than 10,000 years, the glaciers are expected to be completely gone in approximately 20 years (Cousteau 2008). When the snow on the mountaintop disappears, the water supply for hundreds of thousands of people and animals will disappear (Maoncha 2013). One British NGO bringing about change in this area is WaterAid, launched in 1981. It has grown to become an international NGO

FIGURE 14.6   Open-System Model

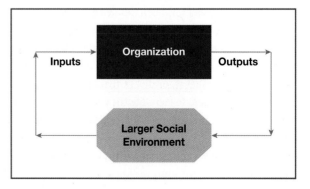

that focuses entirely on water and sanitation issues, including hygiene. WaterAid now assists communities throughout the world to develop the most appropriate technologies for clean water, given the geographical features and changes in resources in their areas. This is an issue that requires careful planning and strategic use of resources if change is to be effective and have positive outcomes.

Using planned change, WaterAid reached 2 million people with safe water, 3.1 million people with sanitation, and an estimated 8.2 million people with hygiene promotion in 2014–2015 (WaterAid 2015). Some sociologists use their understanding of social processes to improve access to safe water and water management.

The process of planned change is like a puzzle with a number of pieces that differ for each organization but must fit together for the smooth operation of the organization. The goal of most organizations is to remain balanced and avoid threats or conflict. Most organizations and countries prefer to bring about change in a slow, carefully planned way because unplanned change can be disruptive to the system.

At the societal and global macro levels, individuals and events outside the chambers of power often stimulate change, and there is much less control over how change evolves. We turn next to an exploration of change at the macro level.

SOCIAL MOVEMENTS: MACRO-LEVEL CHANGE

Sochi, Russia, hosted the prestigious 2014 Winter Olympics. The Olympics purport to promote peace and goodwill around the globe. The Olympic torch, a symbol of peace and goodwill, traveled from Moscow to Sochi through 2,900 towns and villages to prepare for and celebrate the event. However, its journey and the opening of the games were far from peaceful and full of goodwill. Protests about Russia's policies toward gay rights dogged the torch and pregame political commentary, and major political leaders refused to attend the opening ceremonies. Russian legislation denigrating LGBTQ individuals and those spreading "propaganda" that "promotes" same-sex relationships sparked protests and demonstrations around the world ("Sochi" 2014). Was this a social movement? In this section, we define social movements and discuss how social movements form and how they affect the larger society.

This photo shows Russian police attacking members of the Russian punk band Pussy Riot as they mock Russian antigay policies. This was one of hundreds of protests against the Russian policy prior to and during the Winter Olympic Games in Sochi.

What Is a Social Movement?

From human rights and women's rights to animal rights and environmental protection, individuals seek ways to express their concerns and frustrations. **Social movements** are *consciously organized attempts outside of established institutions to enhance or resist change through group action.* Movements focus on a common interest of members, such as abortion policy. They have an organization, defined leadership, and one or more goals that aim to correct some perceived wrongs existing in society or even around the globe. Social movements are most often found in industrial or postindustrial societies although they can occur anywhere groups of people have a concern or frustration.

Social movements entail large groups of people who hold little power individually but do have power as united groups that promote or resist social change. The problems leading to social movements often result from the way resources—human rights, jobs, income, housing, money for education and health care, and power—are distributed. In turn, *countermovements*—social movements against the goals of the original movement—may develop, representing other opinions (J. McCarthy and Zald 1977).

Many individuals join social movements to change the world, or their part of the world, and affect the direction of history. In fact, some social movements have been successful in doing just that. Consider the movements around the world that have protected lands, forests, rivers, and oceans, seeking environmental protection for the people whose survival depends on these natural resources. For example, the Chipko movement (meaning "embrace") has been fighting the logging of forests by commercial industries in a number of areas in India. Villagers, mostly women, who depend on the forests, use Gandhi-style nonviolent methods to oppose the deforestation. Governor Dr. K. K. Paul relates, "Our festivals, religious rituals and ceremonies, weddings, and birth and death rituals give ample importance to trees and plants. Worshipping trees and water has been part of our rich social and religious traditions" (Uttarakhand Community 2015). These women have set an example for environmentalists in many parts of the world who wish to save our ecosystem (Scribd 2011).

Stages of Social Movements

Why do people become involved in social movements such as PETA (People for the Ethical Treatment of Animals), pro-choice or pro-life movements, or political demonstrations against governments and their policies? Social movements begin because of cultural conflicts in society and because people who want to create—or resist—social change come together. Movements take the time and energy of individual volunteers, and these human resources must be focused as the movement evolves.

The first stage of a social movement involves setting the purpose of the movement. Long-standing problems or very recent events may create dissatisfaction and discontent in the general public or a part of the public. This discontent can galvanize people through a single event.

Sociologists have identified four conditions that give rise to the *preliminary stage*:

1. Individuals must *share some basic values and ideals*. They often occupy similar social statuses or positions and share concerns.
2. Social movements need to have a *preexisting communication network* that allows alienated or dissatisfied people to share their discontent (Farley 2011). Several recent political movements, such as MoveOn.org and Crossroads GPS, were carried out primarily on the Internet.
3. A *strain and a precipitating event* galvanize people around the issue. Effective leadership emerges— leaders who can mobilize people, organize the movement, and garner resources to fund the movement.
4. The people in the movement develop a *sense of efficacy*, a sense of confidence that they actually can be successful and change the system. Sometimes, as in the case of the civil rights movement, a sense of efficacy comes from a religious conviction that God will not let the movement fail (Farley 2011).

The *second stage* in the development of a movement is popularization, in which individuals coalesce their efforts, define their goals and strategies, develop recruitment tactics, and identify leaders. The social movement enters the public arena. The leaders present the social problems and solutions as seen by the members of the social movement. Now, the social movement enters the *third stage*: becoming institutionalized and a formal organization. This organized effort generates the resources and members for the social change efforts.

In some movements, the final *fourth stage* is fragmentation and demise. The group may or may not have achieved its goals, but fragmentation breaks apart the organization because the resources may be exhausted, the leadership may be inept or have lost legitimacy, or the leaders may be co-opted to join powerful mainline organizations. In the latter case, radical renewal movements may arise among those still strongly committed to the original cause (Mauss 1975).

Social movements sometimes focus on regional or even organizational modification, but typically, their focus is on national or global issues. For example, Amnesty International's primary interest is challenging countries with human rights violations. It publishes information on violations around the world and encourages supporters to advocate for those who face government persecution. One way to classify social movements is by their purpose or goals, as seen in the following section.

Types of Social Movements

Stonewall is a gay, lesbian, and bisexual rights movement that began when patrons of the Stonewall gay bar fought back against a police raid in New York in 1969. After that incident, the concern about gay rights erupted from a small number of activists into a widespread movement for rights and acceptance. Stonewall now has gone global, with chapters in many other countries and continents.

Proactive social movements such as Stonewall advocate moving forward with a new initiative—proposing something that did not exist before. Another example is the effort by the Nonhuman Rights Project to give mammals such as chimpanzees legal rights of personhood. The Supreme Court ruled in the *Citizens United* case that corporations can be considered "persons." Now, the Nonhuman Rights Project and Harvard professor Steven Wise argue that dogs, cats, elephants, and other animals should be protected with rights of persons (such as the right to bodily integrity) because they are aware, thinking, feeling, compassionate, communicating beings (Nonhuman Rights Project 2016). Regardless of whether you think this is an idea whose time has come or a harebrained notion, it would clearly change many aspects of society and move us in an entirely new direction.

Reactive social movements resist change, reacting against something that exists or against new trends or new social policies. The climate change countermovement provides an example of a reactive social movement. It comprises 91 groups that have spent more than $1 billion from 141 nonprofit organizations and think tanks trying to debunk the conservation movement and climate change claims (Brulle 2014). They aim to counter the environmental movement and the changes in policies that would result if that movement were successful in passing legislation and action.

Note that both liberals and conservatives can be involved in a reactive movement. When businesses want to build a corporation or plant in an area that will wipe out a native forest or destroy a historic area, liberals can be at the forefront of fighting "progress." The designation proactive or reactive only tells us whether a group supports or resists a particular change. There are other aspects of social movements and other ways of thinking about movements, as expressed in the five main types of social movements: expressive, social reform, revolutionary, resistance or regressive, and globalized.

Expressive movements take place in groups, but they *focus on changing individuals and saving people from lifestyles the movement considers corrupt.* Many expressive movements are religious, such as the born-again Christian movements, Zen Buddhism, Scientology, and the Christian Science Church. Expressive movements also include secular psychotherapy movements and self-help or self-actualization groups.

Social reform movements *seek to change some specific dimension of society, usually involving legislative policy modification or appeals to the courts.* They are typically proactive. Movement members generally support the society as a whole but think things could be better if attention were given to issues such as environmental protection, women's rights, same-sex marriage, "just and fair" globalization, reducing the national debt, or abortion policy.

Social reform movements are not interested in disrupting the functioning of the entire society: They have one issue they think needs reform. For example, many individuals with disabilities are given little attention, hope, or opportunity to get ahead and may be institutionalized or left to languish. However, social reform movements have advocated for legislation to promote the rights of the differently abled. One such movement is Special Olympics International, begun by Eunice Kennedy Shriver in 1968 to give those with intellectual or physical disabilities an opportunity to excel in sports. Over 3 million athletes from 150 countries now participate in these games (see www.specialolympics.org). The 2017 Special Olympics World Winter Games were held in Austria, featuring athletes with physical, mental, and sensorial disabilities. These events bring attention to the movement and issues faced by those with disabilities. Of particular interest were the advances the movement has helped to stimulate in physical adaptations for amputees, such as ice hockey using two sticks.

Revolutionary movements *attempt to transform society to bring about total change in society by overthrowing existing power structures and replacing them with new ones; these movements often resort to violent means to achieve goals.* These movements are always proactive. When we read in the paper that there has been a coup, we are learning about the ousting of an existing government, such as when the military in Thailand declared martial law and seized power from the interim prime minister in May 2014.

Resistance or regressive movements *try to protect an existing system, protect part of that system, or return to what a system had been by overthrowing current laws and practices.* They see societal change as a threat to values or practices and wish to maintain the status quo or return to a former status by reversing the change process (Eitzen and Zinn 2012; Inglehart and Baker 2001). Thus, they are always reactive. ISIS, or ISIL as it is sometimes called, has spread throughout the Middle East and parts of Africa, using terror to spread its message. It is a regressive movement against modernization, especially against the Western pattern of giving freedom and autonomy to women. The movement was successful in gaining power in the mid-2000s, imposing a harsh brand of Islamic law in the areas under its control. ISIS, like the Taliban in Afghanistan, insists that its version of Islam is pure in that it follows a literal understanding of the Muslim holy book.

Members of the movement maintain that someone who commits adultery should be stoned to death; the hands or arms of thieves should be amputated; and women who deviate from the Taliban interpretation of Muslim law should be mutilated, publicly beaten, and sometimes executed (G. Wood 2015).

Global transnational movements are *mobilized groups that take place across societies as international organizations.* Such groups focus on issues that affect the global community, such as the status of women, child labor, the rights of indigenous peoples, environmental degradation, global climate change, and disease pandemics. Free the Slaves, an antislavery movement started by sociologist Kevin Bales, provides one example of a global transnational movement. Members of this movement have researched and written about the plight of the 27 million slaves in the world, "forced to work without pay, under threat of violence and unable to walk away" (Bales 2012, 2015; Free the Slaves 2016).

Often these transnational movements are proactive—but not always. The movement by environmental and some international justice groups to stop the Trans Pacific Partnership involving the United States and dozens of other countries and supported by President Obama is resisting this change. They argue that this free-trade agreement would undermine *fair* trade and would be devastating to the environment. So progressive organizations like 350.org and Doctors Without Borders are deeply involved in a movement to resist this change (350.org 2016; Doctors Without Borders 2016b; MoveOn.org 2016).

Figure 14.7 summarizes the types of movements and the focus of each, from the micro to the macro level.

FIGURE 14.7 Types of Movements

Globalization and Social Movements

Social movements provide compelling evidence that humans make choices and are capable of countering macro- and meso-level forces. As Stanley Eitzen and Maxine Baca Zinn put it,

> Powerful social structures constrain what we do, but they can never control (us) entirely. Human beings are not passive actors. . . . Individuals acting alone, or with others, can shape, resist, challenge, and sometimes change the social structures that impinge on them. These actions constitute *human agency*. (Eitzen and Zinn 2012:269)

Since World War II, power in the global system has been dominated by a group of industrial powers that now call themselves the Group of Seven (or the G7). These nations control world markets and regulate economic and trading policies. Included among these elites are the dominant three—Japan from the East, Germany from Central Europe, and the United States from the American continents. The other four members, important but somewhat less powerful, are Canada, France, Great Britain, and Italy.

Although some politicians say they believe in a free-market economy, uninhibited by governmental interference, government officials use international agencies to intervene regularly in the global market. The G7 nations have the most power in the World Trade Organization, the World Bank, the IMF, and other regulatory agencies that preside over the global economy. These agencies have required poor countries to adhere to their demands or lose the right to loans and other support. The policies they have imposed, however, have sometimes been disastrous for poor countries, leading to debt burdens impossible to pay off.

Indigenous people (like the Garifuna and the Lenca of Honduras), laborers, and human rights workers are arising in poor countries and often joining forces across national boundaries to fight the influence of groups like the World Bank and the IMF (Eitzen and Zinn 2012; Ferree 2012; Muchhala 2012; Rights Action 2016). Even some groups within the G7 nations—labor unions, college student groups, nonprofit organizations like Rights Action and Witness for Peace, and religious bodies concerned about social justice—are joining the movements. Global South nations, calling themselves the G77, have now united, rather like a labor union seeking collective unity among workers, in an attempt to gain some power and determine their own destinies (Brecher et al. 2012).

Figure 12.3 on page 365 displays the location of G7 and G77 countries.

Although workers risk losing jobs by participating in protests for higher wages and better working conditions, one result of globalization has been a rise in countermovements. *Globalization from below* refers to the efforts by common people in small groups and protest movements to fight back (Della Porta et al. 2006; Eitzen and Zinn 2012). These countermovements seek to protect workers, defend the environment, and combat the bone-crunching poverty that plagues so much of the Global South. The argument goes like this:

> It is the activity of people—going to work, paying taxes, buying products, obeying government officials, staying off private property—that continually re-creates the power of the powerful. . . . [The system, for all its power and resources, is dependent on common people to do the basic jobs that keep the society running.] This dependency gives people a potential power over the society—but one that can be realized only if they are prepared to reverse their acquiescence. . . . Social movements can be understood as the collective withdrawal of consent to established institutions. (Brecher et al. 2012:279)

The movement against globalization can be understood as individuals and countries withdrawing consent for globalization dominated by the most powerful nations and global corporations (Brecher et al. 2012). There are thousands of small resistance actions against what are sometimes perceived to be the oppressive policies of G7 transnational corporations (Hearn 2012). They involve micro-level actions to bring change at the macro level. Consider the following example:

> Under heavy pressure from the World Bank, the Bolivian government sold off the public water system of its third-largest city, Cochabamba, to a subsidiary of the San Francisco–based Bechtel Corporation, which promptly doubled the price of water for people's homes. Early in 2000, the people of Cochabamba rebelled, shutting down the city with general strikes and blockades. The government declared a state of siege, and a young protester was shot and killed. Word spread all over the world from the remote Bolivian highlands via the Internet. Hundreds of e-mail

REUTERS/Adrees Latif

This photo shows a statue of Nelson Mandela, who voted for the first time in South Africa in 1994. He had been a political prisoner for 26 years before becoming president of South Africa and winning the Nobel Peace Prize. Mandela provides a model for those committed to nonviolent revolutionary change.

messages poured into Bechtel from all over the world, demanding that it leave Cochabamba. In the midst of local and global protests, the Bolivian government, which had said that Bechtel must not leave, suddenly reversed itself and signed an accord accepting every demand of the protesters. (Brecher et al. 2012:284)

Thinking Sociologically

Many concerned citizens in the Global North now buy fair-trade certified goods, such as coffee, cocoa, and fruits. This is an effort by individuals to support globalization from below—a different model of how to change the world. Activists believe that actions by individuals and small groups—globalization from below—can have a real impact on global problems.

In summary, some social change is planned by organizations (planned change), some is initiated by groups outside the organizational structure (social movements), and some is unplanned and spontaneous (collective behavior). The most important point, however, is that actions taken by individuals affect the larger social world, sometimes even having global ramifications. Likewise, national and international changes and social movements influence the lives of individuals.

The following "Sociologists in Action" presents an example of someone who helps others bring about social change.

SOCIOLOGISTS IN ACTION
ELLIS JONES

Empowering Everyday People: Democratizing Access to Social Change

On April 22, 1990, something changed for me. It was a Sunday. I was a student at the University of Southern California, and a friend invited me to walk down to a fair that was going on nearby. I did not have any plans, so I decided to join him. Apparently, it was something called Earth Day. There were tables and booths everywhere, and people were excitedly milling about from one to the next. Every booth I visited offered me a different way to make a positive environmental impact: recycling, composting, conserving water, reusing old clothes, and the list went on and on.

At the end of that day, I felt absolutely inspired to make the world a better place. In my mind, the environmental movement had experienced a stroke of true genius. They were not asking people to join groups, attend meetings, or organize rallies. Instead, they had opened up a completely new realm of action for people—their own everyday lives. By engaging people in microactivism rather than asking them to commit to the much more intensive work undertaken by full-time activists, they were essentially democratizing access to social change. It was a way to expand the environmental movement to almost anyone, despite their limits of time, money, skills, or circumstances.

The more I thought about this potential, the more I became convinced that what people really needed was a book that would collect as many of these actions as possible around environmental protection, human rights, social justice, animal rights, feminism, and LGBTQ issues into a single resource.

I was absolutely sure that someone would write it and that I, in turn, would be first in line to buy it. Ten years later, I was a sociology graduate student at the University of Colorado, Boulder. I had waited, patiently, for the imaginary author of this hypothetical book to appear, and she or he had yet to step forward.

I decided right then that I had waited long enough. So I roped in two of my closest friends (also fellow sociology grad students), and we spent the next year writing a book that collected all of the actions we could find, from every source we could get our hands on, and distilled the results into a single book. We added a section summarizing the latest data on some of the most significant social and environmental problems we seemed to be facing at the beginning of the 21st century, and the result was *The Better World Handbook: Small Changes That Make a Big Difference.* It has since sold 25,000 copies, been added to more than 300 college and university libraries worldwide, and been adopted in sociology classrooms across the country. The website (betterworldhandbook.com) has had over 550,000 unique visitors since it was created. In a very practical sense, sociology provided the three of us with the tools we needed to uncover, understand, and translate our world's social and environmental problems into a form that allows each of us to personally contribute to their resolution.

• •

Ellis Jones received his doctorate from the University of Colorado at Boulder and is now an assistant professor of sociology at College of the Holy Cross in Worcester, Massachusetts.

TECHNOLOGY, ENVIRONMENT, AND CHANGE

A lot is at stake for businesses, workers, environmentalists, policymakers, and others when considering the need for more energy sources. From renewable energy such as solar and wind power to gas and oil from fracking, strong opinions abound. The push for renewable green energy sources such as solar and wind power are changing the landscape as mountaintop removal to mine coal and the controversial practice of fracking are giving way to wind farms and solar arrays.

Technology refers to *the practical application of tools, skills, and knowledge to meet human needs and extend human abilities.* Technology and the environment cannot be separated, as we see from the debate over green energy sources versus oil pumping and coal mining. The raw products that fuel technology come from the environment, the waste returns to the environment, and technological mistakes affect the environment. This section discusses briefly the development and process of technology, the relationship between technology and the environment, and the implications for change at each level of analysis.

Throughout human history, there have been major transition periods when changes in the material culture brought about revolutions in human social structures and cultures (Toffler and Toffler 1980). For example, the agricultural revolution, which resulted from the use of the plow to till the soil, established new social arrangements and created food surpluses that allowed cities to flourish. With the Industrial Revolution came machines powered by steam and gasoline, resulting in mass production, population increases, urbanization, the division of labor in manufacturing, social stratification, and the socialist and capitalist political-economic systems. Today, postindustrial technology, based on the microchip, fuels the spread of information, communication, and transportation on a global level—and even exploration of outer space. It also allows us to store and retrieve masses of information in seconds. However, each wave of innovation initially affects only a portion of the world, leaving other people and countries behind and creating divisions between the Global North and the Global South.

Sociologist William Ogburn has argued that change is brought about through three processes: discovery, invention, and diffusion. *Discovery* is a new way of seeing reality. The material objects or ideas have been present, but they are seen in a new light when the need arises or conditions are conducive to the discovery. It is usually accomplished by an individual or a small group, a micro-level activity (Ogburn [1922] 1938, 1961, 1964).

Invention refers to combining existing parts, materials, or ideas to form new ones. There was no light bulb or combustion engine lying in the forest waiting to be discovered. Human ingenuity was required to put together something that had not previously existed. Technological innovations often result from research and the expansion of science, increasingly generated in meso-level institutions and organizations in society.

Diffusion is the spread of an invention or discovery from one place to another. The spread of ideas such as capitalism, democracy, and religious beliefs has brought about changes in human relationships around the world. Likewise, the spread of various types of music, film technology, telephone systems, and computer hardware and software across the globe has had important ramifications for global interconnectedness. Diffusion often involves expansion of ideas across the globe (macro level), but it also requires individuals to adopt ideas at the micro level.

Technology and Science

Science is *the systematic process of producing human knowledge; it uses empirical research methods to discover facts and test theories.* The question, "How do we know what we know?" is often answered: "It's science." Whether social, biological, or physical, science provides a systematic way to approach the world and its mysteries. It uses empirical research methods to discover facts and test theories. Today, technology applies scientific knowledge to solve problems. Early human technology was largely the result of trial and error, not based on scientific knowledge or principles. Since the Industrial Revolution, many inventors and capitalists have seen science and technology as routes to human betterment and happiness. Science has become a major social institution in industrial and postindustrial societies, providing the bases of information and knowledge for sophisticated technology.

Indeed, one of the major transformations in modern society is the result of science becoming an institution. Prior to the 18th century, science was an avocation. People like Benjamin Franklin experimented in their backyards with whatever spare cash they had to satisfy their own curiosity.

Technological innovation is now providing us with electricity through wind farms. The one depicted here is the first complete high-sea wind farm on the North Sea coast of Germany.

Uber CEO Travis Kalanick wants robots to replace human drivers in his taxi service—and in 2015, Arizona governor Doug Ducey opened the door for the first driverless taxis on public roads. This automated vehicle is taking a test drive in Pittsburgh. As a society, we have little idea how such technological innovations may stimulate change to the larger society and our social structure.

Science in the contemporary world is both a structure and a social process. *Institutionalization* means creation of the organized, patterned, and enduring sets of social structures that provide guidelines for behavior and help the society meet its needs. Within these structures, actions are taken—the processes within the structure—that accomplish a goal such as conducting research. Innovation resulting in change will be very slow until a society has institutionalized science—providing extensive training and paying some people simply to do research. Modern science involves mobilizing financial resources and employing the most highly trained people (which, in turn, requires the development of educational institutions).

Specialization in science speeds up the rates of discovery. A researcher focuses on one area and gets much more in-depth understanding. Also, effective methods of communication across the globe mean that we do not need to wait several years for a research manuscript to cross the ocean and to be translated into another language. Competition in science (now global) means that researchers move quickly on their findings. The first to create new drugs, devices, and other inventions tend to reap the most recognition and compensation.

We would not have automobiles, planes, missiles, space stations, computers, the Internet, and many of our modern conveniences without the institutionalization of science and without scientific application (technology). Science is big business, funded by industry and government. Most university researchers and some government-funded science institutes engage in *basic research* designed to discover new knowledge. Industry and some governmental agencies such as the military and the Department of Agriculture employ scientists to do *applied research* and discover practical uses for existing knowledge.

Scientific knowledge is usually cumulative, with each study adding to the existing body of research. However, radical new ideas can result in scientific revolutions (T. Kuhn 1970). Galileo's finding that Earth revolves around the sun and Darwin's theory of evolution are two examples of radical new ideas that changed history. More recently, cumulative scientific knowledge has resulted in energy-efficient engines that power cars and computer technology that has revolutionized communication.

Thinking Sociologically

Imagine what your life would have been like before home computers, e-mail, and the Internet. What would be different? (Note that you are imagining the world from only 30 years ago.) Ask your parents or grandparents what this recent past was like.

Technology and Change

A nation's research and development (R&D) is an important measure of investment in the future. For many years the biggest investors have been the European Union, the United States, and Japan, accounting in 2014 for $1.6 trillion, or 78%, of global R&D expenditures. However, by 2022, China is expected to surpass the United States in R&D spending. Whereas U.S. industry continues to support R&D, the government is under pressure to pare down federal spending and now contributes less than in previous budgets.

This lack of U.S. investment in research is especially troubling, given what we know about the relationship between economic growth and R&D (Battelle 2013). For example, technological revolution in communications would not have come about without research and development. R&D has resulted in fiber-optic cable, wireless microwave cell phones, and satellite technologies that make it easier to communicate with people around the world. A cable starting in Europe is now circling Africa; the capabilities for high-speed Internet will enhance opportunities for businesses, health care to remote areas, and educational advances in countries that have few textbooks. We now live in a global village, a great boon for those fortunate enough to have the education and means to take advantage of it (Drori 2006).

However, changes in technology do not always have a positive effect on less affluent countries. Consider, for example, the effects of the invention of artificial sweeteners and the demand for sugar. Sugar is the major source of income for the 50 million people who work in the beet and cane sugar industries around the globe. Their jobs are threatened by artificial sweeteners. As new technologies bring substantial benefits to many in the world, these results can also harm people in other parts of the interconnected world. Changes in technology and the economy have forced many individuals to leave their native villages in search of paid labor positions in urban factories and the tourism industry, disrupting family lives.

Rapid technological change has affected generational relationships as well. It is not uncommon for younger generations to have more technological competence than their elders, and this sometimes creates a generational digital divide in competencies regarding use of computers, cell phones, and other electronic devices. In some settings, younger people are looked to for their expertise, whereas in the past, the elders were the source of knowledge and wisdom. Often, the older members of a business or group feel devalued and demoralized late in their careers because those with technical competence view the older members as "outdated has-beens."

Popular video games such as *Battlefield: Hardline*, *Batman: Arkham Knight*, *Below*, *Bloodborne*, *Dying Light*, *Evolve*, and *Game of Thrones* are but a few of the relatively new offerings in the video game pantheon, and forms of entertainment such as the Wii-U and Nintendo 3DS further the social distance between generations (Erik Kain 2015). With the changes brought about by technology come changes in the nonmaterial culture—values, political ideologies, and human relationships. Clearly, technology can have a variety of social impacts—both positive and negative.

You now know the answer is a resounding "Yes!" This final "Engaging Sociology" provides a plan you can follow if you would like to make an impact on your local community and larger society.

ENGAGING SOCIOLOGY

Making a Difference

Because bringing about change requires cooperation, working in a group context is often essential. Flexibility, openness to new ideas, and willingness to entertain alternative suggestions are also key factors in successful change-making. The following steps provide a useful strategy for planning change.

1. *Be specific, and focus on what is to be changed.* Without clear focus, your target for change can get muddied or lost in the attempt.

2. *Research the issue and use those findings.* Learn as much as you can about the situation

or problem to be changed. Use informants, interviews, written materials, observation, existing data (such as U.S. Census Bureau statistics), or anything that helps you understand the issues. That will enable you to find the information you need to thoroughly understand the issue you wish to address.

3. *Find out what has already been done and by whom.* Other individuals or groups may be working on the same issue. Be sure you know what findings and interventions have already taken place. This can also help determine

(Continued)

(Continued)

whether attempts at change have been tried, what has been successful, and whether further change is needed.

4. *Change must take into account each level of analysis.* When planning a strategy, you may focus on one level of analysis, but be sure to consider what interventions are needed at other levels to make the change effective or to anticipate the effects of change on other levels.

5. *Determine the intervention strategy.* Map out the intervention and the steps to carry it out. Identify resources needed, and plan each step in detail.

6. *Evaluate the plan.* Get feedback on the plan from those involved in the issue and from unbiased colleagues. If possible, involve those who will be affected by the intervention in the planning and evaluation of the change. When feasible, test the intervention plan before implementing it.

7. *Implement the intervention.* Put the plan into effect, watching for any unintended consequences. Ask for regular feedback from those affected by the change.

8. *Evaluate the results.* Assess what is working, what is not, and how the constituents that experience the change are reacting.

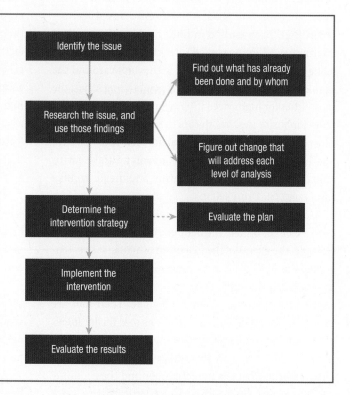

Sociological knowledge and skills should help guide this process.

* * * * * * *

Engaging With Sociology

1. Use the steps to plan how you might bring about a change that would make a difference in your community, in your country, or in the world.

2. Go to "Contributing to Our Social World: What Can We Do?" at the end of this and other chapters to find ways in which you can be actively involved in bettering society.

WHAT HAVE WE LEARNED?

Sociology teaches us that the choices we make facilitate change at each level in our social world. It also helps us to learn how to work with groups to make a difference.

As you face individual challenges to bring about change in your social world, keep in mind this message: Change at one level affects all other levels. Sociology, as a discipline, is focused on gathering accurate information about the society in which we live. Sociologists often use their knowledge to advocate for changes that they think will make a better society. We hope that through this book and your course you have gained important sociological insights that will help you contribute to the dialogue about how to make our social world a better, more humane place.

- Social change—variation or alteration over time in behavior patterns, culture, or structure in a society—typically involves change at one level of the social system that ripples through the other levels, micro, meso, and macro.

- *Strains* within an organization or group can induce change, as can *stresses* imposed from the outside environment.

- Sociological theories—whether micro or macro— offer explanations for the causes of change.

- At the micro level, change is often initiated through collective behavior, which can take several forms: crowds, mobs, riots, rumors, fads, and fashions.

- At the meso level, change in organizations is often managed through a planned process.

- Social movements often provide impetus for change at the macro level. Social changes can be induced at the micro level, but they can have impacts even at the global level.

- Science and technology can also stimulate change, but science has its greatest impact for change when it is institutionalized and becomes a part of the society.

- Social structures constrain what we do, but individuals, especially when acting in concert with others, can challenge, resist, and change the social systems that constrain them. We can change our society through *human agency*.

DISCUSSION QUESTIONS

1. What is the latest technological device you or your family has acquired? How has it changed your life? What are the (a) intended and (b) unintended consequences of having it?

2. Every organization must adapt to change. Describe how an organization to which you belong coped with change. Was the adaptation successful? Why, or why not? What was your role? Did you feel as though you had some influence over the adaptation strategy? Why, or why not?

3. Why is it in the self-interest of Global North nations to help Global South nations battling the effects of climate change? How can sociologists impact efforts to address climate change?

4. What type of social movement has helped bring about the dramatic increase in support for same-sex marriage over the past few years? Why? How do the results of this movement indicate the power of social movements to influence society at the micro, meso, and macro levels?

5. If you were to join a social movement today, which would you join? Why? What would you hope to achieve?

KEY TERMS

collective behavior   421

expressive movements   429

global transnational

   movements   430

resistance or regressive

   movements   429

revolutionary movements   429

science   433

social change   408

social movements   427

social reform movements   429

technology   433

CONTRIBUTING TO OUR SOCIAL WORLD: *WHAT CAN WE DO?*

At the Local (Micro) Level

- *Campus-wide movements:* A wide range of social issues, including international peace, environmental issues, human rights, and specific student concerns such as campus safety and the rising cost of higher education, may have movements represented on your campus. Consider participating in such activities. If you feel strongly about an issue for which no movement exists, consider organizing one with a few like-minded students. You can find tools to create a campus movement at www.campusactivism .org/index.php or www.campusactivism.org/dis playresource-471.htm.

- Many *community movements* bring about change at the local level, sometimes with national and even international effects. Check with your professors, service-learning and campus activities offices, and chambers of commerce to find community movements in your area.

At the Organizational/Institutional (Meso) Level

- *Invite a movement leader to campus.* Consider inviting movement leaders to your campus for a lecture, or organize a conference that features several experts in a particular field. The environment, civil rights, and modern slavery are topics that have wide appeal. Professors who teach classes that cover these issues may be able to help you find a good speaker. Work with your sociology club or student government to provide funding for the speaker.

- *Volunteer Match* seeks to connect individuals with movements of interest to them. Its website (www .volunteermatch.org) has suggestions for getting involved in your local area.

- *Katimavik's* mission is to develop diverse youth as engaged, caring citizens and contributors and leaders for a better Canada. Diverse, engaged, and empowered youth work together to create just relationships. Located in Quebec, opportunities include eco-internships and socio-internships. Visit katima vik.org/en/we-offer.

At the National/Global (Macro) Levels

- *The Jubilee Movement* promotes international debt forgiveness for the world's poorest countries—a solution that the U.S. government has embraced in principle. Named for the principle offered in the Hebrew scriptures that creditors are to cancel all debt owed to them every jubilee year (once every 49 years), the organization sponsors legislative programs, research work, and educational outreach activities throughout the world. The website of Jubilee USA (www.jubileeusa.org/about-us) provides information on ways in which you can get involved and includes information about international debt, activities, and the history of the movement.

$SAGE edge™

Get the edge on your studies. **edge.sagepub.com/ballantinecondensed5e**

- Take a quiz to find out what you've learned.
- Review key terms with eFlashcards.
- Watch videos that enhance chapter content.

Glossary

Ability grouping. Places students into different-level groups within classes, 308

Absolute poverty. Not having resources to meet basic needs, 203

Achieved status. Social status that is chosen or earned by decisions one makes and sometimes by personal ability, 119

Achieved stratification systems. Societal systems that allow individuals to earn positions through their ability, efforts, and choices, 200

Agents of socialization. The transmitters of culture—the people, organizations, and institutions that help us define our identity and teach us how to thrive in our social world, 98

Anomie. The state of normlessness that occurs when rules for behavior in society break down under extreme stress from rapid social change or conflict, 122

Arranged marriages. A pattern of mate selection in which someone other than the couple—such as elder males, parents, or a matchmaker—selects the marital partners, 290

Ascribed status. Social status that is often assigned at birth and that does not change during an individual's lifetime; gender, race, and ethnic status group are examples, 119

Ascribed stratification systems. Societal systems in which characteristics beyond the control of the individual—such as family background, age, sex, and race—determine one's position in society, 200

Assimilation. The structural and cultural merging of minority and majority groups in society, 230

Authoritarian governments. Governments in which power is concentrated in the hands of an absolute monarch, dictator, or small group not accountable to the people, 355

Authority. Power that people consider legitimate and that is recognized as rightful by those subject to it, 346

Bureaucracies. Specific types of large formal organizations that have the purpose of maximizing efficiency; they are characterized by formal relations between participants, clearly laid-out procedures and rules, and pursuit of shared goals, 125

Caste systems. The most rigid ascribed-stratification systems. Individuals are born into a status, which they retain throughout life. That status is deeply embedded in religious, political, and economic norms and institutions, 200

Collective behavior. Actions that are spontaneous, unstructured, and disorganized and that may violate norms; this behavior arises when people are trying to cope with stressful situations and under unclear or uncertain conditions, 421

Conflict theory. Theory that conflict is inevitable in any group or society and that inequality and injustice are the source of the conflicts that permeate society, 32

Consensus crimes. Crimes for which members of society are in general agreement about the seriousness, 141

Counterculture. A group with expectations and values that contrast sharply with the dominant values of a particular society, 75

Crime. Deviant actions for which there are formal penalties imposed by the government, such as fines, jail, or prison sentences, 138

Cultural capital. The knowledge, skills, language mastery, style of dress, and values that provide a person with access to a particular status in society, 181

Cultural relativism. Requires setting aside cultural and personal beliefs and prejudices to understand another group or society through the eyes of its members and using its own community standards, 67

Culture. The way of life shared by a group of people—the knowledge, beliefs, values, rules or laws, language, customs, symbols, and material products within a society that help meet human needs, 54

Democratic governments. Governments characterized by accountability to citizens and a large degree of control by individuals over their own lives, 355

Democratic socialism. Collective or group planning of the development of society but within a democratic political system; the good of the whole is paramount, 359

Demographic transition theory. Links trends in birth rates and death rates with patterns of economic and technological development, 384

Demography. The study of human populations, 378

Dependency ratio. The ratio of those in both the young and aged groups compared with the number of people in the productive age group from age 15 through age 64, 381

Dependent variable. The variable in a cause-and-effect relationship that is affected by and comes after the independent variable in time sequence, 39

Deprofessionalization. The process through which a professional occupation loses autonomy, respect, and service orientation because the professionals come to be controlled by nonprofessionals and outside forces such as financial concerns, government regulations, technological changes, and administrators or management, 330

Deviance. The violation of social norms, 138

Differential association theory. Emphasizes the learning of deviant behavior from those with whom we interact (e.g., family, peers, and fellow employees), 143

Discrimination. Differential treatment and harmful actions against minorities, 222

Dysfunctions. Actions that undermine the stability or equilibrium of society, 31

Empirical knowledge. Founded on information gained from evidence (facts), rather than intuition, 37

Endogamy. Norms that require individuals to marry inside certain human boundaries, whatever the societal members see as protecting the homogeneity of the group, 289

Environment. The setting in which the social unit operates, including everything that influences the social unit, such as its physical and organizational surroundings and technological innovations, 15

Environmental racism. When environmental pollution disproportionately affects racial and ethnic minorities, 385

Equal educational opportunity. A system in which children are provided with equal facilities, financing, and access to school programs, 306

Estate systems. Characterized by the concentration of economic and political power in the hands of a small minority of political-military elite, with the peasantry tied to the land, 201

Ethnic group. A group within the human species that is based on cultural factors: language, religion, dress, foods, customs, beliefs, values, norms, a shared group identity or feeling, and sometimes loyalty to a homeland, monarch, or religious leader, 219

Ethnocentrism. The tendency to view one's own group and its cultural expectations as right, proper, and superior to others, 65

Exogamy. Norms governing the choice of a mate that require individuals to marry outside of their own immediate group, 289

Expressive movements. Focus on changing individuals and saving people from lifestyles the movement considers corrupt, 429

Extended family. Two or more adult generations that share tasks and living quarters. This may include brothers, sisters, aunts, uncles, cousins, and grandparents, 288

Family of orientation. The family into which we are born or adopted, 288

Family of procreation. The family we create ourselves, 288

Feminist theory. Critiques the hierarchical power structures that disadvantage women and other minorities, 35

Fertility. Demographic processes referring to the birth rate, 387

Formal agents of socialization. Official or legal agents (e.g., families, schools, teachers, and religious organizations) whose purpose it is to socialize the individual into the values, beliefs, and behaviors of the culture, 99

Formal education. Schooling that takes place in a formal setting with the goal of teaching a predetermined curriculum, 299

Formal organizations. Modern rational organizations composed of complex secondary groups deliberately formed to pursue and achieve certain goals, 125

Free-choice marriage. A pattern of mate selection in which the partners select each other based primarily on romance and love, 290

Game stage. Stage in the process of developing a social self when a child develops the ability to take the role of multiple others concurrently (norms, values, and expectations of the generalized other) and conform to societal expectations, 95

Gender. A society's notions of masculinity and femininity—socially constructed meanings associated with being male or female—and how individuals construct their identity in terms of gender within these constraints, 251

Gender roles. Those commonly assigned tasks or expected behaviors linked to an individual's sex-determined statuses, 251

Generalized other. A composite of societal expectations that a child learns from family, peers, and other organizations, 95

Genocide. The systematic effort of one group, usually the dominant group, to destroy a minority group, 229

Glass ceiling. Processes that limit the progress of women and other minorities from the highest job or status positions because of invisible barriers that bar promotion within an organization, 262

Global culture. Behavioral standards, symbols, values, and material objects that have become common across the globe, 76

Global transnational movements. Mobilized groups that take place across societies as international organizations seek change in the status of women, child labor, rights of indigenous peoples, environmental degradation, global warming, disease pandemics, and other issues that affect the global community, 430

Globalization. The process by which the entire world is becoming a single interdependent sociocultural entity, more uniform, more integrated, and more interdependent, 76

Groups. Units involving two or more people who interact with each other because of shared common interests, goals, experiences, and needs, 121

Hate crimes. Criminal offenses committed against a person, property, or group that are motivated by the offender's bias against a religious, ethnic, or racial group; national origin; gender; or sexual orientation, 153

Health. A state of physical, mental, and social well-being or the absence of disease, 316

Heterosexism. An assumption that every person is heterosexual, thereby legitimizing heterosexuality as the only normal lifestyle and marginalizing persons who do not identify as heterosexual, 271

Hidden curriculum. The implicit messages learned in school through the other three *R*s of school: rules, routines, and regulations, 302

Homophobia. Intense fear and hatred of homosexuality and homosexuals, whether male or female, 271

Hypothesis. An educated guess or prediction, 37

I. The spontaneous, unpredictable, impulsive, and largely unorganized aspect of the self, 94

Ideal culture. Consists of practices, beliefs, and values that are regarded as most desirable in society and are consciously taught to children, 69

Illness. Lack of health, 316

Imitation stage. A period when children under 3 years old are preparing for role-taking by observing others and imitating their behaviors, sounds, and gestures, 94

Income. Money received from work or investments, 187

Independent variable. The variable in a cause-and-effect relationship that comes first in a time sequence and causes a change in another variable, 39

Inequality. A social condition in which privileges, opportunities, and substantial rewards are given to people in some positions in society but denied to others, 176

Informal agents of socialization. Unofficial influential agents that shape values, beliefs, and behaviors in which socialization is not the express purpose, 99

In-group. A group to which an individual feels a sense of loyalty and belonging; it also may serve as a reference group, 124

Institutional racial discrimination. Any meso-level institutional arrangement that favors one racial group over another; this favoritism may result in intentional or unintentional consequences for minority groups, 225

Institutions. Organized, patterned, and enduring sets of social structures that provide guidelines for behavior and help each society meet its basic survival needs. Whereas institutions operate mostly at the meso level, they also act to integrate micro and macro levels of society, 280

Interaction. The exchange of verbal and nonverbal messages, 87

Labeling theory. Explains how people can be labeled deviant after committing a deviant act, which can then lead them to carry out further acts that reflect that label, 143

Latent functions. Unplanned or unintended consequences of actions or of social structures, 31

Levels of analysis. Social groups from the smallest to the largest, 13

Life expectancy. The average number of years a person in a particular society can expect to live, 377

Lifestyle. Includes attitudes, values, beliefs, behavior patterns, and other aspects of one's place in the world, shaped by socialization, 191

Looking-glass self. A reflective process that develops our self based on our interpretations and internalization of the reactions of others to us, 92

Macro-level analysis. Analysis of the largest social units in the social world, including entire nations, global forces, and international social trends, 17

Manifest functions. The planned outcomes of interactions, social organizations, or institutions, 31

Market or capitalist economic system. An economic system driven by the balance of supply and demand, allowing free competition to reward the efficient and the innovative with profits; stresses individual planning and private ownership of property, 357

Master status. An individual's social status that becomes most important and takes precedence over other statuses, 119

Material culture. Includes all of the objects we can see or touch; all of the artifacts of a group of people, 67

Me. The part of the self that has learned the rules of society through interaction and role taking; it controls the *I* and its desires, 94

Mechanical solidarity. Social cohesion and integration based on the similarity of individuals in the group, including shared beliefs, values, and emotional ties between members of the group, 57

Medicaid. The government-run insurance plan of low-income families, 325

Medicalization. Handling of some forms of deviance, as well as some normal human functions (such as pregnancy and childbirth), in the health care system rather than the family, legal, or religious arenas, 318

Medicare. A government-run health insurance system for those 65 and older in the United States, 315

Meritocracy. A society in which positions are allocated in social groups or organizations according to individuals' abilities and credentials, 196

Meso-level analysis. Analysis of intermediate-size social units, smaller than the nation but large enough to encompass more than the local community or region, 16

Microculture. A culture that develops at the micro level in groups or organizations and affects only a segment of one's life or influences a limited period of one's life, 72

Micro-level analysis. Analysis with a focus on individual or small-group interaction in specific situations, 16

Migration. In terms of demographic processes, refers to the movement of people from one place to another, 387

Minority groups. Groups in a population that differ from others in some characteristics and are therefore subject to less power, fewer privileges, and discrimination, 214

Monogamy. The most familiar form of marriage in industrial and postindustrial societies; refers to marriage of two individuals, 289

Mortality. In terms of demographic processes, refers to the death rate, 387

National culture. Common values and beliefs that tie citizens of a nation together, 76

National society. Includes a population of people, usually living within a specified geographic area, connected by common ideas and subject to a particular political authority, 14

Nonmaterial culture. The thoughts, language, feelings, beliefs, values, and attitudes that make up much of our culture, 68

Norms. Rules of behavior shared by members of a society and rooted in the value system, 69

Nuclear family. Consists of two parents and their children—or any two of the three, 288

Organic solidarity. Refers to social cohesion (glue) based on division of labor, with each member playing a highly specialized role in the society and each person being dependent on others due to interdependent, interrelated tasks, 57

Organized crime. Ongoing criminal enterprises by an organized group whose ultimate purpose is economic gain through illegitimate means, 154

Out-group. A group to which an individual does not belong and a group that competes with or acts in opposition to an in-group, 124

Past-in-present discrimination. Practices from the past that may no longer be allowed but that continue to have consequences for people in the present, 227

Peer group. A group of people who are roughly equal in some status within the society, such as the same age or the same occupation, 99

Planned (or centralized) economic systems. Economic systems in which the government or another centralized group oversees production and distribution, 358

Play stage. Involves a child, usually ages 3 to 5, having the ability to see things (role-take) from the perspective of one person at a time; simple role-taking or play-acting, 94

Pluralism. Occurs when each ethnic or racial group in a country maintains its own culture and separate set of institutions but has recognized equality in the society, 230

Pluralist power theorists. Argue that power is not held exclusively by an elite group but is shared among many power centers, each of which has its own self-interests to protect, 202

Polygamy. Marriage of one person to more than one partner at the same time, 289

Population pyramids. Pyramid-shaped diagrams that illustrate sex ratios and dependency ratios over time, 382

Population transfer. The removal, often forced, of a minority group from a region or country, 230

Populations. Permanent societies, states, communities, adherents of a common religious faith, racial or ethnic groups, kinship or clan groups, professions, and other identifiable categories of people, 378

Power. Ability of a person or group to realize its own will in groups, even against the resistance of others, 343

Power elite. Power held by top leaders in corporations, politics, and military; this interlocking elite makes major decisions guiding the nation, 201

Prejudice. Attitudes of prejudgment about a group, usually negative and not based on facts, 222

Primary deviance. A violation of a norm that may be an isolated act or an initial act of rule breaking, 143

Primary groups. Groups characterized by cooperation among close, intimate, long-term relationships, 123

Public-order crimes. See *victimless crimes*. 152

Public sociologists. Strive to better understand how society operates and to make practical use of their sociological findings, 43

Race. A socially created concept that identifies a group of individuals as "different" based on certain biologically inherited physical characteristics. This allows them to be singled out for dissimilar treatment, 215

Rational choice (exchange) theory. A theory that focuses on humans as fundamentally concerned with self-interests, making rational decisions based on weighing costs and rewards of the projected outcome, 29

Rationalization of social life. The attempt to maximize efficiency by creating rules and procedures focused solely on accomplishing goals, 125

Real culture. The way things in society are actually done, 69

Recidivism rates. The likelihood that someone who is arrested, convicted, and imprisoned will later be a repeat offender, 167

Reference groups. Groups composed of members who act as role models and establish standards against which members evaluate their conduct, 124

Relative poverty. Occurs when one's income falls below the poverty line, resulting in an inadequate standard of living relative to others in the individual's country, 204

Reproduction of class. The socioeconomic positions of one generation passing on to the next, 305

Resistance or regressive movements. Try to protect an existing system, protect part of that system, or return to what a system had been by overthrowing current laws and practices. They see societal change as a threat to values or practices and wish to maintain the status quo or return to a former status by reversing the change process, 429

Resocialization. The process of shedding one or more positions and taking on others; it involves learning new norms, behaviors, and values suitable to the newly acquired status, 97

Revolution. Social and political transformations of a nation that result when states fail to fulfill their expected responsibilities, 361

Revolutionary movements. Attempt to transform society to bring about a total change in society by overthrowing existing power structures and replacing them with new ones; these movements often resort to violent means to achieve goals, 429

Role conflict. Conflict between the roles of two or more social statuses, 121

Role strain. Tension among roles within a social status, 120

Roles. The expected behaviors, rights, obligations, responsibilities, and privileges assigned to a social status, 29

Role-taking. The process by which individuals take others into account by imagining themselves in the position of the other, 92

Sample. A group of systematically chosen people who represent a much larger group, 37

Science. The systematic process of producing human knowledge; it uses empirical research methods to discover facts and test theories, 433

Secondary deviance. Occurs when an individual continues to violate a norm and begins to take on a deviant identity *because* of being labeled as deviant, 144

Secondary groups. Groups characterized by formal, impersonal, and businesslike relationships; often temporary, based on a specific limited purpose or goal, 123

Self. Refers to the perceptions we have of who we are, 91

Self-fulfilling prophecy. Occurs when a belief or a prediction becomes a reality, in part because of the prediction, 144

Sex. A biological term referring to ascribed genetic, anatomical, and hormonal differences between males and females, 250

Sexuality. Culturally shaped meanings both of sexual acts and of how we experience our own bodies—especially in relation to the bodies of others, 250

Shadow education. Learning opportunities outside of school, such as tutoring, test prep, and summer programs, 306

Sick role. A special position in society in which one is temporarily relieved of responsibilities and accepts a position of dependence, 323

Side-effect discrimination. Practices in one institutional area that have a negative impact because they are linked to practices in another institutional area; because institutions are interdependent, discrimination in one results in unintentional discrimination in others, 225

Significant others. Parents, guardians, relatives, siblings, or important individuals whose primary and sustained interactions with the individual are especially influential, 94

Slavery. When an individual or a family is bound in servitude as the property of a person or household, bought and sold, and forced to work, 177

Social capital. Access to people who can help us get jobs or favors, 113

Social change. Variations or alterations over time in the behavior patterns, culture (including norms and values), and structure of society, 408

Social class. The wealth, power, and prestige rankings that individuals hold in society; a large group with similar rankings, 100

Social construction of reality. The process by which individuals and groups shape reality through social interaction, 77

Social control theory. Examines the processes a society or a group uses to ensure conformity to its norms and expectations, 146

Social institutions. Organized, patterned, and enduring sets of social structures that provide guidelines for behavior and help each society meet its basic survival needs, 14

Social interaction. Consists of two or more individuals purposefully relating to each other, 115

Social mobility. The extent of individual movement up or down in the class system, changing one's social position in society—especially relative to one's parents, 193

Social movements. Consciously organized attempts outside of established institutional mechanisms to enhance or resist change through group action, 427

Social networks. Refer to individuals linked together by one or more social relationships, connecting us to the larger society, 113

Social processes. Take place through actions of people in institutions and other social units or structures, 14

Social reform movements. Seek to change some specific dimension of society, usually involving legislative policy modification or appeals to the courts, 429

Social stratification. How individuals and groups are layered or ranked in society according to their access to and possession of valued resources, 179

Social structure. The stable patterns of interactions, statuses (positions), roles (responsibilities), and organizations that provide stability for the society and bring order to individuals' lives, 13

Social units. Interconnected parts of the social world, ranging from small groups to societies, 13

Social world model. The levels of analysis in our social surroundings as an interconnected series of small groups, organizations, institutions, and societies, 13

Socialization. The lifelong process of learning to become a member of the social world, beginning at birth and continuing until death, 86

Socialized medicine. Provides a government-supported consumer service that ensures equal access to health care for all citizens of a country, 326

Society. An organized and interdependent group of individuals who live together in a specific geographical area and who interact more with each other than they do with outsiders; they cooperate for the attainment of common goals and share a common culture over time, 54

Sociological imagination. The recognition of the complex and interactive relationship between micro-level individual experiences and macro-level public issues, 8

Sociology. The scientific study of social life, social change, and the social causes and consequences of human behavior, 5

Status. A social position in society, 119

Stigma. Social disapproval that discredits a person's claim to a "normal" identity, 36

Strain theory. Contends that the opportunity or limitations embedded in the structures of society may contradict and undermine the goals and aspirations society encourages for its members, creating strains that lead to deviance, 147

Structural-functional theory. Assumes that all parts of the social structure (including groups, organizations, and institutions), the culture (values and beliefs), and social processes (social change or child-rearing) work together to make the whole society run smoothly and harmoniously, 30

Subculture. The culture of a meso-level subcommunity that distinguishes itself from the dominant culture of the larger society, 73

Subjugation. The subordination of one group to another that holds power and authority, 229

Symbolic interaction theory (also called social constructionism or interpretative theory). Sees humans as active agents who create shared meanings of symbols and events and then interact on the basis of those meanings, 29

Technology. The practical application of tools, skills, and knowledge to meet human needs and extend human abilities, 433

Terrorism. The planned use of random, unlawful (or illegal) violence or threat of violence against civilians to create (or raise) fear and intimidate citizens in order to advance the terrorist group's political or ideological goals, 158

Theories. Statements or explanations regarding how and why two or more facts are related to each other and the connections between these facts, 28

Totalitarian government. Any form of government that almost totally controls people's lives, 355

Transgender. Refers to those who challenge or change the gender assigned to them at birth, 250

Urbanization. The pattern of movement from rural areas to cities, 378

Variables. Concepts (ideas) that can vary in frequency of occurrence from one time, place, or person to another, 37

Victimless crimes. Acts (also called *public-order crimes*) committed by or between consenting adults, 152

War. Armed conflict occurring within, between, or among societies or groups, 365

Wealth. The worth of a person based on his or her financial holdings (e.g., stocks, bank accounts, and investment income) and property (e.g., homes and cars) minus debt, 187

White-collar (occupational) crime. The violation of law committed by an individual or group in the course of a legitimate, respected occupation or financial activity, 156

References

AAANativeArts. 2011. "Facts About Alaskan Natives." Retrieved April 19, 2011 (www.aaanativearts.com/alaskan-natives/index.html).

AAUW. 2016. "The Simple Truth About the Gender Pay Gap: Spring 2016." Retrieved May 30, 2016 (www.aauw.org/research/the-simple-truth-about-the-gender-pay-gap/).

Abadi, Ponta. 2013. "Kids' Toys: More Gendered Than Ever." *Ms. Magazine*, June 5. Retrieved January 16, 2014 (http://msmagazine.com/blog/2013/06/05/kids-toys-more-gendered-than-ever).

Abrams, Rachel. 2015. "Blue Bell Knew About Listeria Issues, F.D.A. Says." *New York Times*, May 7. Retrieved June 30, 2015 (www.nytimes.com/2015/05/08/business/blue-bell-knew-about-listeria-issues-fda-says.html?ref=topics).

Abu-Lughod, Janet L. 1991. *Changing Cities: Urban Sociology*. New York: HarperCollins.

Abu-Lughod, Janet L. 2001. *New York, Chicago, Los Angeles: America's Global Cities*. Minneapolis: University of Minnesota Press.

ACT. 2013. "National and State Scores." Retrieved September 12, 2014 (http://www.act.org/newsroom/data/2013).

Adams, Rebecca. 2016. "Proof Traditional Masculinity May Actually Be Dangerous." *Huffington Post*, February 22. Retrieved May 30, 2016 (www.huffingtonpost.com/entry/proof-traditional-masculinity-may-be-dangerous-us-55db7a17e4b04ae497040e07).

Addictionblog.org. 2011. "Why Do People Have Different Pain Tolerances?" July 2. Retrieved July 17, 2012 (http://drug.addictionblog.org/why-do-people-have-different-pain-tolerances/).

"African Undersea Cables." 2013. *Many Possibilities*. Retrieved February 13, 2014 (http://manypossibilities.net/african-undersea-cables).

Agius, Silvan. 2013. "Third Gender: A Step Toward Ending Intersex Discrimination." Retrieved January 16, 2014 (Spiegel.de/international/Europe/third-gender-option-in-germany-a-small-step-for-intersex-recognition-a-917650.html).

Aguirre, Jessica Camille. 2012. "Generic Drugs Make Dent in Global AIDS Pandemic." NPR, July 13. Retrieved July 3, 2013 (www.npr.org/blogs/health/2012/07/11/156612196/generic-drugs-make-dent-in-global-aids-pandemic).

Ahmad, Nehaluddin. 2009. "Sati Tradition—Widow Burning in India: A Socio-Legal Examination." *Web Journal of Current Legal Issues* 2. Retrieved April 7, 2011 (http://webjcli.ncl.ac.uk-/2009/issue2/almad2/html).

Ahuja, Masuma. 2013. "Teens Are Spending More Time Consuming Media, on Mobile Devices." *Washington Post*, March 13. Retrieved December 6, 2013 (http://articles.washingtonpost.com/2013-03-13/news/37675597_1_teens-cellphones-video-games).

Alarcon, Arthur L. and Paula M. Mitchell. 2011. "Executing the Will of the Voters? A Roadmap to Mend or End the California Legislature's Multi-Billion Dollar Death Penalty Debacle." *Loyola of Los Angeles Law Review* 44(June):S41.

Alatas, Syed Farid. 2006. "Ibn Khaldun and Contemporary Sociology." *International Sociology* 21(6):782–95.

Alexander, Dan 2015. "Bill Clinton Honors Paul Farmer, the Doctor Out to Save the World." *Forbes*, January 4. Retrieved July 1, 2015 (www.forbes.com/sites/randalllane/2013/10/03/this-guy-may-have-solved-the-health care-model-for-1-billion-people).

Alexander, Michelle. 2010. *The New Jim Crow: Mass Incarceration in the Age of Color Blindness*. New York: New Press.

Alexander, Michelle. 2011. "More Black Men Are in Prison Today Than Were Enslaved in 1850." *Huffington Post*, October 10. Retrieved April 15, 2012 (www.huffingtonpost.com/2011/10/12/michelle-alexan der-more-Black-men-are-in-prison-today-than-were-enslaved-in-1850_n_1007368.html).

Alpert, Emily. 2013. "More Americans Consider Themselves Multiracial." *Los Angeles Times*, June 13. Retrieved June 17, 2013 (www.latimes.com/news/local/la-me-multiracial-growth-20130613,0,6580186.story).

Alter, Charlotte. 2014. "Voter Turnout in Midterm Elections Hits 72 Year Low." *Time*, November 10. Retrieved January 27, 2016 (http://time.com/3576090/midterm-elections-turnout-world-war-two).

Altheide, David, Patricia A. Adler, Peter Adler, and Duane Altheide. 1978. "The Social Meanings of Employee Theft." P. 90 in *Crime at the Top*, edited by John M. Johnson and Jack D. Douglas. Philadelphia: Lippincott.

Amato, Paul R. 2000. "The Consequences of Divorce for Adults and Children." *Journal of Marriage and the Family* 62(November):1269–87.

Amato, Paul R. 2011. *Interpreting Divorce Rates, Marriage Rates, and Data on the Percentage of Children With Single Parents*. National Healthy Marriage Resource Center.

American Association of Medical Colleges. 2015. *2015 State Physician Workforce Data Book*. Retrieved March 14, 2017 (https://members.aamc.org/eweb/upload/2015StateData Book%20(revised).pdf).

American Civil Liberties Union. 2013. *The War on Marijuana in Black and White*. Retrieved June 5, 2013 (www.aclu.org/files/assets/aclu-thewaronmarijuana-rel2.pdf).

American Hospital Association. 2015. "Economic Contribution Often Overlooked." January 21. Retrieved July 2, 2015 (file:///C:/Users/Kathleen/Downloads/econcontribution.pdf).

American Medical Association. 2015. *Physician Characteristics and Distribution in the United States*. Washington, DC: Author.

American Sociological Association. 2009. *21st Century Careers With an Undergraduate Degree in Sociology*. Washington, DC: Author.

Amnesty International. 2012. "Death Penalty 2011: Alarming Levels of Executions in the Few Countries That Kill." March 27. Retrieved April 16, 2012 (www.amnesty.org/en/news/deasth-penalty-2011-alarming-level-executions-few-countries-kill-2012-03-27).

Amnesty International. 2014. "Death Penalty 2013: Small Number of Countries Trigger Global Spike in Executions." Retrieved April 25, 2014 (www.amnesty.org/en/news/death-penalty-2013-small-number-trigger-global-spike-executions-2014-03-27).

Amnesty International. 2016. "Private Prisons." Retrieved September 19, 2016 (www.aclu.org/issues/mass-incarceration/privatization-criminal-justice/private-prisons). ·

ANAD. 2015. "Eating Disorders Statistics." Retrieved September 6, 2015 (www.anad.org/get-information/about-eating-disorders/eating-disorders-statistics).

Anderson, Benedict. 2006. *Imagined Communities: Reflections on the Origin and Spread of Nationalism*, rev. ed. London: Verso.

Anderson, D. Mark and Daniel I. Rees. 2013. "The Legalization of Recreational Marijuana: How Likely is the Worst-Case Scenario?" *Journal of Policy Analysis and Management*. Retrieved October 17, 2013 (http://dmarkanderson.com/Point_Counterpoint_07_31_13_v5.pdf).

Anderson, David A. and Mykol Hamilton. 2005. "Gender Role Stereotyping of Parents in Children's Picture Books: The Invisible Father." *Sex Roles: A Journal of Research* 52(3/4):145.

Anderson, Elijah. 2000. *Code of the Street: Decency, Violence, and the Moral Life of the Inner City*. New York: Norton.

Anderson, Margaret and Patricia Hill Collins. 2016. *Race Class and Gender: An Anthology*, 4th ed. Belmont, CA: Wadsworth.

Anderson, Monica. 2015. "A Rising Share of the U.S. Black Population Is Foreign Born." Pew Research Center, April 9. Retrieved June 18, 2015 (www.pewsocialtrends.org/2015/04/09/a-rising-share-of-the-u-s-black-population-is-foreign-born).

Angier, Natalie. 2013. "The Changing American Family." *New York Times*, November 25. Retrieved January 17, 2014 (www.nytimes.com/2013/11/26/health/families.html?_r=0).

Antoun, Richard T. 2008. *Understanding Fundamentalism: Christian, Islamic, and Jewish Movements*, 2nd ed. Walnut Creek, CA: AltaMira.

Archer, Dale. 2013. "Could America's Wealth Gap Lead to a Revolt?" *Forbes*, September 4. Retrieved January 4, 2014 (www.forbes.com/sites/dalearcher/2013/09/04/could-americas-wealth-gap-lead-to-a-revolt).

Armstrong, Karen. 2000. *The Battle for God*. New York: Knopf.

Arnold, David O., ed. 1970. *The Sociology of Subcultures*. Berkeley, CA: Glendessary.

Arrighi, Barbara A. 2000. *Understanding Inequality: The Intersection of Race, Ethnicity, Class, and Gender*. Lanham, MD: Rowman & Littlefield.

Aseltine, Robert H., Jr. 1995. "A Reconsideration of Parental and Peer Influences on Adolescent Deviance." *Journal of Health and Social Behavior* 36(2):103–21.

Ashley, David and David Michael Orenstein. 2009. *Sociological Theory*, 7th ed. Boston: Allyn & Bacon.

Aslan, Reza. 2011. *No God but God: The Origins, Evolution, and Future of Islam*, updated ed. New York: Random House.

"Assisted Suicide: Over My Dead Body." 2012. *The Economist*, October 20. Retrieved March 13, 2017 (http://www.economist.com/news/international/21564830-helping-terminally-ill-die-once-taboo-gaining-acceptance).

Association of American Colleges and Universities and Hart Research Associates. 2013. *It Takes More Than a Major: Employer Priorities for College Learning and Student Success*. Washington, DC: Author. Retrieved May 22, 2013 (www.aacu.org/leap/documents/2013_EmployerSurvey.pdf).

Aulette, Judy Root. 2010. *Changing American Families*. Boston: Allyn & Bacon.

Azize, Pary M., Ruth Endacott, Allegra Cattani, and Ann Humphreys. 2013. "Cultural Responses to Pain in UK Children of Primary School Age: A Mixed-Methods Study." *Nursing and Health Sciences* 16(2): 1–8.

Babbie, Earl. 2014. *The Basics of Social Research*, 6th ed. Belmont, CA: Thomsen/Wadsworth.

BabyCenter. 2016. "Popular Baby Names for 2016." Retrieved August 18, 2016 (http://www.babycenter.com/popularBaby Names.htm?year=2016).

Baker, Peter. 2015. "Obama Extends Options for Retaliating Against Foreign Hackers." *New York Times*, April 1. Retrieved June 8, 2015 (www.nytimes.com/2015/04/02/us/politics/us-expands-foreign-cyberattack-retaliation-options.html).

Bales, Kevin. 2000. *New Slavery: A Reference Handbook*, 2nd ed. Santa Barbara, CA: ABC-CLIO.

Bales, Kevin. 2007. *Ending Slavery: How We Free Today's Slaves*. Berkeley: University of California Press.

Bales, Kevin. 2012. *Disposable People: New Slavery in the Global Economy*, 3rd ed. Berkeley: University of California Press.

Bales, Kevin. 2015. "New Slavery in the Global Economy." Center for Civil and Human Rights. Retrieved September 13, 2015 (Humanrights.nd.edu/events/2015/11/18/36216-kevin-bales-new-slavery-in-the-global-economy).

Bales, Kevin and Zoe Trodd. 2008. *To Plead Our Own Cause: Personal Stories by Today's Slaves*. Ithaca, NY: Cornell University Press.

Ball, James. 2013. "Women 40% More Likely Than Men to Develop Mental Illness, Study Finds." *The Guardian*, May 22. Retrieved September 6, 2015 (www.theguardian.com/society/2013/may/22/women-men-mental-illness-study).

Ballantine, Jeanne H., Floyd M. Hammack, and Jenny Stuber. 2017. *The Sociology of Education: A Systematic Analysis*, 8th ed. Lanham, MD: Rowman and Littlefield.

Barber, Benjamin R. 2006. "The Uncertainty of Digital Politics: Democracy's Relationship With Information Technology." Pp. 61–69 in *Globalization: The Transformation of Social Worlds*, edited by D. Stanley Eitzen and Maxine Baca Zinn. Belmont, CA: Wadsworth.

Barrera, Juliana. 2013. "Asian Immigrants Surpass Hispanics as Biggest Immigrant Wave to U.S." *Huffington Post* Latino Voices, June 15. Retrieved March 17, 2014 (www.huffingtonpost.com/2013/06/15/asian-immigrants-surpass-hispanics_n_3446441html).

Basso, Keith H. 1996. *Wisdom Sits in Places: Landscape and Language Among the Western Apache*. Albuquerque: University of New Mexico Press.

Battelle. 2013. "2014 Global R&D Funding Forecast." December. Retrieved February 24, 2014 (www.battelle.org/docs/tpp/2014_global_rd_funding_forecast.pdf).

Beaubien, Jason. 2011. "In Haiti, Cell Phones Serve as Debit Cards." NPR, January 30. Retrieved June 8, 2013 (www.npr.org/2011/01/30/133305663/in-haiti-cell-phones-serve-as-debit-cards).

Beaver, David. 2012. "Sally Ride: Beauty of the Earth Is Only Half of It." Overview Institute. Retrieved June 29, 2013 (www.overviewinstitute.org/featured-articles/45-sally-ride-beauty-of-the-earth-is-only-half-of-it).

Beck, Allen, Marcus Berzofsky, Rachel Caspar, and Christopher Krebs 2014. "Sexual Victimization in Prisons and Jails Reported by Inmates, 2011–12 Update." Bureau of Justice Statistics, December 9. Retrieved June 8, 2015 (www.bjs.gov/index.cfm?ty=pbdetail&iid=4654).

Beckwith, Carol. 1993. *Nomads of Niger*. New York: Harry N. Abrams.

Beeman, Angie. 2015. "Walk the Walk but Don't Talk the Talk: The Strategic Use of Color-Blind Ideology in an Interracial Social Movement Organization." *Sociological Forum* 30(1):127–147.

Belding, Theodore C. 2004. "Nobility and Stupidity: Modeling the Evolution of Class Endogamy." Retrieved August 7, 2008 (http://arxiv.org/abs/nlin.AO/0405048).

Bell, Daniel. 1973. *The Coming of Post-Industrial Society: A Venture in Social Forecasting*. New York: Basic Books.

Bell, Daniel. 1989. "The Third Technological Revolution and Its Possible Socioeconomic Consequences." *Dissent* 36(2):164–176.

Bell, Michael Mayerfeld. 2012. *An Invitation to Environmental Sociology*, 4th ed. Thousand Oaks, CA: Sage/Pine Forge.

Bennis, Warren G., Kenneth D. Benne, and Robert Chin. 1985. *The Planning of Change*, 4th ed. New York: Holt, Rinehart and Winston.

Benokraitis, Nijole V. 2015. *Marriages and Families: Changes, Choices, and Constraints—2010 Census Update*, 8th ed. Englewood Cliffs, NJ: Prentice Hall.

Beran, Tanya. 2012. "Bullying: What Are the Differences Between Boys and Girls?" *Education.com*, January 24. Retrieved January 17, 2014 (www.education.com/reference/article/Ref_Bullying_Differences).

Berger, Michael L. 1979. *The Devil Wagon in God's Country: The Automobile and Social Change in Rural America, 1893–1929*. Hamden, CT: Archon.

Berger, Peter L. and Thomas Luckmann. 1966. *The Social Construction of Reality*. Garden City, NY: Doubleday.

Bergthaler, Wolfgang, Kenneth Kang, Yan Liu, and Dermot Monaghan. 2015. "Tackling Small and Medium Sized Enterprise Problem Loans in Europe." *International Monetary Fund*, March. Retrieved September 11, 2015 (www.imf.org/external/pubs/ft/sdn/2015/sdn1504.pdf).

Berk, Richard A. 1974. *Collective Behavior*. Dubuque, IA: Brown.

Berman, Bruce J. 2011. "Of Magic, Invisible Hands and Elfs: How Not to Study Ethnicity in Africa." Presented at the ECAS4, Uppsala, Sweden, June 14–18.

Berman, Jillian. 2015. "Soon, Not Even 1 Percent of Fortune 500 Companies Will Have Black CEOs." *Huffington Post*, January 29. Retrieved June 3, 2015 (www.huffingtonpost.com/2015/01/29/black-ceos-fortune-500_n_6572074.html).

Bernhardt, Annette, Ruth Milkman, Nik Theodore, Douglas Heckathorn, Mirabai Auer, James DeFilippis, Ana Luz González, Victor Narro, Jason Perelshteyn, Diana Polson, and Michael Spiller. 2009. *Broken Laws, Unprotected Workers*. Retrieved June 3, 2013 (http://labor.ucla.edu/publications/reports/brokenlaws.pdf).

Berrey, Ellen. 2013. "Breaking Glass Ceilings, Ignoring Dirty Floors: The Culture and Class Bias of Diversity Management." *American Behavioral Scientist*, October 11. Retrieved January 17, 2014 (http://abs.sagepub.com/content/eas rly/2013/10/11/0002764213503333.abstract).

Berry, Brian J. L. and John Kasarda. 1977. *Contemporary Urban Ecology*. New York: Macmillan.

Bettie, Julie. 2003. *Women Without Class: Girls, Race, and Identity*. Berkeley: University of California Press.

Billig, Michael. 1995. *Banal Nationalism*. Thousand Oaks, CA: Sage.

Blau, Peter M. 1956. *Bureaucracy in Modern Society*. New York: Random House.

Blau, Peter M. 1964. *Exchange and Power in Social Life*. New York: John Wiley.

Blau, Peter and Otis Dudley Duncan. 1967. *The American Occupational Structure*. New York: John Wiley.

Blee, Kathleen M. 2008. "White Supremacy as Extreme Deviance." Pp. 108–17 in *Extreme Deviance*, edited by Erich Goode and D. Angus Vail. Thousand Oaks, CA: Pine Forge.

Bloom, Barbara, Lindsey I. Jones, and Gulnur Freeman. 2013. "Summary Health Statistics for U.S. Children: National Health Interview Survey, 2012." *Vital and Health Statistics* 10(258). Retrieved February 6, 2015 (http://www.cdc.gov/nchs/data/series/sr_10/sr10_258.pdf).

Blumer, Herbert. 1986. *Symbolic Interactionism: Perspective and Method*. Berkeley: University of California Press.

"Body Parts for Sale." 2008. ABC News, May 6. Retrieved January 11, 2010 (blogs.abcnews.com/scienceandsociety/2008/05/body-parts-for.html).

Boger, John Charles and Gary Orfield. 2009. *School Resegregation: Must the South Turn Back?* Chapel Hill: University of North Carolina Press.

Bonacich, Edna. 1972. "A Theory of Ethnic Antagonism: The Split Labor Market." *American Sociological Review* 37(October):547–59.

Bonacich, Edna. 1976. "Advanced Capitalism and Black–White Race Relations in the United States: A Split Labor Market Interpretation." *American Sociological Review* 41(February):34–51.

Bond, Jeff. 2010. "The Anthropology of Garbage." *Columns*, March. Retrieved August 15, 2013 (www.washington.edu/alumni/columns/march10/garbage.html).

Bonilla-Silva, Eduardo. 2003. *Racism Without Racists: Color-Blind Racism and the Persistence of Racial Inequality in the United States*. Berkeley: University of California Press.

Bonilla-Silva, Eduardo. 2009. *Racism Without Racists: Color-Blind Racism and the Persistence of Racial Inequality in America*, 3rd ed. Lanham, MD: Rowman & Littlefield.

Bonilla-Silva, Eduardo and David G. Embrick. 2005. "Black, Honorary White, White: The Future of Race in the United States?" In *Negotiating the Color Line: Doing Race in the Color-Blind Era and Implications for Racial Justice*, edited by David Brunsma and Lynne Rienner. Boulder, CO: Lynne Rienner.

Borenstein, Seth. 2013. "U.S. Scientists Report Big Jump in Heat-Trapping CO2." Phys.org, March 5. Retrieved June 20, 2013 (phys.org/news/2013-03-scientists-big-heat-trapping-co2.html).

Borg, Marcus. 2001. *Reading the Bible Again for the First Time*. New York: HarperCollins.

Bosomworth, Danyl. 2015. "Statistics on Mobile Usage and Adoption Inform Your Mobile Marketing Strategy." *Smart Insights*, July 2015. Retrieved August 31, 2015 (www.smartinsights.com/mobile-marketing-analytics/mobile-marketing-statistics).

Bottomore, Tom. 1979. *Political Sociology*. New York: Harper & Row.

Bourdieu, Pierre and Jean-Claude Passeron. 1977. *Reproduction in Education, Society and Culture*. London: Sage.

Bowles, Samuel and Herbert Gintis. 2002. "Schooling in Capitalist America Revisited." *Sociology of Education* 75(1):1–18.

Bozelko, Chandra. 2015. "Why We Let Prison Rape Go On." *New York Times*, April 17. Retrieved June 8, 2015 (www.nytimes.com/2015/04/18/opinion/why-we-let-prison-rape-go-on.html).

Brandon, Mark E. 2005. "War and American Constitutional Order." In *The Constitution in Wartime: Beyond Alarmism and Complacency*, edited by Mark Tushner. Durham, NC: Duke University Press.

Brecher, Jeremy, Tim Costello, and Brendan Smith. 2012. "Globalization and Social Movements." Pp. 272–90 in *Globalization: The Transformation of Social Worlds*, 3rd ed., edited by D. Stanley Eitzen and Maxine Baca Zinn. Belmont, CA: Wadsworth.

Brettell, Caroline B. and Carolyn F. Sargent. 2012. *Gender in Cross-Cultural Perspective*, 6th ed. Englewood Cliffs, NJ: Prentice Hall.

Brill, Steven. 2013. "Bitter Pill: Why Medical Bills Are Killing Us." *Time*, March 4. Retrieved July 15, 2013 (www.time.com/time/covers/0,16641,20130304,00.html).

Briner, Raphaël. 2015. "The New 2015 Top 500 NGOs Is Out." *Global Journal*, February 14. Retrieved January 25, 2016 (www.theglobaljournal.net/article/view/1171).

Brinkerhoff, David B., Lynn K. White, Suzanne T. Ortega, and Rose Weitz. 2014. *Essentials of Sociology*, 9th ed. New York: Cengage Learning.

Brookover, Wilbur B. and Edsel L. Erickson. 1975. *Sociology of Education*. Homewood, IL: Dorsey.

Broom, Leonard and Philip Selznick. 1963. *Sociology: A Text With Adapted Readings*, 3rd ed. New York: Harper & Row.

Brown, Emma. 2015. "In 23 States, Richer School Districts Get More Local Funding Than Poor Districts." *Washington Post*, March 2. Retrieved June 23, 2015 (www.washingtonpost.com/news/local/wp/2015/03/12/in-23-states-richer-school-districts-get-more-local-funding-than-poorer-districts).

Brulle, Robert J. 2014. "Institutionalizing Delay: Foundation Funding and the Creation of U.S. Climate Change Counter-Movement Organizations." *Climactic Change* 122(4):681–94.

Bruner, Jerome. 1996. *The Culture of Education*. Cambridge, MA: Harvard University Press.

Brunn, Stanley D., Maureen Hays-Mitchell, and Donald J. Zeigler. 2011. *Cities of the World: World Regional Urban Development*, 4th ed. Lanham, MD: Rowman and Littlefield.

Brunn, Stanley D., Jack F. Williams, and Donald J. Zeigler. 2003. *Cities of the World: World Regional Urban Development*, 3rd ed. Lanham, MD: Rowman & Littlefield.

Brunsma, David. 2006. *Mixed Messages: Doing Race in the Color-Blind Era*. Boulder, CO; Lynne Rienner.

Brym, Robert J. and John Lie. 2007. *Sociology: Your Compass for a New World*, 3rd ed. Belmont, CA: Wadsworth.

Buchmann, Claudia, Dennis J. Condron, and Vincent J. Roscigno 2010. "Shadow Education, American Style: Test Preparation, the SAT and College Enrollment." *Social Forces* 89(2): 435–61.

Burn, Shawn Meghan. 2011. *Women Across Cultures: A Global Perspective*, 3rd ed. New York: McGraw-Hill.

BushTV. 2010. "Kowanyama Keeping Culture Alive." Retrieved September 12, 2014 (http://www.youtube.com/watch?v=QCcBaVEUFlo).

Business Insider. 2012. "Hundreds of Suicides in India Linked to Microfinance Organizations." Retrieved January 16, 2014 (www.businessinsider.com/hundreds-of-suicides-in-India-linked-to-microfinance-organizations-2012-2).

Byanyima, Winnie. 2015. "Richest 1% Will Own More Than All The Rest by 2016." Oxfam International, January 19. Retrieved January 29, 2015 (www.oxfam.org/en/pressroom/pressreleases/2015-01-19/richest-1-will-own-more-all-rest-2016).

Cahalan, Margaret, Laura Perna, Mika Yamashita, Roman Ruiz, and Khadish Franklin. 2016. "Indicators of Higher Education Equity in the United States." Pell Institute for the Study of Opportunity in Higher Education, Council for Opportunity in Education. Retrieved November 17, 2015 (www.pellinstitute.org/downloads/publications-Indicators_of_Higher_Education_Equity_in_the_US_45_Year_Trend_Report.pdf).

Cahill, Spencer E., Kent Sandstrom, and Carissa Froyum. 2013. *Inside Social Life*, 7th ed. New York: Oxford University Press.

Caldwell, John C. 1982. *Theory of Fertility Decline*. New York: Academic Press.

Calhoun, Craig, ed. 2007. *Sociology in America: A History*. Chicago: University of Chicago Press.

Cambodian Genocide Program. 2015. "The CGP, 1994–2015." Yale University. Retrieved January 28, 2016 (www.yale.edu/cgp).

Cameron, Charley. 2015. "10 Solutions to Tackle the California Drought." *Environmental Testing Lab*. Retrieved September 11, 2015 (inhabitat.com/possible-solutions-to-tackle-the-california-drought).

Canadian Health Care. 2010. "Introduction." Retrieved May 14, 2011 (www.canadian-healthcare.org).

Cancian, Francesca M. 1992. "Feminist Science: Methodologies That Challenge Inequality." *Gender and Society* 6(4):623–42.

Carson, E. Ann and William J. Sabol. 2012. "Prisoners in 2011." Bureau of Justice Statistics, December. Retrieved June 2, 2013 (www.bjs.gov/content/pub/pdf/p11.pdf).

Casasanto, Daniel. 2008. "Who's Afraid of the Big Bad Whorf? Crosslinguistic Differences in Temporal Language and Thought." *Language Learning* 58(1):63–79.

Casey, Timothy and Laurie Maldonado. 2012. "Worst Off—Single-Parent Families in the United States: A Cross-National Comparison of Single Parenthood in the U.S. and Sixteen Other High-Income Countries." Women's Legal Defense and Education Fund, December. Retrieved October 4, 2014 (www.legalmomentum.org/sites/default/files/reports/worst-off-single-parent.pdf).

Cashmore, Ellis and Barry Troyna. 1990. *Introduction to Race Relations*. London: Routledge.

Castiello, Umberto, Cristina Becchio, Stefania Zoia, Cristian Nelini, Luisa Sartori, Laura Blason, Giuseppina D'Ottavio, Maria Bulgheroni, and Vittorio Gallese. 2010. "Wired to Be Social: The Ontogeny of Human Interaction." *PLoS ONE* 5(10). Retrieved October 19, 2010 (www.plosone.org/article/info%3Adoi%2F10.1371%2Fjournal.pone.0013199).

Catalyst. 2014. "Women CEOs of the Fortune 1000." Equity in Business Leadership, August 27. Retrieved September 2, 2014 (http://www.catalyst.org/knowledge/women-ceos-fortune-1000).

Catalyst. 2016. "Women CEOs of the S & P 500." Retrieved April 7, 2016 (www.catalyst.org/knowledge/women-ceos-sp-500).

CBS News. 2014. "Texas Hospital Removes Brain-Dead Pregnant Woman Marlise Munoz From Life Support." January 26. Retrieved August 26, 2016 (www.cbsnews.com/news/texas-hospital-to-remove-brain-dead-pregnant-woman-marlise-munoz-from-life-support).

Center for Constitutional Rights. 2013. "Report: Torture and Cruel, Inhuman, and Degrading Treatment of Prisoners at Guantanamo Bay." March 19. Retrieved April 25, 2014 (http://ccrjustice.org/learn-more/reports:-torture-and-cruel,-inhuman,-and-degrading-treatment-prisoners-quantanamo).

Center for Responsive Politics. 2012a. "Overview: Stats at a Glance." Retrieved June 7, 2013 (www.opensecrets.org/overview/index.php?cycle =2012&type=A&display=A).

Center for Responsive Politics. 2012b. "2012 Presidential Race." Retrieved June 7, 2013 (www.opensecrets.org/pres12/#out).

Center for Responsive Politics. 2015. "2014 Election Overview." *Open Secrets*, April 6. Retrieved June 11, 2015 (www.opensecrets.org/overview/index.php?cycle=2014&type=A&display=A).

Centers for Disease Control and Prevention. 2013. "National Marriage and Divorce Rate Trends." Retrieved February 26, 2014 (www.cdc.gov/nchs/nvss/marriage_divorce_tables.htm).

Centers for Disease Control and Prevention. 2015a. "Births—Method of Delivery" January 22. Retrieved July 1, 2015 (www.cdc.gov/nchs/fastats/delivery.htm)

Centers for Disease Control and Prevention 2015b. *Epidemiology and Prevention of Vaccine-Preventable Diseases*, 13th ed. Retrieved March 14, 2017 (https://www.cdc.gov/vaccines/pubs/pinkbook/downloads/appendices/e/reported-cases.pdf).

Centers for Disease Control and Prevention. 2015c. "Health Expenditures." April 29. Retrieved July 2, 2015 (www.cdc.gov/nchs/fastats/health-expenditures.htm).

Centers for Disease Control and Prevention. 2015d. "Life Expectancy." April 29. Retrieved August 31, 2015 (www.cdc.gov/nchs/fastats/life-expectancy.htm).

Centers for Disease Control and Prevention. 2016a. "Areas With Active Mosquito-Borne Transmission of Zika Virus." January 22. Retrieved May 31, 2016 (www.cdc.gov/zika/geo).

Centers for Disease Control and Prevention. 2016b. "Alcohol and Public Health: Frequently Asked Questions." (https://www.cdc.gov/alcohol/faqs.htm).

Centers for Medicare and Medicaid Services. 2014. "National Health Expenditure Projections 2012–2022." Retrieved March 10, 2014 (www.cms.gov/Research-Statistics-Data-and-Systems/Statistics-Trends-and-Reports/NationalHealthExpendData/downloads/proj2012.pdf).

Century Foundation. 2014. "What Can We Learn From States That Ban Affirmative Action?" Retrieved June 18, 2015 (www.tcf.org/work/education/detail/what-can-we-learn-from-states-that-ban-affirmative-action).

Chamberlain, Houston Stewart. [1899] 1911. *The Foundations of the Nineteenth Century*, translated by John Lees. New York: John Lane.

Chambliss, William J. 1973. "The Saints and the Roughnecks." *Society* 11(December):24–31.

Charities Aid Foundation. 2012. "World Giving Index 2012." December. Retrieved June 15, 2013 (www.cafonline.org/PDF/WorldGivingIndex2012WEB.pdf).

Charles, Camille Z., Vincent J. Roscigno, and Kimberly C. Torres. 2007. "Racial Inequality and College Attendance: The Mediating Role of Parental Investments." *Social Science Research* 36(1):329–52.

Charon, Joel. 2010. *Symbolic Interactionism: An Introduction, an Interpretation, an Integration*, 10th ed. Englewood Cliffs, NJ: Prentice Hall.

Chase, Cheryl. 2000. "Genital Surgery on Children Below the Age of Consent: Intersex Genital Mutilation." In *Psychological Perspectives on Human Sexuality*, edited by Lenore Szuchman and Frank Muscarella. New York: Wiley.

Chase-Dunn, Christopher and E. N. Anderson. 2006. *The Historical Evolution of World-Systems*. New York: Palgrave Macmillan.

Cheng, Cecilia. 2005. "Processes Underlying Gender-Role Flexibility: Do Androgynous Individuals Know More or Know How to Cope?" *Journal of Personality* 73(3):645–73.

Cheng, Siwei and Yu Xie. 2013. "Structural Effect of Size on Interracial Friendship." *Proceedings of the National Academy of Sciences*, April 15.

Cherlin, Andrew. 1978. "Remarriage as an Incomplete Institution." *American Journal of Sociology* 84(3):634–50.

Cherlin, Andrew J. 2010. *The Marriage-Go-Round: The State of Marriage and the Family in America Today*. New York: Random House.

Cherry, Kendra. 2012. "Understanding Body Language." *About.com Psychology*. Retrieved September 25, 2012 (http://psychology.about.com/od/nonverbalcommunication/ss/understanding-body-language.htm).

Chetty, Raj and Nathaniel Hendren. 2015. "Executive Summary: The Impacts of Neighborhoods on Intergenerational Mobility Childhood Exposure Effects and County-Level Estimates." April. Retrieved June 25, 2015 (www.equality-of-opportunity.org/images/nbhds_exec_summary.pdf).

Chetty, Raj, Nathaniel Hendren, Patrick Kline, and Emmanuel Saez. 2014. "Where Is the Land of Opportunity? The Geography of Intergenerational Mobility in the United States." The Equality of Opportunity Project, June. Retrieved June 11, 2015 (www.equality-of-opportunity.org/images/mobility_geo.pdf).

Chetty, Raj, Michael Stepner, Sarah Abraham, Shelby Lin, Benjamin Scuderi, Nicholas Turner, Augustin Bergeron, and David Cutler. 2016. "The Association Between Income and Life Expectancy in the United States, 2001–2014." Journal of the American Medical Association. Retrieved April 11, 2016 (http://jama.jamanetwork.com/article.aspx?articleid=2513561).

Cheung, Cecilia Sin-Sze and Eva M. Pomerantz. 2012. "Why Does Parents' Involvement Enhance Children's Achievement? The Role of Parent-Oriented Motivation." Journal of Educational Psychology 14(3):820–32.

ChildStats.gov. 2013. "America's Children: Key National Indicators of Well-Being, 2013." Retrieved February 25, 2014 (www.childstats.gov/americaschildren/famsoc2.asp).

ChildStats.gov. 2015. "America's Children: Key National Indicators of Well-Being, 2015." Retrieved September 9, 2015 (www.childstats.gov/americaschildren/family1.asp).

Child Trends. 2013. "Child Support Receipt." Retrieved February 19, 2014 (www.childtrends.org/wp-content/uploads/212/07/84_Child_Support_Receipt.pdf).

Child Trends Data Bank. 2015. "Family Structure." December. Retrieved January 10, 2015 (www.childtrends.org/?indicators=family-structure).

Children's Defense Fund. 2013. "Cradle to Prison Pipeline Campaign." Retrieved January 15, 2014 (www.childrensdefense.org/programs-campaigns/cradle-to-prison-pipeline).

Churchill, Winston. 2009. Churchill by Himself: The Definitive Collection of Quotations, edited by Richard Langworth. Jackson, TN: Public Affairs.

Cisco. 2014. "Cisco Visual Networking Index: Global Mobile Data Traffic Forecast Update, 2013." Retrieved May 10, 2014 (www.cisco.com/c/en/us/solutions/collateral/service-provider/visual-networking-index-vni/white_paper_c11-520862.html).

Clark, Lara, Dylan B. Millet, and Julian D. Marshall. 2014. "National Patterns in Environmental Injustice and Inequality: Outdoor NO_2 Air Pollution in the United States." PLOS One 9(4). Retrieved July 6, 2015 (www.plosone.org/article/fetchObject.action?uri=info:doi/10.1371/journal.pone.0094431&representation=PDF).

Clarke, Ronald R., ed. 1997. Situational Crime Prevention: Successful Case Studies, 2nd ed. New York: Harrow and Heston.

Clausen, John A. 1986. The Life Course: A Sociological Perspective. Englewood Cliffs, NJ: Prentice Hall.

Clement, Scott. 2015. "Do Cubans Like the Castros?" Washington Post, April 9. Retrieved January 28, 2016 (www.washingtonpost.com/news/worldviews/wp/2015/04/09/do-cubans-like-the-castros).

Clymer, Floyd. 1953. Those Wonderful Old Automobiles. New York: Bonanza.

CNBC. 2010. "Mob Money: An American Greed." July 7. Retrieved February 8, 2013 (www.cnbc.com/id/37593299/mob_money).

Cockerham, William C. 2015. Medical Sociology, 12th ed. Englewood Cliffs, NJ: Prentice Hall.

Coghlan, Andy and Debora MacKenzie. 2011. "Revealed—The Capitalist Network That Runs the World." NewScientist. Retrieved June 23, 2013 (www.newscientist.com/article/mg21228354.500-revealed—the-capitalist-network-that-runs-the-world.html).

Cohen, Patricia. 2016. "Wealth Inequality Rising Fast, Oxfam Says, Faulting Tax Havens." New York Times, January 18. Retrieved February 15, 2016 (http://nyti.ms/1JVJKdp).

Cohn, D'Vera. 2015. "How Many Same-Sex Married Couples in the U.S.? Maybe 170,000." Pew Research Center, June 24. Retrieved September 9, 2015 (www.pewresearch.org/fact-tank/2015/06/24/how-many-same-sex-married-couples-in-the-u-s-maybe-170000).

Cohn, D'Vera, Paul Taylor, Mark Hugo Lopez, Catherine A. Gallagher, Kim Parker and Kevin T. Maass. 2013. "Gun Homicide Rate Down 49% Since 1993 Peak; Public Unaware." Pew Research Social & Demographic Trends, May 7. Retrieved June 1, 2013 (www.pewsocialtrends.org/2013/05/07/gun-homicide-rate-down-49-since-1993-peak-public-unaware).

Coleman, James S. 1968. "The Concept of Equality of Educational Opportunity." Harvard Education Review 38(Winter):7–22.

Coleman, James S. 1975. "What Is Meant By 'An Equal Educational Opportunity'?" Oxford Review of Education 1(1):27–29.

Coleman, James S. 1990. Equality and Achievement in Education. Boulder, CO: Westview.

Coleman, James William. 2006. The Criminal Elite: Understanding White Collar Crime, 6th ed. New York: Worth.

Coleman-Jensen, Alisha, Christian Gregory, and Anita Singh. 2014. "Household Food Security in the United States in 2013." ERR-173, U.S. Department of Agriculture, Economic Research Service, September.

College Board. 2013. "SAT Total Group Profile Report." Retrieved May 16, 2014 (http://media.collegeboard.com/digitalServices/pdf/research/2013/TotalGroup-2013.pdf).

Collins, Patricia Hill. 2005. Black Sexual Politics: African Americans, Gender and the New Racism. New York: Routledge.

Collins, Patricia Hill. 2008. Black Feminist Thought: Knowledge, Consciousness, and the Politics of Empowerment. New York: Routledge.

Collins, Randall. 1971. "A Conflict Theory of Sexual Stratification." Social Problems 19(Summer):2–21.

Collins, Randall. 2004. "Conflict Theory of Educational Stratification." American Sociological Review 36:47–54.

Commonwealth Fund. 2015a. "Mirror, Mirror on the Wall, 2014 Update: How the U.S. Health Care System Compares Internationally." Retrieved April 21, 2016 (www.commonwealthfund.org/publications/fund-reports/2014/jun/mirror-mirror).

Commonwealth Fund. 2015b. "U.S. Health Care From a Global Perspective: Spending, Use of Services, Prices, and Health in 13 Countries." Retrieved April 21, 2016 (www

.commonwealthfund.org/publications/issue-briefs/2015/oct/us-health-care-from-a-global-perspective).

ComScore. 2010. "Social Networking Sites Reach a Higher Percentage of Women Than Men Worldwide." July 28. Retrieved May 25, 2012 (www.comscore.com/Press_Events/Press_Releases/2010/7/Social_Networking_Sites_REach_a-Higher_Percentage_of_Women_than_Men_).

Comte, Auguste. [1855] 2003. *The Positive Philosophy of Auguste Comte*, freely translated and condensed by Harriet Martineau. Whitefish, MO: Kessinger.

Conley, Dalton. 2014. "Recognizing When Kids Benefit From Their Parents' Divorce." *The Atlantic*, April 16. Retrieved January 15, 2016 (www.theatlantic.com/health/archive/2014/04/recognizing-when-kids-benefit-from-their-parents-divorce/284589).

Conrad, Peter. 2007. *The Medicalization of Society: On the Transformation of Human Conditions Into Treatable Disorders*. Baltimore, MD: Johns Hopkins University Press.

Cook, Karen S., Jodi O'Brien, and Peter Kollock. 1990. "Exchange Theory: A Blueprint for Structure and Process." Pp. 158–81 in *Frontiers of Social Theory: The New Syntheses*, edited by George Ritzer. New York: Columbia University Press.

Cook Political Report. 2016. "2016 National Popular Vote Tracker." Retrieved December 15, 2016 (http://cookpolitical.com/story/10174).

Cooke, Jennifer G. 2012. "Polio in Nigeria: The Race to Eradication." Center for Strategic and International Studies, February 10. Retrieved July 16, 2012 (http://csis.org/publication/polio-nigeria).

Cooley, Charles Horton. [1909] 1983. *Social Organization: A Study of the Larger Mind*. New York: Schocken Books.

Coontz, Stephanie. 2011. "What Is the 'Traditional American Family'? Interview With Stephanie Coontz." *The Mother Company*, November 22. Retrieved May 25, 2012 (www.themotherco.com/2011/1/what-is-the-traditional-family).

Coontz, Stephanie. 2016. *The Way We Never Were: American Families and the Nostalgia Trap*, rev. ed. New York: Basic Books.

Copp, Jennifer E., Peggy C. Giordano, Monica A. Longmore, and Wendy D. Manning. 2013. "Stay/Leave Decision-Making in Non-Violent and Violent Dating Relationships." 2013 Working Paper Series. Center for Family and Demographic Research. Retrieved January 17, 2014 (www.bgsu.edu/organizations.cfdr).

Coser, Lewis A. 1956. *The Functions of Social Conflict*. New York: Free Press.

Council on Foreign Relations. 2014. "NAFTA's Economic Impact." Retrieved February 23, 2014 (www.cfr.org/trade/naftas-economic-impact/p15790).

Council on Foreign Relations. 2016. "The Group of Seven (G7)." Retrieved January 29, 2016 (www.cfr.org/international-organizations-and-alliances/group-seven-g7/p32957).

Council of Graduate Schools. 2014. "Doctoral Degrees by Field and Gender, 2012." Retrieved May 11, 2014 (www.aei-ideas.org/2013/09/women-earned-majority-of-doctoral-degrees-in-2012-for-4th-straight-year-and-outnumber-men-in-grad-school-141).

Cousteau, Jacques-Yves. 2008. "The Great Ocean Adventure." Lecture at Hanover College, January 15.

Covert, Bryce. 2014. "Getting More Women Into Japan's Workforce Could Grow Its Economy by 13 Percent." *Think Progress*, May 7. Retrieved September 6, 2015 (thinkprogress.org/economy/2014/05/07/3435262/japan-women-gdp).

Cowen, Nick and Nigel Williams. 2012. "Comparisons of Crime in OECD Countries." *Civitas Crime*. Retrieved May 2, 2013 (www.civitas.org.uk/crime/crime_stats_oecdjan2012.pdf).

Cox, Wendell. 2016. "Largest Cities in the World: 2016." Demographia World Urban Areas, April 16. Retrieved May 30, 2016 (www.newgeography.com/content/005219-largest-cities-world-2016).

Crary, David and Denise Lavoie. 2013. "As Boston Buries Its Dead, More Evidence Gathered." AP, April 23. Retrieved August 23, 2014 (http://bigstory.ap.org/article/more-details-sought-mute-boston-bomb-suspect).

Crosby, Faye J. 2004. *Affirmative Action Is Dead; Long Live Affirmative Action*. New Haven, CT: Yale University Press.

Cuddy, Alice. 2015. "Rule of Law Rank Near Bottom." *Phnom Penh Post*, June 2. Retrieved October 5, 2016 (www.phnompenhpost.com/national/rule-law-rank-near-bottom)

Cultural Survival. 2010. "Wodaabe." Retrieved July 7, 2013 (www.culturalsurvival.org/publications/cultural-survival-quarterly/cameroon/wodaabe).

Curtiss, S. 1977. *Genie: A Psycholinguistic Study of a Modern-Day "Wild Child."* New York: Academic Press.

Cuzzort, R. P. and Edith W. King. 2002. *Social Thought Into the Twenty-First Century*, 6th ed. Belmont, CA: Wadsworth.

"Cybercrime: Smoking Gun." 2013. *The Economist*, February 23. Retrieved June 2, 2013 (www.economist.com/news/china/21572228-evidence-mounting-chinas-government-sponsoring-cybertheft-western-corporate).

DaCosta, Kimberly McClain. 2007. *Making Multiracials: State, Family, and Market in the Redrawing of the Color Line*. Stanford, CA: Stanford University Press.

Dahl, Robert A. 1961. *Who Governs?* New Haven, CT: Yale University Press.

Dahrendorf, Ralf. 1959. *Class and Class Conflict in Industrial Societies*. Palo Alto, CA: Stanford University Press.

Daley, Suzanne, and Nicholas Kulish. 2013. "Germany Fights Population Drop." *New York Times*, August 13. Retrieved March 17, 2014 (www.nytimes.com/2013/08/14/world/europe/germany-fights-population-drop.html).

Dalton, Harlon. 2012. "Failing to See." Pp. 15–18 in *White Privilege*, edited by Paula S. Rothenberg. New York: Worth.

Danielsson, Sarah K. and Frank Jacob, eds. 2017. *War and Geography: The Spatiality of Organized Mass Violence*. Paderborn, Germany: Ferdinand Schoningh.

D'Arcy, Yvonne. 2009. "The Effect of Culture on Pain." *Nursing Made Incredibly Easy!* 7(3):5–7.

Das, Udaibir S., Michael G. Papaioannou, and Christoph Trebesch. 2012. "Sovereign Debt Restructurings 1950–2010: Literature Survey, Data, and Stylized Facts." International Monetary Fund, August. Retrieved September 8, 2014 (www.un.org/esa/ffd/ecosoc/debt/2013/IMF_wp12_203.pdf).

Daucher, Brian. 2015. "CMS Proposes Payment Reform/Cap Adjustments." SheppardMullin, May 7. Retrieved June 30, 2015 (www.sheppardhealthlaw.com/2015/05/articles/centers-for-medicare-and-medicaid-services-cms/cms-proposes-payment-reformcap-adjustments).

Davenport, Coral and Marjorie Connelly. 2015. "Most Americans Support Government Action on Climate Change, Poll Finds." *Environmental Economics*, January 30. Retrieved September 13, 2015 (www.env-econ.net/2015/01/

most-americans-support-government-action-on-climate-change-poll-finds.html).

Davis, Alyssa and Lawrence Mishel. 2014. "CEO Pay Continues to Rise as Typical Workers Are Paid Less." *Economic Policy Institute*, June 12. Retrieved June 9, 2015 (www.epi.org/publication/ceo-pay-continues-to-rise).

Davis, Kingsley. 1940. "Extreme Social Isolation of a Child." *American Journal of Sociology* 45:554–65.

Davis, Kingsley. 1947. "A Final Note on a Case of Extreme Isolation." *American Journal of Sociology* 52:432–37.

Davis, Kingsley and Wilbert Moore. 1945. "Some Principles of Stratification." *American Sociological Review* 10(April):242–45.

Death Penalty Information Center. 2015. "States With and Without the Death Penalty." Retrieved June 7, 2015 (www.deathpenaltyinfo.org/states-and-without-death-penalty).

Death Penalty Information Center. 2016. "States With and Without the Death Penalty." November 9. Retrieved February 27, 2017 (http://www.deathpenaltyinfo.org/states-and-without-death-penalty).

Death Penalty Information Center. 2017. "Deterrence: States Without the Death Penalty Have Had Consistently Lower Murder Rates." Retrieved March 23, 2017 (http://www.deathpenaltyinfo.org/deterrence-states-without-death-penalty-have-had-consistently-lower-murder-rates#stateswithvwithout).

Death with Dignity. 2017. "Death With Dignity Laws." Retrieved March 13, 2017 (https://www.deathwithdignity.org/learn/access).

Debenham, Lucy. 2014. "Communication—What Percent Is Body Language?" August 18. Retrieved August 29, 2014 (www.bodylanguageexpert.co.uk/communication-what-percent age-body-language.html).

Deerwester, Karen. 2013. "Boy Toys or Girl Toys: Children Are What They Play." *Examiner*, November 8. Retrieved January 16, 2014 (www.examiner.com/article/boy-toys-or-girl-toys-children-are-what-they-play).

Della Porta, Donatella, Massimillano Andretta, Lorenzo Mosca, and Herbert Reiter. 2006. *Globalization From Below: Transnational Activists and Protest Networks*. Minneapolis: University of Minnesota Press.

Deming, David J. 2015. "The Growing Importance of Social Skills in the Labor Market." NBER Working Paper No. 21473. National Bureau of Economic Research, August. Retrieved October 19, 2015 (www.nber.org/papers/w21473).

DeMitchell, Todd A. and John J. Carney. 2005. "Harry Potter and the Public School Library." *Phi Delta Kappan* (October):159–65.

Demographics Livability. 2014. "Why Do People Move? Here Are the Top Reasons for Relocation." June 12. Retrieved September 8, 2014 (http://livability.com/blog/demographics/why-do-people-move-here-are-top-reasons-relocation).

Denali Commission. 2001. "Telecommunications Inventory Survey." Retrieved June 29, 2006 (www.commonwealth.north.org/transcripts/denalicom.html).

DeNavas-Walt, Carmen and Bernadette D. Proctor. 2014. *U.S. Census Bureau, Current Population Reports, P60-249, Income and Poverty in the United States: 2013*. Washington, DC: U.S. Government Printing Office.

DeNavas-Walt, Carmen and Bernadette D. Proctor. 2015. "Income and Poverty in the United States: 2014." U.S. Census Bureau. Retrieved April 13, 2016 (www.census.gov/hhes/socdemo/education/data/cps/2014/tables.html).

DeParle, Jason and Sabrina Tavernise. 2012. "For Women Under 30, Most Births Occur Outside Marriage." *New York Times*, February 17. Retrieved June 5, 2012 (www.nytimes.com/2012/02/18/us/for-women-under-30-most-births-occur-outside-marriage.html?pagewanted=all).

DeSantis, Carol. 2013. "Cancer Statistics About African Americans Released." American Cancer Society, February 4. Retrieved July 15, 2013 (http://www.cancer.org/cancer/news/expert voices/post/2013/02/04/cancer-statistics-about-african-americans-released.aspx).

Desilver, Drew. 2015. "Women Have Long History in Congress, but Until Recently There Haven't Been Many." Pew Research Center Fact Tank, January 14. Retrieved September 2, 2015 (www.pewresearch.org/fact-tank/2015/01/14/women-have-long-history-in-congress-but-until-recently-there-havent-been-many).

De Waal, Frans. 2016. "Are We Smart Enough to Know How Smart Animals Are?" New York: W. W. Norton.

Dews, C. L. Barney and Carolyn Leste Law, eds. 1995. *This Fine Place So Far From Home: Voices of Academics From the Working Class*. Philadelphia: Temple University Press.

Diamond, Jared. 1999. *Guns, Germs, and Steel: The Fates of Human Societies*. New York: Norton.

Diamond, Jared. 2005. *Collapse: How Societies Choose to Fail or Succeed*. New York: Viking.

Diamond, Larry. 1992. "Introduction: Civil Society and the Struggle for Democracy." Pp. 1–28 in *The Democratic Revolution: Struggles for Freedom and Pluralism in the Developing World*, edited by Larry Diamond. New York: Freedom House.

Diamond, Larry. 2009. *The Spirit of Democracy: The Struggle to Build Free Societies Throughout the World*. New York: Times Books/Henry Holt & Co.

Diekman, Amanda B. and Sarah K. Murmen. 2004. "Learning to Be Little Women and Little Men: The Inequitable Gender Equality of Nonsexist Children's Literature." *Sex Roles: A Journal of Research* 50(5/6):373.

Diggs, Nancy Brown. 2011. *Hidden in the Heartland*. East Lansing: Michigan State University Press.

Dilon, Michele. 2009. *Introduction to Sociological Theory: Theorists, Concepts, and Their Applicability to the Twenty-First Century*. Malden, MA: Wiley-Blackwell.

DiPrete, Thomas A. and Claudia Buchmann. 2013. *The Rise of Women: The Growing Gender Gap in Education and What It Means for American Schools*. New York: Russell Sage Foundation.

Doane, Beth. 2013. "Beijing Pollution Forces Children to Play Under Dome." CBS News, July 17. Retrieved July 9, 2015 (www.cbsnews.com/news/beijing-pollution-forces-students-to-play-under-dome).

Dobbs, David. 2013. "The Social Life of Genes." *Pacific Standard*, September 3. Retrieved December 17, 2013 (www.psmag.com/health/the-social-life-of-genes-64616).

Dockterman, Eliana. 2014. "Chore Wars: How the Division of Domestic Duties Really Affects a Couple's Sex Life" *Time*, February 18. Retrieved February 28, 2014 (http://healthland.time.com/2014/02/18/chore-wars-how-the-division-of-domestic-duties-really-affects-a-couples-sex-life/#ixzz2udTcoUJ0).

Dockterman, Eliana. 2015. "22 Movies Featuring Women We're Excited to See in 2015." *Time*, January 6. Retrieved January 5, 2016 (time.com/3653495/movies-2015-featuring-women).

Dollars and Sense Collective. 2012. Pp. 81–91 in *Globalization: The Transformation of Social Worlds*, 3rd ed., edited by D. Stanley Eitzen and Maxine Baca Zinn. Belmont, CA: Wadsworth.

Domhoff, G. William. 2008. "Who Rules America.net: Power, Politics, and Social Change." Retrieved March 24, 2008 (http://sociology.ucsc.edu/whoruleeesamerica).

Domhoff, G. William. 2009. *Who Rules America: Challenges to Corporate and Class Dominance*, 6th ed. Upper Saddle River, NJ: Prentice Hall.

Domhoff, G. William. 2014. *Who Rules America: The Triumph of the Corporate Rich*, 7th ed. New York: McGraw-Hill.

Dotinga, Randy. 2011. "Fewer Med Students Training as Primary Care Doctors—Study." U.S. News.com, April 26. Retrieved July 15, 2013 (http://health.usnews.com/health-news/managing-your-healthcare/healthcare/articles/2011/04/26/fewer-med-students-training-as-primary-care-doctors-study).

Doyle, Alister. 2015. "China to Surpass US as Top Cause of Modern Global Warming." *Reuters*, April 13. Retrieved February 10, 2016 (http://uk.reuters.com/article/climatechange-china-idUKL5N0XA1JD20150413).

Drafke, Michael. 2008. *The Human Side of Organizations*. Englewood Cliffs, NJ: Prentice Hall.

Drori, Gili S. 2006. *Global E-Litism: Digital Technology, Social Inequality, and Transnationality*. New York: Worth.

Du Bois, W. E. B. [1899] 1967. *The Philadelphia Negro: A Social Study*. New York: Schocken.

Du Bois, W. E. B. [1899] 1996. *The Philadelphia Negro*. Philadelphia: The University of Pennsylvania Press.

Dufur, Mikaela J. and Seth L. Feinberg. 2007. "Artificially Restricted Labor Markets and Worker Dignity in Professional Football." *Journal of Contemporary Ethnography* 36(5):505–36.

Duhigg, Charles and David Kocieniewski. 2013. "How Apple Sidesteps Billions in Taxes." *New York Times*, April 28. Retrieved May 31, 2013 (www.nytimes.com/2012/04/29/business/apples-tax-strategy-aims-at-low-tax-states-and-nations.html?pagewanted=all&_r=0).

Durkheim, Émile. [1893] 1947. *The Division of Labor in Society*, translated by George Simpson. New York: Free Press.

Durkheim, Émile. [1893] 1997. *The Division of Labor in Society*. New York: Free Press.

Durkheim, Émile. [1895] 1982. *The Rules of the Sociological Method*, edited by Steven Lukes and translated by W. D. Halls. New York: Free Press.

Durkheim, Émile. [1897] 1964. *Suicide*. Glencoe, IL: Free Press.

Dusenbery, Maya and Jaeah Lee. 2012. "Charts: The State of Women's Athletics, 40 Years After Title IX." *Mother Jones*, June 22. Retrieved May 2, 2013 (www.motherjones.com/politics/2012/06/chasrts-womens-athletics-title-nine-ncaa).

Dworkin, Anthony Gary and Rosalind J. Dworkin. 1999. *The Minority Report: An Introduction to Racial, Ethnic, and Gender Relations*, 3rd ed. Fort Worth, TX: Harcourt Brace.

Dworkin, Anthony Gary and Pamela F. Tobe. 2012. "Teacher Burnout in Light of School Safety, Student Misbehavior, and Changing Accountability Standards." Pp. 199–211 in *Schools and Society: A Sociological Approach to Education*, edited by Jeanne H. Ballantine and Joan Z. Spade. Thousand Oaks, CA: Sage Pine Forge.

Dye, Thomas, R. 2002. *Who's Running America? The Bush Restoration*, 7th ed. Upper Saddle River, NJ: Prentice Hall.

Dye, Thomas, R. 2014. *Who's Running America? The Obama Reign*, 8th ed. Upper Saddle River, NJ: Prentice Hall.

Dye, Thomas and Harmon Zeigler. 1983. *The Irony of Democracy*. North Scituate, MA: Duxbury Press.

Dyer, Richard. 2012. "The Matter of Whiteness." Pp. 9–14 in *White Privilege*, edited by Paula S. Rothenberg. New York: Worth.

Dynarski, Susan M. 2015. "For the Poor, the Graduation Gap Is Even Wider Than the Enrollment Gap." *New York Times*, June 2. (www.nytimes.com/2015/06/02/upshot/for-the-poor-the-graduation-gap-is-even-wider-than-the-enrollment-gap.html?_r=0).

Earls, Felton M. and Albert J. Reiss. 1994. *Breaking the Cycle: Predicting and Preventing Crime*. Washington, DC: National Institute of Justice.

Edelson, Josh. 2014. "Most Americans Think It's Illegal to Fire Someone for Being Gay. They're Wrong." *Bloomberg Businessweek*, June 26. Retrieved September 6, 2014 (www.businessweek.com/articles/2014-06-23/discrimination-at-work-is-it-legal-to-fire-someone-for-being-gay).

Education Law Center. 2013. "Funding Formulas, and Fairness." Retrieved June 19, 2015 (www.elc-pa.org/wp-content/uploads/2013/02/ELC_schoolfundingreport.2013.pdf).

Edwards, Harry. 2000. "Crisis of the Black Athlete on the Eve of the 21st Century." *Society* 37(3):9–13.

Ehrlich, Paul and Ann Ehrlich. 1990. *The Population Explosion*. New York: Simon and Schuster.

Eitzen, D. Stanley and Maxine Baca Zinn. 2012. "Changing Global Structures: Resistance and Social Movements." Pp. 269–71 in *Globalization: The Transformation of Social Worlds*, 3rd ed., edited by D. Stanley Eitzen and Maxine Baca Zinn. Belmont, CA: Wadsworth.

Ellison, Christopher G. and Daniel A. Powers. 1994. "The Contact Hypothesis and Racial Attitudes Among Black Americans." *Social Science Quarterly* 75(2):385–400.

"Ending the Cycle of Racial Isolation." 2015. *New York Times*, October 17. Retrieved December 8, 2015 (www.nytimes.com/2015/10/18/opinion/sunday/ending-the-cycle-of-racial-isolation.html?smid=nytcore-ipad-share&smprod=nytcore-ipad&_r=0).

Engels, Friedrich. [1884] 1942. *The Origin of the Family, Private Property, and the State*. New York: International Publishing.

England Church Records. 2014. "Introduction." Retrieved September 10, 2014 (https://familysearch.org/learn/wiki/en/England_Church_Records#Introduction).

Environmental Protection Agency. 2016. "Climate Change: Basic Information." Retrieved February 10, 2016 (www3.epa.gov/climatechange/basics).

Erickson, Fritz and John A. Vonk. 2012. "100 People: A World Portrait." Retrieved January 4, 2014 (www.100people.org/statistics_100stats.php).

Eshleman, J. Ross and Richard A. Bulcroft. 2010. *The Family*, 12th ed. Boston: Allyn & Bacon.

Esperitu, Yen Le. 1992. *Asian American Panethnicity: Bridging Institutions and Identities*. Philadelphia: Temple University Press.

Espo, David. 2009. "$797 Billion Stimulus Plan Ok'd in Victory for Obama." *Los Angeles Daily News*, February 14.

Retrieved February 24, 2009 (www.dailynews.com/search/ci_11703066).

Estrellado, Alicia F. and Jennifer (M. I.) Loh. 2013. "Factors Associated With Battered Filipino Women's Decision to Stay in or Leave an Abusive Relationship." *Journal of Interpersonal Violence*, November 7. Retrieved January 17, 2014 (http://jiv.sagepub.com/content/early/2013/11/07/0886260513505709.abstract).

Etounga-Manguelle, Daniel. 2000. "Does Africa Need a Cultural Adjustment Program?" Pp. 65–77 in *Culture Matters: How Values Shape Human Progress*, edited by Lawrence E. Harrison and Samuel P. Huntington. New York: Basic Books.

European Commission. 2014. "EU Anti-Corruption Report." February 3. Retrieved April 25, 2014 (http://ec.europa.eu/dgs/home-affairs/e-library/documents/policies/organized-crime-and-human-trafficking/corruption/docs/acr_2014_en.pdf).

European Commission. 2016. "Climate Action." Retrieved August 12, 2016 (http://ec.europa.eu/clima/policies/international/negotiations/paris/index_en.htm).

Eurostat. 2015. "Mortality and Life Expectancy Statistics." Retrieved August 31, 2015 (ec.europa.eu/eurostat/statistics-explained/index.php/Mortality_and_life_expectancy_statistics).

"Every Woman Who Has Served in the U.S. Senate." 2015. *New York Times*, March 2. Retrieved September 2, 2015 (www.nytimes.com/interactive/2015/03/02/us/politics/women-in-the-senate.html?_r=0).

Ewert, Stephanie. 2013. "The Decline in Private School Enrollment." SEHSD Working Paper Number FY12-117. U.S. Census Bureau, January. Retrieved July 10, 2013 (www.census.gov/hhes/school/files/ewert_private_school_enrollment.pdf).

FactCheck. 2016. "Presidents Winning Without Popular Vote." Retrieved November 15, 2016 (www.factcheck.org/2008/03/presidents-winning-without-popular-vote).

Farley, John E. 2011. *Majority–Minority Relations*, 6th ed. Englewood Cliffs, NJ: Prentice Hall.

Farrer, Claire R. 2011. *Thunder Rides a Black Horse: Mescalero Apaches and the Mythic Present*, 3rd ed. Long Grove, IL: Waveland.

Fathi, David C. 2009. "Prison Nation." Human Rights Watch, April 9. Retrieved April 15, 2009 (www.hrw.org/en/news/2009/04/09/prison-nation).

Fausto-Sterling, Anne. 1992. *Myths of Gender: Biological Theories About Women and Men*, 2nd ed. New York: Basic Books.

Fausto-Sterling, Anne. 2000. "The Five Sexes, Revisited." *Sciences* 40(July/August):118.

FBI. 2014. "Table 16 Rate: Number of Crimes Per 100,000 Inhabitants by Population Group, 2013." Retrieved June 8, 2015 (www.fbi.gov/about-us/cjis/ucr/crime-in-the-u.s/2013/crime-in-the-u.s.-2013/tables/table-16/table_16_rate_by_population_group_2013.xls).

FBI. 2015. "Bias Breakdown." Retrieved April 5, 2016 (www.fbi.gov/news/stories/2015/november/latest-hate-crime-statistics-available/latest-hate-crime-statistics-available).

Feagin, Joe R. 2012. *The White Frame: Centuries of Racial Framing and Counter-Framing*, 2nd ed. New York: Routledge.

Feagin, Joe R. and Clairece Booher Feagin. 1986. *Discrimination American Style: Institutional Racism and Sexism*. Malabar, FL: Krieger.

Feagin, Joe R. and Clairece Booher Feagin. 2010. *Racial and Ethnic Relations*, 9th ed. Englewood Cliffs, NJ: Prentice Hall.

Featherman, David L. and Robert Hauser. 1978. *Opportunity and Change*. New York: Academic Press.

Federal Communication Commission. 2015. "Broadband Availability in America." January 30. Retrieved June 18, 2015 (http://transition.fcc.gov/Daily_Releases/Daily_Business/2015/db0130/DOC-331734A1.pdf).

Feeding America. 2015. "Hunger in America." Retrieved January 5, 2014 (www.feedingamerica.org/hunger-in-america/?_ga=1.80958743.1235139451.1434032482).

Ferhansyed. 2008. "Fundamental Terminology of Planned Change." Retrieved December 21, 2009 (http://organizationdevelopment.wordpress.com/2008/08/10/fundamental-terminology-of-organization-development).

Ferree, Myra Marx. 2012. "Globalization and Feminism: Opportunities and Obstacles for Activism in a Global Arena." Pp. 291–320 in *Globalization: The Transformation of Social Worlds*, 3rd ed., edited by D. Stanley Eitzen and Maxine Baca Zinn. Belmont, CA: Wadsworth.

Fields, Julian. 2015. "Speaking Without Words: Body Language and Non-Verbal Cues in Communication." *Lifesize*, June 23. Retrieved August 29, 2015 (www.lifesize.com/video-conferencing-blog/speaking-without-words).

FindLaw. 2015. "Death With Dignity." *Laws by State*. Retrieved June 30, 2015 (http://healthcare.findlaw.com/patient-rights/death-with-dignity-laws-by-state.html).

Florida, Richard. 2004. *Cities and the Creative Class*. New York: Routledge.

Florida, Richard. 2012. "Creative Class Group." March 2. Retrieved March 5, 2012 (www.creativeclass.com/richard_florida).

Flynn, Simone I. 2014. "Social Movement Theory: Value-Added Theory." *Research Starters*. Retrieved February 24, 2014 (http://connection.ebscohost.com/c/essays/36268048/social-movement-theory-value-added-theory).

Foner, Nancy. 2005. *In a New Land: A Comparative View of Immigration*. New York: New York University Press.

Foster, Brooke Lea. 2015. "What Is It Like to Be Poor at an Ivy League School?" *Boston Globe*, April 9. Retrieved June 11, 2015 (www.bostonglobe.com/magazine/2015/04/09/what-like-poor-ivy-league-school/xPtql5uzDb6r9AUFER8R0O/story.html).

Foundation for Women. 2012. "Eliminating Global Poverty Through Microcredit." Retrieved May 21, 2012 (www.foundationforwomen.org).

Frank, Mark G. and Thomas Gilovich. 1988. "The Dark Side of Self- and Social Perception: Black Uniforms and Aggression in Professional Sports." *Journal of Personality and Social Psychology* 54(1):74–85.

Frankal, Elliot. 2011. "Compulsory Voting Around the World." *The Guardian*, October 4. Retrieved May 21, 2014 (politics.guardian.co.uk).

Freese, Jeremy, Brian Powell, and Lala Cara Steelman. 1999. "Rebel Without a Cause or Effect: Birth Order and Social Attitudes." *American Sociological Review* 64(2):207–231.

Free the Children. 2015. "Our Story: A Connection a World Away." Retrieved November 25, 2015 (www.freethechildren.com).

Free the Slaves. 2015. "Slavery Is Everywhere." Retrieved June 10, 2015 (www.freetheslaves.net/about-slavery/slavery-today).

Free the Slaves. 2016. "Our Mission." Retrieved August 28, 2016 (www.freetheslaves.net).

Frey, Bruno S. 2004. *Dealing With Terrorism: Stick or Carrot?* Cheltenham, UK: Edward Elgar.

Frezzo, Mark. 2015. *The Sociology of Human Rights*. Malden, MA: Polity Press.

Frost, Aja. 2014. "As Competition Among Chinese International Students for U.S. Schools Grows, So Does Fraud." *USA Today*, April 22. Retrieved June 9, 2015 (http://college.usatoday.com/2015/04/22/as-competition-among-chinese-international-students-for-u-s-schools-grows-so-does-fraud).

Galanti, Geri-Ann. 2008. *Caring for Patients From Different Cultures*, 4th ed. Philadelphia: University of Pennsylvania Press.

Gallagher, Charles. 2004. "Transforming Racial Identity Through Affirmative Action." Pp. 153–70 in *Race and Ethnicity: Across Time, Space and Discipline*, edited by Rodney D. Coates. Leiden, Holland: Brill.

Ganley, Colleen and Sarah Lubienski, 2016. "Current Research on Gender Differences in Math." National Council of Teachers of Mathematics, May 9. Retrieved May 30, 2016 (www.nctm.org/Publications/Teaching-Children-Mathematics/Blog/Current-Research-on-Gender-Differences-in-Math).

Gannon, Shane Patrick. 2009. *Translating the Hijra: The Symbolic Reconstruction of the British Empire in India*. PhD thesis, University of Alberta, Edmonton, Alberta, Canada.

Gans, Herbert J. 1962. *The Urban Villagers: Group and Class in the Life of Italian-Americans*. New York: Free Press.

Gans, Herbert J. 1971. "The Uses of Poverty: The Poor Pay All." *Social Policy* 2(2):20–24.

Gans, Herbert J. 1994. "Positive Functions of the Undeserving Poor: Uses of the Underclass in America." *Politics and Society* 22(3):269–83.

Gans, Herbert J. 1995. *The War Against the Poor*. New York: Basic Books.

Gans, Herbert J. 2007. "No, Poverty Has Not Disappeared." Reprinted in *Sociological Footprints*, edited by Leonard Cargan and Jeanne Ballantine. Belmont, CA: Wadsworth.

Gardner, Howard. 1987. "The Theory of Multiple Intelligences." *Annual Dyslexia* 37:19–35.

Gardner, Howard. 1999. *Intelligence Reframed: Multiple Intelligences for the 21st Century*. New York: Basic Books.

Garfield, Rachel, Anthony Damico, Jessica Stephens, and Saman Rouhani. 2015. "The Coverage Gap: Uninsured Poor Adults in States That Do Not Expand Medicaid—An Update." Kaiser Family Foundation. Retrieved June 27, 2015 (http://kff.org/health-reform/issue-brief/the-coverage-gap-uninsured-poor-adults-in-states-that-do-not-expand-medicaid-an-update/).

Gellner, Ernest. 1983. *Culture, Identity, and Politics*. Cambridge, UK: Cambridge University Press.

Gellner, Ernest. 1993. "Nationalism." Pp. 409–11 in *Blackwell Dictionary of Twentieth Century Thought*, edited by William Outhwaite and Tom Bottomore. Oxford, UK: Basil Blackwell.

Gellner, Ernest and John Breuilly. 2009. *Nations and Nationalism*, 2nd ed. Ithaca, NY: Cornell University Press.

Gender Bias Against Women of Color in Science. 2015. "Executive Summary." Retrieved September 3, 2015 (www.uchastings.edu/news/articles/2015/01/double-jeopardy-report.pdf).

Gender Equity Resource Center. 2013. "Definition of Terms: Heterosexism." Retrieved February 10, 2014 (http://geneq.berkeley.edu/lgbt_resources_definiton_of_terms#heterosexism).

"Gender Stereotypes Easing More for Girls than Boys." 2011. *USA Today*. Retrieved May 21, 2012 (www.usatoday.com/news/health/wellness/teen-ya/story/2011/05/Gender-stereotypes-easing-more-for-girls-than-boys/46886846/1).

"Gendercide: The War on Baby Girls." 2010. *The Economist*, March 4. Retrieved May 2, 2010 (www.economist.com/node/15606229).

"Getting Married in Japan." 2014. Retrieved September 8, 2014 (http://japanese.about.com/library/weekly/aa080999.htm).

"The Ghost in Your Genes." 2009. BBC's Science and Nature. Retrieved November 12, 2009 (www.bbc.co.uk/sn/tvradio/programmes/horizon/ghostgenes.shtml).

Gibler, John. 2012. "Mexico's Ghost Towns." Pp. 68–72 in *Globalization: The Transformation of Social Worlds*, 3rd ed., edited by D. Stanley Eitzen and Maxine Baca Zinn. Belmont, CA: Wadsworth.

Giddens, Anthony. 1986. *The Constitution of Society*. Berkeley: University of California Press.

Gilbert, Dennis. 2011. *The American Class Structure in an Age of Growing Inequality*, 8th ed. Thousand Oaks, CA: Sage.

Gilleard, Chris and Paul Higgs. 2015. "Connecting Life Span Development With the Sociology of Life Course: A New Direction." *Sociology*, May 12. Retrieved August 31, 2015 (soc.sagepub.com/content/early/2015/05/12/0038038515577906,full).

Gillis, Justin. 2015. "Naomi Oreskes, a Lightning Rod in a Changing Climate." *New York Times*, June 15. Retrieved September 13, 2015 (www.nytimes.com/2015/06/16/science/naomi-oreskes-a-lightning-rod-in-a-changing-climate.html).

Gillis, Justin. 2016. "Seas Are Rising at Fastest Rate in Last 28 Centuries." *New York Times*, February 23. Retrieved February 27, 2016 (www.nytimes.com/2016/02/23/science/sea-level-rise-global-warming-climate-change.html?smid=nytcore-ipad-share&smprod=nytcore-ipad).

Gillis, Justin and Nicholas St Fleur. 2015. "Global Companies Joining Climate Change Efforts." *New York Times*, September 23. Retrieved February 15, 2016 (www.nytimes.com/2015/09/23/science/global-companies-joining-climate-change-efforts.html?emc=eta1).

Gilman, Azure. 2015. "Work Conditions for Japanese Women May Be Affecting Marriage, Birth Rates." *Aljazeera*, June 26. Retrieved September 6, 2015 (www.america.aljazeera.com/articles/2015/6/26/japans-maternity-harassment-and-the-case-of disappearing-babies.html).

Giridharadas, Anand. 2014. "The Immigrant Advantage." *New York Times Sunday Review*, May 25, pp. 1, 5.

Girls Health. 2009. "Bullying." Retrieved May 21, 2012 (www.girlshealth.gov/bullying).

Givens, David B. 2012. "Nonverbal Communication." Center for Nonverbal Studies. Retrieved September 25, 2012 (http://center-for-nonverbal-studies.org).

Glasberg, Davita Silfen and Deric Shannon. 2011. *Political Sociology: Oppression, Resistance, and the State*. Thousand Oaks, CA: Sage.

"The Glass-Ceiling Index." 2015. *The Economist*, March 5. Retrieved September 4, 2015 (www.economist.com/blogs/graphicdetail/2015/03/daily-chart-1).

Glasscock, C. B. 1937. *The Gasoline Age: The Story of the Men Who Made It*. Indianapolis, IN: Bobbs-Merrill.

Global Journal. 2013. *Top 100 NGOs*. Retrieved June 28, 2013 (http://theglobaljournal.net/top100NGOs).

Global Security. 2009. "Guantanamo Bay Detainees." Retrieved April 14, 2012 (www.globalsecurity.org/military/facility/guantanamo-bay_detainees.htm).

Global Sports Development. 2013. "Steroid Use Among High School Athletes: Research Articles." November 12. Retrieved January 17, 2014 (http://globalsportsdevelopment.org/steroid-use-among-high-school-athletes).

"Global Warming and Climate Change." 2013. *New York Times*, January 8. Retrieved February 5, 2013 (http://topics.nytimes.com/top/news/science/topics/globalwarming/index.html).

Globe Women. 2013. "WEXPO: Women's Online Marketplace." Retrieved January 23, 2013 (http://www.wexpo.biz).

Goffman, Erving. 1961. *Asylums: Essays on the Social Situation of Mental Patients and Other Inmates*. New York: Anchor.

Goffman, Erving. 1967. *Interaction Ritual*. New York: Anchor.

Goffman, Erving. [1959] 2001. *Presentation of Self in Everyday Life*. New York: Harmondsworth, UK: Penguin.

Goldstein, Matthew, Nicole Perloth, and David E. Sanger. 2014. "Hackers' Attack Cracked Ten Firms in Major Assault." *New York Times*, October 3. Retrieved August 26, 2016 (http://dealbook.nytimes.com/2014/10/03/hackers-attack-cracked-10-banks-in-major-assault/?_r=0).

Gonzalez-Perez, Margaret. 2011. "The False Islamization of Female Suicide Bombers." *Gender Issues* 28(1/2):50–65.

Goode, Erich. 1992. *Collective Behavior*. New York: Harcourt Brace Jovanovich.

Goode, William J. 1970. *World Revolution and Family Patterns*. New York: Free Press.

Goodman, Marc D. and Susan W. Brenner. 2002. "The Emerging Consensus on Criminal Conduct in Cyberspace." *International Journal of Law and Information Technology* 10(2):139–223.

Goodstein, Laurie. 2012. "Ugandan Gay Rights Group Sues U.S. Evangelist." *New York Times*, March 14. Retrieved May 27, 2012 (www.nytimes.com/2012/03/15/us/ugandan-gay-rights-group-sues-scott-lively-an-american-evangelist.html).

GoodTherapy.org. 2012. "Complementary and Alternative Medicine (CAM)." Retrieved August 3, 2012 (www.goodtherapy.org/complementary-alternative-medicine.html).

Gordon, Milton. 1970. "The Subsociety and the Subculture." Pp. 150–63 in *The Sociology of Subcultures*, edited by David O. Arnold. Berkeley, CA: Glendessary.

Gore, Al. 2012. "Global Warming Is Real." *EarthSky*, April 30. Retrieved September 7, 2012 (http://earthsky.org/human-world/al-gore-at-hampshire-college-global-warming-is-real).

Gottfredson, Michael R. and Travis Hirschi. 1990. *A General Theory of Crime*. Palo Alto, CA: Stanford University Press.

Gould, Elise. 2012. "U.S. Lags Behind Peer Countries in Mobility." Economic Policy Institute, October 10. Retrieved June 12, 2013 (www.epi.org/publication/usa-lags-peer-countries-mobility).

Gould, Stephen J. 1997. *The Mismeasure of Man*. New York: Norton.

Gouldner, Alvin W. 1960. "The Norm of Reciprocity: A Preliminary Statement." *American Sociological Review* 25(2):161–78.

Gracey, Harry L. 1967. "Learning the Student Role: Kindergarten as Academic Boot Camp." Pp. 215–26 in *Readings in Introductory Sociology*, 3rd ed., edited by Dennis Wrong and Harry L. Gracey. New York: Macmillan.

Grandpa Junior. 2006. "If You Were Born Before 1945." Retrieved July 20, 2006 (www.grandpajunior.com/1945.shtml).

Granovetter, Mark. 2007. "Introduction for the French Reader." *Sociologica* 1(Suppl.):1–10.

Gratton, Lynda. 2012. "The Globalisation of Work—and People." BBC News, September 6. Retrieved June 11, 2015 (www.bbc.com/news/business-19476254).

Gray, Robin Hattersley. 2012. "Sexual Assault Statistics." *Campus Safety Magazine*, March 6. Retrieved January 17, 2014 (www.campussafetymagazine.com/Channel/Public-Safety/articles/2012/03/Sexual-Assault-Statistics-and-Myths.aspx).

Greenan, Matthew. 2013. "New Indian Documentary on the Practice of Sati." Retrieved January 16, 2014 (http://greenanreport.wordpress.com/2013/05/12/new-indian-documentary-on-the-practice-of-sati).

Grieco, Elizabeth M., Yesenia D. Acosta, G. Patricia de la Cruz, Christine Gambino, Thomas Gryn, Luke J. Larsen, Edward N. Trevelyan, and Nathan P. Walters. 2012. "The Foreign-Born Population in the United States: 2010." *American Community Survey Reports*. Retrieved June 17, 2013 (www.census.gov/prod/2012pubs/acs-19.pdf).

Guerino, Paul, Paige M. Harrison, and William J. Sabol. 2011. *Prisoners in 2010*, rev. December 15. Retrieved April 15, 2012 (http://bjs.ojp.usdoj.gov/index.cfm?ty=tp&tid=13).

Guttmacher Institute. 2013. "Contraceptive Use in the United States." August. Retrieved March 17, 2014 (www.guttmacher.org/pubs/fb_contr_use.html).

Hagan, Frank E. 2011. *Introduction to Criminology*, 7th ed. Thousand Oaks, CA: Sage.

"Haiti." 2015. *The Economist*. July 12. Retrieved July 20, 2015 (http://country.eiu.com/haiti).

Hall, Edward T. 1983. *The Dance of Life*. Garden City, NY: Anchor Books/Doubleday.

Hall, Edward T. and Mildred Reed Hall. 1992. *An Anthropology of Everyday Life*. New York: Doubleday.

Hall, Richard H. 2002. *Organizations: Structures, Processes, and Outcomes*, 7th ed. Englewood Cliffs, NJ: Prentice Hall.

Handel, Gerald, Spencer Cahill, and Frederick Elkin. 2007. *Children and Society: The Sociology of Children and Childhood Socialization*. New York: Oxford University Press.

Handwerk, Brian. 2004. "Female Suicide Bombers: Dying to Kill." *National Geographic News*, December 13. Retrieved July 5, 2008 (http://news.nationalgeographic.com/news/2004/12/1213_041213_tv_suicide_bombers.html).

Haniffa, Aziz. 2009. "Financial Crisis Bigger Than Al Qaeda, Says U.S. Intelligence Czar." *Rediff India Abroad*, February 13. Retrieved March 17, 2009 (www.rediff.com/money/2009/feb/15bcrisis-financial-crisis-bigger-threat-than-al-qaeda-says-us-intel-chief.htm).

Hansen, Randall and Katharine Hansen. 2003. "What Do Employers Really Want? Top Skills and Values Employers Seek From Job-Seekers." Quintessential Careers. Retrieved June 23, 2008 (www.quintcareers.com/job_skills_values.html).

Harris, Judith Rich. 2009. *The Nurture Assumption: Why Children Turn Out the Way They Do*, rev. and updated edition. New York: Free Press.

Harris, Marvin. 1989. *Cows, Pigs, War, and Witches: The Riddles of Culture*. New York: Random House.

Harrison, Matthew S. 2010. "Colorism: The Often Un-Discussed '-ism' in America's Workforce." *Jury Expert*, January. Retrieved June 19, 2015 (www.thejuryexpert.com/wp-content/uploads/HarrisonTJEJan2010.pdf).

Harrison, Matthew S. and Keisha M. Thomas. 2009. "The Hidden Prejudice in Selection: A Research Investigation on Skin Color Bias." *Journal of Applied Social Psychology* 39(1):134–68.

Hart, Betty and Todd R. Risley. 2003. "The Early Catastrophe: The 30 Million Word Gap by Age 3." *American Educator* 27(1):4–9.

Haskins, Ron, Julia B. Isaacs, and Isabel V. Sawhill. 2008. *Getting Ahead or Losing Ground: Economic Mobility in America*. Brookings Institute. Retrieved June 7, 2013 (www.brookings.edu/research/reports/2008/02/economic-mobility-sawhill).

Hattery, Angela and Earl Smith. 2012. *African American Families Today: Myths and Realities*. Lanham, MD: Rowman and Littlefield.

Hearn, Kelly. 2012. "Big Oil Wreaks Havoc in the Amazon, but Communities Are Fighting Back." Pp. 313–16 in *Globalization: The Transformation of Social Worlds*, 3rd ed., edited by D. Stanley Eitzen and Maxine Baca Zinn. Belmont, CA: Wadsworth.

Heberlein, Tom. 2016. "Low Taxes? We Get Just What We Pay For." *Cap Times*. Retrieved April 18, 2016 (http://host.madison.com/ct/opinion/column/tom-heberlein-low-taxes-we-get-just-what-we-pay/article_edafbda2-b379-5afc-8836-a482b4312b42.html).

Hegewisch, Ariane, Claudia Williams, Heidi Hartmann, and Stephanie Keller Hudiburg. 2014. "The Gender Wage Gap: 2013." Institute for Women's Policy Research, March. Retrieved May 12, 2014 (www.iwpr.org/publications/pubs/the-gender-wage-gap-2013-differences-by-race-and-ethnicity-no-growth-in-real-wages-for-women).

Heilbroner, Robert L. and William Milberg. 2007. *The Making of Economic Society*, 12th ed. Englewood Cliffs, NJ: Prentice Hall.

Hendry, Joy. 1987. *Becoming Japanese: The World of the Preschool Child*. Honolulu: University of Hawaii Press.

Henley, Jon. 2008. "Did a Pair of Twins Really Get Married by Mistake?" *The Guardian*, January 15. Retrieved August 29, 2015 (www.theguardian.com/lifeandstyle/2008/jan/15/familyandrelationships.jonhenley).

Hensley, Christopher, M. Koscheski, and Richard Tewksbury. 2005. "Examining the Characteristics of Male Sexual Assault Targets in a Southern Maximum-Security Prison." *Journal of Interpersonal Violence* 20(6):667–79.

Hepworth, Kimberly. 2010. "Eating Disorders Today—Not Just a Girl Thing." *Journal of Christian Nursing* (July/September). Retrieved January 17, 2014 (http://nursing.ceconnection.com/nu/public/modules/2224).

Herskovitz, Jon. 2012. "Militant South African Union Tells Lonmin to Pay Up." *Reuters*, September 7. Retrieved September 8, 2012 (www.reuters.com/article/2012/09/07/us-safrica-mines-idUSBRE8860U820120907).

Hewitt, John P. and David Shulman. 2011. *Self and Society: A Symbolic Interactionist Approach to Social Psychology*, 11th ed. Englewood Cliffs, NJ: Prentice Hall.

Hewlett, Sylvia Ann. 2013. "What's Holding Japanese Women Back." *Time*, September 27. Retrieved January 18, 2014 (http://ideas.time.com/2013/09/27/whats-holding-japanese-women-back).

Heyes, J. D. 2012. "Plastic Waste Garbage Floating in Pacific Ocean Has Increased 100-Fold." NaturalNews.com, May 15. Retrieved September 7, 2012 (www.naturalnews.com/035866_garbage_floating_Pacific_Ocean.html).

Hinton, Christopher. 2010. "Global Military Spending to Outpace GDP Growth in 2010." Market Watch, June 18. Retrieved May 10, 2011 (www.marketwatch.com/story/worlds-militaries-see-another-budget-busting-year-2010-06-18).

Hirschi, Travis. [1969] 2002. *Causes of Delinquency*. Berkeley: University of California Press.

Hochschild, Arlie. 1989. *The Second Shift: Working Parents and the Revolution at Home*. New York: Viking.

Holt, Sheila. 2007. *Talk of the Nation*. National Public Radio Interview by Cheryl Covley, March 26.

Homans, George C. 1974. *Social Behavior: Its Elementary Forms*. New York: Harcourt, Brace Jovanovich.

Horowitz, Jason, Shaila Dewan, and Richard A. Oppel. 2015. "On Facebook, Dylann Roof, Charleston Suspect, Wears Symbols of White Supremacy." *New York Times*, June 18. Retrieved June 18, 2015 (www.nytimes.com/2015/06/19/us/on-facebook-dylann-roof-charleston-suspect-wears-symbols-of-white-supremacy.html?hp&action=click&pgtype=Homepage&module=b-lede-package-region&region=top-news&WT.nav=top-news).

Hotchkiss, Gord. 2014. "The Unintended Consequences of Technology." *Media Post*, November 6. Retrieved September 10, 2015 (www.mediapost.com/publications/article/237717/the-unintended-consequences-of-technology.html).

Houlis, Anna Marie. 2011. "Gender Stereotypes in Picture Books Are Blamed for Affecting Children." June 13. Retrieved May 23, 2012 (http://annamariehoulis.wordpress.com/2011/06/13/gender-stereotypes-in-picture-books-are-blamed-for-affecting-children).

"How Finnish Schools Shine." 2012. *The Guardian*, May 21. Retrieved July 8, 2013 (www.guardian.co.uk/teacher-network/teacher-blog/2012/apr/09/finish-school-system).

Howard, Adam. 2007. *Learning Privilege: Lessons of Power and Identity in Affluent Schooling*. New York: Taylor & Francis.

Howard, Adam and Ruben Gaztambide-Fernandez, eds. 2010. *Educating Elites: Class Privilege and Educational Advantage*. Lanham, MD: Rowman and Littlefield.

Hozien, Muhammad. n.d. "Ibn Khaldun: His Life and Work." Retrieved May 7, 2009 (www.muslimphilosophy.com/ik/klf.htm).

Huang, Al. 2011. "'Poster Child' for Environmental Racism Finds Justice in Dickson, TN." NRDC Switchboard, December 8. Retrieved March 14, 2014 (http://archive.is/AsHA).

Huddy, Leonie and Stanley Feldman. 2006. "Worlds Apart: Blacks and Whites React to Hurricane Katrina." *Du Bois Review* 3(1):97–113. Retrieved July 7, 2011 (http://journals.cambridge.org/action/displayAbstract?fromPage=online&aid=462978).

Hudson, Heather E. 2011. "Digital Diversity: Broadband and Indigenous Populations in Alaska." *Journal of Information Policy* 1:378–393. Retrieved September 25, 2012 (jip.vmhost.psu.edu/ojs/index.php/jip/article/download/42/37).

Hughes, Mark. 2015. "Leading Changes: Why Transformation Explanations Fail." *Leadership*, February 9. Retrieved

September 10, 2015 (http://lea.sagepub.com/content/early/2015/02/09/1742715015571393.abstract).

Hugo, Peter. 2010. "A Global Graveyard for Dead Computers in Ghana." *New York Times Magazine*, August 4. Retrieved July 10, 2013 (http://www.nytimes.com/slideshow/2010/08/04/magazine/20100815-dump.html?_r=0).

Huizinga, David, Rolf Loeber, and Terence P. Thornberry. 1994. "Urban Delinquency and Substance Abuse: Initial Findings." OJJDP Research Summary. Washington, DC: Government Printing Office.

Human Planet. 2012. "Wodaabe Flirtation Festival." Retrieved January 16, 2014 (http://dsc.discovery.com/tv-shows/human-planet/videos/wodaabe-flirtation-festival.htm).

Human Rights First. 2015. "Guantanamo by the Numbers." Fact Sheet, January 15. Retrieved January 27, 2015 (www.humanrightsfirst.org/sites/default/files/gtmo-by-the-numbers.pdf).

Human Rights Watch. 2016. "Iraq: Women Suffer Under ISIS." Retrieved August 19, 2016 (https://www.hrw.org/news/2016/04/05/iraq-women-suffer-under-isis).

Hunter College Women's Studies Collective. 2005. *Women's Realities, Women's Choices: An Introduction to Women's Studies*, 3rd ed. New York: Oxford University Press.

Hurst, Charles E. 2013. *Social Inequality: Forms, Causes and Consequences*, 8th ed. Boston: Allyn & Bacon.

Iannelli, Vincent. 2014. "Measles Outbreaks 2014." Retrieved March 10, 2014. (http://pediatrics.about.com/od/measles-outbreaks.htm).

"Ice." 2015. "'Ice': An Exhibition at the Anchorage Museum." Presented in Collaboration with Inuit Elders, Anchorage, Alaska.

"Iceberg Breaks Off From Greenland's Petermann Glacier." 2012. BBC News, July 19. Retrieved February 8, 2013 (www.bbc.co.uk/news/world-europe-18896770).

IMDb. 2015. "Most Popular 'Gay' Feature Films Released in 2015." Retrieved September 6, 2015 (www.imdb.com/search/title?at=0&keywords-gay&sort=moviemeter,asc&title_type=feature&year=2015,2015).

Index Mundi. 2014. "Life Expectancy at Birth." January 1. Retrieved April 11, 2016 (www.indexmundi.com/g/r.aspx?t=50&v=30).

Index Mundi. 2015. "United States Age Structure." Retrieved April 24, 2016 (www.indexmundi.com/united_states/age_structure.html).

Infoplease. 2016. "Median Annual Earnings by Race and Sex, 2013." U.S. Census Bureau, Institute for Women's Policy Research. Retrieved April 14, 2016 (www.infoplease.com/us/census/median-earnings-by-race.html).

Ingersoll, Richard M. and Elizabeth Merrill. 2015. "The Status of Teaching as a Profession." Pp. 170–182 in *Schools and Society: A Sociological Approach to Education*, 5th ed., edited by Jeanne H. Ballantine and Joan Z. Spade. Thousand Oaks, CA: Sage.

Inglehart, Ronald. 1997. *Modernization and Postmodernization: Cultural, Economic, and Political Change in 43 Societies*. Princeton, NJ: Princeton University Press.

Inglehart, Ronald and Wayne E. Baker. 2001. "Modernization's Challenge to Traditional Values: Who's Afraid of Ronald McDonald?" *The Futurist* 35(2):16–22.

Ingraham, Christopher. 2016. "About 100 Million People Couldn't Be Bothered to Vote This Year" *Washington Post*, November 12. Retrieved November 14, 2016 (www.washingtonpost.com/news/wonk/wp/2016/11/12/about-100-million-people-couldnt-be-bothered-to-vote-this-year).

"In Sickness and In Wealth: Health in America." 2008. Unnatural Causes, July 3. Retrieved May 13, 2014 (www.youtube.com/watch?v=w98GSXBEyQw).

Institute for Economics & Peace. 2015. *Global Terrorism Index 2015*. Retrieved April 3, 2015 (http://economicsandpeace.org/wp-content/uploads/2015/11/Global-Terrorism-Index-2015.pdf).

Intergovernmental Panel on Climate Change. 2013. "Working Group I Contribution to the IPCC Fifth Assessment Report." *Climate Change 2013: The Physical Science Basis. Summary for Policymakers*, September 27.

Intergovernmental Panel on Climate Change. 2014. *Climate Change 2014: Mitigation of Climate Change*. Retrieved May 27, 2014 (http://www.ipcc.ch).

International Beliefs and Values Institute. 2012. "Mission." Staunton, VA: Mary Baldwin College. Retrieved March 23, 2012 (www.ibavi.org).

International Center for Prison Studies. 2014. "World Prison Brief." Retrieved May 13, 2014 (www.prisonstudies.org).

"International Digital Divide." 2011. *Science Daily*, February 8. Retrieved May 18, 2012 (www.sciencedaily.com/releases/2011/02/110208121345.htm).

International Institute for Democracy and Electoral Assistance. 2012. *Voter Turnout Since 1945: A Global Report*. Retrieved June 2, 2013 (www.idea.int/vt).

International Institute for Democracy and Electoral Assistance. 2016. "Voter Turnout—Most Recent Parliamentary Elections." Retrieved April 18, 2016 (www.idea.int/vt/field.cfm?field=221).

International Lesbian, Gay, Bisexual, Trans and Intersex Association. 2015. "The Lesbian, Gay and Bisexual Map of World Laws." Retrieved April 11, 2015 (http://old.ilga.org/Statehomophobia/ILGA_WorldMap_2015_ENG.pdf).

International Monetary Fund. 2014. "World Economic Outlook Database, October 2014. 5." Report for Selected Countries and Subjects. Retrieved June 27, 2015 (http://www.imf.org/external/pubs/ft/weo/2014/02/weodata/index.aspx).

Internet World Statistics. 2014. "Internet Usage Statistics: The Internet Big Picture." Retrieved January 30, 2015 (http://www.internetworldstats.com/stats.htm).

Internet World Statistics. 2016. "Internet Usage Statistics: The Internet Big Picture." June 30. Retrieved August 28, 2016 (www.internetworldstats.com/stats.htm).

Inter-Parliamentary Union. 2016. "Women in National Parliaments." Retrieved March 3, 2016 (www.ipu.org/wmn-e/classif.htm).

Interuniversity Consortium for Political and Social Research. 2011. "Voting Behavior: The 2008 Election." Retrieved May 16, 2012 (http://www.icpsr.umich.edu/icpsrweb/SETUPS2008/voting.jsp).

Irvine, Leslie. 2004. *If You Tame Me: Understanding Our Connection With Animals*. Philadelphia: Temple University Press.

Irwin, John. 1985. *The Jail: Managing the Underclass in American Society*. Berkeley: University of California Press.

Irwin, John and Barbara Owen. 2007. *The Warehouse Prison: Disposal of the New Dangerous Class*. New York: Oxford University Press.

Irwin, Neil, Claire Cain Miller, and Margot Sanger Katz. 2014. "America's Racial Divide, Charted." The Upshot, *New York Times*. Retrieved April 14, 2016 (www.nytimes.com/2014/08/20/upshot/americas-racial-divide-charted.html).

Jackson, Jasper. 2016. "Children Spending More Time Online Than Watching TV for the First Time." *The Guardian*, January 26. Retrieved February 26, 2017 (https://www.theguardian.com/media/2016/jan/26/children-time-online-watching-tv).

Jackson, Philip W. 1968. *Life in Classrooms*. New York: Holt, Rinehart & Winston.

Jaeger, Mads Meier. 2011. "Does Cultural Capital Really Affect Academic Achievement? New Evidence From Combined Sibling and Panel Data." *Sociology of Education* 84 (October):281–98.

James, Deanna. 2013. "The Psychology of Eating Disorders." PsychCentral, August 8. Retrieved January 18, 2014 (http://psychcentral.com/blog/archives/2013/08/08/the-psychology-of-eating-disorders).

James, William. [1890] 1934. *The Principles of Psychology*. Mineola, NY: Dover.

Jaschik, Scott. 2013. "Prestige vs. Major." *Inside Higher Education*, December 10. Retrieved January 4, 2014 (www.insidehighered.com/news/2013/12/10/study-examines-impact-major-vs-impact-college-prestige-womens-earnings).

Jaschik, Scott. 2016a. "SAT Scores Drop." *Inside Higher Ed*. September 3. Retrieved April 11, 2016 (www.insidehighered.com/news/2015/09/03/sat-scores-drop-and-racial-gap-remains-large).

Jaschik, Scott. 2016b. "ACT Scores Are Flat." *Inside Higher Ed*, August 26. Retrieved April 11, 2016 (www.insidehighered.com/news/2015/08/26/act-scores-year-flat-and-racial-gaps-persist).

Jaslow, Ryan. 2013. "End of Life Care for Elderly Often Too Aggressive, Study Says." CBS News, February 6. Retrieved July 16, 2013 (www.cbsnews.com/8301-204_162-57567998/end-of-life-care-for-elderly-often-too-aggressive-study-says).

Jellinek, E. M. 1960. *The Disease Concept of Alcoholism*. New Haven, CT: Hillhouse.

Johnson, Carolyn Y. 2012. "Scientists Begin to Unravel the Long-Lasting Biological Effects of Early-Life Adversity, Social Isolation." *Boston Globe*, September 21. Retrieved August 30, 2015 (www.boston.com/news/science/2012/09/21/scientists-begin-unravel-the-long-lasting-biological-effects-early-life-adversity-social-isolation/j28yh2lHWj3P8vYY1CpGPO/story/html).

Johnson, Kevin. 2014. "Thousands of Prisoners Could Qualify for Clemency." *USA Today*, April 21. Retrieved April 25, 2014 (www.usatoday.com/story/news/nation/2014/04/21/prisoners-clemency-holder/7962929).

Johnson, Robert. 2002. *Hard Time: Understanding and Reforming the Prison*. Belmont, CA: Wadsworth/Thompson Learning.

Jordan, Amy B., James C. Hersey, Judith A. MdDivitt, and Carrie D. Heitzler. 2006. "Reducing Children's Television-Viewing Time: A Qualitative Study of Parents and Their Children." *Pediatrics* 118(5):1303–10.

Jordan, Winthrop D. 2012. *White Over Black: American Attitudes Toward the Negro 1550–1812*, 2nd ed. Chapel Hill: University of North Carolina Press.

Jory, Brian and Carry L. Yodanis. 2014. "Family Relationships, Marital Relationships." *Marriage and Family Encyclopedia*. Retrieved February 18, 2014 (http://family.jrank.org/pages/1316/Power.html).

Julian, Tiffany and Robert Kominski. 2011. "Table 1: Annual Earnings by Level of Education and Work Status." *American Community Survey Reports*, September. Retrieved September 9, 2014 (http://www.census.gov/prod/2011pubs/acs-14.pdf).

Kain, Edward L. 2012. "Changes in the MCAT Have Implications for Sociology Department Planning." *ASA Footnotes* 40(9). Retrieved May 31, 2016 (www.asanet.org/footnotes/dec12/mcat_1212.html).

Kain, Erik. 2015. "The Top Video Games of 2015." *Forbes*, December 29. Retrieved September 13, 2016 (www.forbes.com/sites/erikkain/2014/12/29/the-top-video-games-of-2015).

Kaiser Family Foundation. 2015a. "The Global HIV/AIDS Epidemic." November 20. Retrieved April 11, 2016 (kff.org/global-health-policy/fact-sheet/the-global-hivaids-epidemic).

Kaiser Family Foundation 2015b. "What Is Medicare's Role in End-of-Life Care?" November 15. Retrieved May 31, 2016 (kkf.org/medicare/fact-sheet/10-faqs-medicares-role-in-end-of-life-care).

Kaiser Family Foundation. 2016. "Infant Mortality Rate (Deaths per 1,000 Live Births)." Retrieved March 14, 2017 (http://kff.org/other/state-indicator/infant-death-rate/?currentTimeframe=0&sortModel=%7B%22colId%22:%22Location%22,%22sort%22:%22asc%22%7D).

Kamarck, Elaine C. 2016. *Primary Politics*, 2nd ed. Washington DC: Brookings Institution.

Kan, Man Yee, Oriel Sullivan, and Jonathan Gershuny. 2011. "Gender Convergence in Domestic Work: Discerning the Effects of Interactional and Institutional Barriers from Large-Scale Data." *Sociology* 45(2):234–51.

Kanter, Rosabeth Moss. 1977. *Men and Women of the Corporation*. New York: Basic Books.

Kantorová, Vladímira, Ann Biddlecom, and Holly Newby. 2014. "Keeping Pace With Population Growth." *The Lancet* 384(9940):307–308.

Kaplan, Howard B. and Robert J. Johnson. 1991. "Negative Social Sanctions and Juvenile Delinquency: Effects of Labeling in a Model of Deviant Behavior." *Social Science Quarterly* 72(1):117.

Kasperkevic, Jana. 2014. "How Much Can You Get for Selling Your Body (Parts)?" *The Guardian*, January 31. Retrieved May 27, 2014 (www.theguardian.com/money/us-money-blog/2014/jan/31/flu-government-sell-egg-sperm-body).

Katz, Jonathan and Jennifer Bradley. 2013. *The Metropolitan Revolution*. Washington, DC: Brookings Institution.

Kean, Sam. 2007. "What's in a Name?" *New York Times*, October 28. Retrieved May 21, 2012 (www.nytimes.com/2007/10/28/magazine/28wwln-idealab-t.html).

Kennedy, Sheela and Steven Ruggles. 2014. "Breaking Up Is Hard to Count: The Rise of Divorce in the United States, 1980-2010." *Demography* 51:587–598.

Kerbo, Harold R. 2008. *Social Stratification and Inequality*, 7th ed. Boston: McGraw-Hill.

Kessler, Sarah. 2011. "Study: 80% of Children Under 5 Use Internet Weekly." *Technology Live*, March 15. Retrieved April 9, 2013 (http://content.usatoday.com/communities/technologylive/post/2011/03/study-80-percent-of-children-under-5-use-internet-weekly).

Kidder, Tracy. 2004. *Mountains Beyond Mountains*. New York: Random House.

Kielburger, Craig. 2009. *Free the Children*. Toronto: Me to We Books.

Killian, Caitlin. 2006. *North African Women in France: Gender, Culture, and Identity*. Palo Alto, CA: Stanford University Press.

Kim, Min-Sun, Katsuya Tasaki, In-Duk Kim, and Hye-ryeon Lee. 2007. "The Influence of Social Status on Communication Predispositions Focusing on Independent and Inter-dependent Self-Construals." *Journal of Asian Pacific Communication* 17(2):303–329.

Kim, Susanna. 2014. "Target (TGT) Profits Hit by Card Security Hack." ABC News, February 26. Retrieved June 8, 2015 (http://abcnews.go.com/Business/target-profits-hit-card-security-hack/story?id=22680841).

King, Neil, Jr. 2012. "Vote Data Show Changing Nation." *Wall Street Journal*, November 8. Retrieved June 7, 2013 (http://online.wsj.com/article/SB100014241278873240735045781 05360833569352.html#project%3DEXITPOLLS2012%26ar ticleTabs%3Darticle).

Kinsey Institute for Research in Sex, Gender, and Reproduction. 2012. Retrieved May 20, 2012 (www.kinseyinstitute.org).

Kirchhoff, Suzanne M. 2010. "Economic Impacts of Prison Growth." Congressional Research Service, April 13. Retrieved June 2, 2013 (www.bjs.gov/content/pub/pdf/p11.pdf).

Kirkham, C. 2012. "Private Prison Corporation Offers Cash In Exchange For State Prisons." *Huffington Post*, February 14. Retrieved September 16, 2014 (http://www.huffing-tonpost.com/2012/02/14/private-prisons-buying-state-prisons_n_1272143.html).

Kitano, Harry H., Pauline Aqbayani, and Diane de Anda. 2005. *Race Relations*, 6th ed. Englewood Cliffs, NJ: Prentice Hall.

Kleinman, Johathan. 2014. "Top 10 Energy Efficiency Predictions for 2015." Clearesult, December 9. Retrieved August 28, 2015 (www.clearesult.com/insights/top-10-energy-efficient-predictions-2015).

Kliff, Sarah. 2014. "Think America Has the World's Best Health Care System? You Won't After Seeing This Chart." *Washington Post*, January 7. Retrieved March 12, 2014 (www.washingtonpost.com/blogs/wonkblog/wp/2014/01/07/think-america-has-the-worlds-best-health-care-system-you-wont-after-seeing-this-chart).

Kochhar, Rakesh and Richard Fry. 2014. "Wealth Inequality Has Widened Along Racial, Ethnic Lines Since End of Great Recession." Pew Research Center, December 12. Retrieved June 15, 2015 (www.pewresearch.org/fact-tank/2014/12/12/racial-wealth-gaps-great-recession).

Kodish, Bruce I. 2003. "What We Do With Language—What It Does With Us." *ETC: A Review of General Semantics* 60:383–95.

Kohn, Melvin. 1989. *Class and Conformity: A Study of Values*, 2nd ed. Chicago: University of Chicago Press.

Koos, Earl. 1954. *The Health of Regionville*. New York: Columbia University Press.

Korgen, Jeffry and Charles Gallagher. 2013. *The True Cost of Low Prices*. New York: Orbis Books.

Korgen, Kathleen Odell and David Brunsma. 2012. "Avoiding Race or Following the Racial Scripts? Obama and Race in the Recessionary Part of the Colorblind Era." In *Obama and the Biracial Factor: The Battle for a New American Majority*, edited by Andrew Jolivette. Bristol, UK: Policy Press.

Korgen, Kathleen Odell, Jonathan M. White, and Shelley K. White. 2013. *Sociologists in Action: Sociology, Social Change, and Social Justice*, 2nd ed. Thousand Oaks, CA: Sage.

Korte, Charles and Stanley Milgram. 1970. "Acquaintance Networks Between Racial Groups." *Journal of Personality and Social Psychology* 15:101–108.

Koschate-Reis, Miriam. 2009. "The Social Psychology of Embarrassment." Research project at the School of Psychology, University of St. Andrews. Retrieved March 31, 2012 (http://sites.google.com/site/embarrassmentproject/home).

Kost Kathryn. 2015. *Unintended Pregnancy Rates at the State Level: Estimates for 2010 and Trends Since 2002*. New York: Guttmacher Institute. Retrieved July 6, 2015 (www.guttmacher.org/pubs/StateUP10.pdf).

Kotkin, Joel. 2013. "America's Fastest—And Slowest—Growing Cities." *Forbes*, March 18. Retrieved July 1, 2013 (www.forbes.com/sites/joelkotkin/2013/03/18/americas-fastest-and-slowest-growing-cities).

Kotkin, Joel and Wendell Cox. 2011. "Cities and the Census." *City Journal*, April 6. Retrieved July 1, 2013 (www.city-journal.org/2011/eon0406jkwc.html).

Kottak, Conrad Phillip. 2014. *Anthropology: Appreciating Human Diversity*, 16th ed. New York: McGraw-Hill.

Kozol, Jonathan. 2006. *The Shame of the Nation: The Restoration of Apartheid Schooling in America*. New York: Crown.

Kozol, Jonathan. 2012. *Fire in the Ashes: Twenty-Five Years Among the Poorest Children in America*. New York: Random House Crown Publishing Group.

Kramer, Laura and Ann Beutel. 2014. *The Sociology of Gender: A Brief Introduction*, 4th ed. New York: Oxford University Press.

Kreider, Rose M., and Renee Ellis. 2011. "Living Arrangements of Children: 2009." U.S. Census Bureau, June. Retrieved May 4, 2013 (www.census.gov/prod/2011pubs/p70-126.pdf).

Kristof, Nicholas. 2015. "Payday for Ice Bucket Challenge's Mocked Slacktivists." *New York Times*, September 2. Retrieved February 11, 2016 (www.nytimes.com/2015/09/03/opinion/nicholas-kristof-payday-for-ice-bucket-challenges-mocked-slacktivists.html?_r=0).

Kristof, Nicholas and Sheryl WuDunn. 2009. *Half the Sky: Turning Oppression Into Opportunity for Women Worldwide*. New York: Alfred A. Knopf.

Kroenig, Matthew and Barry Pavel. 2012. "How to Deter Terrorism." *Washington Quarterly* 35(2):21–36.

Krueger, Megan. 2015. "Kids Books That Defy Gender Stereotypes." *MetroParent*, January 11. Retrieved September 2, 2015 (www.metroparent.com/daily/parenting/parenting-issues-tips/kids-books-defy-gender-stereotypes).

Kübler-Ross, Elizabeth. 1997. *Death, the Final Stage of Growth*, rev. ed. New York: Scribner.

Kuhn, Manford. 1964. "Major Trends in Symbolic Interaction Theory in the Past Twenty-Five Years." *Sociological Quarterly* 5:61–84.

Kuhn, Thomas. 1970. *The Structure of Scientific Revolutions*, 2nd ed. Chicago: University of Chicago Press.

Kurtz, Lester R. 2007. *Gods in the Global Village*, 2nd ed. Thousand Oaks, CA: Pine Forge Press.

LaFraniere, Sharon and Andrew W. Lehren. 2015. "The Disproportionate Risks of Driving While Black." *New York Times*, October 24. Retrieved December 8, 2015 (www.nytimes.com/2015/10/25/us/racial-disparity-traffic-stops-driving-black.html?smid=nytcore-ipad-share&smprod=nytcore-ipad).

Lake, Nell. 2012. "Labor, Interrupted." *Harvard Magazine*, November–December. Retrieved July 15, 2013 (http://harvardmagazine.com/2012/11/labor-interrupted).

Lake, Robert. 1990. "An Indian Father's Plea." *Teacher Magazine* 2(September):48–53.

Langfitt, Frank. 2011. "Mobile Money Revolution Aids Kenya's Poor, Economy." NPR, January 5. Retrieved June 8, 2013 (http://www.npr.org/2011/01/05/132679772/mobile-money-revolution-aids-kenyas-poor-economy).

Langlois, Chistine. 2015. "The Accidental Activists: Craig and Marc Kielburger." *Canadian Living*. Retrieved November 25, 2015 (www.canadianliving.com/life/community/the_accidental_activists_craig_and_marc_kielburger.php).

Langton, Lynn, Michael Planty, and Nathan Sandholtz. 2013. "Hate Crime Victimization, 2003–2011." Bureau of Justice Statistics, March 21. Retrieved June 1, 2013 (www.bjs.gov/index.cfm?ty=pbdetail&iid=4614).

Lareau, Annette. 2003. *Unequal Childhoods: Class, Race, and Family Life*. Berkeley: University of California Press.

Lasch, Kathryn E. 2002 "Culture and Pain." *Pain: Clinical Updates* X(5):1–9.

Lashbrook, Jeffrey. 2009. "Social Class Differences in Family Life." P. 224 in *Our Social World*, 2nd ed., edited by Jeanne H. Ballantine and Keith A. Roberts. Thousand Oaks, CA: Sage.

Lavy, Victor and Edith Sand. 2015. "On the Origins of Gender Human Capital Gaps: Short and Long Term Consequences of Teachers' Stereotypical Biases." National Bureau of Economic Research, January 15. Working Paper No. 20909. Retrieved September 3, 2015 (www.nber.org/papers/w20909).

Lawrence, Alison. 2009. "Cutting Correction Costs: Earned Time Policies for State Prisoners." National Conference of State Legislatures. Retrieved June 2, 2013 (www.ncsl.org/documents/cj/earned_time_report.pdf).

Lazare, Aaron. 2004. *On Apology*. New York: Oxford University Press.

Lazaridis, Gabriella. 2011. *Security, Insecurity and Migration in Europe*. Farnham, UK: Ashgate.

LeBon, Gustave. [1895] 1960. *The Crowd: A Study of the Popular Mind*. New York: Viking.

Lebow, R. N. 1981. *Between Peace and War: The Nature of International Crisis*. Baltimore, MD: Johns Hopkins University Press.

Lechner, Frank J. and John Boli. 2005. *World Culture: Origins and Consequences*. Malden, MA: Blackwell.

Lederman, Josh. 2012. "Voter Turnout Shaping Up to Be Lower Than 2008." *Huffington Post*, November 7. Retrieved November 11, 2012 (http://www.huffingtonpost.com/2012/11/07/voter-turnout_n_2088810.html).

Lee, Jennifer and Frank D. Bean. 2004. "America's Changing Color Lines: Immigration, Race/Ethnicity, and Multiracial Identification." *Annual Review of Sociology* 30(August):222–42.

Lee, Jennifer and Frank D. Bean. 2007. "Redrawing the Color Line?" *City and Community* 6(1):49–62.

Lee, Richard B. 1984. *The Dobe!Kung*. New York: Holt, Rinehart & Winston.

Lee, Suevon. 2012. "By the Numbers: The U.S.'s Growing For-Profit Detention Industry." ProPublica, June 20. Retrieved June 3, 2013 (www.propublica.org/article/by-the-numbers-the-u.s.s-growing-for-profit-detention-industry).

Leeder, Elaine J. 2004. *The Family in Global Perspective: A Gendered Journey*. Thousand Oaks, CA: Sage.

Legters, Nettie E. 2001. "Teachers as Workers in the World System." Pp. 417–26 in *Schools and Society: A Sociological Approach to Education*, edited by Jeanne H. Ballantine and Joan Z. Spade. Belmont, CA: Wadsworth.

Lemert, Edwin M. 1951. *Social Pathology*. New York: McGraw-Hill.

Lemert, Edwin M. 1972. *Human Deviance, Social Problems, and Social Control*, 2nd ed. Englewood Cliffs, NJ: Prentice Hall.

Lenhart, Amanda. 2015. "Teens, Technology and Friendships." Pew Research Center, August 6. Retrieved September 3, 2015 (www.perinternet.org/2015/08/06/chapter-3-video-games-are-key-elements-in-friendships-for-many-boys).

Lenski, Gerhard E. 1966. *Human Societies*. New York: McGraw-Hill.

Leonhardt, David. 2015. "Middle-Class Black Families, in Low-Income Neighborhoods." *New York Times*, June 24. Retrieved June 25, 2015 (www.nytimes.com/2015/06/25/upshot/middle-class-black-families-in-low-income-neighborhoods.html?abt=0002&abg=1).

Lerner, Richard M. 1992. "Sociobiology and Human Development: Arguments and Evidence." *Human Development* 35(1):12–51.

Leslie, Gerald R. and Sheila K. Korman. 1989. *The Family in Social Context*, 7th ed. New York: Oxford University Press.

Levinson, Stephen C. 2000. "Yeli Dnye and the Theory of Basic Color Terms." *Journal of Linguistic Anthropology* 1:3–55.

Levitt, Peggy. 2001. *The Transnational Villagers*. Berkeley: University of California Press.

Levitt, Peggy. 2007. *God Needs No Passport: Immigrants and the Changing American Religious Landscape*. New York: New Press.

Levitt, Peggy and Mary Waters, eds. 2006. *The Changing Face of Home: The Transnational Lives of the Second Generation*. New York: Russell Sage Foundation.

Lieber, Jessica. 2015. "Introducing The Bridge, The Innovation Hub of New York City's $2 Billion Tech Campus." FastCompany. Retrieved July 8, 2015 (www.fastcoexist.com/3047388/introducing-the-bridge-the-innovation-hub-of-new-york-citys-2-billion-tech-campus).

Lieberson, Stanley, Susan Dumais, and Shyon Bauman. 2000. "The Instability of Androgynous Names: The Symbolic Maintenance of Gender Boundaries." *American Journal of Sociology* 105(5):1249–87.

Lindberg, Richard and Vesna Markovic. N.d. "Organized Crime Outlook in the New Russia: Russia Is Paying the Price of a Market Economy in Blood." Retrieved January 4, 2001 (www.search-international.com/Articles/crime/russiacrime.htm).

Lindow, Megan. 2009. "South Africa's Rape Crisis: 1 in 4 Men Say They've Done It." *Time*, June 20. Retrieved February 27, 2012 (www.time.com/time/world/article/0,8599,1906000,00.html).

Lindsay, James M. 2006. "Global Warming Heats Up." Pp. 307–13 in *Globalization: The Transformation of Social Worlds*, edited by D. Stanley Eitzen and Maxine Baca Zinn. Belmont, CA: Wadsworth.

Lindsey, Linda L. 2015. *Gender Roles: A Sociological Perspective*, 6th ed. Englewood Cliffs, NJ: Prentice Hall.

Lino, Mark. 2014. "Expenditures on Children by Families, 2013." U.S. Department of Agriculture, Center for Nutrition Policy and Promotion. Retrieved April 3, 2016 (www.cnpp.usda.gov/sites/default/files/expenditures_on_children_by_families/crc2013.pdf).

Linton, Ralph. 1937. *The Study of Man*. New York: D. Appleton-Century.

Lips, Hilary M. 2010. *Sex and Gender: An Introduction*, 9th ed. Boston: McGraw-Hill.

Lips, Hilary. 2013. *Gender: The Basics*. New York: Routledge.

Liptak, Adam. 2008. "U.S. Prison Population Dwarfs That of Other Nations." *New York Times*, April 23. Retrieved April 15, 2012 (www.nytimes.com/2008/04/23/world/americas/23iht-23prisons.12253738.html).

Liptak, Adam. 2013. "Justices Step Up Scrutiny of Race in College Entry." *New York Times*, June 24. Retrieved June 25, 2013 (www.nytimes.com/2013/06/25/us/affirmative-action-decision.html?pagewanted=1&_r=0&hp).

Liptak, Adam. 2015. "Supreme Court Ruling Makes Same-Sex Marriage a Right Nationwide." *New York Times*, June 26. Retrieved October 23, 2015 (www.nytimes.com/2015/06/27/us/supreme-court-same-sex-marriage.html?_r-0).

Liptak, Adam. 2016. "Supreme Court Upholds Affirmative Action Program at University of Texas." *New York Times*, June 23. Retrieved July 20, 2016 (www.nytimes.com/2016/06/24/us/politics/supreme-court-affirmative-action-university-of-texas.html).

Lofgren, Orvar. 1999. *On Holiday: A History of Vacationing*. Berkeley: University of California Press.

Lofgren, Orvar. 2010. "The Global Beach." Pp. 37–55 in *Tourists and Tourism*, 2nd ed., edited by Sharon Bohn Gmelch. Long Grove, IL: Waveland Press.

Loftsdottir, Kristin. 2004. "When Nomads Lose Cattle: Wodaabe Negotiations of Ethnicity." *African Sociological Review* 8(2):55–76.

Lombard, Hamilton. 2014. "Ancestry: Who Do You Think You Are?" Stat Chat From the Demographics Research Group at UVA. Retrieved September 5, 2014 (http://statchatva.org/2014/03/13/ancestry-who-do-you-think-you-are/).

"Lonmin Profit Plunges on South Africa Platinum Strike." 2014. BBC News, May 12. Retrieved September 7, 2014 (www.bbc.com/news/business-27369966).

"Looking for a Home." 2016. *The Economist*, May 28. Retrieved June 6, 2016 (www.economist.com/news/special-report/21699307-migrant-crisis-europe-last-year-was-only-one-part-worldwide-problem-rich).

Lopez, Mark Hugo and Ana Gonzalez-Barrera. 2014a. "Women's College Enrollment Gains Leave Men Behind." Pew Research Center. Retrieved April 25, 2016 (www.pewresearch.org/fact-tank).

Lopez, Mark Hugo and Ana Gonzalez-Barrera. 2014b. "Women Outpace Men in College Enrollment." Pew Research Fact Tank, March 6. Retrieved May 16, 2014 (www.pewresearch.org/fact-tank/2014/03/06/womens-college-enrollment-gains-leave-men-behind).

Lorber, Judith. 2009. *Gender Inequality: Feminist Theories and Politics*. New York: Oxford University Press.

Lorber, Judith and Lisa Jean Moore. 2011. *Gendered Bodies: Feminist Perspectives*, 2nd ed. New York: Oxford University Press.

Lorillard, Didi. 2011. "What's Going on With the Venerable State of Marriage?" GoLocal Lifestyle. Retrieved June 4, 2012 (www.golocalprov.com/lifestyle/modern-manners-etiquette-sharing-household-chores).

Loveless, Tom. 2013. "The Resurgence of Ability Grouping and Persistence of Tracking." Brookings. Retrieved June 23, 2015 (www.brookings.edu/research/reports/2013/03/18-tracking-ability-grouping-loveless).

Loy, Irwin. 2012. "Observers: Cambodian Vote Improved but Problems Remain." Voice of America. Retrieved July 25, 2012 (www.voanews.com/content/observers-cambodian-elections-improved-but-problems-remain/1146999.html).

Luckerson, Victor. 2014. "Fewer People Than Ever Are Watching TV." *Time*, December 3.

Lucas, Samuel R. and Mark Berends. 2002. "Sociodemographic Diversity, Correlated Achievement, and De Facto Tracking." *Sociology of Education* 75(4):328–48.

Luhman, Reid and Stuart Gilman. 1980. *Race and Ethnic Relations: The Social and Political Experience of Minority Groups*. Belmont, CA: Wadsworth.

Lutz, Ashley. 2012. "These 6 Corporations Control 90% of the Media in America. *Business Insider*, June 14. Retrieved June 30, 2016 (www.businessinsider.com/these-6-corporations-control-90-of-the-media-in-america-2012-6).

Ma, Yngyi and Gokhan Savas. 2014. "Which Is More Consequential: Fields of Study or Institutional Selectivity?" *Review of Higher Education* 37(2):221–47.

Machalek, Richard and Michael W. Martin. 2010. "Evolution, Biology, and Society: A Conversation for the 21st Century Classroom." *Teaching Sociology* 38(1):35–45.

Machiavelli, Niccolò. [1532] 2010. *The Prince*. Hollywood, FL: Simon & Brown.

Macionis, John. 2016. *Sociology*, 16th ed. Upper Saddle River, NJ: Prentice Hall.

MacLeod, Jay. 2008. *Ain't No Makin' It: Aspirations and Attainment in a Low-Income Neighborhood*, 3rd ed. Boulder, CO: Westview.

Madden, Mary, Amanda Lenhart, Maeve Duggan, Sandra Cortesi, and Urs Glasser. 2013. "Teens and Technology." Pew Internet and American Life Project, March 13. Retrieved December 6, 2013 (www.pewinternet.org/Reports/2013/Teens-and-Tech/Main-Findings/Teens-and-Technology.aspx).

Madden, Mary and Kathryn Zickuhr. 2011. "65% of Online Adults Use Social Networking Sites." Pew Internet. Retrieved May 25, 2012 (http://pewinternet.org/Reports/2011/Social-Networking-Sites.aspx).

"The Madoff Case: A Timeline." 2009. *Wall Street Journal*, March 12. Retrieved November 5, 2009 (http://online.wsj.com/article/SB112966954231272304.html?mod=googlenews.wsj).

Maglaty, Jeanne. 2011. "When Did Girls Start Wearing Pink?" *Smithsonian Magazine*, April 7. Retrieved May 9, 2013 (www.smithsonianmag.com/arts-culture/When-Did-Girls-Start-Wearing-Pink.html).

Magnus, George. 2009. "Malthus, Marx and the Globalization Debate." *The Globalist*, February 28. Retrieved February 16, 2015 (www.theglobalist.com/malthus-marx-and-the-globalization-debate).

Makhmalbaf, Mohsen, producer. 2003. *Kandahar: The Sun Behind the Moon* (Film).

"Mali 'at War' With Tuareg Rebels." 2014. *Al Jazeera*, May 19. Retrieved August 29, 2014 (http://www.aljazeera.com/news/africa/2014/05/mali-at-war-with-tuareg-reb els-2014518 15152681548.html).

Malthus, Thomas R. [1798] 1926. *First Essay on Population*. London: Macmillan.

Maniac Agenda. 2016. "6 New Music Genres You Need to Hear Coming in 2016." Retrieved June 3, 2016 (www.maniamusic.net/home/blog/6-new-music-genres-you-need-to-hear-coming-in-2016)

Mann, Charles C. 2005. *1491: New Revelations of the Americas Before Columbus*. New York: Alfred A. Knopf.

Manning, Jennifer E. 2015. "Membership of the 114th Congress: A Profile." Congressional Research Service Report to Congress, October 31. Retrieved August 24, 2016 (https://www.fas.org/sgp/crs/misc/R43869.pdf).

Maoncha, Merculine. 2013. "Sustainability: Lake Nakuru in the Great Rift Valley." Thomson Reuters, April 22. Retrieved February 24, 2014 (http://sustainability.thomsonreuters.com/2013/04/19/youth-perspective-lake-nakuru-in-the-great-rift-valley).

Marcotte, Amanda. 2015. "Teen Girls Love Video Games, but They're Really Quiet About It." *Slate*, August 18. Retrieved September 3, 2015 (www.slate.com/blogs/xx_factor/2015/08/18/teen_girls_play_video_games_but_they_minimize_their_contact_with_other_players.html).

Marger, Martin N. 2012. *Race and Ethnic Relations: American and Global Perspectives*, 9th ed. Belmont, CA: Wadsworth.

Markoff, John and Somini Sengupta. 2011. "Separating You and Me? 4.74 Degrees." *New York Times*, November 21. Retrieved September 25, 2012 (www.nytimes.com/2011/11/22/technolgoy/between-you-and-me-4-74-degrees.html).

Martin, Jenny Beth and Mark Meckler. 2012. *Tea Party Patriots: The Second American Revolution*. New York: Henry Holt and Company.

Martinez, Martha A. 2008. "Split Labor Market." Pp. 1275–1277 in *Encyclopedia of Race, Ethnicity, and Society*, edited by Richard T. Schaefer. Thousand Oaks, CA: SAGE.

Martineau, Harriet. [1837] 1962. *Society in America*. Garden City, NY: Doubleday.

Martineau, Harriet. 1838. *How to Observe Manners and Morals*. London: Charles Knight & Co.

Martorell, Gabriela, Diane Papalia, and Ruth Feldman. 2014. *A Child's World: Infancy Through Adolescence*, 13th ed. New York: McGraw Hill.

Marty, Martin E. and R. Scott Appleby, eds. 2004. *Accounting for Fundamentalism: The Dynamic Character of Movements*. Chicago: University of Chicago Press.

Marx, Karl. [1844] 1963. "Contribution to the Critique of Hegel's Philosophy of Right." Pp. 43–59 in *Karl Marx: Early Writings*, translated and edited by T. B. Bottomore. New York: McGraw-Hill.

Marx, Karl. [1844] 1964. *The Economic and Philosophical Manuscripts of 1844*. New York: International Publishers.

Marx, Karl. [1844] 2009. *Economic & Philosophic Manuscripts of 1844*. Retrieved February 12, 2015 (www.marxists.org/archive/marx/works/download/pdf/Economic-Philosophic-Manuscripts-1844.pdf).

Marx, Karl and Friedrich Engels. [1848] 1969. *The Communist Manifesto*. Baltimore: Penguin.

Marx, Karl and Friedrich Engels. 1955. *Selected Work in Two Volumes*. Moscow: Foreign Language Publishing House.

Marx, Karl and Friedrich Engels. 1975. *Selected Correspondence*. Moscow: Progress Publishers. Retrieved February 12, 2015 (www.marxists.org/archive/marx/works/1881/letters/81_02_01.htm).

Massey, Douglas S. and Nancy A. Denton. 1998. *American Apartheid: Segregation and the Making of the Underclass*. Cambridge, MA: Harvard University Press.

Massey, Douglas S., Len Albright, Rebecca Casciano, Elizabeth Derickson, and David N. Kinsey. 2013. *Climbing Mount Laurel: The Struggle for Affordable Housing and Social Mobility in an American Suburb*. Princeton, NJ: Princeton University Press.

Mathews, T. J., Marian F. MacDorman, and Marie E. Thoma. 2015. "Infant Mortality Statistics From the 2013 Period Linked Birth/Infant Death Data Set." *National Vital Statistics Reports* 64(9). Retrieved April 21, 2016 (www.cdc.gov/nchs/data/nvsr/nvsr64/nvsr64_09.pdf).

Matson, John. 2013. "Women Are Earning Greater Share of STEM Degrees, but Doctorates Remain Gender-Skewed." *Scientific American*, April 23. Retrieved January 18, 2014 (www.scientificamerican.com/article.cfm?id=women-earnings-greater-share-stem-degrees-doctorates-remain-skewed).

Matthews, Chris. 2014. "Fortune 5: The Biggest Organized Crime Groups in the World." *Fortune*, September 14.

Matthews, Chris. 2015. "Millionaires Now Control an Even Bigger Share of the World's Wealth." *Fortune*, June 15. Retrieved June 27, 2015 (http://fortune.com/2015/06/15/millionaires-wealth-china).

Mauss, Armand. 1975. *Social Problems as Social Movements*. Philadelphia: Lippincott.

Mawani, Vrushti. 2011. "Marriage Majestic. William-Kate Wedding to Cost $70 Million." *Industry Leaders Magazine*, April 29. Retrieved June 5, 2013 (www.industryleadersmagazine.com/marriage-majestic-william-kate-wedding-to-cost-70-million).

Mayeda, David. 2013. "Preventing Violence Against Women and Girls." *Sociology in Focus*, April 3. Retrieved July 18, 2015 (www.sociologyinfocus.com/2013/04/03/preventing-violence-against-women-girls-steubenville-sport).

Mayflower Church. 2016. "Social Justice: Earthwise Congregation." Retrieved February 10, 2016 (www.mayflowermpls.org/social-justice/earthwise).

Mayoux, Linda, ed. 2008. *Sustainable Learning for Women's Empowerment: Ways Forward in Micro-Finance*. Warwickshire, UK: ITDG Publishing.

McBride, James. 2015. "Prospects for the Global Economy in 2016." Council on Foreign Relations, December 23. Retrieved February 11, 2016 (www.cfr.org/global/prospects-global-economy-2016/p37400).

McCabe, Janice, Emily Fairchild, Liz Grauerholz, Bernice A. Pescosolido, and Daniel Tope. 2011. "Gender in Twentieth-Century Children's Books: Patterns of Disparity in Titles and Central Characters." *Gender and Society* 25(2):197–226.

McCarthy, Niall. 2015. "The Countries Where Gay Marriage Is Legal (map)." *Forbes*, June 29. Retrieved September 8, 2015 (www.forbes.com/sites/niallmccarthy/2015/06/29/the-countries-where-gay-marriage-is-legal-map/).

McCarthy, John D. and Mayer N. Zald. 1977. "Resource Mobilization and Social Movements: A Partial Theory." *American Journal of Sociology* 82(6):1212–41.

McCoy, Terrence. 2014. "India's Gang Rapes—and the Failure to Stop Them." *Washington Post*, May 30. Retrieved May 28, 2015 (www.washingtonpost.com/news/morning-mix/wp/2014/05/30/indias-culture-of-gang-rape-and-the-failure-to-stop-it).

McCrone, David. 1998. *The Sociology of Nationalism*. London: Routledge.

McCrummen, Stephanie. 2008. "Women Run the Show in a Recovering Rwanda." *Washington Post*, October 27. Retrieved May 6, 2011 (www.washingtonpost.com/wpdyn/content/article/2008/10/26/AR2008102602197.html).

McIntosh, Peggy. 2002. "White Privilege: Unpacking the Invisible Knapsack." Pp. 97–101 in *White Privilege: Essential Readings on the Other Side of Racism*, edited by Paula S. Rothenberg. New York: Worth.

McKelvie, Samuel R. 1926. "What the Movies Meant to the Farmer." *Annals of the American Academy of Political and Social Science* 128(November):131.

McKenzie, David. 2015. "For China, Three Decades of One-Child Policy Proves Hard to Undo." CNN, March 30. Retrieved July 6, 2015 (www.cnn.com/2015/03/30/asia/china-one-child-policy-undo).

Mead, George Herbert. [1934] 1962. *Mind, Self, and Society*. Chicago: University of Chicago Press.

Mears, Bill. 2014. "Michigan's Ban on Affirmative Action Upheld by Supreme Court." CNN Justice, April 23. Retrieved May 11, 2014 (www.cnn.com/2014/04/22/justice/scotus-michigan-affirmative-action).

Mehan, Hugh. 1992. "Understanding Inequality in Schools: The Contribution of Interpretive Studies." *Sociology of Education* 65(1):1–20.

Mehrabian, Albert. 1972. *Silent Messages: Implicit Communication of Emotions and Attitudes*. Belmont, CA: Wadsworth.

Mehsud, Saud. 2012. "Pakistani Girl Shot by Taliban Defied Threats for Years." *Reuters*, October 10. Retrieved October 11, 2012 (www.reuters.com/article/2012/10/10/us-pakistan-girl-family-idUSBRE8990T720121010).

Meier, Robert F. 2016. "Sociological Perspectives on Criminal Behavior." In *The Cambridge Handbook of Sociology*. Cambridge, UK: Cambridge University Press.

Meixell, Brady and Ross Eisenbrey. 2014. "An Epidemic of Wage Theft Is Costing Workers Hundreds of Millions of Dollars a Year." Economic Policy Institute, September 11. Retrieved June 7, 2015 (www.epi.org/publication/epidemic-wage-theft-costing-workers-hundreds).

Meltzer, Bernard. 1978. "Mead's Social Psychology." Pp. 15–27 in *Symbolic Interactionism: A Reader in Social Psychology*, 3rd ed., edited by Jerome Manis and Bernard Meltzer. Boston: Allyn & Bacon.

Meltzer, Bernard N., John W. Petras, and Larry T. Reynolds. 1975. *Symbolic Interactionism: Genesis, Varieties and Criticism*. London: Routledge & Kegan Paul.

Merriam-Webster. 2014. "Black." Retrieved April 9, 2014 (www.merriam-webster.com/dictionary/black).

Merton, Robert K. 1938. "Social Structure and Anomie." *American Sociological Review* 3(October):672–82.

Merton, Robert K. 1948. "The Self Fulfilling Prophecy." *Antioch Review* 8(2):193–210.

Merton, Robert K. 1968. *Social Theory and Social Structure*, 2nd ed. New York: Free Press.

Merton, Robert K. [1942] 1973. *The Sociology of Science: Theoretical and Empirical Investigations*. Chicago: University of Chicago Press.

Meyer, Ali. 2014. "Women Now 33% More Likely Than Men to Earn College Degrees." CNS News, March 31. Retrieved April 8, 2016 (cnsnews.com/news/article/ali-meyer/women-now-33-more-likely-men-earn-college-degrees).

Meyer, Elaine. 2012. "Is the Wealth Gap Creating a Health Gap?" 2x2 Project, December 5. Retrieved May 13, 2014 (http://the2x2project.org/health-gap-wealth-gap/).

Michels, Robert. [1911] 1967. *Political Parties*. New York: Free Press.

Mikkelson, Barbara and David P. Mikkelson. 2012. "Urban Legends." Snopes. Retrieved January 1, 2012 (www.snopes.com/college/college.asp).

Milgram, Stanley. 1967. "The Small World Problem." *Psychology Today* 1:61–67.

Miller, Claire Cain. 2015. "More Than Their Mothers, Young Women Plan Career Pauses." *New York Times*, July 22. Retrieved September 14, 2015 (http://nyti.ms/1JxIeIa).

Miller, Claire Cain and Liz Alderman. 2014. "Why U.S. Women Are Leaving Jobs Behind." *New York Times*, December 12. Retrieved September 14, 2015 (http://nyti.ms/1zJZTL6).

Mills, C. Wright. 1956. *The Power Elite*. New York: Oxford University Press.

Mills, C. Wright. 1959. *The Sociological Imagination*. New York: Oxford University Press.

Mills, Theodore M. 1984. *The Sociology of Small Groups*, 2nd ed. Englewood Cliffs, NJ: Prentice Hall.

"Mobility, Measured." 2014. *The Economist*, February 1. Retrieved August 24, 2016 (http://www.economist.com/news/united-states/21595437-america-no-less-socially-mobile-it-was-generation-ago-mobility-measured).

Molotch, Harvey. 2003. *Where Stuff Comes From: How Toasters, Toilets, Cars, Computers, and Many Other Things Come to Be as They Are*. London: Routledge.

Monir, Malak. 2015. "Half the States Look at Right-to-Die Legislation." *USA Today*, April 16. Retrieved June 30, 2015 (www.usatoday.com/story/news/politics/2015/04/15/death-with-dignity-laws-25-states/25735597/_).

Morey, Peter and Amina Yaqin. 2011. *Framing Muslims: Stereotyping and Representation After 9/11*. Cambridge, MA: Harvard University Press.

Morgan, David. 2012. "One in Four Americans Without Health Coverage." *Reuters*, April 19. Retrieved August 1, 2012 (www.reuters.com/article/2012/04/19/us-usa-healthcare-insurance-idUSBRE83117420120419).

Morris, Aldon D. 2015. *The Scholar Denied: W.E.B. Du Bois and the Birth of Modern Sociology*. Berkeley: University of California Press.

Morris, Joan M. and Michael D. Grimes. 1997. *Caught in the Middle: Contradictions in the Lives of Sociologists From Working Class Backgrounds*. Westport, CT: Praeger.

Morris, Lloyd R. 1949. *Not So Long Ago*. New York: Random House.

Morrison, Maureen. 2010. "New Data Shed Light on Women's Internet Usage." *Ad Age*, August 3. Retrieved May 25, 2012 (http://adage.com/article/adagestat/data-research-women-s-internet-usage/145224).

Motel, Seth. 2015. "6 Factors about Marijuana." Pew Research, April 14. Retrieved June 7, 2015 (www.pewresearch.org/fact-tank/2015/04/14/6-facts-about-marijuana).

Mou, Yi and Wei Peng. 2009. "Gender and Racial Stereotypes in Popular Video Games." IGI Global OnDemand.

MoveOn.Org. 2016. "Stop the Trans-Pacific Partnership." Retrieved February 12, 2016 (www.petitions.moveon.org/sign/stop-the-trans-pacific).

Muchhala, Bhumika. 2012. "Students Against Sweat Shops." Pp. 303–12 in *Globalization: The Transformation of Social Worlds*, 3rd ed., edited by D. Stanley Eitzen and Maxine Baca Zinn. Belmont, CA: Wadsworth.

Münchener, Rückversicherungs-Gesellschaft. 2016. "Natural Loss Events Worldwide 2015." Retrieved April 8, 2016 (www.munichre.com/site/wrap/get/documents_E1656163460/mram/assetpool.munichreamerica.wrap/PDF/07Press/2015_World_map_of_nat_cats.pdf).

Mydans, Seth. 2002. "In Pakistan, Rape Victims Are the 'Criminals." *New York Times*, May 17, p. A3.

Myers, Steven Lee and Nicholas Kulish 2013. "Growing Clamor About Inequities of Climate Crisis." *New York Times*, November 16. Retrieved February 24, 2014 (www.nytimes.com/2013/11/17/world/growing-clamor-about-inequities-of-climate-crisis.html?_r=0).

Myrdal, Gunnar. 1964. *An American Dilemma*. New York: McGraw-Hill.

Nagel, Joane. 1994. "Constructing Ethnicity: Creating and Recreating Ethnic Identity and Culture." *Social Problems* 41(1):152–76.

Nagourney, Adam and Rick Lyman. 2013. "Few Problems With Cannabis for California." *New York Times*, October 26. Retrieved October 27, 2013 (www.nytimes.com/2013/10/27/us/few-problems-with-cannabis-for-california.html?_r=0).

National Center for Complementary and Alternative Medicine. 2013. "Complementary, Alternative or Integrative Health: What's in a Name?" National Institutes of Health, May. Retrieved March 10, 2014 (http://nccam.nih.gov/health/whatiscam).

National Conference of State Legislatures. 2011. "The Affordable Care Act: A Brief Summary." Retrieved July 13, 2013 (www.ncsl.org/portals/1/documents/health/hraca.pdf).

National Conference of State Legislatures. 2015. "State Laws Regarding Marriages Between First Cousins." Retrieved January 17, 2015 (www.ncsl.org/issues-research/human-services/state-laws-regarding-marriages-between-first-cousi.aspx).

National Consumers League. 2013. "Parents: Take Control Over Your Child's Viewing, Surfing, and Texting Habits." Retrieved December 6, 2013 (www.ncinet.org/technology/149-parental-controls/537-parental-controls).

National Partnership for Women and Families. 2015. "An Unlevel Playing Field: America's Gender-Based Wage Gap, Binds of Discrimination, and a Path Forward." April. Retrieved September 5, 2015 (www.nationalpartnership.org/research-library/workplace-fairness/fair-pay/an-unevel-playing-field-americas-gender-based-wage-gap-binds-if-discrimination-and-a-path-forward.pdf).

National Public Radio. 2013. "Closing the 'Word Gap' Between Rich and Poor." Retrieved January 5, 2014 (www.wbur.org/npr/257922222/closing-the-word-gap-between-rich-and-poor).

NationMaster. 2011. "United States Population Pyramids." Retrieved May 19, 2011 (www.nationmaster.com/country/us/Age_distribution).

NationMaster. 2014. "Physicians per 1,000 People." Retrieved September 15, 2014 (http://www.nationmaster.com/country-info/stats/Health/Physicians/Per-1%2C000-people).

Neuman, Michelle J. 2005. "Global Early Care and Education: Challenges, Responses, and Lessons." *Phi Delta Kappan* (November):188–92.

New America Foundation. 2014. "School Finance: Federal, State, and Local K–12 School Finance Overview." April 21. Retrieved May 13, 2014 (http://febp.newamerica.net/background-analysis/school-finance).

Newman, David. 2009. *Families: A Sociological Perspective*. New York: McGraw-Hill.

Newman, Matthew L., Carla J. Groom, Lori D. Handelman, and James W. Pennebaker. 2008. "Gender Differences in Language Use: An Analysis of 14,000 Text Samples." *Discourse Process* 45: 211–36.

New Media Trend Watch. 2013. "Demographics: Percentage of Population Online." Retrieved December 6, 2013 (www.newmediatrendwatch.com/markets-by-country/17-usa/123-demographics).

Nielsen. 2014. "The Total Audience Report." Retrieved September 14, 2015 (ir.nielsen.com/files/doc_presentations/2015/total-audience-report-q4-2014.pdf).

Nixon, Ron. 2012. "New Rules for School Meals Aim at Reducing Obesity." *New York Times*, January 25. Retrieved February 7, 2015 (www.nytimes.com/2012/01/26/us/politics/new-school-lunch-rules-aimed-at-reducing-obesity.html?_r=0).

Noack, Rick. 2014. "The World's 36 Million Slaves." *Washington Post*, November 18. Retrieved April 7, 2016 (https://www.washingtonpost.com/news/worldviews/wp/2014/11/18/map-the-worlds-36-million-slaves/?utm_term=.c74c1e2e01ef).

Noel, Donald. 1968. "A Theory of the Origin of Ethnic Stratification." *Social Problems* 16(Fall):157–72.

Noesselt, Nele. 2014. "China and Socialist Countries: Role Change and Role Continuity." German Institute of Global and Area Studies, August 2014. Retrieved August 26, 2016 (www.giga-hamburg.de/en/system/files/publications/wp250_noesselt.pdf).

Noguera, Pedro A. 2011. "A Broader and Bolder Approach Uses Education to Break Cycle of Poverty." *Phi Delta Kappan* 93(3):9–14.

Noguera, Pedro and Robby Cohen. 2006. "Patriotism and Accountability: The Role of Educators in the War on Terrorism." *Phi Delta Kappan* 87(8):573–78.

Nolan, Cathal J. 2002. "Terrorism" and "War." Pp. 1648–49 in *The Greenwood Encyclopedia of International Relations*. London: Greenwood.

Nolan, Patrick and Gerhard Lenski. 2014. *Human Societies: An Introduction to Macrosociology*, 12th ed. New York: Oxford University Press.

Nolan, Patrick D., Jennifer Triplett, and Shannon McDonough. 2010. "Sociology's Suicide: A Forensic Autopsy." *American Sociologist* 41:292–305.

Nonhuman Rights Project. 2016. "About Us." Retrieved February 12, 2016 (www.nonhumanrightsproject.org/about-us-2).

Norton, Michael and Dan Ariely. 2011. "Building a Better America—One Wealth Quintile at a Time." *Perspectives in Psychological Science* 6(1):9–12.

Nossiter, Adam. 2014. "Wielding Whip and a Hard New Law, Nigeria Tries to 'Sanitize' Itself of Gays." *New York Times*, February 8. Retrieved February 8, 2014 (www.nytimes.com/2014/02/09/world/africa/nigeria-uses-law-and-whip-to-sanitize-gays.html?hp&_r=0).

Oakes, Jeannie, Amy Stuart Wells, Makeba Jones, and Amanda Datnow. 1997. "Detracking: The Social Construction of Ability, Cultural Politics, and Resistance to Reform." *Teacher's College Record* 98(3):482–510.

O'Brien, Denise. 1977. "Female Husbands in Southern Bantu Societies." In *Sexual Stratification: A Cross-Cultural View*, edited by Alice Schlegel. New York: Columbia University Press

O'Brien, Jody. 2011. *The Production of Reality*, 5th ed. Thousand Oaks, CA: Sage

O'Connor, Liz, Gus Lubin, and Dina Spector. 2013. "The Largest Ancestry Groups in the United States." *Business Insider*, August 13. Retrieved September 5, 2014 (www.business insider.com/largest-ethnic-groups-in-america-2013-8).

Ogburn, William F. 1933. *Recent Social Trends*. New York: McGraw-Hill.

Ogburn, William F. [1922] 1938. *Social Change, With Respect to Culture and Original Nature*. New York: Viking.

Ogburn, William F. 1961. "The Hypothesis of Cultural Lag." Pp. 1270–73 in *Theories of Society: Foundations of Modern Sociological Theory*, Vol. 2, edited by Talcott Parsons, Edward Shils, Kaspar D. Naegele, and Jesse R. Pitts. New York: Free Press.

Ogburn, William F. 1964. *On Culture and Social Change: Selected Papers*, edited by Otis Dudley Duncan. Chicago: University of Chicago Press.

Olsen, Lauren D. 2016. "It's on the MCAT for a Reason: Premedical Students and the Perceived Utility of Sociology." *Teaching Sociology* 44(2):72–83.

Organisation for Economic Co-operation and Development. 2013. "Health at a Glance 2013: OECD Indicators." Retrieved May 28, 2014 (http://dx.doi.org/10.1787/health_glance-2013-en).

Organisation for Economic Co-operation and Development. 2014a. "OECD Family Database—Trends in Parental Leave Policies Since 1970." Retrieved February 27, 2014 (www .oecd.org/els/family/PF2.5%20Trends%20in%20leave%20 entitlements%20around%20childbirth%20since%20 1970%20-%2010%20oct%202012%20-%20FINAL.pdf).

Organisation for Economic Co-operation and Development. 2014b. *PISA 2012 Results: What Students Know and Can Do: Student Performance in Mathematics, Reading and Science* (Vol. 1), rev. ed., February.

Organisation for Economic Co-operation and Development. 2015a. "Employment: Gender Wage Gap." Retrieved September 6, 2015 (stats.oecd.org/index.aspx?queryid=54751).

Organisation for Economic Co-operation and Development. 2015b. "Health at a Glance 2015: OECD Indicators." Retrieved April 21, 2016 (www.keepeek.com/Digital-Asset-Management/oecd/social-issues-migration-health/health-at-a-glance-2015_health_glance-2015-en).

Organisation for Economic Co-operation and Development. 2016. "Time Spent in Paid and Unpaid Work, by Sex." Retrieved February 27, 2016 (http://stats.oecd.org/index. aspx?queryid=54757).

Ortutay, Barbara, and Brett Zongker. 2011. "Newspapers See Big Demand From Bin Laden News." *Seattle Times*, May 3. Retrieved August 8, 2016 (www.seattletimes.com/business/newspapers-see-big-demand-from-bin-laden-news).

Ostroff, Stephen M. 2013. "Perspectives: The Role of the Traveler in Translocation of Disease." Chapter 1 in *Travelers' Health*. Retrieved March 10, 2014 (www.cdc.gov/travel/yellow book/2014/chapter-1-introduction/perspective-the-role-of-the-traveler-in-translocation-of-disease).

Otieno, Christine. 2013. "Nigeria Polio." Immunising the Vaccine Fears." BBC News, April 26. Retrieved July 13, 2013 (www.bbc.co.uk/news/world-africa-22307412).

Oxfam. 2016. "An Economy for the 1%." Oxfam Briefing Paper, January 18. Retrieved February 15, 2016 (www.oxfam .org/sites/www.oxfam.org/files/file_attachments/bp210-economy-one-percent-tax-havens-180116-en_0.pdf).

Pager, Devah, Bruce Western, and Bart Bonikowski. 2009. "Discrimination in a Low Wage Labor Market: A Field Experiment." *American Sociological Review* 74(October):777–99.

Papalia, Diane, Ruth Feldman, and Gabriela Mastorell. 2015. *Experience Human Development*, 13th ed. New York: McGraw-Hill.

Pareto, Vilfredo. [1911] 1955. "Mathematical Economics." In *Encyclopedie des Sciences Mathematique*. New York: Macmillan.

Park, Robert Ezra, Ernest W. Burgess, and Roderick D. McKenzie. [1925] 1967. *The City*. Chicago: University of Chicago Press.

Parker, Kim, and Wendy Wang. 2013. "Time in Work and Leisure, Patterns by Gender and Family Structure." Pew Research Social and Demographic Trends. Retrieved February 28, 2014 (www.pewsocialtrends.org/2013/03/14/modern-parent hood-roles-of-moms-and-dads-converge-as-they-balance-work-and-family/7).

Parlapiano, Alicia, Robert Gebeloff, and Shan Carter. 2015. "The Shrinking American Middle Class." *New York Times*, January 26. Retrieved July 20, 2015 (www.nytimes.com/ interactive/2015/01/25/upshot/shrinking-middle-class .html?abt=0002&abg=0).

Parsons, Talcott. 1951. *The Social System*. New York: Free Press.

Parsons, Talcott. 1971. *The System of Modern Societies*. Englewood Cliffs, NJ: Prentice-Hall.

Parsons, Talcott, and Robert F. Bales. 1953. *Family, Socialization, and Interaction Process*. Glencoe, IL: Free Press.

Partners in Prepaid. 2012. "Haiti Leads in Mobile Payments." April 23. Retrieved June 8, 2013 (www.partnersinprepaid. com/topics/articles/haiti-leads-in-mobile-payments.html).

Pasternak, Susan. 2013. "Of That $554 Billion, Medicare Spent 28 Percent, or About $170 Billion, on Patients' Last Six Months Of Life." Medicare Newsgroup, June 3. Retrieved July 13, 2013 (www.medicarenewsgroup.com/context/ understanding-medicare-blog/understanding-medicare-blog/2013/06/03/end-of-life-care-constitutes-third-rail-of-u.s.-health-care-policy-debate).

Paxton, Pamela and Melanie M. Hughes. 2007. *Women, Politics, and Power: A Global Perspective*. Thousand Oaks, CA: Pine Forge.

Paxton, Pamela and Tess Pearce. 2009. "How Does Social Class Affect Socialization Within the Family?" Exploring Social Science Research, April 24. Retrieved March 1, 2011 (http:// ibssblog.wordpress.com/2009/04/24/how-dues-social-class-affect-socialisation-within-the-family/).

Payne, Ed. 2014. "Doctors Keep Brain-Dead Pregnant Woman on Life Support Until Baby's Birth." CNN, February 4. Retrieved February 3, 2014 (www.cnn.com/2014/02/04/ world/americas/canada-brain-dead-woman).

Pearson, Michael and Joe Sutton. 2015. "Black Football Players at Missouri: We'll Sit Out Until System President Resigns." CNN, November 9. Retrieved December 8, 2015 (www.cnn .com/2015/11/08/us/missouri-football-players-protest).

Peek, Lori. 2011. *Behind the Backlash: Muslim Americans After 9/11*. Philadelphia: Temple University Press.

Pelaez, Vicky. 2014. "The Prison Industry in the United States: Big Business or a New Form of Slavery?" Global Research,

March 31. Retrieved August 27, 2016 (www.globalresearch.ca/the-prison-industry-in-the-united-states-big-business-or-anew-form-of-slavery/828).

Pellow, David Naguib. 2002. *Garbage Wars: The Struggle for Environmental Justice in Chicago*. Cambridge, MA: MIT Press.

Pemberton, David. 2015. "Statistical Definition of 'Family' Unchanged Since 1930." U.S. Census, January 28. (http://blogs.census.gov/2015/01/28/statistical-definition-of-family-unchanged-since-1930).

Perez, Marvin G. 2013. "Coffee Consumption Increases in U.S., Association Survey Shows." *Bloomberg News*, March 22. Retrieved February 14, 2014 (www.bloomberg.com/news/2013-03-22/coffee-consumption-increases-in-u-s-association-survey-shows.html).

Perkins, Lucy. 2015. "California Governor Signs School Vaccination Law." National Public Radio, June 30. Retrieved July 2, 2015 (www.npr.org/sections/thetwo-way/2015/06/30/418908804/california-governor-signs-school-vaccination-law).

Perlroth, Nicole and David E. Sanger. 2013. "Cyberattacks Seem Meant to Destroy, Not Just Disrupt." *New York Times*, March 28. Retrieved June 3, 2013 (http://www.nytimes.com/2013/03/29/technology/corporate-cyberattackers-possibly-state-backed-now-seek-to-destroy-data.html).

Persell, Caroline Hodges. 2005. "Race, Education, and Inequality." Pp. 286–24 in *Blackwell Companion to Social Inequalities*, edited by M. Romero and E. Margolis. Oxford, UK: Blackwell.

Persell, Caroline Hodges and Peter W. Cookson Jr. 1985. "Chartering and Bartering: Elite Education and Social Reproduction." *Social Problems* 33(2):114–29.

Pescosolido, Bernice A., 1992. "Beyond Rational Choice: The Social Dynamics of How People Seek Help." *American Journal of Sociology* 97(4):1113.

Pescosolido, Bernice A. and Carol A. Boyer. 2010. "The American Health Care System: Beginning the 21st Century With High Risk, Major Challenges, and Great Opportunities." Pp. 391–411 in *The New Blackwell Companion to Medical Sociology*, edited by William C. Cockerham. Malden, MA: Wiley-Blackwell.

Pescosolido, Bernice A., Jack K. Martin, Jane D. McLeod, and Anne Rogers, eds. 2011. *The Sociology of Health, Illness, and Healing: Blueprint for the 21st Century*. New York: Springer.

"Petermann Glacier." 2015. Department of Geological Sciences, Stockholm University. Retrieved September 10, 2015 (wwwgeo.su.se/index.php/en/expedition-logs/1276-petermann-glacier-2015).

Pettigrew, Thomas F., Linda R. Troppb, Ulrich Wagner, and Oliver Christ. 2011. "Recent Advances in Intergroup Contact Theory." *International Journal of Intercultural Relations* 35(May):271–80.

Pew Charitable Trusts. 2012. *Pursuing the American Dream: Economic Mobility Across Generations*. Retrieved June 7, 2013 (www.pewstates.org/uploadedFiles/PCS_Assets/2012/Pursuing_American_Dream.pdf).

Pew Research Center. 2010. "The Decline of Marriage and Rise of New Families." Pew Social & Demographic Trends, November 18. Retrieved March 8, 2012 (www.pewsocialtrends.org/2010/11/18/the-decline-of-marriage-and-rise-of-new- families).

Pew Research Center. 2015a. "Changing Attitudes on Gay Marriage." July 29. Retrieved September 6, 2015 (www.pewforum.org/2015/07/29/graphics-slideshow-changing-attitudes-on-gay-marriage/).

Pew Research Center. 2015b. "College Enrollment, by Race and Ethnicity: 2013." Table 20: Statistical Portrait of Hispanics in the United States, 2013. March 11. Retrieved May 12, 2017. http://www.pewhispanic.org/2016/04/19/statistical-portrait-of-hispanics-in-the-united-states/ph_2015-03_statistical-portrait-of-hispanics-in-the-united-states-2013_current-20/

Pew Research Center. 2015c. "Teens, Social Media & Technology Overview 2015." April 8. Retrieved September 3, 2015 (www.pewinternet.org/2015/04/09/teens-social-media-technology-2015/pi_2015-04-09_teensandtech_16/).

Pew Research Center. 2016. "Social Networking Fact Sheet." Retrieved April 12, 2016 (http://www.pewinternet.org/fact-sheets/social-networking-fact-sheet).

Pew Research Center Internet and American Life Project. 2012. "Teens Fact Sheet." Retrieved August 29, 2014 (http://www.pewinternet.org/fact-sheets/teens-fact-sheet/).

Pew Research Center Internet and American Life Project. 2014a. "Internet User Demographics." Retrieved January 17, 2015 (http://www.pewinternet.org/data-trend/internet-use/latest-stats).

Pew Research Center Internet and American Life Project. 2014b. "Social Networking Fact Sheet." Retrieved May 11, 2014 (www.pewinternet.org/fact-sheets/social-networking-fact-sheet).

Phillips, Richard. 2013. "Animal Communication" Lecture at Tuesdays with a Liberal Arts Scholar, University of Minnesota, May 6.

Phillips, Tom. 2015. "China Ends One-Child Policy After 35 Years." *The Guardian*, October 29. Retrieved January 4, 2015 (www.theguardian.com/world/2015/oct/29/china-abandons-one-child-policy).

Phys.Org. 2009. "Humans Spread Out of Africa Later." Retrieved October 9, 2012 (http://phys.org/news171286860.html).

Piaget, Jean. 1989. *The Child's Conception of the World*. Savage, MD: Littlefield, Adams Quality Paperbacks.

Pickard, Ruth, and Daryl Poole. 2007. "The Study of Society and the Practice of Sociology." Previously unpublished essay.

Picker, Les. 2014. "The Effects of Education on Health." National Bureau of Economic Research, October 28. Retrieved October 28, 2014 (www.nber.org/digest/mar07/w12352.html).

Pinker, Steven. 2002. *The Blank Slate: The Modern Denial of Human Nature*. New York: Viking.

Plato. [ca. 350 BCE] 1960. *The Laws*. New York: Dutton.

Political Geography Now. 2015. "How Many Countries Are There in the World in 2015?" September 12. Retrieved January 28, 2016 (www.polgeonow.com/2011/04/how-many-countries-are-there-in-world.html).

Population Reference Bureau. 2013a. "Rate of Natural Increase." Retrieved March 17, 2014 (www.prb.org/DataFinder/Topic/Rankings.aspx?ind=16).

Population Reference Bureau. 2013b. "Total Fertility Rate, 2012." Retrieved February 7, 2013 (http://www.prb.org/DataFinder/Topic/Rankings.aspx?ind=17).

Population Reference Bureau. 2015. "2015 World Population Data Sheet." Retrieved April 22, 2016 (www.prb.org/pdf15/2015-world-population-data-sheet_eng.pdf).

Population Reference Bureau. 2016. "Human Population: Women." Retrieved March 18, 2017 (www.prb.org/Publications/Lesson-Plans/HumanPopulation/Women.aspx).

Porter, Eduardo. 2015. "Gender Gap in Education Cuts Both Ways." *New York Times*, March 11. Retrieved September 4, 2015 (www.nytimes.com/2015/03/11/business/gender-gap-in-education-cuts-both-ways.html?_r=0).

Potok, Mark. 2013a. "DOJ Study: More Than 250,000 Hate Crimes a Year, Most Unreported." Southern Poverty Law Center, March 26. Retrieved June 1, 2013 (www.splcenter.org/blog/2013/03/26/doj-study-more-than-250000-hate-crimes-a-year-a-third-never-reported).

Potok, Mark. 2013b. "Editorial: Boston and Beyond." Intelligence Report 150. Retrieved June 17, 2013 (www.splcenter.org/get-informed/intelligence-report/browse-all-issues/2013/summer/boston-and-beyond).

Potok, Mark. 2013c. "The Year in Hate and Extremism." Intelligence Report 149. Retrieved July 20, 2016 (www.splcenter.org/fighting-hate/intelligence-report/2013/year-hate-and-extremism).

Poushter, Jacob. 2014. "What's Morally Acceptable? It Depends on Where in the World You Live." Pew Research Center, April 15. Retrieved August 29, 2015 (www.pewresearch.org/fact-tank/2014/04/15/whats-morally-acceptable-it-depends-on-where-in-the-world-you-live).

Pradhan, Elina. 2015. "The Relationship Between Women's Education and Fertility." World Economic Forum. Retrieved April 3, 2016 (www.weforum.org/agenda/2015/11/the-relationship-between-womens-education-and-fertility).

Pramis, Joshua. 2013. "Number of Mobile Phones to Exceed World Population by 2014." February 28. Retrieved January 6, 2014 (www.digitaltrends.com/mobile/mobile-phone-world-population-2014).

ProCon.org. 2016. "32 States With the Death Penalty and 18 States With Death Penalty Bans." December 9. (www.deathpenaltyprocon.org/view.resource.php?resourceID=001172).

Proudman, Charlotte Rachael. 2012. "Sex and Sharia: Muslim Women Punished for Failed Marriages." *The Independent*, April 2. Retrieved May 24, 2012 (http://blogs.independent.co.uk/2012/04/02/sex-and-sharia-muslim-women-punished-for-failed-marriages).

Putt, Gina 2014. "Life Events and the Life Cycle: Crises of Adulthood." Decoded Science, March 3. Retrieved August 31, 2015 (www.decodedscience.com/life-events-life-cycle-crises-adulthood/43230).

Quinney, Richard. 2002. *Critique of Legal Order: Crime Control in Capitalist Society*. New Brunswick, NJ: Transaction.

Radcliffe-Brown, A. R. 1935. "On the Concept of Functional in Social Science." *American Anthropologist* 37(3):394–402.

Radelet, Michael L. and Traci L. Lacock. 2009. "Do Executions Lower Homicide Rates? The Views of Leading Criminologists." *Journal of Criminal Laws and Criminology* 99(2).

Rauniyar, Ishwar and Jason Burke. 2015. "Nepal Earthquake Survivors Get Self-Defence Classes after Sexual Assaults." *The Guardian*, June 7. Retrieved June 8, 2015 (www.theguardian.com/world/2015/jun/07/nepal-earthquake-survivors-get-self-defence-classes-after-sexual-assaults).

Real Clear Politics. 2016. "Republican Delegate Count" and "Democratic Delegate Count." Retrieved March 18, 2016 (www.realclearpolitics.com/elections/2016).

Reardon, Sean F., Lindsay Fox, and Joseph Townsend. 2015. "Neighborhood Income Composition by Household Race and Income, 1990–2009." *Annals of the American Academy of Political and Social Science* 660(1):78–97.

Reason. 2011. "In-Depth Study: After Divorce, 44% of Women Fell Into Poverty." Family Research Council, May 31. Retrieved June 6, 2012 (http://primacyofreason.blogspot.com/2011/05/in-depth-study-after-divorce-44-of_31.html).

Reference.com. 2016. "What Countries Have a Planned Economy?" Retrieved August 26, 2016 (www.reference.com/government-politics/countries-planned-economy-3f07e563b79708ba).

Reich, Ashley. 2013. "U.S. Divorce Rate." *Huffington Post*, November 11. (www.huffingtonpost.com/news/us-divorce-rate).

Reid, Scott A. and Sik Hung Ng. 2006. "The Dynamics of Intragroup Differentiation in an Intergroup Social Context." *Human Communication Research* 32:504–525.

Reiman, Jeffrey and Paul Leighton. 2012. *The Rich Get Richer and the Poor Get Prison*. London: Routledge.

Religious Tolerance. 2014. "Stem Cell Research: All Viewpoints." Retrieved March 4, 2014 (www.religioustolerance.org/res_stem.htm).

Renick, Oliver. 2011. "Disconnected: 70 Percent of World Doesn't Have Internet, Despite Rising Phone Usage." Laptop, October 31. Retrieved May 18, 2012 (http://blog.laptopmag.com/disconnected-70-percent-of-world-doesn%E2%80%99t-have-internet-despite-rising-phone-usage).

Rhoades, Kimberley. A. 2008. "Children's Responses to Interparental Conflict: A Meta-Analysis of Their Associations With Child Adjustment." *Child Development* 79(6):1942–56.

Rice, William. 2013. "Types of Terrorism." Prezi, March 8. Retrieved May 13, 2014 (http://prezi.com/zyhuxjslaame/copy-of-types-of-terrorism).

Riegle-Crumb, Catherine and Chelsea Moore. 2013. "The Gender Gap in High School Physics: Considering the Context of Local Communities." *Social Science Quarterly* 95(1):253–68. Retrieved Jan. 17, 2014 (http://onlinelibrary.wiley.com/doi/10.1111/ssqu.12022/abstract).

Rights Action. 2016. "The Emperor Isn't Wearing Anything at All." *Rights Action Newsletter*, December. Retrieved March 19, 2017 (rightsaction.org/rights-action-newsletter-december-2016-the-emperor-isnt-wearing-anything-at-all).

Riley, Michael, Ben Elgin, Dune Lawrence, and Carol Matlack. 2014. "Missed Alarms and 40 Million Stolen Credit Card Numbers: How Target Blew It." *Bloomberg Business Week*, March 13. Retrieved June 8, 2015 (www.businessweek.com/articles/2014-03-13/target-missed-alarms-in-epic-hack-of-credit-card-data).

Riley, Robin. 2014. *Journey of Hope: The Mayflower Carbon Neutral Story* [Video]. Retrieved February 16, 2015 (www.youtube.com/watch?v=_Qx1UGTEWMA&list=UUfUaer6k7cf-z6RV2JjAUOA).

Riordan, Cornelius. 2004. *Equality and Achievement: An Introduction to the Sociology of Education*. Upper Saddle River, NJ: Prentice Hall.

Risman, Barbara J. and Pallavi Banerjee. 2013. "Kids Talking About Race: Tween-agers in a Post-Civil Rights Era." *Sociological Forum* 28(2):213–35.

Ritzer, George. 2007. *The Globalization of Nothing*, 2nd ed. Thousand Oaks, CA: Pine Forge.

Ritzer, George. 2011. *Globalization: The Essentials*. Malden, MA: Wiley.

Ritzer, George. 2013. *Introduction to Sociology*. Thousand Oaks, CA: Sage.

Ritzer, George. 2015. *The McDonaldization of Society*, 8th ed. Thousand Oaks, CA: Sage.

Ritzer, George and Douglas J. Goodman. 2004. *Sociological Theory*, 6th ed. New York: McGraw-Hill.

Roberts, Christine. 2012. "Most 10 Year-Olds Have Been on a Diet." *New York Daily News*, July 3. Retrieved January 17, 2014 (www.nydailynews.com/news/national/diets-obsess-tweens-study-article-1.1106653).

Roberts, Judith C. and Keith A. Roberts. 2008. "Deep Reading, Cost/Benefit, and the Construction of Meaning: Enhancing Reading Comprehension and Deep Learning in Sociology Courses." *Teaching Sociology* 36(April):125–40.

Roberts, Keith A. and Karen A. Donahue. 2000. "Professing Professionalism: Bureaucratization and Deprofessionalization in the Academy." *Sociological Focus* 33(4):365–83.

Roberts, Keith A. and David Yamane. 2016. *Religion in Sociological Perspective*, 6th ed. Thousand Oaks, CA: Sage/Pine Forge Press.

Robertson, Roland and Jan Aart Scholte, eds. 2007. *Encyclopedia of Globalization*. London: Routledge.

Robinson, Melian and Skye Gould. 2016, November 9. "This Map Shows Every State That Legalized Marijuana on Election Day." *Business Insider*. Retrieved May 4, 2017 (http://www.businessinsider.com/where-is-marijuana-legal-2016-11).

Robles, Frances, Jason Horowitz, and Shaila Dewan. 2015. "Dylann Roof, Suspect in Charleston Shooting, Flew the Flags of White Power." *New York Times*, June 18. Retrieved June 19, 2015 (www.nytimes.com/2015/06/19/us/on-facebook-dylann-roof-charleston-suspect-wears-symbols-of-white-supremacy.html).

Robson, David. 2013. "There Really Are 50 Eskimo Words for 'Snow.'" *Washington Post*, January 14. Retrieved October 1, 2015 (www.washingtonpost.com/national/health-science/there-really-are-50-eskimo-words-for-snow/2013/01/14/e0e3f4e0-59a0-11e2-beee-6e38f5215402_story.html).

Roethlisberger, Fritz J. and William J. Dickson. 1939. *Management and the Worker*. Cambridge, MA: Harvard University Press.

Roisen, Ron. 2012. "Mrs. Marty Mann and the Early Medicalization of Alcoholism." *The Atlantic*, February 22. Retrieved July 16, 2012 (www.theatlantic.com/health/archive/2012/02/mrs-marty-mann-and-the-early-medicalization-of-alcoholism/252286).

Rosenbaum, James E. 1999. "If Tracking Is Bad, Is Detracking Better? A Study of a Detracked High School." *American Schools* (Winter):24–47.

Rosenberg, Matt. 2015. "The Number of Countries in the World." About.com, April 30. Retrieved January 28, 2016 (http://geography.about.com/od/politicalgeography/a/taiwancountry.htm).

Rosenthal, Elisabeth. 2013. "As Drug Costs Rise, Bending the Law Is One Remedy." *New York Times*, October 22. Retrieved March 12, 2014 (http://nyti.ms/17HuF6G).

Roser, Max. 2016. "Future World Population Growth." Our World In Data. Retrieved April 24, 2016 (http://ourworldindata.org/future-world-population-growth).

Rosman, Abraham, Paula G. Rubel, Maxine Weisgrau. 2009. *The Tapestry of Culture: An Introduction to Cultural Anthropology*, 9th ed. Lanham, MD: AltaMira Press.

Rossi, Alice S. 1984. "Gender and Parenthood." *American Sociological Review* 49(February):1–19.

Rothenberg, Paula S. 2014. *Race, Class, and Gender in the United States: An Integrated Study*, 9th ed. New York: Worth.

Rothenberg, Paula S. 2015. *White Privilege: Essential Readings on the Other Side of Racism*, 5th ed. New York: Worth Publishers.

Rothkopf, David. 2012. "Two Septembers." Pp. 100–103 in *Globalization: The Transformation of Social Worlds*, 3rd ed., edited by D. Stanley Eitzen and Maxine Baca Zinn. Belmont, CA: Wadsworth.

Rothman, Robert A. 2005. *Inequality and Stratification: Race, Class, and Gender*, 5th ed. Englewood Cliffs, NJ: Prentice Hall.

Royal Society. 2012. *People and the Planet*. April. Retrieved July 31, 2012 (royalsociety.org/uploadedFiles/Royal_Society_Content/policy/projects/people-planet/2012-04-25-People Planet.pdf).

Rumbaut, Ruben G. and Alejandro Portes. 2001. *Ethnicities: Children of Immigrants in America*. Los Angeles: University of California Press.

Rupar, Terri. 2014. "Here Are the 10 Countries Where Homosexuality May Be Punished by Death." *Washington Post*, February 24. Retrieved September 6, 2015 (www.washingtonpost.com/news/worldviews/wp/2014/02/24/here-are-the-10-countries-where-homosexuality-may-be-punished-by-death).

Ryan, Camille L. and Kurt Bauman. 2016. "Educational Attainment in the United States: 2015." U.S. Census Bureau. Retrieved March 30, 2015 (www.census.gov/content/dam/Census/library/publications/2016/demo/p20-578.pdf).

Rydgren, Jens. 2004. "Mechanisms of Exclusion: Ethnic Discrimination in the Swedish Labour Market." *Journal of Ethnic and Migration Studies* 30(4):687–716.

Sachs, Jeffrey. 2011. "With 7 Billion on Earth, a Huge Task Before Us." CNN, October 17. Retrieved July 10, 2013 (www.cnn.com/2011/10/17/opinion/sachs-global-population).

Sachs, Jeffrey D. 2015. "Financing Education for All." Project Syndicate. Retrieved July 6, 2015 (www.project-syndicate.org/commentary/financing-education-poor-children-by-jeffrey-d-sachs-2015-03).

Sack, Kevin and Megan Thee-Brenan. 2015. "Poll Finds Most Hold Dim View of Race Relations." *New York Times*, July 23. Retrieved October 8, 2015 (www.nytimes.com/2015/07/24/us/poll-shows-most-americans-think-race-relations-are-bad.html?smid=nytcore-iphone-share&smprod=nytcore-iphone&_r=0).

Sadker, David Miller and Karen R. Zittleman. 2013. *Teachers, Schools and Society*, 10th ed. New York: McGraw-Hill.

Saez, E. 2012. *Striking It Richer: The Evolution of Top Incomes in the United States* (Updated with 2009 and 2010 estimates). March 2. Retrieved June 18, 2012 (http://elsa.berkeley.edu/~saez/saez-UStopincomes-2010.pdf).

Saha, Lawrence and A. Gary Dworkin. 2006. "Educational Attainment and Job Status: The Role of Status Inconsistency on Occupational Burnout." Paper presented at the Annual Meeting of the International Sociological Association, July 23–29, Durban, South Africa.

Saharan Vibe. 2007. "Wodaabe Beauty Ceremony." February 19. Retrieved November 6, 2009 (saharanvibe.blogspot.com/2007/02/wodaabe-beauty-ceremony.html).

Sample, Ian. 2015. "Hope Raised for New Genetic Therapy to Prevent Inherited Diseases." *The Guardian*, April 23. Retrieved November 22, 2015 (www.theguardian.com/science/2015/apr/23/hopes-raised-for-new-genetic-therapy-to-prevent-inherited-diseases).

Sandberg, Sheryl. 2013. *Lean In: Women, Work, and the Will to Lead*. New York: Alfred A. Knopf.

Sandberg, Sheryl and Adam Grant. 2015. "Speaking While Female." *New York Times*, January 12. Retrieved September 1, 2015 (http://nyti.ms/1A7Xwyw).

Sapir, Edward. 1929. "The Status of Linguistics as a Science." *Language* 5:207–14.

Sapir, Edward. 1949. In *Selected Writings of Edward Sapir in Language, Culture, and Personality*, edited by David G. Mandelbaum. Berkeley: University of California Press.

Sapiro, Virginia. 2003. *Women in American Society: An Introduction to Women's Studies*, 5th ed. Mountain View, CA: Mayfield.

Sapolsky, Robert. 2014. "The Trouble With Testosterone." In *The Kaleidoscope of Gender*, 4th ed., edited by Joan Z. Spade and Catherine G. Valentine. Thousand Oaks, CA: Sage.

Sauter, Michael B. and Alexander E. M. Hess. 2013. "The States Where the Most People Go Hungry: 24/7 Wall St." September 9. Retrieved January 5, 2014 (www.huffingtonpost.com/2013/09/08/states-food-insecurity_n_3890209.html?slide=2885737).

Savage, Charlie and Steven Erlanger. 2015. "Shaker Aamer Is Released From Guantánamo Prison After 13 Years." Retrieved October 30, 2015 (www.nytimes.com/2015/10/31/world/shaker-aamer-released-guantanamo-bay-cuba.html?smid=nytcore-ipad-share&smprod=nytcore-ipad).

Scelfo, Julie. 2015. "A University Recognizes a Third Gender: Neutral." *New York Times*, February 3. Retrieved September 1, 2015 (www.nytimes.com/2015/02/08/education/edlife/a-university-recognizes-a-third-gender-neutral.html?_r=0).

Schaefer, Richard T. 2012. *Racial and Ethnic Groups*, 13th ed. Upper Saddle River, NJ: Prentice Hall.

Schaefer, Richard T. and Jenifer Kunz. 2007. *Racial and Ethnic Groups*. Upper Saddle River, NJ: Pearson/Prentice Hall.

Scheiber, Noam. 2015. "Rising Economic Insecurity Tied to Decades-Long Trend in Employment Practices." *New York Times*, July 12. Retrieved July 13, 2015 (www.nytimes.com/2015/07/13/business/rising-economic-insecurity-tied-to-decades-long-trend-in-employment-practices.html).

Scheiber, Noam and Patricia Cohen. 2015. "For the Wealthiest, a Private Tax System That Saves Them Billions." *New York Times*, December 29. Retrieved April 18, 2016 (www.nytimes.com/2015/12/30/business/economy/for-the-wealthiest-private-tax-system-saves-them-billions.html?emc=eta1).

Scheper-Hughes, Nancy. 2014. "Human Traffic; Exposing the Brutal Organ Trade." *New Internationalist*, May. Retrieved July 2, 2015 (http://newint.org/features/2014/05/01/organ-trafficking-keynote).

Schmalleger, Frank. 2006. *Criminology Today: An Integrative Introduction*, 4th ed. Upper Saddle River, NJ: Prentice Hall.

Schmalleger, Frank. 2012. *Criminology Today: An Integrative Introduction*, 6th ed. Upper Saddle River, NJ: Prentice Hall.

Schoen, Cathy, David Radley, and Sara R. Collins. 2015. "State Trends in the Cost of Employer Health Insurance Coverage, 2003–2013." The Commonwealth Fund, January. Retrieved July 2, 2015 (https://timedotcom.files.wordpress.com/2015/01/1798_schoen_state_trends_2003_2013.pdf?la=en).

Schoepflin, Todd. 2011. "Doing Gender." Creative Sociology, August 10. Retrieved May 25, 2012 (http://creativesociology.blogspot.com/2011/08/doing-gender.html).

Schwartz, Hunter. 2015. "There Are 390,000 Gay Marriages in the U.S. The Supreme Court Could Quickly Make It Half a Million." *Washington Post*, April 28. Retrieved September 9, 2015 (www.washingtonpost.com/news/the-fix/wp/2015/04/28/heres-how-many-gay-marriages-the-supreme-court-could-make-way-for/).

Scott-Montagu, John. 1904. "Automobile Legislation: A Criticism and Review." *North American Review* 179(573):168–77.

Scribd. 2011. "Chipko Movement." Retrieved January 1, 2012 (www.scribd.com/doc/27513230/Chipko-Movement).

Selod, Saher. 2018. "Anti-Muslim Sentiment in the United States." In *Our Social World: Introduction to Sociology*, 6th ed. (p. 236) by Jeanne H. Ballantine, Keith A. Roberts, and Kathleen Odell Korgen. Thousand Oaks, CA: Sage.

Sengupta, Somini. 2014. "U.N. Report Says Progress for Women Is Unequal." *New York Times*, February 12. Retrieved February 20, 2014 (www.nytimes.com/2014/02/13/world/un-report-says-progress-for-women-is-unequal.html?_r=0).

Sentencing Project. 2014. "Facts About Prisons and People in Prison." Retrieved September 4, 2014 (http://www.sentencingproject.org/doc/publications/inc_Facts%20About%20Prisons.pdf).

Sentencing Project. 2015. "Incarceration." Retrieved October 16, 2015 (www.sentencingproject.org/template/page.cfm?id=107).

Senter, Mary S., Roberta Spalter-Roth, and Nichole Van Vooren. 2012. "Table 1: Distribution of Respondents' Job Categories and Percent in Career-Type Jobs." P. 3 in *Jobs, Careers & Sociological Skills: The Early Employment Experiences of 2012 Sociology Majors*. Washington, DC: American Sociological Association. Retrieved July 18, 2015 (www.asanet.org/documents/research/pdfs/Early_Employment.pdf).

Sernau, Scott. 2010. *Social Inequality in a Global Age*. Thousand Oaks, CA: Sage/Pine Forge Press.

Shackle, Samira. 2012. "Mukhtar Mai—the Gang Rape Victim Who Defied Her Attackers." *New Statesman*, October 19. Retrieved April 24, 2014 (www.newstatesman.com/world-affairs/2012/10/mukhtar-mai-gang-rape-victim-who-defided-her-attackers).

Sharp, Henry S. 1991. "Memory, Meaning, and Imaginary Time: The Construction of Knowledge in White and Chipewayan Cultures." *Ethnohistory* 38(2):149–73.

Sharp, Lauriston. 1990. "Steel Axes for Stone-Age Australians." Pp. 410–24 in *Conformity and Conflict*, 7th ed., edited by James P. Spradley and David W. McCurdy. Glenview, IL: Scott Foresman.

Shaw, Clifford R. and Henry D. McKay. 1929. *Delinquency Areas*. Chicago: University of Chicago Press.

Shaw, Susan M. and Janet Lee. 2005. *Women's Voices, Feminist Visions: Classic and Contemporary Readings*, 3rd ed. Boston: McGraw-Hill.

Sheridan, Mary Beth and William Branigin. 2010. "Senate Ratifies New U.S.-Russia Nuclear Weapons Treaty." *Washington Post*, December 22. Retrieved June 28, 2013 (www.washingtonpost.com/wp-dyn/content/article/2010/12/21/AR2010122104371.html?sid=ST2010122205900).

Sherif, Muzafer and Carolyn Sherif. 1953. *Groups in Harmony and Tension*. New York: Harper & Row.

Shreeve, Jamie. 2015. "Oldest Human Fossil Found, Redrawing Family Tree." *National Geographic*, March 5. Retrieved July 25, 2015 (http://news.nationalgeographic.com/news/2015/03/150304-homo-habilis-evolution-fossil-jaw-ethiopia-olduvai-gorge).

Siegel, Larry J. 2011. *Criminology: Theories, Patterns, and Typologies*, 11th ed. Belmont, CA: Thomson/Wadsworth.

Simmel, Georg. [1902–1917] 1950. *The Sociology of Georg Simmel*, translated by Kurt Wolff. Glencoe, IL: Free Press.

Simmel, Georg. 1904. "The Sociology of Conflict." *American Journal of Sociology* 4(January):490–525.

Simmel, Georg. 1955. *Conflict and the Web of Group Affiliation*, translated by Kurt H. Wolff. New York: Free Press.

Simmons, Rachel. 2002. *Odd Girl Out: The Hidden Culture of Aggression in Girls*. Orlando, FL: Harcourt.

Simon, David R. 2006. *Elite Deviance*, 8th ed. Boston: Allyn & Bacon.

Sizer, Theodore R. 1984. *Horace's Compromise: The Dilemma of the American High School*. Boston: Houghton Mifflin.

Skocpol, Theda. 1979. *States and Social Revolutions: A Comparative Analysis of France, Russia, and China*. Cambridge, UK: Cambridge University Press.

Skocpol, Theda and Vanessa Williamson. 2012. *The Tea Party and the Remaking of Republican Conservatism*. New York: Oxford University Press.

Slaughter, Anne-Marie. 2012. "Why Women Still Can't Have It All." *The Atlantic*, July/August. Retrieved January 17, 2014 (www.theatlantic.com/magazine/archive/2012/07/why-women-still-cant-have-it-all/309020).

SlideShare. 2014. "Population Pyramids 2014." Retrieved September 16, 2014 (http://www.slideshare.net/sbsgeog/population-pyramids-2014).

Smelser, Neil J. 1963. Theory of Collective Behavior. New York: Free Press.

Smelser, Neil J. 1988. "Social Structure." Pp. 103–29 in *Handbook of Sociology*, edited by Neil J. Smelser. Newbury Park, CA: Sage.

Smelser, Neil J. 1992. "The Rational Choice Perspective: A Theoretical Assessment." *Rationality and Society* 4: 381–410.

Smith, Aaron. 2015. "U.S. Smartphone Use in 2015." Pew Research Center, June 1. Retrieved June 3, 2015 (www.pewinternet.org/2015/04/01/us-smartphone-use-in-2015).

Smith, Adrian. 2012. "Private vs. Public Facilities: Is It Cost Effective and Safe?" Corrections.com, June 11. Retrieved September 1, 2014 (www.corrections.com/news/article/30903-private-vs-public-facilities-is-it-cost-effective-and-safe).

Smith, Mark K. 2008. "Howard Gardner and Multiple Intelligences." *The Encyclopedia of Informal Education*. Retrieved April 17, 2011 (http://www.infed.org/thinkers/gardner.htm).

Snyder, Denson R. 1971. *The Hidden Curriculum*. New York: Alfred A. Knopf.

Snyderman, Nancy and Chiara Sottile. 2013. "'It's Getting a Lot Harder to Do This': Doctor Shortage Strains Practices." NBC News, May 25. Retrieved July 15, 2013 (http://dailynightly.nbcnews.com/_news/2013/05/25/18042694-it-is-getting-a-lot-harder-to-do-this-doctor-shortage-strains-practices?lite).

Soble, Johathan. 2015. "To Rescue Economy, Japan Turns to Supermom." *New York Times*, January 1. Retrieved September 14, 2015 (http://nyti.ms/1zDywPg).

"Sochi 2014: Gay Rights Protests Target Russia's Games." 2014. BBC News, February 5. Retrieved February 24, 2014 (www.bbc.co.uk/news/world-europe-26043872).

Social Security Administration. 2013. "Social Security Basic Facts." Retrieved July 1, 2013 (www.ssa.gov/pressoffice/basic fact.htm).

Social Security Administration. 2014. "Social Security Basic Facts." Retrieved July 25, 2015 (www.ssa.gov/news/press/basicfact.html).

Social Security and Medicare Boards of Trustees. 2013. "A Summary of the 2013 Annual Reports." Retrieved July 13, 2013 (www.ssa.gov/oact/trsum).

Sommer, Eric. 2014. "How Five American Companies Control What You Think." RT, May 14. Retrieved January 25, 2016 (www.rt.com/op-edge/158920-us-ukraine-media-control).

Sons of Union Veterans of the Civil War. 2010. "The United States' Flag Code." Retrieved December 21, 2011 (http://suvcw.org/flag.htm).

Southern Poverty Law Center. 2016. "Active Hate Groups in the United States in 2015." February 17. Retrieved March 5, 2017 (https://www.splcenter.org/fighting-hate/intelligence-report/2016/active-hate-groups-united-states-2015).

Spacey, John. 2012. "Japan's Crime Rate." *Japan Talk*, June 30. Retrieved April 18, 2013 (www.japan-talk.com/jt/new/japans-crime-rate).

Sperling, Gene B. 2006. "What Works in Girls' Education." PBS Wide Angle. Retrieved July 11, 2009 (www.pbs.org/wnet/wideangle/episodes/time-for-school-series/essay-what-works-in-girls-education/274).

Standler, Ronald B. 2012. "Annotated Legal Cases on Physician-Assisted Suicide in the USA." Carbon Mitigation Initiative, July 12. Retrieved July 16, 2013 (cmi.princeton.edu).

Stanton, Glenn 2015. "What Is the Actual US Divorce Rate and Risk?" December 16. Witherspoon Institute. Retrieved May 12, 2016 (www.thepublicdiscourse.com/2015/12/15983).

Staples, Brent. 2001. "Black Men and Public Space." Pp. 244–46 in *The Production of Reality*, edited by Jodi O'Brien and Peter Kollock. Thousand Oaks, CA: Pine Forge Press.

Statistica. 2014. "Number of Vehicles Registered in the United States from 1990 to 2011." Retrieved February 23, 2014 (www.statistica.com/statistics/183505/number-of-vehicles-in-the-united-stastes-since-1990).

Statistica 2016a. "Number of Monthly Active Facebook Users Worldwide as of 4th Quarter 2016." Retrieved February 26, 2017 (http: www.statistica.com/statistics/264810/number-of-monthly-active-facebook-users-worldwide).

Statistica 2016b. "Reach of Leading Social Media and Networking Sites Used by Teenagers and Young Adults in the United States as of February 2016." Retrieved May 30, 2016 (www.statistica.com/statistics/199242/social-media-and-networking-sites-used-be-us-teenages).

Statistica. 2016c. "Reported Violent Crime Rate in the United States From 1990 to 2014." Retrieved April 5, 2016 (www.statista.com/statistics/191219/reported-violent-crime-rate-in-the-usa-since-1990).

St. Claire, Pat and Karen Smith. 2015. "South African Mine Massacre: Report Says Many Share in the Blame." CNN News, June 25. Retrieved September 11, 2015 (www.cnn.com/2015/06/25/africa/south-africa-mine-massacre-report).

Steele, Tracey L. 2005. *Sex, Self, and Society: The Social Context of Sexuality*. Belmont, CA: Thomson Wadsworth.

Stephen, Eric M., Jennifer Rose, Lindsay Kenney, Francine Rosselli-Navarra, and Ruth S. Weissman. 2014. "Adolescent Risk Factors for Purging in Young Women: Findings From the National Longitudinal Study of Adolescent Health." *Journal of Eating Disorders* 2(1). Retrieved January 16, 2014 (www.jeatdisord.com).

Stewart, Susan D. 2007. *Brave New Stepfamilies: Diverse Paths Toward Stepfamily Living*. Thousand Oaks, CA: Sage.

Stiglitz, Joseph E. 2012. "A Real Cure for the Global Economic Crackup." Pp. 104–109 in *Globalization: The Transformation of Social Worlds*, 3rd ed., edited by D. Stanley Eitzen and Maxine Baca Zinn. Belmont, CA: Wadsworth.

Stockholm International Peace Research Institute. 2016. "Recent Trends in Military Expenditure." April 13. Retrieved January 29, 2016 (www.sipri.org/research/armaments/milex/ recent-trends).

Stoessinger, John. 1993. *Why Nations Go to War*. New York: St. Martin's Press.

Stracansky, Pavol. 2013. "Curbs on Abortion Spread Across East Europe." Inter Press Service, July 12. Retrieved March 17, 2014 (www.ipsnews/net/2013/07/curbs-on-abortion-spread-across-east-europe).

Straus, Murray A., Richard J. Gelles, and Suzanne K. Steinmetz. 2006. *Behind Closed Doors: Violence in the American Family*. New Brunswick, NJ: Transaction.

Stryker, Sheldon. 1980. *Symbolic Interactionism: A Social Structural Version*. Menlo Park, CA: Benjamin Cummings.

Stryker, Sheldon. 2000. "Identity Competition: Key to Differential Social Involvement." Pp. 21–40 in *Identity, Self, and Social Movements*, edited by Sheldon Stryker, Timothy Owens, and Robert White. Minneapolis: University of Minnesota Press.

Stryker, Sheldon and Anne Stratham. 1985. "Symbolic Interaction and Role Theory." Pp. 311–78 in *Handbook of Social Psychology*, edited by Gardiner Lindsey and Eliot Aronson. New York: Random House.

Sullivan, Brian. 2013. "HUD Reports Continued Decline in U.S. Homelessness Since 2010." HUD.gov, November 21. Retrieved February 17, 2014 (http://portal.hud.gov/hudpor tal/HUD?src=/press/press_releases_media_advisories/2013/HUDNo.13-173).

Sutherland, Edwin H., Donald R. Cressey, and David Luckenbil. 1992. *Criminology*. Dix Hills, NY: General Hall.

Sutton, Joe. 2013. "Maryland Governor Signs Death Penalty Repeal." CNN, May 2. Retrieved June 2, 2013 (www.cnn .com/2013/05/02/us/maryland-death-penalty).

Svrluga, Susan. 2015. "U. Missouri President, Chancellor Resign over Handling of Racial Incidents." *Washington Post*, November 9. Retrieved December 8, 2015 (www .washingtonpost.com/news/grade-point/wp/2015/11/09/missouris-student-government-calls-for-university-presi-dents-removal).

Swank, Eric, Breanne Fahs, and David M. Frost. 2013. "Region, Social Identities and Disclosure Practices as Predictors of Heterosexist Discrimination against Sexual Minorities in the United States." *Sociological Inquiry* 83(2):238–58.

Swing, William Lacy. 2015. "Migration Comes of Age." International Organization for Migration, July 6. Retrieved July 8, 2015 (http://weblog.iom.int/migration-comes-age).

Tanner, Lindsey. 2014. "AMA Officially Designates Cheerleading a Sport." *USA Today*, June 10. Retrieved September 4, 2015 (www.usatoday.com/story/news/nation/2014/06/10/ama-cheerleading-sport/10272941).

Taseer, Shehrbano. 2011. "True Survivor." *Daily Beast*, May 1. Retrieved April 12, 2012 (www.thedailybeast.com/news-week/2011/05/01/true-survivor.html).

Taub, Diane E. and Penelope A. McLorg. 2010. "Influences of Gender Socialization and Athletic Involvement on the Occurrence of Eating Disorders." Pp. 73–82 in *Sociological Footprints: Introductory Readings in Sociology*, 11th ed., edited by Leonard Cargan and Jeanne H. Ballantine. Belmont, CA: Wadsworth Cengage Learning.

Tavernise, Sabrina. 2015. "Colorado's Effort against Teenage Pregnancies Is a Startling Success." *New York Times*, July 5. Retrieved July 6, 2015 (www.nytimes.com/2015/07/06/science/colorados-push-against-teenage-pregnancies-is-a-startling-success.html).

Tavernise, Sabrina. 2016. "Disparity in Life Spans of the Rich and the Poor Is Growing." *New York Times*, February 12. Retrieved February 15, 2016 (www .nytimes.com/2016/02/13/health/disparity-in-life-spans-of-the-rich-and-the-poor-is-growing .html?smid=nytcore-ipad-share&smprod=nytcore-ipad).

Tea Party. 2016. "About Us." Retrieved January 25, 2016 (www. teaparty.org/about-us).

Teixeira, Ruy and John Halpin. 2012. "The Obama Coalition in the 2012 Election and Beyond." Center for American Progress, December. Retrieved November 19, 2013 (www .americanprogress.org/wp-content/uploads/2012/12/Obama Coalition-5.pdf).

Terra Networks. 2013. "Kony 2012 Viral Campaign Sheds Light on Ugandan Violence." Retrieved March 30, 2012 (http://en.terra.com/latin-in-america/news/kony_2012_viral_campaign_sheds_light_on_ugandan_violence/hof18171/ECID=US_ENGLISH_terrausa_SEMSearch_Kony).

Testa, Maria Rita. 2014. "On the Positive Correlation Between Education and Fertility Intentions in Europe: Individual- and Country-Level Evidence." *Advances in Life Course Research*, September 21, pp. 28–42.

Theroux, David J. 2012. "Secular Theocracy: The Foundations and Folly of Modern Tyranny." The Independent Institute, January 11. Retrieved July 13, 2012 (www.independent.org/newsroom/article.asp?id=3206).

Thomas, Villani J. and F. D. Rose. 1991. "Ethnic Differences in the Experience of Pain." *Social Science and Medicine* 32(9):1063–66.

Thompson, A. C. 2009. "Katrina's Hidden Race War." *The Nation*, January 5. Retrieved July 7, 2011 (www.thenation .com/article/katrinas-hidden-race-war).

Thompson, Andrea. 2017. "Both NASA and NOAA Declare That Our Planet Is Experiencing Record-Breaking Warming for the Third Year in a Row." *Scientific American*, January 17. Retrieved March 19, 2017 (www.scientific.american.com/article/2016-was-the-hottest-year-on-record).

Thomson, Helen. 2015. "Study of Holocaust Survivors Finds Trauma Passed on to Children's Genes." *The Guardian*, August 21. Retrieved November 16, 2015 (www.theguardian.com/science/2015/aug/21/study-of-holocaust-survivors-finds-trauma-passed-on-to-childrens-genes?CMP=share_btn_fb).

Thorne, Barrie. 1993. *Gender Play: Girls and Boys in School*. New Brunswick, NJ: Rutgers University Press.

350.Org. 2016. "Tell Congress: Stop the Trans-Pacific Partnership." Retrieved February 12, 2016 (https://act.350 .org/sign/congress-tpp/?gclid=CMzdmMXL8soCFYsCaQod EBwMOg).

Title IX. 2015. "Athletics Under Title IX." Retrieved September 4, 2015 (www.titleix.info/10-key-areas-of-title-ix/athletics .aspx).

Toffler, Alvin and Heidi Toffler. 1980. *The Third Wave*. New York: Morrow.

Tolbert, Pamela S. and Richard H. Hall. 2008. *Organizations: Structures, Processes, and Outcomes*, 10th ed. Upper Saddle River, NJ: Prentice Hall.

Townsend, Sarah. 2015. "Saudi Drafts Law to Allow Women to Vote for First Time." *Arabian Business*, May 24. Retrieved September 2, 2015 (www.arabianbusiness.com/saudi-draft-law-allow-women-vote-for-first-time-593738.html).

Transparency International. 2012. "Global Corruption Barometer 2010/11." Retrieved October 6, 2012 (http://gcb.transparency.org/gcb201011/infographic).

"Trash-Mapping Expedition Sheds Light on 'Great Pacific Garbage Patch.'" 2015. *The Guardian*, August 23. Retrieved February 10, 2016 (www.theguardian.com/us-news/2015/aug/23/pacific-ocean-plastic-trash-mapping-mission).

Travers, Jeffrey and Stanley Milgram. 1969. "An Experimental Study of the Small World Problem." *Sociometry* 32:425–43.

Trust in Education. 2013. "Life as an Afghan Woman." Retrieved January 16, 2014 (www.trustineducation.org/why-afghanistan/life-as-an-afghan-woman).

Tull, Matthew. 2012. "The Consequences of Male Gender Role Stress." About.com. Retrieved February 6, 2014 (http://ptsd.about.com/od/relatedconditions/a/MaleGenderRoleStres.htm).

Turner, Bryan S. 1991a. "Politics and Culture in Islamic Globalism." Pp. 161–81 in *Religion and Global Order*, edited by Roland Robertson and William R. Garrett. New York: Paragon.

Turner, Bryan S. 1991b. *Religion and Social Theory*. London: Sage.

Turner, Jonathan H. 2003. *The Structure of Sociological Theory*, 7th ed. Belmont, CA: Wadsworth.

Turner, Ralph H. and Lewis M. Killian. 1993. "The Field of Collective Behavior." Pp. 5–20 in *Collective Behavior and Social Movements*, edited by Russell L. Curtis Jr. and Benigno E. Aguirre. Boston: Allyn & Bacon.

UNICEF. 2005. "Convention on the Rights of the Child." Retrieved July 23, 2012 (www.unicef.org/crc/index_30229.html).

UNICEF. 2014. "Update on Haiti's Children." Retrieved February 23, 2014 (www.unicefusa.org/work/emergencies/Haiti/?gclid=CJ6zxOK847wCFdE-Mgodt1IANg).

United Nations Department of Economic and Social Affairs. 2014. "World Urbanization Prospects: 2014 Revision." Retrieved April 24, 2016 (http://esa.un.org/unpd/wup/Publications/Files/WUP2014-Highlights.pdf).

United Nations Framework Convention on Climate Change. 2015. "Status of Ratification of the Kyoto Protocol." United Nations Framework Convention on Climate Change. Retrieved August 2016 (http://unfccc.int/meetings/paris_nov_2015/meeting/8926.php)

United Nations High Commissioner for Refugees. 2015. "Syria Regional Refuge Response." Retrieved July 8, 2015 (http://data.unhcr.org/syrianrefugees/regional.php).

United Nations News Center. 2010. "Senior UN Official Cites Evidence of Growing Support for Abolishing Death Penalty." February 24. Retrieved March 8, 2011 (www.un.org/apps/news/story.asp?NewsID=33877&Cr=death+penalty&Cr1=).

United Nations Office on Drugs and Crime. 2013. "Global Study on Homicide 2013: Trends, Contexts, Data." Retrieved October 16, 2014 (www.unodc.org/documents/gsh/pdfs/2014_GLOBAL_HOMICIDE_BOOK_web.pdf).

United Nations Office on Drugs and Crime. 2014a. "Human Trafficking FAQs." Retrieved September 5, 2014 (http://www.unodc.org/unodc/en/human-trafficking/faqs.html#How_widespread_is_human_trafficking).

United Nations Office on Drugs and Crime. 2017. "Trafficking for Organ Trade." Global Initiative to Fight Human Trafficking. Retrieved March 10, 2017 (www.ungift.org/knowledgehub/en/about/trafficking-for-organ-trade.html).

United Nations Water. 2015. "International Decade for Action 'Water for Life' 2005–2015." Retrieved September 10, 2015 (www.un.org/waterforlifedecade/scarcity.shtml).

United Nations Women. 2015. "Facts and Figures: Ending Violence Against Women." Retrieved February 28, 2017 (www.unwomen.org/en/what-we-do/ending-violence-against-women/facts-and-figures).

United States Elections Project. 2016. "Turnout 1980–2012." Retrieved January 27, 2016 (http://elections.gmu.edu/voter_turnout.htm).

University of Michigan Documents Center. 2003. "Documents in the News—1997/2003: Affirmative Action in College Admissions." Retrieved April 17, 2010 (www.lib.umich.edu/files/libraries/govdocs/pdf/affirm/pdf).

University of Pennsylvania. 2010. "Body Modification." Retrieved November 18, 2010 (penn.museum/sites/body_modification/bodmodpierce.shtml).

UPI. 2014. "OECD: Switzerland Tops 34 Nations for Life Expectancy at 82.8." Health News UPI. Retrieved January 2014 (www.upi.com/Health_News/2014/01/07/OECD/Switzerland-tops-34-nations-for-life-expectancy-at-828/UPI-32701389078243).

U.S. Bureau of Labor Statistics. 2014a. "Injuries, Illnesses, and Fatalities." Retrieved September 4, 2014 (www.bls.gov/iif/).

U.S. Bureau of Labor Statistics. 2014b. *Registered Nurses: Occupational Outlook Handbook*. Retrieved March 14, 2017 (http://www.iun.edu/career-services/docs/Registered%20Nurses%20-Occupational%20Outlook%20Handbook%20-U.S.%20Bureau%20of%20Labor%20Sta.pdf_).

U.S. Bureau of Labor Statistics. 2015. "Earnings and Unemployment Rates by Educational Attainment." April 2. Retrieved June 11, 2015 (www.bls.gov/emp/ep_chart_001.htm).

U.S. Bureau of Labor Statistics. 2016. "Table 1: Time Spent in Primary Activities and Percent of the Civilian Population Engaging in Each Activity, Averages per Day by Sex, 2015 Annual Averages." (https://www.bls.gov/news.release/atus.t01.htm).

U.S. Bureau of Labor Statistics. 2017. "Household Data Annual Averages 37. Median Weekly Earnings of Full-Time Wage and Salary Workers by Selected Characteristics." February 8 (https://www.bls.gov/cps/tables.htm#weekearn).

U.S. Census Bureau. 2011. "Income (in Dollars) by Educational Level and Race/Ethnicity (Table 228)." Retrieved April 19, 2011 (http://www.census.gov/compendia/statab/2011/tables/11s0228.pdf).

U.S. Census Bureau. 2012. "Educational Attainment by Race and Hispanic Origin 1970–2010 (Table 229)." Retrieved June 17, 2013 (www.census.gov/compendia/statab/2012/tables/12s0229.pdf).

U.S. Census Bureau. 2014. "State & County Quick Facts." Retrieved August 22, 2014 (http://quickfacts.census.gov/qfd/states/00000.html).

U.S. Census Bureau. 2015a. "Current Population Survey, 2015: Educational Attainment—People 25 Years Old and Over by Median Income and Sex 1991–2014." Retrieved January 6, 2016 (www.census.gov/hhes/www/income/data/historical/people).

U.S. Census Bureau. 2015b. "U.S. and World Population Clock." Retrieved February 6, 2015 (www.census.gov/popclock).

U.S. Census Bureau. 2016. "Detailed Years of School Completed by People 25 Years and Over by Sex, Age Groups, Race and

Hispanic Origin: 2015." Retrieved March 30, 2016 (www.census.gov/hhes/socdemo/education/data/cps/2015/tables.html).

U.S. Debt Clock. 2016. "U.S. National Debt Clock." Retrieved January 25, 2016 (www.usdebtclock.org).

U.S. Department of Commerce. 2011. "Commerce Department's U.S. Census Bureau Reports 55 Percent of Americans Have Married Once in Their Lifetimes." Retrieved February 19, 2014 (www.commerce.gov/blog/2011/05/18/commerce-department%E2%80%99s-us-census-bureau-reports-55-percent-americans-have-married-onc).

U.S. Department of Defense. 2011. *Dictionary of Military and Associated Terms*, January 31. Retrieved January 19, 2013 (http://ra.defense.gov/documents/rtm/jp1_02.pdf).

U.S. Department of Defense. 2012. "Department of Defense Antiterrorism Program Memo: Instruction No. 2000.12." March 1. Retrieved July 28, 2012 (www.dtic.mil/whs/directives/corres/pdf/200012p.pdf).

U.S. Department of Health and Human Services. 2015a. "2015 Poverty Guidelines." September 3. Retrieved September 8, 2015 (aspe.hhs.gov/woa5-poverty-guidelines).

U.S. Department of Health and Human Services. 2015b. "Health Insurance Coverage and the Affordable Care Act." May 5. Retrieved July 2, 2015 (http://aspe.hhs.gov/health/reports/2015/uninsured_change/ib_uninsured_change.pdf).

U.S. Department of Housing and Urban Development. 2014. "The 2014 Annual Homeless Assessment Report (AHAR) to Congress." October. Retrieved June 11, 2015 (www.hudexchange.info/resources/documents/2014-AHAR-Part1.pdf).

U.S. Department of Interior Office of Education. 1930. *Availability of Public School Education in Rural Communities* (Bulletin No. 34, edited by Walter H. Gaummitz). Washington, DC: Government Printing Office.

U.S. Department of Justice. 2015. "2011 Crime Clock Statistics." Retrieved April 6, 2016 (www.fbi.gov/about-us/cjis/ucr/crime-in-the-u.s/2014/crime-in-the-u.s.-2014/offenses-known-to-law-enforcement/browse-by/national-data).

U.S. Department of Labor. 2011. "Highlights of Women's Earnings in 2010." Report 1031. Retrieved June 5, 2012 (www.bls.gov/cps/cpswom2010.pdf).

U.S. Department of Labor. 2013. "Employee Rights and Responsibilities Under the Family and Medical Leave Act." Retrieved February 19, 2014 (www.dol.gov/whd/regs/compliance/posters/fmlean.pdf).

U.S. Department of Labor. 2014. "Ratio of Women's to Men's Earnings and Wage Gap by Occupation." Women's Bureau—Chart 15. Retrieved April 11, 2016 (www.dol.gov/wb/stats/earnings.htm).

U.S. Department of State. 2015. South Africa 2015 Crime and Safety Report. Retrieved May 28, 2015 (www.osac.gov/pages/ContentReportDetails.aspx?cid=17042).

U.S. Flag Code. 2008. "U.S. Flag Code (4 US Code 1)." Retrieved August 28, 2008 (http://suvcw.org/flag.htm).

U.S. Government Accountability Office. 2015. "Financial Audit: Bureau of the Fiscal Service's Fiscal Years 2015 and 2014 Schedules of Federal Debt." November 13. Retrieved January 25, 2016 (www.gao.gov/products/GAO-16-160).

"U.S. Life Expectancy Ranks 26th in the World, OECD Report Shows." 2013. *Huffington Post*, November 21. Retrieved December 5, 2013 (www.huffingtonpost.com/2013/11/21/us-life-expectancy-oecd_n_4317367.html).

U.S. Trade Representative. 2012. "Joint Stats From 2012 NAFTA Commission Meeting." Retrieved September 8, 2012 (www.ustr.gov).

Uttarakhand Community. 2015. "Chipko Movement Harbinger of Environmental Protection." *The Tribune* (India), September 13. Retrieved September 13, 2015 (www.tribuneindia.com/news/uttarakhand/community/chipko-movement-harbinger-of-environment-protection-gov/102784.html).

Uzoma, Kay. 2015. "How Much TV Does the Average Child Watch Each Day?" Livestrong, May 25. Retrieved September 14, 2015 (www.livestrong.com/article/222032-how-much-tv-does-the-average-child-watch-each-day).

Van der Voet, Joris. 2015. "Change Leadership and Public Sector Organizational Change." *American Review of Public Administration*, March 22. Retrieved September 10, 2015 (http://arp.sagepub.com/content/early/2015/03/18/0275074015574769.abstract).

Varul, Matthias Zick. 2010. "Talcott Parsons, the Sick Role and Chronic Illness." *Body Society* 16(2):72–94.

Veblen, Thorstein. 1902. *The Theory of the Leisure Class: An Economic Study of Institutions*. New York: Macmillan.

Verbeek, Stjin and Rinus Penninx. 2009. "Employment Equity Policies in Work Organisations." Pp. 69–94 in *Equal Opportunity and Ethnic Inequality in European Labour Markets: Discrimination, Gender, and Policies of Diversity*, edited by Karen Kraal, Judith Roosblad, and John Wrench. Amsterdam: University of Amsterdam Press.

Victor, Barbara. 2003. *Army of Roses: Inside the World of Palestinian Women Suicide Bombers*. Emmaus, PA: Rodale Books.

Vinograd, Cassandra. 2013. "Teen Pregnancy: 7.3 Million Teenage Births in Developing World, UN Says." *Huffington Post*, October 30. Retrieved March 12, 2014 (www.huffingtonpost.com/2013/10/30/teen-pregnancy-developing-world_n_4176898.html).

von Grebmer, Klaus, Alex de Waal, Jill Bernstein, Nilam Prasai, Sandra Yin, Yisehac Yohannes. 2015. *2015 Global Hunger Index: Armed Conflict and the Challenge of Hunger*. "Global Hunger Index" map. Bonn: Welthungerhilfe; Washington, DC: International Food Policy Research Institute; Concern Worldwide: Dublin (http://www.ifpri.org/sites/default/files/gfpr/2015/feature_3154.html).

Wade, Lisa. 2012. "The New Elite: Attributing Privilege and Class vs. Merit." Sociological Images: Inspiring Sociological Imaginations Everywhere, June 21. Retrieved September 14, 2012 (http://thesocietypages.org/socimages/2012/06/21/the-new-elite-attributing-privilege-to-class-vs-merit).

Wade, Lisa. 2013a. "The Number of People in Private Prisons Has Grown by 1,664% in the Last 19 Years." PolicyMic, January 25. Retrieved April 26, 2014 (www.policymic.com/articles/24142/the-number-of-people-in-private-prisons-has-grown-by-1-664-in-the-last-19-years).

Wade, Lisa. 2013b. "The Truth About Gender and Math." *Sociological Images*, March 7. Retrieved Jan. 17, 2014 (http://thesocietypages.org/socimages/2013/03/07/the-truth-about-gender-and-math).

Walk Free Foundation. 2013. "The Global Slavery Index 2013." Retrieved January 2, 2014 (www.globalslaveryindex.org).

Wallenstein, Peter. 2002. *Tell the Court I Love My Wife: Race, Marriage, and Law—An American History*. New York: Macmillan

Wallerstein, Immanuel. 1974. *The Modern World System*. New York: Academic Press.

Walters, Joanna. 2015. "Tablets and Smartphones May Affect Social and Emotional Development, Scientists Speculate." *The Guardian*, February 2. Retrieved August 30, 2015 (www .theguardian.com/technology/2015/feb/01/toddler-brains-research-smartphones-damage-social-development).

Wang, Julia and Morgan Currier. 2015. "Students Force 16 Universities to End Sweatshop Contracts" *Popular Resistance*, February 3. Retrieved February 10, 2016 (www .popularresistance.org/students-force-16-universities-to-end-sweatshop-contracts).

War Child. 2014. "Child Soldier: Some Words Don't Belong Together." Retrieved August 21, 2014 (www.warchild.org.uk/ issues/child-soldiers?gclid=CJ_78cL7bYCFSdgMgod11wAmQ).

Ward, Martha C. and Monica Edelstein. 2014. *A World Full of Women*, 6th ed. Boston: Allyn & Bacon.

WaterAid. 2012. "Annual Review 2010/11." Retrieved September 9, 2012 (www.wateraid.org/uk/about_us/annual_report/default.asp).

Water.org. 2015. "Millions Lack Safe Water." Retrieved September 10, 2015 (water.org/water-crisis/water-facts/water).

Waters, Tony. 2012. *Schooling, Childhood, and Bureaucracy: Bureaucratizing the Child*. Basingstoke, UK: Palgrave Macmillan.

Weaver, Janelle. 2010. "Social Life Starts in the Womb." *Science*, October 12. Retrieved October 19, 2010 (http://news .sciencemag.org/sciencenow/2010/10/scienceshot-social-life-starts-in.html?rss=1&utm_source=twitterfeed&utm_ medium=twitter).

Weber, Max. 1946. *From Max Weber: Essays in Sociology*, translated and edited by Hans H. Gerth and C. Wright Mills. New York: Oxford University Press.

Weber, Max. 1947. *The Theory of Social and Economic Organization*, translated and edited by A. M. Henderson and Talcott Parsons. New York: Oxford University Press.

Weber, Max. [1904–1905] 1958. *The Protestant Ethic and the Spirit of Capitalism*, translated by Talcott Parsons. New York: Scribner.

Webster's Unabridged English Dictionary. 1989. New York: Gramercy Books.

Weeks, John R. 2012. *Population: An Introduction to Concepts and Issues*, 11th ed. Belmont, CA: Wadsworth.

Weinberg, George. 1972. *Society and the Healthy Homosexual*. New York: St. Martin's Press.

Weiss, Gregory L. and Lynne E. Lonnquist. 2015. *The Sociology of Health, Healing, and Illness*, 7th ed. Englewood Cliffs, NJ: Prentice Hall.

Weiss, Robin Elise. 2010. "Pregnancy and Childbirth." Retrieved January 9, 2010 (pregnancy.about.com/od/cesareansections/ ss/cesarian.htm).

Weissmann, Jordan. 2014. "Americans Have No Idea How Bad Inequality Really Is." *Slate*, September 26. Retrieved April 8, 2016 (www.slate.com/articles/business/moneybox/2014/09/ americans_have_no_idea_how_bad_inequality_is_new_ harvard_business_school.html).

Wells, Amy Stuart and Jeannie Oakes. 1996. "Potential Pitfalls of Systemic Reform: Early Lessons From Research on Detracking." *Sociology of Education* 69(Extra Issue):135–43.

Wells, Cheryl. 2008. "Suns, Moons, Clocks, and Bells: Native Americans and Time." USC History Seminar, December, SOS 250, Department of History, University of Wyoming.

West, Candace and Don H. Zimmerman. 1987. "Doing Gender." *Gender and Society* 1(2):125–51.

Whitney, Lance. 2012. "2011 Ends With Almost 6 Billion Mobile Phone Subscriptions." CNET News. Retrieved May 18, 2012 (http://news.cnet.com/8301-1023_3-57352095-93/2011-ends-with-almost-6-billion-mobile-phone-subscriptions).

Whorf, Benjamin Lee. 1956. *Language, Thought, and Reality*. New York: John Wiley.

Whoriskey, Peter and Dan Keating. 2015. "The Business of Hospice." *Washington Post*, December 26. Retrieved June 30, 2015 (www.washingtonpost.com/business/economy/2014/12/ 26/a7d90438-692f-11e4-b053-65cea7903f2e_story.html).

Whyte, William H. 1956. *The Organization Man*. New York: Simon and Schuster.

Wike, Richard, Bruce Stokes, and Jacob Poushter. 2015. "America's Global Image." Pew Research Center, June 23. Retrieved August 29, 2015 (www.pewglobal .org/2015/06/23/1-americas-global-image).

Wilhoit, Sarah 2014. "Demand That U.S. Coffee Companies Stop Using Child and Slave Labor Overseas." Retrieved February 14, 2014 (http://forcechange.com/62236/demand-that-u-s-coffee-companies-stop-using-child-and-slave-labor-over seas).

Wilkerson, Isabel. 2010. *The Warmth of Other Suns: The Epic Story of America's Great Migration*. New York: Vintage/ Random House.

Williams, Brian K., Stacey C. Sawyer, and Carl M. Wahlstrom. 2013. *Marriages, Families, and Intimate Relationships*, 3rd ed. Boston: Allyn & Bacon.

Williams, Christine L. 2006. *Inside Toyland: Working, Shopping, and Social Inequality*. Berkeley: University of California Press.

Williams, Christine L. 2013. "The Glass Escalator, Revisited: Gender Inequality in Neoliberal Times." *Gender and Society* 27(5):609–29.

Williams, Robin Murphy, Jr. 1970. *American Society: A Sociological Interpretation*, 3rd ed. New York: Alfred Knopf.

Willis, Paul. 1979. *Learning to Labor: How Working Class Kids Get Working Class Jobs*. Aldershot, Hampshire, England: Saxon House.

Wilson, Edward O. 1980. *Sociobiology*. Cambridge, MA: Belknap.

Wilson, Edward O. 1987. *The Coevolution of Biology and Culture*. Cambridge, MA: Harvard University Press.

Wilson, Edward O. 2000. *Sociobiology: The New Synthesis*, 25th ann. ed. Cambridge, MA: Harvard University Press.

Wilson, Kate, Vlad Lavrov, Martina Keller, Thomas Jajer, and Gerard Ryle. 2012. "Skin, Bones and Tissue for Sale: How the Dead Are Being Used for Grisly Trade in Human Body Parts." *Daily Mail*, July 17. Retrieved August 2, 2012 (www .dailymail.co.uk/news/article-2175006/Skin-bones-tissue-sale-How-dead-used-grisly-trade-human-body-parts.html).

Wilson, Megan. 2012. "Big Business Sides With Obama on Affirmative Action Case Before High Court." *The Hill*, October 28. Retrieved May 31, 2013 (http://thehill.com/ homenews/administration/264329-big-business-sides-with-obama-on-affirmative-action-case-before-supreme-court).

Wilson, Reid. 2015. "In Major Cities, Murder Rates Drop Precipitously." *Washington Post*, January 2. Retrieved June 7, 2015 (www.washingtonpost.com/blogs/ govbeat/wp/2015/01/02/in-major-cities-murder-rates-drop-precipitously).

Winders, Bill. 2004. "Changing Racial Inequality: The Rise and Fall of Systems of Racial Inequality in the U.S."

Paper presented at the Annual Meeting of the American Sociological Association, San Francisco.

Wing, Nick. 2013. "Countries With the Largest Number of Prisoners per 100,000 of the National Population, as of 2013." *Huffington Post*, August 13. Retrieved April 25, 2014 (www.huffingtonpostcom/2013/08/13/incarceration-rate-per-capita_n_3745291.html).

Winslow, Robert W. and Sheldon X. Zhang. 2008. *Criminology: A Global Perspective*. Upper Saddle River, NJ: Pearson Prentice Hall.

Witness for Peace. 2016. "Free Trade Agreements." Retrieved February 10, 2016 (www.witnessforpeace.org/section.php?id=99).

Wolf, Arthur P. and William H. Durham, eds. 2004. *Inbreeding, Incest, and the Incest Taboo: The State of Knowledge at the Turn of the Century*. Palo Alto, CA: Stanford University Press.

Wong, Alia. 2015. "Where Girls Are Missing Out on High-School Sports." *The Atlantic*, June 26. Retrieved September 4, 2015 (www.theatlantic.com/education/archive/2015/06/girls-high-school-sports-inequality/396782).

Wong, Edward. 2013. "In China, Breathing Becomes a Childhood Risk." *New York Times*, April 22. Retrieved July 1, 2013 (www.nytimes.com/2013/04/23/world/asia/pollution-is-radically-changing-childhood-in-chinas-cities.html?pagewanted=all).

Wood, Graeme. 2015. "What ISIS Really Wants?" *The Atlantic*, March. Retrieved September 13, 2015 (www.theatlantic.com/magazine/archive/2015/03/what-isis-really-wants/384980/).

Wood, Julia. 2008. *Gendered Lives: Communication, Gender, and Culture*, 8th ed. Belmont, CA: Wadsworth.

Wood, Julia T. and Nina M. Reich. 2006. "Gendered Communication Styles." Pp. 177–86 in *Intercultural Communication*, 11th ed., edited by Larry A. Samovar, Richard E. Porter, and Edwin R. McDaniel. Belmont, CA: Wadsworth.

World Almanac and Book of Facts. 2015. New York: World Almanac Books. p. 716.

World Bank. 2012. "Girls' Education: Learning for All." Retrieved September 14, 2012 (http://web.worldbank.org/WBSITE/EXTERNAL/TOPICS/EXTEDUCATION/o,,contentMDK:20298916~menuPK:617572~pagePK:148956~piPK:216618~theSitePK:282386,00.html).

World Bank. 2013a. "Featured Conversation: Slums and Service Delivery for the Urban Poor." Striking Poverty. Retrieved July 1, 2013 (www.forbes.com/sites/joelkotkin/2013/03/18/americas-fastest-and-slowest-growing-cities/).

World Bank. 2013b. "Population Density (People per Square KM of Land Area)." Retrieved June 9, 2013 (http://data.worldbank.org/indicator/EN.POP.DNST).

World Bank. 2014. "Sub-Saharan Africa (Developing Only)." Retrieved September 16, 2014 (http://data.worldbank.org/region/sub-saharan-africa).

World Bank. 2015. "Haiti Overview." Retrieved June 9, 2015 (www.worldbank.org/en/country/haiti/overview).

World Bank. 2016a. "GNI Per Capita, Atlas Method (Current US$)." Retrieved April 16, 2016 (http://data.worldbank.org/indicator/NY.GNP.PCAP.CD/countries?display=map).

World Bank. 2016b. "The World Bank 2016 Internet Users (per 100 People)." Retrieved April 12, 2016 (http://data.worldbank.org/indicator/IT.NET.USER.P2/countries/1W?display=map3).

World Bank. 2017. "Poverty Overview." Retrieved March 3, 2017 (www.worldbank.org/en/topic/poverty/overview).

World Coalition. 2012. "World Database." World Coalition Against the Death Penalty. Retrieved May 29, 2012 (http://www.worldcoalition.org/worldwide-database.html).

World Economic Forum. 2015. "The Global Information Technology Report 2015." Retrieved June 11, 2015 (http://reports.weforum.org/global-information-technology-report-2015/report-highlights/#keyfindings).

World Economic Forum. 2016. *The Global Gender Gap Index 2015*. Retrieved April 3, 2016 (http://reports.weforum.org/global-gender-gap-report-2015/the-global-gender-gap-index-2015/).

World Factbook. 2014a. "China." Retrieved September 15, 2014 (https://www.cia.gov/library/publications/the-world-factbook/geos/ch.html).

World Factbook. 2014b. "Congo, Democratic Republic of the." Retrieved September 15, 2014 (https://www.cia.gov/library/publications/the-world-factbook/geos/cg.html).

World Factbook. 2014c. "India." Retrieved September 15, 2014 (https://www.cia.gov/library/publications/the-world-factbook/geos/in.html).

World Factbook. 2014d. "Kenya." Retrieved September 15, 2014 (https://www.cia.gov/library/publications/the-world-factbook/geos/ke.html).

World Factbook. 2014e. "Life Expectancy at Birth." Retrieved April 18, 2014 (https://www.cia.gov/library/publications/the-world-factbook/rankorder/2102rank.html).

World Factbook. 2014f. "Niger." Retrieved September 15, 2014 (https://www.cia.gov/library/publications/the-world-factbook/geos/ng.html).

World Factbook. 2014g. "Uganda." Retrieved September 15, 2014 (https://www.cia.gov/library/publications/the-world-factbook/geos/ug.html).

World Factbook. 2015a. "Afghanistan: People and Society." Retrieved July 3, 2015 (www.cia.gov/library/publications/the-world-factbook/geos/af.html).

World Factbook. 2015b. "Chad: People and Society." Retrieved July 8, 2015 (www.cia.gov/library/publications/the-world-factbook/geos/cd.html).

World Factbook. 2015c. "China: People and Society." Retrieved July 6, 2015 (www.cia.gov/library/publications/resources/the-world-factbook/geos/sn.html).

World Factbook. 2015d. "France: People and Society." Retrieved July 3, 2015 (www.cia.gov/library/publications/the-world-factbook/geos/fr.html).

World Factbook. 2015e. "Germany: People and Society." Retrieved July 3, 2015 (www.cia.gov/library/publications/the-world-factbook/geos/gm.html).

World Factbook. 2015f. "United Kingdom: People and Society." Retrieved July 3, 2015 (www.cia.gov/library/publications/the-world-factbook/geos/uk.html).

World Factbook. 2016a. "Country Comparison: GDP Per Capita." Retrieved April 14, 2016 (www.cia.gov/library/publications/resources/the-world-factbook/rankorder/2004rank.html).

World Factbook. 2016b. "Country Comparison: Infant Mortality Rate." Retrieved April 14, 2016 (www.cia.gov/library/publications/resources/the-world-factbook/rankorder/2091rank.html).

World Factbook. 2016c. "Country Comparison: Life Expectancy at Birth." Retrieved April 14, 2016 (www.cia.gov/library/publications/resources/the-world-factbook/rankorder/2102rank.html).

World Factbook. 2017a. "Country Comparison: Infant Mortality Rate." Retrieved March 14, 2017 (https://www.cia.gov/library/publications/the-world-factbook/rankorder/2091rank.html).

World Factbook. 2017b. "Country Comparison: Life Expectancy at Birth." Retrieved March 14, 2017 (https://www.cia.gov/library/publications/resources/the-world-factbook/rankorder/2102rank.html).

World Famine Timeline. 2016. "Famine." Retrieved April 4, 2016 (www.mapreport.com/subtopics/d/0.html#2013).

World Food Programme. 2013. "10 Things You Need to Know About Hunger in 2013." January 2. Retrieved January 5, 2014 (www.wfp.org/stories/10-things-you-need-to-know-about-hunger-2013).

World Health Organization. 2013. "Urban Population Growth."

World Health Organization. 2014a. "Adolescent Pregnancy." Maternal, Newborn, Child, and Adolescent Health. Retrieved March 17, 2014 (www.who.int/maternal_child_adolescent/topics/maternal/adolescent_pregnancy/en/).

World Health Organization. 2014b. "Children: Reducing Mortality." September. Retrieved June 8, 2015 (www.who.int/mediacentre/factsheets/fs178/en).

World Hunger Education Service. 2013. "2013 World Hunger and Poverty Facts and Statistics." Retrieved September 16, 2014 (http://www.worldhunger.org/articles/Learn/world%20hunger%20facts%202002.htm).

Worldometers. 2014. "Current World Population." Retrieved March 18, 2014 (www.worldometers.info/world-population).

WorldWideLearn. 2007. "Guide to College Majors in Sociology." Retrieved June 23, 2008 (www.worldwidelearn.com/online-education-guide/social-science/sociology-major.htm).

Yablonski, Lewis. 1959. "The Gang as a Near-Group." *Social Problems* 7(Fall):108–117.

Yardley, Jim. 2013. "Report on Deadly Factory Collapse in Bangladesh Finds Widespread Blame." *New York Times*, May 23. (http://www.nytimes.com/2013/05/23/world/asia/report-on-bangladesh-building-collapse-finds-widespread-blame.html).

Yehuda, Rachel, Nikolaos P. Daskalakis, Linda M. Bierer, Heather N. Bader, Torsten Klengel, Florian, Holsboer, and Elisabeth B. Binder. 2015. "Holocaust Exposure Induced Intergenerational Effects on FKBP5 Methylation." *Biological Psychiatry*, August 6. Retrieved November 16, 2015 (www.biologicalpsychiatryjournal.com/article/S0006-3223(15)00652-6/abstract).

Yinger, J. Milton. 1960. "Contraculture and Subculture." *American Sociological Review* 25(October):625–35.

Yoon, Mi Yung. 2005. "Sub-Saharan Africa." Chapter 7 in *Sharing Power: Women, Parliament, Democracy*, edited by Manon Tremblay and Yvonne Galligan. Aldershot, UK: Ashgate.

Yoon, Mi Yung. 2011a. "More Women in the Tanzanian Legislature: Do Numbers Matter?" *Journal of Contemporary African Studies* 29(January):83–98.

Yoon, Mi Yung. 2011b. "Factors Hindering 'Larger' Representation of Women in Parliament: The Case of Seychelles." *Commonwealth and Comparative Politics* 49(February):98–114.

Yu, Tianyi, Gregory S. Pettit, Jennifer E. Lansford, Kenneth A. Dodge, and John E. Bates. 2010. "The Interactive Effects of Marital Conflict and Divorce on Parent–Adult Children's Relationships." *Journal of Marriage and Family* 72(2):282–292.

Zahniser, Steven, Sahar Angadjivand, and Thomas Hertz. 2015. "NAFTA at 20: With Regional Trade Liberalization Complete, Focus Shifts to Other Methods of Deepening Economic Integration." U.S. Department of Agriculture, April 6. Retrieved February 10, 2016 (www.ers.usda.gov/amber-waves/2015-april/nafta-at-20-with-regional-trade-liberalization-complete,-focus-shifts-to-other-methods-of-deepening-economic-integration.aspx).

Zapotosky, Matt and Chico Harlan 2016. "Justice Department Says It Will End Use of Private Prisons." *Washington Post*, August 18. Retrieved September 19, 2016 (www.washingtonpost.com/news/post-nation/wp/2016/08/18/justice-department-says-it-will-end-use-of-private-prisons/?utm_term=.b3a308b2daa7).

Zarya, Valentina. 2015. "Here's One Big Reason Men's Earnings Are Growing Twice as Fast as Women's." *Fortune*, October 21. Retrieved January 8, 2016 (http://fortune.com/2015/10/21/pay-gap-widens).

Zborowski, Mark. 1952. "Cultural Components in Response to Pain." *Journal of Social Issues* 8(4):16–30.

Zeleny, Jeff. 2009. "Obama Vows, 'We Will Rebuild' and 'Recover.'" *New York Times*, February 25. Retrieved February 25, 2009 (www.nytimes.com/2009/02/25/us/politics/25obama.html?scp=1&sq=obama%20vows%20we%20will%20rebuild&st=cse).

Ziel, Magda. 2013. "Sati Widow Burning Still Going On." HubPages. Retrieved January 16, 2014 (http://whitemuse.hubpages.com/hub/Sati-Still-Being-Done-in-India).

Zimbardo, Philip C. 2004. "Power Turns Good Soldiers Into 'Bad Apples.'" *Boston Globe*, May 9. Retrieved July 5, 2008 (www.boston.com/news/globe/editorial_opinion/oped/articles/2004/05/09/power_turns_good_soldiers_into_bad_apples).

Zimbardo, Philip C., Craig Haney, Curtis Banks, and David Jaffe. 1973. "The Mind Is a Formidable Jailer: A Pirandellian Prison." *New York Times Magazine*, April 8, pp. 38–60.

Zull, James E. 2002. *The Art of Changing the Brain: Enriching the Practice of Teaching by Exploring the Biology of Learning.* Sterling, VA: Stylus.

Index

About the Authors

Jeanne H. Ballantine is emerita professor of sociology at Wright State University, a state university of about 17,000 students in Ohio. She has also taught at several 4-year colleges, including an "alternative" college and a traditionally Black college and at international programs in universities abroad. She has been teaching introductory sociology for more than 30 years, with a mission to introduce the uninitiated to the field and to help students see the usefulness and value in sociology. She has been active in the teaching movement, shaping curriculum, writing and presenting research on teaching, and offering workshops and consulting in regional, national, and international forums. She is a Fulbright Senior Scholar and serves as a Departmental Resources Group consultant and evaluator.

Jeanne has written several textbooks, all with the goal of reaching the student audience. As the original director of the Center for Teaching and Learning at Wright State University, she scoured the literature on student learning and served as a mentor to teachers in a wide variety of disciplines. Local, regional, and national organizations have honored her for her teaching and for her contributions to helping others become effective teachers. In 1986, the American Sociological Association's Section on Undergraduate Education (now called the Section on Teaching and Learning in Sociology) recognized her with the Hans O. Mauksch Award for Distinguished Contributions to Teaching of Sociology. In 2004, she was honored by the American Sociological Association with its Distinguished Contributions to Teaching Award. In 2010, the North Central Sociological Association awarded her the J. Milton Yinger Award for Distinguished Career in Sociology.

Keith A. Roberts is emeritus professor of sociology at Hanover College, a private liberal arts college of about 1,100 students in Indiana. He has taught introductory sociology for 35 years, with a passion for active-learning strategies and a focus on deep learning by students that transforms the way they see the world. Prior to teaching at Hanover, he taught at a 2-year regional campus of a large university.

He has been active in the teaching movement, writing on teaching and serving as a consultant to sociology departments across the country in his capacity as a member of the American Sociological Association Departmental Resources Group. He has written a very popular textbook in the sociology of religion, has coauthored a book on writing in the undergraduate curriculum, has published and led many workshops on the "Scholarship of Teaching and Learning," and for 22 years ran an annual workshop for high school sociology teachers. He has chaired the Selection Committee for the SAGE Innovations and Professional Development Awards since the program's inception. He has been honored for his teaching and teaching-related work at local, state, regional, and national levels. The American Sociological Association's Section on Teaching and Learning awarded him the Hans O. Mauksch Award for Distinguished Contributions to Teaching of Sociology in 2000. He was honored with the American Sociological Association's Distinguished Contributions to Teaching Award in 2010. In 2012, the North Central Sociological Association awarded Keith the J. Milton Yinger Award for Distinguished Career in Sociology.

Kathleen Odell Korgen is professor of sociology at William Paterson University, a comprehensive university in Wayne, New Jersey. In addition to her research on racial identity and race relations, she has written extensively in support of the public sociology movement. Kathleen enjoys teaching her students that sociology is a remarkably useful discipline and highlights how "Sociologists in Action" make a positive impact on society. Her published works on race relations and racial identity include *Race Policy and Multiracial Americans* (2016), *Multiracial Identity and Social Class* (2010), *Crossing the Racial Divide: Close Friendships Between Black and White Americans* (2002), and *From Black to Biracial: Transforming Racial Identity Among Americans* (1998, 1999). Her works on public sociology include *Sociology in Action* (with Maxine Atkinson, 2018), *The Engaged Sociologist: Connecting the Classroom to the Community* (with Jonathan White, 2007, 2009, 2011, 2014), *Sociologists in Action: Sociology, Social Change, and Social Justice* (2011, 2014), and *Sociologists in Action on Inequalities: Race, Class, and Gender* (with Jonathan White and Shelley White, 2015). Kathleen is also the editor of *The Cambridge Handbook of Sociology* (2017).

Kathleen works as a consultant for other sociology departments as a member of the American Sociological Association Departmental Resources Group and received William Paterson University's award for Excellence in Scholarship/Creative Expression in 2006 and the university's award for Excellence in Teaching in 2014.